CHILDREN'S
ILLUSTRATED
DICTIONARY

CHILDREN'S
ILLUSTRATED
DICTIONARY

DP
DEMPSEY
PARR

Authors
John Grisewood, Neil Morris, Ting Morris

Designer
Diane Clouting

Cover Design
Jo Brewer

Design Management
Angela Ashton

Editor
Linda Sonntag

Additional Editorial help from
Cindy Leaney

Project Management
Sarah Eason

Editorial Assistant
Helen Parker

Artwork Commissioning
Susanne Grant

Picture Research
Lesley Cartlidge, Libbe Mella

Production
Jenni Cozens and Ian Paulyn

Editorial Director
Paula Borton

Art Director
Clare Sleven

Director
Jim Miles

This edition is for Books are Fun
This is a Dempsey Parr Book
This edition published in 2000

Dempsey Parr is an imprint of Parragon
Parragon
Queen Street House
4 Queen Street
Bath BA1 1HE, UK

Copyright © Parragon 1998

Produced by Miles Kelly Publishing Ltd
11, Bardfield Centre, Great Bardfield, Essex CM7 4SL

ISBN 1-84084-422-1

Printed in Indonesia

Introduction

Have you ever played the game in which you try to describe something in words only —without using any gestures—and other people have to work out what you are describing? How would you describe a horse or a television?

This dictionary describes a horse as follows: 'a big, four-legged animal with hooves, a long mane and a tail, which can be used for riding or for pulling things like carts and plows'. The television is described as 'a box-shaped instrument that receives programs that have been broadcast, and shows them on a screen as moving pictures with sound'.

That is exactly what a dictionary does— tells us what words mean. A good dictionary should describe things well by being clear and concise. If a word has two or more meanings, it should tell us. 'Post', for example, has two quite different meanings: firstly, mail (letters, parcels etc.) and secondly, a pole, like a telegraph pole. The noun 'bear' is an animal but the verb means 'to carry or support'.

A good dictionary has certain other features:

It tells you how words are spelled ('accommodation' has two 'c's and two 'm's).

It tells you how awkward words are pronounced ('gnome', 'handkerchief', 'scythe', 'qualm', 'typhoon', for example).

It tells you what the part of speech is. Is it a noun, verb, adjective or adverb?

This is useful. For instance, the noun 'object' meaning 'a thing' is pronounced '**ob**-ject' but the verb, meaning 'to protest' is pronounced 'ob-**ject**'.

It provides example sentences or phrases to help you understand how a word should be used. For instance: 'This is just (exactly) the color I'm looking for' and 'There's just about (almost not) enough to eat.'

To be really useful, a dictionary must be up-to-date. New words enter the language and old words may die or acquire a new meaning. If you looked at a dictionary that is only a few years old, you probably would not find the second definition of mouse: 'a small device on your desk that you move on the surface with your hand to control the position of the cursor on a computer screen'. And the word 'cursor' in the definition would probably not be in the dictionary.

This dictionary has some other features that make it rather special:

- It is superbly illustrated with photographs, diagrams and drawings that complement the definitions and add more visual information.

- Special notice-board panels provide fascinating facts on such things as word histories, spelling, grammar and homophones plus much general information associated with a particular word.

We hope you will find this dictionary both useful and interesting. How would you describe it—without using gestures?

John Grisewood, Neil Morris, Ting Morris

How to use this dictionary

All the entries are in alphabetical order. A page letter or thumb-index shows you the pages on which all the entries beginning with the same letter appear. A guide word at the top outside corner of each page also helps you find the word you're looking for. The guide word on the left-hand page gives the first word on that page and the guide word on the right gives the last.

Headwords

Headwords or entries are printed in bold, black type. Other forms of the same word (related words) are in less bold type, for example: **baptize** *verb*. **baptism** *noun*. **baptismal** *adjective*.

Derivatives

Derivatives or other irregular forms of the headword are shown in brackets as in the verb give (give, gives, giving, gave), the noun goose (geese) and the adjective big (bigger, biggest). Regular forms are not given, for example, dog (dogs).

Pronunciation

For some of the more difficult words there is a guide to how to say it correctly, for example **gnash** *verb* (say nash).

Definition

This tells you what a word means. If a word has more than one meaning, each meaning is numbered. For example: temple noun 1 a building... 2 the flat part on either side of your head...

Parts of speech

These show how words behave in a sentence. They are: adjective, adverb, conjunction, noun, preposition, pronoun, verb. Look up the entry in the dictionary to find out more about each of these parts of speech.

chariot

C

Around 1200 BC the Hittites, who lived in modern-day Turkey, used chariots for warfare.

charity *noun* 1 an organization that helps those who need it. *A charity for stray cats.* 2 kindness towards others.

charm *noun* 1 the ability to be attractive and to please. *He used all his charm to win her over.* 2 an act, saying or object that has magical powers. 3 an ornament on a bracelet or chain. **charm** *verb* 1 *He charmed her with his flattery.* 2 to control something by using magical powers.

charming *adjective* delightful, pleasing. *She is a charming person.*

chart *noun* 1 a map of the sea and coast or sky and stars. 2 a map with special information in curves and graphs. *A weather chart.* 3 a list of information in a particular order. *The charts list the most popular records.* **chart** *verb*. *Explorers charted the coastline.*

chase *verb* to go after somebody or something in order to try and catch them or make them go away. *The cat chased the mouse.* **chase** *noun*.

chasm *noun* 1 a deep crack in the ground. 2 a large difference between two things or groups. *The chasm between us widened.*

chat *noun* a friendly talk. **chat** *verb*. *We chatted all afternoon.*

chat show *noun* a TV or radio programme in which famous people are interviewed.

chatter *verb* 1 to talk non-stop about unimportant things. 2 to make a rattling sound. *His teeth were chattering with cold.*

chauffeur *noun* (say **shoh**-fer) a person employed to drive somebody's car.

The chauffeur wears a smart uniform and waits by his employer's car.

AMAZING FACT

Cheetahs can reach speeds of up to 60 mph (100kph) over short distances when chasing gazelles.

Tartan is a traditional Scottish fabric pattern, based on colourful overlaid checks.

WORD HISTORY

The original 'chauffeur', in French, was not a driver but a stoker or fireman, who put coal on the furnace of a steam engine. Early motor cars gave off a lot of smoke and steam, so their drivers were jokingly called stokers.

chauvinist *noun* (say **shoh**-vin-ist) a person who shows great prejudice, especially against women. *He's a real male chauvinist.*

cheap *adjective* 1 not costing very much. *Food is cheaper in Portugal than in Spain.* 2 of poor quality, not very good. *Cheap housing is hard to come by.*

cheat *verb* to lie or trick somebody, often in order to do well. *He always cheats in exams.* **cheat** *noun* 1 a person who cheats. 2 a dishonest action.

check *noun* 1 an examination to find out if something is correct. *He made a thorough check.* 2 keeping somebody or something under control. *It's impossible to keep the disease in check.* 3 in chess the position of the king when under attack.

check *noun* a pattern of squares in different colours. **checked** *adjective*.

check *verb* 1 to make sure something is correct or satisfactory. *Have you checked the bill?* 2 to hold back or stop doing something. *The bad weather checked their progress.* **check in** to register at a hotel or report at an airport. *You have to check in an hour before take-off.* **check out** to pay the bill and leave a hotel.

checkout *noun* a place in a supermarket where goods are packed and paid for.

check-up *noun* a medical examination.

cheek *noun* the side of the face below the eye. *Rosy cheeks are a sign of health.*

cheek *noun* rude behaviour. **cheeky** *adjective*. *Don't be cheeky to your mother!*

cheer *noun* 1 a shout of praise or happiness. *The crowd gave a big cheer.* 2 If you are full of cheer, you are very happy. **cheer** *verb*. *The fans cheered wildly throughout the match.* **cheer up** to become happy and stop feeling sad.

cheerful *adjective* 1 looking, sounding and feeling happy. 2 something pleasant, that makes you happy. **cheerfully** *adverb*.

cheese *noun* a soft or hard food made from milk. *Let's have bread and cheese for lunch.*

cheetah *noun* a wild animal, like a big spotted cat. Cheetahs are the fastest land animals in the world.

72

Illustrations

The illustrations have been carefully selected to extend and complement the definitions. All have informative captions or labels. 'A good picture,' they say, 'is worth a thousand words.'

Phrasal verbs

Phrasal verbs are included as a distinct part of many definitions. They are simple verbs like make, get, go, together with an adverb or preposition (as in get up, get away, get on etc.). They function like a single word but the meaning cannot be worked out from the literal meaning of the words. The ability to use and understand phrasal verbs is very important in writing and speaking clear English.

Examples of use

A sentence or phrase may be given to show how to use the word correctly.

---

chip

C

chef *noun* a cook in a restaurant.

A chef has to deal with many pans at once. His job is both hot and demanding.

chemical *adjective* used in, made by or connected with chemistry. **chemical** *noun*. **chemically** *adverb*.

chemist *noun* 1 a trained person who makes up and sells medicines. 2 a shop selling medicines and toilet articles. 3 a scientist who specializes in chemistry.

chemistry *noun* the study of how substances are made up and how they react with other substances.

cheque *noun* a printed form telling the bank to pay money from your account to the person you have written the cheque to. *Can I pay by cheque?*

cherry (cherries) *noun* 1 a small round fruit with a stone. Ripe cherries are red. 2 the tree on which cherries grow.

chess *noun* a game for two players in which each player moves pieces on a chessboard.

chest *noun* the upper front part of the body enclosing the heart and the lungs.

chest *noun* a big, strong box for keeping things in. *A treasure chest.*

chestnut *noun* 1 a reddish brown nut inside a prickly green case. 2 the tree on which these nuts grow. **chestnut** *adjective* having a reddish-brown colour. *Chestnut hair.*

chest of drawers *noun* a piece of furniture with a set of drawers.

chew *verb* to move food about in your mouth and grind it with your teeth, so it is easy to swallow. **chew over** to think about something very carefully.

chewing gum *noun* a sweet gum that you chew and don't swallow.

chick *noun* a young bird.

Chile is a long thin country that runs along the backbone of South America.

DID YOU KNOW

China has a population of more than 1,200 million, more people than any other country in the world. Yet China has a smaller area than either Russia or Canada.

When the chestnut is ripe, the case falls to the ground and splits open. The shiny nuts roll out.

chicken *noun* 1 a young bird, especially a hen. 2 the bird's meat used as food. *We had chicken for dinner.* 3 (slang) a coward or frightened person. **chicken out** not to do something because you are frightened.

chickenpox *noun* a disease with red itchy spots on the skin.

chief *noun* a leader or highest official. **chief** *adjective* most important. **chiefly** *adverb*.

chilblain *noun* a painful swelling or sore in the fingers or toes caused by extreme cold.

child (children) *noun* 1 a young boy or girl. 2 a son or daughter.

childhood *noun* the time when you are a child. *Now he's old, he often thinks back to his childhood.*

childish *adjective* behaving like a child, often in silly way. *It's very childish to shout and scream like that.*

children plural of child.

Chile *noun* a country in South America.

chill *noun* 1 an unpleasant coldness. *In the morning there is often a chill in the air.* **chilly** *adjective*. 2 an illness caused by cold in which you might have a temperature, a headache and feel shivery. 3 a feeling of fear and doom. **chill** *verb* 1 to make something colder. 2 to become cold with fear. **chilling** *adjective*. *A chilling film.*

chimney *noun* a hollow passage in a roof through which smoke goes up into the air.

chimpanzee *noun* an African ape.

chin *noun* the front of the lower jaw.

china *noun* 1 a kind of fine white clay. 2 cups, saucers, plates and ornaments made of china. *The china cupboard.*

China *noun* a country in East Asia.

Chinese *noun* a person who comes from China. **Chinese** *adjective*. *An excellent Chinese restaurant.*

chip *noun* 1 a fried strip of potato. *We bought fish and chips.* 2 a small piece of wood, brick or paint, broken off something. 3 a crack that has been left in a cup or glass, when a small piece has been broken off. 4 a flat plastic counter used as money in games. 5 a very small electronic circuit in a computer. *A silicon chip.* **have a chip on your shoulder** to be rude or behave badly, because you think you have been treated unfairly in the past. **chip** (chipping, chipped) *verb* to damage something by breaking off a small piece of it. *I'm afraid I've chipped a plate.* **chip in** 1 to interrupt a conversation. 2 to give money to a fund, so that something can be paid for by a number of people.

Gazetteer

The dictionary is also a useful mini-gazetteer. It includes as 'definition' all the countries of the world and their capitals, from Abu Dhabi, capital of the United Arab Emirates, to Zimbabwe, a country in Africa.

Notice-board

The narrow center column has been used as a kind of notice-board on which to 'pin' different kinds of notes—tips, words of advice and warnings about problem words and how to use them well. There are notes on grammar and spelling, on confusable words ('lightening' and 'lightning', for example), on how to make new words by building them with prefixes, as well as notes on the history of words and an interesting series of asides called 'Did you know'.

73

Aa

aardvark *noun* an African mammal with a long snout and a long sticky tongue that it uses for catching insects.

abacus (abacuses) *noun* a frame with beads that slide along wires, used for counting.

abandon *verb* 1 to leave someone or something without returning. *They abandoned the sinking boat.* 2 to stop doing something. *She abandoned her search when it got dark.*

abbey *noun* a church and a group of buildings where monks or nuns live, work and pray.

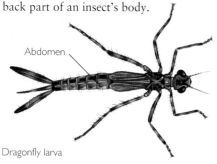

Some large abbeys were like walled towns, where the monks or nuns lived in seclusion from the rest of the world.

abbot *noun* the head of an abbey of monks.

abbreviation *noun* a short way of writing a word or group of words. *Math is an abbreviation for mathematics.* **abbreviated** *adjective.*

abdicate *verb* to give up a position, especially that of king or queen. **abdication** *noun.*

abdomen *noun* 1 the part of the body that contains the stomach. 2 the back part of an insect's body.

Abdomen

Dragonfly larva

WORD HISTORY

Dutch settlers in South Africa gave the aardvark its name. It means 'earth pig', although an aardvark is really a type of anteater.

DID YOU KNOW

Abbreviations such as Mr and Dr that end in the final letter of the word do not need a period after them. Abbreviations of names of countries and organizations, e.g. USA and UN, do not usually have periods either.

An insect's body is clearly divided into head, thorax and abdomen.

---

abhor (abhors, abhorring, abhorred) *verb* to look on something with horror and hate. **abhorrence** *noun.*

ability *noun* the power or skill to do something. *Cats have the ability to see in the dark.*

able *adjective* 1 having the power, time, opportunity etc. to do something. *I wasn't able to leave work early.* 2 clever or skilled. *An able cook.* **ably** *adverb.*

abnormal *adjective* strange, peculiar and not normal. *It's abnormal for it to snow in summer.* **abnormality** *noun.*

aboard *adverb, preposition* in or on a ship, bus, train or airplane. *The train is leaving. All aboard!*

abolish (abolishes, abolishing, abolished) *verb* to get rid of or put an end to. *Capital punishment was abolished years ago.* **abolition** *noun.*

abominable *adjective* bad and very unpleasant. **abominably** *adverb. He was rude and noisy and behaved abominably.*

aborigine (or now preferred) **aboriginal** *noun* (say ab-or-ij-in-ee and ab-or-ij-in-ul) one of the original people who lived in Australia. **aboriginal** *adjective.*

The art of Australian aboriginals often recalls their ancient myths and legends with bold patterns and pictures of animals.

abortion *noun* ending a woman's pregnancy by removing the fetus from her womb. **abort** *verb.*

abortive *adjective* unsuccessful. *An abortive attempt to seize power.*

about *preposition* 1 concerning, in connection with. *The movie is about a family that leaves the city and moves to a farm.* 2 near to. *I'll call you at about six o'clock.* 3 all around. *Old papers were scattered about the room.* **about** *adverb* all over the place.

above *preposition* 1 higher than. *A bee is buzzing above my head.* 2 more than. *Above normal temperature.* **above** *adverb* overhead. *The sky above was gray.*

abreast *adverb* side by side and facing the same way. *The boys marched four abreast.*

abridge *verb* to make a book etc. shorter. **abridged** *adjective. The abridged novels of Dickens.* **abridgement** *noun.*

abroad *adverb* in another country. *Vacations abroad.*

abrupt *adjective* 1 sudden and unexpected. *The bus came to an abrupt stop.* 2 rude and unfriendly. *An abrupt answer.*

abscess *noun* (say ab-sess) a swelling on the body containing a yellow liquid called pus.

abseil *verb* (say ab-sail) to lower yourself down a cliff by holding on to ropes. Rappel.

Henry abseiled slowly down the cliff face.

absent *adjective* not there but away. *Anne was absent from school because she had a cold.* **absence** noun.

absent-minded *adjective* forgetful or not paying attention.

absolute *adjective* 1 complete. *I'm telling the absolute truth.* 2 unlimited. *Dictators have absolute power to do what they want.*

absorb *verb* 1 to soak up a liquid. *Sponges absorb water.* **absorbent** *adjective.* 2 to take up somebody's attention. *She is absorbed in her work.* **absorbing** *adjective.*

Litmus paper absorbs liquid and turns pink if the liquid is acid. It turns blue if the liquid is alkaline. This experiment is called the litmus test.

abstain *verb* 1 to keep yourself from doing something, especially if it is something you enjoy. *She abstained from drinking alcohol.* **abstinence** *noun.* 2 to choose not to vote in an election. **abstention** *noun.*

abstract *adjective* concerned with thoughts and ideas rather than real things.

WORD BUILDER

The suffix '-able' can be added to certain verbs and nouns to form adjectives, e.g. 'adaptable' and 'advisable'. But some adjectives end in '-ible', e.g. 'audible', 'credible' and 'edible'. This has given rise to a lot of confusion and misspellings!

AMAZING FACT

In the 1950s a group of playwrights founded a type of drama called the Theater of the Absurd which examined the meaning of life. They included Beckett, Ionesco and Pinter.

---

abstract *noun* a noun that is concerned with qualities and ideas. *Love and courage are abstract nouns.* The opposite of 'abstract' is 'concrete'.

absurd *adjective* stupid and ridiculous. **absurdity** *noun.*

Abu Dhabi *noun* the capital of the United Arab Emirates.

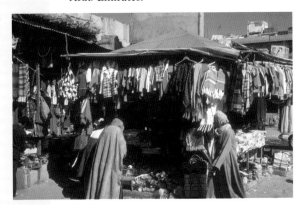

Shoppers hunt for bargains in this bazaar in Abu Dhabi, United Arab Emirates.

Abuja *noun* the capital of Nigeria.

abundant *adjective* available in large amounts, plentiful. *Abundant supplies of fruit.* **abundance** *adjective.*

abuse *verb* (say a-bewz) 1 to treat a person or an animal in an unkind or violent way. 2 to misuse or use in a wrong way.

abuse *noun* (say a-bewss) 1 rude or cruel words. 2 the wrong and harmful use of something. *Drug abuse.* **abusive** *adjective.*

abysmal *adjective* very bad. *What an abysmal play!*

abyss *noun* a very deep pit.

academic *adjective* concerned with education and learning. *Academic studies.* **academic** *noun.*

Academics wearing traditional gowns talk outside a college at Oxford University.

academy *noun* a school, college or group that trains or examines a particular field. *The American Academy of Science.*

accelerate *verb* to go faster and faster. **acceleration** *noun.*

accelerator *noun* a pedal that you press with your foot to make a motor vehicle go faster.

accent *noun* (say ak-sent) 1 a way of pronouncing a language in a particular region or country. *An Australian accent.* 2 a mark that is put above or below a letter of the alphabet in some languages to show you how to pronounce it. **accent** *verb* (say ak-sent) to pronounce a syllable in a word with more force. *You accent the second syllable in 'tomato'.*

accentuate *verb* to emphasize or to make more noticeable.

accept *verb* 1 to take something that is offered. 2 to agree to or say yes to something. *I accept your decision.* 3 to believe something to be true. *You must accept that snowboarding is dangerous.* **acceptance** *noun.*

acceptable *adjective* satisfactory. *Your homework is not acceptable.*

access *noun* a way to get into a place. *The access to the castle is over the drawbridge.*

accessible *adjective* easy to approach or to reach.

accessory *noun* 1 an extra part that goes with the main part. 2 somebody who helps to carry out a crime.

accident *noun* an unexpected and usually unpleasant happening, especially one in which people are hurt. *An airplane accident.*

accidental *adjective* by chance and not on purpose. **accidentally** *adverb.*

accommodate *verb* to provide a place for somebody to live. **accommodation** *noun.*

accompany (accompanies, accompanying, accompanied) *verb* 1 to go along with somebody or something. 2 to play a musical instrument while somebody else sings or dances. **accompanist** *noun.*

People must cross a drawbridge to gain access to this fortress.

The accordion is a popular musical instrument in Madeira, Portugal.

accomplice *noun* a person who helps somebody commit a crime.

accomplish *verb* to succeed in completing something. **accomplishment** *noun.*

A student who has accomplished a degree is awarded a certificate.

accomplished *adjective* talented or skillful at something. *An accomplished violinist.*

according to *preposition* 1 as said by or in the opinion of somebody. *According to Jack, the visit has been postponed.* 2 in a suitable way. *You will be paid according to the amount of work that you do.*

accordingly *adverb* therefore, as a result.

accordion *noun* a portable musical instrument that you play by pressing keys and squeezing bellows to force air through reeds. *My cousin played the accordian at the wedding reception.*

account *noun* 1 a description of something. *There was a full account of the accident in the paper.* 2 the money that a person keeps in a bank. *Which bank is your account with?* 3 a bill or a record of money received or owed. **on account of** because of. *She stayed at home on account of the strike.* **by all accounts** according to what other people say.

account *verb* To account for means to give an explanation or reason for something. *How do you account for this broken window?*

accountant *noun* a person whose job it is to take care of money and the accounts of businesses or people.

Accra *noun* the capital of Ghana.

accumulate *verb* to collect things in large quantities or to let things pile up. *Dad has accumulated a pile of magazines over the years.* **accumulation** *noun*.

accurate *adjective* correct and exact. **accuracy** *noun*.

For accurate measurement of time, athletes use a stopwatch.

accuse *verb* to blame and say that somebody has done something wrong. **accusation** *noun*.

accustomed *adjective* used to something. *It will take a little time to get accustomed to your new computer.*

ace *noun* 1 a playing card with a single symbol on it. *The ace of spades.* 2 a person who is very skilled at something. *He was a diving ace.*

ache *noun* a pain that goes on hurting for a long time. **ache** *verb* to hurt. *I'm aching badly all over.*

achieve *verb* to do or finish something successfully, especially after trying hard. **achievement** *noun*.

acid *noun* a chemical substance that can dissolve metals and turn blue litmus paper pink. **acidic** *adjective*.

acid *adjective* a sharp, sour taste. *Lemons have an acid taste.*

acid rain *noun* rain that contains chemicals from factories and cars and that damages plants and rivers.

Trees damaged by acid rain are unable to produce leaves, and so slowly die.

DID YOU KNOW
Some common acronyms are 'laser' (light amplification by stimulated emission of radiation), 'Nato' (North Atlantic Treaty Organization), 'radar' (radio detection and ranging) and 'sonar' (sound navigation ranging).

acknowledge *verb* to admit or agree that something is true. *She acknowledged that she'd been mistaken.* **acknowledgment** *noun*.

acne *noun* a lot of red pimples on the face, especially common in young people.

acorn *noun* the nut or seed of an oak tree.

Acorns are a favorite food of squirrels. They bury them to provide a stock of winter food.

acoustics *plural noun* 1 the science of sound. 2 the effect a room has on the quality of sounds you hear in it. **acoustic** *adjective*. *The acoustics in the auditorium are great.*

acquaintance *noun* 1 a person you know, but not a close friend. 2 a knowledge of something. *I have some acquaintance with the Japanese language.*

acquire *verb* to get something, especially by your own efforts.

acre *noun* an area of land equal to 4,840 square yards or 4,047 square meters.

acrobat *noun* a person who is skilled in doing difficult and exciting gymnastic actions (acrobatics), especially at a circus. **acrobatic** *adjective*.

Trapeze artists are among the most daring of circus acrobats, swinging high over the ring, often without a safety net.

acronym *noun* a word made from the first letter of other words, such as 'scuba' (self-contained underwater breathing apparatus).

acrophobia *noun* a fear of great heights.

across *adverb, preposition* from one side of something to the other. *It measures almost 3 yards across.*

act *verb* 1 to do something. *She acted quickly to rescue the child from the blazing car.* 2 to perform a part in a play or film. **acting** *noun*. 3 to behave. *He's acting strangely.*

act *noun* 1 something that somebody does. *A kind act.* 2 a part of a play. *We left before the last act was over because we were bored.*

action *noun* 1 something that is done. *His fast action prevented the fire from spreading.* 2 a gesture or physical movement. 3 a law suit. 4 a battle. *He was killed in action.* **take action** to do something. **out of action** not working.

active *adjective* busy and full of energy. The opposite of 'active' is 'inactive'.

activity *noun* 1 lively action and movement. *The city is full of activity.* 2 something that people do, for example a hobby or playing games.

actor *noun* a man who performs in plays, in movies or on television.

actress *noun* a woman who performs in plays, in movies or on television.

actually *adverb* really, in fact. *Did you actually talk to the manager?*

acute *adjective* 1 severe and great. *An acute shortage of water.* 2 sharp. *Acute toothache.*

acute accent a sloping symbol placed over a vowel in some languages to show how it is pronounced, e.g. é in café.

acute angle an angle of less than 90°.

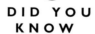

'Acute' also means sharp, and an acute angle has a narrow point.

AD *abbreviation* Anno Domini, the Latin words meaning 'in the year of our Lord', used for all dates after the birth of Jesus Christ.

adamant *adjective* unwilling to change your mind. *He's adamant that he will go.*

AMAZING FACT

Some species of adder, although they are poisonous, are so small that they can only bite humans in very delicate places, such as the skin between the toes or fingers.

The adder has a distinctive zigzag pattern along its back.

These actors are performing on stage against a painted backdrop.

If the address on a letter contains a zipcode, it can get to its destination more quickly.

DID YOU KNOW

By tradition the abbreviation 'AD' is placed before the year number, e.g. AD 2006, whereas 'BC' (standing for Before Christ) follows the year number, e.g. 20 BC.

---

adapt *verb* to change or make something suitable for a new situation or purpose. *We adapted the old garage to make an office.* **adaptable** *adjective.*

adaptor *noun* a device that can connect two or more electrical plugs to one socket.

add *verb* to put two or more things together. *If you add four and three you get seven.* **addition** *noun.* The opposite of 'add' is 'subtract'.

adder *noun* a small snake, also sometimes known as a viper.

addict *noun* somebody who likes or needs something (especially harmful drugs) so much that they cannot give it up.

addiction *noun* something that people find it hard to do without, especially harmful drugs. **addictive** *adjective.*

Addis Ababa *noun* the capital of Ethiopia.

additional *adjective* extra, more than usual. *It was so cold she put on an extra sweater.*

address *noun* the name of the house, street and town where somebody lives. **address** *verb* to write an address on an envelope, package etc.

adenoids *plural noun* soft lumps of flesh at the back of your nose, which sometimes swell and make it difficult to breathe.

adequate *adjective* just enough, suitable. *Adequate food supplies.*

adhere *verb* to stick. *Please adhere strictly to the rules.*

adhesive *noun* a substance, like glue, that sticks things together. **adhesive** *adjective* sticky. *Adhesive tape.*

adjacent *adjective* very close or next to. *The playground is adjacent to the school.*

The settlers built their wooden homes adjacent to each other.

adjective *noun* a word that tells us something about nouns. In the phrase 'big, brown bear' the words 'big' and 'brown' are adjectives that describe the noun 'bear'.

adjust *verb* to arrange or change something slightly so as to improve it. *She adjusted the curtains.* **adjustment** *noun.*

administer *verb* 1 to be in charge of and manage. *She administers the company's finances.* 2 to give out. *The nurse who was on duty always administered the medicine at the correct time.*

administration *noun* 1 the management of a company etc. 2 the government of a country. *The Democratic administration.* **administrate** *verb* to admininster.

admirable *adjective* very good and worthy of being admired. *An admirable achievement.*

admiral *noun* a very senior officer in the navy.

Admiral Lord Nelson was the hero of the Battle of Trafalgar.

admire *verb* 1 to like and to think somebody or something is very good, to respect. *They admired him for his courage.* 2 to look at something with pleasure. *We admired the view.* **admiration** *noun.*

This boat has broken free of its moorings and is adrift near dangerous rocks.

admission *noun* 1 permission to enter somewhere. *Admission is by invitation only.* 2 the price charged to enter a place. *Admission is free.* 3 a statement that something is true. *She was guilty by her own admission.*

Tickets give admission to the National Theater.

admit (admits, admitting, admitted) *verb* 1 to agree or say that something is true. *They admitted they were wrong.* 2 to let somebody enter.

adobe *noun* 1 a clay brick hardened in the Sun. 2 a building made of such brick.

adolescent *noun* a young person who is changing from a child to an adult. **adolescence** *noun.*

adopt *verb* to take somebody's child into your home and make it legally your own son or daughter. **adoption** *noun.*

adore *verb* to love and admire somebody very much. **adoration** *noun.*

adorn *verb* to decorate something to make it look pretty.

adrift *adverb* floating and drifting without being secured. *The sailboat was adrift.*

adult *noun* a grown-up person or animal. **adult** *adjective* grown-up. **adulthood** *noun.*

adulterate *verb* to spoil something by adding to it something that is less good or harmful. **adulteration** *noun.*

advance *verb* 1 to move forward. *The army advanced towards the enemy.* **advance** *noun.* 2 to suggest an idea. *The detective advanced a new theory.*

advance *noun* 1 progress. *Medicine has made great advances.* 2 a loan of money. **in advance** before a certain date.

advantage *noun* something that helps you to succeed and perhaps do better than others. *It's a great advantage to be able to speak Japanese.* **take advantage of** to make use of a person or situation to help yourself.

advent *noun* 1 the beginning or arrival of something. *The advent of television.* 2 the four weeks before Christmas in the Christian Church.

adventure *noun* a happening that is exciting and perhaps dangerous. **adventurous** *adjective. She led an adventurous life in Africa.*

The South Pole was first reached by a Norwegian, Roald Amundsen, in 1911. The expedition was the greatest adventure of his life.

adverb *noun* a word that tells us more about a verb, an adjective or another adverb. In the sentence 'My grandmother talks very quickly,' the words 'very' and 'quickly' are adverbs.

advertise *verb* to tell people in a newspaper, on television etc. about something that is for sale.

advertisement *noun* a notice in a newspaper, on a billboard, on television etc. that advertises something.

advice *noun* a helpful suggestion made to somebody about what they should do.

A television mast or aerial placed on high ground ensures good reception for viewers in the surrounding area.

advisable *adjective* sensible and worth doing. *It's advisable to go to bed early on school nights.*

advise *verb* to recommend and tell somebody what you think they ought to do. *The dentist advised me to brush my teeth twice a day.* **adviser** *noun.*

aerial *noun* a device such as a metal rod or wire that transmits or receives radio or television signals.

aerobics *plural noun* energetic physical exercises performed to music.

aerodynamics *plural noun* the science of objects moving through the air. **aerodynamic** *adjective.*

The aerodynamic shape of the Bullet train enables it to reach an average speed of 100 mph.

aeronautics *plural noun* the science of designing and building aircraft.

aerospace *adjective* involving the design and building of aircraft and space vehicles. *My dad works in the aerospace industry.*

aerosol *noun* a container that holds a liquid such as paint under pressure and lets it out as a fine spray.

affair *noun* 1 an event. *A barbecue is usually an informal affair.* 2 a relationship between two people, usually temporary. *A passionate love affair.*

affairs *plural noun* business and things that have to be done.

affect *verb* to influence or to cause a change in something. *The cold weather affects her health really badly.*

affected *adjective* pretended, not natural or sincere. *An affected smile.*

affection *noun* a feeling of love for somebody. **affectionate** *adjective*.

affluent *adjective* wealthy. **affluence** *noun*.

afford *verb* to have enough money to buy something.

afforestation *noun* the covering of land with forest. The opposite of 'afforestation' is 'deforestation'.

Afghanistan *noun* a country in central Asia.

afloat *adjective, adverb* floating on water or another liquid.

afraid *adjective* 1 frightened. *Are you afraid of the dark?* 2 apologetic. *I'm afraid you'll have to wait outside.*

Africa *noun* one of the Earth's seven continents.

Africa is a vast continent with deserts, high mountains, lush rainforests and grassy plains.

African *noun* a person who comes from Africa. **African** *adjective*. *An African landscape.*

aft *adverb* towards the back or stern of a ship or an aircraft. *The captain went aft.*

Aft

The plan shows the two flagpoles at the aft of the boat.

after *preposition* 1 later. *Come over after school.* 2 following behind. *The puppy ran after her.* **after** *adverb* later. *I met her the day after.*

SPELLING NOTE

'Agenda' is a noun with a Latin plural ending (the singular form is 'agendum'). However, it is used as a singular noun. 'What's on the agenda for today?'

---

afternoon *noun* the part of the day between noon and the evening.

afterwards *adverb* later. *We swam first and had breakfast afterwards.*

again *adverb* once more. *Please sing it again.*

against *preposition* 1 touching or next to something. *She propped the ladder against the wall.* 2 opposed to *They are against all hunting.* 3 in opposition to. *Which team are you playing against tomorrow?*

agate *noun* a semi-precious stone striped with different colors.

age *noun* 1 the length of time that somebody has lived or that something has existed. *What age are you?* 2 a length of time in history. *The Iron Age.* **age** *verb* to become old.

This flint was used as a tool during the Iron Age.

aged *adjective* 1 (say **ay**-jid) very old. *An aged witch.* 2 (rhymes with 'paged') having a certain age. *A woman aged 50.*

ageism *noun* unfair treatment of somebody because of their age.

ageless *adjective* showing no signs of getting old.

agenda *noun* a list of things that are to be discussed at a meeting.

agent *noun* 1 a person who organizes things and does business for other people. *A travel agent.* 2 a spy.

The secret agent has a glamorous image thanks to fictional characters like James Bond.

aggression *noun* forcefulness, or an attack without being provoked.

aggressive *adjective* violent and likely to attack people. *An aggressive dog.* **aggressor** *noun.*

agile *adjective* nimble. Moving quickly and easily. **agility** *noun.*

The ballet dancer displayed astonishing agility.

agitate *verb* 1 to make somebody nervous or worried. *She was agitated because she was late.* 2 to campaign or argue strongly for something. *They agitated for bigger salaries.* **agitator** *noun.*

agitation *noun* 1 a strong feeling of worry. 2 a campaign or protest.

ago *adverb* in the past. *Napoleon lived many years ago.*

agonizing *adjective* very painful.

agony *noun* great pain or suffering.

agoraphobia *noun* (say agra-**foh**-bee-uh) a great fear of open spaces.

agree *verb* 1 to say 'yes' to something. *Angela agreed to babysit.* 2 to share the same ideas or opinions about something. *We all agree that cruelty is wrong.* **agree with** to be good for or to suit. *Spicy food doesn't agree with him.*

agreeable *adjective* pleasant. *An agreeable evening.* The opposite of 'agreeable' is 'disagreeable'.

agreement *noun* a promise or an understanding between two or more people, countries etc.

agriculture *noun* farming. **agricultural** *adjective.*

DID YOU KNOW

Do not use 'ago' with 'since' – you should use either one or the other. 'It's years since I last went to Greece,' or 'It was years ago that I last went to Greece.'

Agriculture began when humans realized that sowing seeds would yield food crops. They settled to farm because it was more efficient than gathering food. Agriculture has shaped our land – not always for the better.

aground *adverb* If a boat runs aground, it touches the bottom of the sea or lake and cannot move.

ahead *adverb* 1 in front of. *She walked ahead.* 2 in the future. *Plan ahead.*

aid *verb* to help. **aid** *noun* 1 help or support, something that helps you do something. *He walks with the aid of a cane.* 2 money, food etc. for people in need.

Aids *noun* (short for or an acronym for acquired immune deficiency syndrome) a serious illness that destroys the body's natural defenses (immunity) against disease and infection.

ailment *noun* an illness that is not very serious.

aim *verb* 1 to point at something, especially with a weapon. *He aimed the gun at the target.* 2 to plan or try to do something. *Alan aims to be the finest athlete in his school.* **aim** *noun* line of sighting. *He took aim.*

An archer takes careful aim. He fires arrows that are stored in a quiver belted to his waist.

aimless *adjective* without any purpose. *An aimless existence.*

air *noun* 1 the invisible mixture of gases that surrounds us and which we breathe. 2 general appearance or impression. *You have an air of calm about you.* 3 a tune. *The Londonderry Air.*

air-conditioning *noun* a system of controlling a building's temperature and keeping it cool in summer. **air-conditioner** *noun.* **air-conditioned** *adjective.*

aircraft any machine that flies, such as an airplane, glider or helicopter.

aircraft carrier *noun* a warship with a large deck from which aircraft can take off and land.

airfield *noun* a place where aircraft take off and land.

A plane lifts off the runway at an airfield. In the background are the airport buildings, including the control tower.

airforce *noun* the part of a country's forces that uses aircraft for fighting.

airline *noun* a company that owns aircraft and provides a regular service.

airplane *noun* a machine with wings that flies through the air carrying passengers or freight, driven by one or more engines.

airport *noun* a place you leave from or arrive at when traveling by airplane.

airscrew *noun* an aircraft's propeller.

airtight *adjective* tightly sealed so that no air can get in or out. *Food can be preserved in airtight containers.*

airy (airier, airiest) *adjective* full of fresh air. *A large, airy room.*

The window is open, so a breeze can blow in, making the room cool and airy.

aisle *noun* (rhymes with 'pile') 1 a narrow passage where you can walk between rows of seats in an airplane, theater etc., or rows of shelves in a supermarket.

> **AMAZING FACT**
>
> HMS Hermes, which was completed in 1913, was the first purpose-designed aircraft carrier.

> **WORD HISTORY**
>
> *'Alcohol' is one of a number of words that we have taken from Arabic. Others include 'algebra', 'assassin' and 'sofa'.*

---

ajar *adverb, adjective* When a door or window is slightly open, it is ajar.

alarm *verb* to make somebody suddenly afraid or anxious that something bad will happen. *They were alarmed to see smoke pouring out of their house.*

alarm *noun* 1 a sudden fear or danger. 2 a bell, buzzer etc. that warns people of danger. *A fire alarm.*

Albania *noun* a country in southeastern Europe.

The Albanian flag shows a black eagle against a red ground.

Albanian *noun* a person who comes from Albania. **Albanian** *adjective*. *Albanian wine.*

albatross (albatrosses) *noun* a large white seabird with long wings.

album *noun* 1 a blank book in which to keep photographs, stamps etc. 2 a CD or tape or record with a collection of songs.

Keeping a photograph album is a good way to record your family's history.

alchemy *noun* (say al-kem-ee) the medieval science of trying to turn metals into gold. **alchemist** *noun*.

alcohol *noun* 1 a colorless chemical liquid that catches fire quickly. 2 drinks such as beer, whisky and wine that contain alcohol and which can make people drunk.

alcoholic *adjective* containing alcohol. *alcoholic drink*. **alcoholic** *noun* a person who is addicted to alcohol and cannot stop drinking it.

alcove *noun* a recess or a small part of a room with the wall set back.

ale *noun* a kind of beer.

alert *verb* to warn people of a possible danger. *The doctor alerted her to the danger of eating too much.*

alert *adjective* quick-thinking and watchful of what is going on. **on the alert** ready for any possible danger.

algae *noun* (say al-gee) water plants such as seaweed that have no root or stem.

algebra *noun* a branch of mathematics that uses symbols and letters to represent numbers. $3X + Y = 10$ is an example of an algebraic equation.

Algeria *noun* a country in Africa.

The Algerian flag shows a red star and crescent moon against a green and white ground.

Algiers *noun* the capital of Algeria.

alias *noun* (say ail-ee-uss) a false or pretended name. **alias** *adverb* also known as. *Ron Chalky, alias Ronald White.*

alibi *noun* (say al-i-beye) a proof or claim that a person charged with a crime was somewhere else when it was committed.

alien *noun* 1 a foreigner or stranger. 2 a creature from space. **alien** *adjective. An alien being.*

It's difficult to imagine what an alien creature from outer space might look like....

alight *adjective* on fire, burning.

alike *adjective* similar. *The brothers are very alike.* **alike** *adverb* equally. *She treats them all alike.*

alive *adjective* living, not dead. **alive** *adverb* full of life.

alkali (alkalis) *noun* a chemical substance that can turn pink litmus paper blue. It reacts with acid to form a salt.

SPELLING NOTE

'Allege' is a word that is often misspelt. People often put '–edge' at the end instead of just '–ege'.

Some people suffer from allergies that cause them difficulty in breathing. They can often get relief by using an inhaler to breathe in a fine spray of medicine.

all *adjective* the whole amount or number. *All babies sleep a lot.* **all** *adverb* completely. *He was dressed all in black.* **all along** all the time. **all at once** 1 suddenly. *All at once the house shook.* 2 all at the same time. *Try not to spend it all at once.* **after all** all things considered. *After all he is a criminal.*

Allah *noun* the name given to God in the Islamic religion.

allege *verb* (say al-edge) to say that something is true or that somebody has done something, usually without having any proof. **allegation** (say al-eg-ay-shun) *noun.*

allergy *noun* an illness caused by substances such as dust, fur or certain foods, which do not normally make people ill. **allergic** *adjective* reacting badly to. *Andy is really allergic to eggs.*

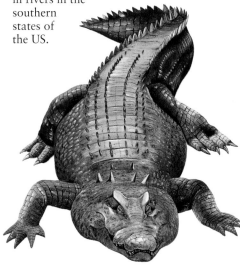

alley (alleys) *noun* a very narrow street or a lane that passes behind houses. **a blind alley** a situation without a way out.

alliance *noun* a union or friendly agreement between two or more different countries, political parties etc.

alligator *noun* a large reptile with a long body and tail, sharp teeth and strong jaws. Alligators are similar to crocodiles and live in rivers in the southern states of the US.

You can tell an alligator from a crocodile, because when an alligator shuts its mouth, the fourth pair of teeth on the lower jaw disappears into pits in the upper jaw. A crocodile's teeth stick out when its mouth is shut!

alliteration *noun* the repetition of the same sound at the beginning of each word in a phrase or sentence. *The Sun sank slowly.*

allocate *verb* to share out or to set aside something for a particular purpose. *The charity allocated $1,000 for the children's home.* **allocation** *noun.*

allow *verb* to permit or let somebody do something. *Nobody is allowed to smoke in the library.*

allowance *noun* a fixed amount of money that is paid to somebody regularly. *I only get an allowance if I do all my chores.* **make allowances for** to take someone's circumstances into account.

alloy (alloys) *noun* a metal made from mixing other metals. **alloy** *verb* to mix metals together.

Some knives and forks are made of alloy.

all right *adjective* If you are all right, you are not ill, hurt or in difficulties. **all right** *interjection* a phrase you can say when you agree to something. *'Will you do the dishes?' 'Oh, all right.'*

allude *verb* to talk about something in an indirect way or to mention it in passing. **allusion** *noun.*

alluring *adjective* very attractive, appealing and charming.

alluvium *noun* fertile soil washed down by rivers and floods.

ally *noun* (say al-eye) a country or person that helps and supports another. *America, France and Great Britain were allies in World War II.*

almanac *noun* a kind of calendar or book with information about the movements of the Moon and stars.

Almaty *noun* the capital of Kazakhstan.

almond *noun* the oval nut that grows on the almond tree.

Almonds are a nutritious source of food.

AMAZING FACT

Alliteration is a powerful poetic device but many of familiar phrases and cliches are also examples of alliteration.

For example:
She's 'cool as a cucumber'.
He's 'fit as a fiddle'.

WORD HISTORY
The word 'alphabet' comes from the first two letters of the Greek alphabet, 'alpha' and 'beta'.

Our alphabet has 26 letters.

SPELLING NOTE
Don't confuse 'already' with 'all ready' – 'Are you all ready to go?'

almost *adjective* nearly but not quite. *Ben is almost as tall as Amy.*

alone *adjective, adverb* with no other people, by yourself.

along *preposition, adverb* 1 from one end to the other. *They drove along the road.* 2 in the company of. *He brought his sister along.*

alongside *preposition, adverb* next to and by the side of. *He put the bench alongside the pool.*

aloud *adverb* in a voice loud enough to be heard. *Archie read the letter aloud.*

The teacher is reading aloud from a storybook to a group of children.

alphabet *noun* all the letters we use to write words, arranged in order. *Our alphabet begins with A and ends with Z.*

Aa Bb Cc Dd Ee
Ff Gg Hh Ii Jj
Kk Ll Mm Nn
Oo Pp Qq Rr Ss
Tt Uu Vv Ww
Xx Yy Zz

alphabetical *adjective* in order according to the alphabet. *The words in this dictionary are arranged in alphabetical order.*

alphabetize *verb* to put words in the order of the alphabet.

already *adverb* before this time. *I've already had lunch.*

alsatian *noun* a large wolf-like breed of dog, also called a German Shepherd, often used as a guard dog and by the police.

also *adverb* as well, too. *He can play and also sing, but not very well.*

altar *noun* a table used for religious ceremonies in a church or temple.

A cross and two candlesticks stand on the altar.

alter *verb* to change or to become different. *The plans have been altered slightly.*

alternate *verb* (say **awl**-ter-nate) to happen by turn or to change first one way and then the other. *Barbara alternates between being happy and sad.* **alternate** *adjective* (say awl-ter-nat) *Alternate weeks of good weather and bad weather.* **alternately** *adverb*.

alternative *noun* 1 a choice between two or more things or possibilities. *The alternative to flying is to travel by train.* 2 different from what is usual. *Alternative medicine can involve taking herbs to cure illness.*

although *conjunction* even if, in spite of the fact. *Although it was snowing, we drove through the mountains.*

altitude *noun* the height above sea level.

altogether *adverb* 1 completely. *Are you altogether pleased with the plan?* 2 counting everybody or everything. *There are eight of us altogether.*

aluminum *noun* a lightweight silver-colored metal.

Because aluminum is a very lightweight metal, it is often used in building planes.

always *adverb* something that always happens, happens all the time or very often. *Sally is always smiling.*

> **SPELLING NOTE**
>
> *Try not to confuse 'alternate' with 'alternative'.*

Amateur dramatics can be fun for anyone who likes dressing up.

> **SPELLING NOTE**
>
> *Try not to confuse 'altogether' with 'all together'. 'The puppies sat all together in a line. It was altogether an amusing sight.'*

a.m. *abbreviation* the initial letters of the Latin words 'ante meridiem', which mean before noon. *7 a.m. is 7 o'clock in the morning.*

amalgam *noun* a mixture of metals. *Dentists use an amalgam of mercury and silver to fill teeth.*

amalgamate *verb* to combine to make something bigger. *The two companies have amalgamated.* **amalgamation** *noun*.

amateur *noun* a person who does something such as paint or play games just for pleasure and not for payment. **amateur** *adjective*. *Amateur dramatics.*

amateurish *adjective* not professional or skillful. *Debbie turned in a very amateurish design job.*

amaze *verb* to surprise or astonish somebody very much. **amazement** *noun*. *We watched the bungee jumping with fear and amazement.*

amazing *adjective* surprising. *What amazing tricks!*

ambassador *noun* an important official who represents his or her country abroad.

amber *noun* a hard yellowish-red fossil substance that you can see through, used in making jewellery. 2 the yellowish-red color of amber.

Sometimes you can be lucky enough to find pieces of amber on the beach.

ambi- *prefix* meaning 'both'. **ambidextrous** able to use both hands equally well.

ambiguous *adjective* not clear, having more than one possible meaning. 'They are eating apples' is an ambiguous sentence. It could mean 'the apples are for eating', or 'those people are eating apples.' **ambiguity** *noun* of uncertain meaning.

ambition *noun* a very strong wish to do something well or to have success and fame. *Her burning ambition is to be a vet.* **ambitious** *adjective*.

amble *verb* to walk slowly. **amble** *noun*.

ambulance *noun* a vehicle for carrying people who are sick or injured.

You can often recognize an ambulance by a red cross on a white background.

ambush *verb* to wait in hiding in order to attack somebody by surprise. **ambush** *noun*.

amend *verb* to change or correct something slightly in order to improve it. *Some laws are out of date and need to be amended.* **amendment** *noun*.

American *noun* a person who comes from the United States. **American** *adjective* belonging to the United States.

amiable *adjective* pleasant and friendly. **amiably** *adverb*.

Amman *noun* the capital of Jordan.

ammonia *noun* a strong-smelling gas that dissolves in water.

ammonite *noun* a fossilized shell shaped like a flat coil.

Ammonites were molluscs, related to squid. This is a fossilized ammonite.

DID YOU KNOW

The preposition 'among' or 'amongst' is used when talking about more than two people: 'The teacher handed the books among the pupils.' Use 'between' when talking of two people. 'The twins shared the candy between them.'

Frogs are amphibians. This is the poison arrow frog that lives in South American rainforests. The bright colors warn predators that they are poisonous and should be left alone.

ammunition *noun* things such as bullets and shells that can be fired from a gun or other weapon.

amnesia *noun* loss of memory.

amnesty *noun* a general pardon given by the state to, usually political, prisoners.

amoeba *noun* a microscopic, one-celled animal that moves around by constantly changing its shape.

Amoeba live in fresh water or soil.

among or **amongst** *preposition* 1 in the middle of, surrounded by. *She lived among the islanders.* 2 one of. *Canada is among the biggest countries in the world.* 3 between. *We shared the work among all of us.*

amount *noun* the quantity of something, or how much there is. *A large amount of money was spent on remodeling the palace.*

amount *verb*. to add up to or be equal to. *The bill amounts to $50.*

ampersand *noun* the sign '&' that means 'and'.

amphibian *noun* an animal that lives mainly on land and breathes air but breeds in water. Frogs and newts are amphibians. **amphibious** *adjective*.

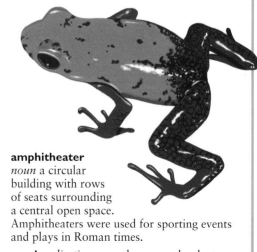

amphitheater *noun* a circular building with rows of seats surrounding a central open space. Amphitheaters were used for sporting events and plays in Roman times.

ample *adjective* more than enough, plenty. *The car has ample room for five passengers.*

amplifier *noun* an electrical device for making sounds louder.

Small electrical signals from the pickup of a record player are strengthened in the amplifier before being passed to the loudspeaker.

amplify (amplifies, amplifying, amplified) *verb* to make louder. **amplification** *noun*.

amputate *verb* to cut off a limb because it is diseased or badly broken. *He had his leg amputated in the war.* **amputation** *noun*.

amputee *noun* a person who has had a limb amputated.

Amsterdam *noun* the capital of the Netherlands.

amuse *verb* to make somebody laugh or smile or to keep them happy and busy. *They amused themselves by drawing, reading and listening to records.*

amusement *noun* 1 the feeling of being amused. 2 something that gives enjoyment or entertainment.

WORD HISTORY

The word 'anemia' comes from Greek words for 'no' ('an') and 'blood'. 'Anesthetic' comes from the Greek for 'no' and 'feeling', and 'anarchy' from the words 'no' and 'ruler'.

DID YOU KNOW

Coats of arms of the Middle Ages gave a lot of information about each person. A woman's 'arms' said whether she was married or not.

Amsterdam is a city of fine old buildings and many canals.

In the Middle Ages a knight's shield displayed his coat of arms and stated something about his ancestry.

---

amusing *adjective* something that is funny. *The museum guide told us an amusing story about the families that used to live in the house.*

anagram *noun* a word made by changing all the letters of another word. 'Horse' is an anagram of 'shore'.

analyst *noun* a person who analyses something. *The financial analysts predict an increase in public spending.*

analytical *adjective* using methods or techniques that help you examine things closely and carefully. *She has a very analytical approach to problems. We used analytic methods in all our research.*

analyze *verb* to examine something in great detail, often to find what it is made of. *She analyzed the water and found that it was polluted.* **analysis** *noun*.

anarchist *noun* a person who believes there should be no government and no laws.

anarchy *noun* disorder and lack of control by the government.

anatomy *noun* 1 the structure of the body of an animal or person. 2 the study of the structure of the body of living things.

This cutaway drawing shows the anatomy of the arm.

ancestor *noun* Your ancestors are members of your family who lived before you. **ancestral** *adjective*.

ancestry *noun* all your ancestors, the people you are descended from. *Many Canadians have Scottish ancestry.*

anchor *noun* a heavy metal hook that is lowered on a long chain from a boat to lodge in the seabed and stop the boat from moving. *They threw the anchor overboard.*

ancient *adjective* (say **ane**-shunt) 1 very old. *Ancient ruins.* 2 of a time long ago. *Ancient Rome was the center of a great empire.*

The arrangement of the seats and the cages for the wild animals in the Coliseum can tell us a lot about life in ancient Rome, where visiting the amphitheatre was a popular entertainment.

Andorra *noun* a small country in Europe.

Andorra la Vella *noun* the capital of Andorra.

anecdote *noun* a very short, amusing story.

anemia *noun* (say a-**neem**-ya) a shortage of red cells in the blood. **anemic** *adjective*.

anesthetic *noun* (say an-iss-**thet**-ik) a drug given to stop patients feeling pain. **anesthetize** *verb*.

An angel descended from heaven and appeared to the shepherds.

angel *noun* 1 a heavenly spirit . 2 a very kind person. **angelic** *adjective*.

anger *noun* a strong feeling of being very displeased with someone.

angle *noun* a corner, the space between two straight lines that meet.

Angola *noun* a country in Africa.

The civil war in Angola has left a great many children orphaned.

angry (angrier, angriest) *adjective* annoyed and feeling full of anger. *I'm very angry with her for being so late.* **angrily** *adverb*.

anguish *noun* a very great feeling of sorrow or pain. **anguished** *adjective*.

animal *noun* 1 any living creature that is not a plant. 2 all mammals except human beings. **animal kingdom** one of the three basic groups into which all things in nature are divided. The other two are the mineral kingdom and the plant kingdom.

animate *adjective* (say **anny**-mut) alive. Animals and plants are animate. The opposite is 'inanimate'. Stones and metals are inanimate.

animation *noun* a kind of film, e.g. a cartoon in which photographs or a series of drawings of people and things are shown in quick succession and appear to move.

These three pictures form part of an animation sequence.

DID YOU KNOW

You are usually 'angry' or 'annoyed' with somebody, but you are 'angry' or 'annoyed' at or about something.

AMAZING FACT

Wedding anniversaries have different materials connected to them. The first anniversary is cotton, the fifth is wood and the twentieth is china.

Ankara *noun* the capital of Turkey.

ankle *noun* the joint that connects your leg to your foot.

annexation *noun* the act of annexing a territory or of taking possession of it. *The annexation of Poland.*

annex *noun* an additional building joined on to or near the main building. **annex** *verb* to seize or take possession of.

annihilate *verb* to destroy completely. *The volcano annihilated all the farms for miles around.* **annihilation** *noun*.

anniversary *noun* a day each year when you remember something special that happened on the same day in a previous year. *A wedding anniversary.*

announce *verb* to make known publicly something important. *The king announced his abdication over the radio.* **announcement** *noun*.

announcer *noun* a person who makes an announcement. *A radio announcer.*

annoy *verb* to irritate or make somebody angry. **annoyance** *adjective*.

annual *adjective* happening every year or once a year. *Annual medical check-up.* **annual** *noun* 1 a plant that lives for one year only. 2 a book or magazine that appears once a year. **annually** *adverb*.

anoint *verb* to put oil on somebody, usually as part of a religious ceremony.

anonymous *adjective* without the name being known or given. *The charity received a huge donation from an anonymous donor.* **anonymity** *noun*.

anorexia *noun* an illness that makes the sufferer afraid of becoming fat and so not want to eat anything. **anorexic** *adjective*.

another *adjective* 1 one more *He had another helping of everything on the table.* 2 different. *Can you find me this dress in another color?*

He already had one piece of candy but his friend gave him another.

answer *verb* 1 to speak or write in reply to a question or to something that somebody has said. *'Where are you going?' 'To the stables,' she answered.* 2 to respond to a signal etc. *'Can you answer the phone?'*

answer *noun* 1 reply. *Have you had an answer to your letter?* 2 a solution. *I can't find the answer to this problem.* **answer back** to give a rude reply to somebody.

answerable *adjective* responsible for.

A birthday is an annual event. Most people are given presents on their birthday.

Antelopes are fast running animals that live in South Africa's grassy savanna.

answering machine *noun* a machine that records telephone messages from people who call you when you are out.

ant *noun* a small sociable insect that lives with other ants in an underground colony. **anthill** *noun* a heap of earth made by ants above their nest.

Ants are industrious creatures that work as a team.

antagonist *noun* an enemy or opponent.

antagonize *verb* to make somebody angry, unfriendly or hostile to you. **antagonism** *noun*. **antagonistic** *adjective*.

Antananarivo *noun* the capital of Madagascar.

Antarctic *noun* the area around the South Pole. **Antarctic** *adjective*. *An Antarctic expedition with sleds and husky dogs.*

Antarctica *noun* one of the Earth's seven continents, situated at the South Pole.

ante- *prefix* before. 'Antenuptial' means before marriage and 'antenatal' means before birth.

anteater *noun* a toothless mammal from South America that uses its long snout and long sticky tongue to catch ants and other insects on which it feeds.

antelope *noun* any one of several kinds of deer-like animals of Africa and Asia. They include gazelles, impala and springboks.

antenna (antennae) *noun* 1 one of the feelers on an insect's head. 2 an aerial.

anthem *noun* a hymn or a song written for special occasions. *'The Star-Spangled Banner' is the US national anthem.*

anther *noun* part of a flower's stamen where pollen matures.

anthology *noun* a collection of poems, stories etc.

anthropology *noun* the study of human beings, especially their customs and beliefs.

anti- *prefix* against, opposed to, opposite. *Anti-Communist demonstrations.*

antibiotic *noun* a powerful medicine that kills harmful bacteria that cause diseases.

AMAZING FACT

In 1928, Alexander Fleming dicovered that penicillin could kill harmful germs. It was first used extensively in WWII on soldiers with serious wounds and saved many lives.

It is important not to take antibiotics too often, or the body will get immune to them.

anticipate *verb* to look forward to or expect something to happen. *We anticipated that these books would sell well, so we stocked up.* **anticipation** *noun.*

anticyclone *noun* air moving away from an area of high pressure, usually bringing calm weather. The opposite of 'anticyclone' is 'cyclone'.

antidote *noun* a medicine that acts against the harmful effects of poison. *We were lucky that the hospital had some of the antidote in stock.*

antifreeze *noun* a chemical that you put in a car's radiator to stop the water freezing. *It gets so cold in the fall that you have to put antifreeze in your car in October.*

Antigua and Barbuda *noun* a country in the West Indies.

The colorful flag of Antigua and Barbuda shows that the Sun and the sea are part of everyday life.

antiquated *adjective* old and out of date. *The new principal was amazed at the antiquated rules when he got to the school.*

DID YOU KNOW

The opposite of 'antique' is 'modern'. Another word meaning old is 'antiquated', but whereas 'antique' is old and valuable, 'antiquated' is old and almost laughably useless.

antique *noun* something that is old and also very valuable. **antique** *adjective* valuable, old. *Antique furniture.*

Valuable antiques, like this chest of drawers, are often passed down through generation after generation.

antiquity *noun* ancient times, especially the times of Ancient Greece and Rome.

antiseptic *noun* a substance that kills harmful germs and prevents infection and disease. **antiseptic** *adjective* clean and germ-killing. *Antiseptic soap.*

antler *noun* one of the branching horns on a deer's head.

During the mating season, stags fight by locking antlers until one brings the other to its knees.

antonym *noun* a word that has the opposite meaning to another word. 'Hot' is the antonym of 'cold'.

anus *noun* the opening at the end of the bowels through which solid food waste leaves the body.

anxious *adjective* 1 worried, concerned. **anxiety** *noun.* 2 eager. *Annie is extremely anxious to help.*

any *adjective* 1 one of. *Take any one you want.* 2 some. *Is there any cake left?* 3 at all. *Are you any happier?* 4 every. *Any athlete could jump that.* (**anybody anyhow anyone anything anytime anyway anywhere**).

apart *adverb* 1 separate and at a distance away from each other. *The two villages are about a mile apart.* 2 into parts or pieces. *Andrea took her bike apart.* **apart from** except for. *Apart from a few showers the weather is lovely.*

apartment *noun* a place to live, usually rooms in a large building.

apathy *noun* a lack of interest or feeling.

ape *noun* an animal like a monkey but with no tail. Gorillas and chimpanzees are apes.

Gorillas are apes that live in the rainforests of West and Central Africa.

ape (apes, aping, aped) *verb* to imitate how somebody behaves, usually in a silly way.

aperture *noun* a small hole or opening.

apex (apexes) *noun* the highest point.

aphid or **aphis** *noun* a tiny insect that damages or kills plants by sucking juices from them.

Apia *noun* the capital of Samoa.

apologize *verb* to say that you are sorry for doing something. *We apologized sincerely for causing so much trouble.* **apology** *noun.* **apologetic** *adjective.*

apostle *noun* one of the original twelve disciples or followers of Christ.

The apostles listened to Christ's teachings and spread the Christian message after his death.

apostrophe *noun* (say a-**poss**-tra-fee) a punctuation mark (') that shows that letters have been left out of a word (*we've* for *we have*) or to show the ownership of something (*Margaret's pencil*).

appall (appalls, appalling, appalled) *verb* to cause horror or shock. *I was appalled by the chairman's rude and unkind remarks.* **appalling** *adjective.*

apparatus *noun* the tools or equipment needed for a particular purpose.

DID YOU KNOW

Apostrophes are often used – for clarity – to form the plural of a number of short words, e.g. do's and dont's, but dos and donts are acceptable too.

Inflammation of the appendix is common. The usual treatment is to remove the appendix by surgery.

apparent *adjective* 1 obvious and easily seen. *It was quite apparent that she was bored.* 2 seeming to be true or real.

apparition *noun* a ghost or something that you think you have seen.

appeal *verb* 1 to ask for something urgently and seriously. *They appealed for help for the orphans.* 2 to be interesting or attractive. *The plan doesn't appeal to me at all.* **appealing** *adjective.* 3 to ask for a legal decision to be changed by going to a higher court. **appeal** *noun.*

appear *verb* 1 to come into view. *He suddenly appeared from behind the wall.* 2 to seem. *They appear to be quite happy.* 3 to take part in. *Actors appear in films and plays.*

appearance *noun* 1 the act of coming into view. *The sudden appearance of the bull frightened everybody.* 2 the way somebody or something looks.

appendicitis *noun* painful inflammation of the appendix.

appendix (appendixes or appendices) *noun* 1 a small tube inside the body at the end of the intestines. 2 additional information after the main text at the end of a book.

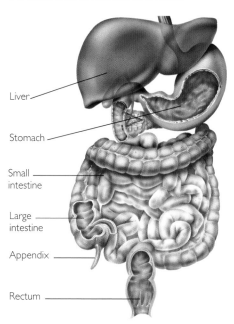

Liver

Stomach

Small intestine

Large intestine

Appendix

Rectum

appetite *noun* 1 hunger or a desire for food. 2 a desire or enthusiasm.

appetizing *adjective* smelling and looking so good that you want to eat it.

applaud *verb* to show that you like something by clapping your hands. **applause** *noun.*

apple *noun* the hard, round fruit of the apple tree. **in apple pie order** in perfect order.

The Golden Delicious is the most popular apple in the world.

appliance *noun* a tool or piece of equipment designed to do a specific job, especially in the home, such as a vacuum cleaner.

The steam iron is one of the most commonly owned electrical appliances.

applicant *noun* a person who applies or asks for something. *There were lots of applicants for the job.*

apply (applies, applying, applied) *verb* 1 to ask for something formally. *She applied for the job of editor.* 2 to be relevant or suitable to a person or situation. *These rules apply to everyone.* 3 to spread on. *She applied the ointment to the cut.* **application** *noun*.

appoint *verb* to choose somebody to do a job. *Mrs Bartholomew has been appointed chief accountant.*

appointment *noun* 1 a time and place that you have arranged to see somebody. 2 a job.

appreciate *verb* 1 to know about and understand the value or good points of something. *She appreciates good food.* 2 to be grateful for something. *I appreciate all the valuable help you've given me.* 3 to rise in value. *House prices have appreciated.* **appreciation** *noun*.

appreciative *adjective* showing gratitude.

approach *verb* 1 to come nearer. *She approached the stray dog.* 2 to speak to somebody about a request or an offer. *Dean approached his uncle to ask for some money to buy a new car.*

approach *noun* 1 a road or path leading somewhere. 2 the course followed by an airplane before landing.

WORD HISTORY

Like all the months of the year, 'April' comes from a Latin word. It is named after 'Aprilis', meaning to open. April was the second month in the early Roman calendar.

Write your appointments down to help you remember them.

approachable *adjective* easy to talk to and willing to listen. The opposite of 'approachable' is 'unapproachable'.

appropriate *adjective* suitable and correct for a certain place or event. *Walking boots are appropriate footwear for the hike.*

approval *noun* 1 good opinion. *Does this plan meet with your approval?* 2 permission. *You have to get approval from the council to build a summerhouse.*

approve *verb* to agree to, to be in favor of something. *She doesn't approve of my clothes.* The opposite is disapprove.

approximate *adjective* nearly but not exactly correct. *What is the approximate length of the Nile?*

apricot *noun* a yellowish-orange fruit like a small peach.

Apricots grow best in a warm climate. This fruit is rich in vitamin A.

April *noun* the fourth month of the year. April has 30 days. **April fool** somebody who has been fooled by a trick played on them on the morning of April 1, April Fools' Day.

apron *noun* a piece of clothing you wear around the front of your body to protect the clothes underneath when you are cooking or cleaning etc.

apt *adjective* 1 suitable. *An apt time to leave.* 2 likely to do something. *He's apt to fall asleep when he's bored.*

aptitude *noun* an ability to learn and do something well.

aqualung *noun* equipment that divers wear to breathe underwater.

aquarium *noun* a glass tank for keeping fish and other water animals, or a building (in a zoo) where many such tanks are kept.

It is fun to keep tropical fish in an aquarium at home.

aquatic *adjective* living or growing in water, or to do with water. *Aquatic plants.*

aqueduct *noun* a bridge with a canal or pipes for carrying water across a valley etc.

Arab *noun* a person who comes from Arabia and other parts of the Middle East and North Africa. **Arabian** *adjective*.

Arabic *noun* the language spoken by the Arabs. **Arabic numerals** the numerical figures 1 to 9.

arable *adjective* plowed and suitable for growing crops. *Arable land.*

arbitrary *adjective* decided by a person's random opinion and not according to reason or rules. *An arbitrary decision.*

arc *noun* 1 a curved line. 2 in geometry, a section of the circumference of a circle.

arcade *noun* 1 a row of arches supported on columns. 2 a covered passageway usually with small shops on either side. 3 a place where there are machines for playing video games etc.

arch *noun* a curved part of a building, bridge or wall. *verb* to form the shape of a curve. *The rainbow arches across the sky.*

This spectacular arch leads to the Murder Corridor in Alnwick Castle, Northumberland.

arch- *prefix* chief or most important. *archbishop.*

archaic *adjective* (say ar-**kay**-ik) very old or antiquated.

archeology *noun* (say ar-kee-**ol**-oh-jee) the study of the past and how people lived, by the examination of remains of buildings, tools etc. **archeological** *adjective*. *An archeological dig.* **archeologist** *noun*.

Stonehenge is a site of special archaeological interest. The stones are said to have been brought across the River Severn to the south of England from the Preselli Mountains in Wales.

archer *noun* a person who shoots with a bow and arrow. *We went on a tour of the castle and saw the windows the archers used to fire their arrows from.*

archery *noun* a sport in which people shoot at a target with a bow and arrow.

This archer is using a longbow. Nowadays, archery is a popular competitive sport, testing concentration and steadiness of aim.

archipelago *noun* (say ar-kee-**pel**-agoh) a group of small islands.

architect *noun* a person who designs and plans buildings.

architecture *noun* 1 the skill or activity of designing buildings. 2 a style of architecture. *Greek architecture.*

Arctic *noun* the region around the North Pole. **Arctic** *adjective*.

The Arctic Circle is an imaginary line around the northern part of the globe.

arduous *adjective* difficult and tiring to do. *Arduous work.*

area *noun* 1 the size of a flat surface. *The barn has an area of 15 square meters.* 2 a part of a place. *The residential area of Boston.* 3 a part of somewhere used for a special purpose. *Non-smoking areas.*

arena *noun* a large area with seats around it where you can watch sports and various other entertainments.

Argentina *noun* a country in South America.

Argentinian *noun* a person who comes from Argentina. **Argentinian** *adjective.*

argue *verb* 1 to talk angrily with somebody you disagree with, to quarrel. 2 to give your reasons for or against something. *Mrs Earnshaw argued against joining the club.* **argument** *noun.*

argumentative *adjective* often arguing and tending to disagree for the sake of it.

arid *adjective* very dry and having little rainfall. Deserts are arid.

aristocracy *noun* the nobility, the social class that aristocrats belong to.

aristocrat *noun* a person of high social rank and with a title, a nobleman or noblewoman.

arithmetic *noun* the study and use of numbers, especially addition, subtraction, division and multiplication.

ark *noun* a ship in the Bible that Noah built for his family and animals to live in during the Great Flood.

arm *noun* 1 the part of your body between your shoulder and your hand. 2 anything shaped like an arm. *The arm of a chair.* **arm in arm** with arms joined in friendship.

arm *verb* to supply with weapons (arms). **armed** *adjective* carrying weapons. *The armed forces.*

armada *noun* a fleet of ships, especially the fleet that was sent from Spain to attack England in 1588.

armadillo (armadillos) *noun* a South American mammal covered with a shell of bony plates.

WORD HISTORY

'Arena' comes from the Latin word for sand. Sand was put on central areas of amphitheaters where Roman gladiators fought.

Tradition tells that one pair of each species of Earth's animals went aboard the ark and survived the flood.

WORD HISTORY

'Armadillo' is a Spanish word meaning a small armoured man.

armaments *plural noun* guns, ammunition and other war supplies.

armchair *noun* a comfortable chair with supports for the arms.

Armenia *noun* a country in West Asia.

armor *noun* 1 a strong metal or leather covering that protects a soldier's body in battle. *Knights in armor.* 2 a metal protection for tanks, ships etc. **armored** *adjective.*

This suit of armor is made of shaped metal plates fitted carefully together. It dates from around 1450. The most expensive suits of armor were decorated with engraved patterns or polished gold.

armory (armories) *noun* a place in which to store arms.

armpit *noun* the hollow place under your shoulder.

arms *plural noun* 1 weapons. 2 a coat of arms, a symbol or design on a shield etc. used as the badge of a noble family, city etc. **up in arms** very angry and ready to fight.

army *noun* a large number of soldiers who have been trained to fight on land.

aroma *noun* a pleasant, distinctive smell. **aromatic** *adjective. The chef liked to use plenty of aromatic herbs.*

around *adverb* on all sides. *He looked around but there was nobody there.* **around** *preposition* in all directions, in a circle. *She walked around the room.*

arouse *verb* 1 to stir up or excite feelings. *The terrible news aroused great anger in everybody.* 2 to wake somebody up.

arrange *verb* 1 to put in a certain order or position. *He arranged his books in alphabetical order.* 2 to plan or prepare something. *Can you arrange a meeting for next week?* **arrangement** *noun.*

arrest *verb* 1 to hold somebody as a prisoner. *The police arrested her for shoplifting.* 2 to stop or prevent. *Progress was arrested because of the weather.* **arrest** *noun.* **arresting** *adjective* attractive, holding your attention.

arrival *noun* 1 the act of arriving or reaching a place. 2 a person or thing that has arrived. *The new arrivals were welcomed by the committee.*

arrive *verb* to reach somewhere. *They arrived home last night.*

arrogant *adjective* having an unpleasantly high opinion of yourself. **arrogance** *noun*.

arrow *noun* 1 a stick with a point at one end that you shoot from a bow. 2 a sign that tells you which way to go.

The head of an arrow points in the direction you need to go. An arrow is also a useful symbol meaning 'this way up'.

arsenic *noun* a very powerful poison made from a metallic element.

arson *noun* the crime of deliberately setting fire to a house etc. **arsonist** *noun* someone who intends criminal damage by fire. *The arsonist was sent to jail.*

art *noun* 1 the ability to create beautiful paintings, sculpture, music, poetry etc. 2 an activity requiring a great skill. *The art of good conversation.* **artful** *adjective* 1 skillful. 2 cunning.

artery *noun* one of the thick-walled tubes that carries blood from your heart to all parts of your body.

An Australian road train is a very powerful articulated truck that often has several trailers.

Artery

The heart's job is to pump blood to the lungs and then all round the body. The right side of the heart takes in blood from the body and pumps it to the lungs. The left side of the heart takes blood filled with oxygen from the lungs and pumps it to the rest of the body.

DID YOU KNOW

'An' is the form of the indefinite article used before words beginning with a vowel, as in 'an apple', and before words beginning with a vowel sound, as in 'an hour'.

This Russian artist has set up his easel outside and is painting from life.

arthritis *noun* a disease that makes joints painful and swollen. **arthritic** *adjective*.

arthropod *noun* an animal such as an insect, spider or crab, with a skeleton on the outside of its body.

article *noun* 1 an object of some kind. *A belt is an article of clothing.* 2 a piece of writing published in a newspaper etc. 3 the words 'a' or 'an' (indefinite articles) and 'the' (definite article).

articulate *adjective* able to express thoughts and feelings clearly in words. *My little brother is extremly articulate for his age.* **articulate** *verb* to pronounce words clearly.

artificial *adjective* not found in nature but made by people. *These flowers are artificial because they are made of plastic.*

artillery *noun* large guns used by the army.

artist *noun* a person who can paint, draw or produce other works of art.

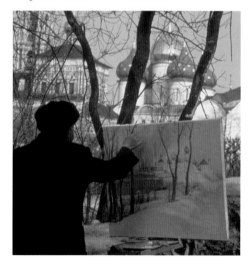

artistic *adjective* liking art or showing skill in creating art. *Everyone in that family is artistic.*

artistry *noun* the skill of an artist. *This pianist's artistry is much admired.*

a.s.a.p. *abbreviation* as soon as possible.

ascend *verb* (say az-**send**) to go or move up, to climb. *The plane ascended quickly after take-off.* **ascent** *noun*. The opposite of 'ascend' is 'descend'.

ASCII *abbreviation* American Standard Code for Information Interchange (a computer term).

ash (ashes) *noun* the gray powder that is left after something has burned completely. *Wood ash is good for the garden.*

ash *noun* a hardwood tree with a silver-gray bark. *A whole forest of ash trees.*

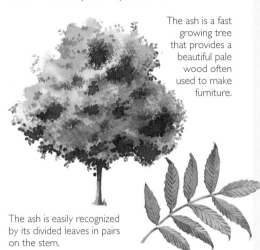

The ash is a fast growing tree that provides a beautiful pale wood often used to make furniture.

The ash is easily recognized by its divided leaves in pairs on the stem.

ashamed *adjective* feeling guilty or embarrassed about something.

Ashkhabat *noun* the capital of Turkmenistan.

ashore *adverb* on shore or land. *The sailors stepped ashore on the island.*

Asia *noun* one of the Earth's seven continents.

Asian *noun* a person from Asia. **Asian** *adjective*. *Asian countries include Korea and Viet Nam.*

ask *verb* 1 to speak in order to get the answer to a question. 2 to make a request or to say that you would like somebody to do something for you. 3 to invite. *Have you asked them to your party yet?.*

asleep *adjective* sleeping. *He was still asleep when I called, although it was after lunch.* The opposite of 'asleep' is 'awake'.

When you are asleep you are not aware of what is going on around you. The brain blocks incoming signals unless they are so strong they wake you up.

WORD HISTORY

The word 'assassin' – and note its two double 's's – comes from an Arabic word meaning an eater of the drug hasish. Many people under the influence of the drug in ancient times committed murders.

AMAZING FACT

Although aspirin has been used as a painkiller for many years, it was not known how the drug works until recently.

SPELLING NOTE

Try not to confuse 'assent' (meaning agreement) with 'ascent' (meaning a climb or an act of ascending).

Asmera *noun* the capital of Eritrea.

asp *noun* a small poisonous snake.

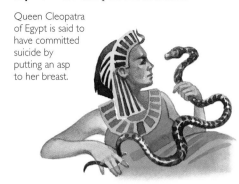

Queen Cleopatra of Egypt is said to have committed suicide by putting an asp to her breast.

aspect *noun* a side, feature or look of something. *Let's consider every aspect of the problem before making a decision.*

asphalt *noun* a tar-like substance that is used for making road surfaces etc.

aspiration *noun* an ambition or goal in life.

aspirin *noun* a medicine that helps to ease pain and reduce fever.

ass (asses) *noun* 1 a wild donkey. 2 a stupid person.

Asses are used in many countries as beasts of burden.

assassin *noun* a person who assassinates or murders. *The assassin was arrested.*

assassinate *verb* to murder somebody, especially an important person like a king or president. **assassination** *noun*.

assault *verb* to attack someone violently. **assault** *noun*. *It was a ferocious assault.*

assemble *verb* 1 to bring or collect together in one place. *A small crowd assembled in the square.* 2 to put or fit the parts of something together.

assembly *noun* 1 a meeting, often regular like a school assembly. 2 putting together different parts of something to make a whole. *A car assembly plant.*

assent *verb* to agree to something. **assent** *noun* agreement. *He gave his assent.*

assert *verb* to declare or state something forcefully so people pay attention. **assertion** *noun*. *He made a false assertion about me.*

assess *verb* to judge the quality or value of something. *He assessed the damages.* **assessment** *noun*.

This wine taster is assessing the quality of a glass of red wine. He must smell the wine as well as taste it.

asset *noun* somebody or something that is useful or valuable. *She is good at languages and this is a great asset to the company.*

assist *verb* to help. **assistance** *noun*. *Can I be of any assistance?*

The girl is giving her mother valuable assistance with the dishes.

assistant *noun* 1 a person who helps. *My aunt is the editor's assistant.* 2 a person who works in a store. *A sales assistant must be polite to the customers.*

associate *verb* 1 to spend time with a group, to work together. *He associates mainly with sports people.* 2 to connect two things in your mind. *He associates snow with skiing.*

association *noun* 1 a club or a group of people working together, an organization. 2 a connection made in your mind.

assorted *adjective* of different kinds. Mixed. *We found assorted pieces of clothing strewn all over the lawn.* **assortment** *noun*.

An assortment of candy usually contains chocolates, toffee and hard candy.

Over 3,200 asteroids have been identified so far. The biggest, Ceres, is 1,000 km across, but most are much smaller.

assume *verb* 1 to accept something as true without question, to suppose. *We assumed she had no money because she dressed so badly.* **assumption** *noun*. 2 to take over. *The vice-president assumed absolute control of the country.*

assurance *noun* 1 a confident statement or promise. *He gave every assurance that the bridge was safe.* 2 confidence. *She is playing the piano now with more assurance.* 3 insurance.

assure *verb* to tell somebody something confidently and definitely. *The nurse assured him that he would be better soon.*

asterisk *noun* a small star (*) used in printing.

astern *adverb* towards the stern or back of a boat.

asteroid *noun* a small planet that orbits the Sun between Mars and Jupiter.

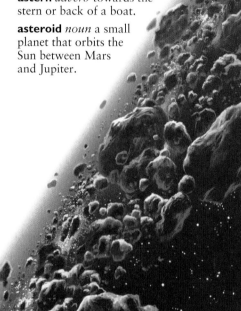

asthma *noun* a chest illness that makes it difficult to breathe. **asthmatic** *adjective*.

astonish *verb* to surprise somebody very much, to amaze. **astonishment** *noun*.

astound *verb* 1 to surprise or shock somebody very much. *She was astounded to hear that he had failed the final examination.*

astride *preposition* with one leg on each side of something. *He sat astride the horse.*

astrologer *noun* a person who studies the stars to try to predict the future. *The astrologer predicted a win.* **astrology** *noun*.

astronaut *noun* a man or woman who travels in a spacecraft.

Astronauts on the Moon could jump high in heavy spacesuits because the Moon is much smaller than Earth and its gravity is weaker.

astronomer *noun* a person who scientifically studies the planets, the stars and other heavenly bodies.

astronomical *adjective* 1 concerned with astronomy. 2 very large. *The house prices were astronomical.*

astronomy *noun* the scientific study of the planets and stars.

People from all over the world compete in athletic championships.

WORD HISTORY

Atlas is named after a Greek god who was made to carry the heavens on his shoulders as a punishment for his rebelliousness.

It is not clear who invented the telescope, but Galileo was the first person to put it to use in the study of astronomy.

astute *adjective* clever and quick of mind, shrewd. *She is an astute businesswoman.*

Asuncion *noun* the capital of Paraguay.

asylum *noun* 1 a refuge or a place to shelter from persecution etc. *The refugees were given political asylum.* 2 in the past, a place for treating people with mental illnesses.

ate *verb* past tense of eat. *He ate too much.*

atheism *noun* the rejection of a belief in God or gods.

atheist *noun* a person who does not believe in God or gods.

Athens *noun* the capital of Greece.

athlete *noun* a person who is good at sports. **athletic** *adjective*.

athletics *plural noun* physical activities such as sports and exercises.

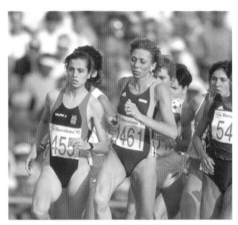

atlas (atlases) *noun* a book of maps.

atmosphere *noun* 1 the air that surrounds and protects the Earth. 2 the air in a particular place. *The atmosphere in this city is badly polluted.* 3 the general feeling of a place. *The hotel has a warm and friendly atmosphere but is very expensive.*

atoll *noun* a coral island in the shape of a ring surrounding a lagoon.

atom *noun* the smallest possible part of a chemical element that can take part in a chemical reaction. An atom consists of a nucleus surrounded by electrons. **atomic** *adjective*. *Atomic energy.*

The atom was first split by the New Zealand-British physicist Ernest Rutherford in 1919.

atrocious *adjective* very bad, terrible. *Atrocious spelling mistakes.*

atrocity *noun* a very cruel act, a crime.

attach *verb* to fasten or join two things together. *She attached another link to the chain.* **to be attached to** to be very fond of somebody or something.

attachment *noun* 1 something extra that can be attached. *The vacuum cleaner has a special attachment for cleaning upholstery.* 2 fondness or friendship.

Electric drills usually come with several attachments designed for different jobs.

attack *verb* 1 to use violence against a person or place. *The army attacked the village.* 2 to criticize or speak strongly against. *The architects were attacked for their bad design.*

attack *noun* 1 a violent attempt to hurt someone or something. 2 a fit or sudden illness. *An asthma attack.*

attain *verb* to reach or achieve something, to succeed. *She attained a ripe old age.* **attainment** *noun.* **attainable** *adjective.*

attempt *verb* to try to do something. *Jo attempted to climb the tree.* **attempt** *noun.*

attend *verb* to be present at a place or happening. *We all attended the public meeting.* **attendance** *noun.* **attend to** 1 to concentrate. 2 to deal with or take care of. *He attended to the accident victims even though he was injured himself.*

SPELLING NOTE

Whether words like 'attendance', 'acquaintance' and 'intelligence' should end in '–ance' or in '–ence' causes people a lot of trouble. There are no easy rules. You just have to learn the spelling!

attention *noun* giving thought or care or being interested in something. *She gave all her attention to studying.* **attract attention** to make somebody notice something.

attentive *adjective* 1 taking care to notice or listen. 2 kind and gentle. *He was very attentive to his grandfather's needs.*

attic *noun* a room just under the roof of a house.

Attics are sometimes full of forgotten treasures.

attitude *noun* an opinion or a way of thinking about somebody or something, a way of behaving. *She has a very strict attitude towards her children.*

attract *verb* 1 to like and find somebody or something interesting. *Katie was attracted to the boy next door.* 2 to catch the attention of. *The elephant caught the child's attention and he stopped crying.* 3 to make something come nearer. *Bright flowers attract butterflies.* **attraction** *noun.*

attractive *adjective* 1 interesting and pleasing. *An attractive idea.* 2 good-looking. *An attractive boy.*

aubergine *noun* another name for eggplant. A vegetable with a shiny purple skin.

A crowd is gathering in the square to attend a public meeting.

Aubergines grow in warm climates. They are a favorite vegetable in Mediterranean lands and in the Middle East.

auburn *adjective* reddish-brown. *Jill had long auburn hair.*

auction *noun* a public sale in which goods are sold to the person who will bid (offer to pay) the highest price. **auction** *verb*.

audible *adjective* loud enough to be heard. The opposite of 'audible' is 'inaudible'.

audience *noun* a group of people who watch or listen to something. *The play is attracting huge audiences.*

audio-visual *adjective* using recorded sound and pictures for teaching etc. *The school's audio-visual equipment includes CDs and videos.*

Audio-visual material such as CDs and videos make learning more fun.

audition *noun* a short performance to test whether an actor, singer or musician is suitable for a particular job.

auditorium *noun* the place in a theater, concert hall etc. where the audience sits. *When we arrived the auditorium was already full and we had to stand in the aisles.*

August *noun* the eighth month of the year. August has 31 days.

aunt *noun* Your aunt is the sister of your father or mother, or the wife of your uncle. *I have an aunt who is only a few years older than I am. She's my mom's sister, the baby of the family.*

An auctioneer is someone in charge of an auction. Items such as paintings are sold to the highest bidder.

WORD HISTORY
August was named in honor of the Roman Emperor, Augustus Caesar.

The archaeologists found an authentic African mask.

SPELLING NOTE
The name 'Australia' comes from the Latin word 'australis', meaning southern.

---

austere *adjective* simple and without luxury, severe. **austerity** *noun*.

Australasia *noun* one of the Earth's seven continents.

Australia *noun* a country in Australasia.

Australian *noun* a person who comes from Australia. **Australian** *adjective*. *The Australian outback.*

Austria *noun* a country in Central Europe.

The red and white stripes of the Austrian flag also appear on the country's eagle crest.

Austrian *noun* a person from Austria. **Austrian** *adjective*. *The Austrian alps.*

authentic *adjective* real, genuine and not copied. *An authentic painting by Picasso.* **authenticity** *noun*.

author *noun* a person who writes a book, article, poem, play etc.

authoritative *adjective* 1 showing power and authority. 2 reliable and coming from somebody in authority. *An authoritative atlas contains up-to-date information.*

authority *noun* 1 the power to tell others what to do. *The police have the authority to stop cars at the gate.* 2 an expert. *She's an authority on dolls' houses.* 3 **the authorities** a group or organization that has the power to control what is going on.

authorize *verb* to give somebody power or permission to do something.

autism *noun* an abnormal condition in children in which they are unable to respond to or communicate with people. **autistic** *adjective*.

auto- *prefix* self, self-caused, or same.

autobiography *noun* a book that somebody writes about her or his own life. **autobiographical** *adjective*.

autograph *noun* a person's name written in their own handwriting, a signature. **autograph** *verb*. *The star of the show autographed our programs.*

automatic *adjective* 1 working by itself without the control of a human being. *An automatic sprinkler system.* 2 done without thinking about it. *Breathing is automatic.* **automatically** *adverb*.

automation *noun* using machines instead of people to do monotonously repetitive jobs in factories etc.

SPELLING NOTE

Try not to confuse 'adverse' (which means harmful or unfavorable) with 'averse' (which means unwilling or disinclined).

The autograph of a famous person could be worth a lot of money some day.

automobile *noun* a motor car .

autopsy *noun* the examination of a body after death, a post-mortem.

autumn *noun* fall, the season of the year between summer and winter.

available *adjective* 1 obtainable and ready to be used. *Raspberries are not available all the year round.* 2 free to see people. *She'll be available to interview you next week.* **availability** *noun*.

avalanche *noun* a huge mass of snow and ice suddenly falling down a mountain.

avenge *verb* to harm or punish somebody in return for a wrong they have done to somebody else. *He avenged his father's murder.* **avenger** *noun*.

average *noun* in math, the sum of several amounts divided by the number of amounts. The average of 4+6+9+13 = 8. (4+6+9+13=32 divided by 4 = 8.) **average** *adjective* 1 normal, ordinary. *It's been a very average week.* 2 not extreme or special. *Her work is about average.*

averse *adjective* opposed to or disliking. *Averse to hard work.*

aversion *noun* a strong dislike. *He has a great aversion to jellyfish.*

aviary *noun* a large cage for keeping birds.

aviation *noun* the science of building and flying aircraft.

Automobiles are produced in a factory by automation. Robots rather than humans put them together.

aviator *noun* (old-fashioned) an aircraft pilot. *The aviator wore flying goggles and a leather hat with earflaps.*

The Sopwith Camel was flown by British aviators in World War I.

avid *adjective* 1 keen, enthusiastic. *An avid reader.* 2 greedy. *The student waved her arm in the air, avid for the teacher's attention.*

await *verb* to wait for, to expect. *We are awaiting the arrival of the president.*

awake *adjective* not sleeping. **awake** (awakes, awaking, awoke, awoken) *verb* to wake up. *I awoke at dawn.*

award *noun* something, such as a prize or money, given to somebody for doing well. **award** *verb* to present. *She was awarded first prize for the high jump.*

She was awarded a gold medal for coming first in the swimming contest.

aware *adjective* knowing about. *Andy wasn't aware of the dangers of mountaineering.* **awareness** *noun.*

away *adverb* 1 not here, not at home. *He's gone away for a few weeks.* 2 at a distance. *The next town is miles away.* 3 into the distance. *The music faded slowly away.* 4 ceaselessly. *She worked away at her exercises.* **do away with** *verb* to get rid of.

awe *noun* a mixture of wonder, fear and respect. *She is in awe of her teacher.* **awe-inspiring** *adjective* causing a feeling of awe. *An awe-inspiring poem.*

SPELLING NOTE

An award is something that you win or are given for a special reason. 'She was awarded the Nobel peace prize.' A reward is something you get for doing something useful or helpful. 'The police are offering a reward for any information about the accident.'

awful *adjective* 1 very bad or unpleasant. *What an awful smell!* 2 very great. *She's done an awful lot of knitting.*

awfully *adverb* very. *I'm awfully sorry.*

awkward *adjective* 1 clumsy and embarrassed. *The boy feels awkward among adults.* 2 not convenient. *We are eating, so this is an awkward time to call.* **awkwardness** *noun.*

awoke past tense of awake. *He awoke when the alarm went off.*

axe ax *noun* a tool with a sharp blade on a long handle used for chopping wood.

An axe can be used for felling trees as well as for splitting timber.

axiom *noun* a statement that everyone generally agrees to be true.

axis *noun* 1 a real or imaginary line through the middle of an object around which it spins. *The Earth rotates on its axis, which passes through the North and South Pole.* 2 a line along the side or bottom of a graph.

The Earth tilts on its axis as it spins through space.

axle *noun* the rod that goes through the centre of a wheel and on which it turns.

Azerbaijan *noun* a country in West Asia.

azure *adjective* bright blue like an unclouded sky.

Bb

babble *verb* to chatter and talk in a confused and excited way.

babe *noun* a baby. *A babe in arms.*

baboon *noun* a large monkey from Africa.

A baboon needs nearly 7,000 kJ of energy from food each day, half the amount of an adult man.

baby *noun* a very young child. *The baby's first smile.* **babyish** *adjective.*

babysitter *noun* a person who is paid to look after children when their parents are away. **babysit** (babysits, babysitting, babysat) *verb.*

bachelor *noun* a man who has never been married. *Mr Lee is a bachelor.*

back *noun* 1 the part of your body along the spine between your shoulders and bottom, also the top part of an animal. *She climbed on to the horse's back.* 2 the opposite side to the front, the part situated behind. **back** *adjective* at the rear. *The back door was wide open and the dog had run away.* **back-breaking** very tiring. *Back-breaking work.*

back *adverb* to an earlier place or time. *He thought back to when he was young.*

SPELLING NOTE

The commonest error in spelling 'bachelor' is to put a 't' before the 'ch'.

The staple food in Southeast Asia is rice. Cultivating the paddy fields is back-breaking work.

back *verb* 1 to move backwards. *She backed away from the fierce dog.* 2 to support or help. *Will you back me?* 3 to put money (bet) on an animal etc. *Uncle Joe backed the winning horse in the race.* **back down** to give up or change your mind. **put your back into** to work hard. **back out** to decide not to keep an agreement. *You promised to come to the party. You can't back out now.*

backbone *noun* the set of joined bones along the back. The spine.

The backbone is made up of individual bones called vertebrae. They interlock with each other in sliding joints.

backfire *verb* to have the opposite result to the one intended. *The plan backfired and the robbery was discovered.*

background *noun* 1 the part of a scene or picture that is behind the main objects or people. *The picture shows a lake with mountains in the background.* 2 the different facts that surround an event and which help to explain it. 3 a person's past experience or family history and education. *She comes from a farming background.*

backpack *noun* a large bag that climbers, campers etc. carry on their backs. **backpacker** *noun.*

This backpack is ready for the hike. It is stuffed with warm clothes and has a bed-roll strapped beneath it.

backward *adjective* 1 towards the back. *A backward look.* 2 slow to learn or develop. *This baby is backward at walking.*

backwards *adverb* 1 towards the back. *She took a step backwards and fell over the rug, breaking her leg.* 2 in the reverse way from normal. *Counting backwards.*

backyard *noun* the land at the back of a house, usually covered in grass. *We built a fort in the backyard.*

bacon *noun* thin slices of salted or dried meat from a pig.

bacteria *plural noun* microscopic living things. Some bacteria cause diseases.

bad (worse, worst) *adjective* 1 not good. Unpleasant. *I've got some bad news.* 2 naughty, wicked. *You're a bad girl to tell so many lies.* 3 harmful. *Eating too much candy is bad for you.* 4 hurt or in bad health. *I've got a bad leg.* 5 rotten and not good to eat. *The food has gone bad.* 6 serious. *A bad accident.* **go bad** to decay.

badge *noun* a piece of cloth, metal or plastic that is pinned or sewn on to clothes, with a picture or message on it. *All employees must wear a badge with their name on it.*

badger *noun* a wild animal with gray fur and a black and white striped head. Badgers live in underground holes called sets and are active at night.

Badgers' hands and feet are broad with wide claws for digging.

badger *verb* to annoy somebody by pestering them to do something.

badminton *noun* a game like tennis that is played by hitting a shuttlecock over a high net with rackets.

baffle *verb* to confuse or puzzle. *I was baffled by so many questions and couldn't think of what to say.* **baffling** *adjective*.

bag *noun* a container for carrying things. *Never put a plastic bag on your head.*

baggage *noun* bags and suitcases that travelers use. Luggage.

Baghdad *noun* the capital of Iraq.

bagpipes *plural noun* a musical instrument. Air is squeezed from a bag into pipes on which the music is played.

baggy *adjective* loose, not tight or fitted. *My favorite clothes are jeans and a baggy old sweatshirt.*

Bahamas *noun* a country in the West Indies.

Bahrain *noun* a country in the Middle East.

WORD HISTORY

'Badminton' is named after Badminton House in England where the game was first played in the middle of the 19th century.

Bagpipe music is traditional in Scotland at Hogmanay, or New Year.

bail *noun* money that is paid to allow somebody accused of a crime to go free until their trial. *She was released on bail of $100,000.*

bail *verb* to scoop water from a boat to prevent it sinking. **bail out** to jump from an aircraft, using a parachute.

bait *noun* 1 a small amount of food used to attract fish, birds or animals to help you catch them. 2 something that is tempting.

bake *verb* to cook in an oven. *He baked a cake for their birthday party.*

baker *noun* a person who works in a bakery and makes and sells bread, cakes etc.

This decorative tile shows a scene in a bakery in Seville, Spain.

Baku *noun* the capital of Azerbaijan.

balance *verb* to keep something steady and not let it fall over. **balance** *noun*. *Jack has good balance. He can stand on one leg without falling over.*

balance *noun* 1 an instrument for weighing things. 2 the amount of money somebody has in the bank.

balcony *noun* a platform on the outside wall of a building with a wall or railings around it.

A beautiful girl stands on the balcony waiting for her lover.

bald *adjective* (rhymes with 'crawled') with little or no hair on the head. **baldness** *noun*.

bale *noun* a large bundle of something soft. *A bale of hay.*

ball *noun* 1 a round object used to play games. 2 something that is round in shape. *A cannon ball.* 3 a grand, formal party at which people dance.

ball bearings *plural noun* very small steel balls that help different parts of a machine move smoothly against each other.

ballad *noun* a poem or song that tells a story. *He sang a romantic ballad.*

ballerina *noun* a female ballet dancer.

ballet *noun* (say bal-**ay**) a form of highly artistic dancing, usually telling a story, and performed on a stage. **ballet-dancer** *noun*.

balloon *noun* 1 a small bag made of thin material such as plastic or rubber and filled with gas. *The children blew up red and blue balloons.* 2 a large bag made of strong material and filled with gas or hot air (hot-air balloon), which carries people in a basket underneath. **balloonist** *noun*.

A colorful hot air balloon drifts through a blue sky.

ballot *noun* a way of voting secretly in an election. *The ballot box was full of votes.*

Bamako *noun* the capital of Mali.

bamboo *noun* a giant tropical grass-like plant with a hollow, woody stem used to make furniture etc.

ban (banning, banned) *verb* to forbid or say that something must not be done. *Smoking is banned in public places.* **ban** *noun*.

banana *noun* a long tropical fruit with soft white flesh and a yellow skin when ripe.

band *noun* a group of musicians or a group of people who get together for a purpose. *I'm going to see my favorite band on my birthday.* **band together** *verb*. *Six families in our neighborhood banded together to protest the new mall.*

band *noun* a narrow strip of material that goes around something. *A head band.*

bandage *noun* a strip of material used to tie around an injury or to cover a wound. **bandage** *verb*. *The nurse bandaged his knee.*

Bandar Seri Begawan *noun* the capital of Brunei.

bandit *noun* a robber who works with others in a group or band. *The travelers were attacked by bandits.*

Gangs of bandits often hide in remote wooded hills and ambush unsuspecting travelers.

bang *noun* 1 a sudden, very loud noise. *She shut the lid with a bang.* 2 a heavy knock. **bang** *verb*. *He banged on the door.* **Get a bang out of something.** to enjoy something very much. *Grandma really got a bang out of seeing you!*

Bangkok *noun* the capital of Thailand.

Visitors to Bangkok often shop for local produce in Thailand's floating markets.

Bangladesh *noun* a country in South Asia.

bangs *noun* hair that is cut across your forehead.

Bangui *noun* the capital of the Central African Republic.

banish *verb* to send somebody away, usually from their own country, as a punishment. **banishment** *noun*.

banister or **bannister** *noun* a hand-rail along the side of a staircase.

Banjul *noun* the capital of Gambia.

bank *noun* 1 a place that takes care of money for people and which provides financial services. **bank** *verb*. *She banked all her savings.* 2 a place for storing things. *A blood bank.* **bank on** to rely on. *You can bank on me. I'll be there.*

bank *noun* 1 the sides of a river, lake or canal. 2 a piece of raised, sloping land.

bankrupt *adjective* unable to pay debts. **bankruptcy** *noun*.

banner *noun* a large flag with a design or message on it, hung up or carried on a pole or between two poles.

The suffragettes carried banners demanding votes for women.

banquet *noun* a large, formal dinner, usually for a special occasion. *The mayor held a banquet in honor of the Governor.*

baptize *verb* in the Christian religion, to sprinkle or pour water over a person as a sign that they have become a Christian. To christen. **baptism** *noun*. **baptismal** *adjective*.

bar *noun* 1 a long, straight piece of metal or wood. *A cage with iron bars.* 2 a room or a long table or counter in a place at which drinks etc. are served. 3 a solid block of something. *A bar of soap.* 4 the equal sections into which music is divided.

bar (bars, barring, barred) *verb* 1 to keep out. *Children are barred from the premises.* 2 to block. *She barred the door.*

Barbados *noun* a country in the West Indies.

Neptune's trident appears on the flag of the island nation of Barbados.

barbarian *noun* a cruel, rough, uncivilized person. In the ancient world barbarians were people who were not Greek or Roman.

barbaric or **barbarous** *adjective* brutally cruel. **barbarity** *noun*.

barbecue *noun* an outdoor party at which food is cooked on a grill over a charcoal fire. **barbecue** *verb*.

barbed wire *noun* fencing wire with sharp spikes sticking out of it.

barber *noun* a men's hairdresser.

bar code *noun* an arrangement of thick and thin lines and spaces printed on goods in stores, containing information about price, size etc., and which can be 'read' by a computer.

9 781863 095471

bare *adjective* 1 uncovered, naked. *bare arms.* 2 empty. *The moving van has gone and the house is bare.* **bare** *verb* to expose. *The dog bared its teeth.*

barely *adverb* scarcely. *She could barely lift the heavy box.*

bargain *noun* 1 something that you buy at a price that is cheaper than usual. *This book is a real bargain!* 2 an agreement between two people in return for something.

bargain *verb* to haggle or argue over the price of something.

barge *noun* a long boat with a flat bottom, used on rivers and canals mainly to carry heavy goods.

barge *verb* to push your way into a place. To bump clumsily into people or things. *Jim barged into our meeting.*

WORD HISTORY

'Barbarian' comes from the Greek word 'barbaros', meaning foreign. The Greeks invented the word because it resembled the strange sounds of the languages spoken by non-Greeks.

Bar codes save time at a supermarket checkout.

SPELLING NOTE

Try not to confuse the spellings of 'bare', meaning naked, and 'bear', the verb meaning to support.

A barricade hastily put together out of any objects to hand blocks the road.

bark *noun* the sharp sound made by a dog, fox etc. **bark** *verb*. *The dog barked at the mailman and then bit his leg.*

bark *noun* the rough, hard covering of the trunk and branches of trees.

barley *noun* a grain used for food and in making beer.

bar mitzvah *noun* a religious ceremony that takes place on a Jewish boy's 13th birthday to celebrate his becoming an adult.

barn *noun* a farm building for keeping animals or storing crops.

barnacle *noun* a shellfish that attaches itself firmly to rocks and the sides of boats.

barometer *noun* an instrument that measures the air pressure and shows changes in the weather.

The barometer was invented in 1643 by Italian scientist Torricelli, who discovered air pressure.

baron *noun* a nobleman or peer of the lowest rank.

baroness *noun* the wife of a baron or a noblewoman or peer of the lowest rank.

baroque *noun* a highly ornate style of European architecture of the late 16th to early 18th century.

barracks *plural noun* buildings where soldiers live.

barrage *noun* 1 continuous heavy gunfire. 2 a huge number of something. *We received a barrage of complaints about the new parking meters.*

barrel *noun* 1 a large container with curved sides for storing liquids such as beer. *The beer barrels are in the cellar.* 2 the tube of a gun through which a bullet is fired.

barren *adjective* the soil of barren land is so poor that crops cannot grow.

barricade *noun* a barrier that has been quickly put up to block a road. **barricade** *verb* to block. *The demonstrating students barricaded the streets.*

B

barrier *noun* 1 a fence, railing or some other obstacle designed to stop people or things getting past. 2 a rule or situation that stops people from doing something. *Trade barriers.*

barrow, wheel barrow *noun* a cart that you can push or pull.

The wheel barrow is full of sand.

barrow *noun* a prehistoric mound of earth and stones over a grave.

barter *noun* to exchange goods for other goods rather than for money. To swap.

base *noun* 1 the lowest part of something, especially the part on which it stands. *The base of the lamp.* 2 the headquarters or main place from which things are controlled. *The expedition returned to base.* **base** *verb. The company is based in Cleveland.*

base *verb* to use something as a basis or starting point. *The new musical is based on a famous novel.*

baseball *noun* an American game played with a bat and ball by two teams of nine players.

Baseball players use thick gloves when they are in the field because the balls are hit with such force.

basement *noun* a room or an area below the level of the street.

bashful *adjective* shy and lacking in confidence. **bashfulness** *noun.*

basic *adjective* 1 the most important and necessary. *The basic rules of grammar.* 2 very simple, essential. *Basic needs.*

basically *adverb* 1 concerned with what is basic or fundamental. 2 most important.

basil *noun* a herb used to flavor food.

basin *noun* 1 a large bowl for mixing food. 2 a sink on a wall in a bathroom where you can wash. 3 A river basin is the area of land it gets its water from.

AMAZING FACT

Bats are the only mammal that is capable of genuine flight.

There is great variety among the 2000 + species of bats. Some have wingspans of only about 10 inches while others have a wingspan of up to four or five feet.

Bats have leathery wings and very poor eyesight. They hunt and navigate using ultrasonics and echo-location.

DID YOU KNOW

'Basically' is far too often used nowadays to mean simply 'importantly' – or even nothing at all. Try to avoid sentences like: 'Basically, I think it's time I went to bed.'

basis (bases) *noun* the main principle or idea behind something.

basket a woven container with a handle.

basketball *noun* a game for two teams in which the players try to score points by throwing a ball through a high net at each end of the court.

bass *adjective* 1 the lowest sounds in music. *Deep bass notes.* 2 A double bass is a very large violin-shaped instrument that plays very low notes.

Basseterre *noun* the capital of St Kitts and Nevis.

bat *noun* a mouse-like animal with wings that flies at night hunting for insects.

bat *noun* a piece of wood or metal that players use to hit a ball in games like baseball. **bat** (bats, batting, batted) *verb. Nick batted in the players on all three bases and slid into home.*

batch *noun* a group of things that were made at one time or have to be dealt with together. *A large batch of letters arrived for my grandmother this morning.*

bathe *verb* 1 to wash a part of the body very gently. *The nurse bathed the wound.* 2 to take a bath or to bath.

bathroom *noun* a room with a bath or shower and usually a basin and toilet.

bathtub *noun* a long, deep container that you fill with water and sit in to wash your whole body. **(take a) bath** *verb.*

batik *noun* an Eastern way of printing designs on cloth by covering parts of the cloth with wax patterns and dyeing the rest. *We made batiks in art class last semester.*

Cotton and silk can be dyed with brilliant colors to make batiks.

baton *noun* 1 a short, thin stick the conductor uses to beat time for an orchestra or choir. 2 a metal stick that is spun and thrown into the air.

battalion *noun* an army unit made up of smaller units called companies.

batter *noun* (in baseball) the player whose turn it is to hit the ball. *Mark is the best batter on our team this year.* **batting** *adjective. Batting average.* **bat** *verb.*

batter *noun* a mixture of flour, milk and eggs for making pancakes etc.

battery *noun* 1 a container that makes and stores electricity. You put batteries in things like radios and flashlights to make them work. 2 a number of big guns. 3 the crime of beating someone.

battle *noun* a fight between two armies or opposing groups. **battle** *verb. She battled against poor health.*

battleship *noun* a large, heavily armed warship. *Battleship gray.*

bay (bays) *noun* a part of the ocean shore that curves inwards. An inlet. **bay window** a window that forms a recess by sticking out from the wall of a house. **at bay** facing an enemy and fighting them off.

bay *adjective* a reddish-brown color of a horse. **bay** *noun. This horse is a bay.*

bayonet *noun* a knife that can be attached to the end of a rifle.

bazaar *noun* 1 a market in Eastern countries. 2 a sale to raise money for something. *Our class had a bazaar to raise money for poor children in other countries.*

Men selling beaten metalware wait for their customers. When buying goods at a bazaar it is customary to haggle over the prices.

WORD HISTORY

The word 'bayonet' is named after the town of Bayonne in France, where the weapons were originally made.

BC *abbreviation* Before Christ, used for dates before the birth of Jesus Christ. *Alexander the Great died in 323* BC.

beach *noun* the area of sand or pebbles where the land meets the ocean.

beacon *noun* a light or fire used as a guide or warning. *A beacon was lit on the hilltop.*

bead *noun* a small piece of glass or other material with a hole through it, which can be threaded on string or wire to make a necklace etc.

beak *noun* the hard pointed outer part of a bird's mouth. *The eagle has a hooked beak.*

beaker *noun* a glass vessel used for pouring liquids in a laboratory.

beam *noun* a large, heavy bar of wood, metal or concrete used for supporting the roof or floors of a building.

beam *noun* a band or ray of bright light. *The beam of the headlights dazzled the rabbit.*

bean *noun* a plant that produces seeds (beans) that grow in a pod and are eaten as a vegetable. **full of beans** full of energy, lively.

Beans are one of the world's most nutritious foods. Young Lima beans can be eaten raw, and even the pods can be made into a soup. Older beans are lightly steamed or boiled.

bear *noun* a large wild animal with thick fur and hooked claws.

bear (bears, bearing, bore, borne) *verb* 1 to support the weight of something. *That little chair won't bear your heavy weight.* 2 to carry from one place to another. *Seeds borne by the wind.* 3 to produce. *The plum tree bears fruit in the fall.* 4 to accept or tolerate something unpleasant. *She cannot bear rudeness.* **bear with** to be patient with. *Bear with me and I'll tell you.*

beard *noun* the hair on a man's face.

beast *noun* 1 a large wild animal. 2 (slang) a cruel, unpleasant person. **beastly** *adjective.*

beat (beats, beating, beat, beaten) *verb* 1 to hit somebody or something hard and often. *The hail beat against the window.* 2 to stir something with a whisk or fork. *The chef beat the batter.* 3 to defeat or win against somebody. *He always beats me at chess.* 4 to make a regular sound or movement. *The bird was beating its wings.* **beat** *noun* rhythmic knocking. *The beat of the music.*

beauty *noun* the quality of something that makes it attractive to look at or listen to. Loveliness. *The inspiring beauty of the lakes and mountains.* **beautiful** *adjective.* **beautifully** *adverb.*

beaver *noun* a North American furry wild animal with a broad flat tail and strong front teeth. Beavers cut branches to build dams and homes called lodges in rivers.

A beaver gnaws at a stick in front of its dam. The beaver's staple food is fish.

because *conjunction* for the reason that. *The tennis match stopped because it had started to rain.*

become (becomes, becoming, became, become) *verb* 1 to come to be. To start feeling. *We became very good friends.* 2 to change into. *Caterpillars become moths and tadpoles develop into frogs.*

bed *noun* 1 a piece of furniture to sleep on. 2 the bottom of the sea or a river. 3 an area for growing flowers etc. *Flower bed.*

A bee takes nectar from a flower. At the same time, it pollinates the flower by carrying pollen on its legs from one bloom to the next.

WORD HISTORY

The word beauty – and be careful how you spell it! – comes via the French from the Latin 'bellus'. We usually use the word 'beautiful' to describe women, children and things, but not men. It is more usual to call a man 'handsome' or 'good-looking'.

There are over 300,000 species of beetle worldwide.

bedridden *adjective* permanently in bed because of illness or old age.

bedroom *noun* a room to sleep in. *The twins share a bedroom.*

bedspread *noun* a large cloth to cover a bed.

bee *noun* a flying insect with a yellow and black body that lives in large groups and makes honey. Some bees can sting.

beech *noun* a hardwood tree with a smooth bark. Beeches are deciduous, so their leaves drop off in the fall.

beef *noun* the meat of cattle.

beefy (beefier, beefiest) *adjective* A beefy person is big and has strong muscles.

beehive or **hive** *noun* the place that bees make to live in or a small wooden house in which bees are kept.

beeline *noun* a straight line between two places. **make a beeline for** to go directly and swiftly towards something. *The boys made a beeline for the beach.*

beer *noun* an alcoholic drink brewed from malt, barley and hops.

beeswax *noun* the wax produced by bees to build the combs in which they store honey.

beet or **sugarbeet** *noun* 1 a plant with a bulbous root that can be eaten as a vegetable 2 the root that is cooked as a vegetable or that can be used to make sugar.

beetle *noun* an insect with hard covers for its wings.

bedding *noun* 1 blankets, sheets etc. for a bed (also bedclothes). 2 straw etc. for animals to lie on.

Water beetles, snails and small fishes are some of the creatures that feed on the bed of the river.

before *preposition* 1 earlier than or sooner than now. *The day before yesterday.* 2 in front of. *She stood before the statue.* **before** *adverb* previously. *We've never met before.*

beg (begs, begging, begged) *verb* 1 to ask somebody for money or food, especially in the street. *She begged for enough money to buy a bowl of soup.* **beggar** *noun*. 2 to ask for something very earnestly and eagerly. *He begged to be allowed to go swimming.*

begin (begins, beginning, began, begun) *verb* to start. *The meeting began at 7 o'clock.* The opposite of 'begin' is 'end'.

beginner *noun* a person who is just starting to do or learn something.

When you begin to learn to ride a bike, training wheels can give you confidence.

beginning *noun* the start of something, the origin. *At the beginning of the week.*

behave *verb* 1 the way we act or do things is how we behave. *She's been behaving in a funny way lately.* 2 to act in a good or proper way. *You can come with me only if you behave.*

behavior *noun* a way of behaving.

behind *preposition* 1 on the other side of or towards the back. *She hid behind the curtain.* 2 not making good progress. *He's behind with his studies.* 3 supporting or encouraging somebody. *We're behind you in your campaign.* **leave behind** *verb* to leave without something. *Peter was always leaving his keys behind.*

Beijing *noun* the capital of China.

being *noun* a living creature. *The first human beings lived in Africa.*

Beirut *noun* the capital of Lebanon.

Belarus *noun* a country in eastern Europe.

This is the flag of Belarus, which used to be part of the Soviet Union. The capital of Belarus is Minsk.

WORD HISTORY

The word 'beggar' may have come from an Old French word 'bégard', a begging monk, named after Lambert e Begue, the founder of an order of nuns.

AMAZING FACT

Belize was the last British mainland colony in the Americas. It gained independence in 1981. Both English and Spanish are spoken in Belize.

belch *verb* 1 to let wind from your stomach come noisily out of your mouth, to burp. *It is rude to belch at the table.* 2 to send out gases, fire smoke etc. like a volcano.

Belfast *noun* the capital of Northern Ireland.

belfry (belfries) *noun* a tower attached to a church, where the bells are hung.

Belgian *noun* a person from Belgium. **Belgian** *adjective. Belgian chocolates.*

Belgium *noun* a country in Northwest Europe.

Belgrade *noun* the capital of Yugoslavia.

belief *noun* 1 the things you believe to be true. The feeling that something is true.

believe *verb* 1 to think or feel strongly that something is true or real. *I believe in ghosts.* 2 to think that somebody is telling the truth. 3 to think or have an opinion. *I believe he's coming tomorrow.*

Belize *noun* a country in Central America.

bell *noun* a hollow metal object shaped like an upside-down cup that makes a ringing sound when struck. Any device that makes a ringing sound. *The front door bell.*

A brass hand bell was used to call children to school.

bellow *noun* a deep roaring sound made by a bull. **bellow** *verb. The bull bellowed with rage and the children ran for cover.*

bellows *plural noun* an instrument used for pumping air into a fire.

To get a fire to light, people used to pump air under it with bellows.

belly (bellies) *noun* the abdomen or the part of a person's or animal's body containing the stomach and intestines. *He ate until his belly was full.* **belly button** the navel.

Belmopan *noun* the capital of Belize.

belong *verb* 1 to be the property of somebody. *This book belongs to you, it is yours.* 2 to be a member of a group. *Brian belongs to the bowling club.* 3 to have its right place. *Put the tools back in the cupboard where they belong.*

belongings *plural noun* all the things that are yours and which you own.

below *preposition* 1 lower than. *Your chin is below your mouth.* 2 less than. *The temperature is below freezing.* **below** *adverb* beneath. *He looked down at the moat below.* The opposite of 'below' is 'above'.

belt *noun* 1 a long strap of leather or other material that you wear around your waist. 2 a narrow area of land. *The corn belt.* **belt** *verb* to hit. *He belted me in the shoulder.*

bench *noun* 1 a long wooden seat that two or more people can sit on. 2 a table that people put things on when they work. *A work bench.*

A work bench is an essential piece of furniture for the home improvement enthusiast.

bend *verb* 1 to change the shape of something straight so that it curves or is at an angle. 2 something that bends changes direction. *The trees bend in the wind.* 3 to move the top part of your body downwards. *Ben bent down to examine the beetle.*

beneath *preposition, adverb* 1 under, below. *The cat was asleep all day beneath the bed.* 2 not worthy or not good enough. *The business executive thought it was beneath him to do the housework.*

benefit *noun* 1 an advantage or something that helps you. 2 money that the government pays to people who are ill, unemployed, or very poor. **benefit** (benefits, benefiting, benefited) *verb. She benefited from her vacation and felt much better.*

Benin *noun* a country in Africa.

beret *noun* (say **bare**-ay) a soft, round, flat cap made of wool.

Berlin *noun* the capital of Germany.

Berne *noun* the capital of Switzerland.

berry *noun* a small, round, juicy fruit with lots of seeds such as a strawberry, blackberry or gooseberry.

Blueberries, raspberries and strawberries make a lovely dessert.

berserk *adjective* **go berserk** *verb* to become violently angry.

berth *noun* 1 a bed in a ship or train. 2 a place in a port where a ship can be moored.

beside *preposition* at the side of, next to. *A house beside the sea.*

besides *adverb* as well as. *What games can you play besides poker?*

besiege *verb* to lay siege to a place or surround it with soldiers in order to make it surrender. *The soldiers besieged the castle.*

best *adjective, adverb* better than all the others. *The best film I've ever seen.* **best man** a friend of the bridegroom who helps him at his wedding. **best-seller** *noun* a book that sells a very large number of copies.

bet (bets, betting, bet or betted) *verb* 1 to forecast the result of a race etc. and to risk money on the result. *She bet $3 on the bay horse.* **bet** *noun* the money risked. 2 to be certain. *I bet I can swim farther than you.*

betray *verb* 1 to let somebody down and hurt them by being disloyal. *She betrayed me by giving away all my secrets.* 2 to show signs of your real feelings etc. *His face betrayed his sadness.*

better *adjective* 1 something that is better has more good about it but is not the best. 2 recovered from an illness. *When you're better you can go back to school again.*

The patient is sitting up in bed reading, so he must be getting better.

between *preposition* 1 in the space or time after one thing and before another. *Between the school and the hospital is a field where we play football between dinner and bedtime.* 2 in shares or parts. *They shared the money between them.* 3 used in comparing. *What's the difference between jam and jelly?*

beverage *noun* a drink.

beware *interjection* be careful and look out for something dangerous. *Beware of the bull!*

Bulls can be dangerous, so beware of entering a field with a bull in it.

bewilder *verb* to confuse and worry somebody. *He was bewildered by all the street signs.* **bewildering** *adjective*.

beyond *preposition* 1 on the other side or farther than. *Don't drive beyond the crossroads.* 2 outside the limit of, past. *The camera is beyond repair.* 3 too difficult or confusing. *Algebra is beyond me.*

Bhutan *noun* a Himalayan country in South Asia.

bi- *prefix* two or twice. **biannual** happening twice a year. **bilateral** with two sides. **bilingual** speaking two languages.

biased *adjective* unfairly preferring one side to another, prejudiced. *She's biased against all foreigners.* **bias** *noun*.

bib *noun* a cloth or piece of plastic tied under a child's chin to protect its clothes when it is eating.

Bible *noun* A sacred book that has two main parts. First, the Old Testament, the holy book of the Jewish religion. Second, the New Testament, which, with the Old Testament, is the holy book of the Christian religion. **biblical** *adjective*.

A bicycle provides an environmentally friendly way of getting about.

Labels: Saddle, Handlebars, Frame, Tire, Pedal, Gears, Spokes

AMAZING FACT

Although we have a saying, 'like a red rag to a bull', it is misleading. Bulls, like most mammals, are color-blind.

Television is banned in mountainous Bhutan and the people are required by law to wear national costume.

WORD HISTORY

'Billabong' is an Australian aboriginal word that means 'dead river'.

bicker *verb* to quarrel continuously over unimportant things.

bicycle *noun* a two-wheeled vehicle that you ride by pushing pedals and steering with handlebars. The short form of bicycle is bike. *I love riding my new bike.*

bid (bids, bidding, bid) *verb* to offer to pay a certain amount of money for something, especially at an auction. *What am I bid for this vase?* **bid** *noun*.

bid *noun* an attempt to achieve something. *She's going all out in her bid to become ice-dance champion.*

big (bigger, biggest) *adjective* 1 large in size. *Elephants are big.* 2 important. *Today is the big game.* The opposites of 'big' are 'small' and 'unimportant'.

bigot *noun* a bigot is somebody who has strong and usually unreasonable views, which they obstinately refuse to change.

bike *noun* a bicycle or motorcycle.

bill *noun* 1 a piece of paper on which is written how much you owe for something. *The phone bill.* 2 a piece of paper money. *A ten dollar bill.* 3 a written statement of a proposed new law.

bill *noun* a bird's beak.

billabong *noun* in Australia, a pool of water that is left when a river has run dry.

billiards *noun* a game played with balls and long sticks (cues) on a cloth-covered table with pockets along the sides and at the corners. *Let's have a game of billiards.*

billion *noun* a thousand million.

billygoat *noun* a male goat.

bin *noun* a container for storing things.

binary *adjective* consisting of two parts.
binary system *noun* a number system used in computers in which only two numbers, 0 and 1, are used.

bind (binds, binding, bound) *verb* 1 to tie or fasten together. *He bound the magazines into a bundle with string.* 2 to wrap. *She bound the bruise with a bandage.* 3 to join the pages of a book together and put a cover or binding on it.

binder *noun* a stiff cover or folder for holding papers.

binoculars *plural noun* an instrument with lenses you look through to make distant things seem closer.

The craters on the surface of the Moon are clearly visible through binoculars.

biodegradable *adjective* Things that are biodegradable decay naturally. *Paper is biodegradable.*

biography *noun* the story of somebody's life written by somebody else. **biographical** *adjective*. **biographer** *noun* someone who writes a biography.

biologist *noun* a person who studies biology. *The biologist examined the newt.*

biology *noun* the scientific study of living things. *Human biology.* **biological** *adjective*. **biological warfare** the use of germs as weapons in warfare.

biped *noun* an animal with two feet. *Birds and humans are bipeds.*

biplane *noun* an airplane with two sets of wings. *The biplane looped the loop.*

bird *noun* a creature that is covered with feathers, has two legs, two wings and a beak. All female birds lay eggs and most birds can fly. **bird of prey** any bird that kills other birds and small animals for food. *Eagles are birds of prey.* **bird-watcher** *noun* a person who studies birds.

The toucan is a bird that lives in the rainforests of South America.

WORD HISTORY
The word 'biscuit' – a French word – means 'twice cooked' – from the two Latin words 'bis coctus'. Remember the 'u' in the spelling.

WORD HISTORY
The prefix 'bio–' in words like 'biology', 'biography' and 'biopsy' comes from the Greek word 'bios', meaning 'life'.

birth *noun* being born, the beginning of anything. *The birth of the universe.*

birth control *noun* ways of preventing a woman becoming pregnant.

birthday *noun* the anniversary or day each year when you celebrate the day you were born. *Birthday cake.*

biscuit *noun* a type of bread that is baked in small round shapes.

bisect *verb* to divide into two equal parts.

Bishkek *noun* the capital of Kyrgyzstan.

bishop *noun* 1 a high-ranking priest in some Christian churches. 2 a chesspiece in the shape of a bishop's hat.

bison *noun* (*plural* bison) a wild ox (the buffalo of North America).

The bison has been saved from extinction and lives in protected wildlife parks.

Bissau *noun* the capital of Guinea-Bissau.

bit *noun* a very small piece.

bit *noun* the metal bar part of a bridle that fits into a horse's mouth.

bit *noun* the smallest unit of information, expressed in binary numbers, in a computer.

bitch *noun* a female dog.

bite (biting, bit, bitten) *verb* 1 to grasp and cut through something with your teeth. 2 to sting. *The gnats have bitten me.* **bite** *noun*. *The insect bite has left a red mark.*

bitter *adjective* 1 having a sharp, nasty taste. *Bitter medicine.* 2 angry and full of hatred. *Bitter enemies.* 3 very cold. *We expect bitter weather in the winter months.*

bizarre *adjective* strange and unusual.

black *adjective* the darkest of colors. *I've got a small darkroom at home where I can develop black and white film.*

Black *noun* a dark-skinned person.

blackberry *noun* a small sweet wild fruit.

blackbird *noun* a common American and European bird.

blackboard *noun* a large board painted in a dark color for writing on with chalk.

A cat is drawn in white chalk on this child's blackboard.

blackbox *noun* an electronic machine on an aircraft that automatically records details of the flight.

blacken *verb* to make or become black. *Soot from the fire has blackened the bricks.*

blackmail *noun* the crime of trying to get money from somebody by threatening to reveal a secret. **blackmail** *verb*. *He was arrested for blackmail.* **blackmailer** *noun*.

blacksmith *noun* a person who makes things out of metal, including horseshoes.

bladder *noun* a bag-like organ in your body where urine collects until it leaves your body.

Kidney

Ureter

Bladder

Urethra

blade *noun* 1 the sharp part of an axe, knife, sword etc. 2 a narrow leaf. *A blade of grass.* 3 the flat, thin parts of oars, propellers etc.

WORD HISTORY

The 'mail' in 'blackmail' is a Scottish word meaning 'payment', 'tax' or 'tribute'. Blackmail was the tribute in money, corn or cattle demanded by rebel chiefs in the 16th century in return for their protection.

Urine leaves the bladder through the urethra when a circle of muscle relaxes to open the entrance to the tube.

blame *verb* to say that somebody has done something wrong and that it is their fault. *She blamed me for spilling the paint all over the sofa.* **blame** *noun*. *My sister took the blame.* **blameless** *adjective*.

blank *adjective* 1 unmarked, with nothing on it. *A book of blank pages.* 2 empty. *My mind went blank.*

blanket *noun* 1 a thick warm covering for a bed. 2 any sort of covering. *A thick blanket of snow lay over the fields.*

blare *verb* to make a loud, harsh, unpleasant noise. *The taxi horn blared.*

blaspheme *verb* (say blass-**feem**) to speak without respect about God or people's religious beliefs. **blasphemy** *noun*. **blasphemous** *adjective*.

blast *noun* 1 a sudden strong gust of air or wind. 2 a sudden loud noise, especially the noise of an explosion. *He gave a deafening blast on the trumpet.*

blast-off *noun* the moment when a rocket or spacecraft takes off. **blast off** *verb*.

It is always a thrilling moment when a rocket blasts off the launchpad.

blaze *noun* a very bright light or fire. *The blaze of the headlights.* **blaze** *verb* to give off bright light. *The fire is blazing.*

blazer *noun* a suit jacket that doesn't have matching pants.

bleach *noun* a strong chemical liquid used to kill germs and to make things such as cloth white. **bleach** *verb* to make white. *He bleached his gray shirt.*

bleak *noun* 1 cold, bare and miserable. *The landscape is windswept and bleak.* 2 not very hopeful. *Bleak prospects.*

bleat *verb* the noise a sheep or goat makes. *We could hear the sheep bleating high upon the mountain.* **bleat** *noun*.

bleed (bleeds, bleeding, bled) *verb* to lose blood. *My nose was bleeding.*

blend *verb* 1 to mix things together. *He blended the ingredients into a smooth paste.* 2 When things like colors or sounds come together in a pleasing way, they blend. **blend** *noun*. *A nice blend of coffee.*

bless (blesses, blessing, blessed *or* blest) *verb* to ask God to protect someone or something from harm.

blew past tense of blow.

blind *adjective* not able to see. *Seeing eye dogs for the blind.* **blindness** *noun.*

blind *noun* a screen or covering for a window. *Pull up the blind to let in the Sun.*

A venetian blind is made up of slats that tilt to allow more or less light into a room.

blindfold *noun* a piece of cloth tied over someone's eyes. **blindfold** *verb.*

blink *verb* to close and open your eyes again very quickly. *He blinked in the bright light.*

blinkers *plural noun* leather flaps placed at the side of a horse's eyes so that it can only see ahead.

blister *noun* a sore swelling like a bubble on your skin, filled with liquid, caused by a burn or by rubbing. *I have blisters from these new boots.*

blizzard *noun* a heavy snowstorm with strong winds. *They were lost in the blizzard.*

block *verb* to be in the way of, or put something in the way of so that nothing can pass. *A broken-down tractor blocked the road and stopped us from getting home.*

block *noun* 1 a lump or solid piece of something with flat sides like a block of wood. 2 the distance between two streets. *We live two blocks from school.*

blockade *verb* to isolate or cut off a place and stop supplies getting through.

blockage *noun* something in, e.g. a pipe, that stops anything passing through.

blond, blonde *adjective* having light-colored hair.

blood *noun* the red liquid that flows around inside the bodies of humans and animals.

Red blood cell

White blood cell

DID YOU KNOW

In Australia and New Zealand a 'block' is also a plot of land or settlement. And 'to do your block' means to get very angry.

AMAZING FACT

Wind blows when some air masses are warmer than others.

Each drop of your blood contains up to 5 million red blood cells that give blood its color.

It used to be thought that the winds had personalities, both kind and unkind.

blood-curdling *adjective* terrifying.

blood donor *noun* a person who gives some blood to be stored in a blood bank to be given to others in operations etc.

bloodhound *noun* a large dog with a very good sense of smell.

bloodshed *noun* the loss or spilling of blood in war etc.

blood-thirsty *adjective* keen for violence or killing. *A bloodthirsty film.*

blood vessel *noun* one of the tubes in your body that blood flows along.

bloom *noun* a flower. **bloom** *verb. The roses are blooming.*

The bright red blooms of the poppy are very short-lived.

blossom *noun* the flowers that grow on trees in spring. **blossom** *verb* 1 to grow blossom. 2 to grow and improve. *The girl blossomed into a beautiful woman.*

blot *noun* 1 a mark or spot made by a spilled drop of ink or paint. 2 a stain or fault that spoils something. **blot** *verb.*

blouse *noun* a loose shirt, usually worn by girls and women.

blow (blows, blowing, blew, blown) *verb* 1 to push air quickly through your mouth. 2 to move about in or be moved by the wind. *The wind blew the gate shut.* **blow over** to pass or become forgotten. *The fuss will soon blow over.* **blow up** 1 to destroy with an explosion. *They blew up the wrecked ship because it was dangerous.* 2 to enlarge. *She blew up the photo.*

blow *noun* 1 a hard hit. *A blow to the head.* 2 a cause of unhappiness or disappointment. *Her dad's death was a terrible blow.*

blubber *noun* the fat from whales.

blubber or **blub** *verb* to cry.

blue *noun* the pure color of a cloudless sky. **blue** *adjective* 1 of the color blue. 2 sad and miserable. **out of the blue** suddenly. *The money arrived out of the blue.*

The blue hamlet is one of the world's most beautiful fish.

blues *noun* a slow, sad kind of music.

blunder *noun* a bad and stupid mistake. **blunder** *verb* to stumble or make a clumsy mistake. *He blundered into the room.*

blunt *adjective* 1 not sharp. *A blunt knife.* 2 plain and to the point. *The language my father used was very blunt.*

blur (blurs, blurring, blurred) *verb* to make something indistinct or less clear. To smear. *The photograph is very blurred.* **blur** *noun* a smear, something that is unclear. *In my memory, the accident is all a blur.*

The sign is blurred. It is not shown in clear focus.

blurb *noun* a publisher's description praising a book.

blurt out *verb* to say something suddenly and without thinking.

blush *verb* to go red in the face, usually because you are shy, embarrassed or ashamed.

boa constrictor *noun* a large South American snake that crushes its prey to death by winding its body around it.

boar *noun* 1 a male pig. 2 a wild pig.

board *noun* 1 a plank or long flat piece of wood or card. 2 a piece of wood or card used for playing games etc. *A chess board.* 3 a group of people who manage an organization. *The company's board of directors met to discuss the merger.*

board *verb* to get on an aircraft, ship or train. *We got on board ship and set sail.*

boarding school *noun* a school where students eat and sleep.

boast *verb* to talk proudly about what you possess and how good and smart you think you are in order to impress people, to brag. **boast** *noun.* **boastful** *adjective.*

boat *noun* a small vessel for carrying people and things on water. **in the same boat** in the same difficult or unpleasant situation.

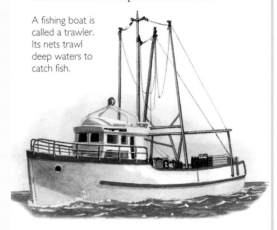

A fishing boat is called a trawler. Its nets trawl deep waters to catch fish.

body *noun* 1 all the physical parts of a person or animal, both inside and outside. 2 the main part of a body without the limbs. 3 a dead body, a corpse. 4 the main part of something. 5 a group of people. **bodily** *adjective.*

bodyguard *noun* a person or group of people who protects someone.

bog *noun* soft, wet ground. A marsh.

bogged down *adjective* stuck and unable to make progress. *Bogged down with work.* **bog down** *verb.*

The body moves by means of its muscles. The body has about 650 muscles, and they work in pairs.

Bogota *noun* the capital of Colombia.

bogus *adjective* false, not genuine.

boil *verb* 1 When a liquid boils, it becomes so hot that it bubbles and steams. 2 to cook food in boiling water. *He prefers to eat boiled beef and carrots, like his mother used to make.* **boiling point** the temperature at which a liquid boils.

boil *noun* a red, painful lump under your skin. *He had horrible boils all over his face.*

boisterous *adjective* noisy, cheerful and lively. *The children were too boisterous.*

bold *adjective* 1 showing no fear, brave. 2 clear, easy to see and impressive. *Bold lettering.* **boldness** *noun*.

Bolivia *noun* a country in South America.

bollard *noun* a short, thick post in a road to keep traffic away from the area.

bolt *noun* 1 a metal bar that slides across to lock a door, window etc. **bolt** *verb*. *She bolted the door every night.* 2 a metal pin with a screw that fits into a part called a nut to hold things together.

The bolt screws into the nut to make a secure fastening.

bolt *verb* 1 to run away suddenly. *The horses bolted.* 2 to eat something very quickly. *Don't bolt your food!*

bomb *noun* a weapon containing explosive chemicals that is used to destroy buildings etc. **bomb** *verb*. *Coventry was badly bombed in the war.* **bombshell** *noun* a surprise. *The news that she had been chosen for the job came as a bombshell.*

bombard *verb* 1 to attack with gunfire. 2 to attack or overwhelm. *They bombarded the chairman with difficult questions, but he was able to give satisfactory answers.*

The pan of boiling water is steaming up the mirror.

This is what it looks like inside a bone.

Spongy bone

Blood vessel

Red marrow jelly

Outer compact bone

bone *noun* any of the hard, white pieces forming the skeleton of a person or animal. **bone idle** very lazy.

bonfire *noun* an outdoor fire. *We made a massive bonfire yesterday to burn all the leaves.*

bonnet *noun* 1 the part of a car that covers the engine (US hood). 2 a hat tied under the chin, worn by women or babies.

bonus *noun* a reward or extra payment added to your pay.

bony (bonier, boniest) *adjective* 1 thin and with little flesh. *A bony cow.* 2 having large bones. 3 full of bones. *This fish is very bony.*

book *noun* a set of pages, usually printed, bound together in a cover. *A leather-bound book of poems.*

book *verb* to reserve or arrange a place in a theater, hotel, airline etc. before you need it. *Let's book up to go to Spain.* **booking** *noun*.

bookcase *noun* a piece of furniture with shelves for books.

bookmaker or **bookie** *noun* a person whose job is to take bets on horses etc.

bookworm *noun* a person who likes reading books a lot.

boom *noun* 1 a deep, loud sound. *The boom of the guns.* 2 a period of sudden increase. *A boom in computer sales.*

boomerang *noun* a curved stick used by Australian aboriginals as a weapon. It is thrown at its target and returns to the thrower if it misses.

Boomerangs are often decorated by aboriginal hunters with beautiful patterns.

boost *verb* to increase, push up or encourage. *The advertisement has boosted sales considerably.* **boost** *noun*.

boot *noun* 1 a shoe with high sides covering the ankle and sometimes lower leg. *Cowboy boots.* 2 **to boot** a phrase used at the end of a list to emphasize the last item. *She's tall, blonde and intelligent, to boot!*

boot up *verb* to turn on a computer.

booty *noun* valuable things stolen after a battle. Plunder.

border *noun* 1 the line along which two countries meet. **border** *verb. Canada borders the US.* 2 a strip along an edge.

The border between France and Spain runs along the Pyrenees mountains.

bore *verb* 1 to pierce or drill a hole into something. 2 to tire through lack of interest. **boring** *adjective* dull. *What a boring book!*

bore *noun* a dull person who makes you feel weary. *The boss is a real bore.*

bore past tense of bear. *The knight bore a coat of arms on his helmet.*

boredom *noun* tiredness caused by dull or monotonous work etc.

born *verb* When people or animals are born they start a life of their own. *Mum was born in Singapore in 1970.*

borrow *verb* to take something belonging to somebody else and use it for a short time before returning it. **borrower** *noun.* The opposite of 'borrow' is 'lend'.

Bosnia-Herzegovina *noun* a country in Southeast Europe.

The flag of Bosnia-Herzegovina shows a blue shield with yellow fleurs-de-lys on a white ground.

bosom *noun* a woman's chest or breasts. **bosom friend** a very close friend.

boss *noun* a person in charge of workers. **boss** *verb* to tell people what to do.

bossy *adjective* enjoying giving orders and telling people what to do. **bossiness** *noun.*

SPELLING NOTE

Try not to confuse 'borne', past participle of the verb 'bear', with 'born', which means giving birth.

---

botany *noun* the scientific study of plants. **botanist** *noun. She's studying to become a botanist.* **botanical** *adjective.*

Botanical drawings are very delicate and show every detail of the plant.

both *adjective, pronoun* the two together, not only one. *Both Jane's grandparents are now dead.*

bother *verb* 1 to feel worried or disturbed about something. 2 to be a nuisance or worry somebody. **bother** *noun* nuisance. *I'm sorry to be a bother.* 3 to take care, time and trouble over something. *He can't be bothered to do his homework.*

Botswana *noun* a country in Africa.

bottle *noun* a container made of glass or plastic for holding liquid. **bottle** *verb. He bottled the delicious homemade lemonade.*

This beautiful blue glass bottle has been hand-blown. You can tell this because of irregularities in the glass.

bottleneck *noun* a place where a road becomes narrower and traffic cannot flow freely. Anything that slows down work or progress.

bottle up *verb* to keep your feelings and thoughts to yourself.

bottom *noun* 1 the lowest part or underside of something. *The bottom of the sea.* 2 the part of your body that you sit on. **get to the bottom of** *verb* to solve or explain a mystery etc. *Let's get to the bottom of the problem.*

bough *noun* (rhymes with 'how') a large branch of a tree. *An apple bough.*

bought past tense of buy.

boulder *noun* a large, round rock.

bounce *verb* to spring back after hitting something. *The ball hit the floor and bounced back.* **bounce** *noun.* **bouncy** *adjective. A bouncy castle.*

bound *verb* to move along by making large leaps. **bound to** certain to. *You're bound to win the competition.* **out of bounds** a place where you are not allowed to go.

boundary *noun* a line that marks an edge.

bouquet *noun* (say boo-**kay**) a gift of a bunch of flowers.

The bouquet is made up of lovely summer flowers.

bout *noun* a short period of something. *A serious bout of the flu.*

bow *noun* (rhymes with 'so') 1 a piece of wood curved by a string attached at each end, used in shooting arrows. 2 a long thin stick used for playing stringed instruments such as violins. 3 a knot with loops. *He tied his shoelaces in a neat bow.*

bow *noun* (rhymes with 'cow') the front part of a ship.

bow *verb* (rhymes with 'cow') 1 to bend your head or the top part of your body forwards. *At the end of the show the actors bowed.* 2 to give in. *They refused to bow to his unreasonable demands.*

bowels *plural noun* the intestines in the lower part of your body, which carry waste matter from your body.

bowl *noun* a deep, uncovered dish. *A sugar bowl.*

bowl *verb* 1 to roll a ball towards pins, usually in a bowling alley. 2 to throw a ball towards a batsman in the game of cricket.

The bowler runs up to the wicket and bowls the cricket ball to the batsman.

box *noun* a wooden or cardboard container with straight sides and usually with a lid.

WORD HISTORY
Modern boxing began in 1867, when the first set of rules was drawn up by the Marquess of Queensberry.

WORD HISTORY
'Boycott' is named after a British estate manager in Ireland whose tenants refused to pay unreasonable rents.

DID YOU KNOW
Braille was invented in the 19th century by a Frenchman called Louis Braille.

box *verb* to punch or fight with your fists wearing heavy leather gloves in a sport called boxing. **boxer** *noun. He is a not a heavyweight but a middleweight boxer.*

boxer *noun* a short-haired breed of dog related to the bulldog.

Boxing Day *noun* In Britain, the first weekday after Christmas Day.

boy (boys) *noun* a male child. **boyhood** *noun* the childhood of a man. *In my boyhood things were different.*

boycott *verb* to refuse to have any dealings with somebody, as a protest or to bring about a change.

boyfriend *noun* 1 a girl or woman's usual and regular male friend. *She lives with her boyfriend.* 2 a gay man's partner.

bra or **brassiere** *noun* a piece of underwear that supports a woman's breasts.

brace *noun* 1 something that straightens or supports. *My mom had to wear a brace on her leg when she was little.* 2 a carpenter's tool for drilling holes. 3 two things of the same kind. 4 **braces** *plural noun* wires put on your teeth to straighten them.

The brace gives the carpenter a good grip for drilling holes.

brace *verb* to prepare yourself for something nasty. *He braced himself to go to the dentist and have six fillings.*

bracelet *noun* an ornamental band worn around the arm or wrist.

bracing *adjective* fresh and strength-giving. *Bracing sea breezes are good for the health.*

bracket *noun* a support fixed to a wall for a shelf etc. **bracket** *verb* to group together.

brag (brags, bragging, bragged) *verb* to boast and talk too proudly about yourself. **braggart** *noun* boaster.

braid *noun* 1 a narrow strip of decorative material used for trimming. 2 hair (or rope) that is separated into three parts and woven. **braid** *verb.*

Braille *noun* a system of printing for blind people using raised dots that can be felt and read with the fingers.

brain *noun* the part inside your head that controls how your body works and which enables you to think and feel.

The brain controls the body and processes the information collected by the senses.

Cerebral cortex

Cerebellum

Hypothalamus

Pituitary gland

brainchild *noun* a person's favorite invention, idea etc.

brainstorm *noun* a good idea that comes suddenly. *I've just had a brainstorm, I know what we can do!*

brainteaser *noun* a difficult problem or puzzle. *This crossword is a real brainteaser.*

brainy (brainier, brainiest) *adjective* smart and intelligent. *Tom is probably the brainiest person in our class.*

brake *noun* the part of a vehicle that you use to slow it down or to stop it. *The brakes failed and the car crashed.* **brake** *verb.*

bran *noun* what is left after flour has been made from the grain of wheat, the husks or outside parts of the seed.

branch *noun* 1 a part of a tree that sticks out from the trunk. 2 a division of a group or subject. 3 a bank, office, etc. belonging to a big organization. *The bank has branches in most towns.* **branch** *verb* to divide. *The path branches here.* **branch out** to strike out in a new direction. *They've branched out on their own.*

In spring, the branch sprouts new leaves.

brand *noun* a particular kind or make of goods. *An expensive brand.* **brand new** *adjective* unused and completely new.

brandy *noun* a strong alcoholic drink.

WORD HISTORY

'Brandy' is the shortened form of a Dutch word, 'brandewijn', meaning 'burnt wine'. In fact the wine was not burned but distilled over a fire.

Brasilia *noun* the capital of Brazil.

brass *noun* a yellow metal made from mixing two other metals, copper and zinc. **brass band** a group of musicians who play instruments made of brass.

Bratislava *noun* the capital of Slovakia.

brave *adjective* willing to do dangerous things and face danger, fearless. **bravery** *noun. He was awarded a medal for bravery.*

brave *noun* a Native American warrior.

brawl *noun* a rowdy quarrel or rough fight. *A drunken brawl.* **brawl** *verb.*

brawn *noun* great physical and muscular strength. **brawny** *adjective.*

bray *noun* the loud sound that a donkey makes. **bray** *verb.*

brazen *adjective* without shame. *A brazen lie.*

Brazil *noun* a country in South America.

Brazilian *noun* a person from Brazil. **Brazilian** *adjective. Brazilian coffee.*

Brazzaville *noun* the capital of the Republic of the Congo.

Brazil is the largest country in South America. It has the world's greatest rainforest, the Amazon.

bread *noun* a food made from flour, water and yeast and baked in an oven. **breadwinner** the person who earns money for a family to live on.

Brown bread is healthier than white bread because it contains more roughage.

breadth *noun* how wide something is from one side to the other.

break *verb* 1 to split into pieces, to smash. *The glass fell off the table and broke.* **breakages** *plural noun* things that are broken. *All breakages must be paid for.* 2 to damage something so it does not work. *The radio is broken.* 3 to fail to keep. *He broke his promise.* **break down** 1 If a car breaks down, it stops going because something has gone wrong. 2 If somebody has a breakdown, they cry and are overcome by nervous exhaustion. **break into** to enter a building with force. **break off** to stop doing something. *They broke off for lunch.*

break *noun* 1 a rest. *You've worked long enough. Take a break.* 2 a sudden change. *A lucky break that was well deserved.*

breaker *noun* a large wave that crashes against the rocks.

breakfast *noun* the first meal of the day. *I like cereal for breakfast.* **breakfast** *verb*.

breakthrough *noun* an important achievement or discovery.

breakwater *noun* a wall or barrier protecting a harbour or shore from the full force of waves.

breast *noun* 1 one of the two soft parts on a woman's chest that produces milk when she has had a baby, the bosom. 2 the chest.

breath *noun* the air that you draw in and let out of your lungs. **out of breath** panting. **under your breath** very quietly. *She said it under her breath so they wouldn't hear.*

breathalyzer *noun* a device that the police ask a person to breathe into to find out how much alcohol is in their blood. **breathalyze** *verb*. *He was breathalyzed by the police.*

breathe *verb* to draw air into your lungs through your nose and mouth and send it out again. *Breathe deeply and calm down.*

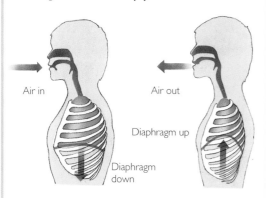

Air in   Air out

Diaphragm up

Diaphragm down

breed *verb* 1 to mate and produce young. 2 to raise animals to sell. *Tom and Mary breed dogs.* **breed** *noun* animals that mate and produce others of the same kind. *Bloodhounds and collies are breeds of dog.*

The collie is a very popular breed of dog.

WORD HISTORY

The 'groom' in 'bridegroom' has nothing to do with horses. It is a misspelling of an original word 'gome' that simply meant 'man'.

The diaphragm and the muscles between the ribs make you breathe in and out.

WORD HISTORY

'Breathalyzer' is a 'blend' word made up of two words put together – 'breath' and 'analyzer'. ('Motel' - 'motor' + 'hotel' and 'smog' - 'smoke' and 'fog' are other examples.)

breeze *noun* a soft wind. **breezy** *adjective*.

brewery *noun* a place where beer is made (brewed). *Malt is delivered to the brewery.*

bribe *noun* a gift or money given to somebody to persuade them to do something unlawful or dishonest. *He gave them a bribe to keep them quiet.* **bribe** *verb*.

brick *noun* a small block of hardened clay used for building.

bride *noun* a woman who is about to get married. **bridal** *adjective*.

bridegroom *noun* a man who is about to get married. *The bridegroom is nervous.*

bridesmaid *noun* a girl or young woman who helps the bride on her wedding day.

bridge *noun* 1 a structure built over a canal, river, road etc. so that people and vehicles can cross from one side to the other. 2 a high platform from which a ship is steered. *The captain stands on the bridge.* 3 a piece of wood that holds up the strings stretched along a violin, guitar etc. **bridge** *verb*.

A bridge goes across the river.

bridge *noun* a card game for four players.

Bridgetown *noun* the capital of Barbados.

bridle *noun* the leather straps that fit over a horse's head and to which the reins are attached. *The bridle is part of the tack.*

brief *adjective* lasting or taking only a short time. *A brief encounter.*

brief *verb* to give instructions, information or advice. *She briefed her staff on the best tactics.* **briefing** *noun*.

briefcase *noun* a flat case for papers etc.

briefs *plural noun* short men's or women's underpants.

bright *adjective* 1 giving out a lot of strong light. 2 a clear, strong color. *Bright orange.* 3 smart. *A bright student.* **brightness** *noun*. *The brightness of the Sun.* The opposite of 'bright' is 'dull' or 'dim' or 'dark'.

brighten *verb* to make or become brighter or more cheerful.

brilliant *adjective* 1 shining very brightly. *Brilliant stars.* 2 very intelligent or able. *A brilliant scientist.* **brilliance** *noun.*

The dancers wear brilliant flowers round their necks, heads and ankles.

brim *noun* 1 the top of a container. *The glass is full to the brim.* 2 the part of a hat that sticks out.

brine *noun* salty water.

bring (brings, bringing, brought) *verb* 1 to carry something or to take somebody with you. *Can you bring your CDs when you come?* 2 to cause or start something happening. *The sad story brought tears to his eyes.* **bring back** to cause to return. *This song brings back memories.* **bring up** 1 to look after and educate a child. 2 to mention a subject. *Don't bring up your report card.*

brink *noun* the edge of a steep place such as a cliff.

brisk *adjective* 1 lively and efficient. *Brisk manner.* 2 fast. *A brisk walk by the sea.*

bristle *noun* a short, stiff hair on a brush, an animal or on a man's unshaven face. **bristly** *adjective.*

British *adjective* relating to Great Britain and its people.

brittle *adjective* hard and easily broken. *Brittle twigs.*

broad *adjective* measuring a lot from one side to the other, wide. **broaden** *verb* to make wider. *They plan to broaden the road.*

broadcast (broadcasts, broadcasting, broadcast) *verb* to send out a program by radio or television. **broadcast** *noun.*

When a television program is broadcast, the signal leaves the studios and is sent via a transmitter to a satellite in space. The satellite beams the signal to a receiver on your house and into your television set.

broad-minded *adjective* tolerant and accepting opinions and behavior that you may not agree with.

broccoli *noun* a vegetable like a cauliflower with a green stalk and small green flowerheads. *Broccoli is very good for you.*

brochure *noun* a pamphlet or small book containing information.

broke, broken past and past participle of break.

bronchitis *noun* an illness of the lungs that makes you cough a lot.

bronco *noun* (US) a wild or half-tamed pony. *The bucking bronco threw off the cowboy who was trying to break him in.*

bronze *noun* a reddish-brown metal made by mixing copper and tin. **bronze** *adjective.*

Bronze Age *noun* a time in history when people made tools of bronze.

These urns were made by people who lived in the Bronze Age.

brooch *noun* (rhymes with 'poach') an ornament that you can pin to your clothes.

brood *noun* a family of young birds hatched at the same time. *The mother hen sat on her brood of chicks.* **brood** *verb* 1 to sit on eggs to hatch them. 2 to worry about things for a long time. *Helen was brooding over her bad grades.*

brook *noun* a small stream. *The brook rushed down the mountainside.*

broom *noun* a large brush with a long handle for sweeping floors. *A new broom sweeps away old problems.*

broth *noun* a soup made from vegetables or meat which are then removed. *The doctor recommended chicken broth.*

brother *noun* a boy or man who has the same parents as you. A half-brother has only one parent the same as you. **brotherly** *adjective. Brotherly love.*

brother-in-law *noun* the brother of a person's husband or wife.

brought past tense of bring.

B

brow *noun* 1 the part of your face between your eyes and the top of your head, forehead. 2 the arch of hair over each eye, eyebrow. 3 the top of a hill.

Eyebrow

Eyebrows protect the eyes from sweat running into them down the brow.

brown *noun, adjective* the color of wood or chocolate. *She has big, brown eyes and long, black hair.*

browse *verb* to glance at things such as books or goods in a shop in a casual way. *He browsed through the catalogues.* **browser** *noun.*

bruise *noun* a bluish-black mark on your skin caused by a knock. **bruise** *verb. She bruised her knee when she fell.*

Brunei *noun* a country on the island of Borneo, in Southeast Asia.

The flag of Brunei has a red crest on a yellow, black and white ground.

brush *noun* a tool with stiff hairs called bristles used for sweeping, painting etc. *A hairbrush.* **brush** *verb* 1 to use a brush. *He brushed the dog.* 2 to touch gently while passing. *The cat brushed against her legs.*

Brussels *noun* the capital of Belgium.

brutal *adjective* cruel, violent and without feeling. **brutality** *noun.*

brute *noun* 1 a cruel person. 2 a wild, savage animal.

bubble *noun* a thin ball of liquid filled with air or gas, especially one that floats. *A soap bubble.* **bubble** *verb. The water is bubbling on the stove.* **bubbly** *adjective. Bubbly lemonade.*

buccaneer *noun* an old word for pirate.

The buccaneers boarded the ship wielding their daggers. Then they took all the valuables on board.

SPELLING NOTE

Be careful with the spelling of 'Buddha' and 'Buddhism' and note the double 'd' and the position of the 'h'. The word 'Buddha' means 'the enlightened one'.

The young Buddhist monks are praying in the temple. Their heads are shaved and they wear robes dyed with saffron, a valuable crocus flower.

Bucharest *noun* the capital of Romania.

buck *noun* 1 a male deer or rabbit. 2 (slang) a dollar. *That will cost you several bucks.*

buck *verb* When a horse bucks it leaps into the air with its head down.

bucket *noun* a container with a handle for carrying water etc.

buckle *noun* a metal fastener for joining the ends of a belt. **buckle** *verb.*

bud *noun* a small, round swelling on a plant that will grow into a leaf or flower. **bud** *verb. The trees are starting to bud.* **budding** *adjective.* **nip in the bud** *expression* to deal with a problem etc. while it is still small.

Budapest *noun* the capital of Hungary.

Buddhism *noun* the religion founded by the Buddha in the 500s BC. **Buddhist** *adjective, noun. Buddhist monks.*

buddy *noun* an informal word for friend. *Hi, buddy, how's it going?*

budge *verb* to move a little.

budget *noun* a plan of how money should be spent. **budget** *verb.*

Buenos Aires *noun* the capital of Argentina.

buff *noun* 1 a dull yellow color. 2 (informal) a person who knows a lot about a subject. *An opera buff.*

buffalo *noun* 1 one of a variety of wild oxen from Asia and Africa with long curved horns. 2 a North American bison.

buffet *noun* (say buh-**fay**) a meal set out on a table from which guests help themselves.

bug *noun* 1 an insect, especially an unpleasant one. *Bed bugs.* 2 a germ causing a minor illness. *A tummy bug.* 3 a fault in a computer program. 4 a hidden microphone that records conversations.

bugle *noun* a brass musical instrument like a small trumpet used mainly in the armed forces. **bugler** *noun*.

build (builds, building, built) *verb* to make something by joining different pieces together. *The house that Jack built.*

The truck is at the construction site, pouring concrete into the foundations.

build *noun* the shape and size of a person. *A woman of slender build.*

building *noun* a construction such as a house or supermarket with walls and a roof.

built-in *adjective* built as part of something larger. *Our room has built-in bunkbeds.*

built-up *adjective* A built-up area is covered with houses, shops and other buildings.

Bujumbura *noun* the capital of Burundi.

bulb *noun* 1 the roundish part of plants like daffodils and tulips from which the flowers grow. 2 (or **light bulb**) the pear-shaped glass part of an electric lamp that gives the light.

The pressure of the electric current through the bulb's thin wire filament makes it glow.

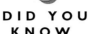

Wire filament

Bulgaria *noun* a country in eastern Europe.

bulge *verb* to swell or stick out. *His sack was bulging with presents.*

bulk *noun* 1 great in size. 2 most of. *The bulk of the work has been done.* **bulky** *adjective*. *A bulky package.*

bull *noun* a male cow, elephant, seal or whale. *A bull elephant has huge tusks.*

bulldog *noun* a strong breed of dog. *The fierce bulldog bit the mail carrier.*

bulldozer *noun* a powerful vehicle with a big metal blade in front for moving earth and clearing land.

A bulldozer clears up after logging in a sustainable plantation.

bullet *noun* the small pointed piece of metal that is fired from a gun.

bullion *noun* large bars of gold or silver.

bull's eye *noun* the small round center of a target. *Peter hits the bull's eye every time.*

bully *noun* somebody who tries to frighten or hurt a weaker or smaller person. **bully** *verb*. *The bully was expelled from school.*

bump *verb* to collide or knock into something. *Things that go bump in the night.* **bump** *noun*. **bump into** to meet accidentally. *I bumped into Adam.*

bump *noun*. a round lump caused by something hitting you. **bumpy** *adjective*. *A very bumpy road.*

bumper *noun* a bar fixed to the front and back of a car or truck to protect it from bumps. Fender.

bumptious *adjective* A bumptious person is full of self-importance.

bun *noun* 1 small, round bread. 2 a round coil of hair at the back of a woman's head.

Hamburger buns are usually made of white flour.

bunch *noun* 1 a group of things of the same kind tied or joined together. *An enormous bunch of keys.* 2 a group of people. *A nice bunch of kids.* **bunch** *verb*.

bundle *noun* a number of things tied loosely together or wrapped in a cloth. *A bundle of old newspapers.* **bundle** *verb* 1 to tie up loosely. 2 to push or hurry away. *The children were bundled into the bus.*

bungalow *noun* a house with all the rooms on the ground floor.

bungee jumping *noun* a sport in which a person jumps from a great height with elastic ropes tied to their legs to stop them hitting the ground.

bungle *verb* to do something awkwardly and badly. **bungler** *noun*.

bunk *noun* 1 a narrow bed attached to a wall on a ship, train etc. 2 **bunkbeds** a bed that has one or more beds above or below it. *The children slept in bunkbeds.*

bunny *noun* a child's name for a rabbit.

buoy *noun* a floating, anchored marker in the sea that warns ships of danger etc.

buoyant *adjective* 1 able to float. 2 A buoyant person is cheerful.

The life jacket saved his life by keeping him buoyant.

burden *noun* 1 a heavy load. 2 something that is difficult to carry or put up with. *The responsibility is a great burden to him.* **burden** *verb*.

burglar *noun* a person who breaks into a building to steal things. **burglary** *noun*. **burgle** *verb*.

A bundle of towels was tied together with a blue ribbon.

WORD HISTORY

'Bungalow' comes from a Hindi word 'bangla', meaning 'a house in the style of Bengal', a region in Northeast India where thatched, single-storey houses are common.

burial *noun* the act of putting a dead body in a grave. *The burial was a sad affair.*

Burkina Faso *noun* a country in Africa.

The flag of Burkina Faso has a gold star on a red and green ground.

burn (burns, burning, burned or burnt) *verb* 1 to set fire to something. To be destroyed by fire. *We burn logs in the fireplace at the cabin.* 2 to hurt or damage with fire. *He burned his hand very badly while cooking.* **burn** *noun*. *She has a nasty burn right across her face.*

burp *verb* to let wind from your stomach come noisily out of your mouth, to belch. **burp** *noun*. *He let out a loud burp.*

burrow *noun* a hole made in the ground by an animal as a shelter. **burrow** *verb* to dig or make a tunnel. *Lots of rabbits have been burrowing in the field.*

burst (burst, bursting, burst) *verb* to explode. To break apart suddenly. *The balloons burst in the heat.* **burst into** *He burst into the room. She burst into tears.*

Burundi *noun* a country in Africa.

bury (buries, burying, buried) *verb* 1 to put a dead body or thing in the ground. *The dog buried its bone in the garden.* 2 to hide. *He wept and buried his head in his hands.*

bus *noun* a large road vehicle for carrying a lot of passengers.

bush *noun* a shrub or large plant like a small tree with many branches. **bushy** *adjective*. *Bushy eyebrows.* **the bush** wild, uncultivated land, especially in Australia. **bushman** a native of the African bush.

The burning bush threw out such a lot of light that the shepherd was blinded.

business *noun* (say **biz**-ness) 1 buying and selling goods and services. The company or organization that makes, buys or sells things. *Business is very good at the moment.* 2 concerns, events or situations in general. *What she did is none of your business.*

businesslike *adjective* efficient, methodical.

businessman, businesswoman a man or woman who works in a business or who owns a business.

bus station *noun* the place where buses start and finish their routes.

bust *noun* 1 a statue of a person's head and the top part of the chest. 2 a woman's breasts.

This bust of William Lyon Mackenzie can be seen in Queen's Park, Toronto, Canada.

bust *verb* (slang) to break something. *I busted my sister's bike the very first day she had it.*

bustle *verb* to hurry because you are busy. *He bustled about putting things away.* **bustle** *noun. The bustle of the supermarket.*

busy (busier, busiest) *adjective* 1 If you are busy, you have a lot to do. *I'm too busy to see you today.* 2 full of people or activity. *A busy office.* **busily** *adverb.* **busybody** *noun* a person who interferes with other people's business and gives unwanted advice.

butcher *noun* a person who cuts up meat and sells it.

butler *noun* the chief male servant in a house. *The butler's pantry.*

butt *verb* to push or hit with the head or horns like a bull or goat, to ram. **butt in** to interrupt. *Don't butt in when I'm talking.*

butt *noun* 1 a large barrel. 2 the thick end or handle of a gun etc. 3 the end of a finished cigarette. 4 a person that others joke about or criticize. *I am the butt of all his jokes.*

butter *noun* a soft yellow food made from cream and milk. **butter** *verb. Please butter the bread and pass it to your Aunt Maud.*

WORD HISTORY

'Butler' comes from the French 'bouteillier', a man who puts wine into bottles. The Normans took the word to England at the time of the conquest in 1066.

---

buttercup *noun* a small plant with yellow petals that grows in fields.

butterfly *noun* an insect with large white or colorful wings.

The habitat of many butterflies is under threat because of urban development.

buttocks *plural noun* the fleshy parts of your body on which you sit.

button *noun* 1 a small, round thing sewn on to clothes to hold them together. 2 a small thing or device that you press to make a machine work. *Which button do I press to get this machine to start printing?*

buttress *noun* a support for an outside wall. **buttress** *verb.*

buy (buys, buying, bought) *verb* to get something by paying money for it, to purchase. *He bought a new car.*

buzz *verb* to make a low humming sound like a bee. *The buzz of many flies.*

buzzard *noun* a large bird of prey that hunts other animals for food.

A buzzard glides on a warm air current, waiting to spot its prey.

by *preposition* near.

bypass *noun* a road that takes traffic around a town etc. and not through it. **bypass** *verb.*

bystander a person who looks on at something but takes no part in it, a spectator. *The bystanders cheered loudly.*

byte *noun* a group of bits or units of information in a computer's memory.

Cc

cab *noun* 1 a taxi. 2 the front part of a truck, train or crane in which the driver sits.

cabbage *noun* a large round vegetable with thick green leaves. *A red cabbage has purple leaves that turn blue when cooked.*

cabin *noun* 1 a small wooden house. *A log cabin.* 2 a room or compartment in a ship or plane.

A log cabin in the pine forests makes an ideal vacation home.

cabinet *noun* 1 a piece of furniture for storing things in. *We keep our documents in a filing cabinet.* 2 **Cabinet** the group of senior officials who decide on government policy.

cable *noun* 1 a thick rope of fibers or wire. 2 a bundle of wires inside a plastic casing through which electricity flows. *An electric cable.* 3 a telegram.

cable car *noun* 1 a vehicle that is pulled along by a cable and runs along roads 2 a cabin hanging from a cable which carries people up and down a mountainside.

cable television *noun* a system in which TV programs are sent to sets along electric cables instead of as radio waves.

cackle *verb* to laugh in a loud and nasty way. *The witch cackled as she cast her spell.*

cactus (cacti) *noun* a fleshy plant covered with spines that grows in hot countries.

café *noun* (say kaf-**ay**) a small restaurant that serves refreshments and light meals.

cafeteria *noun* (say kaf-it-**eer**-ee-uh) a self-service restaurant.

cage *noun* a container with wires or bars in which animals or birds are kept.

Cairo *noun* the capital of Egypt.

cajole *verb* to persuade somebody into doing something by flattering them. *He cajoled her into giving him the information.*

AMAZING FACT

The forerunner of today's calculator was the abacus – invented about 5000 years ago!

SPELLING NOTE

'Café' is the French word for 'coffee' or 'coffee house' and is usually spelled with an acute accent on the 'e' (é).

---

cake *noun* a sweet mixture of flour, eggs and sugar baked in an oven. *I had a piece of her birthday cake.* **a piece of cake** really easy.

This gorgeous cake is layered with jam and topped with pink icing, cherries and cream.

calamity *noun* a disaster, such as losing all your money. **calamitous** *adjective*.

calcium *noun* a chemical substance found in limestone, teeth and bones.

calculate *verb* 1 to work out an amount by using numbers. *We calculated that we'd arrive at about 10 o'clock.* 2 to plan. *The ads are calculated to attract students.* **calculation** *noun*.

calculator *noun* a small electronic machine that adds, subtracts, multiplies and divides.

calendar *noun* a list that shows the days, weeks and months of the year, so you can look up the date. Calendars also list important events in the year.

calf (calves) *noun* a young cow, elephant or whale.

A calf learns to walk in the first couple of hours after birth.

calf (calves) *noun* the back part of your leg that is between the knee and the ankle.

call *verb* 1 to shout or speak in a loud voice, usually to attract somebody's attention. 2 to tell somebody to come to you. *Why don't you come when I call you?* 3 to telephone. 4 to give a name to somebody or something. *Her brother is called John.* 5 to describe something or somebody. *I wouldn't call her fat.* 6 to get somebody to come. *We had to call the doctor.* 7 to wake somebody up. *Call me at seven in the morning.* **call** *noun* 1 a shout or cry. 2 a telephone call. *We had a call from school.* **call for** to collect somebody. *I'll call for you on my way to school.* 2 to require. *This calls for prompt action.* **call off** to stop something. *The meeting was called off.* **call out** 1 to shout. 2 to summon in an emergency. *The doctor was called out twice last night.* 3 to order workers to strike.

calling *noun* an occupation, especially a profession that involves helping others.

callous *adjective* not caring about other people's feelings. *His behavior was selfish and callous.*

calm *adjective* 1 not windy. 2 When the sea is calm, it is still and without waves. 3 not excited and not showing any worry. *Please stay calm when we land.* **calm** *noun.*

calorie *noun* 1 a unit for measuring the energy that food produces. *One slice of brown bread has 95 calories, which is less than a slice of cake.* 2 a unit of heat.

calves plural of calf.

Cambodia *noun* a country in Southeast Asia.

camcorder *noun* a video camera and recorder all in one.

came past tense of come.

camel *noun* an animal with a long neck and one or two humps on its back. Camels are used in the desert for riding and carrying goods. *A camel train.*

camera *noun* an apparatus for taking photographs or making films and television pictures. *Smile for the camera, please!*

Cameroon *noun* a country in Africa.

camouflage *noun* (say **kam**-off-lahzh) a way of hiding things by making them blend in with their surroundings. *A polar bear's white fur is good camouflage in the snow.* **camouflage** *verb. The enemy camp was well camouflaged behind the bushes.*

camp *noun* a place where people live in tents, huts or caravans, usually for a short time. **camp** *verb* to make a camp. **camping** *noun. Scouts and Brownies go camping.*

Canada's northern lands reach deep into the frozen Arctic, but most Canadians live in the south, close to the US border.

With a camcorder you can film family events such as weddings.

DID YOU KNOW

A one-humped camel is called an Arabian camel or a dromedary. The two-humped animal is a Bactrian camel.

Bedouins sit inside a tent made of camel skin at their camp in the North African desert.

campaign *noun* a series of planned activities to achieve a particular result. *A successful advertising campaign.* **campaign** *verb. He's campaigning for president.*

campus *noun* the grounds of a university or college. *Most freshmen live on campus.*

can *noun* a metal container for holding food or drink. *I hate cooking, let's just open a can of soup.*

can (could) *verb* 1 to be able to. *Can you carry that heavy box?* 2 to know how to do something or have the ability to do it. *She can speak German.* 3 to be allowed to do something. *The teacher says we can go home after lunch.* 4 a polite way of asking somebody to do something. *Can you tell me the time?*

Canada *noun* a country in North America.

Canadian *noun* a person who comes from Canada. **Canadian** *adjective. A Canadian film.*

canal *noun* 1 a man-made waterway for boats to travel along or to bring water to an area. 2 a tube in a plant or an animal that carries food.

canary (canaries) *noun* a small yellow bird that sings.

Canberra *noun* the capital of Australia.

cancel (canceling, canceled) *verb* 1 to say that a planned activity will not take place. *The concert was cancelled because the singer had the flu.* 2 to stop an instruction for something. *I decided not to go and cancelled the reservation.* 3 to mark a ticket or stamp to stop it from being used again. When you cancel a check, it is no longer valid. **cancelation** *noun.* **cancel out** to balance and be equal to each other.

cancer *noun* 1 a serious disease in which abnormal growths form in the body. *Smoking can cause lung cancer.* 2 **Cancer** a sign of the zodiac (21 June to 22 July).

candid *adjective* honest. If you're candid, you tell the truth even when it is unwelcome. **candor** *noun.*

candidate *noun* 1 a person who wants to be chosen for a special position. *The obvious candidate was elected.* 2 a person taking an examination.

candle *noun* a stick of wax with a piece of string (a wick) through it, which gives light when it burns.

candlestick *noun* a holder for a candle. *Brass candlesticks.*

candy (candies) *noun* a sweet food.

cane *noun* a long thin stick. Cane is the hollow stem from a plant such as bamboo.

cannabis *noun* 1 a kind of hemp plant. 2 a drug made from the plant.

cannibal *noun* 1 a person who eats other people. 2 an animal that eats its own kind. **cannibalism** *noun*.

cannon *noun* a big gun that fires cannon balls.

Cannons were the first guns and appeared in the early 14th century.

cannot = can not, see can. *Unfortunately we cannot come to the party.*

canoe *noun* a light, long and narrow boat that is moved by using a paddle. **canoe** *verb* to go in a canoe. **canoeing** *noun*.

can't short for cannot, see can.

canteen *noun* 1 a portable container for carrying water 2 a restaurant in a movie studio on on a military base.

canter *noun* the movement of a horse, faster than a trot but slower than a gallop. **canter** *verb*.

canvas *noun* 1 a strong, rough cloth used for tents, sails and bags. *We spent the night under canvas.* 2 a stretched piece of cloth on which oil paintings are done. 3 an oil painting on canvas. 4 the floor of a boxing or wrestling ring.

canvass *verb* to go to people to ask for their vote, support or opinion. *They canvassed the neighbors for support.*

canyon *noun* a deep, steep valley, usually with a river running through it.

America's Grand Canyon is regarded as one of the seven natural wonders of the world.

cap *noun* 1 a hat with a small brim. 2 a lid or top on a bottle or tube. 3 a piece of paper covered with a tiny amount of explosive that makes a bang when used in a toy gun. **cap** *verb* to put a cap or top on something.

capable *adjective* having the ability to do something. **capability** *noun*.

SPELLING NOTE

Note that the cloth called canvas has one 's' at the end, while the verb asking for support has two – to canvass. The two words sound exactly the same.

AMAZING FACT

The main difference between a canoe and a kayak is that kayak paddles are double-bladed – one on each side, and canoe paddles are single-bladed.

---

capacity *noun* 1 the amount that can be held. *The stadium has a capacity of 30,000. A place is filled to capacity is completely full.* 2 the ability to do something. *Algebra is beyond my capacity.* 3 a position. *In my capacity as head librarian.*

cape *noun* a loose cloak without sleeves and fastened at the neck.

cape *noun* a large piece of land going out into the sea. *The Cape of Good Hope is in South Africa.*

Cape Town *noun* the legal capital of South Africa.

Cape Verde *noun* a country in the Atlantic Ocean off West Africa.

The flag of Cape Verde has a circle of yellow stars on a striped red, blue and white background.

capital *noun* 1 a city where the government of a country is. *Paris is the capital of France.* 2 a letter written or printed in a large form (A, B, C), used at the beginning of a sentence or a name. *Write your name in capitals.* 3 a sum of money used to start up a business, as well as money or property used to make more money. *He put up the capital for the new company.* **capital** *adjective*.

capitalism *noun* (say **kap**-it-ul-izm) a system in which a country's trade and industry are controlled by the owners of capital and are run for profit.

capitalist *noun* 1 a person who lends his money to businesses, to make more money. 2 a person who supports capitalism. **capitalist** *adjective*.

capital punishment *noun* punishment in which the criminal is killed.

capitulate *verb* to admit that you have lost and give in under agreed conditions. **capitulation** *noun*.

capsize *verb* to overturn in water. *The boat capsized in deep water.*

The friends wait to be rescued on top of the capsized boat.

capsule *noun* 1 a pill containing medicine. 2 the seed case of a plant. 3 the part of a spaceship that holds the crew and instruments and can be separated from the craft in space.

captain *noun* 1 the leader of a team or group. *Who's the captain of your football team?* 2 a person in command of a ship or an aircraft. 3 an officer in the army or navy. **captain** *verb* to be captain of a sports team.

Captain James Cook and the crew of the *Endeavour* step ashore in New Zealand and meet the Maoris for the first time.

caption *noun* 1 words put with a picture to explain what it is about. 2 a heading or short title in a newspaper or magazine.

captive *noun* a person or an animal taken prisoner. If you are taken captive, you are taken as a prisoner. **captive** *adjective* kept as a prisoner. **a captive audience** a group of people who have to listen to somebody. *TV viewers are a captive audience for advertisers.* **captivity** *noun*.

capture *verb* 1 to make a person or an animal a prisoner. 2 to get something by force, skill, attraction or trickery. *Her beauty captured his heart.* 3 to put data into a computer. 4 to describe something in words or pictures. *The film captures the loneliness of old age.* **capture** *noun* 1 the act of capturing. 2 somebody or something that has been taken by force.

car *noun* 1 a car has four wheels and an engine and room for a driver and passengers. Cars drive on roads and interstates. *We usually go by car.* 2 a railroad carriage. *This train has a dining car.*

Most cars have the engine at the front.

Caracas *noun* the capital of Venezuela.

carat *noun* 1 a unit for measuring the weight of precious stones such as diamonds, equal to 0.2 grams. *That diamond is huge, it must be four carats!* 2 a unit for measuring gold. Pure gold is 24 carats. *The gold leaf on this statue is 24 carat gold.*

caravan *noun* 1 a group of people traveling across the desert.

carbon *noun* 1 a substance that is found in all living things. Diamonds and coal are made of carbon. 2 a thin piece of paper with a colored coating on one side which is put between two sheets of paper for making copies of what is written or typed, also called carbon paper. 3 a copy made by using carbon paper, a carbon copy.

carbon dioxide *noun* a gas that is present in the air and is also formed when animals and people breathe out.

carbon monoxide *noun* a poisonous gas produced especially by car engines.

carburetor *noun* the part of a car engine in which gas and air are mixed to provide power. *The carburetor needs to be checked.*

carcass (carcasses) *noun* the body of a dead animal.

Bearded vultures gather at a carcass to feed.

card *noun* 1 a folded piece of stiff paper with a picture on the front and a message inside which you send to somebody on special occasions. *A birthday card.* 2 a piece of stiff paper fthat has information on it. 3 a postcard. 4 a small piece of printed plastic which you use if you have an account at a bank or a store. *I paid with my credit card.* 5 one of a pack of 52 playing cards, used for games like bridge or poker. *We played cards all afternoon.* **on the cards** likely or possible. **put your cards on the table** to make your plans known.

cardboard *noun* thick stiff paper used for making boxes. *A cardboard box.*

Cardiff *noun* the capital of Wales.

cardigan *noun* a sweater that usually buttons up at the front.

care *verb* to be interested and feel that something is important. *We care about the environment.* If you don't care about something, it doesn't matter to you and you don't worry. **care** *noun* 1 serious attention, in an effort to avoid making any mistakes. *She plans her essays with great care.* 2 If you take care of somebody or something, you look after them. 3 a person or object you are responsible for. *I take my babysitting jobs very seriously – the children are in my care.* 4 worry and sorrow. 5 **care of** (c/o *abbreviation*) written when sending a letter or package to somebody who is living at another address.

care for 1 to look after somebody or something. 2 to like a person. *Although he's nasty to her, she still cares for him.* If you care for something, you like or enjoy it. *I don't care for liver.*

The boy was caring for the orphan lamb.

careen *verb* to move very fast and in an uncontrolled way. *The car careened into a wall.*

career *noun* 1 a job or profession that you do for a long time and hope to be successful in. *He's chosen a career in teaching.* 2 the development and progress through a person's working life.

careful *adjective* 1 paying attention to what you do in order to avoid danger or damage. *Be careful.* 2 done with care and thought. *A careful report.* **carefully** *adverb.* **carefulness** *noun.*

careless *adjective* 1 not paying attention or taking care about something and making mistakes. 2 thoughtless. *Careless driving costs lives.* 3 untroubled and not worried. *She's careless with money.* **carelessly** *adverb.*

caress *verb* to stroke or kiss somebody to show your love for them. **caress** *noun* a loving touch.

cargo (cargoes) *noun* goods carried in a ship or plane.

Supertankers designed to carry oil are among the world's biggest cargo ships.

caricature *noun* an amusing picture or description of somebody, so that parts of his character seem odder than they really are. **caricature** *verb* to make a caricature of a person. *He's very good at caricaturing all sorts of politicians.*

carnation *noun* a scented garden flower.

carnival *noun* a public festival with music, dance and processions of people in wild make-up and costumes.

In the 18th century Russians traveled the snowy roads in sled carriages drawn by a team of horses.

WORD BUILDING

The suffix '-ful' means full of. It is usually spelled with just one 'l'. 'Careful' means full of care or taking care. The suffix '-less' means without, e.g. careless.

carnivore *noun* an animal that eats meat. Lions and tigers are carnivores. **carnivorous** *adjective.*

carol *noun* a Christmas song.

carpenter *noun* a person who makes or repairs wooden things.

carpet *noun* a thick woven covering for floors and stairs. **sweep something under the carpet** to keep something secret.

carriage *noun* 1 a section of a train for passengers. 2 an old-fashioned passenger vehicle pulled by horses. *They rode to their wedding in a horse-drawn carriage.* 3 the way a person stands or walks. 4 the movable part of a machine. *The typewriter carriage holds the paper.*

carrier *noun* 1 a construction usually fixed to a car or bicycle for carrying things. 2 a person who has a disease and passes it on to others without suffering from it.

carrion *noun* the flesh of dead animals.

carrot *noun* a plant with an orange root grown as a vegetable.

carry (carries, carrying, carried) *verb* 1 to hold something or somebody and go from one place to another. *The porter carried my suitcase.* 2 to hold something up, e.g. a roof or ceiling. 3 to pass something like a disease from one person to another. *Mosquitoes can carry dangerous diseases.* 4 to make sound move through the air. *Her voice carried right to the back of the arena.* 5 to win the support of others in a debate when voting is involved. *The motion was carried by 20 votes to 10.* 6 to print something. *The newspapers carried pictures of the funeral.* 7 to have as a result. *In some countries murder still carries the death penalty.* 8 to keep goods in stock. 9 If somebody carries weight, people respect that person's opinion. **get carried away** to be very excited. **carry on** 1 to continue. *I tried to speak to him but he just carried on reading.* 2 to complain and make a fuss about something. *My mother carried on all day about the noise from the football game.* 4 (old-fashioned) If a person is carrying on with somebody, they are having an affair.

carry out *verb* to fulfil, to do what you have promised or have been told to do. *We carried out our plan and explored the cave.*

cart *noun* a vehicle for carrying goods, usually drawn by a horse. **cart** *verb* 1 to carry in a cart. 2 to carry something heavy and find it tiring. *I don't want to cart those bags around town.*

carton *noun* a plastic or cardboard container for food or drink.

cartoon *noun* 1 an amusing drawing or set of drawings, often showing something of interest in the news. *There was a funny cartoon about the strike in the newspaper.* 2 an animated film. *Have you seen the latest Disney cartoon?* **cartoonist** *noun*.

cartridge *noun* 1 a container holding film for a camera, a tape, a typewriter ribbon or ink for a pen or printer. 2 a tube holding explosive for a bullet. 3 a small case that holds the stylus of a record-player.

carve *verb* 1 to make something by cutting a special shape out of wood or stone. *This statue is carved from marble.* **carving** *noun*. *An African wood carving.* 2 to cut up cooked meat into slices.

cascade *noun* a waterfall. **cascade** *verb* to fall in a cascade.

case *noun* 1 a container. *A case of wine.* 2 a suitcase. *I packed my case and left.*

Lightweight suitcases are ideal for air travel.

case *noun* 1 an event or a situation of a particular kind. *In this case I wouldn't pay the fee.* 2 an event the police are investigating or a question which will be decided on in court. *A murder case.* 3 an example of something bad, or of a disease. *A case of the flu.* 4 a patient, a lawyer's client, or a person looked after by a social worker. 5 facts and arguments for and against a plan used in a discussion. *The case for giving up smoking.* 6 in grammar, the change in the form of a word showing how it relates to other words in the sentence. *Emma's is the possessive case of Emma.* **in case** an action taken in advance referring to a particular thing that might happen. *I've brought a map in case we get lost.* **in any case** anyway. *I'll come in any case.*

Most cassette recorders are manufactured in the Far East.

cash *noun* money in coins and notes. *Please pay in cash.* **cash** *verb* When you cash a check you get money for it. *We wanted to go to shopping but Mom couldn't get to the bank to cash a check.*

cashier *noun* a person who takes in or pays out money in a bank, restaurant or store. *The cashier has to stand behind that little counter all day long, it must be a pretty boring job.*

cask *noun* a container like a barrel for holding liquids.

casket *noun* a small box for jewelry or other valuable things.

cassette *noun* a small flat plastic container with tape or film inside it. *We have a CD player and I hardly ever listen to cassettes.*

cassette recorder *noun* a machine for recording and playing music and other sounds on cassettes.

cast *noun* 1 all the actors in a film or play. 2 an object made from liquid metal, plastic or plaster poured into a mold. 3 a hard covering made of plaster that keeps a broken bone in place while it is healing. **cast** *verb* 1 to throw. *The fishermen cast their nets into the sea.* 2 To cast doubt on something means that you're not sure about it. 3 to give your vote in an election. *Have all the votes been cast?* 4 to choose actors for a film or play. 5 to make an object by pouring liquid into a mold and leaving it to harden. *A beautiful figure cast in bronze.*

cast off 1 to get rid of something. 2 to set off in a boat by untying the rope. 3 In knitting, you cast off when you take the stitches off the needle to finish a piece. **cast on** You cast on when you start knitting something and put the first stitches on to the needle.

castaway *noun* a shipwrecked person.

castle *noun* 1 a large, strong building with high walls that was built to protect kings, queens and others from their enemies. 2 a chesspiece, also called a rook.

Robinson Crusoe is the world's most famous fictional castaway.

C

Castries *noun* the capital of St Lucia.

casual *adjective* 1 happening by chance, without planning. *A casual remark.* 2 relaxed and not doing things very seriously, sometimes seeming uninterested. *The teacher didn't like his casual attitude.* 3 informal. *I wear casual clothes at home.* 4 not permanent or regular. *Casual work.* **casually** *adverb.*

casualty *noun* a person who is injured or killed in a war or an accident. *There were five casualties in the car crash.*

cat *noun* 1 a small furry pet animal. 2 a large wild animal of the cat family. Lions, tigers and leopards are all big cats. **let the cat out of the bag** to tell a secret.

Today's domestic cat is believed to have originated in Egypt.

catalog *noun* a list of names, places, goods and other things put in a particular order so that they can be found easily. *I buy all my clothes from a catalog.* **catalog** *verb* to list something in a catalogue. *The library catalogs each book as it comes in.*

catalyst *noun* (say **kat**-uh-list) something that causes a change or speeds up an event. One person's actions can also act as a catalyst to others.

catapult *noun* an ancient military machine used to hurl stones and rocks at the enemy. **catapult** *verb* to launch, as if from a catapult. *She was catapulted to stardom overnight.*

cataract *noun* a large waterfall.

cataract *noun* a growth over the eyeball that blurs a person's vision. *My grandfather had a cataract removed by laser.*

catarrh *noun* (say ku-**tar**) an inflammation of the nose and throat similar to a cold.

catastrophe *noun* (say ku-**tass**-trof-ee) a disastrous event that causes suffering and great damage. **catastrophic** *adjective. A catastrophic mistake.* **catastrophically** *adverb. It went catastrophically wrong.*

Fishermen often tend to exaggerate the size of the fish they catch.

WORD HISTORY

The expression 'to let the cat out of the bag' probably started in market places hundreds of years ago. Traders would sometimes secretly put a cat in a bag and pretend it was a pig, which was worth much more.

The cataract is rushing down the mountainside.

Caterpillars are voracious eaters and can do a lot of damage to crops.

catch (catches, catching, caught) *verb* 1 to get hold of an object that is moving through the air. *He threw the ball and I caught it.* 2 to capture an animal or a person after chasing them. *You can catch fish in a net and mice in a trap.* 3 to be in time for a bus or train. *Leave now if you want to catch the train.* 4 to suddenly discover a person doing something wrong. *The teacher caught them smoking.* 5 to become stuck. *I caught my shirt on a nail.* 6 to manage to hear. *I didn't catch his name.* 7 to become infected by an illness. *The baby caught a cold.* 8 to overtake. *He's only just left, you can still catch him.* 9 If you catch sight of somebody or something, you see them for just a moment. **catch fire** to start burning. **catch somebody's eye** to attract their attention. **catch the drift** to understand something.

catch *noun* 1 catching something like a ball. *He saved the game with a brilliant catch.* 2 something caught or worth having. *She's a good catch, marry her if you can.* 3 a trick, a hidden difficulty. *That car's too cheap, there must be a catch.* 4 a hook or another method of fastening something or locking a door. *The catch on the door is broken.* 5 a game in which children throw a ball to each other. **catch on** 1 to become popular. *The new fashion soon caught on.* 2 to understand. *I didn't catch on at first.* **catch up** 1 to reach somebody who is in front of you. *You go on, I'll catch up with you.* 2 to make up work that you are behind on. *I stayed up late to catch up on my homework.* 3 If something catches up with a person, they have to deal with an unpleasant situation they wanted to avoid. *My laziness caught up with me at last.*

catcher *noun* a person or thing that catches. *Grandpa was a dog catcher.*

catching *adjective* spreading quickly from one person to another. *Is the disease catching?*

category *noun* a division or class.

cater *verb* 1 to provide food and drink for parties. **caterer** *noun.* 2 to provide whatever is needed. *They don't cater for children.*

caterpillar *noun* a small worm-like creature with many legs. *Caterpillars turn into beautiful butterflies.*

cathedral *noun* a large church. The main church of a district.

Catholic *noun* a member of the Roman Catholic Church. **Catholic** *adjective. Their children go to a Catholic school.* **Catholicism** *noun.*

catnap *noun* a short sleep, usually during the day.

These cattle are Friesians. Commercial dairy cows can produce 18 liters of milk a day.

cattle *noun* farm animals, especially cows. Cattle are kept for beef and milk.

caught past tense of catch.

cauliflower *noun* a vegetable with green leaves and a large head of white flower buds. Only the white part is eaten.

cause *noun* 1 a person or thing that makes something happen. *Nobody knows the cause of the fire.* 2 reason. *You've got no cause for complaint.* 3 a purpose for which people work, such as a charity. *The money is for a good cause.* **cause** *verb* to make something happen. *The accident was caused by negligence.*

caution *noun* 1 a warning. 2 the act of taking care to avoid danger or making mistakes. **caution** *verb* to give a warning to somebody. **cautious** *adjective Charlie is a very cautious driver, he never takes chances.*

cavalry *noun* soldiers on horses.

cave *noun* a hollow place, usually in the side of a cliff or hill. **cave in** *verb* to fall down. *The roof caved in.*

caveman *noun* a person living in a cave. *The caveman killed a mammoth.*

caving *noun* exploring caves.

cavity *noun* a hole.

CD *abbreviation* compact disc.

CD-ROM *abbreviation* compact disc read-only memory, a disc used in a computer for reading information.

cease *verb* 1 to end. 2 to stop doing something. *Cease this idle chat!*

ceiling *noun* 1 the top part of a room forming the upper surface. 2 the highest limit of something.

Some people keep wine in their cellars. Others use them for storing junk.

DID YOU KNOW

The Celsius scale was invented by the Swedish astronomer Anders Celsius (1701–1744).

There are 100 cents in a dollar.

The CD has largely replaced vinyl records and cassettes.

celebrate *verb* to do something special to show that a day or an event is important. *We had a party to celebrate Granny's 80th birthday.* **celebration** *noun.*

celebrity *noun* 1 fame. 2 a famous person.

celery *noun* a plant with long stems grown as a vegetable and often eaten raw.

cell *noun* 1 a small room in which a prisoner is kept. 2 a small room in which a monk or a nun lives. 3 the smallest part of humans, plants or animals. 4 one of the compartments of a honeycomb. 5 a unit of an apparatus, such as a battery for producing electric current.

cellar *noun* an underground room of a building, often used for storing things.

cello *noun* (say chel-oh) a musical instrument with strings that looks like a very large violin. **cellist** *noun.*

cellular *adjective* 1 made up of cells. 2 Cellular blankets are loosely woven and very warm. 3 A cellular phone is a mobile phone.

Celsius *adjective* (say sel-see-us) from the Celsius scale for measuring temperature. Water boils at 100° Celsius.

cement *noun* 1 a gray powder, made from lime and clay, used for building. When cement is mixed with water and left to dry, it becomes hard as stone. 2 a strong glue. **cement** *verb* 1 to cover with cement. *Unfortunately the garden has been cemented over, so we can't plant anything.* 2 to strengthen an agreement or a friendship.

cemetery *noun* a place where dead people are buried.

census *noun* the official count of population.

cent *noun* the 100th part of a dollar and some other currencies. *I've only got a few cents left in my pocket.*

centenary *noun* a 100th anniversary.

center *noun* 1 the middle part or point, such as the point around which a circle is drawn. *She likes to be the center of attention.* 2 an important place of interest and great activity. *Harvard is a center of learning.* 3 in sports, a player in a team who plays near the middle of the field. **center** *verb* 1 to put something near or in the middle. 2 to concentrate your thoughts.

centimeter *noun* a measure of length. There are 100 centimeters in a meter.

centipede *noun* a long crawling creature with many legs.

central *adjective* 1 in the middle of something, near the center. 2 most important. *The government's central aim is to improve education.* **centrally** *adverb*.

Central African Republic *noun* a country in Africa.

Central America *noun* a narrow strip of seven countries between Mexico and South America.

centurion *noun* (say sent-**yoor**-ee-un) a commander of 100 men in the ancient Roman army.

century *noun* 1 a period of 100 years. *The 21st century starts in the year 2000.* 2 in cricket, 100 runs made by a batsman.

cereal *noun* 1 any grain such as wheat, rice or maize used for food. 2 a breakfast food made from grain.

ceremony *noun* 1 a special event or occasion, such as a wedding. 2 the things said and done during such an occasion. *I don't like all the ceremony at big church weddings, I prefer something quiet.* **ceremonious** *adjective*.

certain *adjective* 1 sure, having no doubt. *I'm absolutely certain that's right.* If you make certain of something, you find out first. 2 not named. *A certain person was involved in the crime.* 3 some but not much. *He seems to get a certain pleasure out of it.*

certificate *noun* an official document giving facts about a person. *We needed to show our birth certificates when we applied for passports.* **certify** *verb*.

CFC *abbreviation* chlorofluorocarbon. A substance used in things such as fridges and aerosols. CFCs have caused the ozone layer to shrink.

The CAR has diamond mines and rubber plantations, but most of its people are subsistence farmers.

Strong chains such as this one are often used in heavy industry.

SPELLING NOTE

'Cereal' is pronounced the same as 'serial', but the two words have completely different meanings. The word for grain comes originally from Ceres, who was the Roman goddess of agriculture.

A birth certificate gives proof of identity and entitles its owner to a passport.

Chad *noun* a country in Africa.

chaffinch *noun* a small songbird.

chain *noun* 1 metal rings fitted into one another. *She wore a silver chain around her neck.* 2 a number of connected events, or stores, mountains and restaurants. **chain reaction** a number of events in which each causes the next. **chain-smoke** to smoke coninuously. **in chains** kept as a prisoner.

chair *noun* 1 a seat with legs and a back for one person to sit on. 2 a person in control of a discussion. *Who is in the chair?* **chair** *verb* to chair a meeting.

chalk *noun* 1 a soft white stick used for writing and drawing on a blackboard. 2 a soft white rock. Chalk is a common form of limestone.

challenge (challenging, challenged) *verb* 1 to demand to have a fight, play a game or run a race to see who is stronger or better. *I challenged my brother to a game of tennis.* 2 to question the truth or rightness of something. **challenge** *noun* 1 a demand to see who is stronger or better. 2 a difficult project which demands effort and willpower. *Mountaineering is a great challenge.* **challenger** *noun*.

chamber *noun* 1 a large room used for meetings or for a special purpose. 2 A Chamber of Commerce is a group of people in businesses who work together. 3 an enclosed space in a body or a machine. *The human heart has four chambers.* 4 in old use, a room, especially the bedroom.

champion *noun* 1 a person or team who wins a race or game. *Ann has worked hard to become a tennis champion.* 2 somebody who speaks or fights for other people and defends ideas. *She is a champion of women's rights.* **champion** *verb*.

The champion was presented with this fine cup by the mayor.

championship *noun* a competition to find the best player or team. *Wimbledon is the oldest tennis championship.*

chance *noun* 1 something unplanned. *I met her by chance.* 2 the possibility that something might happen. *What are our chances of winning?* 3 an opportunity. *This is your last chance.* If you take a chance, you do something although it might fail. **by any chance** a polite way of asking for something. *Are you Mr Wilson's son by any chance?* **chance it** to take a risk.

chancellor *noun* 1 the head of some universities 2 the leader of some governments. *The Chancellor of the Exchequer is the UK's finance minister.*

change *verb* 1 to become different or make something different. *She's changed a lot since I last saw her.* 2 to take something back and get something else instead. *I changed the jeans because they were too tight.* 3 to put on different clothes or coverings. *I always change when I get home from work.* 4 to get off one bus, train or plane and get on to another. *We changed planes in Dallas.* **change your mind** to come to have another opinion. **change money** to exchange a sum of money for the same amount in coins or bills. **change** *noun* 1 the act of changing or the result of changing. *A change in the weather.* 2 the money returned to the payer when the cost of the goods is less than the amount given. *It costs $4 and you gave her a five dollar bill, so you get a dollar change.* 3 the same amount of money in coins or smaller notes. *Have you got change for a dollar?* 4 A change of clothes is a clean set. **for a change** something different from what usually happens. *A change of scene.*

channel *noun* 1 a stretch of water that connects two seas. *The English Channel.* 2 a passage along which water flows. 3 a wavelength for television or radio programs. *There's a good show on channel 6 I'd like to watch.* **channel** (channeling, channeled) *verb* 1 to form a channel in something. 2 to direct. *He channeled his energy into the new project.*

chant *noun* 1 a word or a group of words that is repeated over and over again. 2 a religious song. **chant** *verb*.

chaos *noun* a state of disorder and confusion. *The accident caused chaos on the tollway in both directions.*

WORD HISTORY

'Chancellor' comes from the Latin word 'cancelli', meaning a lattice or grating. This is because a Roman court official used to stand at a grating to separate the public from judges.

AMAZING FACT

'Chaos theory' is the theory that changes in the physical world, and their consequences, are unpredictable.

The weekend traffic threatened to cause chaos.

chapel *noun* 1 a small church, sometimes as part of a hospital or school. *A Methodist chapel.* 2 a part of a church with its own altar.

chapter *noun* 1 a division of a book, usually with its own number or title. 2 a special period in history. 3 all the members of a religious group. 4 the local section of a group or club. *The Phoenix chapter flew out to play in the tournament.*

char (charring, charred) *verb* to become black from burning.

character *noun* 1 the qualities that make a person or a place what they are. *The twins have quite different characters.* 2 a person in a story, film or play. 3 a character is somebody interesting or different from others. *He's a real character.* 4 a letter, number or other symbol. **characteristic** *adjective*. **characterize** *verb*.

The cartoon character gasped with exhaustion as he continued his journey.

charade *noun* an act that can easily be seen by others to be false or foolish. *The trial was just a charade.*

charades *noun* a game in which players guess words acted out by others.

charge *noun* 1 a price asked or paid for goods or a service. 2 a written or spoken statement blaming a person for breaking the law. *He was arrested on a murder charge.* 3 the care and responsibility for a person or thing. If you are in charge of somebody or something, you are in control of them and responsible for them. 4 a sudden attack. 5 an amount of explosive to be fired. 6 electricity in a battery or other electrical apparatus. **take charge** to become responsible for something. *I'll take charge of the children if you do the dishes.*

charge *verb* 1 to ask a price for something. *He didn't charge me for the phone call.* 2 to accuse somebody of a crime. 3 to rush forward in an attack. *The bull charged at the crowd and killed three children.* 4 When you charge a battery, it lasts longer. 5 If you are charged with something or charged to do something, you are given a duty or task.

chariot *noun* an ancient horse-drawn vehicle with two wheels, used in battles and races.

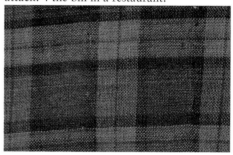

Around 1200 BC the Hittites, who lived in modern-day Turkey, used chariots for warfare.

charity *noun* 1 an organization that helps those who need it. *A charity for orphans.* 2 kindness towards others.

charm *noun* 1 the ability to be attractive and to please. *He used all his charm to win her over.* 2 an act, saying or object that has magical powers. 3 an ornament on a bracelet or chain. **charm** *verb* 1 *He charmed her with his flattery.* 2 to control something by using magical powers.

charming *adjective* delightful, pleasing. *She is a charming person.*

chart *noun* 1 a map of the sea and coast or sky and stars. 2 a map with special information in curves and graphs. *A weather chart.* 3 a list of information in a particular order. *The charts list the most popular records.* **chart** *verb. Explorers charted the coastline.*

chase *verb* to go after somebody or something in order to try and catch them or make them go away. *The cat chased the mouse.* **chase** *noun.*

chasm *noun* 1 a deep crack in the ground. 2 a large difference between two things or groups. *The chasm between us widened.*

chat *noun* a friendly talk. **chat** *verb. We chatted all afternoon.*

chatter *verb* 1 to talk non-stop about unimportant things. 2 to make a rattling sound. *His teeth were chattering with cold.*

chauffeur *noun* (say shoh-**fer**) a person employed to drive somebody's car. *They have a chauffeur who drives them everywhere.* *verb* to drive a car for somebody.

AMAZING FACT

Cheetahs can reach speeds of up to 60 mph (100kph) over short distances when chasing gazelles.

Tartan (or plaid) is a traditional Scottish fabric pattern, based on colorful overlaid checks.

W O R D   H I S T O R Y

The original 'chauffeur', in French, was not a driver but a stoker or fireman, who put coal on the furnace of a steam engine. Early cars gave off a lot of smoke and steam, so their drivers were jokingly called stokers.

The chauffeur wears a uniform and waits by his employer's car.

---

chauvinist *noun* (say **shoh**-vin-ist) a person who shows great prejudice, especially against women. *He's a real male chauvinist.*

cheap *adjective* 1 not costing very much. *Food is cheaper in Portugal than in Spain.* 2 of poor quality, not very good. *Cheap housing is hard to come by.*

cheat *verb* to lie or trick somebody, often in order to do well. *He always cheats in exams.* **cheat** *noun* 1 a person who cheats. 2 a dishonest action.

check *noun* 1 a printed form telling the bank to pay money from your account to the person you have written the check to. *Can I pay by check?* 2 an examination to find out if something is correct. 3 keeping somebody or something under control. *It's impossible to keep the disease in check.* 4 in chess the position of the king when under attack. 4 the bill in a restaurant.

check *noun* a pattern of squares in different colors. **checked** *adjective.*

check *verb* 1 to make sure something is correct or satisfactory. *Have you checked the bill?* 2 to hold back or stop doing something. *The bad weather checked their progress.* **check in** to register at a hotel or report at an airport. *You have to check in an hour before take-off.* **check out** to pay the bill and leave a hotel.

checkout *noun* a place in a supermarket where goods are packed and paid for.

check-up *noun* a medical examination.

cheek *noun* the side of the face below the eye. *Rosy cheeks are a sign of health.*

cheer *noun* 1 a shout of praise or happiness. *The crowd gave a big cheer.* 2 If you are full of cheer, you are very happy. **cheer** *verb. The fans cheered wildly throughout the concert* **cheer up** to become happy and stop feeling sad.

cheerful *adjective* 1 looking, sounding and feeling happy. 2 something pleasant, that makes you happy. **cheerfully** *adverb.*

cheese *noun* a soft or hard food made from milk. *Let's have bread and cheese for lunch.*

cheetah *noun* a wild animal, like a big spotted cat. Cheetahs are the fastest land animals in the world.

chef *noun* a cook in a restaurant.

A chef has to deal with many pans at once. His job is both hot and demanding.

chemical *adjective* used in, made by or connected with chemistry. **chemical** *noun*. **chemically** *adverb*.

chemist *noun* a scientist who specializes in chemistry. *I'd like to be a research chemist someday.*

chemistry *noun* the study of how substances are made up and how they react with other substances.

cherry (cherries) *noun* 1 a small round fruit with a pit. Ripe cherries are red. 2 the tree on which cherries grow. *There's a famous story about George Washington and a cherry tree.*

chess *noun* a game for two players in which each player moves pieces on a chessboard. *Larry plays chess about three times a week and practices all the time.*

chest *noun* the upper front part of the body enclosing the heart and the lungs.

chest *noun* a big, strong box for keeping things in. *We put a plastic treasure chest and a diver in our aquarium.*

chestnut *noun* 1 a reddish brown nut inside a prickly green case. 2 the tree on which these nuts grow. **chestnut** *adjective* having a reddish-brown color.

When the chestnut is ripe, the case falls to the ground and splits open. The shiny nuts roll out.

chest of drawers *noun* a piece of furniture with a set of drawers.

chew *verb* to move food about in your mouth and grind it with your teeth, so it is easy to swallow. **chew out** to scold someone.

chewing gum *noun* a sweet gum that you chew and don't swallow.

chick *noun* a young bird.

Chile is a long thin country that runs along the backbone of South America.

DID YOU KNOW

China has a population of more than 1,200 million, more people than any other country in the world. Yet China has a smaller area than either Russia or Canada.

chicken *noun* 1 a young bird, especially a hen. 2 the bird's meat used as food. *We had chicken for dinner.* 3 (slang) a coward or frightened person. **chicken out** not to do something because you are frightened.

chickenpox *noun* a disease with red itchy spots on the skin.

chief *noun* a leader or highest official. **chief** *adjective* most important. **chiefly** *adverb*.

chilblain *noun* a painful swelling or sore in the fingers or toes caused by extreme cold.

child (children) *noun* 1 a young boy or girl. 2 a son or daughter.

childhood *noun* the time when you are a child. *Now that he's old, he often thinks back to his childhood.*

childish *adjective* behaving like a child, often in silly way. *It's very childish to shout and scream like that.*

children plural of child.

Chile *noun* a country in South America.

chill *noun* 1 an unpleasant coldness. *In the morning there is often a chill in the air.* **chilly** *adjective*. 2 an illness caused by cold in which you might have a temperature, a headache and feel shivery. 3 a feeling of fear and doom. **chill** *verb* 1 to make something colder. 2 to become cold with fear. **chilling** *adjective. A chilling film.*

chimney *noun* a hollow passage in a roof through which smoke goes up into the air.

chimpanzee *noun* an African ape.

chin *noun* the front of the lower jaw.

china *noun* 1 a kind of fine white clay. 2 cups, saucers, plates and ornaments made of china. *The china cabinet.*

China *noun* a country in East Asia.

Chinese *noun* a person who comes from China. **Chinese** *adjective*.

chip *noun* 1 a crispy fried strip of potato. *I bought a bag of potato chips.* 2 a small piece of wood, brick or paint, broken off something. 3 a crack that has been left in a cup or glass, when a small piece has been broken off. 4 a flat plastic counter used as money in games. 5 a very small electronic circuit in a computer. *A silicon chip.* **have a chip on your shoulder** to be rude or behave badly, because you think you have been treated unfairly in the past. **chip** (chipping, chipped) *verb* to damage something by breaking off a small piece of it. *I'm afraid I've chipped a plate.* **chip in** 1 to interrupt a conversation. 2 to give money to a fund, so that something can be paid for by a number of people.

chipmunk *noun* a small American animal like a squirrel with a long bushy tail.

chirp *verb* to make a short, sharp sound like a bird or insect.

Chisinau *noun* the capital of Moldova.

chivalry *noun* (say **shiv**-ul-ree) good manners, helpfulness and polite behavior, in particular by men towards women. **chivalrous** *adjective*.

chocolate *noun* 1 a sweet food made from cocoa beans. *A bar of chocolate.* 2 candy covered with a layer of chocolate. *A box of chocolates.* 3 a hot drink made from the powder of crushed cocoa beans.

choice *noun* 1 a number of things you can choose from. *There is a choice of three films.* 2 the thing or things you have decided on. *The French film was my choice.* 3 the right, act or possibility of choosing. *My friend had no choice but to come.* **choice** *adjective* of high quality, best. *We only sell choice wines.*

choir *noun* a group of people who sing together, e.g. in a church or school.

choke *verb* 1 to be unable to breathe properly because something is blocking the air passages. *He choked on a fish bone.* 2 to stop the breathing by pressing on the throat or squeezing the neck. *The victim was choked to death.* 3 If a place is choked with cars or people, it is so full that it is impossible to move.

choke *noun* a device controlling the amount of air going into the engine that makes it easier to start a car.

cholesterol *noun* (say kol-**est**-er-ol) a fatty substance found in animals and food. Too much cholesterol is bad for the heart.

choose (choosing, chose, chosen) *verb* 1 to pick out a person or thing from a greater number. *I chose my favorite music.* 2 to decide to do something. *We chose to stay.*

chop (chopping, chopped) *verb* to cut wood or food into small pieces with a chopper, an axe or a knife. **chop** *noun* 1 a quick, heavy blow with a chopper or an axe. 2 a slice of meat with a bone in it. *Sometimes we put pork chops on the grill, too.*

Chipmunks are friendly animals. They often come up to visitors in US national parks, looking for treats.

Lots of trees are cut down every year and made into chopsticks. But other chopsticks are made of plastic.

SPELLING NOTE

It's easy to confuse 'chord' and 'cord', which are pronounced the same. Musicians play chords, and mathematicians use them to connect points on a curve. Both words come from the Latin 'chorda', the string of a musical instrument.

Christmas is celebrated in many countries.

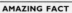
AMAZING FACT

Chocolate originally came from the Aztec people of Mexico who valued it as a drink.

chopper *noun* a heavy tool, like an axe, for cutting wood or meat.

chopsticks *noun* a pair of thin sticks held in one hand and used by the Chinese and others to eat food.

chord *noun* (say kord) a number of musical notes sounded at the same time.

chord *noun* (say kord) in geometry, a straight line connecting two points on a curve.

chore *noun* (say chor) a small everyday task or duty that is usually boring.

choreography *noun* (say ko-ree-**og**-ru-fee) the art of planning and arranging dances for the stage. **choreographer** *noun*.

chorus *noun* 1 a group of people who sing together. 2 a part of a song that is repeated after each verse by all the singers. 3 a group of singers or dancers who act together in a show. *She dances in the chorus.* **in chorus** at the same time. **chorus** *verb* to sing or say something at the same time.

chose past tense of choose.

chosen past participle of choose.

Christian *noun* a person who believes in Jesus Christ and his teachings. A member of the Christian Church. **Christian** *adjective* believing in the Christian religion. **Christianity** *noun*.

Christmas (Christmases) *noun* the day when people celebrate the birth of Jesus Christ, 25 December. **Christmas Eve** the day before Christmas Day. **Christmas tree** a tree decorated at Christmas time.

chrome *noun* (say krohm) a hard, silver-coloured metal used for covering objects such as faucets.

chronic *adjective* lasting for a long time. *A chronic illness kept him away from work.*

chronological *adjective* arranged in the order in which things happened, according to time. *I've listed the events in strict chronological order.* **chronologically** *adverb.*

chrysalis *noun* 1 a butterfly or moth in the stage between being a caterpillar and the time when it flies, also called a pupa. 2 the hard covering of a chrysalis during that time.

church *noun* 1 a building in which Christians pray. 2 a religious service in a church. 3 The Church is a group of people within the Christian religion. *The Pope is head of the Catholic Church throughout the world.*

cigar *noun* a roll of dried tobacco leaves that people smoke. *Cigars are usually much bigger than cigarettes.*

cigarette *noun* finely cut tobacco wrapped in a roll of thin paper which people smoke.

cinema *noun* 1 the art of movie making 2 **old-fashioned** a movie theater. *Let's go to the cinema tonight.*

cipher *noun* (say **sy**-fer) a secret way of writing. *Inscribed with strange ciphers.*

circa *preposition* about, approximately. *He died circa 1850.*

circle *noun* 1 a round flat shape enclosed by a line. Every part of the line is the same distance from the center. 2 something that makes the shape of a circle. 3 a group of people who like the same thing or have similar interests. *He is well respected in political circles.* **circle** *verb* to go around and around in a circle.

circular *adjective* 1 round, shaped like a circle. 2 moving in a circle, starting from a point and ending up in the same place. *A circular route.*

circular *noun* a printed notice sent to a large number of people.

circulation *noun* 1 the process of passing something round a number of people. *When will the new coin be put into circulation?* 2 the flow of blood through the body. *She's got poor circulation.* 3 the movement of any substance around a system. *Air circulation.* 4 the number of sold copies of a newspaper or magazine. *This magazine has a high circulation.* **circulate** *verb.*

Inside this chrysalis a beautiful butterfly is waiting to emerge.

AMAZING FACT

Inside the chrysalis, the caterpillar's body is broken down by hormones and is gradually replaced with the butterfly's body.

The diameter of a circle is twice the length of its radius.

diameter

radius

Lemons and other citrus fruit grow around the warm Mediterranean Sea.

circumcision *noun* cutting off the foreskin of the penis for medical or religious reasons. **circumcise** *verb.*

circumference *noun* the line that marks out a circle or the distance all the way around a circular object.

circumstance *noun* the conditions connected with an event or person and influencing a particular situation. *Mysterious circumstances surrounded her disappearance.* **in the circumstances** because of the way things are. *I decided it was the best thing to do in the circumstances.* **under no circumstances** never.

circus (circuses) *noun* a show with clowns, animals and acrobats in a big tent. *The circus travels from one town to another.*

The large tent that houses a circus is called a big top.

cistern *noun* a tank for storing water.

citizen *noun* 1 a member of a state. *She's a Canadian citizen.* 2 the inhabitant of a city.

citrus fruit *noun* a fruit, such as a lemon, orange, lime or grapefruit, with a sour-sweet taste.

city *noun* a large town. *I've lived in this city all my life.*

civil *adjective* 1 belonging to the people. *Civil rights include freedom and equality.* 2 Used to describe things in a country that are not controlled by military or religious organizations. *A civil ceremony.* 3 polite and helpful. *He gave me a civil response.* **civility** *noun.*

civilian *noun* a person who is not a member of the armed forces.

civilization *noun* 1 a society that has reached a high level of education and culture. *The Greek civilization.* 2 the state of making or becoming civilized.

civilize *verb* to educate and bring culture to people. *The civilized world.*

civil war *noun* a war between people of the same country.

The Battle of Bull Run, which took place in Virginia in 1861, was the first major battle of the American Civil War. Confederate forces (right) defeated the Union army (left).

claim *verb* 1 to say that something belongs to you and ask for it. *Who claimed the lost umbrella?* 2 to say that something is a fact. *He claims to have written to me, but I haven't received the letter.* **claim** *noun* 1 *His claim to have written is a lie.* 2 a demand for something you have a right to. *A pay claim.* 3 a piece of ground or property belonging to somebody. **lay claim to something** to say that something belongs to you.

clan *noun* a group of families who all come from one common family. *The whole Evans clan got together for Thanksgiving.*

clap (clapping, clapped) *verb* 1 to hit your hands together loudly, to show that you are pleased or to attract attention. *Everybody clapped when the music started.* 2 to hit somebody in a friendly way. *He clapped him on the shoulder and said, 'Hello!'* **clap** *noun* 1 the sound of people clapping. 2 a friendly slap. 3 a clap of thunder.

clarinet *noun* a wooden musical instrument, shaped like a tube, which you blow into.

The clarinet is a wind instrument that gives a lovely mellow sound.

clarity *noun* clearness. *He explained it with such clarity that I understood immediately.*

clash *verb* 1 to fight, argue or disagree with somebody. *Street gangs clashed with the police.* 2 When colors clash, they don't look good together. 3 to take place at the same time and therefore be difficult. *The football clashes with the tennis.* 4 to make a loud sound, like the noise of metal objects being hit together. **clash** *noun.*

GRAMMAR NOTE

There are two types of clauses in grammar. A main clause stands alone and forms a complete sentence, e.g. 'I switched on the light.' A subordinate clause cannot stand on its own and has to go with a main clause to form a sentence, e.g. 'I switched on the light when it got dark.'

A bird's claws help it grip its perch.

clasp *noun* 1 a metal fastener for holding two things or parts of something together. *I can't close my purse because the clasp has broken.* 2 a tight hold with your fingers or arms. **clasp** *verb* to take something in your hand or arms and hold it tightly.

class (classes) *noun* 1 a group of pupils or students who are taught together. **in class** during the lesson. *We aren't allowed to talk in class.* 2 people of the same social group. *People used to divide society into upper, middle and lower classes.* 3 people, animals or things that are similar. *Dolphins belong to the same class as humans.* 4 good style. *You can see from the way she dresses that she's got class.* **class** *verb* to say that somebody or something belongs to a group of things, to put them in a class. *You can't class all pop music as junk.*

classic *adjective* 1 of very high quality, outstanding. *A classic novel.* 2 well known and serving as a good example for what is expected. *This is a classic case of measles.* **classic** *noun* 1 a book or film of very high quality. 2 classics is the study of ancient Greek and Roman customs, language and literature.

Students of the classics know that Julius Caesar was murdered on the Ides (15) March by Brutus and Cassius.

classical *adjective* 1 thought of as best, because it follows old traditions. Serious and lasting. *I prefer classical ballet to modern dance.* 2 going back to Roman or Greek customs, art and literature. *In classical times, women were often treated as badly as slaves.*

classroom *noun* a room in a school or college in which children or students are taught. *The classroom was full of students.*

clause *noun* 1 a part of a written agreement or legal document. *It was covered by a clause in the contract written in small print.* 2 a group of words with its own verb forming part of a sentence.

claustrophobia *noun* fear of being in a small closed space.

claw *noun* 1 a sharp nail on the toe of an animal or bird. *Cats have sharp claws.* 2 Crabs and lobsters catch and hold things with their claws. 3 an instrument like a hook on machines for lifting things. **claw** *verb* to pull and scratch with a claw or hand. *The cat clawed a hole in my sock.*

clay *noun* a kind of earth that is soft when it is wet and hard when it is dry. Bricks and pots are made from clay.

The first clay pots were made in Japan around 10,500 BC.

clean *adjective* 1 without any dirt or marks. *I put on clean clothes.* 2 not yet used. *Can I have a clean sheet of paper?* 3 fair. *A clean fight.* 4 morally pure, not dirty. *He only tells clean jokes when there are girls around.* **come clean** to decide to be honest about something you've kept as a secret.

clean *verb* to make something clean from dirt or dust. *I finally cleaned my room.* **clean up** 1 to make an area or a person clean and tidy again. *Before my parents came back, we cleaned up the mess.* 2 You clean up when you win a bet and take all the money.

clean *adverb* completely. *I clean forgot about the money.*

clear *adjective* 1 easy to see through. *The water is so clear, you can see the bottom of the lake.* 2 not cloudy. *A clear sky.* 3 easy to understand or hear. 4 empty, free from blocks, unwanted things or dangers. *A clear road ahead.* 5 free from doubt, guilt or difficulty. *I'm quite clear about my plans.* 6 complete. *Allow three clear days for the package to arrive.* **make yourself clear** to say something so that it is understood and there is no doubt. **clearly** *adverb*.

clear *adverb* 1 easily heard or seen. *He said it loud and clear.* 2 out of the way, not near or touching. *Stand clear of the doors.*

clear *verb* 1 to become free of something like clouds, traffic or unwanted objects. *The mist has cleared.* 2 *The tablets will clear your headache.* 3 to get past something without touching it. *The horse cleared the fence.* 4 to state that somebody is not guilty. *The jury cleared him of all charges.* 5 to get somebody's permission for something. *You'll have to clear your plans with the manager.* **clear away** to take away things that are no longer needed. **clear out** to empty out. **clear up** 1 to stop raining or being cloudy. 2 to solve or settle a mystery or misunderstanding.

clench *verb* to close your teeth or fist tightly.

clergy *noun* leaders in religious organizations such as ministers and rabbis.

Waves hollow out caves in a rocky cliff. Blow holes form above the caves.

Ice cubes are sparkling clear lumps of frozen water.

clerk *noun* 1 a person who works in an office or bank and deals with accounts, records and paperwork. 2 a person who deals with people arriving and leaving a hotel. *The desk clerk was very polite.*

clever *adjective* 1 intelligent and able to learn and understand things quickly. 2 showing skill. **cleverness** *noun*.

cliché *noun* a phrase that has been used so much that it has become meaningless.

click *noun* a short, sharp sound. **click** *verb* 1 *I heard the camera click.* 2 to suddenly understand something. *It suddenly clicked that I had met them before.*

cliff *noun* a steep rock-face, usually at the coast. *We stood on the cliff and looked across the bay.*

climate *noun* the weather conditions of a place. *Oranges don't grow in cold climates.*

climax *noun* the most important and exciting moment in a story, usually near the end. *The plot built up to a climax.*

climb *verb* 1 to go up, down or over something. *We climbed over the wall.* 2 to go higher. *Prices have climbed.* 3 to grow upwards. *A rose climbing up the fence.* **climb** *noun*. *It was a hard climb to the top.*

climber *noun* a person or plant that climbs.

cling *verb* to hold on to somebody tightly. If you cling to an idea, you keep it firmly in your head and believe in it.

clinging *adjective* 1 sticking tightly to something. 2 dependant on another person.

clinic *noun* a place where people go to get medical treatment or advice.

clip *noun* a small metal or plastic fastener for holding things together. **clip** *verb*.

clip *noun* a short piece of a film or television program. **clip** *verb* to cut. *Diane clipped the hedge with her shears.*

cloak *noun* 1 a loose coat without sleeves that fastens at the neck. 2 a disguise to hide the truth. *Under the cloak of darkness.* **cloak** *verb* to hide or cover secrets.

clock *noun* an instrument that tells the time. **turn the clock back** to go back to things or ideas how they were a long time ago. **clock in** *verb* to record the time when you start work. **clock out** to record the time you stop work. *The workers clocked out at 4 p.m.*

No one would be able to sleep through the loud ringing of this alarm clock.

clockwise *adjective* moving in the same direction as the hands of the clock. *To switch on, you turn the knob clockwise.*

clockwork *noun* a mechanism with wheels and springs that is wound up. **clockwork** *adjective. Clockwork toys.*

clod *noun* a lump of earth.

clog *noun* a shoe with a wooden sole.

clog (clogging, clogged) *verb* to become blocked with grease or dirt. **clog up** *I need a plunger because the sink is clogged up.*

cloister *noun* a covered path round a square in a monastery or college.

clone *noun* an animal or plant that has been produced in a laboratory from the cells of another animal or plant. A clone looks exactly like the animal it was made from. **clone** *verb.*

close *verb* (say klohz) 1 to shut. *She closed the door.* 2 to end. *The offer closes at the end of the month.* **close down** to stop work. *Most of the coal mines have closed down.* **close in** to come nearer and nearer. *Winter is closing in.* **close** *noun* the end of an activity or a period of time.

close *noun* (say klohss) the end of some activity or block of time. *The summer evening drew to a close.*

close *adjective* (say klohss) 1 near. *My cousins are my close relatives.* 2 trusted and liked. *Sophie is my closest friend.* 3 tight, with little space between, especially in competitions and games. *It was a close contest.* 4 thorough and careful. *A close examination of the document showed that it was a forgery.* 5 warm and stuffy. **closely** *adverb.* **closeness** *noun.*

close *adverb* (say klohss) 1 near. *I live quite close.* 2 almost. *Close to 30 years ago.*

The section of the caterpillar that is under the magnifying glass is seen in close-up.

closed *adjective* 1 not open. *We could hardly breathe with all the windows closed.* 2 not open to the public, especially a store or museum. *Closed on Mondays and Wednesdays.* **behind closed doors** in secret.

closet *noun* a tall cupboard for storing things, especially clothes. *Instead of really cleaning my room, I just threw all the clothes into the closet.*

close-up *noun* a photograph or film that is taken from very near.

closure *noun* the closing down of a factory or other business. *The closure of the hospital was a blow to the local community.*

cloth *noun* 1 woven fabric used for making clothes, coverings and other things. 2 a piece of material for cleaning, e.g. a dish cloth.

clothes *plural noun* things you wear, such as pants, shirts and dresses.

clothing *noun* the clothes people wear. *You'll need waterproof clothing for sailing.*

cloud *noun* 1 a mass of small drops of water that floats in the sky. *Clouds are usually white or gray.* 2 a mass of smoke or dust in the air. **under a cloud** out of favour, in disgrace. *He had a fight and left under a cloud.* **cloud** *verb* to become unclear. **cloudy** *adjective.*

cloud over *The sky clouded over.*

It was a bright summer's day, but now the sky is beginning to cloud over.

clover *noun* a small plant with three leaves on each stalk.

clown *noun* 1 a person in a circus or pantomime who wears funny clothes and make-up, and says and does silly things to make people laugh. 2 a person who acts like a clown. **clown** *verb.*

club *noun* 1 a group of people who meet because they have the same interests. *My brother has joined the chess club.* 2 the place where the club members meet.

club *noun* 1 a big, heavy stick with a thick end that can be used for fighting. 2 a specially shaped stick for hitting a golf ball. 3 a playing card with black clover leaves on it. *The king of clubs.* **club** *verb* to hit somebody with a heavy stick. **club house** the building where a club meets.

clue *noun* something that helps you to find the answer to a question or problem. *The footprints provided a clue.* **not to have a clue** not to know much about something.

clump *noun* a group. *A clump of daffodils.* **clump** *verb* to walk with heavy footsteps. *Don't clump around in those big heavy boots.*

Daffodils grow in clumps as the bulbs under the ground multiply.

clumsy *adjective* 1 A clumsy person moves about awkwardly, walks into things, knocks things over and breaks them. 2 tactless and not very skillful. *A clumsy explanation.*

cluster *noun* a small group of people or things close together. *A cluster of bright stars.* **cluster** *verb* to form a tight group.

clutch (clutches) *noun* 1 a tight hold. If you are in somebody's clutches, they have control over you. 2 the pedal you press in a car while changing gear.

clutch *verb* to hold tightly.

coach (coaches) *noun* 1 the economy seats on a plane or train. 2 a four-wheeled horse-drawn carriage that was used to carry passengers and mail.

coach (coaches) *noun* 1 a person who trains sportspeople. *The football team has a new coach.* 2 a teacher who gives private lessons. **coach** *verb.* *She was coached by her dad.*

coal *noun* 1 a hard black or brown mineral substance from under the earth that gives heat when it is burned. Coal is dug out of mines. 2 a piece of coal.

coarse *adjective* 1 rough, not smooth. 2 rude, vulgar. **coarseness** *noun.*

coast *noun* land right next to the ocean. **coastal** *adjective.* **the coast is clear** there is nobody around to see you or catch you out.

coastline *noun* the outline of the coast. *The hotel is on a cliff that looks out over a rocky coastline.*

Inside a coconut there is white flesh and a thin milk that makes a refreshing drink.

This coastline has rocky headlands, sandy beaches and two rivers running down to the sea.

coat *noun* 1 a piece of clothing with sleeves that you wear over other clothes when you go out. 2 an animal's fur or hair. 3 a layer of paint or varnish. *A coat of paint.* **coat** *verb.*

coating *noun* a thin covering or layer spread over a surface.

coax *verb* to gently try to talk somebody into doing something.

cobra *noun* (say **koh**-bruh) a poisonous snake. *A cobra was coiled up in the grass.*

cobweb *noun* a spider's web.

cockerel *noun* a young male bird.

A cockerel has a bright red comb and shiny tail feathers. A male is usually more colorful than a hen.

cockney *noun* 1 a person born in East London. 2 the way people from East London speak.

cockpit *noun* a compartment for the pilot of a plane or the driver of a car.

cocoa *noun* 1 a brown powder made from cocoa seeds. 2 a hot drink made from cocoa powder and water or milk.

coconut *noun* 1 a large round nut with a hard, hairy shell from the coconut palm. 2 the white flesh inside the nut, which is used in cooking and baking.

cocoon *noun* a covering of silky threads produced by a caterpillar before it develops into an adult insect.

cod (cod) *noun* a large sea-fish. *We had cod and salad for dinner.*

code *noun* 1 a set of signals or a system of words, letters or numbers used to write messages. *You can only crack a code if you know the system.* 2 a set of laws or rules. *There is a strict dress code at our school - no jeans or tee-shirts.* **code** *verb* You code a message by replacing the letters or numbers in it with other letters or numbers. **coded** *adjective.* *A coded message.*

coffee *noun* 1 a drink made by pouring hot water on to the roasted and ground seeds, called coffee beans, of a tropical plant. *A cup of strong coffee.* 2 the coffee beans or powder the drink is made from.

coffin *noun* a box in which a dead person is buried. *A vampire rose up out of the coffin.*

cog *noun* one of a number of teeth round the edge of a wheel which is used to move another wheel or part in a machine.

Cogs like these are found in watches as well as in gear boxes.

cogwheel *noun* a wheel with cogs.

coil *noun* a loop of rope or wire or a series of loops wound into a spiral. **coil** *verb* to wind into a coil. *The snake coiled its body around a tree.* **coil up** to wind round and round.

coin *noun* a piece of metal money. **coin** *verb* 1 to manufacture coins. 2 to invent a new word or phrase.

coincide *verb* to happen at the same time as something else. *Her vacation coincided with his trip to Italy.*

coincidence *noun* a remarkable set of events. *By coincidence they met on the plane to New York.*

cold *adjective* 1 not warm, having a low temperature. 2 unfriendly or unkind. *She seems very cold and unloving.* If something leaves you cold, you can't get excited about it. **coldness** *noun.*

cold *noun* 1 low temperature, cold weather. *Wear a hat if you're going out in the cold.* 2 an infectious illness that makes you sneeze and cough. *Have you got a cold?*

cold-blooded *adjective* Cold-blooded animals change their body temperature according to the temperature around them. Reptiles are cold-blooded. A cold-blooded person is cruel.

Reptiles like this iguana are cold-blooded. They need to sit on a rock to warm up in the Sun before they get active.

cold sore *noun* a blister on the lips or in the mouth.

colic *noun* a stomach-ache.

collaborate *verb* to work together or with someone else on a job. **collaboration** *noun.*

collapse *verb* 1 to fall down suddenly. *The roof collapsed in the storm.* 2 If you collapse, you become weak or ill. 3 If a plan collapses, it doesn't work out. 4 to fold up, e.g. a table or chair. **collapse** *noun. Disagreements on both sides caused the collapse of the talks.* **collapsible** *adjective.*

Colombia was named by its Spanish conquerors after Christopher Columbus, the first European to discover it.

collar *noun* 1 the part of a shirt, dress or coat that stands up or folds down round the neck. 2 a leather band round the neck of a dog, cat or horse. **collar** *verb* to catch somebody. *I collared him just as he was leaving the office.*

colleague *noun* a person you work with.

collect *verb* 1 to gather from various places. *We collected wood for the fire.* 2 If you collect things, you are interested in them. *I collect comics.* 3 to come together. *People collected around the singer.* 4 to ask for money from people. 5 When you collect your thoughts, you prepare and calm yourself. **collection** *noun. My dad gave me his old stamp collection.*

collector *noun* a person who collects things. *A coin collector.*

college *noun* a place where people can carry on studying after they have left school.

collide *verb* to crash into something. *The two cars collided.* **collision** *noun.*

Colombia *noun* a country in South America.

Colombo *noun* the capital of Sri Lanka.

colon *noun* a mark (:), often put before listing a number of things.

colon *noun* the large part of the intestine.

colonel *noun* (say ker-nul) an army officer in charge of a regiment.

colony *noun* 1 a country that is controlled by another more powerful country. 2 a group of people of the same kind living close together. 3 a group of animals living together. *A colony of bees.*

color *noun* 1 Color is what you see when light is broken up into parts. Red, blue and green are colors. 2 something seen in all its colors, not just in black and white. 3 the quality that makes things interesting or more exciting. *He'll add a bit of color to the party.* **color** *verb* 1 to color in a picture with crayons. 2 to influence somebody's opinion or feelings. 3 to become red in the face. **colored** *adjective.*

colossal *adjective* very large. *It's a colossal project.*

Red, blue and yellow are the primary colors from which all other colors can be made.

colt *noun* a young male horse.

column *noun* 1 a tall stone structure holding up part of a building or standing on its own. A pillar. 2 a long, narrow shape. *A column of smoke.* 3 an article usually written by the same person in a newspaper or magazine. 4 part of a page. *There are three columns on this page.* 5 a group of people or animals that move in a long line.

coma *noun* (say koh-muh) a state of unconsciousness from which it is difficult to wake up, usually due to illness or an accident.

comb *noun* a piece of plastic or metal with a row of teeth for fixing your hair. **comb** *verb* 1 to comb your hair. 2 to search thoroughly. *We combed the house for clues.*

Viking comb

combination *noun* 1 a mixture of things. *The members are a good combination of young and old.* 2 a code of numbers or letters for opening a lock.

combine *verb* to join together. *It's not always easy to combine work and play.*

combine harvester *noun* a machine that reaps and threshes grain.

combustion *noun* the process of burning.

come (coming, came, come) *verb* 1 to move towards a place or the speaker. 2 to arrive at a particular place or reach something like a decision. *I've come to the conclusion that I don't like meat.* 3 to happen. *How did you come to be invited to the party?* 4 to exist. *The tee-shirts come in all colors.* 5 to become. *My laces have come undone.* **come about** to happen. **come across** to meet or find. **come by** to get. **come in** 1 to enter. 2 to become fashionable. 3 to be received. *A report of the accident has just come in.* **come in for** to get a share of something. *She's come in for some criticism.* **come into** to inherit. **come off** 1 to take place or succeed. *Our field trip didn't come off.* 2 to become unfastened. *A button has come off.* 3 **Come off it!** said when someone is being silly or unreasonable. **come through** to survive a difficult situation. **come to** 1 *The bill came to $20.* 2 to wake up after having been unconscious. *I was in the hospital when I came to.* **come up** 1 to come to attention, be mentioned or discussed. *My question came up at the meeting.* 2 to happen. *An interesting job has come up.* 3 to win. *Your number might come up next time.* **come up against** to meet something, such as a difficult situation. **come up with** to think of. *He came up with a solution.*

comedian *noun* an actor who plays a funny part or a person who makes people laugh.

comedy *noun* a funny play, film or situation.

comet *noun* an object traveling across the sky that looks like a star with a bright tail of light.

Cats usually like to sit in the most comfortable chair in the house.

Napoleon was in command of the French navy as well as the French army.

Spectacular comets are just dirty iceballs a few kilometers across.

comfort *noun* 1 a pleasant and relaxed situation or feeling. 2 kindness and sympathy given to a person who is unhappy. 3 a person or thing that gives hope or makes pain easier for an unhappy person. **comfort** *verb* to make somebody less unhappy. *I tried to comfort her after the accident.* **comforting** *adjective*.

comfortable *adjective* 1 relaxing and pleasant to be in or on. *A comfortable chair.* 2 having enough money. *We are comfortable and can afford most things now.* 3 free from pain or worry. *I don't feel comfortable with people I don't know.*

comic *noun* 1 a magazine with picture stories. 2 a person who makes people laugh or an actor who plays funny parts. **comic** *adjective*. *A comic strip.*

comma *noun* a mark (,) used in writing to show a pause or separate items in a list. *Oranges, apples and pears are all fruit.*

command *noun* 1 an order, telling people what to do. *The soldier obeyed the officer's commands.* 2 control. *The troops are under the general's command.* 3 knowledge and ability. *She has a good command of French.* **command** *verb* 1 to order. 2 to be in control and responsible for a person or group. 3 to deserve and get. *Her position commands respect.* **commanding** *adjective*.

commence *verb* to begin.

comment *noun* an opinion or explanation about an event, a book or a person. **comment** *verb*. *Would you like to comment on the recent election?*

commentary *noun* 1 opinions and descriptions spoken during an event. *I listened to the commentary on the big game.* 2 a collection of written opinions and explanations on an event, book, etc.

commerce *noun* the buying and selling of goods on a large scale.

commercial *adjective* 1 used in commerce. 2 profitable, out to make money. *His film is a commercial success.* 3 Commercial television and radio are paid for by advertisements.

commercial *noun* an advertisement on television or radio.

Some people enjoy the commercials on television more than the programs.

commit (committing, committed) *verb* 1 to do something wrong or bad. To commit a crime. 2 to put somebody into care or prison. 3 If you commit yourself to something, you promise to do it. **commitment** *noun*.

committee *noun* a group of people chosen by others to carry out special duties.

common *adjective* 1 shared by two or more. *It is our common aim to stop the war.* If people have something in common, they share the same interest or are somehow the same. 2 ordinary or happening often. *Smith is a common name.* 3 generally known. *It is common knowledge that smoking is bad for you.* 4 If something is done for the common good, it is done for all people. **common law** unwritten law based on customs. **common sense** good sense and the ability to make the right decision, gained from experience.

common *noun* a park where everybody is allowed to go.

communicate *verb* to make news, information or your feelings known to other people. *She communicates very well.*

communication *noun* 1 sharing and exchanging news or information. 2 a message. 3 Communications are the links between people and places, such as television, radio, telephone, fax, e-mail, roads and railroads.

communism *noun* a political system in which production is owned and controlled by the state. **communist** *noun*. **communist** *adjective*.

community (communities) *noun* 1 people living in one particular place or area. 2 a group of people living together and sharing interests, religion or nationality.

You should always take a compass when walking in the mountains, in case a fog descends and you lose your way.

The Muslim community prays to Allah five times a day, not always at a mosque. The most important worship is at noon on Friday.

commuter *noun* a person who travels regularly between home and work. **commute** *verb*. *I commute by train.*

Comoros *noun* a country in the Indian Ocean off East Africa.

compact *adjective* closely packed and neatly fitted together. *A compact kitchen.*

compact disk *noun* a disc from which recorded sound is reproduced. CD stands for compact disk.

companion *noun* a person you spend time with. *A traveling companion.*

company *noun* 1 being with other people. When you keep somebody company, you stay or go with them. 2 visitors. 3 a business firm. *He works for a toy company.*

comparative *adjective* judged by looking and thinking about things, by comparing. *Despite the war raging around them, they live in comparative peace.* **comparatively** *adverb*. **comparative** *noun* the form of an adjective or adverb that shows 'more'. The comparative of 'good' is 'better'.

compare *verb* to look at and examine things or people to find out in what ways they are similar or different. *It's cold compared to yesterday.* **comparison** *noun*.

compartment *noun* a separate place in something larger. *There's a flashlight in the glove compartment.*

compass (compasses) *noun* (say **kum**-puhss) an instrument used for finding directions. The needle of a compass always points north.

compasses *noun* a V-shaped instrument used for drawing circles.

compatible *adjective* able to exist together or work well with another. *Good vacations at prices compatible with most people's income.* The opposite of compatible is incompatible.

compel (compelling, compelled) *verb* to make somebody do something they don't want to do.

compensate *verb* to make up for loss, injury or damage, usually by paying money. **compensation** *noun*. *They asked for compensation for their injuries.*

C

compete *verb* to take part in a game, race or examination.

The fastest cars in the world compete against each other at a Grand Prix race.

competent *adjective* able to do something. *She is a competent teacher.*

competition *noun* 1 a game, race or other test that people try to win. 2 the act of trying to win or get something. *I was in competition with two other applicants for the job.* In business, competition means trying to get people to buy one thing rather than another. *Competition helps to keep prices down.*

competitive *adjective* 1 wanting to succeed or be better than other people or companies. 2 Competitive prices are low. *Selling at competitive rates.*

competitor *noun* a person, firm or product competing with others.

compile *verb* to collect information and put it together in a list or book. *Lots of people helped to compile this dictionary.*

complain *verb* to say that you are not happy about something. *The neighbors complained about the noise.*

complaint *noun* 1 a statement expressing unhappiness with a particular situation. 2 an illness.

complete *adjective* 1 whole. 2 finished. *When will work be complete?* 3 total, full. *The party was a complete surprise.* **complete** *verb* to finish doing something or add what is needed. **completion** *noun*.

complex *adjective* difficult to understand or explain. *A complex problem.*

$$X^2 = 109(a + b), (x + y)$$

complex *noun* 1 a group of buildings or things connected with each other. *A new housing complex.* 2 an emotional problem that influences a person's behavior. *If you keep blaming me, I'll get a guilt complex.*

complexion *noun* the natural color and quality of the skin of your face. *She has a beautiful complexion.*

WORD HISTORY

The ancient Greeks believed that the body contained four vital fluids, or humors – blood, phlegm, yellow bile and black bile. Your complexion, from the Latin 'weaving together', showed how your humors were combined.

Simon could not figure out the complex equation his teacher set him.

complicated *adjective* difficult. *A complicated problem.* **complication** *noun*.

compliment *noun* an expression of praise and admiration. *He paid her a compliment on her new dress.* **compliment** *verb*.

component *noun* a part of a larger object or machine. *The bike's components are made in southern Italy.*

A spark plug is one of the components of a car's engine.

compose *verb* 1 to make up or form something. *The firm is composed of managers, secretaries and builders.* 2 to write music or poetry. 3 to make yourself calm. *Compose yourself before you speak.*

composer *noun* a person who writes music.

composition *noun* 1 a piece of music. 2 an essay or story written at school. 3 the various parts something is made up of. *A chemical composition.*

comprehend *verb* to understand. *I don't comprehend.* **comprehension** *noun*.

comprehensive *adjective* including everything needed. *The chairman gave a comprehensive explanation of his plans.*

compress *verb* (say kum-press) to squeeze something together so it takes up less space. *New techniques make it possible to compress data so that a huge amount fits onto a disk.*

A car crusher can compress a whole car into a small cube for recycling purposes.

compromise *noun* the settlement of an argument or differences of opinion by each side accepting less than it had asked for. *After a long discussion we reached a compromise.* **compromise** *verb* 1 *We compromised and went by bus.* 2 If you compromise yourself, you act unwisely or make people doubt you.

compulsive *adjective* not being able to stop yourself from doing something, even though it is wrong or harmful. *Compulsive liars rarely tell the truth.* **compulsion** *noun*.

compulsory *adjective* having to do something. If something is compulsory, it must be done. *Education is compulsory for all children in Europe.* The opposite of compulsory is optional.

computer *noun* an electronic machine that can make calculations, store information or control other machines. **computerize** *verb* 1 to store information on a computer. 2 to equip a business with computers.

Businesses and schools have all benefitted from the invention of the computer.

Conakry *noun* the capital of Guinea.

concave *adjective* curved inwards, like the inside of a hollow ball. The opposite of concave is convex.

conceal *verb* to hide or keep secret. *The scarf concealed the hideous scar.*

conceited *adjective* being too proud of yourself and your abilities. **conceit** *noun*.

concentrate *verb* 1 to give all your attention to something. *You must concentrate more on your homework.* 2 to bring or come together. *Industry is concentrated in the north.* **concentrated** *adjective. Concentrated orange juice has to be diluted with water.*

concentration *noun* 1 If something needs concentration, it requires all your attention. 2 a gathering. *A concentration of troops at the border.*

concept *noun* an idea.

concern *noun* 1 something that is very important to you. *Her diet is no concern of mine.* **concern** *verb*. 2 a business. *A very profitable concern.*

concert *noun* a musical performance. *They played a symphony at the concert.*

WORD HISTORY

'Concave' comes from the Latin 'cavus', a cave. 'Convex' comes from the Latin 'convexus', arched.

The type on the right has been squashed up, or condensed.

CONDENSED

The concert is in full swing, with the conductor directing.

concise *adjective* short and to the point, not saying anything unnecessary.

conclude *verb* 1 to end. 2 to come to believe something after having thought it over. To decide. *When they didn't call back, he concluded that they had gone away.*

conclusion *noun* 1 an ending. 2 an opinion or judgement. *The jury reached the conclusion that he was guilty.*

concrete *noun* building material made by mixing together cement, sand, gravel and water. *A concrete bridge.*

concrete *adjective* definite, real. *Can you give me a concrete example?*

condemn *verb* 1 to say that you find something wrong and unacceptable. *We condemn violence.* 2 to judge a person guilty or sentence a criminal. 3 to force somebody to suffer. *After her husband's death, she was condemned to a life of loneliness.*

condense *verb* 1 to make a speech or piece of writing shorter. *He condensed his report to a few sentences.* 2 to change from gas or vapor into liquid. 3 to become thicker. **condensed** *adjective. Condensed milk.*

condition *noun* 1 the state somebody or something is in. *My bike is in very good condition.* 2 The conditions people live or work in are the surroundings that affect their well-being. *It is impossible to work under these conditions.* 3 something that is dependent on another thing, or necessary for something else. *You can come to stay on condition that you help with the baby.*

condom *noun* a rubber covering for the penis used as a means of birth control or to prevent infection.

conduct *verb* (say kun-**dukt**) 1 to behave. *They conducted themselves well.* 2 to lead or guide a person. 3 to control or manage a group. *To conduct a meeting.* 4 to direct. *To conduct an orchestra.* 5 to act as a path for electricity or heat.

conduct *noun* (say **kon**-dukt) 1 behavior. *Conduct at school has improved.* 2 the manner in which something is managed.

conductor *noun* 1 a person who conducts musicians in an orchestra. 2 a person who is in charge of buses or trains. 3 something that conducts heat or electricity. *Copper is a good conductor.*

cone *noun* 1 a shape with a round base ending in a point at the top. 2 the fruit of pine or fir trees. 3 an ice-cream cone.

Cones are the seed pods of conifers or evergreen trees.

confuse *verb* 1 to make a person feel puzzled. To make something difficult to understand. *He confused me with his long explanation.* 2 to get things mixed up. *I'm always confusing her with her sister.*

confusion *noun* 1 mixing a thing, person or situation up. 2 a situation where nobody knows what is going on. **confusing** *adjective*. *A confusing explanation.*

Congo *noun* one of two countries in Africa; the Republic of the Congo is also called Congo-Brazzaville; the Democratic Republic of the Congo was fomerly called Zaire.

The flag of the Congo has a diagonal yellow stripe on a green and red ground.

congratulate *verb* to tell a person that you are pleased about their success or something that they have done. *My friend congratulated me for scoring a touchdown.* **congratulation** *noun*.

conifer *noun* (say **kon-if-er**) a type of tree that has needle-like leaves and bears its fruit in cones. *A conifer plantation.*

conjure (say **kun-juh**) *verb* to do magic tricks. *The magician conjured a large white rabbit out of a hat.* **conjuror** *noun*. a person who does magic tricks. **conjure up** to make something appear.

conk out *verb* (slang) to go to sleep.

connect *verb* 1 to join together. 2 to link by telephone. *Don't hang up, I'm trying to connect you.* 3 to be related or linked. *The families are connected.* **connection** *noun*.

conquer *verb* 1 to defeat and take over. To conquer a country. 2 to overcome an illness or a difficult situation. **conqueror** *noun*.

conquest *noun* 1 the conquering of something. *The conquest of Mount Everest.* 2 overcoming something.

conscience *noun* the part of your mind that tells you if what you are doing is right or wrong. *You have a guilty conscience when you do something wrong.*

conscious *adjective* 1 noticing what is happening. *He was conscious of everybody looking at him.* 2 awake. *The patient is not conscious.* **consciousness** *noun*.

consent *verb* to agree to do something. **consent** *noun* permission given. *She left school without her parents' consent.*

DID YOU KNOW

Except for the larch, nearly all conifer trees are evergreen. This means they don't lose their leaves in the fall. Trees that drop their leaves are called deciduous.

Many of the constellations, such as the Great Bear, were named after mythical creatures.

consequence *noun* something that happens as a result of something else. *He dreaded the consequences of his actions.*

conserve *verb* to store up, or keep from going bad or being wasted. *We need to conserve energy.* **conservation** *noun*.

consider *verb* 1 to think about something in order to make a decision. *I'm considering quitting my job.* 2 to regard as. *I consider him an idiot.* **consideration** *noun*. **take into consideration** to allow for something. *I will take your illness into consideration when giving you a final grade.*

considerable *adjective* fairly large. *We had to pay a considerable amount of money for the lot.*

consist *verb* to be made up of. *Europe consists of many different countries.*

The Low Countries consist of many islands.

console *verb* to give somebody sympathy to make them less sad. **consolation** *noun*.

consonant *noun* any of the letters of the alphabet except for the vowels a, e, i, o and u. *How many consonants are in your name?*

conspiracy *noun* a secret plan to do something that is against the law. A plot.

conspirator *noun* a person who takes part in a conspiracy.

constant *adjective* 1 unchanging, fixed. *We were driving at a constant speed.* 2 loyal and faithful. **constancy** *noun*.

constellation *noun* a group of stars.

constipated *adjective* If you are constipated, you are unable to empty your bowels. **constipation** *noun*.

constituency *noun* an area that has elected officials.

constitution *noun* 1 the system of laws that states how a country is governed. *The Constitution of the United States of America.* 2 the general condition of a person's body. 3 the way in which something is made up.

construct *verb* to build or put together.

construction *noun* 1 a building. 2 the process of building. *The bridge is under construction.* 3 words put together to form a phrase or sentence. *The construction of a sentence.* 4 an explanation. *The wrong construction was put on his behavior.*

constructive *adjective* helpful.

consult *verb* to go to a person or book for information. *Consult a doctor about your illness before it gets any worse.*

consultant *noun* a person who gives advice.

consume *verb* 1 to eat or drink something. 2 to use up. *The car consumes a lot of gas.* 3 to destroy. *Fire consumed the entire village in a matter of hours.*

consumer *noun* a person who buys and uses goods and services.

contact *noun* 1 the process of touching or coming together. Communication. *I'm not in contact with him.* 2 a person. **contact** *verb. He's got some useful contacts.*

contact lens *noun* a tiny piece of plastic shaped to fit over the eye to make you see better. *Disposable contact lenses.*

contagious *adjective* spreading from person to person. *A contagious disease.*

contain *verb* to hold. *The book contains all the information you need.*

container *noun* 1 a box, barrel or bottle to hold things in. 2 a large metal box used for transporting goods.

Different shaped plastic containers are useful for storing food.

contemporary *adjective* 1 happening now, modern. 2 belonging to the past and happening at the same time as something else. *Some contemporary politicians were critical of Lincoln.* **contemporary** *noun. Our fathers were contemporaries at school.*

contempt *noun* lack of respect, thinking that somebody or something is not important. *I hold him in contempt.*

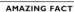

Cranes work from above to finish the construction of this skyscraper.

GRAMMAR NOTE

Words like 'I've', 'won't' and 'shouldn't' are called contractions. These shorter forms (for 'I have', 'I will not' and 'I should not') use an apostrophe to show where letters have been missed out.

content *adjective* (say kun-**tent**) happy, satisfied. *She was content with her life.*

content *noun* (say **kon**-tent) something contained. *The contents were damaged.*

contents *plural noun* things contained. *He emptied the contents of the package.*

contest *noun* (say **kon**-test) a struggle or fight in which people take part in order to win. *It was an even contest.*

contest *verb* (say kun-**test**) to compete or fight for a place. *To contest an election.*

continent *noun* one of Earth's huge land masses. *Europe, Asia and Africa are continents.*

The continent of Antarctica surrounds the South Pole.

continual *adjective* without stopping.

continue *verb* 1 to go on doing or being something without stopping. 2 to start again after stopping. **continuation** *noun.*

continuous *adjective* without a break. **continuity** *noun.*

contract *noun* (say **kon**-trakt) a written agreement between people. **contract** *verb* (say kun-**trakt**) 1 *We have been contracted to do the music.* 2 to get a disease. *My sister has contracted German measles.*

contract *verb* (say kun-**trakt**) to make or become smaller or shorter. *'Has not' is often contracted to 'hasn't'.* **contraction** *noun.*

contradict *verb* to say that something said or written is wrong. *Don't contradict me.* **contradiction** *noun.*

contrast *noun* (say **kon**-trast) the difference seen between things when they are compared. *There was a big contrast between their results.* **contrast** *verb* (say kun-**trast**).

contribute *verb* 1 to join with others in doing things or giving money to help make something successful. *She contributed towards my success.* 2 to write an article for a newspaper or magazine. **contribution** *noun. He made a contribution of $100.*

control *noun* the power to influence, make decisions or give orders. **control** *verb* to have control of something. *The teacher can't control the class.*

convenience *noun* 1 ease of use. *I always buy frozen food for convenience when I'm busy at work.* 2 a useful appliance, such as a dishwasher.

convenient *adjective* 1 easy to use or suitable. 2 easy to get to. *The supermarket is a convenient place to shop.*

convent *noun* a place where nuns live.

converge *verb* to come together towards the same point. *The crowds converged on the stadium.*

conversation *noun* a talk between people.

converse *verb* to talk. *Let's converse.*

convex *adjective* curved outward, like the outside of a ball. The opposite of convex is concave. *A convex mirror.*

convey *verb* 1 to carry from one place to another. 2 to make known. *Words cannot convey my sympathy.*

convict *verb* (say kun-**vikt**) to find somebody guilty of a crime. *He was convicted of murder.* **convict** *noun* (say **kon**-vikt) a person who has been found guilty.

convoy *noun* a group of ships or vehicles traveling together.

A convoy of vehicles is heading for the ferry.

cook *verb* to make food. **cook** *noun*. *She's a wonderful cook.*

cookie *noun* a small, flat sweet cake. *We're making oatmeal, peanut butter and chocolate chip cookies for the party.*

cool *adjective* 1 between warm and cold. 2 calm. *She manages to keep cool even when she is annoyed.* **cool** *verb* to make or become cool.

cooperate *verb* to work together for a common purpose. **cooperation** *noun*.

cooperative *adjective* 1 helpful. 2 owned by its members. *A cooperative business.*

cope *verb* to deal with something successfully. *She manages to cope with all the family's problems.*

Copenhagen *noun* the capital of Denmark.

The roads converged just south of the mountains.

copper *noun* a reddish-brown metal. Wires are often made of copper. **copper** *adjective*. *Ann's new bike is a copper color.*

copy *noun* 1 a thing that looks exactly like another. *Can I have a copy of the picture?* 2 an example of a book, newspaper or magazine of which there are many others. *His copy of the book was torn.* **copy** *verb* 1 to make a copy of something. 2 to do the same as another person. *He's always copying me.*

coral *noun* a hard red, pink or white substance formed from the skeletons of tiny sea animals. *We went snorkeling on the coral reef.*

A coral reef is a fascinating place for underwater explorers to observe tropical fish.

cord *noun* 1 a thick string. 2 wires inside a plastic casing for electrical equipment. 3 a part of the body. *We use our vocal cords to make sounds.* 4 corduroy.

corduroy *noun* thick velvety cotton material with ridges. *A corduroy jacket.*

core *noun* 1 the hard middle of an apple or pear which contains the pips. 2 the central, most important part of something.

cork *noun* 1 the soft, light bark of the cork oak. Cork tiles are used as a floor covering. 2 a stopper for a bottle made of cork or other material.

corn *noun* maize. *Corn on the cob is my sister's favorite food.*

corn *noun* a painful, hard lump of skin on the foot. *He stepped on my corn.*

corner *noun* 1 the place where two edges, lines, walls or streets meet. 2 a kick from the corner of a soccer field. *They scored from a corner.* 3 a region. *The four corners of the world.* **in a corner** in a difficult situation. **corner** *verb* 1 to drive round a corner. 2 to force somebody into a difficult situation. *He finally cornered me about the mistake.*

cornflakes *noun* toasted flakes made from corn, usually eaten with milk for breakfast.

coronation *noun* the crowning of a king or queen. *We watched the coronation of the new king on television.*

WORD BUILDING

The prefix 'co-' gives a sense of together. People who cooperate (sometimes spelled with a hyphen, co-operate), work together.

corporal punishment *noun* punishing a person by beating them.

corpse *noun* a dead body.

correct *adjective* 1 without any mistakes. 2 proper, most suitable in a particular situation. **correct** *verb* 1 to put something right and mark the mistakes. 2 to point out a person's faults in order to improve their behavior. **correction** *noun*.

correspond *verb* 1 to write letters to each other. 2 to be the same or in agreement with something. *Her report of the accident doesn't correspond with his.* 3 to be like or match closely. *Our president corresponds to their prime minister.*

correspondence *noun* 1 writing and exchanging letters. 2 the letters you receive. *A pile of correspondence.* 3 likeness or relationship between particular things.

corridor *noun* a passage in a building.

A cart waits outside the door to one of the rooms in a hospital corridor.

corrode *verb* to destroy by chemical action or by rust. *Acid corrodes metal.* **corrosion** *noun.* **corrosive** *adjective.*

corrugated *adjective* shaped into ridges or folds. *Corrugated paper is used for packing.*

corrupt *adjective* immoral or wicked. *The newspaper exposed the corrupt politicians.*

corrupt *verb* to make somebody change from good to bad. *Power corrupts.* **corruption** *noun.*

cosmetics *noun* substances such as lipstick and eyeshadow, used to beautify the face.

cosmic *adjective* related to the universe. *Cosmic rays from outer space.*

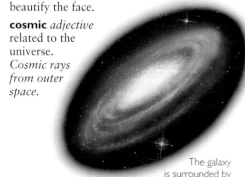

The galaxy is surrounded by cosmic dust.

cosmonaut *noun* a Russian astronaut.

cosmos *noun* (say **koz**-moss) the universe.

cost *noun* the price of something. **at all costs** no matter what the cost may be. **cost** (costing, cost) *verb* 1 to have a certain price. 2 to cause a loss or disadvantage to somebody. *Drunken driving costs many lives.* 3 to estimate. *The garage costed the repairs at about $200.*

Costa Rica *noun* a country in Central America.

The flag of Costa Rica has a colored emblem on a striped red, blue and white background.

costly *adjective* expensive.

costume *noun* clothes worn by actors or at a particular time in history. *National costume is worn on historic occasions.*

cot *noun* a light, narrow bed.

cottage *noun* a small house, especially in the country.

cotton *noun* 1 cloth made from the soft white fibers covering the seeds of the cotton plant. 2 a tall tropical plant. 3 cotton thread.

cotton ball *noun* balls of soft, fluffy cotton for putting cream on your skin or cleaning wounds.

couch *noun* a sofa. *Sit on the couch.*

cough *verb* to push air out of your throat and make a harsh noise. **cough** *noun* 1 the sound of coughing. 2 an illness that makes you cough. *The baby had a nasty cough.*

could past tense of can.

council *noun* a group of people chosen to make laws and decisions and run a town or organization. *The UN Security Council first met in London.*

councillor *noun* a member of a council.

counsel *noun* 1 advice. 2 a group of lawyers acting for somebody in court. **counsel** (counselling, counselled) *verb. She counsels families who have problems.*

counsellor *noun* a person trained to give advice and help.

count *verb* 1 to say numbers in order. *He counted up to 10.* 2 to say or name objects or people to find the total number in a collection. *The teacher counted the children.* 3 to include. *There are four of us, counting me.* 4 to have importance or value. *It's the thought that counts.* 5 to consider. *I count myself lucky.* **count** *noun* 1 counting. 2 a number reached by counting. 3 one of a number of crimes somebody is accused of. *He was found guilty on all counts.* **lose count** not know the exact number.

count *noun* a European nobleman equal to an earl. *The count married the countess.*

counter *noun* 1 a flat surface like a table in the kitchen for working and preparing food or in stores on which goods are shown and where customers are served in a shop or bank. 2 a small, flat, round piece of plastic or wood used in board games.

counter *verb* 1 to act against something. 2 to meet an attack by hitting back.

counterfeit *noun* a copy of something made in order to deceive, a fake. **counterfeit** *adjective. Counterfeit money.* **counterfeit** *verb. It is illegal to counterfeit money.*

country *noun* 1 a land with its own people, government and language. 2 all the people who live in a particular country. *The floods paralyzed the country.* 3 land away from towns. *We live in the country.*

county (counties) *noun* a region that has its own local government.

couple *noun* 1 two people or things. 2 two people who are married or live together.

couple *verb* to connect or link together.

coupon *noun* a ticket or piece of printed paper allowing the holder to receive goods or information or pay less money for something than usual.

courage *noun* the ability to control fear and face danger or difficulty. **courageous** *adjective.*

courier *noun* 1 a messenger who takes letters and packages from one place to another. 2 a person who works for a travel company and takes care of tourists.

course *noun* 1 lessons or lectures on a particular subject. 2 a series of events or things you can do in a particular situation. 3 the direction or route in which something goes. 4 part of a meal. *What would you like for your main course?* 5 a ground for certain games. *A golf course.* **in the course of** during. **of course** certainly, naturally.

court *noun* 1 a place where law cases are heard and judged. 2 a place where a king or queen, their family and officials live. 3 an area for games. *A tennis court.*

court *verb* to try and win somebody's love. *He courted her for many years.*

courtesy *noun* (say ker-tuh-see) polite behavior. **courteous** *adjective.*

They bathed in the sea in the beautiful cove.

DID YOU KNOW

Your mother's or father's cousin is your cousin once removed. Your grandmother's or grandfather's cousin is your cousin twice removed.

The lion is known as the king of the jungle because of its great courage.

cousin *noun* the child of your uncle or aunt.

cove *noun* a small bay on the coast.

cover *verb* 1 to put something on or around something else to protect or hide it. *I covered my eyes.* 2 to spread over. *Snow covered the fields.* 3 to travel a certain distance. 4 to be enough money for something. *$10 should cover the gas.* 5 to deal with or discuss a subject or topic. *The book covers the whole of modern history.* 6 to insure against damage or loss. *The policy doesn't cover jewelry.*

cover *noun* 1 a thing put on to cover another thing. 2 the binding of a book or magazine. If you read a book from cover to cover, you read it from beginning to end. 3 something that hides something illegal or shelters you from bad weather. *We had to spend the whole day under cover.* 4 a guarantee from an insurance company against loss or damage. **take cover** to hide or protect yourself.

cow *noun* 1 a fully grown female animal that farmers keep for its milk. 2 a female elephant, whale or seal.

coward *noun* a person who shows fear and avoids dangerous situations. *Cowards lack courage.* **cowardly** *adjective.*

cowardice *noun* cowardly behavior.

cowboy *noun* a man who takes care of cattle.

A cowboy on horseback rounds up a steer that has strayed from the herd.

cowgirl *noun* a woman who takes care of cattle.

coy *adjective* pretending to be shy and modest. *She gave him a coy smile.*

crab *noun* a sea animal with a shell-covered body and five pairs of legs.

crack *verb* 1 to split or make something split. *The hot water cracked the glass.* 2 to make a sudden loud noise. *To crack a whip.* 3 to break down. *After days of questioning, he finally cracked.* **crack a problem** to finally solve a problem. **crack a joke** to tell a joke. **crack up** to break down. **crack** *noun* 1 a thin line on the surface of a glass or plate, for example, where they have cracked but not come completely apart. 2 a narrow gap. 3 a sudden loud noise. **at the crack of dawn** very early in the morning. **have a crack at something** to try to do something difficult.

cracker *noun* a thin, flat, dry type of bread. *My favorite snack is cheese and crackers.*

cradle *noun* a small bed for a baby. **from the cradle to the grave** from birth to death.

cradle *verb* to hold gently.

craft 1 a job that needs skill, especially making things skillfully with your hands. 2 the skill of tricking people. **crafty** *adjective. I wouldn't trust him, he's very crafty.*

craft *noun* a ship, boat or plane. *A spacecraft is a craft for traveling in space.*

Sputnik was the first craft ever to be sent into space. It was launched on 4 October 1957.

cram (cramming, crammed) *verb* 1 to push lots of things or people into a small space. 2 to fill. *His head was crammed with facts.*

crane *noun* 1 a machine for lifting and moving heavy objects. 2 a large bird with a long neck and long legs.

crane *verb* to stretch out your neck in order to see something better.

crash *noun* 1 a loud noise made by something falling or breaking. 2 a bad accident. 3 a business failure. **crash** *verb* 1 to make a loud noise when falling, or hitting something violently. 2 to hit something and be damaged. *She crashed the car.* 3 to move noisily or break through something with force. *He crashes through the house like an elephant.* 4 to fail, especially in business or money matters. *The stock market crashed.*

crate *noun* a box made of wood for putting goods in. *A crate of oranges.*

crater *noun* 1 a round hole in the top of a volcano. 2 a round hole in the ground or on the surface of another planet.

crawl *verb* 1 to move on your hands and knees with the body close to the ground. 2 to move slowly. *The traffic was crawling along.* 3 to be full of or covered with crawling things. *Don't sit on the grass, it's crawling with ants.* 4 If something makes your skin crawl, it gives you a nasty feeling. **crawl** *noun* 1 a slow crawling movement. 2 a fast swimming stroke.

Babies learn to crawl before they can walk.

crayon *noun* a pencil or stick of colored wax for drawing.

crazy *adjective* 1 foolish, mad. 2 very interested or excited. *Crazy about football.* **crazily** *adverb.* **craziness** *noun.*

creak *verb* to make a sound, usually when something is moved or moves. **creak** *noun* the sound of wood bending or an unoiled door opening.

cream *noun* 1 the fatty part of milk. *We had strawberries and cream.* 2 food that looks and tastes like cream. *Ice-cream.* 3 a soft substance that you put on your skin to make it soft or soothe it. 4 the best part of something. *The cream of society.* **creamy** *adjective.* **cream** *verb* to mix food until it is like cream. **cream** *adjective* a cream color.

Cream and fruit are two common ingredients of ice-cream.

crease *noun* 1 a line made on cloth, paper or clothes by folding, crushing or pressing. 2 a line or a wrinkle on someone's skin.

create *verb* 1 to make something new. *They have created a garden in the desert.* 2 to produce or cause something to happen. *His film created a lot of controversy.*

creation *noun* 1 making something. *The creation of great works of art.* 2 a thing created. *This is not a recipe from a book, it is all my own creation.*

creative *adjective* able to invent and produce new ideas and things.

creator *noun* a person who makes or invents something.

creature *noun* a living or an imaginary being. *The spaceship landed and we were surrounded by weird alien creatures.*

credit *noun* 1 the practice of allowing somebody to buy something and pay for it later. 2 the money a bank or business has agreed somebody can borrow. 3 the time you are allowed to pay a debt. *They gave us a month's credit.* 4 somebody with a good reputation. *He's a credit to the school.* 5 trust. *Don't give any credit to what he says.* 6 Credits are the list of people who helped to make a film or program. **credit** *verb* 1 to believe. 2 to say that somebody has done something. *She is credited with many achievements.* 3 to increase an account with a sum of money. *We will credit your account with the refund.*

credit card *noun* a plastic card you can use to buy goods on credit.

Credit cards make spending money even easier than it used to be.

creditor *noun* a person money is owed to.

creed *noun* a set of beliefs or opinions.

creek *noun* a small river or stream.

creep (crept) *verb* 1 to move slowly and quietly. *She creeps around the house.* 2 to move slowly towards or across something. **creep** *noun* an unpleasant person you dislike. *Get out, you creep!* If someone or something gives you the creeps, they make you feel nervous. **creepy** *adjective.*

cremate *verb* to burn a dead body to ashes. **cremation** *noun.*

crematorium *noun* a place where people are cremated.

crescent *noun* a curved shape like a crescent moon.

crevice *noun* an opening or crack in a rock.

crew *noun* 1 all the people working on a ship, plane or spacecraft. 2 a group of people working together. *A film crew.*

The air crew greets the passengers as they board the plane.

crib *noun* a baby's bed. *Harry stood up in his crib and cried.*

crib sheet *noun* a piece of paper that you use to cheat in an exam.

cricket *noun* an outdoor game for teams played with a ball, bats and two wickets.

cricket *noun* an insect like a grasshopper.

On warm summer nights you can hear the crickets chirping.

cried past tense of cry.

crime *noun* 1 an unlawful activity. 2 an action that is wrong, but not a matter for the police. *It would be a crime not to enjoy the sunshine.*

criminal *noun* a person who has committed a crime. **criminal** *adjective. A criminal act.*

crimson *adjective* purplish red.

cringe *verb* to move back with fear.

The poor creature cringed with fear when he heard the man's voice.

crisis *noun* a serious or dangerous situation.

crisp *adjective* 1 dry and easily broken. *Crisp pastry.* 2 fresh or newly made. *A crisp shirt.* 3 fresh and cold. *A crisp morning.* 4 quick and clear. *A crisp hello.*

critic *noun* 1 a person who gives his opinion about books, films, music or art. 2 a person who points out mistakes.

critical *adjective* 1 finding faults or mistakes. *He made critical remarks about my work.* 2 very important or dangerous. *A critical illness.* **critically** *adverb.*

criticism *noun* 1 pointing out faults and mistakes. 2 a critic's opinion on books, films, music or art. **criticize** *verb.*

croak *verb* to make a deep low sound. *Frogs croak in spring.* **croak** *noun* a deep hoarse sound.

Croatia *noun* a country in Southeast Europe.

The flag of Croatia has a colorful crest on a striped red, blue and white background.

crockery *noun* cups, plates and other dishes. *He smashed all their crockery.*

crocodile *noun* a large reptile with a long body. Crocodiles live in rivers.

crocus *noun* a small plant with white, yellow or purple flowers that grows in spring. *Crocuses grew on the lawn in spring.*

croissant *noun* (say **krwah**-sahn) a crescent-shaped bread roll.

crook *noun* 1 a shepherd's stick. 2 a dishonest person. 3 the inside of your elbow or knee. *The crook of my arm.*

crooked *adjective* 1 not straight, twisted. 2 dishonest, criminal.

crop *noun* 1 plants such as grain, fruit or vegetables grown for food. 2 the plants collected at harvest time. 3 a group of things appearing at the same time. *A crop of questions.* **crop** *verb* to cut short. *Cropped hair.* **crop up** to appear or happen. *A problem has cropped up.*

cross *noun* 1 a mark that looks like an X. *He marked the place with a cross.* 2 an upright post with another shorter bar across the top or any similar design used for decoration or as jewellery. The cross is an important Christian symbol. 3 a mixture of two animals or plants. *A mule is a cross between a horse and a donkey.*

Christian relics were highly prized in the Byzantine Empire, which began in AD 476. This gold crucifix, or cross, is an example.

WORD HISTORY

In crossword puzzles, words have to fit both across and down and so cross each other. The first crossword was published in a New York magazine called 'World' in 1913, so the puzzle is not as old as you might think.

cross *verb* 1 to go across something, or move from one side to another. 2 to draw a line or lines across something. 3 When roads or railways cross, they meet and go across each other. 4 to put one arm, leg or finger on top of the other. *I crossed my fingers for luck.* 5 to mix one animal or plant with another. 6 to oppose somebody's plans or go against somebody's wishes. *If you cross me, I'll get angry.* **cross out** to draw a line through something to show that it is wrong or not wanted.

cross *adjective* angry.

crossing *noun* 1 a journey by ship to the other side of an ocean. 2 a place where people can cross a road or railroad. 3 a place where two roads or railroads cross.

crossroads *noun* a place where two roads meet and cross each other.

crossword *noun* a puzzle in which you work out answers to clues and write the answers into numbered squares.

crouch *verb* to lower your body close to the ground by bending your knees and back.

crow *noun* a large black bird with a loud cry. **as the crow flies** in a straight line. **crow** *verb* to make a loud cry like a crow.

crowd *noun* a large group of people in one place. **crowd** *verb* 1 to come together in a large group. 2 to fill completely. *The new museum was crowded with tourists carrying cameras.* 3 to cram in.

crown *noun* 1 a headdress like a ring made of gold and jewels, worn by a king or queen. 2 The Crown is the governing power of a monarchy. 3 the top part of your head. **crown** *verb* 1 to put a crown on somebody who has become king or queen. 2 to complete something successfully. *Crowned with glory.*

The crown was made of gold and studded with precious jewels.

crucial *adjective* (say **kroo**-shuhl) extremely important. *A crucial appointment.*

crucify (crucifying, crucified) *verb* to punish by nailing or binding a person to a cross and leaving them to die. **crucifixion** *noun.* The Crucifixion is the death of Jesus Christ on the Cross.

crude *adjective* 1 in a raw or natural state. *Crude oil.* 2 rough, not skillfully made. *A crude drawing.* 3 not showing sensitive feeling, vulgar. *Crude jokes.*

cruel (crueller, cruellest) *adjective* causing pain or suffering to people or animals. **cruelty** *noun.*

cruise *noun* a holiday on a ship visiting a number of places. **cruise** *verb* to move in a car or ship at a comfortable speed.

A cruise in the warm blue waters of the Mediterranean makes a luxurious vacation.

crumb *noun* a very small piece of bread, cake or biscuit.

crumble *verb* 1 to break or fall into lots of small pieces. 2 to come to an end or to nothing. *Her hopes soon crumbled.* **crumble** *noun* cooked fruit covered with a mixture of flour, butter and sugar.

crumple *verb* to become full of creases and folds. *She crumpled up the invoice.*

crunch *verb* 1 to crush hard food noisily with your teeth. *The dog was crunching a bone.* 2 to make a crushing or breaking noise. **crunch** *noun* 1 crunching. 2 a crunching noise. *The crunch of footsteps on the gravel drive frightened me.* **come to the crunch** to reach a point when a difficult decision has to be made.

crusade *noun* 1 an expedition to Palestine made by Christian knights in the Middle Ages. 2 a movement against something bad or for something good. *A crusade against smoking in public places.*

crust *noun* 1 the hard surface of something baked, such as bread. 2 a hard surface. *The Earth's crust.*

crustacean *noun* (say krust-**ay**-shuhn) an animal with a shell. Crabs and lobsters are crustaceans.

Crabs and crustaceans have delicately flavored meat.

AMAZING FACT

Cuckoos live in all the continents of the world except Antarctica. There are 136 species of cuckoo in all and 45 of these lay their eggs in the nests of other birds. Their eggs are then incubated, and hatched by the 'adopted' parent.

crutch *noun* a stick, with a piece that fits under the arm, which people who have difficulty walking use as a support.

cry (cried) *verb* 1 to shed tears from your eyes, because you are unhappy or in pain. 2 to shout or say something loudly. *She cried for help.* **cry** (cries) *noun* 1 a sound you make when you feel excited or frightened. *A cry of pain.* 2 a shout to attract somebody's attention. 3 weeping.

crypt *noun* an underground room in a church.

crystal *noun* 1 a natural mineral that looks like ice. 2 a shaped piece of this mineral used in jewelry or decoration. 3 high-quality glass, often cut. **crystal** *adjective.*

Crystals are prized for their brilliance and clarity. Some people believe they have the power to heal illness.

cub *noun* a young wild animal. *Tiger cubs.*

Cuba *noun* a country in the West Indies.

cube *noun* 1 an object with six square sides which are all the same size. *A cube of sugar.* 2 the number made by multiplying a number by itself twice. The cube of 2 is 2 x 2 x 2, which makes 8. **cube** *verb* 1 to multiply a number by itself twice. 2 to cut something into cubes. **cubed** *adjective.*

cubicle *noun* a small room, for changing clothes.

cuckoo *noun* 1 a bird that lays its eggs in other birds' nests. 2 the sound a cuckoo makes.

cucumber *noun* a long thin vegetable with a green skin, eaten raw in salads.

Cucumbers can be served with salads or sandwiches.

cud *noun* the half-eaten food that cows and sheep bring up a number of times, before finally swallowing it.

cuddle (cuddled, cuddling) *verb* to hold somebody or something closely in your arms. **cuddle** *noun.* **cuddly** *adjective.*

cue *noun* a signal for somebody to do or say something.

cue *noun* a long stick for hitting the ball in snooker or pool.

culprit *noun* a person who has done something wrong.

cultivate *verb* 1 to use land to grow crops on. 2 to develop something and make it strong. *He has cultivated a love of art.* **cultivation** *noun*.

In the Philippines rice is cultivated in terraces that were dug out 2,000 years ago.

culture *noun* 1 an understanding of literature, art, music and other activities of the mind. 2 the shared customs and traditions of a group of people at a particular time. *He studied the Inca culture.* 3 a group of cells grown in a laboratory for medical study. 4 raising animals and growing plants. **cultural** *adjective*.

cultured *adjective* well educated, with good manners and a knowledge of the arts.

cunning *adjective* clever in deceiving others. *He's as cunning as a fox.* **cunning** *noun*.

The fox is an animal renowned for its cunning.

cup *noun* 1 a container with a handle for drinking from, or its contents. 2 a metal trophy given as a prize to a winning team or player. 3 anything shaped like a cup. **cup** *verb* to make your hands into a cup shape.

cupboard *noun* a piece of furniture with shelves and a door for keeping things in.

curb *verb* to keep something under control. *The government has curbed the powers of the police.* **curb** *noun*.

cure (cured, curing) *verb* 1 to make an illness disappear or a person well again. *There are still many diseases that drugs cannot cure.* 2 to stop something bad. *It is impossible to cure his stinginess.* 3 to preserve something to make it last longer. *Fish and meat can be cured by drying, smoking or salting.* **cure** *noun*. *Doctors are searching for a cure for Aids.*

AMAZING FACT

'Amp' or 'ampere' is the unit of electric current. Our muscles respond to electric impulses from our nerves. The current necessary to raise an arm is about one hundred thousandth of an amp.

Most of the world's currencies are made up of paper bills and metal coins.

SPELLING NOTE

'Currant' and 'current' sound the same but are spelt differently. Currants get their name from Corinth, in Greece, where they grew in ancient times. 'Current' comes from the Latin word for to run or flow.

---

curious *adjective* 1 interested in things and wanting to find out. *I'm curious to know what he said to my mother the other day.* 2 unusual and interesting. *That's a curious story!* **curiosity** *noun*.

curl *noun* 1 hair shaped into curves and circles. *Goldilocks had golden curls.* 2 a spiral shape. *A curl of smoke.* **curl** *verb* to twist hair into curls or be in curls. **curl up** 1 to form curls or twists. *The leaves have turned brown and curled up.* 2 to lie with your arms and legs drawn close to the body. *She curled up in front of the fire.*

curler *noun* a pin or roller put in the hair to make it curly.

curly *adjective* full of curls.

currant *noun* 1 a small dried grape used in baking and cooking. 2 a soft red, black or white berry.

currency (currencies) *noun* 1 the money used in a country. *The value of foreign currencies is always changing.* 2 the common use of something. If an idea gains currency, more people get used to it and accept it.

current *adjective* happening or being used now. *The current fashion for body piercing.*

current *noun* 1 water or air moving in one direction. *The river has a strong current.* 2 the flow of electricity. *An electric current.*

curry (curries) *noun* food cooked with hot-tasting spices. *An Indian curry.*

curse *noun* a word, phrase or sentence asking supernatural powers to harm somebody or something. *There must be a curse on our family, because everything is going wrong.* **curse** *verb* 1 to swear or say rude words because you are angry. 2 to use a curse against somebody.

cursor *noun* a small movable point on a computer screen used to identify a position.

curtain *noun* 1 a piece of material hung up at a window or door. 2 the heavy sheet of material lowered in front of a theater stage. 3 something that covers or hides. *A curtain of mist descended on the hills.*

curve *verb* to bend. *The road curves at the top of the hill.* **curve** *noun* a bending line, like the edge of a circle. *A curve in the road.* **curvy** *adjective*.

cushion *noun* 1 a case filled with soft material to sit on or lean against. 2 anything soft or springy in the shape of a cushion. *We floated on a cushion of air.* **cushion** *verb* to protect from shock, a knock, hardship or change. *The branches must have cushioned his fall.*

Big soft cushions add to the comfort of any home.

custody *noun* 1 the legal right of caring and looking after a child. *The mother was given custody of the children.* 2 imprisonment. **take into custody** to arrest.

custom *noun* 1 something which is accepted behavior among people or that people of a particular society always do. *Different countries have different customs.* 2 regular business given to a shop by customers. *The convenience store lost most of its custom to the new supermarket.*

At the spring festival of Holi, it is the custom for Hindu children to throw colored powder over each other.

customer *noun* a person who buys goods from a shop or uses a bank or other business. *The customer is always right.*

customs *plural noun* a place where government officers check your luggage for goods on which you need to pay duty (tax) when your enter or leave a country. *We were stopped at customs.*

cut (cutting, cut) *verb* 1 to make an an opening in your skin with something sharp. *I cut my finger.* 2 to divide, break or make something shorter with a knife, scissors or another sharp instrument. *I've cut some flowers.* 3 to reduce time, size or quantity. *Stores are cutting prices.* 4 to shorten something. *The film was cut by twenty minutes.* 5 to make a recording. *We cut a record.* **cut and dried** already decided and impossible to change. **cut back** to reduce. *Factories are cutting back on staff.* **cut in** to interrupt. **cut off** 1 to stop a person while speaking. *He cut me off when I was in the middle of asking a question.* 2 to stop a telephone connection. *We were cut off and the line went dead.* 3 to cut off a flower. 4 to stop the supply. *The electricity was cut off because we couldn't pay the bill.* **cut** *noun* 1 the act of cutting. 2 the result of cutting. *There's a cut in the counter.* 3 an opening or small wound. 4 a reduction. *A price cut.* 5 a part that is cut out. *I noticed quite a few cuts in the film.* 6 a style or shape. *A good hair cut.* 7 a share. *She promised me a cut of her winnings.*

cute *adjective* 1 pretty, attractive. *She's a cute little girl.* 2 clever. *That's a cute idea.*

cutlery *noun* knives, forks and spoons.

cycle (cycling, cycled) *verb* to ride a bicycle or tricycle. *I usually cycle to school, but today I'm walking.* **cyclist** *noun*.

cyclone *noun* (say **seye**-klohn) a tropical storm that moves very fast round a calm central area, a hurricane.

cygnet *noun* (say **sig**-nit) a young swan.

cylinder *noun* an object or container with a long tubular body.

cynic *noun* (say **sin**-ik) a person who sees no good in anything and believes that people always behave in a selfish way. **cynical** *adjective*.

Cypriot *noun* a person who comes from Cyprus. **Cypriot** *adjective*. *A Cypriot dance.*

Cyprus *noun* an island country in the eastern Mediterranean Sea.

The island of Cyprus appears in yellow on the country's flag.

czar *noun* (say zar) the title of the former emperor of Russia.

Czech *noun* (say chek) 1 the language spoken in the Czech Republic. 2 a person who comes from the Czech Republic. **Czech** *adjective*. *A Czech tennis player.*

Czech Republic *noun* a country in eastern Europe.

Dd

dab (dabs, dabbing, dabbed) *verb* to touch quickly and gently with something soft. *She dabbed the dirty mark with a damp cloth.*

dachshund *noun* a small black or brown dog with a long body and short legs.

dad *or* **daddy** (daddies) *noun* an informal word for father.

daddy-long-legs *noun* also known as a cranefly, a flying insect with very long legs.

daffodil *noun* a tall plant with a yellow, bell-shaped flower that grows from a bulb in spring.

daft *adjective* silly or foolish. *You really look daft in that hat!*

dagger *noun* a weapon for stabbing that looks like a short, pointed knife.

Dáil *noun* the lower house in the parliament of the Republic of Ireland, the equivalent of the British House of Commons.

daily *adjective* happening or done every day. **daily** *adverb*. **daily** (dailies) *noun* a newspaper that is published every day except on Sunday.

dainty (daintier, daintiest) *adjective* small, pretty and delicate. *Dainty feet.* **daintiness** *noun*. **daintily** *adverb*.

dairy (dairies) *noun* a place where milk is put into bottles and where milk products such as butter and cheese are made and sold. **dairy** *adjective*.

daisy *noun* a wild flower with a yellow center and white petals.

Dakar *noun* the capital of Senegal.

dam *noun* 1 a strong barrier or concrete wall built across a river to hold back the water. 2 the water held back. **dam** (dams, damming, dammed) *verb*.

damage *verb* to harm or spoil something. **damage** *noun*. **damaging** *adjective*.

The Aswan Dam in Egypt provides the country with hydroelectric power.

Graceful Balinese dancers enact a traditional story. Their elaborate costumes are decorated with gold threadwork.

damages *noun* money that somebody is paid for injury or harm done to them.

Damascus *noun* the capital of Syria.

damp *adjective* moist or slightly wet. **dampness** *noun*. **dampen** *verb*.

dance *verb* to move your feet and body to the rhythm of music. **dancer** *noun*.

dance *noun* 1 a style of dancing with special set steps e.g. a waltz or gavotte. 2 a party at which there is dancing.

dandelion *noun* a wild plant with a yellow flower.

dandruff *noun* small flakes of dead skin found on the scalp of some people.

danger *noun* 1 the chance that something may happen that will cause harm or injury. 2 a situation that is not safe. *The tunnel is in danger of collapsing.* **danger** *interjection*. *Danger! Falling rocks.* **dangerous** *adjective*.

dangle *verb* to swing to and fro or to hang down loosely. *He dangled his legs over the side of the pool.*

Danish *adjective* of Denmark or its people. *A Danish ship.* **Danish** *noun*. The language spoken in Denmark.

dank *adjective* damp and cold.

dappled *adjective* marked with patches or spots of dark and light colors.

dare *verb* 1 to be brave enough or rude enough to do or try to do something. *How dare you contradict me!* 2 to challenge somebody to do something brave. *I dare you to jump.* **dare** *noun*.

daring *adjective* brave and not afraid to take chances. **daring** *noun*.

dark *adjective* 1 with little or no light. **dark** *noun* darkness. 2 not light or fair in colour. *She has dark hair.* **in the dark** not knowing about something. **a dark horse** somebody who may have unexpected, hidden abilities.

darken *verb* to make or become dark.

darn *verb* to mend a hole in a piece of clothing by sewing threads across it.

dart *noun* a small arrow that players throw at a round board marked with numbers in a game called darts.

dart *verb* to move suddenly and quickly. *She darted across the road.*

dash *verb* to rush somewhere. **dash** *noun.*

dash *noun* a short line (–) used in writing.

dash *noun* a small amount. *A dash of salt.*

data *noun* facts and information.

database *noun* a large amount of information stored on a computer.

date *noun* 1 the day, month and/or year of a particular event. 2 an appointment to meet somebody, particularly a boyfriend or girlfriend. **date** *verb* 1 to put a date on a letter etc. 2 to guess or give a date when something was made. *This church dates from 1400.* **out of date** 1 old-fashioned. 2 no longer valid. *An out of date ticket.* **up to date** modern.

date *noun* the brown, sticky fruit of the date palm.

daughter *noun* somebody's female child.

daughter-in-law *noun* the wife of somebody's son.

daunt *verb* to make somebody afraid that they won't be able to do something. *He was daunted by the huge task that lay ahead of him.* **daunting** *adjective.*

dawdle *verb* to waste time by moving or doing something very slowly.

dawn *noun* the beginning of the day when the Sun rises.

day (days) *noun* 1 the 24 hours from one midnight to the next midnight. 2 the part of the day from sunrise to sunset when it is light. **call it a day** to stop doing something in order to return to it later.

daybreak *noun* dawn.

daydream *noun* pleasant, distracting thoughts that some people have when they are awake. **daydream** *verb.*

All the data about the new business venture was presented in a huge sheaf of papers.

At dawn the sky was full of warm apricot colored light.

dazed *adjective* bewildered and unable to think clearly, perhaps because of a shock.

dazzle *verb* 1 to blind briefly or make somebody dazed with a bright light. 2 to amaze or impress somebody. *She was dazzled by his wit.* **dazzling** *adjective.*

de- *prefix* By adding de- to a noun or verb it changes the meaning to its opposite or negative. **defrost** to remove ice from something. *Please defrost the fridge.*

dead *adjective* no longer alive.

deadline *noun* a time or date by which some work or a job must be finished.

deadlock *noun* a situation in which people cannot settle a disagreement. *The talks ended in deadlock.*

deadly (deadlier, deadliest) *adjective* fatal or likely to kill. *Deadly poison.*

deaf *adjective* unable to hear well or to hear at all. **deafness** *noun.*

deafen *verb* to make unable to hear because the noise is so loud. **deafening** *adjective.*

deal (deals, dealing, dealt) *verb* 1 to do business by buying and selling. *They deal in silver.* 2 to give out cards to people in a card game. **dealer** *noun.* **deal with** 1 to take action to sort out a problem. 2 to be about or concerned with. *This book deals with tribal customs in Africa.*

The cards were dealt into four piles.

deal *noun* 1 a business agreement. 2 a bargain. *I got a good deal on this car.*

dear *adjective* 1 loved very much. 2 the way of beginning a letter before putting the name of the person you are writing to. *Dear Mrs Smith.* 3 (old-fashioned) costing a lot of money. Expensive.

dear *noun* 1 a person you love or who is loveable. 2 an interjection, used when surprised or angry. *Oh dear, I'm late!*

death *noun* the end of life. **put to death** to kill, execute. **frightened/sick to death** very scared/fed up.

death penalty *noun* the punishment of death for a person who has committed a crime such as murder.

death trap *noun* a building, vehicle or something else that is very dangerous.

deathly *adjective, adverb* like death. *Deathly cold hands.*

debate *noun* a discussion, especially at a public meeting. **debate** *verb.*

debris *noun* (say **deb**-ree) scattered pieces of things that have been destroyed, or rubbish. *The debris left after the bomb attack.*

The beach was littered with all kinds of debris.

debt *noun* (say det) 1 money you owe somebody. *Pay off your debts before you buy a new car.* If you are in debt, you owe money. 2 a feeling that you owe somebody for something they have done for you. *A debt of gratitude.*

debtor *noun* a person who owes money. The opposite of debtor is creditor.

debug (debugging, debugged) *verb* 1 to remove faults or problems from a computer. 2 to remove a listening device.

decade *noun* a period of ten years. *The first decade of the 21st century.*

decaffeinated *adjective* with the caffeine removed. *My grandmother has a heart problem, so she drinks decaffeinated coffee.*

decapitate *verb* to cut off someone's head.

decathlon *noun* a competition in which athletes take part in ten different events, including running, jumping, hurdling, shot put, discus, pole vault and javelin.

decay *verb* 1 to go bad. *Sugar can decay your teeth.* 2 to lose health or power, to become weak. **decay** *noun. The building is falling into decay.* **decayed** *adjective.*

Decaying fruit attracts wasps and other insects.

deceased *noun* a person who has recently died. *The deceased was a very rich man.*

deceit *noun* being dishonest by making people believe something that is not true. **deceitful** *adjective.*

deceive *verb* to make somebody believe something that is not true. *He deceived everybody with his terrible lies.*

December *noun* the twelfth month of the year. December has 31 days.

decent *adjective* 1 socially acceptable, honest and respectable. 2 acceptable, good. *A decent wage.* **decency** *noun. He had the decency to apologize.*

deception *noun* deceiving somebody or being deceived. **deceptive** *adjective. Her charm is very deceptive.*

decibel *noun* (say **dess**-ib-el) a unit for measuring the loudness of sound.

decide *verb* 1 to do something after thinking about it; to make up your mind. *I've decided to go away.* 2 to settle something or bring it to an end. *Lack of money decided the issue.*

decided *adjective* clear and definite, easily seen. *You have a decided advantage.*

deciduous *adjective* (say dis-**id**-yoo-us) deciduous trees shed their leaves every fall. (Trees that never shed their leaves are called evergreen.)

decimal *adjective* counting units in tens. *Dewey Decimal System.* The dot in a decimal fraction (such as 1·5) is called a decimal point. **decimal** *noun.*

decipher *verb* (say dis-**eye**-fer) to work something out that is difficult to read or understand. *I can't decipher his writing.*

Morse code is deciphered after it has been transmitted on this machine.

decision *noun* 1 a choice made about what should be done. Deciding. *She made the right decision.* 2 the ability to decide and act quickly.

decisive *adjective* 1 full of decision and acting quickly. 2 having a definite result or making certain that there will be a particular result. *A decisive victory.* **decisively** *adverb.*

deck *noun* 1 a floor on a ship or bus. 2 a piece of equipment for playing records on or tapes in. *A tape deck.* 3 a pack. *A deck of playing cards.*

declaration *noun* something declared. *A declaration of war.*

declare *verb* 1 to make known or say something clearly. *I have declared my support.* 2 to tell Customs that you have bought goods overseas or tell the tax office about your income.

decline *verb* 1 to refuse politely. *We declined the invitation.* 2 to become smaller, weaker or worse. *Her health is declining rapidly.* **decline** *noun* a gradual loss of strength or importance.

decode *verb* to work out the meaning of a code. *He tried to decode the message.*

decompose *verb* to rot or decay after having died. **decomposition** *noun.*

decorate *verb* 1 to make something look more attractive by adding things to it. *The cake was decorated with candy.* 2 When you decorate a room, you paint or wallpaper it. 3 to give somebody a medal. *The soldier was decorated for bravery.* **decoration** *noun.*

decorator *noun* a person who paints houses or paints and wallpapers rooms.

The decorator is wearing rubber gloves to protect her hands against the paint.

decrease *verb* to become smaller or weaker. *The number of voluntary workers is sadly decreasing.* **decrease** *noun.* **decreasing** *adjective.*

decree *noun* an official order or decision, especially by a ruler or a government. **decree** *verb.* *The king decreed an end to the war.*

decrepit *adjective* very old and in bad condition. *A decrepit old man.*

dedicate *verb* 1 to give a lot of time and effort to something. *She dedicates her life to prayer.* 2 to declare a book or performance to be in honor of somebody. *I dedicated this book to my mother.* **dedication** *noun.*

dedicated *adjective* devoted to something or somebody. *Dedicated to her job.*

deduce *verb* to work something out by looking at the facts and reaching a conclusion. *They have been silent all year, and from this I deduce that they must have moved away.* **deduction** *noun.*

deed *noun* 1 something done, especially a good deed. 2 The deeds of a house are the official documents given to its owner.

deep *adjective* 1 going a long way down from the surface. *A deep hole.* 2 measured from back to front. *The drawers are 20 inches deep.* 3 serious, strong or to a great extent. *Deep feelings* 4 low. *A deep voice.* **deeply** *adverb.* **deep in thought** thinking very hard about something.

deep-freeze *noun* a refrigerator for keeping frozen food in, a freezer.

deer (*plural* deer) *noun* a large fast animal. Male deer usually have antlers.

Two of these pots are perfect, but the middle one is cracked and broken. This may be due to a defect in manufacturing techniques.

DID YOU KNOW
Male deer (note that the plural word stays the same, like sheep) are called stags, bucks or harts. Female deer are called hinds or does. Deer range in size from the small Pudu of South America to the huge elk of northern Europe, Asia and North America.

A male red deer has magnificent antlers. It uses them to attract a mate and to fight off other stags.

deface *verb* to spoil something, especially a wall or a notice, by scribbling all over it. *The white wall was defaced with graffiti.*

default *verb* to fail to do something you have agreed to do. **default** *noun.* If you win a game by default, you have won because the other player has not turned up.

defeat *verb* 1 to beat. *Chelsea were defeated in the final.* 2 to cause to fail. *My hopes were defeated.* 3 to be too difficult to solve. *The problem defeated me.* **defeat** *noun.*

defect *noun* (say dee-fekt) a fault or imperfection. *His radio had a defect.*

defect *verb* (say di-fekt) to leave your own country, party or army and join the other side. **defector** *noun.*

defective *adjective* having faults, not working properly.

defence *noun* 1 something used for defending or protecting. *The trees act as a defence against the wind.* 2 the act or action of defending. 3 the arguments put forward by a defendant in court. 4 the lawyers representing an accused person in a trial. 5 a group of players in a team who try to stop the opposition from scoring.

defend *verb* 1 to protect, guard or speak in support, especially when attacked. *She is always defending her little brother.* 2 to try to prove in court that an accused person is not guilty. 3 to play in a position that stops an opponent from scoring points or goals. If a champion defends her title, she wants to win to keep it. **defender** *noun.*

defendant *noun* a person who has been accused of a crime.

defensive *adjective* 1 used for defending. *Defensive weapons.* 2 behaving in an unsure or threatened way. *She is very defensive about her friends.* **on the defensive** behaving as if expecting an attack.

defer (defers, deferring, deferred) *verb* 1 to arrange that something will take place at a later date. *She deferred her studies for a year.* 2 to agree with a person or an opinion out of respect.

defiance *noun* openly refusing to obey. If you act in defiance of something, you do something although it is forbidden. **defiant** *adjective. Defiant teenagers stay out late.*

deficient *adjective* lacking in a particular thing, short of something. **deficiency** *noun. A deficiency in vitamin C.*

define *verb* to say exactly what something is or explain what a word means. *Let's define the problem.* **definition** *noun*.

definite *adjective* firm and unlikely to change. *I need a definite answer.* **definite article** the word 'the' is the definite article. ('A' and 'an' are indefinite articles.) **definitely** *adverb*.

deforestation *noun* the cutting down of forests.

Deforestation is a huge problem in the Amazon, where more trees are felled every day to make way for building and farming land.

deformed *adjective* abnormally shaped. **deformity** *noun*.

defrost *verb* 1 to get rid of ice or frost, especially in a refrigerator or on a windshield. 2 When you defrost food, it becomes unfrozen.

defuse *verb* 1 to remove the fuse from an unexploded bomb so it cannot explode. 2 to make a situation less dangerous. *He defused the situation by apologizing.*

defy (defies, defying, defied) *verb* 1 to refuse to obey. *Criminals defy the law.* 2 to challenge somebody to do something that seems impossible. *I defy you to swim across the river.* 3 to be impossible to understand or solve. *The problem defies solution.*

degree *noun* 1 a unit for measuring temperature, usually written with a degree sign (°). 2 a unit of measurement of angles. *A right angle is a 90° angle.* 3 the extent or amount of feeling. *I admire him to a degree.* 4 an academic grade given by a university or a college to a person who has finished a course or passed an examination. *A bachelor's degree.* **by degrees** gradually.

deity (deities) *noun* (say **day**-it-ee) a god or goddess. *They worshipped several deities.*

delay *verb* 1 to put something off until later. *We have decided to delay the meeting until the middle of this afternoon.* 2 to make somebody or something late.

delete *verb* to cross out something written or printed.

deliberate *adjective* (say dil-ib-er-ut) 1 planned, done on purpose and not by accident. *A deliberate lie.* 2 slow and careful, especially when moving or speaking. **deliberately** *adverb*.

deliberate *verb* (say dil-ib-er-**ayt**) to think carefully. **deliberation** *noun* careful consideration of a subject.

delicacy (delicacies) *noun* 1 something soft, fine and graceful. 2 something that needs careful and tactful handling. *He didn't appreciate the delicacy of the situation.* 3 delicious and often expensive food.

delicate *adjective* 1 soft, fine and graceful. *Delicate silk.* 2 fragile, easily broken or becoming ill easily. *A delicate child.* 3 not strong, especially when talking about color, taste or smell. *A delicate flavor.* 4 needing careful treatment or tactful handling. *Don't mention her old boyfriend, it's a delicate subject.* **delicately** *adverb*.

Lace is a strong yet very delicate fabric.

delicatessen *noun* a store or section of a supermarket selling cooked meats, cheeses and other prepared foods.

delicious *adjective* giving great pleasure, having a pleasant taste or smell. *The food was delicious.*

delight *noun* great pleasure. *To our delight the exam was cancelled.* **delight** *verb* to give or feel a lot of pleasure. **be delighted** *I'd be delighted to come to Marianne's party.* **delightful** *adjective*.

deliver *verb* 1 to take something, especially goods or messages, to somebody's house or office. *The mailman delivered the letters.* 2 to give a speech. 3 to help with the birth of a baby. *The baby was delivered this morning.* **delivery** *noun*.

delta *noun* 1 the Greek letter D (written Δ). 2 the fan-shaped area at the mouth of a river, where it splits up into many channels. *The Nile delta.*

WORD HISTORY

The delta of a river got its name from its triangular shape. It was named after the shape of the Greek letter D.

At the delta of a river a lot of silt flows into the sea.

deluge *noun* 1 a heavy fall of rain, a great flood. 2 things arriving in large numbers. *We had a deluge of applications for the job we advertised.* **deluge** *verb*.

demand *verb* 1 to ask for something firmly, as if ordering it. *I demand an explanation.* 2 to need. *Teaching demands a lot of patience.* **demand** *noun* 1 a firm request. 2 a desire to buy or get something. **in demand** wanted. *Mobile phones are in great demand even though expensive to run.*

demanding *adjective* needing attention, time or energy. *Looking after small children is a very demanding job.*

demo (demos) *noun* a demonstration.

democracy *noun* 1 a system of government in which people elect the leaders of their country. 2 a country governed by democracy. **democrat** *noun*. **democratic** *adjective*. *A democratic decision.*

demolish *verb* to pull down old buildings or destroy something. **demolition** *noun*. *Demolition work began early.*

demon *noun* a devil or evil spirit.

demonstrate *verb* 1 to show how something works or prove a point by giving examples. 2 to take part in a march or meeting, to show support for a cause. *The students are demonstrating against human rights violations.* **demonstration** *noun*.

demonstrative *adjective* showing your feelings. *He rarely kisses his children, he is not a very demonstrative father.* 'This', 'that', 'these', 'those' are **demonstrative adjectives**. They are used to point out a person or thing.

den *noun* 1 the home of a fox or wolf. 2 a person's private room. *He invited me to watch TV in his den.*

denial *noun* 1 denying or refusing something. *A denial of justice.* 2 saying that something somebody is accused of is not true. *He printed a denial in the newspaper.*

Denmark *noun* a Scandinavian country in Europe.

The flag of Denmark has a white cross against a red background.

The crane operator began the demolition work and soon the old house began to crumble.

denounce *verb* to speak or write against somebody. *He was denounced as a traitor.* **denunciation** *noun*.

dense *adjective* 1 thick, crowded together or difficult to see through. *A dense forest.* 2 stupid. **density** *noun*.

dent *noun* a hollow in a hard surface made by a collision or by pressure. *There was a big dent in the side of the car.* **dent** *verb* to make a dent.

dental *adjective* of or for the teeth. *We were campaigning for free dental treatment for children.*

dentist *noun* a person trained to treat people's teeth.

dentures *plural noun* false teeth.

Some people take out their dentures and put them in a glass beside the bed overnight.

depart *verb* to go away, leave. *The train to Boston is about to depart from platform three.* **departure** *noun*.

department *noun* a part of a large business, government, college or store.

department store *noun* a large store in which all sorts of goods are sold in different departments.

depend *verb* 1 If you depend on somebody or something, you need them. *Our group depends on your help.* 2 to trust somebody or rely on something. *You can always depend on me.* 3 to vary according to circumstances. *The success of the trip will depend on the weather.* **it depends** said when you are not sure about what will happen. *'Are you going to the game?' 'I don't know. It depends.'*

deport *verb* to send an unwanted person out of a country. **deportation** *noun*.

deposit *noun* 1 a sum of money paid into a bank account. *I'd like to make a deposit, please.* 2 money paid as part payment for something. *If you want to order the goods, you will have to pay a deposit.* 3 a layer of a substance left somewhere. *There were deposits of sugar at the bottom of the bottle.* 4 a natural layer of sand, coal or rock. **deposit** *verb* 1 to put something down. *Sand was deposited by the wind.* 2 to pay money as a deposit.

depot *noun* (say deep-oh) 1 a place for storing goods. 2 a place where buses or trains are parked and repaired.

depressed *adjective* very sad. **depression** *noun*. *She felt depressed and anxious.*

deprive *verb* to take or keep something away from somebody. *The children have been deprived of love.*

depth *noun* the distance between the top and bottom surfaces or the distance from the front to the back of something. How deep something is. **in depth** thoroughly, looking at all aspects. **out of your depth** 1 to be in water that is too deep to stand in. 2 to try and do something that is too difficult.

Divers wear special breathing apparatus so they can explore the ocean depths.

derive *verb* 1 to get from. *She derives great satisfaction from her work.* 2 to come from. *The word democracy derives from the Greek for 'people'.*

descend *verb* to go down. **be descended from** to be related to and come from a certain family. **descent** *noun*.

descendant *noun* a person or an animal related to another who lived a long time ago. *We're descendants of Martin Luther King.*

describe *verb* 1 to say what something or somebody is like. 2 to mark out. **description** *noun*. **descriptive** *adjective*.

desert (say dez-urt) *noun* a large sand-covered area of land where very little rain ever falls.

The cactus can survive in the harsh conditions of the desert. It stores water in its thick stems and its spines protect it against getting eaten by animals.

SPELLING NOTE

They sound almost the same but they are spelled differently: 'desert' is an empty area, 'dessert' (with two 's's) is something sweet to eat.

desert (say diz-ert) *verb* 1 to go away with no intention of returning, to abandon. *He deserted his wife and children.* 2 to run away from military service. **desertion** *noun*. *The soldier was accused of desertion.* **deserter** *noun*. **deserted** *adjective* empty, abandoned.

deserts *plural noun* what somebody deserves. *He got his just deserts.*

deserve *verb* to be worthy of something. *He deserves to win after all the hard training he has done.*

desiccate *verb* to dry. *Desiccated coconut.*

design *noun* 1 a drawing that shows how something is to be made or built. *He showed the designs for his new fashion collection.* 2 the way something is made or built. *I don't like the design of the car.* 3 a pattern of shapes to decorate something. *Curtains with a floral design.* 4 a thought-out plan. **design** *verb* 1 to invent the look of something. *He designs for a jeweler.* 2 to plan. *This dictionary is designed for children.* **designer** *noun*.

desire *noun* a strong wish for something. *I have no desire to meet him.* **desire** *verb*.

desk *noun* a table at which you sit to read, write and work.

despair *noun* a complete loss of hope. **despair** *verb*. *He despaired of ever seeing her again.*

despatch see dispatch.

despise *verb* If you despise somebody, you think that they are worthless.

dessert *noun* (say diz-ert) sweet food eaten at the end of a meal.

destination *noun* the place to which a person or thing is going.

destiny *noun* 1 Your destiny is what will happen to you in your life. *It was her destiny to marry the king.* 2 the force that controls your life. Fate. **destine** *verb*. *They were destined to meet again.*

destroy *verb* to ruin something, or break it to pieces. *The criminals destroyed all the vital evidence before their capture.* **destruction** *noun*. **destructive** *adjective*.

detail *noun* a small point or fact. *The police officer wrote down the essential details.* **detailed** *adjective*.

detective *noun* a person, especially a police officer, whose job it is to find out what has happened in a crime.

deteriorate *verb* to become worse. *Her health has deteriorated within the last year.* **deterioration** *noun.*

determined *adjective* having firmly decided to do something in order to be successful. *She is determined to win the tennis tournament.* **determination** *noun.*

devastate *verb* 1 to destroy or damage. *The floods have devastated the whole area.* 2 to shock. *I was devastated when he gave me the terrible news.* **devastation** *noun.*

develop *verb* 1 to grow or become bigger. *Her small company soon developed into a major business.* 2 to come into existence, to become more serious. *She has developed a huge appetite.* 3 to make prints from a photographic film. 4 to use an area of land for building. **development** *noun.*

device *noun* something made or built for a particular purpose. *She has invented an unusual listening device.*

A corkscrew is a device for opening bottles.

devise *verb* to invent or think up. *He devised a cunning plan.*

devote *verb* to spend time or energy on something or somebody. *He devotes all his spare time to football.* **devotion** *noun.*

devour *verb* to eat greedily.

dew *noun* tiny drops of water that form during the night on the ground or cool surfaces. *Dew lay on the grass.*

Dhaka *noun* the capital of Bangladesh.

diabetes *noun* (say die-uh-**bee**-teez) an illness in which there is too much sugar in a person's blood. **diabetic** *adjective* (say die-uh-**bet**-ik). *Diabetic marmalade.*

diagnose *verb* to find out what is wrong with a person and what illness they might have. *The doctor diagnosed a case of measles.* **diagnosis** *noun.*

diagonal *adjective* (say die-**ag**-un-ul) A diagonal line goes in a slanting direction, joining opposite corners. **diagonal** *noun* a straight line going diagonally across.

diagram *noun* a simple drawing that shows the parts of something, often used to explain how things work.

dial *noun* an indicator, like a clock face or a meter, with numbers or letters around it. **dial** (dials, dialling, dialled) *verb* to ring a telephone number by turning a dial or pressing buttons.

Dice are used in many games of chance.

dialect *noun* a form of language spoken in a particular region, which has different words and pronunciation from other forms of the same language.

dialysis *noun* (say die-**al**-iss-iss) a process of removing harmful products from the blood, especially when the kidneys are not functioning properly.

diameter *noun* (say die-**am**-it-er) the length of a straight line going from side to side through the centre of a circle or sphere.

diamond *noun* 1 a very hard precious stone that looks like cut glass. 2 a shape with four straight sides of equal length that stands on one of its points. 3 a playing card with red diamond shapes on it. *The ace of diamonds.* **diamond** *adjective.*

A diamond is a beautiful clear and sparkling stone.

diaphragm *noun* (say **die**-uh-fram) 1 a large, dome-shaped muscle that stretches from your backbone to the front and sides of your ribcage. Your diaphragm rises and falls when you breathe in and out. 2 a hole that controls the amount of light passing through a camera lens.

diary (diaries) *noun* 1 a book with spaces for each day of the year used for writing down appointments. 2 a book for keeping a record of daily events.

dice *noun* ('Dice' is the plural of 'die', but is used as both singular and plural.) a small six-sided cube marked with dots from one to six on each of its sides, used in board games and gambling.

dice *verb* to cut something, especially food, into cubes.

dictate *verb* 1 to say aloud what somebody should write down. *She dictated a letter to her secretary.* **dictation** *noun.* 2 to give orders. *I won't be dictated to by my parents.*

dictator *noun* a ruler who has total power over a country. Most dictators take power by force. *A ruthless dictator ran the country.*

dictionary *noun* a book in which words are listed in alphabetical order, from A to Z. You look up a word in the dictionary to find out what it means and how to spell it.

did past tense of do.

die singular of dice.

die *noun* a block of hard metal for pressing coins and other metal or plastic objects into shape. *This component was cast in a die.*

die (dies, dying, died) *verb* 1 to stop living. *She died of cancer.* 2 to come to an end or disappear. *My love will never die.* **die down** to become less strong. *The noise eventually died down.* **die for** to want something very much. *I'm dying for a glass of water.*

diesel *noun*
1 a vehicle that has a diesel engine. 2 fuel for a diesel engine.

A diesel engine is more economical and less polluting than a gasoline engine.

diet *noun* 1 the sort of food usually eaten by a person or an animal. *A healthy diet.* 2 special kinds of food eaten in order to be healthy or to lose weight. *I'm on a very strict diet.* **diet** *verb*.

difference *noun* 1 being different. A way of being unlike each other. *The difference between boys and girls.* 2 the amount left between two numbers when one is subtracted from the other. *The difference between 10 and 4 is 6.* 3 When people have their differences, they have a disagreement. 4 When something makes a difference, it is important. *It makes no difference to me.*

different *adjective* 1 not the same. *Every time I see her, she has a different boyfriend.* 2 various. *The dress comes in different colors.*

These two houses are the same, but they have different colored doors and different windows.

difficult *adjective* 1 not easy, hard to do or understand. 2 a difficult person is somebody who is not easily pleased and hard to get along with. **difficulty** (difficulties) *noun*.

dig (digs, digging, dug) *verb* 1 to make a hole in the ground, usually by moving soil. *To dig the garden.* 2 to poke or push in. *Don't dig your knife into the cake.* **dig up** 1 to remove something from the soil. *I dug up the bush.* 2 to discover something. *The newspapers have dug up another scandal.*

WORD HISTORY

A diesel (car or locomotive) has a diesel engine that burns diesel oil. They were all named after Rudolf Diesel (1858–1913), a German engineer.

dig *noun* 1 a small push or poke. *She gave him a dig in the ribs.* 2 an archeological site. 3 a remark against a person, intended to upset. *That teacher loves having a dig at me.*

digest (say die-jest) *verb* 1 to make food change so the body can use it. *Fruit is easy to digest.* 2 to take in information and think it over. **digestion** *noun*.

digest (say die-jest) *noun* a summary of information or news.

digit *noun* 1 any of the numbers from 0 to 9. 2 a finger or toe.

digital *adjective* 1 giving a reading by displaying numbers rather than by moving hands. *A digital clock.* 2 working with signals or information represented by numbers. *A digital recording.*

The watch is digital. It has no hands.

dilemma *noun* a difficult situation in which you have to choose between two or more possible actions.

dilute *verb* to make a liquid weaker or thinner by mixing it with water or other liquid. *I like to dilute my orange juice.*

dim (dimmer, dimmest) *adjective* 1 not bright or clear, difficult to see. *The light was very dim.* 2 stupid.

dim (dims, dimming, dimmed) *verb* to make something dim. *Dim the lights.*

dime *noun* a US coin worth ten cents.

dimension *noun* 1 a measurement, especially of length, height or width. *The exact dimensions of the room.* 2 The dimensions of a problem are the extent and importance of it.

diminish *verb* to become smaller.

din *noun* a loud, annoying noise.

dine *verb* to have dinner. **dine out** to eat in a restaurant or at friends.

dinghy (dinghies) *noun* (say **ding**-ee) a small boat, especially an inflatable rubber boat.

dingy (dingier, dingiest) *adjective* (say **din**-jee) dark, depressing and dirty-looking. *He's got a dingy little room.*

dining room *noun* a room where people have their meals.

dinner *noun* the main meal of the day.

dinner party *noun* a party at which guests eat dinner together.

dinosaur *noun* a large extinct reptile that lived in prehistoric times.

dip (dips, dipping, dipped) *verb* 1 to put into a liquid. *He dipped his cracker in the soup.* 2 to move downward or drop slightly. *The Sun dipped below the horizon.*

dip *noun* 1 a downward slope or slight drop. 2 a quick swim or bathe. *A dip in the sea.* 3 a creamy mixture that is eaten with raw vegetables or chips.

diplomacy *noun* 1 the building of relations between countries and different people. 2 the skill of doing and saying the right thing at the right time. *She handled the delicate situation with tact and diplomacy.*

diplomat *noun* 1 a government official who represents their country in another country. Diplomats usually work in an embassy. 2 a tactful person. **diplomatic** *adjective.* **diplomatically** *adverb.*

direct *adjective* 1 straight towards a place. *A direct flight.* 2 honest and frank. *Please give me a direct answer.* 3 exact. *The direct opposite.* **directly** *adverb.*

direct *verb* 1 to tell somebody the way. *Can you direct me to the station?* 2 to order somebody to do something. 3 to organize and manage something. *Who is directing the new Batman film?* **director** *noun.*

direction *noun* 1 the course in which a person or thing is moving or the line they are pointing in. *What direction is the reform taking?* 2 control or management. *The film was made under his direction.*

directions *plural noun* instructions on how to do, use or find something. *Can you give me directions?*

The arms of the signpost point in the directions of some of the world's most famous cities.

dirt *noun* earth, soil, or anything that is not clean.

dirty (dirtier, dirtiest) *adjective* 1 not clean. *My hands are dirty.* 2 vulgar. *Dirty jokes.* 3 mean, unfair. *That was a dirty trick.*

dis- *prefix* forming the opposite of a word. Dishonest is the opposite of honest.

disabled *adjective* physically or mentally unable to do something. *There are special parking places reserved for disabled people.* **disability** *noun.*

disadvantage *noun* a condition that causes problems and makes success difficult. The opposite of advantage. *You are at a disadvantage if you can't use a computer.*

disagree *verb* to have different opinions and so not agree. *The more we talk, the more we seem to disagree.* **disagreement** *noun.*

disappear *verb* to stop being seen, to go out of sight. **disappearance** *noun.*

disappoint *verb* to fail to come up to somebody's hopes or expectations. *My parents were disappointed in me.* **disappointment** *noun.*

disaster *noun* 1 an unexpected event that causes great damage and suffering. *Floods and earthquakes are natural disasters.* 2 a failure, something unsuccessful. *Our party was a disaster.* **disastrous** *adjective.*

disc or **disk** *noun* 1 a record. 2 a round flat object. 3 a layer of cartilage between the bones in your back. *She's got a slipped disk.*

disc jockey or usually **DJ** *noun* a person who plays records and tapes on radio, TV, or in discos and clubs.

disciple *noun* a person who believes in and follows the teachings of a leader. *Jesus and all his disciples sat in a circle.*

discontinue (discontinues, discontinuing, discontinued) *verb* to stop something.

discover *verb* 1 to find or find out. 2 to be the first person to find something. *Christopher Columbus was the first European to discover America.* **discovery** *noun.*

Marco Polo is believed to have discovered spaghetti. He ate it in the form of noodles while exploring China.

discreet *adjective* 1 tactful in what you say or do. 2 not attracting a lot of attention. *Discreet pastel colors.* **discretion** *noun.*

discriminate *verb* 1 to notice a difference between two or more things. *We must discriminate between right and wrong.* 2 to treat things or people differently. If you discriminate against somebody, you treat them unfairly. **discrimination** *noun. Racial discrimination is a crime.*

discuss *verb* to talk about something. *I often discuss politics while drinking coffee with my friends.* **discussion** *noun.*

disguise *verb* to make somebody or something look or sound different so they are not recognized by other people. *The prince disguised himself as a servant.* **disguise** *noun. She wore a red wig as a disguise.* **in disguise** **disguised.**

If you wear this cunning disguise to school, none of your friends will know who you are.

disgust *noun* a feeling of strong dislike caused by an unpleasant smell, sight or sound. *He left the meeting room in utter disgust.* **disgust** *verb.*

disgusting *adjective* very unpleasant. *Wendy noticed a truly disgusting smell.*

dish (dishes) *noun* 1 a shallow bowl for food. 2 part of a meal. **do the dishes** to wash the dishes. **dish up** to serve food.

disheveled *adjective* (say di-shev-uld) untidy, especially somebody's hair or clothes. *The bed was disheveled.*

dishonest *adjective* not honest. *It is dishonest to cheat.* **dishonestly** *adverb.*

dishwasher *noun* a machine that automatically washes dishes.

disinfectant *noun* a substance used to destroy germs.

disk *noun* a flat round object for storing information, used in computing.

dislike *verb* to not like. *I dislike long car journeys intensely.* **dislike** *noun.*

disloyal *adjective* not loyal. *He was disloyal to his regiment.* **disloyally** *adverb.*

dismay *noun* a feeling of worry and disappointment. **dismay** *verb.* **dismayed** *adjective. I was dismayed at her truly pathetic attitude.*

dismiss *verb* 1 to send somebody away or tell a person that they will no longer have a job. *He was dismissed for constantly being late for work.* 2 to stop thinking about something or somebody or considering an idea. *We dismissed the idea.* **dismissal** *noun.*

disobedience *noun* not doing what you are told to. Not obeying. **disobedient** *adjective.*

dispatch *verb* to send somebody or something off to a destination. *The message was dispatched early this morning.*

dispatch *noun* an official report.

dispense *verb* to give out. *The pharmacist dispenses medicines.* **dispenser** *noun. A cash dispenser outside the bank.*

From one side of North America to the other is a huge distance to travel.

---

display *verb* 1 to put something in a place so it can easily be seen. *The store displayed the new range in the window.* 2 to show. *He displayed his ignorance.* **display** *noun.*

dispute *noun* a quarrel between people. *The dispute over zoning laws.* **in dispute** being argued about.

dispute *verb* 1 to argue or quarrel. 2 to say that something is not true, to raise objections. *I don't dispute that the homeless need our support.*

disqualify (disqualifies, disqualifying, disqualified) *verb* to stop somebody from doing something because they have broken the rules. **disqualification** *noun. He took his disqualification badly.*

disrupt *verb* to bring into disorder and prevent something from continuing normally. **disruption** *noun.*

dissatisfied *adjective* not satisfied.

dissect (say dis-sekt) *verb* to cut something up in order to examine it, especially a dead animal or plant. **dissection** *noun.*

Part of the botanist's job was to dissect the plants for research purposes.

distance *noun* the amount of space between two places. *My new house is within easy walking distance of school.* **in the distance** far away. **from a distance** a long way away from something in space or time. **distant** *adjective.*

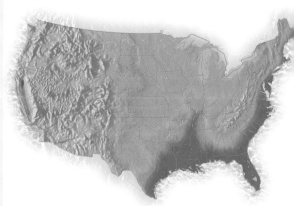

distinct *adjective* 1 easily heard or seen. *I noticed a distinct bruise on his leg.* 2 clearly different. **distinctly** *adverb.*

distinction *noun* 1 a clear difference. 2 excellence. *The mark of distinction.*

distinguish *verb* 1 to make or notice differences between things. *I can't distinguish one from the other.* 2 to show excellence. *He distinguished himself by his bravery in the face of the enemy.*

district *noun* a part of a town or country.

disturb *verb* 1 to spoil somebody's rest or interrupt what they are doing. *That noise disturbs my concentration.* 2 to cause somebody to be upset or worried. 3 to move things from their position. *Nothing in the room had been disturbed.* **disturbance** *noun.*

ditch (ditches) *noun* a channel dug in the ground for water to flow along.

ditch *verb* to get rid of or leave behind. *The robbers ditched their get-away car.*

dive *verb* 1 to plunge head first into the water. *She dove off the top board.* 2 to swim under water. *They went diving for pearls.* 3 to go down steeply. *The eagle dove from a great height.* 4 to move quickly and suddenly. *He dove for cover.* **diver** *noun.*

WORD HISTORY

'Diwali' comes from the ancient Sanskrit for 'row of lights'. During the festival, which is celebrated in October or November, lamps are lit in honor of the Hindu god Rama.

Diving is a skill that requires courage and stamina. It can sometimes be dangerous.

divert *verb* 1 to turn something in another direction. 2 to turn somebody's attention away from something else. to amuse or entertain. **diversion** *noun. The bank robbers staged a bomb scare on the other side of town as a diversion.*

divide *verb* 1 to split up or be separated into smaller parts. *We divided the candy between us.* 2 in maths, to find out how many times one number is contained in another. *Divide 12 by 3.*

division *noun* 1 the process or result of dividing or being divided. *We have a fair division of work in our family.* 2 in maths, the process of dividing one number by another. 3 a disagreement between members of a group. *There are serious divisions within the Republican party.* 4 a group having a special purpose within an organization.

divorce *noun* the legal ending of a marriage. **divorce** *verb* 1 to end a marriage. 2 to separate things.

Diwali (say di-**wah**-lee) *noun* a Hindu religious festival.

This girl is celebrating Diwali by burning candles.

dizzy (dizzier, dizziest) *adjective* feeling that everything is going around and around or that you are going to faint. *I felt dizzy after the roller-coaster ride.*

Djibouti *noun* a country in Africa, and its capital city.

The flag of Djibouti is blue, green and white with a red star.

do (does, doing, did, done) *verb* 1 to carry out or deal with something, perform an action or activity. *I'm doing the cooking.* 2 to be enough. *That will do.* 3 in questions with another verb. *Do you know him?* 4 in statements with 'not' forming the negative. *I do not know him.* 5 to stress something. *He hasn't received the invitation, but I did send him one.* 6 instead of repeating a verb that has already been used. *We earn as much money as they do.* 7 at the end of a statement to form a question. *He won the match, didn't he?* **do away with** to get rid of. **do up** to fasten.

d.o.b. *abbreviation* date of birth.

dock *noun* a place where ships are loaded and unloaded or repaired. **docker** *noun* a worker at the docks.

dock *verb* 1 to come or go into dock. *The ship docked at New York for seven days and then went on to Miami.* 2 to join with another spacecraft in space. 3 to take money away, especially wages. *Our pay was docked.*

dock *noun* a plant with broad leaves that grows as a weed.

doctor *noun* 1 a person who treats people who are ill. 2 an academic title, a high university degree. *A Doctor of Law.*

document (say dock-you-munt) *noun* an official piece of paper giving proof or information about something. **document** (say dock-you-ment) *verb*. *To document the past we have used records from the library.*

dodge *verb* to move away quickly in order to avoid being hit or seen.

Dodoma *noun* the capital of Tanzania.

doe *noun* a female deer, rabbit or hare.

dog *noun* an animal that is kept as a pet. Dogs bark.

Doha *noun* the capital of Qatar.

dole out *verb* to give something out to a lot of people, usually in small amounts.

doll *noun* a child's toy that looks like a person. *A Barbie doll.*

dollar *noun* money used in the USA, Canada and some other countries.

dolphin *noun* a sea animal like a small whale with a long nose. Dolphins are mammals and breathe through a blowhole.

dome *noun* a round roof on a building. A dome is shaped like half a ball.

Dominica *noun* a country in the West Indies.

Dominican Republic *noun* a country in the West Indies. The eastern part of the island of Hispaniola.

The flag of the Dominican Republic has a white cross on a red and blue quartered ground. A colorful crest lies at its center.

domino *noun* a small rectangular piece of wood or plastic marked with two sets of spots used for playing an old game called dominoes. *She beat me at dominoes.*

donate *verb* to give something, especially money, to a good cause. *I donated some money to charity.* **donation** *noun*.

The dormous was a delicacy roasted with honey in Roman times.

Dolphins are among the most friendly and intelligent of animals.

done past tense of do.

done *adjective* finished or completed.

donkey (donkeys) *noun* an animal like a small horse with long ears.

door *noun* a movable flat surface that opens or closes the entrance to a building, room or cupboard. **answer the door** to open the door to a visitor.

door-to-door *adjective* visiting homes to sell something. *A door-to-door salesman.*

dormant *adjective* not active. *A dormant volcano is no longer dangerous.*

dormitory (dormitories) *noun* a room with a number of beds for people to sleep in, especially in a school or hostel.

dormouse (dormice) *noun* a woodland animal like a large mouse with a long furry tail. *As sleepy as a dormouse.*

DOS *abbreviation* disk operating system (in a computer).

dose *noun* the amount of medicine to be taken at one time. **dose** *verb*. *I dosed myself with aspirin against the flu.*

dot *noun* a small spot. **dot** *verb* to mark or cover with dots. **dotted** *adjective*.

double *adjective* 1 twice as much or twice as many. *A double portion of spaghetti.* 2 for two people or things. *A double bed.* 3 having two parts. *Double barrel.* 4 having two different uses. *A word with a double meaning.* **doubly** *adverb*.

double *noun* 1 a double thing, an amount or size that is twice as large. *I paid $5 for it and sold it for double.* 2 a person or thing that looks exactly like another. *He's his father's double.* **double** *verb* 1 to become twice as large, strong or fast. *Sales have doubled in the last year.* 2 to have a second use. *My bedroom doubles as a study.*

doubt *noun* a feeling of not being sure about something. *There's no doubt that he'll pass the exam.* **doubt** *verb* to feel doubt. **doubtful** *adjective*.

doughnut *noun* a round cake or ring fried in hot fat and covered with sugar.

dove *noun* a bird like a pigeon.

dowdy (dowdier, dowdiest) *adjective* not fashionable, dull. *Dowdy clothes.*

down *adverb, preposition* 1 towards, at or into a lower position. *Could you get the book down from the shelf?* 2 in a lower place or from one place to another. *We walked down to the park.* 3 to a smaller size, grade or standard. *Prices are down.* 4 to put something in writing. *To take down notes.* 5 on to a surface. *Sit down.*

down *noun* 1 a bird's soft feathers. 2 fine soft hair. *The down on the baby's head.*

downcast *adjective* 1 sad, depressed. 2 looking downwards, especially when feeling sad. *With downcast eyes.*

downfall *noun* 1 a fall from power, ruin. *Greed was his downfall.* 2 a fall of rain, a downpour.

downstairs *adverb, adjective* to, at or in a lower floor. *I'll wait downstairs.*

Downstairs there is a living room that leads off the kitchen.

doze *verb* to sleep lightly or be half asleep.

dozen *noun* 1 twelve. *A dozen eggs.* 2 lots of. *I've asked him dozens of times.*

Dr *abbreviation* doctor.

drab (drabber, drabbest) *adjective* not colorful, dull.

drag (drags, dragging, dragged) *verb* 1 to pull a heavy load along or pull somebody roughly. *He dragged the crate across the street.* 2 to go on slowly, to seem to last a long time. *The meeting dragged on.* 3 to move along while touching the ground or search for something by pulling a heavy net along the bottom of a river or lake. *Her dress dragged in the mud.*

dragon *noun* an imaginary animal or monster in children's stories that has scales and wings and breathes fire.

dragonfly (dragonflies) *noun* an insect with a long body and two pairs of large thin wings. *The dragonflies darted and hovered over the pond in the warm summer sun.*

The wings of a dragonfly shimmer in the sunlight with rainbow colors.

drain *noun* 1 a pipe that carries away water or other unwanted liquid. 2 something that uses up time, money or energy. *Her sons are a drain on her energy.* **drain** *verb* 1 to flow away slowly. 2 to make weak or take away strength. 3 to empty or become dry or empty. *He drained the glass in one gulp, then threw it in the fireplace and made a wish.*

drake *noun* a male duck.

drama *noun* 1 a play for the theater, television or radio. 2 the study of plays, their writing, presentation and performance. 3 exciting real-life events or an emotional situation. *Our visit turned into a big drama when the house caught fire.*

dramatic *adjective* 1 impressive, exciting. *The new government has made some dramatic changes.* 2 showing feeling in a lively way. *His speech was very dramatic, but not many people appreciated it.*

drank past tense of drink.

drastic *adjective* having a strong and often violent effect. *A drastic decision had to be made to save the day.*

The dragon is a mythical beast that can fly and breathe fire.

draw (draws, drawing, drew, drawn) *verb*
1 to make pictures, patterns or diagrams with a pencil or pen. 2 to pull something heavy along. *Two horses drew the carriage.* 3 to pull something out of a place, to take out. *To draw money out of the bank.* 4 to attract. *The concert drew a large crowd.* 5 to come or move in the direction mentioned. *Our vacation is drawing to an end.* 6 to end a game or contest with the same points on both sides. *It was a draw.* 7 to form an idea. *To draw a conclusion.*
draw ahead to move in front of somebody. **draw the curtains** to open or close the curtains. **draw up** 1 to come near and stop. *A car drew up outside my door.* 2 to prepare, especially a report or document.

draw *noun* 1 equal marks in a game or contest. 2 the drawing of lottery tickets. *The luck of the draw.*

drawback *noun* a disadvantage, something that can cause trouble or difficulty. *The high price is a drawback.*

drawbridge *noun* a bridge over a moat or river that can be pulled up by chains to protect a castle or let ships pass.

drawer *noun* a box-like container which is part of a dresser or a table that slides in and out.

drawing *noun* 1 making pictures with a pen or pencil. 2 a picture made by drawing.

drawing board *noun* back to the drawing board means to develop a new plan.

drawn past tense of draw.

dread *noun* great fear. **dread** *verb* to fear something greatly. *I dread the exam.* **dreadful** *adjective. A dreadful headache.*

dreadlocks *plural noun* hair worn in tight plaits. *Bob Marley's dreadlocks.*

DID YOU KNOW

When you are dreaming, your eyes move rapidly behind your closed eyelids. Experts believe that most people dream every night, but they do not always remember their dreams.

This Bulgarian woman is wearing national dress.

I pinned the drawing of our house on the wall.

AMAZING FACT

In drawing, the point where receding parallel lines seem to meet when you look at them in perspective is called the Vanishing Point.

dream *noun* 1 thoughts, feelings and pictures you see or live through while you are asleep. A bad dream is called a nightmare. 2 something ideal you think about and that you would like to come true. *It's my dream to sail around the world.* 3 something beautiful. *She dances like a dream.* **dream** (dreams, dreaming, dreamt or dreamed) *verb* 1 to have a dream or dreams while sleeping. 2 to imagine that something you want might happen. *I dream of winning the lottery.* **dreamer** *noun.*

dredge *verb* to dredge a river means to clear it by removing mud. **dredger** *noun* a boat or barge used for dredging.

drench *verb* to make or be very wet. *We were caught in a storm and got drenched.*

dress (dresses) *noun* 1 a piece of clothing with a top and a skirt for a woman or a girl. 2 clothing in general. *The children wore national dress.*

dress *verb* 1 to put on clothes. 2 to wear clothes. *She was dressed in black.* 3 to cover with a bandage. *To dress a wound.* 5 to arrange goods for display. *To dress a shop window.* **dress up** 1 to put on smart clothes. 2 to wear something else for fun, to put on clothes in a game. *The children dressed up as pirates.* **get dressed** to put on clothes.

dresser *noun* 1 a chest of drawers or a kitchen cupboard with shelves over it. 2 a person who is employed to help actors and actresses to dress for the stage.

The jugs, plates and dishes were displayed on the kitchen dresser.

dressing *noun* 1 a bandage for covering a wound. 2 a sauce for food.

dressing gown *noun* a robe worn over pajamas or a nightie.

drew past tense of draw.

dribble *verb* 1 to let drops of spit (saliva) trickle out of your mouth. *Babies dribble.* 2 to move the ball forward with short bounces in basketball.

dried past tense of dry.

drier *noun* a device for drying hair or clothes. *The hair drier blows hot or cold.*

drift *verb* 1 to float or be carried along gently by the wind or waves. 2 to move around without a plan. *She just drifts from one job to another.*

drift *noun* 1 sand or snow that the wind has blown into a pile. 2 a general movement or the direction in which something is moving. *There is a drift away from higher education.* 3 the meaning of something, especially a speech. *I didn't catch the drift of their discussion.*

drill *noun* 1 a tool for making holes. *A dentist's drill.* 2 practising an emergency routine. *We had a fire drill this morning.* 3 training by repeating an exercise. *They have a lot of drills in the army.* **drill** *verb* 1 to drill a hole. 2 to do something repeatedly. *We were drilled to say 'thank you'.*

The driver pulled the lever and the powerful drill began to bite into the road.

drink (drinks, drinking, drank, drunk) *verb* 1 to swallow liquid. *You should drink plenty of water.* 2 to drink alcohol. *He drinks too much.* **drink** *noun* 1 something you drink. *A drink of water.* 2 alcohol, an alcoholic drink.

drip (drips, dripping, dripped) *verb* to fall slowly or let something fall in small drops. *The faucet is dripping.* **drip** *noun* 1 a drop of liquid falling, the sound of falling drops. 2 an apparatus for dripping liquid into a blood vessel.

drive (drives, driving, drove, driven) *verb* 1 to travel in a vehicle or make it go. *My brother drives a tractor.* 2 to take somebody in a car. *I'll drive the children home.* 3 to force to go. *She drives all the customers away.* 4 to make somebody do something. *His illness has driven him crazy.* 5 to direct force into or on to something. *To drive a nail into the wall. The engine is driven by steam.* **driver** *noun.*

drive *noun* 1 a trip in a car or bus. 2 a private road to a house or garage. 3 energy and enthusiasm. *People with a lot of drive are often very successful.* 4 the act of hitting a ball or the force with which it is hit, especially in golf. 5 a planned effort by a group for a particular purpose. *We are having an economy drive.*

The drive to our house sweeps through the gates and up to the front door.

drizzle *noun* light rain. **drizzle** *verb.*

drone *noun* 1 a male bee. 2 a low humming sound. **drone** *verb* 1 to make a low humming sound. 2 to talk in a low, boring voice. *He droned on and on.*

drool *verb* 1 If you drool over something, you are very excited and show foolish pleasure in looking at it. 2 to dribble.

droop *verb* to bend or hang down. *The flowers were drooping after the heavy rain.*

drop *noun* 1 a small spot of liquid, a small amount. *Drops of rain.* 2 a fall. *A drop in temperature. A drop of 100 meters.*

drop (drops, dropping, dropped) *verb* 1 to fall. *Water dropped into the bucket.* 2 to let fall. *I dropped my spoon on the floor.* 3 to become less. *Prices have dropped.* 4 to let somebody get out of the car. *Could you drop me off at the station?* 5 to stop doing something or meeting somebody. *He's dropped his girlfriend for someone else.* 6 to not select somebody for a team. *The goalkeeper let the ball into the net too many times and was dropped for the next match.* **drop in** to visit somebody without warning. **drop out** to stop taking part in something or doing something. *She dropped out of the race.*

The girl dropped the ball to see how high it would bounce.

GRAMMAR NOTE

Be careful to use 'drank' and 'drunk' correctly. 'Drank' is the past tense of 'drink'. 'He drank the whole can.' 'Drunk' is the past participle and goes with have. 'I've drunk my milk.' A person who is drunk has had too much alcohol.

drove past tense of drive.

drown *verb* 1 to die under water by not being able to breathe. *Hundreds drowned in the* Titanic *disaster.* 2 to cover something with water or make something very wet. *The peaches were drowned in brandy.* 3 to make a sound impossible to hear by making more noise. *Her voice was drowned by the children's shouting.*

drowsy *adjective* sleepy. **drowsiness** *noun.*

drug *noun* 1 a medicine. 2 a substance that affects your mind and feelings and is addictive. **drug** (drugs, drugging, drugged) *verb.* When you drug somebody, you give them a drug to make them unconscious.

drug addict *noun* somebody addicted to drugs, who cannot stop taking them.

drugstore *noun* a store where you can buy medicines and other goods. You can also sometimes have drinks and snacks in a drugstore.

drum *noun* 1 a musical instrument made of a hollow round frame with a skin stretched tightly over it. 2 a round container for liquids. **drum** (drums, drumming, drummed) *verb* 1 to play a drum. 2 to tap. *He drummed his fingers on the table.* **drummer** *noun.*

drumstick *noun* a stick for beating a drum.

He beat the bongo drums with his hands.

drunk *adjective* having had too much alcohol. *He drank too much beer and got extremely drunk.* **drunk** *noun* a person who often gets drunk.

dry (drier, driest) *adjective* 1 not wet. Without water. *The washing is dry.* 2 not rainy. *It was a dry day.* 3 uninteresting, boring. *The play was slow and pretty dry.* 4 witty. *She has a dry sense of humor.*

dry (dries, drying, dried) *verb* to make or become dry.

dry-clean *verb* to clean clothes with chemicals, without using water.

dry-cleaner's *noun* a shop where clothes are taken to be dry-cleaned.

dual *adjective* having two parts or two functions.

There is all sorts of stuff at the dump, including old furniture and carpets.

Dublin *noun* the capital of Ireland.

duck *noun* a water-bird with a wide beak.

duck *verb* 1 to bend down quickly, to avoid being seen or hit. *When he saw the policeman, he ducked behind a wall.* 2 to dip under water. *My brother ducked me in the swimming pool.* **duck out of** to avoid doing something.

duel *noun* a fight with guns or swords between two people in order to settle a quarrel. **duel** *verb* to fight a duel. **duellist** *noun.*

The fencing champion challenged his friend to a duel.

duet *noun* 1 a performance by two singers or musicians. 2 a piece of music for two singers or players. *A piano duet.*

dug past tense of dig.

dull *adjective* 1 not bright, clear or shining. *A dull color. The weather was dull.* 2 slow in understanding, stupid. *Some of his pupils are rather dull.* 3 uninteresting, boring. *A dull lesson.* 4 not sharp. *He felt a dull pain. It made a dull sound.* **dullness** *noun.*

dumb (say dum) *adjective* 1 unable to speak. 2 unwilling to speak, silent. *He remained dumb throughout the trial.* 3 stupid. *You aren't really that dumb.*

dump *noun* 1 a place where garbage is left. 2 an unpleasant, dull and dirty place. *I couldn't live in such a dump.*

dump *verb* 1 to get rid of something unwanted. *People shouldn't dump dangerous chemicals at sea.* 2 to leave or put something down carelessly. *She dumped her things in the hall.*

dune *noun* a sand hill on a beach or in the desert piled up by the wind.

dung *noun* solid waste matter from the bowels of large animals, especially cattle.

dungeon *noun* (say **dun**-jun) a dark underground prison cell in a castle.

The prisoner was thrown into the filthy dungeon without food or water.

duplicate *adjective* exactly the same. *Duplicate keys.* **duplicate** *noun* something that is exactly the same as something else; an exact copy. *Luckily I had a duplicate of the missing photograph.* **duplicate** *verb* to make or be a duplicate.

during *preposition* 1 throughout, something that happens continuously within a period. *We never go to the movies during the week.* 2 at some point within a period. *He rang twice during the morning.*

Dushanbe *noun* the capital of Tajikistan.

dusk *noun* the time when it is not completely dark, just before nightfall.

dust *noun* tiny specks of earth, sand or dirt that look like dry powder. *There is a lot of dust on the books.* **dust** *verb* 1 to wipe away dust. *She dusts her room every day.* 2 to cover with dust or fine powder. *Dust the cake with powdered sugar.*

duster *noun* a cloth for dusting.

dusty (dustier, dustiest) *adjective* 1 covered with dust. 2 like dust. *A dusty brown.*

Dutch *noun* the language spoken in Holland. **Dutch** *adjective. Dutch people.* **go Dutch** to share expenses. *We always go Dutch when I go out with my boyfriend.* **Dutch courage** so-called courage that comes from being drunk.

WORD HISTORY

'Duvet' comes from an Old French word for down, a bird's soft feathers that are used inside the quilt. A duvet is also called a continental quilt.

duty (duties) *noun* 1 something a person must do because they think it right. *It's my duty to look after my sick uncle.* 2 a task, something you have to do as part of your job. *He told me what my duties would be.* 3 a tax on certain goods. *A duty on cigarettes.* **on duty** at work. *The doctor is on duty tonight.* **off duty** not at work.

duvet *noun* a thick soft quilt used as a bed covering.

dwarf (dwarfs or dwarves) *noun* a very small person, animal or plant. **dwarf** *verb* to make something seem very small by comparison. *The new office block dwarfs the other buildings.*

dwell (dwells, dwelling, dwelt) *verb* to live. *Strange creatures dwell in the forest.* **dwell on** to think or talk about something for a long time. *It's no good dwelling on the past.*

dwelling *noun* a place to live in.

High in the mountains of South America, people make their dwellings from reeds.

dwindle (dwindles, dwindling, dwindled) *verb* to get gradually smaller or fewer. *Numbers are dwindling.*

dye (dyes, dyeing, dyed) *verb* to color something, especially hair or cloth, by soaking it in a colored liquid. *I want to dye my hair red.* **dye** *noun* the substance used for dyeing things.

dynamo *noun* a machine that turns mechanical power into electricity.

dynasty (dynasties) *noun* (say **die**-na-stee) a line of rulers of a country who all belong to the same family. *The Tudor dynasty.*

dyslexia *noun* (say dis-**leks**-ee-a) great difficulty with reading and spelling. **dyslexic** *adjective.*

Windmills are a major feature of the Dutch landscape. The wind blows fiercely across the flat land and its power used to be harnessed to grind the corn into flour.

Ee

each *adjective, pronoun* 1 every person or thing in a group. *Each student.* 2 for one. *The tickets are $10 each.* **each other** one another. *They loved each other.*

eager *adjective* wanting to do something very much, keen. **eagerly** *adverb*.

eagle *noun* a large meat-eating bird, or bird of prey, with very good eyesight.

ear *noun* the organ of hearing. You have two ears, one on either side of your head. **all ears** listening with great interest. *Tell us what she did, we're all ears.* **play it by ear** to act from moment to moment, without making plans in advance.

Cochlea

Eardrum

ear *noun* the part at the top of a corn plant that contains the seeds. *Ears of corn ripened in the summer sun.*

early (earlier, earliest) *adjective, adverb* 1 before the expected time. *The train was 10 minutes early.* 2 happening near the beginning. *Early last week.*

earn *verb* 1 to get money in return for working. 2 to get something, especially praise, because you deserve it. *That will earn him our respect.* **earnings** *plural noun*.

earnest *adjective* very serious. **in earnest** very seriously.

earring *noun* a piece of jewelry worn on the ear.

earth *noun* 1 the planet we live on. *The spacecraft has returned to Earth.* 2 the soil in which plants thrive and grow. 3 the ground. 4 a wire that passes from electrical equipment to the ground and makes the equipment safe.

The compass shows North, South, East and West.

Sound waves travel down the ear canal to the eardrum. The ear is also the body's organ of balance.

SPELLING NOTE

The planet we live on can be spelt with or without a capital 'e' ('Earth' or 'earth'). When you use it together with the names of other planets, such as Mars and Venus, write 'Earth'.

Here the Earth, with clouds above it, is seen from space.

earth *verb* to connect a piece of electrical equipment to the ground.

earthquake *noun* a sudden violent shaking of the Earth's surface.

earthworm *noun* a long thin worm that lives under the ground.

earwig *noun* a crawling insect.

easily *adverb* 1 without difficulty or very likely. *I'll easily finish my essay by tonight.* 2 without doubt. *I'm easily the fastest runner in the class.*

east or **East** *adjective, adverb* to or in the direction in which the Sun rises (the opposite of west). *An east wind.* **east** *noun* 1 *The Sun rises in the east.* 2 the eastern part of a country or continent. *Good news from the east.*

Easter *noun* a religious festival when Christians remember the death and resurrection of Christ.

easterly *adjective* towards or in the east. *We walked in an easterly direction.*

eastern *adjective* in or from the east. *A small village in eastern Russia.*

easy (easier, easiest) *adjective, adverb* 1 not difficult, not needing much effort. *It was easy to persuade him to come.* 2 without any problems. *She has an easy life.* **take it/things easy** to relax and not do or work too much. **go easy on something** to avoid using too much of it.

easy-going *adjective* not easily worried or upset. *My parents are very easy-going, they don't mind what I do.*

eat (eats, eating, ate, eaten) *verb* 1 to put food in your mouth and swallow it. 2 to have a meal. 3 to damage or destroy, especially by chemical action. *The acid has eaten a hole in the metal.* **eat in** to have a meal at home. **eat out** to have a meal in a restaurant. **eat up** to finish a meal.

eavesdrop (eavesdrops, eavesdropping, eavesdropped) *verb* to listen secretly to somebody else's conversation.

ebb *verb* 1 to flow back from the land to the sea. 2 to become weaker or grow less. *Her strength is ebbing.* **ebb** *noun* 1 *The ebb and flow of the tides.* 2 a low mood. *He felt at a very low ebb.*

ebony *noun* a hard black wood. **ebony** *adjective. Ebony skin.*

eccentric (say ek-sen-trik) *adjective* behaving strangely, having odd habits. **eccentric** *noun* an eccentric person. **eccentricity** *noun*.

echo (echoes) *noun* a sound that is heard again as it is sent back from a wall or inside a cave. **echo** (echoes, echoing, echoed) *verb* 1 to make an echo. *Our footsteps echoed in the tunnel.* 2 to repeat somebody else's words or actions. *His views echoed those of his elder sister.*

eclipse *noun* the disappearance of the Sun's or Moon's light when the Moon or the Earth is in the way. *A total eclipse of the Sun.* **eclipse** *verb* to do or be much better than somebody or something. *His paintings eclipsed all the other exhibits.*

ecology *noun* the pattern of relationships between plants, animals and people to each other and their surroundings. **ecologist** *noun.* **ecological** *adjective.*

economic *adjective* 1 relating to economics. 2 making a profit. *It's not economic to run buses all night.*

economical *adjective* using money, time or goods carefully, not wasteful. *He's very economical with the stationery.* **economically** *adverb.*

economics *noun* the science of the production and distribution of wealth.

economy (economies) *noun* 1 the system by which a country spends its money and organizes its industry and trade. 2 the careful spending of money or use of goods in order to save money.

ecosystem *noun* a system relating all the plants, animals and people in an area to their surroundings.

ecstasy (say ek-stuh-see) *noun* a feeling of extreme joy and happiness. **ecstatic** *adjective.* **ecstatically** *adverb.*

Ecuador *noun* a country in South America.

edge *noun* 1 the thin cutting part of a knife or another cutting tool. 2 the place or line where something stops and something else begins. The side of something. *The edge of the cliff.* **on edge** nervous.

This solar eclipse was photographed on 16 February 1980, over Africa.

The Galapagos Islands in the Pacific Ocean belong to Ecuador, a country on the west coast of South America.

SPELLING NOTE

The noun 'effect' goes with the verb 'affect'. 'It had no effect on me; it didn't affect me.' The verb 'effect' has a different meaning, to make happen.

edge *verb* 1 to form the edge of something or put an edge on something. *The lawn was edged with flowers.* 2 to move slowly and carefully. *He edged towards me.*

edible *adjective* fit to be eaten, eatable.

edifice (say ed-if-iss) *noun* a large building.

Edinburgh *noun* the capital of Scotland.

edit *verb* 1 to plan and work on a newspaper, magazine or book. *This manuscript needed a lot of editing.* 2 to choose, arrange and put parts of a film or recording together.

edition *noun* 1 the form in which a book or magazine is printed. *A paperback edition.* 2 the number of copies of a book or magazine printed. *The first edition has already sold out.*

editor *noun* 1 a person who edits a book, magazine or newspaper. 2 the person who is in charge of a newspaper.

educate *verb* to teach or train somebody. **education** *noun.*

eel *noun* a long thin fish that looks like a snake.

The young of the eel is called an elver.

effect *noun* 1 a condition caused by something, a result. *He could feel the effects of the drink.* 2 an impression produced on the mind. *Sound effects are very important in a film.* **effect** *verb* to produce or make something happen. *The changes in the law will be effected soon.* **in effect** really. *In effect the reply told her nothing.* **take effect** to start happening.

effective *adjective* 1 impressive. 2 producing the result you set out to achieve. *Baking soda can be an effective stain remover.* 3 actual or real. *She took effective control.* **to become effective** to come into force. *The new hours become effective on Tuesday.* **effectiveness** *noun.* **effectively** *adverb.*

efficient *adjective* working well without wasting time or effort. *He's very efficient at his job.* **efficiency** *noun.*

effort *noun* trying hard to do something, or the result of it. *I make an effort to be polite.*

egg *noun* 1 an oval object laid by female birds, fishes and reptiles which contains new life. 2 a hen's egg used as food. 3 a female reproductive cell in humans, animals and plants. The scientific term for a human egg is an ovum.

e.g. *abbreviation* for example. *In certain countries, e.g. Italy, France and Holland.*

Egypt *noun* a country in Africa.

Eid (say eed) *noun* a Muslim festival celebrating the end of the fast of Ramadan (Eid ul-Fitr), or the end of a journey to Mecca (Eid ul-Adha).

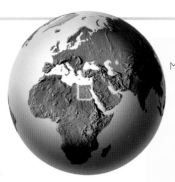

Egypt lies on the Mediterranean Sea in North Africa.

either *adjective, pronoun* 1 one or the other of two. *Both computers work, you can use either one.* 2 one and also the other, both. *'Which do you prefer?' 'I don't like either one.'* **either** *adverb* also (used in negative statements). *I don't like cats and I don't like dogs either.* **either** *conjunction* the first of two or more possibilities. *I'll either write or call you when I feel better.*

eject *verb* 1 to throw somebody out of a place. *They were forcibly ejected from the stadium.* 2 to push out with force. *The machine ejected the coins.*

El Salvador *noun* a country in Central America.

elaborate (say i-**lab**-uh-rut) *adjective* full of detail with a number of complicated parts. *The curtains had an elaborate pattern of flowers.* **elaborate** (say i-**lab**-uh-rate) *verb* When you elaborate on something, you describe or explain it in detail.

elapse *verb* (of time) to pass by. *Three months have elapsed since the wedding.*

elastic *adjective* able to stretch and go back to its original shape. *An elastic band.* **elasticity** *noun.*

elastic *noun* material that stretches.

elbow *noun* the joint where the arm bends.

Joints, such as the elbow joint, are cushioned by soft, squashy cartilage, which is more flexible than bone.

DID YOU KNOW

An element is one of more than 100 substances that consist of atoms of the same type. Everything in the Universe, whether living or non-living, is made up of combinations of chemical elements. For example, water combines the elements hydrogen and oxygen.

elder *noun* a tree with white flowers and red or black berries.

elder *adjective* older. *My elder sister.* **elder** *noun* 1 the older of two people. 2 an older person. *We should respect our elders.*

elect *verb* 1 to choose by voting. *A new government was elected.* 2 to decide to do something. *They elected to stay.*

election *noun* voting to choose a person or party to hold an official position. *She ran for student council in the school elections.*

The elephant uses its trunk for taking food from high in the trees. It can also smell, drink and shower with its trunk.

electric *adjective* 1 producing or produced by electricity. *An electric toothbrush.* 2 very exciting. *The atmosphere at the concert was simply electric.*

electrical *adjective* relating to electricity. *An electrical fault.*

electrician *noun* a person whose job is to fit and repair electrical equipment.

electricity *noun* a form of energy that is used for heating and lighting or for driving machines. Electricity is produced by generators or batteries.

electrode *noun* the point where an electric current enters or leaves a battery.

electron *noun* a tiny particle of matter with a negative electric charge.

electronic *adjective* produced or worked by electrons, usually using microchips. *Electronic music.* **electronics** *noun.*

elegant *adjective* showing good taste in design and style. Graceful and pleasing. *An elegant new dress.* **elegance** *noun.*

element *noun* 1 a single part that combines with others to make a whole. *Listening is an important element of her job.* 2 an amount of something. *There is an element of truth in what she said.* 3 the most important parts or the basics of a subject. *The elements of mathematics.* 4 in science, an element is a substance that consists of only one type of atom. Gold and oxygen are elements. 6 a suitable situation. *He was in his element talking about films.* **the elements** the weather, especially wind and rain.

elementary *adjective* easy, simple. *I took an elementary course.*

elementary school *noun* a school in the US for the first six or eight years of a child's education.

elephant *noun* the largest living land animal, with a trunk and tusks.

elevator *noun* a machine in a building that takes people from one floor to another.

eligible *adjective* 1 entitled to do something. 2 desirable or suitable. *An eligible bachelor.*

elite (say ay-leet) *noun* the most important or powerful group of people.

elm *noun* a tree with broad leaves.

eloquent *adjective* able to make good speeches that persuade and influence others. **eloquence** *noun*.

else *adverb* 1 besides, in addition, other. *What else can I do?* 2 otherwise. *You'd better pay the fine, or else you'll go to jail.*

elusive *adjective* difficult to catch or find. *Success proved elusive.*

e-mail *noun* electronic mail. *I'll send it to you by e-mail.*

emancipate *verb* to free somebody from things that are holding them back. **emancipated** *adjective*. *Today's women are much more emancipated than their grandmothers.* **emancipation** *noun*.

embankment *noun* a wall of stones or earth to hold back a river or support a road or railroad.

embark *verb* to go on board a ship or plane. **embark on** to start. *She embarked on a new life.*

embarrass *verb* to make somebody feel awkward or self-conscious. *The questions embarrassed me so much that I blushed.* **embarrassment** *noun*.

embroider *verb* to sew a design on cloth. *She embroidered the tablecloth with pink flowers.* **embroidery** *noun*.

embryo (say em-bree-oh) *noun* a baby or an animal as it starts to grow in its mother's womb. **embryonic** *adjective* undeveloped.

This sequence of pictures shows the development of the embryo in the womb.

emerald *noun* 1 a green precious stone. 2 a clear green color.

emergency (emergencies) *noun* an unexpected dangerous event that needs immediate action. *Call an ambulance, it's an emergency!*

emigrate *verb* to leave your own country to live in another country. **emigration** *noun*. **emigrant** *noun*.

eminent *adjective* an eminent person is somebody famous and admired.

DID YOU KNOW

An e-mail address is made of a group of letters, numbers and dots, with no spaces in between any of them such as santa@npole.com. E-mail users sometimes call the ordinary postal system 'snail mail', because they think it is so slow.

Emmeline Pankhurst led the campaign to emancipate women. She was arrested and imprisoned several times.

The emu can run very fast but it cannot fly.

SPELLING NOTE

When they start their journey from their original country, people are called emigrants. At the end of the journey, when they arrive in their new country, they are called immigrants.

emotion *noun* a strong feeling. Love and jealousy are emotions. *She was overcome with emotion.* **emotional** *adjective*.

emotive *adjective* causing emotion. *It was a very emotive issue.*

emperor *noun* the ruler of an empire. If the ruler is a woman, she is called an empress.

emphasize *verb* to give special importance to something. *He emphasized that he wanted to be on his own.* **emphasis** *noun*.

empire *noun* 1 a country or group of countries controlled by one person. *The former British Empire.* 2 a large group of firms or shops controlled by one person. *She has built up a huge empire.*

employ *verb* 1 to pay somebody to do work for you. *The firm employs 20 people.* 2 to make use of something or somebody. *He employed all his charm to win her over.*

employee *noun* a person who is paid to work for somebody else.

employer *noun* a person who employs people. *Dad's employer is very fair.*

employment *noun* 1 having a paid job. Employing or being employed. *I have never been out of employment.* 2 a person's regular job.

empty (emptier, emptiest) *adjective* 1 with nothing or nobody in it. 2 with no meaning. *They were empty promises.* **empty** *noun*. *You get your deposit back when you return the empties.* **empty** (empties, emptying, emptied) *verb* to make empty. **emptiness** *noun*. **emptily** *adverb*.

emu *noun* a large Australian bird, like an ostrich.

enable *verb* to make somebody able to do something or give somebody the means to do something.

enamel *noun* 1 a shiny substance that is put on to metal, glass or pottery to decorate and protect it. 2 the outer covering of a tooth. **enamel** *adjective*. *Enamel paint.*

enchant *verb* 1 When you enchant somebody, you charm and delight them. 2 to put somebody or something under a magic spell. **enchanted** *adjective* magic. *An enchanted forest.*

enclose *verb* 1 to put a wall or fence around something to shut it in. 2 to put something with a letter or a package. *I'm enclosing a photograph.* **enclosure** *noun*.

encounter *verb* 1 to meet unexpectedly. 2 to be faced with something bad, especially danger or prejudice. *We encountered many difficulties.* **encounter** *noun.*

encourage *verb* 1 to give courage or hope to somebody. *I encouraged her to take up painting.* 2 to support or help develop. *Don't encourage his laziness.* **encouragement** *noun.* **encouraging** *adjective. Encouraging news from the hospital.*

end *noun* 1 the point or place where something stops, the last part of something. *At the end of the street.* 2 finish. *It was the end of our friendship.* 3 death. *His was a cruel end.* 4 purpose. *He is doing this for his own selfish ends.* **in the end** finally. **make ends meet** to have just enough money to live on. **end** *verb* to finish. *How did the play end?*

endanger *verb* to cause danger to. *Smoking seriously endangers your health.*

endeavor (say en-**dev**-er) *verb* to try. **endeavor** *noun.*

endurance *noun* the ability to endure or bear something. *We were all really impressed by the athlete's skill and endurance.*

The 20,000 men who survived the 9,700 km Long March in China in 1934–35 performed an astonishing feat of endurance. 80,000 men died on the journey.

endure *verb* 1 to put up with, to bear, especially pain or suffering. *After the earthquake, everyone endured great hardship.* 2 to last. *His memory will endure.*

enemy (enemies) *noun* 1 somebody who hates or wants to hurt another person. When two people hate each other, they are enemies. 2 a country or army that is at war with another. *The enemy attacked at night.*

energetic *adjective* full of energy.

energy *noun* 1 the strength and ability to do a lot. 2 the effort put into work. *She concentrated all her energy on her job.* 3 the power that works and drives machines.

engage *verb* 1 to employ. If you are engaged in something, you are doing it or working on it. 2 to attract somebody's attention. 3 to fit into or lock together parts of a machine. *To engage the clutch.*

DID YOU KNOW

English is an official language in 57 countries of the world. But more people speak Mandarin Chinese in China and Hindi in India as their first language. After Mandarin, Hindi and English, the next most common language is Spanish.

engaged *adjective* having agreed to marry. *They have been engaged for five years.*

engagement *noun* 1 an agreement to marry. *She called off their engagement.* 2 the period of time during which two people are engaged. 3 an arrangement to meet somebody or do something. *A dinner engagement is something I look forward to.*

engaging *adjective* attractive, interesting. *He's got a really engaging smile.*

engine *noun* 1 a machine that produces power which makes a vehicle move. 2 a machine that pulls a railroad train, also called a locomotive.

This is a car engine with four cylinders.

engineer *noun* 1 a person who designs machines, roads and bridges. 2 a person who repairs machines or electrical devices. 3 a person in control of an engine or engines, especially on a ship.

engineer *verb* to plan or cause something to happen. *He engineered an interview with the top boss.*

England *noun* a country that is part of the United Kingdom.

England is part of the British Isles. It is separated from the mainland of Europe by the English Channel.

English *noun* 1 the people of England. 2 the language spoken in Great Britain, America, Canada, Australia and elsewhere. **English** *adjective. English customs and traditions.*

enjoy *verb* to get pleasure from something. **enjoyment** *noun.*

enlarge *verb* to make or get bigger. *The house was enlarged by the previous owners.* **enlargement** *noun. I'd like an enlargement of this photograph.*

enormous *adjective* very big.

enough *adverb* having the right amount or to the right degree. *He's not old enough to understand.* **enough** *adjective* as much or as many as necessary. *Have we got enough time for a cup of coffee?* **enough** *pronoun. Not enough is known about the universe.*

enquire, enquirer, enquiry. See inquire, inquirer, inquiry.

enroll (enrolls, enrolling, enrolled) *verb* to become a member, especially on a course. *I have enrolled at the community college.*

ensure *verb* to make certain (of). *This medicine will ensure a good night's sleep.*

enter *verb* 1 to come in or go into. *He entered the room.* 2 to become a member, especially of a university or profession. 3 to write down in a book or type into a computer. *He entered the amount in the cash book.* 4 to take part in a competition.

entertain *verb* 1 to give food and drink to guests at your home. 2 to amuse and interest. *He entertained us with stories about his trip around the world.* 3 to think about. *I didn't even entertain the idea.*

entertainer *noun* a person whose job it is to entertain, especially a comedian or singer. *Elvis Presley was a great entertainer.*

entertainment *noun* 1 the act of being entertained or being entertaining. *He told stories for the children's entertainment.* 2 a performance at a theater, auditorium, etc.

enthusiasm *noun* a strong feeling of interest, liking and excitement. *She was full of enthusiasm.* **enthusiast** *noun.* *He's a sailing enthusiast.* **enthusiastic** *adjective.*

entire *adjective* whole. *They spent the entire evening arguing.* **entirely** *adverb.*

entrance *noun* 1 a way into a place, for example a door or gate. 2 the arrival in a room. *She made a dramatic entrance.* 3 the right to go into a place. *He was refused entrance.*

entry (entries) *noun* 1 coming or going in. 2 the right to enter. *No entry.* 3 something entered in a list or book. *A dictionary entry.*

envelop (say in-**vel**-up) *verb* to cover or surround completely. *The hills were enveloped in mist.*

envelope (say **en**-vuh-lope) *noun* a paper cover for a letter.

envious *adjective* feeling envy. *He was envious of his successful brother.*

environment *noun* the surroundings and conditions in which people, animals and plants live. **environmental** *adjective.* *Environmental pollution.* **environmentalist** *noun.*

The scales are equally balanced.

The main entrance to Mycenae in ancient Greece was through the Lion Gate.

envy (envies, envying, envied) *verb* wishing you had something that somebody else has. *I envied her her beauty.* **envy** *noun* a feeling of resentment towards somebody who has something that you would like. *His car was the envy of all his friends.*

epic *noun* 1 a long poem about heroes and heroic deeds. 2 a historic, grand book or film. **epic** *adjective.* *An epic adventure.*

epidemic *noun* a large number of cases of an infectious disease in one area at the same time. *A flu epidemic has been forecast.*

episode *noun* 1 one separate and important event. *That trip was one of the funniest episodes in my life.* 2 one of several parts of a radio or TV series.

epoch (say ee-pok) *noun* a period of time in history or life. *A new epoch in the history of space travel.*

epoch-making *adjective* very important, remarkable. *An epoch-making discovery.*

equal *adjective* the same amount, size or degree. *Women demand equal rights and opportunities.* **equal to something** having enough strength and courage for something. *Will he be equal to running the business on his own?* **equally** *adverb.*

equal *noun* a person or thing with the same qualities as another. *The two brothers are always treated as equals.*

equal *verb* 1 to be the same as another one in amount, size or value. *His salary doesn't equal mine.* 2 to be as good or do as well as somebody else. *With this win, they have equalled the record.*

equality *noun* being equal, having the same rights and opportunities.

equate *verb* to consider two things or people to be equal. *It is impossible to equate his novels with his films.*

equator *noun* an imaginary circle around the middle of the Earth.

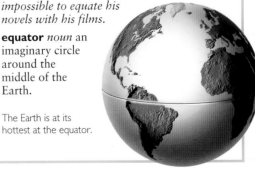

The Earth is at its hottest at the equator.

Equatorial Guinea
noun a country
in Africa.

The flag of Equatorial
Guinea has vertical
red, yellow and
green stripes.

equestrian *adjective*
to do with horses
and horseback-riding.
An equestrian event.

equinox *noun* the time of the year when
day and night are equally long, about 20
March and 22 September.

equip *verb* to supply with what is needed.
*The gym is fully equipped with weights
and exercise machines.*

equipment *noun* things needed for certain
activities. *Office equipment, climbing
equipment, cleaning equipment.*

equivalent *adjective* same, equal in value
or meaning. *That sum of money is almost
equivalent to a day's work.* **equivalent** *noun*.

era *noun* a period of time
that starts from a particular
point. *The Kennedy era.*

eradicate *verb* to get rid
of something or destroy it
completely. *We are determined
to eradicate crime.*

erase *verb* 1 to rub out. 2 to wipe out
a recording. *I erased the tape by mistake.*

eraser *noun* a piecce of rubber used to
erase marks or writing, usually on paper.

erect *adjective* upright. *He stood erect.*

erect *verb* to build or set up. *They erected
a statue in the town.* **erection** *noun*.

Eritrea *noun* a country in Africa.

err *verb* to make a mistake or do something
wrong. *It is better to err on the side of
mercy.*

errand *noun* a short trip that you make to
get something, especially buy things, or to
deliver a message. *Could you run a few
errands for me downtown?*

error *noun* a mistake.

erupt *verb* 1 to explode and spurt out lava.
The volcano erupted. 2 to break out or
happen suddenly. *Violence erupted after the
football game.* **eruption** *noun*.

escalate *verb* to increase by stages. *The
violence soon escalated.*

escalator *noun* a moving staircase that goes
up or down.

escape *verb* 1 to get away from a person
or place, to get out. *Three prisoners escaped
last night.* 2 to avoid, especially something
unpleasant. *They escaped the accident
unhurt. To escape punishment.* **escape**
*noun. They had planned the
escape for weeks.*

**GRAMMAR
NOTE**
*You can use the
word 'to' with
the adjective
'equivalent'. 'That's
equivalent to $10.'
With 'equivalent'
as a noun, use
the word 'of'.
'That's the
equivalent of $10.'*

especially *adverb* specially, in particular.
I love chocolate, especially milk chocolate.

espionage *noun* spying.

essential *adjective* 1 absolutely necessary.
*A knowledge of languages is essential for
foreign correspondents.* 2 most important.
*I only read the essential books on the
reading list.* **essential** *noun. Just tell me
the bare essentials.*

establish *verb* 1 to set up, especially a new
government or business. 2 to place or settle
yourself or somebody else. *Once he has
established himself in the firm, he'll make
progress very quickly.* 3 to find out or make
certain. *We must establish the truth first.*

estate *noun* 1 a large piece of land in the
country owned by one person. 2 everything,
including money and property, that a
person leaves when they die. *The entire
estate was left to the owner's dog.*

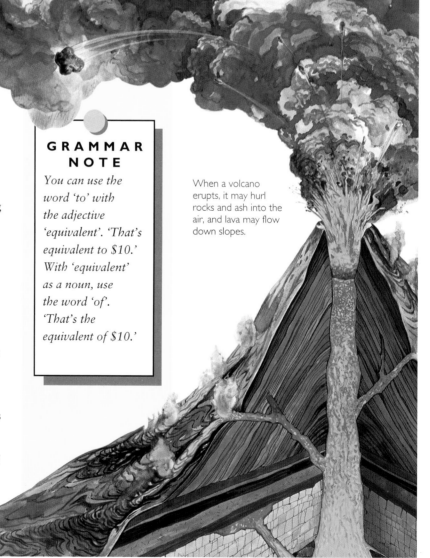

When a volcano
erupts, it may hurl
rocks and ash into the
air, and lava may flow
down slopes.

Estonia *noun* a Baltic country in Europe.

estuary (estuaries) (say ess-tew-uh-ree) *noun* the wide mouth of a river where it flows into the sea.

etc. *abbreviation* et cetera (Latin for 'and other things'), and so on.

eternal *adjective* lasting for ever. *The memorial is marked by an eternal flame.*

Ethiopia *noun* a country in Africa.

ethnic *adjective* relating to people's race or culture. *Ethnic minorities must have the same rights as everybody else.*

etymology (etymologies) *noun* (say et-im-ol-uh-jee) 1 the history and source of a word. *It's fun to find out the etymology of a word.* 2 the study of the origins and meanings of words. **etymological** *adjective*.

EU *abbreviation* European Union.

Europe *noun* one of the Earth's seven continents.

European *adjective* coming from or relating to Europe. *A common European currency.*

evacuate *verb* to leave a place or move people out of a place, especially because of a crisis. *You must evacuate the building immediately. Thousands of people were evacuated after the earthquake.* **evacuation** *noun*.

In England during World War II, many children were evacuated from cities to the country, where they would be safe from bombing.

evade *verb* to avoid a person or thing. *He cleverly evaded the question of money.* **evasion** *noun*. *He was fined for tax evasion.*

evaporate *verb* 1 to change from a liquid into a gas called water vapor. *Water evaporates in the heat of the Sun.* 2 to disappear. *My hopes evaporated.* **evaporation** *noun*.

The flag of the European Union has a circle of 12 gold stars on a blue background.

even *adjective* 1 flat, smooth. *The floor is not very even.* 2 regular, unchanging. *Indoor plants do best in an even temperature.* 3 equal, especially when talking about things that can be measured. *An even distribution of wealth. We both won a game, now we're even.* 4 Even numbers are numbers that can be divided by two. *Four and 26 are even numbers.* **evenly** *adverb*. **evenness** *noun*.

even *adverb* 1 used to stress a word or statement. *Even the teacher was surprised at how difficult the exam was.* 2 used before a comparison, meaning still. *He is even taller than his father.* **even so** nevertheless. *She says she doesn't get on with her parents, but even so, she doesn't want to leave home.* **even though** despite the fact that. *Even though she's upset, she won't say anything.* **even out** to make or become even. *Things even themselves out in the end.*

evening *noun* the end of the day, before nightfall. *We usually go to the movies on Saturday evening.*

event *noun* 1 something that happens, especially something unusual or important. 2 one of the races or other sporting activities in a competition. **in any event** whatever happens.

Russian astronaut Yuri Gagarin was the first man in space. It was a great event in the history of space exploration.

eventual *adjective* happening at last. *He deserved his eventual success.*

ever *adverb* 1 at any time. *Getting a computer was the best thing I ever did.* 2 all the time. *They lived happily ever after.* 3 (used for stress) very. *I had ever such a nice letter from him.* **ever since** since the time. *Ever since I've known him, he has never been late.*

evergreen *adjective* having green leaves all the year round. *Evergreen trees.*

every *adjective* 1 each one. *Every word she says is true.* 2 happening at regular intervals. *Every time I ask her she refuses.* 3 all possible. *He has every reason to be unhappy.* **every now and then** sometimes. *I see my parents every now and then.*

everybody *pronoun* each person or all people. *Everybody wants to come to Marianne's birthday party.*

everyone *pronoun* everybody.

everything *pronoun* each thing or all things. *Money isn't everything.*

everywhere *adverb* in, at or to every place. *I've looked everywhere for it.*

evidence *noun* proof, something that makes a matter or statement clear. *The thieves destroyed the evidence by burning their clothes.* **give evidence** to tell what is known about somebody or something in a court of law.

evil *adjective* very bad, wicked, usually causing harm. *He's an evil man.* **evil** *noun*. *The difference between good and evil.*

evolution *noun* the change and development that takes place over a long period of time, during which animals and plants evolve. **evolutionary** *adjective*.

WORD BUILDING

In words such as 'excavate' the prefix 'ex–' means 'out'. In Latin, 'excavare' means to hollow out, from 'cavus', meaning a hollow or a cave.

As early people evolved, they gradually became less like apes and more like humans.

evolve *verb* to develop gradually.

ewe (rhymes with 'boo') *noun* a female sheep. *Ewe's milk.*

ex- *prefix* former, no longer the thing the noun refers to. *An ex-senator is no longer a senator. My ex-wife has married again.*

exaggerate *verb* to say that something is bigger, better or worse than it really is. *You can't believe his stories, he always exaggerates.* **exaggeration** *noun*.

examine *verb* 1 to test somebody's knowledge. 2 to look at a person or thing carefully. *The doctor examined the patient.* **examination** *noun*.

example *noun* 1 something that shows how a rule works or what others of the same kind are like. *The penguin is an example of a flightless bird.* 2 a person or thing worth copying. *Her courage is an example to us all.* **for example** *Some birds can't fly – penguins, for example.*

exasperate *verb* to annoy or make angry. *Her stupidity is extremely exasperating.* **exasperation** *noun*.

excavate *verb* to dig out. *Archeologists are excavating an ancient Roman site.* **excavation** *noun*.

exceed *verb* to be greater than something. *The whole cost of the trip should not exceed $1000.*

excel (excels, excelling, excelled) *verb* to be extremely good. *He excels at math.*

excellent *adjective* extremely good. *He's an excellent tennis player.*

except *preposition* not including. *The play's all right, except that it's too long.* **except** *verb* to leave out. *No one can be excepted.*

exception *noun* somebody or something that does not follow the general rule. *The exception proves the rule.*

exceptional *adjective* 1 very unusual. *Only in exceptional circumstances.* 2 unusually or extremely good. *Her grades are exceptional this year.*

excess (excesses) *noun* more than is needed, too much of something. **excess** *adjective*. *You will have to pay for excess baggage.*

exchange *verb* to get something else for something. *I exchanged my pounds for pesetas. We exchanged addresses.* **exchangeable** *adjective*.

The penpals exchanged addresses and started a regular correspondence.

exchange *noun* 1 getting something else for something. *They gave us a sandwich in exchange for some fruit.* 2 changing places with somebody. *We went on a study exchange to France.*

The emperor penguin is an example of a bird that cannot fly. The penguin has waterproof feathers and a thick layer of fat to keep out the cold of Antarctica.

excite *verb* to arouse strong feelings. *We were very excited when we got tickets for the concert.* **exciting** *adjective. An exciting adventure.* **excitable** *adjective. He is very nervous and excitable.* **excitement** *noun.*

exclaim *verb* to shout out with strong feeling. *'No!' he exclaimed 'You are never to go there again.'* **exclamation** *noun.*

exclamation mark *noun* the punctuation mark (!) which shows an exclamation.

exclude *verb* to keep or leave somebody or something out. *If you are not a member, you will be excluded from the meeting.* **exclusion** *noun.*

exclusive *adjective* 1 excluding many people and so catering for just a few. *An exclusive club.* 2 not appearing anywhere else. *The newspaper has an exclusive interview with the Brazilian movie star.*

excursion *noun* a short trip. *We went on an excursion to the county museum.*

excuse (say iks-**kewz**) *verb* 1 to forgive. You excuse a person for doing something wrong or inconvenient. *Please excuse me for being late.* 2 to free somebody from a duty. *He asked to be excused from football practice because of injury.* **excuse me** used as an apology or when asking for something or interrupting somebody.

excuse *noun* (say iks-**kewss**) the reason given or an explanation for something that has been done. *That's no excuse.*

execute *verb* 1 to kill somebody as a punishment for a crime. *The murderer was executed.* 2 to perform or carry out something, especially a plan or an order. *This task is not easy to execute.* **execution** *noun.* **executioner** *noun.*

GRAMMAR NOTE

An exclamation mark (!) is used at the end of sentences that express a strong command ('Shut up! Put it down!') or surprise (What an extraordinary idea!). It is also used for warnings (Look out!) and after interjections (Ouch!).

The exclusive interview was the scoop of the year. It was printed on the front page.

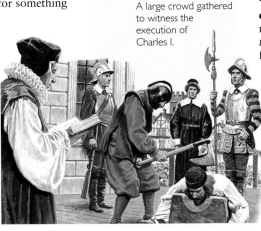

A large crowd gathered to witness the execution of Charles I.

executive *noun* a senior person with authority in a business.

executor *noun* somebody appointed to carry out a person's instructions in their will. *Her son was the executor of her will.*

exercise *noun* 1 movements done to keep healthy or train for a particular sport. *Cycling and swimming are good forms of exercise. Gymnastic exercises.* 2 a short piece of work, especially a set of questions for practice at school. *A grammar exercise.*

exercise *verb* 1 to do exercises to become fit and healthy. *I try to exercise every day.* 2 If a problem exercises your mind, you think a lot about it.

Some people exercise every day to stay healthy.

exert *verb* to use power or influence in order to achieve something. *If you exert yourself, you make an effort.* **exertion** *noun.*

exhaust *verb* 1 to tire out. *I'm exhausted.* 2 to use up completely. *Our food supplies were soon exhausted.* **exhausting** *adjective.*

exhaust *noun* 1 the waste gas produced by an engine. 2 the pipe through which waste gas escapes, also called an exhaust pipe.

exhaustion *noun* the state of being tired out. *Physical and mental exhaustion set in after we had worked all day at a boring job.*

exhaustive *adjective* thorough, comprehensive. *An exhaustive search.*

exhibit *verb* 1 to show in public in a museum or a gallery. *The gallery exhibited the artist's latest paintings.* 2 to show your feelings to other people. *His manner exhibited signs of distress.*

exhibit *noun* something exhibited in a museum or gallery. *Please do not touch the exhibits.*

exhibition *noun* a collection of things shown in a public place.

exile *noun* 1 a person who has been forced to leave his country, usually for political reasons. 2 having to live away from your own country. *He died alone and in exile.* **exile** *verb.*

exist *verb* 1 to be real. *Do you think ghosts really exist?* 2 to stay alive. *She exists on love alone.* **existence** *noun*.

exit *noun* 1 a way out. *Where's the exit?* 2 leaving a room or the stage. *She made a quick exit.* **exit** *verb* to leave.

exorcize *verb* to get rid of an evil spirit. *They had special rituals to exorcize ghosts.* **exorcism** *noun*. **exorcist** *noun*.

exotic *adjective* unusual and interesting. *There are many exotic flowers in the botanical gardens.*

The orchid is a very exotic flower. Orchids grow wild in tropical countries.

expand *verb* to become larger. *Scientists say the universe is expanding.* **expansion** *noun*.

expand *verb* When you expand on something, you tell a story in more detail.

expect *verb* 1 to think that something will happen. *I never expected to win the race. She expects them to make their own beds.* 2 to believe that somebody will come. *We are expecting them at five o'clock.* **expectation** *noun*. *The restaurant didn't really meet our expectations.*

expel (expels, expelling, expelled) *verb* 1 to send somebody away, usually for doing wrong. *He was expelled from school for severe misbehavior.* 2 to force out. *When you breathe out, air is expelled from your lungs.*

expend *verb* to spend or use up. *She expended a lot of energy.*

expenditure *noun* the spending of money or effort.

expense *noun* spending money. *If you spare no expense, you don't worry about the cost of something. I've had a lot of expenses during this past month.*

expensive *adjective* costing a lot of money. *He drives an expensive car.* **expensively** *adverb*. *Expensively dressed.*

experience *noun* 1 knowledge or skill gained from doing or seeing things. *Most stores only employ people with sales experience.* 2 an event that has happened to you. *Riding a camel is a strange and wonderful experience.* **experience** *verb* to have something happen to you. *She has experienced great sadness in her life.*

experiment *noun* a test made in order to learn or prove something. *A scientific experiment.* **experiment** *verb* to try things out and make experiments. *We know that it's dangerous to experiment with drugs.* **experimental** *adjective*.

In this experiment, a can is left on the grass for a few days. Starved of light, the grass under the can turns yellow.

explain *verb* 1 to make something clear so it can be understood. *He explained how to use the computer.* 2 to give a reason for something. *That explains his strange behavior.* **explanation** *noun*.

explode *verb* 1 to blow up, especially of a bomb. 2 to burst out suddenly or show violent feelings. *She exploded with anger.* **explosion** *noun*. **explosive** *adjective*. *Explosive materials.*

exploit (say eks-ploit) *noun* a brave or adventurous deed.

exploit (say iks-**ploit**) *verb* 1 to use or develop, especially a country's natural resources. *Exploiting the country's diamond wealth.* 2 to use unfairly and selfishly for your own profit. *The poor have always been exploited.* **exploitation** *noun*.

explore *verb* 1 to travel to places in order to find out what they are like. 2 to examine something and learn about it. *Have you definitely explored all the possibilities?* **exploration** *noun*.

explorer *noun* somebody who explores. *An Arctic explorer.*

export *verb* to send goods to another country for sale. **export** *noun* 1 exporting goods. *The export of ivory has been banned.* 2 exported goods. *Exports are products sold in another country. Exports are up this year.*

DID YOU KNOW

Exports are sent to and sold in another country, while imports are bought in and sent from another country.

Sir Walter Raleigh first took tobacco and potatoes from South America to Britian. Now tobacco is one of South America's main exports.

expulsion *noun* expelling or being expelled. *The trouble makers faced expulsion.*

extend *verb* 1 to stretch out or make bigger. *They extended the garden.* 2 to offer. *They extended a warm welcome to the delegation of foreign visitors.*

extension *noun* 1 an extra period of time. *I should have handed my essay in today, but the teacher gave me an extension.* 2 something added on. *They announced plans for an extension to the bike trail.* 3 an additional telephone connected to the same line. *I'll take the call on the extension in my office.*

extensive *adjective* covering a large area or amount. *There was extensive damage to the building from the bomb blast.*

exterior *noun* the outside of something. **exterior** *adjective*. *The exterior walls are gradually crumbling away.*

exterminate *verb* to destroy or kill. *Many tribes have been exterminated.* **extermination** *noun*. **exterminator** *noun*.

extinct *adjective* 1 not existing any more. *Dinosaurs have been extinct for millions of years.* 2 no longer active. *An extinct volcano.*

Extinct animals such as dinosaurs can be studied from their fossilized remains.

extra *adjective*, *adverb* more than usual, additional. *She says the vitamins give her extra strength.*

extract (say **iks-trakt**) *verb* 1 to pull or take something out. *The dentist had to extract two teeth.* 2 to obtain, against a person's will. *They used force to extract information.*

extract (say **eks-trakt**) *noun* 1 a small part taken from a book or film. *They printed extracts from the new book in the newspaper.* 2 something that has been extracted. *Vanilla extract.*

extraordinary *adjective* 1 very strange or unusual. *It was an extraordinary sight.* 2 unusually great. *She has an extraordinary musical talent.*

extravagance *noun* 1 spending more money than is reasonable or you can afford. 2 something that is very expensive. *A sports car is a real extravagance.* **extravagant** *adjective*. *She has extravagant tastes.*

exuberant *adjective* full of energy and cheerfulness. *They greeted us noisily with lots of exuberant shouting and waving.* **exuberance** *noun*.

eye *noun* 1 one of two organs in the face to see with. *We close our eyes when we go to sleep.* 2 the power of seeing. *To have sharp eyes.* 3 the hole in a needle through which the thread passes. 4 a dark spot on a vegetable, such as a potato, from which a new plant grows. **eye** *verb* to watch or look at closely. *He eyed her jealously.* **keep an eye on** to watch somebody or something. *Please keep an eye on the house while we're away.*

You see something when light bounces off it and enters your eyes.

Optic nerve

Cornea

Lens

Retina

Eyeball

Tear gland

Tear duct

Tears

eyeball *noun* the whole of the eye, formed like a ball, including the part concealed behind the eyelids.

eyebrow *noun* the line of hairs growing above the eyes.

eyelash *noun* one of the hairs that grow on the edge of your upper and lower eyelids.

eyelid *noun* either of the two pieces of covering skin that move down when you close your eyes or blink.

eyesight *noun* the power to see. *He wears glasses because he has poor eyesight.*

eyewitness *noun* a person who has seen an accident or a crime happen and can describe it. *Will eyewitnesses to the accident please contact the police.*

eyrie (rhymes with 'weary') *noun* an eagle's nest. *The eagle builds its eyrie of large twigs.*

WORD BUILDING

The prefix 'extra–' comes from the Latin for outside or beyond. So something that is extraordinary is 'outside the usual order'.

An eagle builds its eyrie way up in the mountains. The parent birds use the nest every year, and each year they make it a bit bigger.

F

Ff

fable *noun* a short story, usually one with animals, that teaches a lesson about behavior or truth.

fabric *noun* 1 cloth. 2 the structure of a building or the system of a society.

face *noun* 1 the front part of the head. 2 a look or expression on the face. *A sad face.* 3 the front, upper side or surface of something. *The north face of the mountain.* **face to face** looking straight at each other.

face *verb* 1 to have or turn the front towards a certain direction. *Our house faces the park.* 2 to be brave enough to deal with something unpleasant or dangerous. *I can't face the truth.* 3 to cover a surface, such as a wall, with a layer of different material.

facsimile (say fak-**sim**-il-ee) *noun* an exact copy or reproduction.

fact *noun* something that is true or has actually happened. **in fact** really.

factor *noun* 1 one of the things that influences an event and brings about a result. *Money was a very important factor in the decision.* 2 a number by which a larger number can be divided. *2 and 4 are factors of 8.*

factory (factories) *noun* a large building where goods are made, usually by machines.

factual *adjective* based on facts. *She gave a factual account of events.*

faculty *noun* 1 any of the powers of the mind or body, such as speech or understanding. *After the accident her faculties were impaired.* 2 a department in a university.

fade *verb* 1 to become less strong or clear. *The colors have faded in the sunshine.* 2 to disappear gradually.

Fahrenheit *adjective* measuring temperature on a scale where water freezes at 32° and boils at 212°.

Smoke from factories pollutes the atmosphere

---

fail *verb* 1 to try to do something and not succeed. *All my plans failed.* 2 not to do or remember something. *You failed to warn me that she doesn't like dogs.* 3 not to produce the expected result or work as expected. *The brakes failed.* 4 If a teacher fails you, she grades you as not having passed a test. **failed** *adjective* unsuccessful.

failing *noun* a weakness or fault.

failure *noun* 1 lack of success, failing to do something. *After many failures, he has succeeded at last.* 2 an unsuccessful person.

faint *adjective* weak, not clear. *The writing was very faint.*

faint *verb* to lose consciousness suddenly. *He faints at the sight of blood.*

fair *noun* 1 a festival with rides, shows and other amusements. 2 a market or exhibition where goods are displayed and sold. *A trade fair.*

fair *adjective* 1 honest and just. 2 pale or light in color. 3 fine, especially when talking about the weather. 4 fairly good. *After living in France for a year, he has a fair knowledge of French.* **fairness** *noun.*

fairground *noun* the place where a fair is held. *Fairground rides.*

We had fun at the fairground.

fairly *adverb* 1 quite, to some extent. *This restaurant is fairly cheap.* 2 in a fair way. *The election was conducted fairly.*

fairy (fairies) *noun* a small imaginary person with magical powers.

fairy tale *noun* a story about fairies and other creatures with magical powers.

faith *noun* 1 a strong belief or trust. 2 a particular religion. *The Jewish faith.*

faithful *adjective* trustworthy and loyal. **faithfully** *adverb.*

fake *noun* a person or thing that is not what it is supposed to be or looks like. *The painting is a fake.* **fake** *verb* 1 to make something look better or more valuable in order to deceive people. 2 to pretend. *He faked a stomach ache to get out of school.*

falcon *noun* a bird of prey that can be trained to hunt other birds and animals. **falconry** *noun.*

fall (falls, falling, fell, fallen) *verb* 1 to come or go down, to drop to a lower place. *A brick fell on his head.* 2 to become lower. *The temperature fell.* 3 to happen. *Silence fell.* 4 to become or pass into another state. *I have fallen in love.* 5 to die in battle. **fall apart** to break into pieces. **fall behind** to not produce something on time. *The project has fallen behind schedule.* **fall for** 1 If you fall for somebody, you are attracted to them. 2 to be deceived by. *I don't fall for his tricks.* **fall out** to drop out of place. *My tooth fell out last week.* **fall through** to fail.

fall *noun* 1 a drop from a higher to a lower place. 2 getting lower or less. 3 a waterfall. *Niagara Falls.* 4 autumn, the season between summer and winter.

The spectacular Iguaçu Falls are a string of 275 waterfalls on the border between Argentina and Brazil.

false *adjective* 1 not true, wrong. *She gave a false address to the police.* 2 not natural, artificial. *False teeth.*

falsehood *noun* 1 something not true, a lie. 2 telling lies.

fame *noun* being famous. *Her fame soon spread throughout the country.*

familiar *adjective* 1 well known. 2 knowing something well. *Are you familiar with this play?* 3 very friendly.

family *noun* 1 parents and their children, grandparents and other relations. 2 a group of related things, especially animals or plants. *Lions belong to the cat family.*

famine *noun* a severe lack of food in a region. *There is a terrible famine in Africa.*

famous *adjective* well known by many people. *A famous actor.*

fan *noun* something that moves the air to make you or a room cooler.

fan (fans, fanning, fanned) *verb* to make the air move.

fan *noun* an admirer or supporter. *Dean is a football fan.*

fancy (fancies, fancying, fancied) *verb* 1 to want to do or have something. *Do you fancy a game of tennis?* 2 to imagine. *He fancies himself as a dancer.* **fancy** (fancies) *noun* 1 an imagined or unlikely idea. 2 a liking. *I have taken a fancy to that restaurant.* **fanciful** *adjective*.

In summer, a fan is essential in a hot office.

The farmer is at work in the tractor, baling the hay.

fancy *adjective* not ordinary, special. *It's a really fancy restaurant.*

fang *noun* a long sharp tooth.

fantasy (fantasies) *noun* something imagined, a situation that you think about. *His mind is crammed full of fantasies.* **fantastic** *adjective*.

far (farther/further, farthest/furthest) *adverb* 1 at or to a great distance. *I live not far from here.* 2 much. *That's far too expensive.* **far** *adjective* distant, a long way off.

far-fetched *adjective* unlikely or impossible, especially an idea or example. *His story was too far-fetched for us to believe.*

far-reaching *adjective* having wide influence or effect over a long period of time. *Far-reaching reforms.*

farce *noun* 1 a play in which lots of silly things happen. 2 an event that is treated too lightly and becomes ridiculous. *The election was a farce as the winner had already been decided on.* **farcical** *adjective*.

fare *noun* 1 the money paid by passengers for a journey. 2 food and drink.

fare *verb* to get along. If you fare badly, you are unsuccessful or treated badly.

farm *noun* 1 a place where crops are grown and animals are kept. 2 a farmhouse. **farm** *verb* to grow crops or raise animals.

farmer *noun* a person who owns or works on a farm. *My ambition is to be a farmer.*

farther *adjective, adverb* at or to a more distant point. *I'm too tired, I can't walk any farther up the mountain.*

farthest *adjective, adverb* at or to a most distant point.

fascinate *verb* to attract and be very interesting. *He has always been fascinated by space travel.* **fascination** *noun*. **fascinating** *adjective*.

fashion *noun* 1 the style of clothes or the way of doing something at a particular time. *Short skirts are back in fashion this autumn.* 2 a way of doing something. *She walks in a strange fashion.* **fashionable** *adjective*. **fashionably** *adverb*.

fast *adjective* 1 quick. *A fast car.* 2 firmly fixed. *Wash the shirt separately, the colors aren't fast.* 3 showing a time that is later than the real time. *My watch is fast.* **fast food** hot food that is cooked and served quickly after ordering.

fast *adverb* 1 quickly. *He was driving too fast.* 2 fully. *She was fast asleep.*

fast *verb* to eat no food. *Ramadan is the Muslim month of fasting.* **fast** *noun.*

fasten *verb* 1 to fix one thing to another. 2 to close or lock. *Fasten your seatbelts.* **fastener** *noun.* **fastening** *noun.*

fat *noun* 1 the greasy part of human flesh or animal meat. *Fat under the skin keeps us warm.* 2 oil or grease used for cooking.

fat (fatter, fattest) *adjective* 1 Fat people have a lot of flesh on their body. *He is fat because he eats too much.* 2 thick or large. *A fat book.* **fatness** *noun.*

fatal *adjective* bringing or ending in death. *A fatal accident.* **fatally** *adverb.*

fate *noun* 1 the power that is believed to control events. *Fate was against us.* 2 what will happen or has happened to somebody. *It was her fate.*

father *noun* a male parent. *Your father and mother are your parents.*

father-in-law *noun* the father of your wife or husband.

fatigue *noun* 1 a feeling of great tiredness. 2 weakness in metals caused by stress.

fault *noun* 1 something wrong, a mistake or imperfection. *An electrical fault.* 2 a bad point about a person or thing. *He's always finding fault with me.* 3 a crack in the surface of the earth. *Earthquakes usually occur along faults.* **fault** *verb* to find fault with something or somebody. *His attitude can't be faulted.* **faulty** *adjective.*

Earthquakes occur along faults.

fauna *noun* all the wild animals living in a region. *She was studying the flora and fauna of the Alps.*

favor *noun* 1 a liking of somebody or something. *He is trying to win her favor.* 2 If you are in favor of something, you like the idea of it. If somebody is in favor, he is liked. If he is out of favor, he is not liked. 3 a kind act. *Could you do me a favor and take me to the station?* **favor** *verb* 1 to like or support, especially a plan or an idea. *The government favors free school meals.* 2 to be kinder to one person than another. *The teacher tends to favor the girls.*

AMAZING FACT

'Phobia' means 'fear of. There is a state called 'phobophobia' which means 'fear of fear'.

Some people have an irrational fear of spiders.

WORD HISTORY

The phrase 'a feather in your cap' comes from a Native American custom. Indian braves were given a feather for their headdress for every warrior they killed in battle.

WORD HISTORY

Fauna was the name of a Roman goddess of the countryside. She was the sister of Faunus, who was associated with the Greek god Pan.

---

favorable *adjective* good, approving. *The teacher gave her a favorable report.*

favorite *adjective* liked more than all others. *What is your favorite TV program?* **favorite** *noun* 1 a person or thing preferred over others. *This book is my favorite.* 2 in sport, the competitor expected to win.

favoritism *noun* being unfairly kinder to one person than another. *It's not fair if teachers show favoritism.*

fear *noun* 1 an unpleasant feeling that something dangerous or painful might happen. *She has a fear of flying.* 2 danger. *There is no fear of failure.* **fear** *verb* to be afraid or worry about something or somebody. *They feared for their lives.* **for fear of** because of worry about something. *I didn't ring the bell last night for fear of disturbing you.* **never fear** there is no danger of that.

fearful *adjective* old-fashioned 1 causing fear or being afraid. *A fearful storm.* 2 bad, terrible.

fearless *adjective* without fear, not afraid. *She was fearless in the face of danger.* **fearlessly** *adverb.*

fearsome *adjective* terrible or frightening. *The monster was a fearsome sight.*

feasible *adjective* possible, that can be done. *Is it feasible to rebuild the bridge?*

feast *noun* 1 a large and very good meal. *A wedding feast.* 2 a religious festival. **feast** *verb* to eat and drink very well.

feat *noun* a courageous or skillful action that is difficult to do.

feather *noun* one of the many soft, light things that cover a bird's body. **as light as a feather** very light. **a feather in your cap** an achievement that you can be proud of.

feature *noun* 1 an important part. *Sand is a feature of the desert.* 2 an important part of your face. *Your eyes, mouth and nose make up your features.* 3 an article in a newspaper or a special program on the radio or television. *The local TV station is doing a feature on our neighborhood later this summer*

feature *verb* to be an important part of something. *The film features an unknown but very beautiful actress.*

February *noun* the second month of the year. February has 28 days, but in leap years it has 29.

fed past tense of feed.

federation *noun* a united group of states with one government.

fee *noun* a sum of money paid for services. *The agency charges a fee for arranging tours of the ruins.*

feeble *adjective* weak, having very little power. *He made rather a feeble attempt.* **feebly** *adverb.*

feed (feeds, feeding, fed) *verb* 1 to give food to. *Don't forget to feed the cat.* 2 to eat. *Horses feed on hay.* 3 to put something in. *All the data has been fed into the computer.* **feed** *noun* food for animals.

feedback *noun* comments about something that you have done, so that possible changes can be made. *Most businesses welcome feedback from their customers.*

feel (feels, feeling, felt) *verb* 1 to touch something with your fingers or hold it. *Just feel the quality of the fabric.* 2 to be a certain sensation – wet, dry, soft or sticky, for example. *My clothes feel damp.* 3 to be aware of a mood or to know that something is happening to your body. *I'm not feeling well.* 4 to think something or have an opinion. *I feel strongly that the action is wrong.* 5 to search, usually with your hands, feet or a stick. *He felt in his pockets for money.* **feel** *noun. I like the feel of silk.* **feel like** to want. *I feel like a swim.*

feeler *noun* the long, thin part on the front of an insect's head with which it touches things. **put out feelers** to suggest something in order to find out what others think or want to do.

Feelers

An insect uses its feelers to help it find its way.

feeling *noun* 1 the power to feel things. *I'm so cold, I've lost all feeling in my hands.* 2 an emotion or physical sensation. *An itchy feeling.* If you have a feeling for somebody or something, you like them. 3 what you think, an idea. *I have a feeling that he'll do very well in the exams.* 4 sympathy and understanding. *He read the poem with great feeling.*

feet plural of foot. **fall on one's feet** to have good luck. *He's fallen right on his feet with that new job.*

feint (say faynt) *noun* a pretend attack, especially in fencing or boxing. **feint** *verb.*

feline (say fee-line) *adjective* like a cat.

fell past tense of fall.

felt past tense of feel.

female *adjective* 1 referring to a woman or girl. *Male and female workers.* 2 A female animal or plant can have babies, lay eggs or produce fruit. *A ewe is a female sheep.* **female** *noun* a female person or animal.

feminine *adjective* 1 with the qualities of a woman. *She designs very feminine clothes.* 2 in grammar, referring to words that are classed as female. *French nouns are either masculine or feminine.* **femininity** *noun.*

feminist *noun* a person who believes that women should have the same rights and opportunities as men. **feminism** *noun.*

fence *noun* a barrier made of wood or wire round an area or used to divide two areas of land. **fence** *verb* 1 to build a fence round an area or along something. *We fenced in the garden to keep the cows out.* 2 to fight with a long thin sword as a sport. **fencing** *noun.*

ferment (say fer-ment) *verb* to change chemically; to turn liquid into an alcoholic drink by the action of yeast, for example. **fermentation** *noun.*

fern *noun* a plant with green, feathery leaves and no flowers.

ferocious *adjective* fierce, savage. *A ferocious dog guards the entrance to the house.* **ferocity** *noun.*

ferret *noun* a small animal with a pointed nose. Ferrets are used for catching rats and rabbits. **ferret out** *verb* to search for something or find out information.

ferry (ferries) *noun* a boat that goes across a river or other narrow channel of water carrying people and cars. **ferry** (ferries, ferrying, ferried) *verb* to transport people or goods. *She ferried the children to and from school every day.*

fertile *adjective* 1 land or soil is fertile when plants grow well in it. *Silt from the river makes the land very fertile.* 2 able to produce babies or seeds. 3 full of ideas. *My brother has a very fertile imagination.* **fertility** *noun.*

fertilize *verb* 1 to put pollen into a plant or sperm into an egg to make them grow. 2 When you fertilize the soil you add things to it to make it more fertile. **fertilization** *noun.*

A sperm swims towards an egg. In a moment, fertilization will occur.

fertilizer *noun* a natural substance or chemical added to soil to make it more fertile. *Organic fertilizers are best.*

fester *verb* 1 to become infected, especially of a wound or cut. 2 to poison the mind, causing bitterness over a period of time. *Hatred still festers between the brothers.*

festival *noun* 1 a day or time for public celebration which is usually a holiday. *Mardi Gras is an important festival in many countries.* 2 a number of events like concerts, movies, exhibitions etc. *An international music festival.*

festive *adjective* joyful and suitable for a festival. **festivity** *noun*.

fetch *verb* 1 to get and bring back. *Can you fetch me a rope from the garage, please?* 2 to be sold for a certain price. *These old books might well fetch a lot of money.*

fetlock *noun* the back part of a horse's leg near the foot.

fetus *noun* (say **fee**-tus) a young human or animal before birth.

feud *noun* (say fewd) a long-lasting quarrel, especially between families.

feudal *adjective* (say **few**-dal) relating to a method practised in the Middle Ages in which people were given land in exchange for fighting and working for the owner.

fever *noun* 1 a body temperature that is higher than usual, because of illness. 2 an illness that causes a high body temperature. 3 great excitement. *There was a fever of anticipation in the hall.* **feverish** *adjective*.

few *adjective, pronoun* not many, a small number. *A few went home early.* **fewer than** not as many as. *Fewer than ten students passed the exam.*

fiancé *noun* (say fee-**ahn**-say) a man engaged to be married. *She introduced her friends to her fiancé.* **fiancée** *noun* (say fee-**ahn**-say) a woman engaged to be married.

fiasco *noun* (say fee-**ass**-koh) an absurd failure. *Everything went wrong and the program was a complete fiasco.*

fiber *noun* 1 a very thin thread, especially one used to make cloth or rope. 2 parts of plants or seeds which the body cannot digest. Brown bread is high in fiber. 3 a thin piece of flesh in the body. *Muscles are made of fibers.* **fibrous** *adjective*.

These are artificial fibers seen under the microscope.

At New Year the Chinese celebrate by dressing up as a dragon and parading through the streets.

The Earth's magnetic field is called the magnetosphere.

fickle *adjective*. Fickle people always change their mind. They are not loyal in love or friendship. **fickleness** *noun*.

fiction *noun* writing or stories about something that is not true. *Is the report I read in the paper fact or fiction?* **fictional** *adjective*.

fictitious *adjective* imaginary, invented. *He gave the police a fictitious name.*

fiddle *noun* a violin. *He played us a Cajun song on the fiddle.*
as fit as a fiddle in very good health.

fiddle *verb* 1 to play the violin. 2 to touch or move things around with your fingers. *Stop fiddling around with those matches.* **play second fiddle** to be less important. *He gets tired of playing second fiddle to his brother.* **fiddler** *noun*.

fidget *verb* to move around restlessly and never sit still. *Some children fidget a lot.* **fidget** *noun*.

field *noun* 1 a piece of land with grass or crops growing on it. 2 an area of grass marked out for a game. *There's a football field in the park behind our house.* 3 a battlefield. 4 a piece of land where oil, coal, gold or other things might be found. 5 a subject, an area of study or activity. *She is an expert in the field of medical research.* 6 an area of space where something is strong. *A magnetic field.* Your field of vision is the whole area you can see.

field *verb* 1 to catch the ball in baseball or other games. 2 to be on the side whose turn it is to pitch rather than bat in baseball or other games. 3 to answer or respond to complaints or questions *The boss fielded all the questions himself.*

fierce *adjective* 1 angry and violent. 2 very strong. *The plants were wilting in the fierce heat.*

fiery *adjective* flaming, like fire. *He has a fiery temper.*

fig *noun* a soft fruit full of seeds that grows on trees in hot countries. *My grandmother makes fig jam.*

Figs ripened in the Sun are one of the most delicious of all fruits.

fight (fights, fighting, fought) *verb* 1 to use your hands, weapons or words against another in order to try and win. When people fight, they try to hurt each other. 2 to try to overcome or stop something. *We must fight crime.* When you fight for something, you try to get or keep it. 3 to quarrel. **fight** *noun* 1 the act of fighting somebody, using hands or weapons. 2 a struggle to overcome something. *The fight against poverty.*

fighter *noun* 1 a person who fights. 2 a fast military aircraft.

figure *noun* 1 a sign that stands for a number. 1, 3 and 9 are figures. 2 an amount, how much money something costs. *A huge figure.* 3 a diagram or drawing, usually in a book. 4 the shape of the body. *She's got a very good figure.* 5 the shape of a person or an animal in a picture or carved in wood or stone. *A wooden figure of an African tribesman.* 6 a person. *He was a great figure in the world of pop music.* **figure of speech** a word or an expression used to produce an impression, making your meaning stronger. 'As pretty as a picture' is a figure of speech.

figure *verb* 1 to take part in something. *He doesn't figure much in the article.* 2 to believe, imagine or work out. *I figure they'll make him captain.*

Fiji *noun* a country of many islands in the Pacific Ocean.

The flag of Fiji has the Union Jack and a crest against a turquoise blue background.

file *noun* a tool with a rough surface for smoothing, cutting or shaping things. *A nail file.* **file** *verb* to smooth, shape or cut with a file. *The woman sat filing her nails.*

file *noun* 1 a holder for keeping papers and documents in order. 2 a set of papers kept in a file. 3 information stored in a computer. 4 a line of people or things one behind the other. **file** *verb* 1 to put papers or documents in a file. 2 When you file an application, you apply for something officially. 3 to walk one after another. *The class filed into the room.*

fill *verb* 1 to make or become full. 2 to block up. *She pulled the nails out of the wall and filled the holes.*

DID YOU KNOW

There are 176 different kinds of bird in the finch family. They are found in most regions of the world except Australia, and range in size from 10 to 27 cm long. The finch family includes chaffinches, canaries and crossbills.

fillet *noun* a piece of fish or meat without any bone. **fillet** *verb* to remove the bones from meat or fish.

filling *noun* something used to fill something. *I went to the dentist and had two new fillings.*

film *noun* 1 moving pictures taken with a film camera which can be seen at the movies or on television. 2 a roll of thin plastic that is put in a camera for taking photographs or shooting a film. 3 a thin layer. *A film of dust.* **film** *verb* 1 to make a film. 2 to take moving pictures with a film camera.

John took a roll of film to be developed.

filter *noun* 1 a device through which liquids are passed to make them clean. 2 a piece of glass or plastic used on a camera lens to hold back light.

filter *verb* 1 to pass through a filter. *It's a good idea to filter drinking water.* 2 to pass or move slowly, especially of people, traffic or ideas. *Light filtered through the curtains.*

filth *noun* a disgusting amount of dirt. **filthy** *adjective. Your bedroom looks filthy.*

fin *noun* 1 a wing-like part that a fish uses in swimming. 2 something shaped like a fish's fin, such as a swimmer's flipper or the surface of a car or plane.

final *adjective* last, at the end. *The final word on the page.* **final** *noun* the last game in a competition or the last examination. *Are you ready for your finals?* **finalist** *noun.*

finally *adverb* 1 lastly or at last. *Finally, I'd like to thank the teaching staff.* 2 after a long time. *I finally found out where he lives.*

finance *noun* the control and management of money. **finances** *plural noun* money, especially of a business. *How are the firm's finances?* **finance** *verb* to provide money for something. *Who is financing the trip?*

finch *noun* a small songbird.

find (finds, finding, found) *verb* 1 to get or see somebody or something by searching or by chance. 2 to learn by working, experimenting or by experience. *Doctors are hoping to find a cure for Aids.* **find** *noun* something found.

fine *adjective* 1 excellent. *We had a fine time on Sunday.* 2 dry, bright and sunny. *In fine weather.* 3 very thin. *Fine hair.* **fine** *adverb* very well. *That suits me fine.* **cut it fine** to just make it on time.

fine *noun* a sum of money to be paid as punishment. *I had to pay a parking fine.* **fine** *verb* to make somebody pay a fine.

finger *noun* 1 one of the parts of the hand. You have five fingers on your hand. 2 a thin piece of something. **finger** *verb* to touch with your fingers.

fingernail *noun* the hard flat piece at the end of your finger.

fingerprint *noun* the mark made by the lines on the skin of the finger. *The thieves left no fingerprints.*

finish *verb* to reach the end or bring to the end.

finish (finishes) *noun* 1 the end or last part of something. 2 the coating, especially of painted or polished articles.

Everyone has different fingerprints, even identical twins.

Finland *noun* a Scandinavian country in Europe.

Finnish *noun* the language spoken by the Finns. **Finnish** *adjective*.

The capital of Finland is Helsinki.

fir *noun* an evergreen tree with leaves that look like needles. The seeds are formed in cones. *The cabin is surrounded by a forest of firs.*

fire *noun* 1 burning with flames. *The house is on fire.* If you set fire to something, you light it in order to burn it. 2 burning coal or wood or an apparatus using gas or electricity for heating or cooking. 3 the shooting of guns. *The enemy opened fire.* **catch fire** to begin to burn.

fire *verb* 1 to shoot a gun or propel bullets, missiles or arrows. 2 to let off other things. *He fired lots of questions at us.* 3 to bake pottery. *Clay pots are fired in a kiln.* 4 to dismiss somebody from a job. *He was fired for misconduct.* 5 to excite. *His speech fired our enthusiasm.*

firearm *noun* a gun.

fire engine *noun* a large vehicle that carries firefighters and equipment for putting out fires. *The fire engine raced towards the fire.*

firefighter *noun* a person who puts out fires. *The firefighter was awarded a medal.*

fireplace *noun* a place in a room for a fire.

fireproof *adjective* fireproof things cannot be damaged by fire or heat.

fireworks *noun* objects filled with chemical powder that make sparks and noises when lit. *There is always a fireworks display at school on the fourth of July.*

DID YOU KNOW

Finnish is one of two official languages in Finland. The other is Swedish. An English word borrowed from Finnish is 'sauna'. Finland joined the European Union in 1995.

AMAZING FACT

A fish's fins are used primarily for steering and balance. Most fish propel themselves by beating their tail from side to side.

---

firm *adjective* 1 hard, not changing shape when pressed. *Firm muscles.* 2 steady, not shaking or moving. *Keep a firm grip on it.* 3 strong and sure, not likely to change. *We need a firm decision.*

firm *noun* a business or organization. *He works for a computer firm.*

first *adjective, adverb* before all others or everything else. *He came first in the race.* **at first** in the beginning. *They didn't like each other at first.* **first** *noun* the first thing, person or event. *I was the first to know.*

first aid *noun* emergency treatment given to an injured person, usually before a doctor arrives. *She went on a first aid course.*

first name *noun* in English, the name that you are given, not your family name.

first-rate *adjective* excellent. *A first-rate performance.*

fish (fish or fishes) *noun* an animal that lives and breathes in water. Fish use their fins and tail to swim.

fish *verb* 1 to try and catch fish. *We went fishing at the lake.* 2 to try to get something, especially information or compliments. *She is fishing for praise.* 3 to pull something out.

Fin

Gill

Fish breathe through their gills and steer with their fins.

fisherman *noun* a man who catches fish, usually for a living.

fist *noun* a hand with the fingers tightly closed. *In boxing you fight with your fists.*

fit (fitter, fittest) *adjective* 1 right or good enough. *The meal was fit for a king.* 2 healthy. *She goes jogging every day to keep fit.* **fitness** *noun*.

fit (fits, fitting, fitted) *verb* 1 to be the right size or shape. *The shoes don't fit, they're too small.* 2 to make clothes the right size and shape for somebody. *He had a suit fitted.* 3 to put into place. *We had a new lock fitted on the door.* 4 to be or make suitable. *The description fits her well.* **fit in** 1 to feel comfortable among a group of people. 2 to find time to do something. *We'll fit in an extra lesson before the exam.*

fit *noun* 1 the way something fits. 2 a sudden attack of an illness or loss of consciousness. *I had a coughing fit right in the middle of the ceremony.* 3 an outburst. *He hit him in a fit of anger.*

fix *verb* 1 to repair. *He fixed his bike.* 2 to decide or arrange. *We have fixed the date for our wedding.* 3 to make something firm, to attach it. 4 to treat colors or a photographic film with chemicals to protect them from light. 5 to prepare or cook, especially food or a drink. *I'll fix dinner tonight, you go watch TV.* **fix up** to arrange.

fix *noun* 1 something arranged, especially by deception. *The election was a fix.* 2 an injection of illegal drugs. **in a fix** in a difficult situation.

fixture *noun* 1 built-in furniture or equipment. *The light fixtures are all imported from Mexico.* 2 a (permanent) fixture is one that is always present. *The little store has been a permanent fixture in this neighborhood for years.*

fizzy *adjective* bubbling. *A fizzy drink.*

fjord *noun* (say fee-ord) a long narrow inlet of sea between steep cliffs, especially in Norway. *Norwegian fjords.*

flabby *adjective* too soft, fat. *He's a bit flabby around the waist.*

flag *noun* a piece of cloth with a design on it, which is used as a signal or sign of something, especially a country.

flag (flags. flagging, flagged) *verb* 1 to become weak. *My energy is flagging.* 2 to signal with a flag. **flag down** to wave, especially at a car, to make it stop.

flagstone *noun* a stone slab used for paving.

flair *noun* instinctive talent. *She has a real flair for fashion.*

flake *noun* 1 a small, thin piece of something. *Flakes of paint.* 2 a piece of falling snow. **flake** *verb* to come off in flakes. *The paint is starting to flake.*

flame *noun* a portion of fire or burning gas. *The car burst into flames.* **in flames** burning.

Flamingoes, with their soft pink feathers, are among the world's most beautiful birds.

The fjords of Norway were created by glaciers during the Ice Age.

Each country is represented by its own flag.

flamingo (flamingos or flamingoes) *noun* a tropical water bird with long legs and pink feathers. *Flamingo pink.*

flammable *adjective* likely to catch fire or burn easily. Flammable is the same as inflammable. The opposite of flammable is non-flammable.

flank *noun* the side of something, especially an animal. **flank** *verb* to be placed on one or both sides. *The actress was flanked by two tall men in dinner suits.*

flap (flaps, flapping, flapped) *verb* 1 to move up and down or from side to side. *The bird flapped its wings and took off.* 2 to move quickly and make a noise. *The sails flapped against the mast.*

flap *noun* 1 a piece of material or flat part of something that covers an opening. *A cap with ear flaps.* 2 the sound of flapping. **flapjack** *noun* a pancake.

flare *noun* 1 a sudden bright flame or light. 2 a device producing a bright light that is used as a signal. **flare** *verb* to burn with a bright flame for a short time. **flare up** to show sudden anger.

flared *adjective* shaped so as to get wider towards the bottom. *Flared skirt.*

flash (flashes) *noun* 1 a sudden bright light. *Flashes of lightning.* 2 a sudden idea or display of wit. *She had a flash of inspiration.* 3 a device producing a sudden bright light for taking photographs in the dark. 4 a short news report. **flash in the pan** a sudden short-lived success. **in a flash** quickly. *The ambulance was there in a flash.*

flash *verb* 1 to shine brightly once or several times. *Lights flashed across the sky.* 2 to suddenly think of something. *It flashed through my mind that he was lying.* 3 to move very fast or appear suddenly. *Cars flashed past me.* 4 When you flash a look at somebody, you look at them very quickly.

flashback *noun* a scene in a film or story that shows events that happened in the past.

flat (flatter, flattest) *adjective* 1 not curved, smooth with no bumps. 2 spread out. *Lie down flat on the ground and don't make any noise.* 3 dull or boring. *The atmosphere at the party was flat so we left early.* 4 not deep or high. 5 complete or absolute. *A flat refusal.* 6 A flat tire has no air in it. A flat drink is not fizzy. A flat battery no longer produces electricity. **flat** *adverb* 1 exactly. *He arrived in five minutes flat.* 2 If something falls flat, it is unsuccessful. **flat out** 1 at top speed. 2 using all your energy. *I'm working flat out.*

The farmlands of Arizona, USA are flat and featureless.

flashlight *noun* a portable light that runs on batteries. *Let's take a flashlight.*

flatten *verb* to make or become flat.

flatter *verb* 1 to say that a person or thing is better, more important or beautiful than they really are. 2 to show somebody or something as better then they really are. *The picture flatters her.* **flattery** *noun*.

flavor *noun* the taste of something. **flavor** *verb* to give a taste to something. *Flavor it with vanilla.* **flavoring** *noun*.

flaw *noun* something that makes a person or thing imperfect, something wrong. **flawed** *adjective*.

flea *noun* a small jumping insect that bites and sucks blood from people and animals.

fledgling *noun* a young bird.

flee (flees, fleeing, fled) *verb* to run away from something or somewhere. *We had to flee the country.*

fleece *noun* the woolly covering of sheep.

fleece *verb* to trick a person out of their money. *We were fleeced in the market.*

fleet *noun* a group of ships, planes or other vehicles belonging to one country or company. *A fleet of taxis.*

flesh *noun* 1 the soft substance that includes fat and muscle between the bones and the skin of people and animals. 2 the soft part of fruit and vegetables. **fleshy** *adjective*. **in the flesh** in real life. *He doesn't look so tall in the flesh.* **flesh out** to give more details.

AMAZING FACT

Flint was used by Stone Age people to make tools and weapons.

DID YOU KNOW

There are about 1,600 different kinds of fleas around the world. Some are tiny, and the largest is 8 mm long. One of the best jumpers is the cat flea, which is known to have reached a height of 34 cm in a single jump.

---

flew past tense of fly.

flex *verb* to bend or stretch, especially a muscle, leg or arm. *He flexed his muscles.*

flexible *adjective* 1 easily bent. 2 easily changed to suit new conditions, or adaptable. *I prefer flexible working hours.* **flexibility** *noun*.

flicker *verb* 1 to burn or shine unsteadily. 2 to move lightly or jerkily. *His eyelids flickered.* **flicker** *noun*.

flight *noun* 1 flying. 2 a plane trip. 3 a set of stairs. 4 the act of running away and escaping. 5 a group of birds flying together. *A flight of geese.*

flimsy (flimsier, flimsiest) *adjective* thin or light and easily damaged. **flimsily** *adverb*. *Careful, the table is very flimsy.* **flimsiness** *noun*.

fling (flings, flinging, flung) *verb* 1 to throw quickly or carelessly. *She flung a few clothes into a suitcase and left.* 2 to move quickly and violently. *She flung her head back angrily.*

fling *noun* 1 throwing something quickly. 2 a short, wild time of fun and enjoyment. 3 a dance.

flint *noun* 1 a hard gray stone. 2 a small piece of flint or hard metal that can be struck to produce sparks and light things.

Flints were shaped by Stone Age people and used as tools.

flip (flips, flipping, flipped) *verb* 1 to turn something over quickly. 2 to move something into a different position or send it spinning in the air with a quick push or light hit. *She flipped open her diary and searched for the appointment.* **flip** *noun*.

flippant *adjective* not serious, especially when trying to be amusing. *She made some very flippant remarks.* **flippancy** *noun*.

flipper *noun* 1 the flat limb of some sea animals used for swimming. 2 Flippers are attachments you can wear on your feet to help you swim more quickly.

flirt *verb* to behave in a playful way as if you were attracted to somebody. *She flirts with all the boys.* **flirt** *noun* somebody who flirts a lot. **flirtatious** *adjective*.

float *verb* 1 to stay or move in a liquid or in the air. *We floated down the river.* 2 to move aimlessly about. *She floats from one job to another without ever settling down.*

float *noun* 1 a light object, such as a cork, that is used to help somebody or something float. 2 a flat trailer that is decorated and driven through the streets in a parade or festival procession. *Every class in the school built a float for the homecoming parade.* 3 a sum of money kept, especially by waiters, for giving change.

flock *noun* a group of sheep, goats or birds. **flock** *verb* to gather or move in large crowds. *People flocked to the fair.*

floe *noun* (rhymes with glow) a sheet of floating ice. *The ice floes begin to melt in the spring.*

flog (flogs, flogging, flogged) *verb* to beat a person or an animal, especially with a whip or rod. **flogging** *noun.*

flood *noun* 1 a large amount of water in a place that is usually dry. *The village was almost destroyed by the flood.* 2 a large amount. *The radio station received a flood of complaints following the show.* **flood** *verb* 1 to cover with a flood. 2 to arrive in large amounts. *Calls flooded in.*

floor *noun* 1 the surface, especially of a room, that you walk on. 2 all the rooms that are on the same level in a building. *Our apartment is on the second floor.* 3 The ground at the bottom of the ocean, a cave or a valley.

floor *verb* 1 to knock down. *The punch floored him.* 2 to confuse. *His question completely floored me.*

flop (flops, flopping, flopped) *verb* 1 to sit or lie down suddenly and heavily. 2 to fail or be unsuccessful. *The play flopped.* **flop** *noun* 1 a flopping movement or sound. 2 a total failure.

floppy *adjective* not firm, hanging loosely. *They wore floppy hats.*

floppy disk *noun* a disk that can be put into a computer, also called a diskette.

The flood washed away the houses and made the people homeless.

flora *noun* all the plants growing in a region. *Flora and fauna.*

Mountain flora, such as edelweiss and mountain avens, grow well in the poor rocky soil above the tree-line.

florist *noun* a person or store that sells flowers. *The florist's art is arranging flowers.*

flour *noun* a powder made from ground grain, especially wheat, used to make bread and cakes. **floury** *adjective.*

flourish (flourishes, flourishing, flourished) *verb* 1 to grow healthily. 2 to be well and successful. *Business is flourishing, we are going to expand.* 3 to wave something about for people to notice it. *He rushed into the room flourishing a check.* **flourish** *noun.*

flow *verb* 1 to move along smoothly. 2 to hang down loosely, especially of clothing or hair. **flow** *noun.*

flower *noun* 1 the colored or white part of a plant which produces seeds and fruit. 2 the flower and its stem. **flower** *verb* to produce flowers. *Daffodils flower in spring.*

flown past tense of fly.

flu *noun* short for influenza, an illness in which you may have a cold, a temperature and aching muscles.

fluent *adjective* able to speak and write a language easily. *She speaks fluent French.* **fluently** *adverb.* **fluency** *noun.*

fluff *noun* 1 soft bits from woolly material. 2 soft newly grown hair on young animals.

fluff *verb* 1 to shake or push something to make it seem larger and lighter. *The bird fluffed out its feathers.* 2 to do something badly or unsuccessfully. *Tom fluffed the catch and we lost the game.*

fluffy *adjective* like or covered with fluff.

fluid *noun* a substance that can flow, such as a liquid or a gas.

fluid *adjective* 1 able to flow, not solid. 2 not fixed, likely to change. *Her ideas were totally fluid.* 3 smooth and graceful. *The dancer's fluid movements.*

fluke *noun* an unexpected piece of accidental good luck. *He won the tournament, but only by a fluke.* **fluke** *verb.*

flung past tense of fling.

flush *verb* 1 to become red, to blush. 2 to clean something with a sudden flow of water. *Don't forget to flush the toilet every time you use it.* **flush** *noun.*

fluster *verb* to make somebody nervous and confused. *I got flustered when they all started asking me questions.*

flute *noun* a musical instrument shaped like a long tube with holes.

The flute is a woodwind instrument.

flutter *verb* 1 to move quickly and irregularly, up and down or from side to side. *The flags fluttered prettily in the wind.* 2 to move through the air with small quick movements. *Ticker tape fluttered down.*

flutter *noun* 1 a fluttering movement. 2 a feeling of panic or excitement. *There was a flutter of excitement as the winner was announced.*

fly (flies, flying, flew, flown) *verb* 1 to move through the air like a bird or plane. 2 to control a plane or transport passengers in a plane. *A helicopter flew the injured to the nearest hospital.* 3 to make something fly. *To fly a kite.* 4 to move at speed or pass quickly. *Time flies when you enjoy your work.* 5 to move or wave about. *Flags were flying.* **send somebody flying** to hit a person so they fall over. **fly at somebody** to attack a person suddenly and violently.

fly (flies) *noun* 1 a small flying insect. 2 the front opening on pants.

Flies often carry germs and can spread disease.

foal *noun* a young horse.

foam *noun* 1 a mass of small white air bubbles, especially on top of a liquid. 2 rubber with plastic air bubbles inside, used for making mattresses and cushion stuffing, also called foam rubber.

Origami is the Japanese art of folding paper to make models.

focus (focuses) *noun* 1 a point or distance from an eye or lens at which an object is sharpest. *The picture is out of focus.* 2 the point at which beams of light or heat or sound waves meet. 3 the center of interest or attention. **focus** (focused, focusing or focussed, focussing) *verb* 1 to adjust a lens so that things can be seen clearly. *He focused the telescope on the Moon.* 2 to concentrate. *All Jean's attention is focused on her work.*

fodder *noun* food for farm animals.

foe *noun* an enemy.

fog *noun* very thick mist.

foggy *adjective* thick with fog. **I don't have the foggiest idea.** I have no idea at all.

foil *noun* 1 metal sheet as thin as paper, especially for wrapping up food. 2 somebody or something that makes another person or thing look better. *Richard acted as a foil for his friend.*

foil *noun* a long thin sword with a covered point used in the sport of fencing.

foil *verb* to stop somebody from carrying out a plan. *The police managed to foil the robbers after hearing of their plan.*

fold *verb* 1 to turn back a part of something, especially paper or cloth, and cover it with another part. When you fold something, you make it into a smaller shape. *If you fold the clothes as soon as they come out of the dryer, you might not need to iron them.* 2 to bring together or cross, especially your arms or hands. *The old woman folded her hands and smiled.* 3 to bend back or close up furniture or equipment. **fold** *noun* a line where something is folded, a crease. **fold up** 1 to make something into a smaller shape. 2 to fail. *The business has folded up.*

fold *noun* a fenced-in area for sheep.

-fold *suffix* meaning 'by the number of times stated', showing that something has a particular number of parts or kinds. 'Fivefold' means five times. *My problem is twofold. I don't have any money or time.*

folder *noun* a folded piece of cardboard for keeping papers in.

foliage *noun* leaves of plants and trees.

Fall foliage is a beautiful sight, with the leaves turning red and gold.

folk (folk or folks) *noun* people.

follow *verb* 1 to come or go after, to move behind in the same direction. 2 to go in the same direction. *I followed the route on the map.* 3 to come next on a list. *Tuesday follows Monday.* 4 to do what somebody says or suggests. *I followed his advice.* 5 to take an interest in something. *He follows his local football team.* 6 to understand. *I couldn't follow his line of thought.* 7 to be true or logical. *It doesn't follow that because you don't like school, you don't have to go.* **follower** *noun.* **following** *adjective.* **following** *noun. She has a large following of fans.*

fond *adjective* 1 To be fond of somebody or something means liking them. *She is very fond of children.* 2 loving and kind. *His fond parents.* 3 foolishly hopeful. *Fond hopes.* **fondly** *adverb.*

fondle *verb* to stroke gently.

font *noun* a typeface, such as you choose on a computer.

font *noun* a stone water basin in a church that is used for baptisms.

food *noun* something that is eaten by people or animals, or taken in by plants to help them to grow and live.

food chain *noun* a series of animals in a community, in which each member feeds on another in the chain. Humans are at the top of the food chain.

fool *noun* 1 a silly person who acts stupidly. If you make a fool of somebody, you make them look stupid. 2 a clown. **fool** *verb* 1 to trick somebody. *She fooled me into thinking it was her car.* 2 to behave in a silly way. *Please stop fooling around and finsh your dinner right this minute!* **foolish** *adjective* unwise or stupid.

WORD HISTORY

The word 'fool' has a very interesting history. It comes originally from the Latin 'follis', which means bellows – a bag that blows air. It could be that people thought fools were full of hot air and spoke nonsense, or that their heads were full of air, in other words empty.

Delicious-looking food was spread on the table for a wonderful lunch.

foolproof *adjective* Something that is easy to use and cannot go wrong is foolproof. *My plan is absolutely foolproof.*

foot (feet) *noun* 1 the part at the end of the leg below the ankle that people and animals stand on. 2 the lowest part or the bottom end. *At the foot of the hill.* 3 a measurement of length (*abbreviation* ft, equal to 12 inches or 30·5 centimetres). **on foot** walking. *What's the quickest way on foot?* **fall on your feet** to be lucky. **have cold feet** to be nervous. **stand on your own two feet** to be financially independent. **have one foot in the grave** to be very old. **put your foot in your mouth** to say the wrong thing.

football *noun* 1 a game played by two teams of eleven players who kick, carry or throw a ball into an area and score points. 2 the ball used in this game.

footnote *noun* a note at the bottom of a page. *This book has too many footnotes.*

footprint *noun* a mark made by a foot.

The footprints led us to the animal's lair.

for *preposition* 1 to show that something is intended to be given to or aimed towards somebody. *This huge present is for you.* 2 towards, in order to reach. *The plane for Chicago left ten minutes ago..* 3 for the purpose of. *The computer is for my office.* 4 in order to have, get or do something. *I'm doing it for your own good.* 5 to show distance, time or price. *For the first time.* 6 in favor of. *How many people are for a strike and how many are against it?* 7 because of something. *I was told off for being late.* 8 as being or meaning. *What is the Spanish word for 'tomorrow'?.* 9 with reference to something surprising. *She looks young for her age.* 10 being suitable. *The right person for the job.* **for ever** always.

forbid (forbids, forbidding, forbade, forbidden) *verb* to order somebody not to do something. *I forbid you to go out.*

force *noun* 1 power or strength. *He had to use force to open the door.* 2 a power that produces changes of movement in a body. *The force of gravity.* 3 a person, thing, belief, influence or idea that causes changes. *The force of public opinion.* 4 an organized group of police or soldiers. *The police force.* **in force** in large numbers. **join forces** to combine efforts.

F

force *verb* 1 to make somebody do something, although they are unwilling. *He forced the children to clean their room.* 2 to use force to do or get something. *I had to force the lock to get in.* **forced** *adjective. A forced smile.*

ford *noun* a shallow place where you can cross a river. *The ford was liable to flood.*

forecast *noun* a statement that tells you what is likely to happen. *The weather forecast was good.* **forecast** (forecasts, forecasting, forecast) *verb.*

forehand *noun* a stroke played in tennis with the palm turned forward. The opposite of forehand is backhand.

forehead *noun* (say **for**-hed) the part of the face above the eyebrows and below where your hair grows.

foreign *adjective* 1 belonging to a country that is not your own. *Foreign languages.* 2 not natural or belonging. *She is such an honest person, lying is foreign to her.*

foreigner *noun* a person from another country. *Foreigners are always welcome.*

foreman or forewoman *noun* the leader or supervisor of a group of workers.

foresee (forsees, forseeing, forsaw) *verb* to know what is going to happen in the future. *I forsee trouble.* **foresight** *noun.*

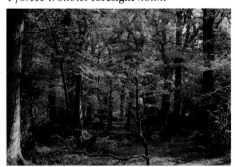

forest *noun* a large area of land covered with trees. *A pine forest.*

forever *adverb* continually. *He was forever complaining about his mother-in-law.*

foreword *noun* an introduction to a book.

forfeit *verb* (say **for**-fit) to lose something because you have done something wrong or broken a rule. *If you don't pay the bill, you forfeit your deposit.* **forfeit** *noun* something lost, a price to be paid.

After heavy rains, the road was impassable at the ford.

SPELLING NOTE

The foreword that sometimes acts as the introduction to a book is spelt differently from 'forward' (meaning to or towards the front). A foreword is often written by a person other than the book's author.

The forest is a mysterious place where many small animals live.

AMAZING FACT

Forests in the United States cover over 700 million acres. The US Government owns and manages about a third of this land.

forge *verb* 1 to copy things, especially banknotes, paintings or documents, in order to deceive people. 2 to shape something by heating and hammering it. *The blacksmith forged an iron staircase and a fire grate.* 3 to form or create something, especially links or a friendship. **forger** *noun.*

forge *noun* a place where metal is heated and shaped. *Horseshoes used to be made in a forge.*

forgery *noun* 1 a crime of forging things like banknotes. 2 something forged. *The painting was discovered to be a forgery.*

forget (forgets, forgetting, forgot, forgotten) *verb* 1 to not remember. 2 to stop thinking about. *Let's forget about the money you owe me.* **forget yourself** to behave thoughtlessly, to lose your temper. *When she kept complaining, he forgot himself and shouted at her.*

forgive (forgives, forgiving, forgave, forgiven) *verb* to say or feel that you are no longer angry with somebody about something. *He still hasn't forgiven his sister for forgetting his birthday.* **forgivable** *adjective. A forgivable error.* **forgiveness** *noun. He begged for forgiveness.*

fork *noun* 1 an instrument with prongs at the end of a handle for eating food. 2 a point, especially in the road, which divides into two parts in the shape of a Y. **fork** *verb* 1 to lift, dig or move with a fork. 2 to divide in a Y-shape. *Turn right where the road forks.* **fork out** to pay out money, usually unwillingly.

fork-lift truck *noun* a truck with a platform at the front for lifting, lowering and moving heavy goods.

A fork-lift truck works by hydraulics.

form *noun* 1 the shape or appearance of something or somebody. *A pencil sharpener in the form of a crocodile.* 2 a particular kind or a particular way of behaving. *Photography is an art form that I admire.* 3 a piece of paper with questions to be answered and filled in. 4 a way in which a word may be spoken, written or spelled. *The irregular forms of verbs are listed.* 4 the way something exists. *You can take the medicine in syrup or tablet form.* **form** *verb* 1 to take shape, develop or come into existence. 2 to shape or create something. *I formed an impression right away.*

formal *adjective* correct, according to accepted rules or customs. *I'm expecting a formal apology from my boss.* **formally** *adverb. We dressed formally for the dance.* **formality** (formalities) *noun.*

format *noun* the shape and size of something, or the way it is presented. *I like the format of this book.*

former *adjective* 1 of an earlier period. *Her former husband has married again, to a very wealthy woman.* 2 the first of two people or things just mentioned. *Extra trains and buses are needed. The former will be more expensive.* (The second of two things just mentioned is called the latter.)

formerly *adverb* in earlier times.

formidable *adjective* very difficult to overcome. *They faced formidable problems in their first year at the new school.*

formula (formulae) *noun* 1 a group of letters, signs or numbers that make up a rule. *The chemical formula for water is H_2O.* 2 a list of substances or directions for making or achieving something. *My formula for success is plenty of sleep.* 3 a set of words or behavior used regularly for a particular occasion. *They changed the formula of the meetings.* 4 a plan, or suggestions worked out to deal with a problem.

forsake (forsakes, forsaking, forsook, forsaken) *verb* to leave. *He has forsaken his wife and children.*

fort *noun* a strong building used as a military base. *There was an ancient fort on the top of the hill.* **hold the fort** to look after things while somebody is away. *Look, will you hold the fort while I'm in the hospital?*

fortify (fortifies, fortifying, fortified) *verb* 1 to strengthen a place against attack. 2 to eat or drink something to make you stronger. **fortification** *noun.*

fortress (fortresses) *noun* a castle or other strong building that is difficult to attack.

Two atoms of hydrogen and one atom of oxygen join together to form a molecule of water (formula H_2O).

DID YOU KNOW

A fossil may be a shell, a bone, a tooth, a leaf, a skeleton or even sometimes a whole animal.

The fortress came under heavy cannon fire and was eventually engulfed in flames.

fortuitous *adjective* by chance, especially by lucky chance, accidental.

fortunate *adjective* lucky. **fortunately** *adverb. Fortunately he didn't notice that I was very late.*

fortune *noun* 1 (good) luck. 2 fate, what will happen in the future. *The old woman told his fortune.* 3 a large amount of money. *She earns a fortune in advertising.*

forward *adjective, adverb* 1 to or towards the front, towards the future. *A step forward.* 2 advanced or early in development. *The boy is very forward for his age.* 3 to be sure or eager in an unpleasant way. *They are a little too forward.* **forward** *noun* one of the two attacking players in a basketball team whose job it is to shoot baskets.

forward *verb* to send on a letter, parcel or information. *Please forward letters to my new address in Spain.*

forwards *adverb* to or towards the front or future. *Let's move forwards.*

fossil *noun* the remains of an animal or a plant that lived long ago and has hardened into rock. *A fossil of a dinosaur tooth.* **fossilize** *verb.*

This fossil was once an ammonite, a creature like a squid.

foster *verb* 1 to bring up a child as if you were her/his father or mother. 2 to help something grow or develop. *Jack is interested in science and we want to foster that interest.*

fought past tense of fight.

foul *adjective* 1 dirty, having a disgusting taste or smell. *Yuk! that garbage smells foul!.* 2 very bad, unpleasant or angry. **foul play** unfair play, actions against the rules. **foul** *noun* an action against the rules in sport. **foul** *verb* 1 to dirty. 2 to commit a foul against another player.

found past tense of find.

found *verb* 1 to establish or give money to start something. *The school was founded by early settlers.* 2 to base on. *Her success was founded on hard work.*

foundation *noun* 1 concrete and stonework that support the walls of a building or other structure, often in the plural, foundations. 2 the things that beliefs and ideas are based on. **be without foundation** to be untrue.

founder *verb* 1 to fill with water and sink. *The ship foundered on the rocks.* 2 to fail or collapse. *The company foundered and went bankrupt.* 3 in horses, to become ill or lame.

fountain *noun* an apparatus, often hidden in a stone figure or pool, that pumps a stream of water up into the air.

The fountain in the courtyard cooled the air.

fox *noun* a wild animal that looks like a dog with a long bushy tail.

foxglove *noun* a tall straight plant that has flowers shaped like the fingers of a glove.

foyer *noun* (say **foy**-er) the entrance hall in a theater or hotel.

fraction *noun* 1 a small part or bit. *For a fraction of a second.* 2 a number that is not a whole number, a part of a whole number. $\frac{1}{2}$ and $\frac{1}{3}$ are fractions.

fracture *noun* a crack or break, especially in a bone. **fracture** *verb*.

fragile *adjective* easily broken or damaged. **fragility** *noun*.

fragment *noun* 1 a small piece that has broken off. *She dropped the vase and it broke into a million fragments.* 2 a small piece or part of something, especially an unfinished work of art.

fragrance *noun* a sweet or pleasant smell. **fragrant** *adjective*.

frame *noun* 1 the border into which something like a picture or window is fitted. 2 the main structure that forms the support for something. *A bicycle frame.* 3 the part that holds the lenses of a pair of glasses in place. 4 the shape or body of a person or animal. *Years of hard work had weakened his powerful frame.* 5 one of a number of small photographs that make up a film. **frame of mind** the mood somebody is in at a particular time. **frame** *verb* 1 to put a frame on or around. 2 to give shape to or express in a particular language, especially words or a plan. 3 to make an innocent person seem guilty and look as if they had committed a crime. *He was framed and sent to prison, but he didn't commit the crime.*

The mirror had an elegant gold frame.

framework *noun* 1 a supporting frame for something. 2 a basic plan or set of rules.

France *noun* a country in western Europe.

France is famous for the excellent food and wine enjoyed in homes across the land.

frank *adjective* honest and direct. The open way in which you say what you think. *I will be frank with you, I don't think he'll pass the exam.* **frankly** *adverb*. **frankness** *noun*.

frank *verb* to stamp a letter or package to show that postage has been paid.

frantic *adjective* wild and desperate; extremely anxious. *He was frantic with worry.* **frantically** *adverb*.

fraud *noun* 1 a swindle, a crime of getting money by trickery. 2 a person who pretends to be something he is not, a swindler. **fraudulent** *adjective*.

freak *noun* 1 an unusual or very strange person, animal, thing or happening. *That was a pure freak, it will never happen again.* 2 a person who takes a fanatical interest in something. *A football freak.* **freak** *adjective*. *A freak storm.* **freakish** *adjective*.

freckle *noun* a small brown spot on the skin, caused by the Sun. **freckly** *adjective*.

The freckles on her face always appear in early summer.

free (freer, freest) *adjective, adverb* 1 able to do what you want, go where you want, not shut up, be held in prison or controlled by anybody. *He set the prisoners free.* 2 without payment, costing nothing. *Entrance to the museum is free.* 3 not fixed on to anything. *The free end of the sail has been torn in the storm.* 4 not busy. *Are you free on Wednesday?* 5 not being used. *Is this seat free?* 6 without obstruction or anything being in the way. *A free flow of water.* **have a free hand** to be able to do things, without having to ask others for permission. **free with** If you are free with something, you are generous and ready to help. **freely** *adverb*. **free** (frees, freeing, freed) *verb* to set free. **freedom** *noun*.

Freetown *noun* the capital of Sierra Leone.

freeze (freezes, freezing, froze, frozen) *verb* 1 to harden into ice or become covered with ice. 2 to preserve food by making it very cold and storing it below freezing point. 3 to be extremely cold. *I'm absolutely freezing.* 4 to stop moving and stand completely still. *The boy froze at the sight of the snake.* 5 to fix prices or wages for a certain time so they cannot be increased. **freeze** *noun.*

The trees look beautiful when they freeze. They are covered with frost and snow.

freezer *noun* a refrigerator in which food can be frozen, because the temperature inside it is below freezing-point.

freezing-point *noun* the temperature at which water freezes into ice. Freezing-point is 32°Fahrenheit or 0° Celsius.

freight *noun* (say frayt) 1 the transportation of goods by trucks, ships, trains or planes. 2 goods. **freight** *verb.*

French *noun* 1 the people of France. 2 the language of France. **French** *adjective. The French flag is red, white and blue.*

French fries *plural noun* thin pieces of potato fried in oil.

frequent *adjective* (say freek-wunt) happening often. *My brother is a frequent visitor, he comes every day.* **frequently** *adverb.* **frequency** *noun.*

frequent (say frik-went) *verb* to be or go somewhere often.

fresh *adjective* 1 newly made, picked, grown or arrived. Not old or stale, tinned or cooked. *I love fresh orange juice.* 2 cool, refreshing and unused. *She put fresh sheets on the bed.* 3 new. *Let's make a fresh start.* 4 Fresh water is not salty. **freshly** *adverb. Freshly caught fish.* **freshness** *noun.*

friction *noun* 1 the rubbing of one thing against another. *Oil is used in machines to stop friction.* 2 disagreement and quarrels. *There is always friction between them.*

Friday *noun* the sixth day of the week, following Thursday.

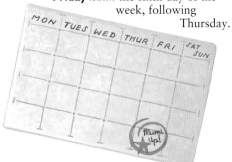

Sarah made an appointment to see the dentist on Friday.

fridge *noun* a refrigerator.

fried past tense of fry.

DID YOU KNOW

Frogs, toads and newts belong to a group of animals called amphibians. They spend part of their lives on land, but always go back to water when it is time to lay their eggs. Most frogs lay between 1,000 and 20,000 eggs.

friend *noun* a person you know and like. *He is our neighbor and our friend.* **make friends** to become somebody's friend. **be friends** If you are friends with somebody, you like spending time together.

friendly *adjective* acting as a friend. *A friendly gesture.* **friendship** *noun.*

frighten *verb* to fill with fear. *The big dog frightened the little girl.* **fright** *noun.*

frill *noun* 1 a pleated strip of paper or cloth attached to something as a decoration. *A frill on a dress.* 2 an unnecessary extra. *We took a no-frills flight and it was just fine.* **frilly** *adjective. A frilly lampshade.*

fringe *noun* 1 a decorative border of many threads hanging down loosely on curtains, clothes, etc. 3 the part furthest from the centre, the edge of something. *They live on the fringes of downtown.* **fringed** *adjective.*

frisk *verb* 1 to run and jump about playfully, especially children or animals. 2 to search somebody with your hands for hidden weapons or goods. *The police frisked the man and found a gun on him.* **frisky** *adjective. A frisky little dog.*

frivolous *adjective* 1 not serious or sensible. *Let's just forget about being sensible and do something frivolous, just for fun.* 2 amusing, not important.

frock *noun* a dress.

frog *noun* a jumping animal, usually brownish-green, that lives in water and on land. Frogs croak.

Frogs develop from tadpoles.

from *preposition* 1 showing a starting point in time, place or number. *We took the bus from Kansas City to Tulsa.* 2 showing who gave or sent something. *He got the money from the bank.* 3 showing what something is made of, what it is based on or where you might find it. *It was cut from cardboard.* 4 out of the possession of, showing separation. *He took the doll from his little sister.* 5 judging by. *From the noise they are making, it must be a party.* 6 showing difference or change. *I can't tell one from the other.* 7 because of, showing the reason for something. *In Africa people are suffering terribly from the famine.*

front *noun* 1 the side that is normally seen and faces forward. *The front of the house.* 2 the part that is ahead of others. *He went to the front of the line.* 3 the place where two armies are fighting in war. 4 a line of separation where masses of cold air meet masses of warm air. *A cold front.* **in front** ahead of others. **in front of** facing somebody or something. *He spends too much time in front of the television.*

frontier *noun* 1 the border where one country meets another country. 2 the limit that is known about something.

The frontiers were clearly marked on the map.

frost *noun* 1 weather at a temperature below freezing-point. *Unfortunately, the frost has killed our new plants.* 2 a thin layer of powdery ice crystals that form on the ground when there is a frost. **frost** *verb* 1 to become covered with frost. 2 to cover with icing, especially a cake.

froth *noun* small white bubbles on liquid that look like foam. **frothy** *adjective.*

frown *verb* to move your eyebrows towards each other and wrinkle your forehead because you are annoyed or worried. **frown** *noun. He frowned with disapproval.*

froze past tense of freeze.

frugal *adjective* 1 careful with money or food, not wasteful. 2 small and costing little. *A frugal meal.* **frugally** *adverb.*

fruit (fruits or fruit) *noun* 1 Fruit grows on trees and bushes, contains seeds and is used for food. *Apples, oranges and strawberries are all kinds of fruit.* 2 good or bad results of something. *Now you can enjoy the fruits of your hard work.* **fruity** *adjective.*

fruitful *adjective* producing good results. *We had a fruitful meeting.*

GRAMMAR NOTE

When 'full' is used as a suffix at the end of a word, it is usually spelt '–ful': 'beautiful', 'useful', 'fruitful', etc. This also applies if the suffix is used to mean 'the amount needed to fill': e.g. 'bucketful', 'handful' etc.

Fresh fruit forms an important part of a healthy diet.

frustrate *verb* 1 to stop you from doing what you would like to do or to stop plans from being carried out. *Our plans for a picnic were frustrated by bad weather.* 2 to make you feel disappointed and angry. *It's frustrating not to be able to see you when I want to.* **frustration** *noun.*

fry (fries, frying, fried) *verb* to cook something in hot fat, usually in a frying pan.

fudge *noun* a soft brown sweet made with butter, sugar and milk.

fudge *verb* to avoid taking firm action or making a clear decision. *The government have fudged the issue.*

fuel *noun* something that is burned to produce heat, especially coal and oil. **fuel** (fuels, fuelling, fuelled) *verb* 1 to supply something with fuel or take in fuel. 2 to make a situation worse or cause an argument. *His anger was fuelled by a tremendous jealousy of his brother.*

fugitive *noun* (say few-jit-iv) somebody who is running away from something. *A fugitive from justice.*

fulcrum *noun* the point on which a bar (called a lever) is fixed or is supported in lifting something.

The weights are perfectly balanced at the fulcrum.

fulfill (fulfills, fulfilling, fulfilled) *verb* 1 to do what was promised, to carry out what is required. *He didn't fulfill his promises.* 2 to make true or come true. **fulfillment** *noun.*

full *adjective* 1 completely filled, holding as much or as many as possible. 2 containing a large number of people or things. *He is always full of ideas.* 3 complete, with nothing missing. *She wrote down her full name and address.* 4 as much or great as possible. *He drove at full speed.* 5 rounded. *She has a full figure.* 6 wide and loosely fitting. *A full skirt.* **full of something** to be talking about something with great enthusiasm. **in full** not leaving out anything. *She told me the story in full.* **full up** with no space left. **fully** *adverb.* **fullness** *noun.*

full moon *noun* the moon when it looks completely round.

fumble *verb* to handle or search for something clumsily. *He fumbled in his pocket for his keys.*

fun *noun* amusement, something enjoyable. **make fun of** to tease or laugh at somebody in an unkind way.

Funafuti *noun* the capital of Tuvalu.

function *noun* 1 a special duty or purpose. What somebody or something is there to do. *One of the chairman's functions is to conduct meetings.* 2 an important party or event. *We were invited to a function at the embassy.* 3 an activity a computer can carry out. **function** *verb* to be in action or work.

fundamental *adjective* very important or basic. **fundamentally** *adverb*.

funeral *noun* the ceremony of burying or cremating a dead person.

fungus (fungi, say **fung**-guy) *noun* a plant-like organism without flowers, leaves or green coloring. Mushrooms, toadstools and mold are all fungi.

Bracket fungus grow on the trunk of a tree.

funnel *noun* 1 a chimney on a steamship or steam engine for letting out smoke. 2 an object with a wide round top and a tube at the bottom used for pouring liquids and powders into a container with a narrow opening. **funnel** *verb* to move as if through a funnel. *Crowds funneled through the gateway and into the square.*

funny (funnier, funniest) *adjective* 1 amusing, making you laugh. 2 strange or unusual. *The car is making a funny noise.*

fur *noun* 1 the thick hair that covers the bodies of many animals. 2 the fur-covered skin used for making clothes, especially fur coats. *The fur traders sold mink and beaver furs.* 3 a coat made from real fur or fabric that looks like fur.

furnace *noun* a container with a very hot fire, used for heating buildings, burning things, melting metal, making glass or producing steam in a factory.

The heat was white hot inside the furnace.

DID YOU KNOW
There are about 50,000 different kinds of fungi. They are different from green plants because they cannot make their own food. They get their food mainly from decaying plants, and sometimes from living plants or animals.

The fuselage of an aircraft can be used for transporting passengers or freight.

furnish *verb* 1 to put furniture in a place. *The house is not furnished.* 2 to supply what is necessary. *Luckily we were furnished with a dictionary for the translation.*

furniture *noun* things like tables, chairs and beds that are put in a room or needed in a place.

furry *adjective* like or covered with fur. *The little boy likes that furry rabbit.*

further *adjective, adverb* 1 at or to a more distant point or greater degree. *We can't walk any further.* 2 more or additional. *He works in further education.* **further** *verb* to help to be successful. *We will do everything to further peace.*

furtive *adjective* done secretly, hoping not to be seen. *The thief gave a furtive glance at my purse.* **furtively** *adverb*.

fury *noun* great anger, rage. **furious** *adjective*. *I am furious that you are late.*

fuse *noun* 1 a short thin piece of wire, e.g. in an electric plug, that acts as a safety device by melting if too much electricity is passed through it. *The lights went out when a fuse blew.* 2 a tube or cord on a bomb or firework used for setting it off. **fuse** *verb* 1 to stop working because a fuse has melted. *Suddenly all the lights in the house fused.* 2 to melt in great heat or become joined by melting. *The wires have fused together.*

fuselage (say few-zuh-lahzh) *noun* the main body of an aircraft.

fuss (fusses) *noun* unnecessary excitement or anger, especially about unimportant things. *Don't make such a fuss.* **make a fuss of somebody** to pay a lot of attention to a person. **fuss** *verb* to behave in an unnecessarily excited or anxious way. **fussy** (fussier, fussiest) *adjective*.

futile (say few-til) *adjective* of no use, not successful. *It's futile to argue with me because I know I'm right.* **futility** *noun*.

future *noun* the time or events that come after the present, the things that will happen. *We all wish you a very happy future.* **in future** from now on. **future** *adjective*. *What are your future plans?*

fuzz *noun* 1 something fluffy and soft, especially from wool. 2 short curly hair. 3 *slang* the police. **fuzzy** (fuzzier, fuzziest) *adjective* 1 not clear in shape, blurred. *Some of the photographs were very fuzzy.* 2 soft and curly. *Fuzzy hair.*

Gg

gabble *verb* to speak so quickly that people cannot understand you.

gable *noun* the triangular outside end of a house between two sloping roofs. **gabled** *adjective. Gabled houses.*

Gabon *noun* a country in Africa.

Gaborone *noun* the capital of Botswana.

gadget *noun* a small, useful instrument or tool for a particular job. *This gadget is called a garlic press.*

gag (gags, gagging, gagged) *verb* 1 to put something over or into somebody's mouth to stop them speaking. **gag** *noun.* 2 to retch or feel like vomiting.

gag *noun* a joke.

gain *verb* 1 to win, earn or obtain something. 2 to increase. *He's gained ten pounds.* **gain** *noun* 1 a profit. 2 an increase.

gala *noun* a special public event or entertainment.

galaxy *noun* a huge group of stars and planets. The Milky Way is a galaxy.

gale *noun* a very strong, violent wind. *It's blowing a gale outside.*

gallant *adjective* 1 brave. *A gallant knight.* 2 honorable and polite.

galleon *noun* a large Spanish sailing ship of the 16th century. *A galleon in full sail.*

gallery *noun* 1 a building or long room for displaying paintings and other works of art. 2 the highest floor of seats in a theater.

galley (galleys) *noun* 1 the kitchen on a ship or aircraft. 2 a single-decked ship of ancient times that was driven by both sails and oars.

gallon *noun* a measure for liquids. There are eight pints or 3.8 liters in a gallon.

gallop *noun* the fastest pace of a horse. **gallop** *verb. We galloped across the field and splashed across the river.*

gallows *singular and plural noun* a wooden structure on which criminals used to be hanged. *The gallows on the hill.*

galore *adverb* in large numbers or amount, in plenty. *The library has got books galore.*

Galaxies are classified according to their shapes. This one is a spiral galaxy.

AMAZING FACT

Our galaxy, the Milky Way, is one of many. The other galaxies are moving away from us. The farther away a galaxy is, the faster it is moving. The most distant galaxies are receding at almost the speed of light.

galvanized *verb* 1 to cover a metal with zinc to protect it from rusting. 2 to shock into doing something. *The threat of flooding galvanized the men into action.* **galvanized** *adjective. A galvanized dustbin.*

Gambia *noun* a country in Africa.

The flag of Gambia has red, blue and green stripes, divided by narrow white stripes.

gamble *verb* to risk something, particularly money, for possible gain, especially on the result of a game or race. *He's gambled away all his family fortune on cards.* **gamble** *noun.* **gambler** *noun.*

game *noun* 1 an activity or contest with rules. Football, baseball, chess and bridge are all different kinds of game. **games** athletic competitions. *The Olympic Games take place every four years.* 2 wild animals and birds that are hunted for food and as a sport.

Many game birds, such as pheasants, are not native to North America.

game *adjective* brave and willing to try something.

gamekeeper *noun* a person who takes care of game animals and birds.

gander *noun* a male goose.

gang *noun* a group of people who regularly go about and do things together.

gangster *noun* one of a gang of criminals.

gangway *noun* 1 a gangplank or movable bridge for passengers between a ship and the shore. 2 a space between rows of seats in an airplane, train or theater, etc.

gap *noun* an opening or empty space.

gape *verb* 1 to stare with your mouth wide open, usually in surprise. 2 to be wide open. *A gaping hole in the ground.*

garage *noun* 1 a place where cars and other motor vehicles are kept. 2 a place that sells gas or where cars can be repaired.

garbage *noun* waste material.

garden *noun* land, usually near a house, where flowers and vegetables are grown. **gardener** *noun.* **gardening** *noun.*

gargle *verb* to wash your throat with a medicated liquid without swallowing it and then to spit it out.

gargoyle *noun* a grotesque carving on a building of a human or animal head forming part of a gutter.

garish *adjective* (say **gair**-ish) over-colored and too bright, gaudy.

garlic *noun* a strong-tasting bulb like an onion that is used in cooking to add flavour to food.

garment *noun* a piece of clothing such as a jacket or skirt.

garnish *verb* to decorate food. *He garnished the vegetables with sprigs of parsley.*

garret *noun* a small room in the attic of a house. *The poet lived in a garret.*

garter *noun* a band of cloth or elastic at the top of a sock or stocking to hold it up.

gas (gases) *noun* 1 any of many substances like air that are neither liquid nor solid. Oxygen and nitrogen are gases. 2 the kind of gas we use as a fuel in our homes for heating and cooking. 3 short for gasoline.

gash *noun* a deep, long cut, a slash. **gash** *verb*. *She gashed her knee on the rock.*

gasoline *noun* fuel that is burned in an internal combustion engine.

gasp *verb* to breathe quickly and noisily through your mouth because you have been running etc. or because you are ill. **gasp** *noun*. *A gasp of surprise.*

gastric *adjective* relating to or belonging to the stomach. *A gastric ulcer.*

gate *noun* 1 a kind of outside door or barrier across an opening in a fence, hedge or wall. 2 the number of people who pay to see a sporting event.

gatecrash *verb* to go to a party when you have not been invited. **gatecrasher** *noun*.

gateway (gateways) *noun* 1 an opening with a gate. 2 an opportunity or an opening to something. *The gateway to stardom.*

gather *verb* 1 to come together as a group, to bring together. *A crowd gathered in the square.* 2 to pick. *He gathered nuts and blackberries.* 3 to understand or find out something. *We gather you're going away.*

gathering *noun* a meeting or coming together of people for some purpose.

gaucho *noun* a cowboy of South America.

gaudy (gaudier, gaudiest) *adjective* too brightly colored and showy.

This gargoyle is on a building at Oxford University in England.

Gauchos wear big hats, baggy trousers and leather boots. They use horses to round up cattle.

gauge *noun* (rhymes with cage) an instrument for measuring. *A fuel gauge.* **gauge** *verb*. *She tried to gauge (measure or estimate) the depth of the pond.*

gaunt *adjective* very thin, bony and haggard. *His gaunt face.*

gauntlet *noun* a long, thick glove with special protection for the wrist, worn by motorcyclists etc. **take up the gauntlet** take up a challenge.

gauze *noun* a thin net-like cloth often used with bandages.

gave past of give.

gay *adjective* 1 homosexual. **gay** 2 bright and cheerful. *Gay colors.* **gaiety** *noun*. **gaily** *adverb*.

gaze *verb* to look steadily at something or somebody for a long time. **gaze** *noun*.

gazelle *noun* a small, graceful antelope of Africa and Asia.

gazetteer *noun* a geographical dictionary that lists and describes places.

gear *noun* a wheel with teeth around the edge which can work with other gears in a machine. Gears in a car or on a bicycle send power to the wheels.

gear *noun* clothes or equipment needed for a special purpose. *Sailing gear.*

geese plural of goose.

gelding *noun* a castrated (neutered) horse.

gem *noun* a precious stone that has been cut. Diamonds and rubies are gems.

gene *noun* one of the parts of a cell of all living things that controls and passes on characteristics from parents to offspring.

The empress built up a huge collection of beautiful gems.

general *noun* a very senior officer in the army. *General Custer.*

general *adjective* 1 concerning several or most people or things. *General knowledge.* 2 not in detail but in broad outline. *A general description.* **in general** mainly, usually. *In general, I prefer cats to people.*

generate *verb* 1 to produce electricity. *Electricity is generated in power stations.* 2 to bring into being, to cause. *The Viking exhibition generated a great deal of interest, both in the period itself and in archeology.*

generation *noun* all the people now living who were born at about the same time. The period of time between generations (about 25 years). *The beat generation.*

generator *noun* a machine that generates (produces) electricity.

generous *adjective* A generous person is kind and helpful and gives freely of their time and money. **generosity** *noun*.

genetic *adjective* concerning the genes or inherited through the genes. *Some diseases are genetic.*

genitals *plural noun* the sexual organs.

genius *noun* an exceptionally intelligent and/or creative person.

gentile *noun* a person who is not Jewish. **gentile** *adjective*.

gentle *adjective* 1 a gentle person is quiet, kind and thinks of others. 2 not rough or violent. 3 not extreme. **gentleness** *noun*. **gently** *adverb*.

genuflect *verb* to bend a knee, especially in a church or temple as a sign of reverence. **genuflection** *noun*.

genuine *adjective* real and not fake or untrue. *A genuine need for help.*

genus (genera) *noun* a group of similar plants or animals but containing different species or kinds. *Foxes and hyenas are two species of the dog genus.*

geography *noun* the study of the Earth, its natural features, its people, resources, weather etc. *World geography.* **geographer** *noun*. **geographic** *adjective*.

geology *noun* the study of the Earth's rocks and layers of soil. **geological** *adjective*. **geologist** *noun*.

geometry *noun* a branch of mathematics concerned with the study of angles, lines, shapes and solids. **geometric** *adjective*.

Georgetown *noun* the capital of Guyana.

Georgia *noun* a country in Southwest Asia.

geranium *noun* a plant with clusters of pink, red or white flowers.

gerbil *noun* a small desert rodent with long back legs, often kept as a pet.

Once the seeds had germinated they began to grow very quickly.

AMAZING FACT

Old Faithful, in Yellowstone National Park in the northwestern United States, is a famous geyser. It is called Old Faithful because it erupts at the same time every day. Yellowstone became the world's first national park in 1872.

The three main types of rock are igneous, sedimentary and metamorphic.

Magma heats water in the ground, producing geysers.

geriatric *adjective* relating to or concerning old people.

germ *noun* a microscopic living thing that can cause diseases.

German *noun* 1 a person who comes from Germany. 2 the language spoken in Germany, Austria and parts of Switzerland. **German** *adjective*. *German music.*

German Shepherd dog another name for an alsatian.

Germany *noun* a country in central Europe.

germinate *verb* when seeds germinate, they begin to sprout.

gesture *noun* 1 a movement of the hand or head intended to mean something. *She wrung her hands in a gesture of despair.* 2 an action that expresses feelings. *He invited them to supper as a friendly gesture.*

get (gets, getting, gotten) *verb* 1 to obtain. *I must get a new book from the library.* 2 to receive. *I got a lot of presents at Christmas.* 3 to bring. *Can you get me a glass of lemonade?* 4 to become. *You'll get wet if you stand in the rain.* 5 to prepare. *Dad got supper ready.* 6 to catch an illness. *I hope you don't get my cold.* 7 to cause to happen. *You must get your watch repaired.* 8 to own something. *Have you got a dog?* 9 to understand. *I don't get the joke.* 10 to ask somebody to do something. *We got the men to move the bricks.* 11 to arrive. *We got home at midnight.* **get ahead** *She got ahead through hard work.* **get along with** *He's friendly and gets along with everybody.* **get around** 1 *How do these stories get around?* 2 *He's over 90 but he still manages to get around.* **get at** 1 *The truth is difficult to get at.* 2 *Why are you always getting at me?* **get by** *He gets by on his salary.* **get down to** *She's getting down to some serious work.* **get off** 1 *Don't get off the train until it has stopped.* 2 *She got off with a small fine.* **get on** 1 *Let's get on with this so we can go home early.* 2 *She's over 80, so she's getting on a bit.* **get on to** *Get on to (contact) the press immediately.* **get over** *He's gotten over his illness.* **get up to** *He's always getting up to mischief.*

geyser *noun* a natural spring from which hot water and steam erupt, often at regular intervals.

Ghana *noun* a country in Africa.

ghastly *adjective* very unpleasant, horrible. *A ghastly accident.* **ghastliness** *noun*.

ghost *noun* the spirit or shape of a dead person that some people believe walks around at night. **ghostly** adjective.

giant *noun* in fairy stories, a huge and often frightening and cruel man. **giant** *adjective*. *A giant-screen TV.*

gibberish *noun* speech that makes no sense at all. *Don't talk gibberish, Gerry.*

gibbon *noun* an ape with very long arms.

giddy (giddier, giddiest) *adjective* feeling dizzy, light-headed and about to fall over. **giddiness** *noun*.

gift *noun* 1 something that you give somebody, a present. 2 a talent. *He has a gift for languages.* **gifted** *adjective*.

gig *noun* a public performance of pop music or jazz. *We went to a great gig in the park.*

gigantic *adjective* (say jie-**gan**-tik) of giant size, enormous.

giggle *noun* a silly, nervous laugh. **giggle** *verb*. *Ellen giggled helplessly.*

gill *noun* an organ on each side of a fish through which it breathes.

gimmick *noun* something clever or unusual that is done to attract attention, especially to advertise something. **gimmicky** *adjective*.

gin *noun* a colorless alcoholic drink.

ginger *noun* 1 a hot spice made from the root of a tropical plant used to flavour food or drinks such as ginger ale and gingerbread. 2 an orange-brown color. **ginger** *adjective*.

gingerbread *noun* a sweet cookie or cake flavored with ginger. *Gingerbread men.*

gingerly *adjective, adverb* carefully and timidly. *Gingerly, he peeled off the label.*

giraffe *noun* an African animal with long legs and a very long neck. It has yellow fur with brown patches as camouflage.

girder *noun* a long metal beam used as a support in buildings, bridges etc.

girl *noun* a female child. **girlish** *adjective*.

girlfriend *noun* 1 a male's usual and regular female friend. 2 a female friend of a woman.

gist *noun* the rough outline or main points of something. *He gave us the gist of the story while we were on the way there.*

AMAZING FACT

Nearly two million years ago, North America was almost completely covered by huge ice sheets. The ice melted, forming rivers and river valleys. The Great Lakes were also formed from ice that melted. Glaciers have given us some of our most dramatic and beautiful scenery.

Snow falls on the mountains. At the highest levels, the snow piles up year on year.

Snow in mountain basins, called cirques, becomes glacier ice.

The ice melts, creating streams that sweep away the glacier's rocky load.

At the end of the glacier the ice melts, creating streams that sweep away the glacier's rocky load.

WORD HISTORY

Until the 17th century giraffes were called 'cameleopards' because of their camel-like necks and leopard-like spots.

---

give (gives, giving, gave, given) *verb* 1 to hand something over to somebody. 2 to bend or collapse. *The fence gave under her great weight.* 3 to organize or present something. *They are giving a concert tonight.* 4 to do something suddenly. *Pat gave sigh of relief.* **give away** *I'm giving away all my money.* **give back** *Jack gave back the tapes he'd borrowed.* **give in** 1 *They gave in their guns to the police.* 2 *He won't give in (succumb) to your threats.* 3 *You don't know the answer, so why don't you give in (admit defeat)?* **give off** 1 *The bonfire is giving off a lot of smoke.* **give out** 1 *She gave out (distributed) the prizes.* 2 *The engine has finally given out (broken).* **give up** 1 *We gave up (renounced) the idea of moving away.* 2 *Mom has given up (stopped) smoking.*

glacial *adjective* 1 concerning ice or glaciers.

glacier *noun* a huge mass of ice that moves slowly like a river down a mountain valley.

glad (gladder, gladdest) *adjective* happy, pleased.

glade *noun* an area of open grass in the middle of a forest or wooded area.

gladiator *noun* a warrior in ancient Rome who fought other gladiators or wild animals for the entertainment of spectators.

glamorous *adjective* exciting and charming. *She has got a glamorous job in the fashion business.* **glamor** *noun*.

glance *verb* 1 to look at something for a moment. *She glanced at her watch.* **glance** *noun*. 2 to hit and then bounce off something at an angle. *The ball glanced off the bat and smashed the window.*

gland *noun* an organ in the body that produces substances for the body to use or that removes unwanted substances. *Sweat glands.* **glandular** *adjective*.

glare *verb* 1 to look at somebody fiercely and angrily. 2 to shine with strong, dazzling light. **glare** *noun*.

glaring *adjective* 1 very bright. *Glaring headlights.* 2 obvious. *There are glaring gaps in your general knowledge.*

glass *noun* 1 a hard, brittle and usually transparent material used in making window panes, bottles, mirrors, etc. 2 a container made of this material, for drinking. 3 a mirror. **glassy** *adjective*.

glasses *plural noun* a pair of lenses in a metal or plastic frame that people with poor eyesight wear over their eyes to help them see better, also called spectacles.

He needed glasses for reading and watching television.

glaze *verb* 1 to put glass into something. *He glazed the windows.* **glazier** *noun*. 2 to cover something with a coating of shiny material called glaze.

gleam *verb* to shine softly. *The furniture is gleaming.* **gleam** *noun*.

glen *noun* a Scottish word for a long narrow valley. *The lochs and glens.*

glide *verb* 1 to move smoothly and silently. 2 to fly smoothly.

glider *noun* a small aircraft without an engine that floats on air currents.

glimmer *verb* to flicker or to shine very faintly. **glimmer** *noun*. *A glimmer of hope.*

glisten *verb* to shine or gleam, especially of a wet or polished surface.

glitter *verb* to sparkle. *The glittering lights of the city.* **glitter** *noun*.

global *adjective* relating to the whole world. *Global issues.*

globe *noun* a ball-shaped object with a map of the Earth on it.

Sheila kept a globe on her desk to remind her of her travels around the world.

WORD HISTORY

The 'g' in most words beginning with 'gn' was once pronounced. We have dropped the 'g' sound in words like 'gnarled', 'gnash' and 'gnat' but kept the spelling.

The gnomes invited the fairies and elves to a tea party under their toadstool.

gloom *noun* 1 near-darkness, dimness. 2 sadness and a feeling of depression. **gloomy** *adjective*. *A gloomy cave.*

glorious *adjective* 1 magnificent, causing great happiness. *A glorious event.* 2 worthy of glory or praise. *A glorious victory was won by the Persians.*

glory *noun* 1 great fame, praise. 2 splendor. *The glory of the mountains.* **glory** *verb*. *They gloried in their achievements.*

glossy *adjective* shiny and smooth. *A glossy magazine.* **gloss** *noun*.

glove *noun* a covering for your hand with parts for each finger and thumb.

glow *verb* to give out a warm, steady light without flames. **glow** *noun*.

glow-worm *noun* an insect that gives out a greenish glow from its tail.

Glow-worms can be seen on summer nights in some parts of the US and Canada.

glucose *noun* a natural sugar found in plants. *Glucose is good for athletes.*

glue *noun* a thick, sticky substance used for sticking things together. **glue** *verb*. *Sue glued the handle on to the cup.*

glum (glummer, glummest) *adjective* gloomy and sad, depressed.

glut *noun* a much greater supply of something than is needed. *A glut of fruit.*

glutton *noun* a person who always eats too much. **gluttony** *adjective*.

GMT *abbreviation* for Greenwich Mean Time.

gnarled *adjective* (say narld) twisted and full of lumpy knots. *A gnarled old oak.*

gnash *verb* (say nash) to grind or strike your teeth together with anger or pain.

gnat *noun* (say nat) any of many small, mosquito-like insects that bite. *A swarm of gnats.*

gnaw *verb* (say naw) to chew on something hard for a long time. *A dog gnaws a bone if it's hungry.*

gnome *noun* (say nowm) a little old man in fairy stories who lives under the ground.

gnu *noun* (say new) an African ox-like antelope, also known as a wildebeest.

go (goes, going, went, gone) *verb* 1 to move away from or to somewhere, to travel. 2 to visit. 3 to leave. 4 to disappear. 5 to do something. *I'm going to mow the lawn.* 6 to become. *This fruit is going bad.* 7 to work correctly. *The car won't go.* 8 to fit or have a place somewhere. *The knives go in that drawer.* 9 to lead somewhere. *The road goes to the coast.* 10 to make a certain sound. *Cats go 'meow'.* **go around** *There's a bug going around.* **go ahead** *Despite the weather, we decided to go ahead with the game.* **go back** *We're going back home to Ireland.* **go for it.** *Don't worry about not finishing the marathon, just go for it!* **go off** 1 *The bomb went off with a bang.* 2 *My alarm didn't go off and I overslept.* **go on** to happen *What's going on this weekend, anything?.* **go with** *Do you think this tie goes with (looks good with) this shirt?*

goal *noun* 1 the space or net between two posts that players have to kick or hit a ball into in games like field hockey and soccer. 2 A goal is something you hope to achieve, an ambition. *Our goal is to raise $2000 for the charity.*

goat *noun* a farm animal with short hair and horns.

The milk of goats is recommended to people who are allergic to cow's milk.

gobble *verb* to eat quickly, noisily and greedily. *Peter gobbled up his Big Mac.*

gobs *noun* (slang) a lot. *We got gobs of candy on Halloween.*

god *noun* any one of many supernatural beings that were thought to control the world. *The gods lived on Mt Olympus.*

God *noun* the creator of the universe in Christianity, Islam and Judaism.

godparent *noun* someone who promises to teach a child religious values.

goggles *plural noun* special glasses that fit tightly around the eyes to protect them.

go-kart *noun* a small racing car.

gold *noun* a very valuable yellow metal that is found in rocks and streams, used for making jewelery. **gold** *adjective.*

golden *adjective* made of gold or of the color of gold. **golden wedding** *noun* the 50th anniversary of a wedding.

goldfish *noun* a small orange fish related to carp. *We have lots of goldfish in our pond.*

AMAZING FACT

Some golf courses in desert areas are all sand, the 'greens' are not green at all!

SPELLING NOTE

Try not to confuse 'goal' with 'gaol', which means 'prison'.

Gondolas operate like buses or taxis in Venice.

SPELLING NOTE

Be careful not to confuse 'gorilla' ('ape)' with 'guerrilla' ('a soldier who fights by surprise attacks'). And notice one 'r' and two 'l's in 'gorilla' and two 'r's and two 'l's in 'guerrilla'.

Rich seams of gold run underground in South Africa.

golf *noun* an outdoor game in which players use long-handled sticks called golf clubs to hit a small ball from one hole to another around a large grassy area called a golf course. **golfer** *noun. Both of my parents are avid golfers.*

gondola *noun* a long narrow boat with high pointed ends used on the canals of Venice. **gondolier** *noun* a person who operates a gondola. *The gondolier earned lots of tips.*

gone past participle of go.

good (better, best) *adjective* 1 of a high quality or standard. 2 kind and helpful. 3 able to do something well. 4 obedient and behaving well. 5 health-giving. 6 enjoyable. **goodness** *noun.* **good-looking** *adjective.*

goodbye *interjection* what we say when we leave somebody.

Good Friday *noun* the Friday before Easter when Jesus was crucified.

goods *plural noun* things that can be bought and sold or that are carried on trains and trucks.

gooey *adjective* (slang) sticky. *This candy bar melted, it's all gooey.* **gooeyness** *noun.*

goose (geese) *noun* a water bird with webbed feet, similar to a large duck. It makes a loud, honking sound. **wild goose chase** a useless trip. **cook someone's goose** to ruin somebody's chances.

gooseberry *noun* the small, round green fruit of the gooseberry bush.

goosepimple *noun* tiny bumps on the skin caused by cold, fear or excitement. *Just thinking about some of the ghoststories we told at camp last summer gives me goosepimples!*

gorilla *noun* the largest and strongest of the apes. *Gorillas are fascinating animals.*

gorge *noun* a deep valley with steep sides.

gorge *verb* to eat your fill greedily.

gorgeous *adjective* 1 very pleasant. 2 beautiful. *It's a gorgeous day. Let's walk.*

gosling *noun* a young goose.

gospel *noun* one of the first four books of the New Testament which describes the life and teachings of Jesus.

gossip *noun* talking about other people's personal affairs and saying things that are sometimes untrue. **gossip** *verb*.

got past tense of get.

gotten past participle of get.

govern *verb* to manage or be in charge of a country or organization and make laws and rules for it.

government *noun* a group of people who govern or rule a country.

governor *noun* a person elected to manage or govern a state in the US. *The Governor of Oklahoma spoke at our graduation.*

gown *noun* 1 a long, formal dress worn by a woman. 2 a long, flowing robe worn on special occasions such as graduation ceremonies.

GPA *abbreviation* Grade point average, The average score that a student gets on all grades. A= 4 points, B= 3 points, C= 2 points, D=1 point.

grab (grabs, grabbing, grabbed) *verb* to take or seize something suddenly and roughly, to snatch. **grab** *noun*. *The mugger made a grab for the old woman's purse.* **how does it grab you?** What do you think about it?

grace *noun* 1 a beautiful and easy way of moving. **graceful** *adjective*. 2 the love and favor of God. 3 a short prayer of thanks sometimes said before meals.

gracious *adjective* pleasant and polite. *A gracious smile.*

grade *noun* 1 a scale that sorts people or things according to quality, rank, size, etc. *Vegetables of the highest grade.* 2 marks given in an exam. 3 a class of a particular level or year. *He's in the fourth grade.* **grade** *verb*. *The eggs are graded according to size.*

gradient *noun* the measure of how steep a slope is. *The gradient was so steep that we practically rolled down the hill.*

gradual *adjective* changing or happening slowly. *A gradual improvement.*

graduate *noun* a person who has finished a course of studies at a school, college, or university. **graduate** *verb*.

graffiti *plural noun* (say gra-fee-tee) drawings and writing scribbled on buildings, trains, etc.

Grain can be ground into flour for making into pasta or bread.

In Britain judges still wear a wig and gown.

DID YOU KNOW

Words that include 'ph' (pronounced 'f') as part of the spelling come from the Greek, as in 'graphic' and 'photograph'.

---

grain *noun* 1 the seed of cereal plants like maize, rice and wheat. 2 tiny bits of something. *Grains of salt, sand and sugar.* 3 the pattern of lines made by the fibers in wood.

gram *noun* a metric unit of weight. There are 1000 grams in a kilogram.

grammar *noun* the rules of a language and how the words are put together correctly.

grand *adjective* 1 large, important and magnificent. *The White House is very grand.* 2 the highest, the top. *We won the grand prize – $1,000!* 3 the final amount. *That comes to a grand total of seventeen dollars.*

grandchild, granddaughter, grandson the child of a person's son or daughter.

grandparent, grandfather, grandmother the parent of one of a person's parents.

grandstand *noun* a covered area at a sports ground with rows of raised seats.

granite *noun* (say **gran**-it) a very hard rock used in building.

granny *noun* grandmother.

grant *verb* to agree to, to give something. *The government granted the island independence.* **take something for granted** to assume something without checking or without appreciating it.

grant *noun* a sum of money given for a particular purpose. *A research grant.*

grape *noun* a small, round green or purple fruit that grows in bunches on a bush called a grapevine. *Wine is made from grapes.*

grapefruit (grapefruit or grapefruits) *noun* a round fruit like a big orange but with a yellow skin.

graph *noun* (rhymes with half) a diagram or chart that shows how numbers, amounts etc. compare or are related.

The graph showed how sales figures had risen dramatically.

graphic *adjective* 1 clear and vivid. *A graphic account.* 2 relating to painting and drawing. *The graphic arts.*

graphics *plural noun* pictures and patterns.

grasp *verb* 1 to hold something tightly, to seize. 2 to understand. **grasp** *noun*. *She has a good grasp of the situation.*

grass *noun* a plant with long, thin, green leaves that grows in fields. **grassy** *adjective*.

grasshopper *noun* a jumping insect with long back legs. It makes a chirping sound by rubbing its wings together.

grate *noun* a metal frame in a fireplace, for holding the burning fuel.

grate *verb* 1 to rub or shred into little pieces against a tool with a rough surface called a grater. 2 to make an unpleasant, scraping sound by rubbing something.

grateful *adjective* pleased and wanting to thank somebody, thankful.

gratitude *noun* a feeling of being grateful, thankfulness. *Helen was full of gratitude.*

grave *adjective* very serious or important. *A grave illness.*

grave *noun* a hole in the ground in which to bury a corpse. **gravestone** a carved stone slab placed over a person's grave. **graveyard** a place where people are buried.

gravel *noun* crushed rock used to cover paths, driveways and roads.

gravity *noun* 1 seriousness. 2 the natural force that draws things to the Earth so that they stay there and do not float away.

gravy *noun* hot sauce made from the juices of cooked meat.

gray *noun* a color that is a mixture of black and white. *Rain clouds are gray.*

graze *verb* 1 when animals graze, they eat grass as it grows. 2 to scrape your skin.

grease *noun* a thick, oily substance. **greasy** *adjective*.

great *adjective* 1 big or heavy. 2 important or famous. *A great composer.* 3 Very good. *It's great to be here.* **greatness** *noun*.

Great Britain *noun* England, Scotland and Wales.

great-grandparents, great-grandfather great-grandmother the grandparents of somebody's father or mother.

The Earth's pull of gravity holds satellites and rockets in orbit around the planet.

Greece *noun* a country in Southeast Europe.

The flag of Greece is blue and white with a cross in the corner.

greed (greedier, greediest) *adjective* a selfish wish to have more of something than you need. **greedy** *adjective*.

Greek *noun* 1 a person who comes from Greece. 2 the language spoken in Greece. **Greek** *adjective*. *Greek civilization.*

green *noun* 1 the color of grass. 2 the flat place around a hole on a golf course. **green** *adjective* 1 A green light means 'go'. 2 *They are interested in such green issues as protecting the environment.* 3 young and without much experience. *When we started working on the ranch we were very green and hardly knew how to do anything practical.*

greenhouse *noun* a building made of glass used for growing plants. *The greenhouse is like an oven this summer.*

A greenhouse is the ideal place for growing flowers and vegetables.

greenhouse effect the effect of the Earth's atmosphere warming up because gases such as methane and carbon dioxide are trapped and become heated by the Sun.

greet *verb* to meet and welcome somebody in a friendly way. **greeting** *noun*.

Grenada *noun* a country in the West Indies.

grew past tense of grow.

greyhound *noun* a thin breed of dog that can run very fast and is used in racing.

grid *noun* 1 a pattern of squares formed by straight lines crossing each other at right angles. 2 the system of squares on a map so that places can be located.

grief *noun* (rhymes with leaf) great sorrow or sadness, especially after a death or misfortune. **grieve** *verb*.

grievance *noun* a reason to complain or be angry about something.

grievous *adjective* very serious or harmful.

grill *noun* a place on a stove or barbeque where food is cooked under or above direct heat. **grill** *verb*. *Let's put these hotdogs back on the grill for a few more minutes.*

grim (grimmer, grimmest) *adjective* 1 stern and unsmiling. *A grim look of disapproval.* 2 unpleasant. *Grim news.*

grime *noun* dirt rubbed deeply into a surface. **grimy** *adjective*.

grin *noun* a broad, cheerful smile. **grin** (grins, grinning, grinned) *verb*. **grin and bear it** to put up with something unpleasant without complaint.

grind (grinds, grinding, ground) *verb* to crush something into very small pieces. *The coffee beans have just been ground.* **grind to a halt** slowly to come to a complete stop.

grip (grips, gripping, gripped) *verb* 1 to hold something very firmly, to grasp. **grip** *noun*. 2 to hold somebody's complete attention. *She was gripped by the news of his death.*

grit *noun* tiny pieces of stone. **grit your teeth** *verb*. try to continue to do something even though it is painful or uncomfortable. **gritty** *adjective*.

groan *noun* a long, deep sound showing pain or unhappiness. **groan** *verb*.

groceries *plural noun* food and other things that you buy in a grocery store or at a supermarket.

groin *noun* the place where the top of your legs meet.

groom *verb* to clean and brush an animal, particularly a horse. **groom** *noun* 1 a person who takes care of horses. 2 a man who is about to get married, a bridegroom.

groove *noun* a long, narrow cut into the surface of something.

grope *verb* to feel your way or search with your hands for something you cannot see.

grotesque *adjective* (say grow-**tesk**) weird and unnatural.

ground *noun* 1 the solid surface of the Earth. The floor. 2 a sports field. **gain ground** to make progress. **break new ground** to do something new or for the first time.

ground past tense of grind.

grounded *adjective* If an aircraft is grounded it is unable to fly. A young person who is grounded is not allowed to go out.

grounds *plural noun* 1 the land around a large building. *The school grounds.* 2 reasons. *What grounds do you have for believing her?* 3 the little bits that fall to the bottom of a drink like coffee.

group *noun* a number of people, animals or things that are together or belong together in some way. A family group. **group** *verb*.

This tadpole may take years to grow into a frog.

AMAZING FACT

The largest North American frog, the bullfrog is very slow to mature. Although the eggs hatch in only about five or six days, it may take from two to five years for the tadpoles to grow into adult bullfrogs.

The groove in this piece of wood has been cut with a chisel.

SPELLING NOTE

Note the 'u' in words like 'guarantee' and 'guard'. Before 'i' and 'e' the 'g' is usually soft, as in 'gem' and 'ginger'. Inserting 'u' makes the 'g' hard as in 'guest' and 'guide'.

---

grovel (grovels, groveling, groveled) *verb* to behave in an over-humble and respectful way to somebody because you think they are important.

grow (grows, growing, grew, grown) *verb* 1 to become larger and taller, to develop. 2 to plant in the ground. *We are growing vegetables this year.* 2 to become. *He's growing stronger every day.* **grow up** to become an adult. **grow out of** *She'll grow out of biting her nails.*

growl *verb* to make a deep, low and angry sound. *The dog growled when I tried to take her bone.*

growth *noun* 1 growing, developing. *The population growth.* 2 a lump growing in a part of person's body.

grown-up *noun* an adult. **grown-up** *adjective*. *He has a grown-up son.*

grub *noun* 1 the larva or worm-like creature that will grow into an insect. 2 (slang) food.

Moles and shrews eat grubs, helping to control pests that could damage crops.

grubby (grubbier, grubbiest) *adjective* dirty. *Wash your grubby hands.*

grudge *noun* a long-lasting feeling of dislike or resentment towards somebody because they harmed you in the past. **grudging** *adjective*. *He gave only grudging praise.*

gruel *noun* a thin porridge eaten by poor or sick people in the past.

gruelling *adjective* very tiring, severe.

gruesome *adjective* revolting and shocking. *A gruesome murder.*

gruff *adjective* unfriendly and rough. *A gruff voice.*

grumble *verb* to mutter and complain in a bad-tempered way. *He's always grumbling about the noise.*

grumpy (grumpier, grumpiest) *adjective* irritable and bad-tempered. **grumpiness** *noun*. *Paul's grumpiness got them down.*

grunt *verb* to make a short, gruff sound like a pig. **grunt** *noun*.

guarantee *noun* 1 a promise by a manufacturer etc that something is of a certain quality and that it will be repaired or replaced if it goes wrong within a certain time. *The computer has a year's guarantee.* 2 a promise that something will definitely happen. **guarantee** *verb*.

Guinea pigs
make ideal pets.

guard *verb* to watch over and protect somebody or something. *Police officers guarded the bank.*

guard *noun* 1 a person or group etc. that guards. *A guard dog.* 2 some device or thing that guards or protects. *A face guard.* **on guard** prepared to defend and protect. **off guard** unprepared.

guarded *adjective* 1 protected. 2 cautious and careful not to say too much. *A guarded reply.*

Guatemala *noun* a country in Central America.

guess *verb* 1 to say what you think is the answer without having enough information to know whether it is really correct. *Joe guessed the weight of the cake.* 2 to think. *I guess I'd better be going.* **guess** *noun.* *My guess is that she is older than she looks.* **guesswork** making guesses or the result of guesses. *He passed the test by guesswork.*

guest *noun* 1 a person who has been invited to stay for a short time in somebody's house, a visitor. *We have guests from overseas.* 2 a person staying in an hotel.

guide *noun* somebody who leads or shows the way; a person who helps or advises. *The guide who showed us around the gallery knew a lot about the paintings and the artists.* **guide** *verb.*

guidebook *noun* a book containing information for visitors to a place. *Sometimes it's nice to get a guidebook and just wander around by yourself.*

guideline *noun* advice or rules on how something should be done. *We wanted to do a good job but we didn't really have any clear guidelines so it was a case of trial and error.*

guillotine *noun* (say gill-uh-teen) a machine used in France to cut off people's heads (behead). It consists of a blade that slides down between two posts.

guilt *noun* 1 the miserable feeling you have when you know you have done something wrong. 2 the fact that you have done something wrong.

guilty *adjective* 1 having done something wrong or committed a crime. *She was guilty of shoplifting.* 2 the feeling of guilt or shame. *I felt really guilty about not showing up for the swim meet but I was exhausted.*

Guinea *noun* a country in Africa.

Guinea-Bissau *noun* a country in Africa.

SPELLING NOTE

The guillotine was first used during the French Revolution (1789–95) and is named after its inventor, Dr Joseph Guillotin.

Marie Antoinette, Queen of France, lost her head on the guillotine.

guinea pig *noun* a furry, tail-less South American rodent, often kept as a pet. 2 somebody used in a scientific experiment.

guitar *noun* a musical instrument with six strings that you pluck with your fingers or with a plectrum. **guitarist** *noun.*

Gujurati *noun* the language spoken in the state of Gujarat in western India.

gulf *noun* a bay or large area of the sea almost surrounded by land.

gull *noun* a large sea bird (seagull) with grey and white feathers and webbed feet.

gum *noun* 1 the firm pink flesh in your mouth that holds your teeth. 2 glue or sticky liquid for sticking things together. **gum** *verb.* 3 chewing-gum.

gun *noun* a weapon that shoots bullets through a metal tube. **gunfire** the repeated firing of guns.

gunpowder *noun* a powder that explodes easily. *Gunpowder is used in fireworks.*

gush *verb* When a liquid such as water gushes, it flows out suddenly and in large quantities. **gush** *noun.*

gust *noun* a strong and sudden rush of wind. **gusty** *adjective.*

guts *plural noun* 1 the intestines. 2 bravery.

gutter *noun* a channel for rainwater to flow along, fixed to the edge of a roof or built along a street.

Guyana *noun* a country in South America.

gym short for gymnasium and gymnastics.

gymnasium *noun* a room or building with special equipment for doing physical exercises. *Sarah goes to the gymnasium at least once a week.*

gymnast *noun* a person who is trained in gymnastics.

gymnastics *noun* highly skilled physical exercises using equipment such as bars, ropes and jumping horses.

Gymnastics is one of the most respected events at the Olympic Games.

gypsy *noun* a member of a dark-haired race of people called Romanies who used to travel from place to place in wagons. *Old gypsy wagons were small and brightly painted.*

Hh

habit *noun* 1 something that you do regularly, usually without thinking about it. A custom. *She has an annoying habit of twisting her hair.* **habitual** *adjective.* 2 the loose clothes worn by a monk or nun.

habitat *noun* the place where an animal or plant naturally lives or grows.

hack *verb* 1 to cut something, roughly, with repeated blows. *He hacked his way through the undergrowth.* 2 to ride a horse in open countryside. 3 to get information from a computer system illegally. **hacker** *noun.*

haddock *noun* an edible sea fish, related to cod. *Smoked haddock is very salty.*

hag *noun* an offensive word meaning ugly old woman.

haggard *adjective* looking thin, ill and tired. *Worry has made her look terribly haggard.*

haggle *verb* to argue over the price of something, to bargain.

hail *noun* frozen rain. **hail** *verb.* **hailstone** *noun* a frozen raindrop.

hail *verb* to call out or wave to get attention. *She hailed a taxi.*

hair *noun* 1 a fine thread that grows on the skin of people and animals. 2 the soft mass of these threads covering a person's head. *Harry has red hair.* **let your hair down** to behave in a very relaxed way. **keep your hair on** to stay calm and not get excited. **split hairs** to argue about unimportant details.

haircut *noun* the act of cutting somebody's hair. The style in which the hair has been cut.

hairdresser *noun* a person who cuts and arranges (styles) hair.

hair-raising *adjective* terrifying.

hairy (hairier, hairiest) *adjective* 1 covered in hair. 2 (slang) exciting and risky. *A hairy ride on the roller-coaster.*

Haiti (say **hay**-tee) *noun* a country in the West Indies, the western part of the island of Hispaniola.

halal *noun* meat from animals that have been killed according to Islam's religious laws. *A halal butcher.*

This section through a hair shaft shows how layers of keratin (a protein) make up the outer coating or cuticle. Inside, more keratin makes up the cortex and the inner layer, or medulla.

half (halves) *noun* one of two equal parts. *Half an apple.* **half** *adverb* partly, not completely. *The meat is still half-frozen.* **half** *adjective A half bottle of wine.* **half-hearted** *adjective* not very keen or enthusiastic. *A half-hearted effort.*

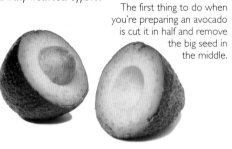

The first thing to do when you're preparing an avocado is cut it in half and remove the big seed in the middle.

half-time *noun* a short break between two halves of a game such as soccer or hockey.

halfmast *noun* the position half-way down a pole at which a flag is flown as a sign that somebody important has died.

hall *noun* 1 a room or passageway at the entrance to a house. 2 a large room or building for public meetings, concerts etc.

Halloween *noun* the evening of 31 October, the day before All Saints Day when some people believe that ghosts and witches roam around.

hallucinate *verb* to hear or see things that are not really there. **hallucination** *noun.*

halt *verb* to come or bring to a stop. *The train halted at the station.* **halt** *noun.*

halve *verb* 1 to divide or cut something into two equal parts. 2 to reduce by half.

ham *noun* 1 salted meat from a pig's back leg. 2 (slang) an actor who is not very good and who overacts.

hamburger *noun* a round bun containing a round patty of chopped beef.

hamlet *noun* a small village (in Britain), usually without a church.

hammer *noun* a tool with a long handle and a heavy head used mainly for hitting (hammering) nails into things. **hammer** *verb.*

hammock *noun* a swinging bed made of strong cloth or rope that is hung up at the ends between two supports.

In the summer, we hang a hammock in the back yard.

hamper *noun* a large basket with a lid, for carrying things. *A picnic hamper.*

hamper *verb* to prevent or make something difficult to do, to hinder. *Her tight jacket hampered her movements.*

hamster *noun* a small, furry, tail-less rodent that can store food in its cheeks. Hamsters are often kept as pets.

Hamsters need plenty of exercise.

hand *noun* 1 the part of your body at the end of your arm and below your wrist with four fingers and a thumb. 2 a pointer on a clock. *My watch has an hour hand, a minute hand and a second hand.* 3 help. *Can you give me a hand, please?* 4 a worker. *A farm hand.* 5 the cards a player holds in his or her hand in a card game. *I had a winning hand.* 6 The measure of the height of horses and ponies (equal to 10 centimeters). **hand** *verb* to give. *She handed me the letter.* **at first hand** directly and not through other people. **in hand** being dealt with, under control. **hand out** to give out, share. **on hand** ready and available. **out of hand** out of control.

handbag *noun* a purse, a small bag usually carried by women for money and personal belongings.

handbook *noun* a book with instructions or useful facts about something.

handcuffs *plural noun* a pair of metal rings joined by a chain and locked around a prisoner's wrists to stop them escaping. **handcuff** *verb*.

handicap *noun* 1 a disadvantage or something that makes it difficult to do what you want to do. *His lack of experience was a handicap.* 2 a disability of the body or mind. *Being deaf can be a terrible handicap.*

handicraft *noun* work such as pottery or weaving that needs skillful use of the hands.

handkerchief *noun* (say **hang-ker-cheef**) a small piece of cloth or paper used for blowing and wiping your nose.

handle *noun* the part of an object that you can hold it by or make it work by. *Turn the handle to open the door.* **handle** *verb* 1 to hold, touch or move something with your hands. 2 to deal with or control. *Grooms handle horses.*

handlebars *plural noun* the bar with a handle at each end at the front of a bicycle or motorcycle that the rider holds and steers with. *Hold on to the handlebars.*

handsome *adjective* attractive, good-looking. *A handsome man.*

handy (handier, handiest) *adjective* 1 nearby and easy to reach. *There's a handy store round the corner.* 2 useful and easy to use. *Penknives are handy tools.* 3 skillful in the use of tools. *He's handy around the house.*

hang (hangs, hanging, hung) *verb* 1 to attach something by its top part so that the lower part is free. *She hung her coat on a hook.* 2 to swing loosely. *The dog's tongue is hanging out of its mouth.* 3 **hang** (hangs, hanging, hanged) to kill somebody by putting a rope around their neck and letting them drop from a support. **hang around** to wait about a place with nothing to do. **hang back** to be unwilling to do something. **hang on** 1 to hold tightly. 2 to wait. *Hang on a second, wait for me!*

hangar *noun* a large building where aircraft are kept. *Aircraft hangar.*

hanger *noun* something on which to hang clothes to be stored in a cupboard.

I hang all my clothes up on hangers on Saturdays.

hang-glider *noun* a kite-like glider to which you are strapped and can then fly from the top of cliffs etc. in the sport of hang-gliding.

hanker *verb* to want something very badly, to long for. *She is hankering after a ride in the helicopter.*

Hanoi *noun* the capital of Vietnam.

Hanukkah *noun* the Jewish festival of lights, which is held in December.

haphazard *adjective* unplanned, happening by accident. *A haphazard arrangement.*

happen *verb* 1 to take place. *What happened next in the story?* 2 to occur by chance. *I just happened to see him.*

happening *noun* an event. *Great happenings in history.*

The space walk was the greatest happening of his life.

happy (happier, happiest) *adjective* 1 the feeling of being pleased and cheerful. 2 willing. *I'd be happy to go instead of you.* **happiness** *noun*. **happily** *adverb*.

Harare *noun* the capital of Zimbabwe.

harass *verb* to annoy or bother somebody repeatedly. **harassment** *noun*. **harassed** *adjective*. *Sarah feels very harrassed today.*

harbor *noun* a place where ships stop to load or unload cargoes and where they can shelter. A port.

hard *adjective* 1 solid and difficult to shape or break, not soft. *Concrete becomes hard when it sets.* 2 difficult. *A hard jigsaw.* 3 severe and tough. *Hard discipline.* **hard** *adverb* with great energy or effort. *Work hard, play hard.* **hardness** *noun*.

hardback *noun* a book with a long-lasting, stiff cover.

harden *verb* to make or to become hard and stiff. *The concrete hardened.*

hard-copy *noun* a printed copy of information created on a computer, also called a printout.

hard-disk *noun* a device inside a computer that holds a large amount of data.

The hard disk contained a lot of memory.

hardly *adverb* almost but not completely, barely. *He was so tired he could hardly keep his eyes open.*

hardship *noun* causing suffering or difficulty. *He suffered great hardship.*

hardware *noun* 1 all the pieces of machinery that make up a computer, e.g. the printer and VDU. 2 tools and equipment used in the home.

hardy *adjective* strong, robust and able to endure severe conditions. *Hardy plants.*

hare *noun* an animal like a large rabbit.

harm *verb* to hurt or damage somebody or something. **harm** *noun*.

harmful *adjective* bad for you. *Too much sugar is harmful to your teeth.*

harmless *adjective* safe and not dangerous or harmful. *A harmless insect.*

harmony *noun* 1 musical notes played at the same time and which sound pleasant. 2 agreement and cooperation. **harmonious** *adjective*. **harmonize** *verb*.

The harp is a favorite instrument in Wales.

SPELLING NOTE

Note the one 'r' and two 's's in 'harass'. But remember that 'embarrass' has two 'r's'.

AMAZING FACT

Some animals have special words for the young, for males, for females, a group of the animal and for the place the animals live.

For example, a young hare is called a leveret, a male hare is a buck, a female is a doe. A group of hares is called a drove and the home of a hare is a form. These specialized words probably developed during the Middle Ages, when hunting was a main source of food.

harness *noun* the leather straps fastened to a horse to control it. The bridle, reins and saddle are parts of the harness. **harness** *verb*.

harp *noun* a musical instrument that you play by plucking its strings. **harpist** *noun*.

harpoon *noun* a spear with a rope attached that is used to hunt whales. **harpoon** *verb*.

harpsichord *noun* a keyboard instrument similar to a piano with strings that are plucked.

harsh *adjective* 1 stern, unkind and severe. *Harsh treatment.* 2 rough and unpleasant. *A harsh sound.*

harvest *noun* the time when grain and other crops are cut and gathered. *Harvest is the busiest time of the year for the farming community.* **harvest** *verb*.

hassle *noun* a bother or a cause of trouble. *It's too much hassle to go by bus.* **hassle** *verb* (slang) to pester or bother somebody. *Stop hassling me!*

haste *noun* a hurry. *She was late and left in great haste.* **hasten** *verb*. *He hastened home.*

hasty (hastier, hastiest) *adjective* done quickly, and sometimes too quickly and without care. *A hasty decision.*

hat *noun* a covering for the head, usually with a brim. *A hat keeps your head warm.* **talk though your hat** to talk nonsense.

Hats can be decorated with feathers, bows and colored bands.

hatch *noun* a movable covering for a hole in a floor, wall or ceiling etc. *An escape hatch on an airplane.* **hatchback car** a car with a door at the back that opens upwards.

hatch *verb* 1 An egg hatches when it breaks open and a chick or reptile comes out. 2 to plan. *What scheme are you hatching?*

hate *verb* to dislike somebody or something very much, to loathe. **hate, hatred** *noun*.

hateful *adjective* causing hatred, unpleasant. *What a hateful person he is.*

haul *verb* to pull or drag something heavy with a lot of effort.

haunt *verb* If a ghost haunts a place, it visits it regularly. **haunted** *adjective*.

Havana *noun* the capital of Cuba.

have (has, having, had) *verb* 1 to own. *She has 20 pairs of shoes.* 2 to experience or enjoy something. *Let's have a party.* 3 to be forced to do something. *I have to go home today.* 4 to receive. *I had a lot of cards on my birthday.*

havoc *noun* great damage, chaos.

hawk *noun* a bird of prey with good eye-sight and sharp talons.

hay *noun* grass that has been cut and dried for feeding to animals. **make hay while the sun shines** to do things while you have the opportunity to.

hayfever *noun* an illness like a bad cold caused by an allergy or bad reaction to breathing in the pollen of grasses or flowers.

hazard *noun* a risk or something that can cause harm. *That loose step is a hazard.*

hazel *noun* 1 a small tree on which hazelnuts grow. 2 a yellowish-brown color. *Hazel eyes glow with a special warmth.*

hazy (hazier, haziest) *adjective* 1 misty. *A hazy day.* **haze** *noun.* 2 not clear, confused. *I have only a hazy idea of how to get there.*

head *noun* 1 the top part of your body above your neck, containing your face, hair and skull. 2 the leader or person in charge of something. *The head of department.* 3 the front or upper part of something. *The head of a letter.* **heads** the side of a coin showing somebody's head. **head** *verb* 1 to move in a direction. *They headed for the beach.* 2 to be in charge of. *She heads the news team.*

headache *noun* 1 a pain in your head. 2 a problem.

headland *noun* a piece of land jutting out into the sea.

headlight *noun* one of the strong lights at the front of a car or truck.

headline *noun* 1 heading or words printed in large, bold print at the head of a story in a newspaper. 2 **headlines** the main items of news. *The news headlines in brief.*

headquarters *noun* the main place from which a business or organization is controlled. *The headquarters of the bank.*

headway *noun* progress. *He's making some headway in learning Japanese.*

heal *verb* to make or become better or healthy again. *The cut healed quickly.*

The hawk is a fearsome predator.

GRAMMAR NOTE

'To hear' means to receive sounds through your ears, and 'to listen' means to pay attention to what you hear.

health *noun* the condition of your body and how well or ill it is.

healthy (healthier, healthiest) *adjective* 1 well and not suffering from any illness or injury, fit. 2 something that is good for you. *Healthy exercise.* **healthily** *adverb.*

heap *noun* 1 an untidy pile or mass of things. *A heap of dirty dishes.* 2 **heaps** a large amount. *There's heaps of time before the train goes.* **heap** *verb.* *She heaped the laundry in the corner.*

Dad left a heap of dirty dishes in the sink.

hear *verb* 1 to receive or pick up sound with our ears, to listen to. 2 to receive information. *We hear you are going away.*

hearing *noun* One of the body's five senses is the ability to hear.

hearing-aid *noun* a small device that makes sounds louder and which people with poor hearing wear in or behind their ears to help them hear better.

hearse *noun* a vehicle for carrying a coffin to a cemetery etc.

heart *noun* 1 the organ inside your chest that pumps blood around your body. 2 the main or most important part. *The heart of the matter.* 3 courage and enthusiasm. *She put her heart into the job.* 4 **hearts** one of the four suits in a pack of playing cards.

The heart is a very strong muscle that works every minute of the day without stopping for a whole lifetime.

heart-attack *noun* a serious condition when the heart suddenly does not work properly and may even stop, causing death.

heart-breaking *adjective* causing great sadness. *I am so sorry to hear the heart-breaking news about your cats.*

heartbroken *adjective. She was heartbroken when her budgie died.*

heart-felt *adjective* very sincere. *My heartfelt thanks to all concerned.*

heartless *adjective* cruel and pitiless. **heartlessness** *noun.*

hearth *noun* the floor of a fireplace.

hearty (heartier, heartiest) *adjective* 1 enthusiastic and friendly. *They gave us a hearty welcome.* 2 strong, big and healthy. *A hearty meal was enjoyed by all.*

heat *adjective* 1 the hotness or warmth of something. *The heat of the fire.* 2 one of a number of races in a competition, the winners of which go forward into the next trial. **heat** *verb* to make something hot. *The fire heated the room.* **heated** *adjective.*

heath *noun* a wild and open area of land covered with grass and shrubs.

heather *noun* an evergreen shrub with pink, purple or white flowers that grows on moors and heaths.

Heather is the national flower of Scotland.

heave *verb* to lift, move or throw something using a lot of effort.

heaven *noun* the place where God or gods live and where good people are said to go when they die.

heavy (heavier, heaviest) *adjective* 1 having great weight and hard to lift. *A heavy suitcase.* 2 great amount or force. *Heavy rain fell in sheets.* 3 (slang) serious, boring and complicated. *Our science teacher makes even the heaviest topics seem interesting.* **heaviness** *noun.* **heavily** *adverb.*

heckle *verb* to interrupt a public speaker by asking rude or difficult questions. **heckler** *noun. The heckler threw a tomato.*

hectare *noun* a measure of an area of land, equal to 10,000 square metres.

hectic *adjective* very busy and full of exciting activity. *A hectic day.*

hedge *noun* a fence around a field or yard made of closely planted shrubs or small trees. **hedge** *verb* 1 to surround land with a hedge. 2 to avoid giving a straight answer. *She hedged around the subject.*

hedgehog *noun* a small animal covered in needle-like prickles. *Hedgehogs come out at night. They roll up into a ball if frightened.*

Hedgehogs are similar to porcupines. Both animals have coats of spines for protection. When they are threatened, they curl up into a ball.

hedgerow *noun* a row or line of bushes forming a hedge around a field or around a park.

heel *noun* 1 the back part of your foot. 2 the part of sock, shoe etc. that covers or supports the heel. *She's wearing shoes with very high heels.*

heifer *noun* (say **heff**-er) a young cow that has not yet had a calf.

height *noun* 1 how high something is from top to bottom. *The height of the room is nearly three meters.* 2 the highest, best or most important point or part of something. *The height of fashion.*

heighten *verb* to make something higher or become greater. *Their excitement heightened as they approached the stadium.*

heir *noun* (say **air**) an heir is a person who will have (inherit) the money, title etc. of somebody when they die.

heiress *noun* (say **air**-ess) a female heir.

heirloom *noun* a special or valuable object that is passed down in a family from one generation to the next.

held past and past participle of hold.

helicopter *noun* an aircraft with a large, fast-turning blade (rotor) on top, which acts as both a propeller and wings.

helium *noun* a colorless gas that is lighter than air and does not burn. It is used to fill balloons and airships.

hell *noun* In Muslim and Chritian religions, the place where bad people go to be punished after they die.

hello *interjection* a word we use to attract somebody's attention or to greet somebody. *'Hello! How have you been?'*

helm *noun* a ship's steering wheel, a tiller.

helmet *noun* a strong, hard covering to protect the head.

Helmets worn into battle were sometimes extremely elaborate and very heavy.

help *verb* 1 to do something that is needed or useful for somebody else, to assist. *'Can you help me move this box, please?'* 2 can't **help** unable to prevent or control. *She can't help sneezing.* **help** *noun.* **helper** *noun.*

helpful *adjective* useful and willing to help. *That was helpful advice.*

helping *noun* a share or amount of food put on your plate. *A big helping of mashed potatoes.*

helpless *adjective* not able to take care of yourself. *Babies are quite helpless.*

Helsinki *noun* the capital of Finland.

hem *noun* the edge of a piece of cloth that is folded over and sewn. **hem** (hems, hemming, hemmed) *verb. She hemmed her skirt.* **hem in** to surround closely and prevent from escaping.

hemisphere *noun* 1 the shape of half a sphere. 2 one half of the Earth. *Europe is in the northern hemisphere.*

hen *noun* a female chicken, especially one kept for its eggs. 2 any female bird. *A hen pheasant.*

A hen that is less than a year old is also called a pullet.

hence *adverb*
1 therefore, for this reason. *There's been no rain, hence it's very dry.*
2 from now on. *From this day hence.*

herald *verb* 1 to say that something is going to happen. 2 to be a sign that something is going to happen. *Dark clouds herald storms.*

heraldry *noun* the study of coats-of-arms and family histories.

herb *noun* a plant used to add flavour in cooking or for making medicines. **herbal** *adjective. Herbal remedies.*

herbivore *noun* an animal that eats only plants. Horses and cattle are herbivores. **herbivorous** *adjective.*

herd *noun* a group of animals of one kind that graze and live together. *A herd of cows.* **herd** *verb* to crowd together.

here *adverb* at or to this place. *Come here immediately!*

hereafter *adverb* in the future, after this time. *Hereafter, things will be different.*

heretic *noun* (say **hair-it-ik**) a person who supports an opinion (usually religious or political) that is against the official view or what most people generally accept. **heretical** *adjective.* **heresy** *noun.*

heritage *noun* traditions, buildings etc. that are passed from one generation to the next.

hermit *noun* somebody who chooses to live alone and away from people, usually for religious reasons.

AMAZING FACT

Herons use their long beaks to grasp their prey rather than to spear it.

AMAZING FACT

Animals hibernate during the cold, winter months when food is scarce. They eat as much as they can before finding a safe place to curl up for the winter. Hibernation isn't the same as sleeping, though. Sleeping takes more energy than hibernation. To conserve energy, the breathing and heartbeat of a hibernating animal slows down so much that they may appear to be almost dead

Florence Nightingale was a heroine during the Crimean War.

hero (heroes) *noun* 1 a man or boy admired for having done something brave or especially good. **heroism** *noun.* **heroic** *adjective. Heroic deeds are related in many myths and fairytales.* 2 the most important male character in a book, film or play.

heroin *noun* a very strong drug that some people become addicted to.

heroine *noun* a woman or girl admired for having done something brave or especially good. **heroism** *noun.* **heroic** *adjective.* 2 the most important female character in a book, film or play.

heron *noun* a bird with long legs and a long thin beak that lives near ponds or rivers.

hesitate *verb* to pause or to stop doing something for a short time because you are uncertain, undecided or worried. **hesitation** *noun. He agreed to help without any hesitation.* **hesitant** *adjective.*

heterosexual *adjective* sexually attracted to people of the opposite sex. **heterosexuality** *noun.*

hew (hews, hewing, hewed, hewn or hewed) *verb* to cut with an axe.

hexagon *noun* a shape with six equal sides. **hexagonal** *adjective.*

A hexagon is a shape with six equal sides.

hibernate *verb* when animals hibernate, they spend the winter in a deep sleep. Bears, hedgehogs and tortoises all hibernate. **hibernation** *noun.*

hiccup *noun* (say **hik-up**) a sudden, repeated sound in your throat which people sometimes make after eating or drinking.

hide (hiding, hid, hidden) *verb* 1 to go to a place where you cannot be seen. *She hid in the attic.* 2 to put something in a place where people will not see it. *She hid the presents in a closet.*

hide *noun* the skin of an animal used for making leather.

hideous *adjective* very ugly, unpleasant. *A hideous smell wafted up out of the drain.*

hieroglyphics *plural noun* (hy-er-uh-glif-iks) the ancient Egyptian system of writing that uses pictures to represent words and sounds.

high *adjective* 1 a long way above the ground. 2 the distance from the top to the bottom of something. *The door is two meters high.* 3 greater than normal. *The police car drove at a high speed.* 4 not deep or low. *Children have high voices.* 5 important or above others in rank.

highlands *plural noun* a hilly region, like the Highlands of northern Scotland, pictured below.

highlight *noun* the most interesting part of something. *Seeing the game park was the highlight of the visit.* **highlight** *verb* 1 to draw attention to something. *He highlighted the importance of good spelling when he spoke to the class.* 2 to use a colored pen to mark important parts of a document.

high-pitched *adjective* shrill and high in sound. *A high-pitched wail.*

high-rise *adjective* High-rise buildings are very tall.

highly-strung *adjective* sensitive and nervous. *The horse is very highly-strung.*

high tech *noun* high technology. The use of advanced computers, electronics etc.

high tide *noun* the time when the sea reaches its highest level.

highway *noun* a main road.

WORD HISTORY

'Hieroglyphics' comes from two Greek words, 'hieros', 'sacred or priestly' and 'glyphe', 'carving' or 'writing'. The Greeks believed that only the Egyptian priests understood and used this system of writing.

In the Highlands of Scotland you can see lochs, mountains and castles.

SPELLING NOTE

The word 'hippopotamus' comes from two Greek words and means 'river horse'. Hippos are in fact more closely related to pigs than horses.

High-rise buildings create an impressive skyline.

highwayman (highwaymen) *noun* in the past, a robber on horseback who stopped travelers at gunpoint.

hijack *verb* to take control of an aircraft, car etc. by force and make it go somewhere. **hijack** *noun*. *The hijack ended in disaster.*

hijacker *noun* a person who hijacks.

hike *verb* to go on a long walk. *We hiked into the hills.* **hike** *noun*. **hiker** *noun*.

hilarious *adjective* very funny in a noisy way. **hilarity** *noun*.

hill *noun* an area of ground that is higher than the ground around it. **hilly** *adjective*. *Hilly countryside.*

hilt *noun* the handle of a sword or dagger. **up to the hilt** completely. *The SWAT team was armed to the hilt.*

hinder *verb* to get in the way and so make things difficult for somebody, to prevent and delay. **hindrance** *noun*.

Hindu *noun* (say hin-**doo**) a follower of Hinduism, an Indian religion which has many gods and teaches that people will return to Earth in a different form after death. **Hindu** *adjective*.

Hindustani *noun* a dialect of the language Hindi, and one of the main languages of India. *Fluent Hindustani.*

hinge *noun* a moving metal joint on which such things as doors, gates, windows and lids to boxes can swing when opened.

hint *verb* to mention something without actually saying it. *Jack hinted that it was time to go by looking at his watch.* **hint** *noun* 1 a suggestion or clue. 2 helpful advice. *Household hints.*

hip *noun* one of the two joints on either side of your body between the top of your legs and your waist.

hippopotamus (hippopotamuses) *noun* a very large African animal with short legs and thick skin that lives in or near lakes and rivers. It is often called a hippo for short.

Hippopotamuses spend most of the day in the water and come out at night to graze along the lakeshores.

hire *verb* to pay money to employ somebody or use something for a short time. *She hired two men to fix the roof.*

hiss *verb* to make a long S sound to show anger or disapproval. **hiss** *verb*. *The audience hissed at the actors.*

historian *noun* a person who studies and writes about history.

historic *adjective* famous or important in the past. *Charleston is full of historic houses.*

historical *adjective* concerned with events and people in history. *Historical documents described a terrible crime.*

history *noun* 1 the study of the people and events of the past. 2 a description of the past. *A history of the southwest.*

hit (hits, hitting, hit) *verb* to strike with a blow, to touch something violently. *She hit the ball with a bat.* **hit** *noun* 1 a blow. 2 a great success. *The show was a big hit.*

hitch-hike *verb* to travel by getting free rides from passing vehicles by holding up your thumb.

HIV short for human immunodeficiency virus, a virus that weakens a person's resistance to diseases and may lead to Aids.

hive *noun* bee-hive, a box-like structure for keeping bees in.

hoard *noun* a secret store of money, valuables, food etc. *Archeologists found a hoard of gold buried in the ruins behind the castle.* **hoard** *verb.* *Squirrels hoard nuts for the winter.* **hoarder** *noun.*

hoarse *adjective* a rough, low voice caused by a sore throat or by shouting too much.

hoax *noun* a practical joke, a trick or deception. *We had to evacuate the building, but the bomb scare was a hoax.* **hoax** *verb.*

hobble *verb* to limp or walk with difficulty. *He twisted his ankle and hobbled around in pain for more than a month.*

hobby *noun* an activity such as model-making that you enjoy doing in your spare time. *His hobby is collecting stamps.*

The Parthenon is a historic building in Athens.

SPELLING NOTE

Try to distinguish between 'historic', meaning 'famous' or 'important in history'; and 'historical', meaning 'having actually happened in history' or 'concerned with history'. 'Hitler is an historical person.'

Bees have been observed 'dancing' as they return to the hive. It is a way of giving directions to food sources.

SPELLING NOTE

Another word that sounds like 'hoarse' is 'horse'.

hockey *noun* a game played on ice with curved sticks by two teams of players who try to score by hitting a puck into a goal.

hoe *noun* a garden tool with a long handle and a short blade, used for weeding.

hog *noun* a male pig that has been neutered.

hog (hogs, hogging. hogged) *verb* to be very selfish and, for example, take much more of something than you can use.

hoist *verb* to raise or lift up something, usually with ropes or a special machine. *The soldiers hoisted the flag.*

hold (holds, holding, held) *verb* 1 to carry something in your hand or mouth, to grasp. 2 to contain a certain amount. *The thermos holds a quart of liquid.* 3 to arrange or carry on. *They held a dance in the gym.* 4 to have in control or in your possession. *Who holds the land speed record?* 5 to support or to keep something steady. *The pillars hold up the roof.* **hold off** to stay away. *I hope the rain holds off for the afternoon.* **hold on** 1 to continue holding something. 2 to wait. *Hold on a minute.* **hold up** 1 to delay or hinder. *The construction held us up for an hour.* 2 to stop and rob somebody with threats. *She was held up at gunpoint.*

hold *noun* a place in a ship or aircraft where cargo is kept.

hole *noun* an opening or gap in something, a hollow space. *There's a hole in my sock. She hit the golf ball into the hole.*

holiday *noun* a day or a longer period of time when you don't have to go to school or work. *We're going to Mexico for the holidays.*

hollow *adjective* not solid, having an empty space inside. *Bottles and pipes are hollow.* **hollow** *noun* 1 a hole. 2 a small valley.

holly *noun* an evergreen tree with shiny, spiky leaves and sometimes red berries in winter. It is often used for decoration at Christmas. *We hung a holly wreath on the front door.*

Holly has beautiful red berries that the birds eat in winter.

hologram *noun* a photograph created by laser beams that appears to be three-dimensional (seeming to have width, depth and height).

holy *noun* relating to or belonging to religion. *Churches and temples are holy places.* **holiness** *noun.*

home *noun* the place where you usually live or where you were brought up. **feel at home** to feel relaxed with somebody or something.

homeless *adjective, noun* without a place to live in. **homelessness** *noun. How can we help the homeless?*

homely *adjective* plain or ugly.

homesick *adjective* unhappy and lonely because you are away from your family and home. *I was homesick for the first few days at camp.*

homework *noun* work that teachers give their students to do at home.

homicide *noun* (say **hom**-uh-side) the killing of a human being.

homosexual *adjective, noun* sexually attracted to somebody of the same sex, gay. **homosexuality** *noun.*

Honduras *noun* a country in Central America.

honest *adjective* (say **on**-est) an honest person is somebody who always tells the truth and whom you can trust. **honesty** *noun. Honesty is always the best policy.*

honey *noun* (rhymes with bunny) the sweet, sticky food made by bees from the nectar of flowers. *Peanut butter and honey sandwich.*

honeycomb *noun* rows of six-sided wax containers made by bees to store their honey and eggs.

honeymoon *noun* a vacation spent together by two people who have just gotten married.

honeysuckle *noun* a climbing shrub with sweet-smelling flowers.

Honiara *noun* the capital of the Solomon Islands.

honor *noun* (say **on**-ur) 1 to give great respect to somebody. *He was honored by everybody for his great achievements.* 2 to praise and reward somebody publicly. 3 to keep an agreement. **honor** *noun* good reputation. **honorable** *adjective. She behaved in an honorable way and told the absolute truth.*

WORD HISTORY
'Hooligan' comes from the name of an unruly Irish family that lived in southeast London in the 19th century.

Bees make the cells of the honeycomb from beeswax.

hood *noun* 1 the metal cover over the engine of a car. 2 a part of a coat that you can pull up to cover your head and neck.

hoodwink *verb* to trick somebody. *He was hoodwinked into paying a lot of money for a worthless clock.*

hoof (hooves or hoofs) *noun* the hard covering on the feet of some animals such as horses, cows and sheep.

hook *noun* 1 a bent piece of metal or plastic for hanging things on. *Hang your raincoat on the hook to dry.* 2 a bent piece of metal for catching fish. **by hook or by crook** by any means possible. **get off the hook** to get out of a difficult situation.

For fly-fishing, anglers use hooks decorated with colorful feathers.

hooked *adjective* 1 shaped like a hook. *A hooked nose.* 2 (slang) fascinated by or addicted to. *He's hooked on bird watching.*

hooligan *noun* a violent, noisy person who gets into trouble and breaks things. **hooliganism** *noun.*

hoop *noun* a large ring made of metal or wood. *At the circus we saw an acrobat jump through a hoop of fire.*

hoot *verb* to make a sound like the horn of a car or the long 'oo' cry of an owl. *We hooted with laughter.* **hoot** *noun. We heard the hoot of the owl.*

hop (hops, hopping, hopped) *verb* 1 to jump on one foot. 2 (of animals) to make short jumps. *The rabbit hopped across the lawn and disappeared under the fence.*

hops *noun* a climbing plant used to flavor beer.

hope *verb* to want something to happen and be expecting it to happen. *I hope you win first prize.* **hope** *noun* a feeling that something you want will happen. *She has no hope of passing her exams.*

hopeful *adjective* feeling confident and full of hope. **hopefulness** *noun.*

hopefully *adverb* in a hopeful way. *'Can we have one of the kittens?' she asked hopefully.*

hopeless *adjective* 1 without hope. *It's a hopeless situation.* 2 very bad, useless.

horde *noun* a large crowd. *Hordes of tourists swarmed into the piazza.*

horizon *noun* the line in the distance where the sky and land or sea seem to meet.

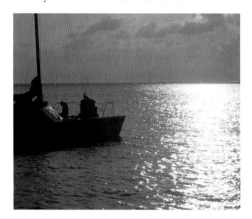

The Sun dropped behind the horizon, leaving a golden path across the sea.

horizontal *adjective* lying flat on the ground in line with the horizon, going from side to side and not up and down.

hormone *noun* a chemical substance produced in your body and that controls particular functions of the body. Some hormones, for example, control growth and others control digestion.

horn *noun* 1 one of the hard, bony growths on the heads of certain animals such as cows and goats. 2 a brass musical instrument that you play by blowing into it. 3 a device on a vehicle that makes a loud, warning sound. *The driver honked her horn, but it was too late.*

horoscope *noun* a forecast of somebody's future, based on the position of the stars at the time of that person's birth.

AMAZING FACT

A horse's height is measured in hands, not feet. A hand is equal to ten centimeters.

When you want to read your horoscope, you have to look up your sign of the zodiac in the newspaper.

horrible *adjective* terrible, very unpleasant. *What a horrible noise!*

horrid *adjective* horrible, unkind or hateful. *What a horrid person she is.*

horrify (horrifies horrifying horrified) *verb* to shock or fill with great horror and disgust. *I was horrified to hear about the earthquake in Armenia.*

horror *noun* a feeling of shock or fear. *He watched the snake slide towards him with horror.*

horse *noun* 1 a big four-legged animal with hooves, a long mane and a tail that can be used for riding or for pulling things like carts or plows. 2 a piece of equipment in a gym used for jumping over and doing exercises.

The horse's coat glowed from so much grooming.

horseback *adjective* 1 horseback riding, riding a horse for pleasure. 2 **on horseback** riding a horse.

horse-play *noun* rough and noisy play by children. *That's enough, knock off the horse-play and settle down!*

horseshoe *noun* a curved piece of iron nailed to a horse's hoof to protect it.

horticulture *noun* the science of gardening and the growing of fruit, flowers and vegetables. **horticultural** *adjective*.

hose *noun* a long rubber or plastic tube that water can go through.

hospice *noun* a hospital where people who are suffering from incurable diseases are taken care of by doctors and nurses.

hospitable *adjective* friendly and generous to guests and strangers. *A most hospitable welcome.* **hospitality** *noun*.

hospital *noun* a place where people who are ill or injured are treated and taken care of.

host *noun* 1 a person who invites guests and organizes a party. 2 a person who introduces guest performers on a TV or radio show. *A talk show host.* 3 a very large number.

hostage *noun* a person who is held prisoner by people who will not release her or him until their demands have been carried out.

hostel *noun* a place where people such as students or hitch-hikers can stay cheaply.

hostile *adjective* behaving in an unfriendly way. *The president was met by a hostile group of students.*

hot (hotter, hottest) *adjective* 1 full of heat and having a high temperature. 2 spicy and strong tasting. *A hot curry.* **in hot water** in serious trouble.

hot dog *noun* a thin, hot sausage in a long bun, a frankfurter. *We camped out and cooked hot dogs and hamburgers.*

We ate delicious hot dogs at the fair.

hotel *noun* a building with many bedrooms where people pay to stay and have meals.

hound *noun* a breed of dog that is used for hunting and racing. Foxhounds, deerhounds and bloodhounds are all different kinds of hound. **hound** *verb* to follow or harass somebody. *The princess was hounded by photographers wherever she went.*

hour *noun* a period of time consisting of 60 minutes. There are 24 hours in a day. **hourly** *adjective, adverb. The hourly rate for the job is very low.*

house *noun* 1 a building where people live. 2 a building used for a particular purpose. *The White House.* **house** *verb* to provide a place for somebody to live.

household *noun* all the people who live together in one house.

householder *noun* the person who owns a house.

househusband *noun* a man who normally takes care of the house for the family.

housekeeper *noun* a person who is paid to take care of a house.

housewife *noun* a woman who normally takes care of the house for the family.

housework *noun* cleaning, washing and cooking and other work that has to be done in a house.

hovel *noun* a small, filthy and broken-down house or hut. *The hermit lived in a hovel.*

hover *verb* 1 to remain in the air over one spot without moving. 2 to linger or to stay near one place.

hovercraft *noun* a boat that can fly over sea or land, lifted up on a cushion of air.

howl *verb* to make a long cry like an animal makes when it is in pain. **howl** *noun.*

howler *noun* a ridiculously funny mistake of fact. *There's a real howler in your essay.*

HQ *abbreviation* Headquarters.

hub *noun* the center part of a wheel.

A cross-section through this house shows all the rooms from the basement to the attic.

SPELLING NOTE

Some howlers! 1 The practice of having only one wife is called monotony. 2 She's at her wick's end. 3 Calm down – don't get so historical. 4 Russia uses the acrylic alphabet.

Hovercrafts run between the islands throughout the tourist season.

huddle *verb* to crowd closely together. *They huddled under the tree to get out of the rain.* **huddle** *noun.*

hue *noun* a color or shade of color.

hug (hugs, hugging, hugged) *verb* to put your arms around somebody and hold them tightly. **hug** *noun. He gave his cousin a big hug to welcome him home.*

huge *adjective* very big, enormous.

hull *noun* the body or frame of a ship.

hum (hums, humming, hummed) *verb* 1 to sing a tune with your mouth shut. 2 to make the low, continuous sound of an insect. **hum** *noun. The hum of the traffic.*

human *noun* human being. A man, woman or child. **human** *adjective* having natural and understandable feelings. *It's only human to cry when you are upset.*

humane *adjective* kind and gentle, not cruel. *Humane treatment of animals.*

humanity *noun* 1 all people. 2 being kind and humane.

humble *adjective* modest and not vain or self-important. *He's very successful, but in spite of his achievements, he's modest too.*

humid *adjective* damp and sometimes warm. *Humid weather.* **humidity** *noun.*

humiliate *verb* to make somebody feel ashamed or appear stupid to other people. **humiliation** *noun.*

hummingbird *noun* a very small, brightly colored bird with a long slender beak. It hovers over flowers, beating its wings so fast that they make a humming sound.

The hummingbird sucked nectar from the flower.

humorous *adjective* funny. *A very humorous book.*

humor *noun* 1 what makes people laugh or smile. 2 a mood. *Is she in a good humor today?* **sense of humor** the ability to see what is funny and to laugh at it.

hump *noun* a small, round lump. A camel has a hump on its back.

hunch *verb* to lean forward with your shoulders raised and your head bent down.

hunch *noun* a feeling about something but not based on facts. *I had a hunch you would be on this train.*

hung past tense of hang.

Hungarian *noun* 1 a person who comes from Hungary. 2 the language spoken in Hungary. **Hungarian** *adjective*. *Hungarian dances.*

Hungary *noun* a country in eastern Europe.

hunger *noun* a strong wish or need to eat. **hunger** *verb*. *She hungered for fame and fortune.*

The Hungarian flag has red, white and green stripes.

hungry (hungrier, hungriest) *adjective* feeling hunger or the need for food. *The hungry dog hurried to eat all its food.* **hungrily** *adverb*.

hunk *noun* a large piece or slice of something. *A hunk of bread.*

hunt *verb* to look for and chase wild animals and then kill them for food or sport. 2 to search carefully for something. *I hunted everywhere for her phone number.* **hunt** *noun*.

Australian aborigines hunted with spears and boomerangs.

hurdle *noun* 1 a small fence a runner jumps over in a race called hurdling. 2 a difficulty or problem to be overcome.

hurl *verb* to throw something with force as far as you can.

hurricane *noun* a violent storm with strong winds. *The hurricane tore off the roof.*

hurry (hurries, hurrying, hurried) *verb* to move quickly or do something as fast as you can. **hurry** *noun*. *Why are you in such a hurry, when we have all day to spare?*

hurt *verb* 1 to cause pain or harm to a person or an animal. *I didn't mean to hurt you.* 2 to feel pain. *My bruised knee hurts.*

husband *noun* a husband is the man that a woman has married.

hush *interjection* Be quiet! **hush** *noun* a sudden silence. *A hush fell over the concert hall and the music began.*

hush-hush *adjective* secret and in confidence. *A hush-hush story.*

husk *noun* the outer covering of some fruits and cereals. *Don't eat the husk.*

husky *adjective* (of a voice) low and rough.

husky *noun* a strong dog used to pull sledges in Arctic regions.

AMAZING FACT

Hyenas have very powerful jaws that they use to crush the bones of their prey, The spotted hyena has the most powerful jaws of any mammal.

Hydrogen is the most abundant element in the whole universe.

WORD HISTORY

'Husband' comes from an Old Norse word meaning 'master of a household'. It was generally applied to all men who were masters of a household whether married or single.

---

hut *noun* a small house or temporary shelter, usually made of wood.

hutch *noun* a wooden cage for pet rabbits or other small animals.

hybrid *noun* a plant or animal produced from two different kinds (species) of plant or animal. A mule is a hybrid of a horse and a donkey. **hybrid** *adjective*. *A hybrid rose.*

hydrant *noun* an outdoor water faucet to which a hose can be attached to supply water for fires or other emergencies.

hydroelectricity *noun* electricity produced by using water power, at a dam or a waterfall, for example.

hydrofoil *noun* a fast, light boat that skims over the surface of water on fin-like foils attached to its hull.

hydrogen *noun* hydrogen is the lightest of all gases and the simplest of all chemical elements. It combines with oxygen to make water.

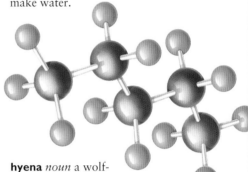

hyena *noun* a wolf-like wild animal from India and Africa that hunts in packs and also scavenges meat from kills made by other animals. *The howl of a hyena is like hysterical laughter.*

hygiene *noun* (say **hy**-jeen) the science and practice of cleanliness and good health. **hygienic** *adjective*.

hymn *noun* (say him) a religious song of praise. *We sang hymns in church.*

hype *noun* exaggerated and excessive publicity about something in order to sell it.

hyphen *noun* a mark (-) used in writing to join two parts of a divided word at the end of a line or to join two words to make a new word. *Stage-coach, self-defence.*

hypocrite *noun* a person who pretends to have feelings, good qualities or beliefs which he or she does not really have.

hypodermic needle *noun* a thin, hollow needle that is used to inject drugs into a vein. *Never re-use a hypodermic needle.*

hysteria *noun* uncontrollable excitement or distress. *She had a fit of hysteria.*

hysterical *adjective* extremely emotional and uncontrollably excited.

hysterics *plural noun* a fit of hysteria.

Ii

ice *noun* water that has frozen hard.

ice *verb* to spread icing on a cake.

ice-age *noun* a time long ago when large areas of the Earth were covered with ice.

iceberg *noun* a huge lump of ice floating in the sea. Most of an iceberg is hidden under the surface of the sea. **the tip of the iceberg** only a small part of a problem.

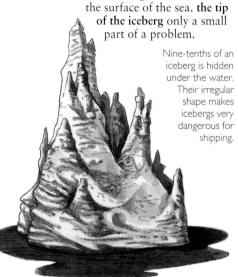

Nine-tenths of an iceberg is hidden under the water. Their irregular shape makes icebergs very dangerous for shipping.

ice cream *noun* a smooth, sweet frozen food usually made with milk or cream.

ice cube *noun* a small block of ice used to cool drinks.

ice hockey *noun* hockey, a game played on ice by two teams in which the skaters try to score goals by hitting a rubber puck with a long stick. *Canada won the ice hockey match.*

Iceland *noun* a Scandinavian country in Europe.

The flag of Iceland shows a red on white cross, on a blue ground.

ice skate *noun* a boot with a metal blade on the bottom for sliding smoothly over the ice. **ice skate** *verb* to move on ice wearing ice skates.

icicle *noun* a long, pointed stick of ice formed by water freezing as it drops.

WORD HISTORY

The shape of the letter I comes from an ancient Egyptian symbol of a hand. The Romans gave the letter its present shape.

SPELLING NOTE

Try not to confuse 'idle', a lazy person, with 'idol', a god.

icing *noun* a mixture that is spread on cakes to decorate them.

icon *noun* 1 a small picture on a computer screen representing a program, file, etc. which can be selected by clicking the mouse. 2 a picture of a holy person painted on wood seen in many Greek or Russian Christian (orthodox) churches.

icy (icier, iciest) *adjective* 1 very cold. *Icy weather.* 2 covered in ice. *Icy roads.*

idea *noun* 1 a thought or picture in your mind. 2 a plan. *She had the idea of becoming a vet.* 3 purpose. *The idea of the game is to score as many goals as possible.*

ideal *adjective* perfect or very suitable. *He's an ideal father.* **ideal** *noun* the best possible person, thing, situation or example.

identical *adjective* exactly the same in every way. *Identical twins.*

identify (identifies, identifying, identified) *verb* to recognize somebody or something and be able to name them. *The police identified the body.* **identification** *noun*.

identity *noun* a person's distinguishing characteristics that make them individual.

idiom *noun* an expression or special way of saying something in which the words have a meaning different from what they appear to have. 'To drop off' means to fall asleep; and 'heads will roll' means that some people will get into trouble.

idiot *noun* a very stupid person. **idiotic** *adjective*. *What an idiotic idea.*

idle *adjective* 1 lazy and work-shy. **idleness** *noun*. 2 not working. *During the strike the machines were left idle.* 3 worthless or not really meant. *Idle threats.*

idol *noun* 1 something, such as a statue, that is worshipped as a god. 2 a famous person who is greatly admired. *A pop idol.*

This statue of Zeus, the Greek king of the gods, was probably worshipped as an idol.

igloo *noun* a house made out of blocks of snow and ice in the shape of a dome by the Inuits of the Arctic region.

ignite *verb* to set fire to or to catch fire.

ignition *noun* a device in a motor vehicle that starts the engine working by igniting the fuel. *Turn the key to start the ignition.*

ignorant *adjective* knowing very little about something, badly educated. *He's ignorant about computers.* **ignorance** *noun*.

ignore *verb* to take no not pay attention to somebody or something, to disregard. *She totally ignored me when I asked her a question.*

il- *prefix* used before many words beginning with l to indicate against or negation. *illiterate* (not literate or able to read), *illegal* (against the law).

ill (worse, worst) *adjective* 1 not in good health, unwell. **illness** *noun*. 2 bad or harmful. *The ill effects of smoking.* **ill at ease** feeling unhappy and uncomfortable with other people. **ill disposed** unfriendly. **ill-founded** without good reasons. *Ill-founded suspicions.* **ill-timed** happening at a bad time. **ill-treat** to treat cruelly.

illegal *adjective* not allowed by the law. *It is illegal to drive faster than 65 mph.*

illegible *adjective* handwriting that is so poor that it is difficult or impossible to read.

illiterate *adjective* unable to read or write. **illiteracy** *noun*.

illogical *adjective* not obeying logic and therefore not making sense.

illness *noun* a disease such as the flu or measles that makes people sick.

illuminate *verb* 1 to light up or shine a light on something. *The castle is illuminated at night.* **illumination** *noun*. the light from a lamp, fire, etc. **illuminating** *adjective*. *An illuminating idea.* 2 to decorate a book with gold and colored letters and pictures. **illumination** *noun*.

In the Middle Ages, monks spent a lot of time copying texts and illuminating the manuscripts with beautiful colors.

Sometimes when people have been traveling for a long time in the desert, they see a mirage. This is an illusion, perhaps brought about by exhaustion or the sand in the air seen through a heat haze. This mirage is of a camel at an oasis, something that desert travelers would dearly love to see.

illusion *noun* a false idea or image of something that is really not there. *An optical illusion.*

im- *prefix* like in-, used before certain words beginning with b, m and p and meaning against, negation or without. *immeasurable* (too great to be measured). *immature* (not mature).

image *noun* 1 a picture or statue. 2 any picture in a book, film, or on television. 3 your reflection in a mirror. 4 a picture of something in your mind. 5 a very close likeness. *He is the image of his twin brother.* 6 a person's image is the general opinion that others have of them.

imagery *noun* the descriptive words used by writers to create pictures in the minds of readers. *Beautiful imagery.*

imaginary *noun* not real but existing only in the mind. Goblins and elves are imaginary creatures.

This imaginary creature is a goblin. He lives underneath the toadstool.

imagination *noun* 1 the ability to create pictures in the mind. *Use your imagination and write a story about space travel.* 2 the ability to create new ideas.

imaginative *adjective* having a lot of imagination. *Imaginative ideas.*

imagine *verb* 1 to have a picture of something in your mind. *Can you imagine life without cars?* 2 to think you see or hear things that are not really there. *You're just imagining there's a ghost under your bed.*

imitate *verb* to copy or behave like somebody or something. *She can imitate her mother's voice perfectly.* **imitation** *noun*. *He does a good imitation of a dog barking.*

immature *adjective* 1 not fully grown or developed, unripe. 2 behaving childishly and not like an adult. **immaturity** *noun*.

immediately *adverb* at once and without delay. *This work needs to be done immediately.* **immediate** *adjective*.

immense *adjective* very big. *The Sahara is an immense desert in North Africa.* **immensity** *noun*.

immerse *verb* to put something into a liquid until it is completely covered. **immerse yourself in** to give all your attention to something. *I'm totally immersed in my work.*

Dishes, and especially pots and pans, immersed in soapy water and left to soak overnight are easier to wash the next day.

immigrant *noun* somebody who immigrates to and goes to settle in a country. **immigration** *noun*.

immigrate *verb* to come to live and settle in a country. *They immigrated quite recently.*

imminent *adjective* Something that is imminent is expected to happen very soon. *The forecast says that snow is imminent.*

immobile *adjective* not moving or able to move. **immobility** *noun*. **immobilize** *verb* to make immobile and unable to move. *All traffic has been immobilized by the snow.*

immoral *adjective* behaving in a way that is considered wrong. **immorality** *noun*.

immortal *adjective* never dying but living and lasting for ever.

immune *adjective* protected against a disease and so unable to catch it. **immunity** *noun*. **immunize** *verb* to give somebody an injection so that they cannot catch a disease.

imp *noun* 1 a mischievous child 2 a creature in fairy tales.

Imps, trolls and goblins are all important characters in fairy tales.

impact *noun* 1 the force of one object colliding with another. 2 the strong effect or impresssion that something has. *Computers have had a great impact on the way we learn, both at home and at school.*

AMAZING FACT

The impala is an extremely fast animal, speed is its main defence. It can also leap as far as ten meters, which it does to escape predators, but also, it seems, because it just enjoys leaping!

SPELLING NOTE

Try not to confuse 'immigrate' (to come from another country) with 'emigrate' (to go to another country).

impala *noun* a small African antelope that lives in large herds.

The impala is a graceful creature that lives in herds across Africa.

impartial *adjective* fair and not favoring one person or side more than another. **impartiality** *noun*.

impassable *noun* not able to be passed through or across. *Heavy snowstorms made the mountain roads impassable.*

impatient *adjective* unwilling to wait and easily annoyed. **impatience** *noun*.

impede *verb* to get in the way of somebody or something and so slow down progress.

impenetrable *adjective* 1 impossible to get through. *An impenetrable forest.* 2 impossible to understand. *His lecture was absolutely impenetrable.*

imperfect *adjective* 1 not perfect and having some fault. **imperfection** *noun*. 2 a verb tense indicating a repeated or incomplete action in the past. *She was sitting in a chair.*

imperial *adjective* 1 of or having to do with an empire or an emperor or empress. 2 The imperial system is the former, non-metric British system of weights and measures.

imperialism *noun* a political system in which one country controls other countries.

impersonal *adjective* unfriendly and showing no personal feelings or warmth. *Her manner was cold and impersonal.*

impersonate *verb* to pretend to be somebody else by copying their behavior. **impersonation** *noun*.

impertinent *adjective* rude and impudent, especially to somebody in authority.

impetuous *adjective* an impetuous person acts suddenly and without thinking first.

implement *noun* a tool or instrument. *Garden implements.*

Gardening tools are a type of implement.

imply (implies, implying, implied) *verb* to suggest or hint at something without actually saying it directly. *By questioning everything he said, she implied that he was lying.* **implication** *noun*.

impolite *adjective* rude and bad-mannered.

import *verb* (say im-**port**) to buy goods from another country to sell in your own country. **import** *noun* (say **im**-port). *One of our main imports is cloth.* The opposite of import is export.

Coffee beans are imported to North America and Europe from South America and Africa.

important *adjective* 1 of great interest and which matters a lot. *Your birthday is an important day for you.* 2 having influence and power. *An important writer.*

imposing *adjective* large and making a great impression. *An imposing palace.*

impossible *adjective* not possible, something that cannot be done or happen.

impostor *noun* someone who pretends to be somebody else in order to deceive and get things they want.

impracticable *adjective* not possible to use or put into practice. *An impracticable idea.*

impractical *adjective* not useful and lacking common sense. *Dad's completely impractical and couldn't boil an egg.*

impress *verb* to cause somebody's admiration or respect. *I was impressed by his knowledge.* **impressive** *adjective*.

impression *noun* 1 the way something appears to you and the effect it has on you. *His kindness made a great impression on us.* 2 a vague idea or belief. *I have the impression I've been here before.* 3 a mark made by something pressing on to a surface. *Our cats, Domino and Max, left the impressions of their paws in the wet concrete.* 4. an impersonation or attempt at copying how somebody talks and behaves, usually in order to entertain people.

impressionable *adjective* very easily influenced or impressed by others. *Some young people are very impressionable.*

WORD BUILDER

You can make many words negative by adding the prefix 'in–' to certain words, as in 'incurable', 'informal'. It is often only necessary to look up the definition of a word to discover its negative meaning.

AMAZING FACT

The system of weights and measures used in the United States is called the English system and is based on the system that was used in Britain until it was officially replaced by the metric system. In 1975, Congress passed the Metric Conversion Act, which called for a voluntary changeover to metric.

The cat, Jez, left the impression of her feet in the wet concrete.

imprison *verb* to put somebody in prison. **imprisonment** *noun. His punishment was imprisonment.*

improve *verb* to become better or to make something better. *Her health is improving.* **improvement** *noun*.

improvise *verb* 1 to do something as you go along without planning or rehearsing beforehand. *She had lost her notes and had to improvise the speech.* 2 to make something quickly with whatever materials are available. *We improvised a table from cardboard boxes.* **improvisation** *noun*.

impudent *noun* rude and showing no respect, insolent. **impudence** *noun*.

in– *prefix* meaning 'not' when added to the beginning of certain words. *inadequate* (not adequate), *inactive* (not active), *inconsistent* (not consistent).

inarticulate *adjective* unable to express yourself well when speaking.

inaudible *adjective* not loud enough to be heard clearly **inaudibility** *noun*.

inborn *adjective* natural and present in a person or animal from birth. *Birds have an inborn ability to build nests.*

Some species of birds, such as weaver-birds, have an inborn ability to construct complicated and distinctive nests.

incapable *adjective* unable to do things expected of you. *She's incapable of getting to school on time.*

incentive *noun* something that encourages you to do something. *He was promised a bike as an incentive to work hard.*

incessant *noun* going on and on and never stopping. *The incessant noise of the traffic.*

inch *noun* a measurement of length, equal to 2.55 centimeters. There are 12 inches in a foot. **inch by inch** very slowly.

incident *noun* a single event or happening.

incidentally *adverb* by the way. *Incidentally, I haven't eaten all day, so I'm really hungry.*

incinerator *noun* a container for burning garbage. *Our apartment builidng has an incinerator chute on each floor.*

incision *noun* a cut into a patient's body made by a surgeon during an operation.

incite *verb* to stir up and encourage people to do something, usually bad and violent. *Despite attempts to incite the crowd to riot, the demonstration remained peaceful.*

inclination *noun* a tendency or slight preference to do something. *My inclination is to try the new system before we buy it.*

incline *verb* 1 to lean or slope towards something, to bend. 2 to have a tendency or preference for doing something. *He's inclined to be a bit slow in the morning.* **incline** *noun* a slope.

include *verb* to consider or count something as a part of a whole or a group of other things. **inclusion** *noun*.

including *preposition* forming part of a larger group. *Everybody went on vacation, including our dog and cat.*

inclusive *adjective* including everything. *The price is inclusive of tax.*

incoherent *adjective* speaking in a rambling way that is not easy to follow or understand. **incoherence** *noun*.

income *noun* the money a person regularly earns. *She has an income of $30,000 a year.* **income tax** a tax that is charged on a person's income.

incompetent *adjective* lacking the ability to do a job well. **incompetence** *noun*.

incomplete *adjective* unfinished, not complete. *An incomplete set of encyclopedias was delivered to the school.*

incongruous *adjective* strange and out of place. *A skyscraper would look incongruous in a small town.*

inconsiderate *noun* thoughtless and not considering the feelings of others.

inconspicuous *adjective* small and not easily noticeable.

incorporate *verb* to include something and make a part of the whole. *The sports wing incorporates a gym and a swimming pool.*

incorrect *adjective* wrong. *We have to go back and change the incorrect answers.*

increase *verb* (say in-**krees**) to make bigger or to become bigger. **increase** *noun* (in-**krees**) *A sharp increase in prices.*

A microscope gives an increased ability to examine the structure of a leaf.

This incubator has a temperature control on the outside.

When Jane left the room, the puzzle was still incomplete.

incredible *adjective* 1 difficult or impossible to believe. *An incredible adventure story.* 2 amazing, very good. *An incredible film.*

incriminate *verb* to show that somebody is guilty of a crime.

incubator *noun* 1 a container in which premature and weak babies are kept alive and safe until they are strong. 2 a heated container for keeping eggs warm until the chicks hatch. **incubate** *verb* to keep eggs warm until they hatch.

incurable *adjective* not able to be cured or made better. *An incurable disease.*

indecent *adjective* shockingly rude and offensive. **indecency** *noun*.

indefinite *adjective* vague, not fixed or limited. *The timescale for the expedition is indefinite. We can't predict how long it will take.* **indefinite article** the adjectives 'a' and 'an'.

independent *adjective* free, not controlled by or needing help from others. *Most colonies have become independent.* **independence** *noun*.

index *noun* a section at the end of some books giving an alphabetical list and page number of all the subjects mentioned in the book. *The index in this book is very useful.*

India *noun* a country in South Asia.

India is the seventh largest country in the world and has the second largest number of people.

Indian *noun* 1 a person who comes from India. 2 a Native American. **Indian** *adjective. An Indian temple.*

indicate *verb* 1 to show or point out something. *Research indicates that vitamin C helps shorten the length of a cold. The conductor indicated a chair in the first row of the string section and invited me to sit down.* 2 to be a sign of. *Dark clouds indicate rain.* **indication** *noun. He gave no indication of his intentions.*

indifferent *adjective* 1 having no feelings and not caring. *She is indifferent to what people think of her.* 2 not very good. *It is an indifferent plot.* **indifference** *noun*.

indigestion *noun* pain you get in your stomach when you have eaten too much and have difficulty in digesting your food. **indigestible** *adjective*.

indirect *adjective* not direct or straightforward. *An indirect route.*

Roads often have to take an indirect route across country.

individual *adjective* 1 relating to one person or thing and not to a group. *She has individual golf lessons from the pro.* 2 having an unusual quality or way of behaving. *He has an individual way of walking.* **individual** *noun* a single person. **individually** *adjective* separately.

individuality *noun* a quality that makes a person or thing different and stand out from others. *It won for its individuality.*

Indonesia *noun* a country in Southeast Asia, made up of Sumatra, Java and many other islands.

indulge *verb* 1 If you indulge in something you take great pleasure in it, even if it is bad for you. 2 To indulge somebody is to let them have or do what they want, to spoil them. **indulgence** *noun*. **indulgent** *adjective*. *They're very indulgent grandparents.*

industrial *adjective* concerning industry and factories. *The industrial regions of Italy.* **Industrial Revolution** the name given to the widespread use of machines in factories during the 18th and 19th centuries, particularly in Britain.

industrialist *noun* a person who owns an industry.

industrious *adjective* hardworking.

industry *noun* 1 work and the making of things in factories. 2 a particular business or branch of industry. *The car industry.* 3 hard work.

inefficient *adjective* not working well and wasting time or energy.

GRAMMAR NOTE

Indirect speech is reported speech and not the exact words of the speaker. 'He said he was happy to be home,' is indirect speech. "I am happy to be home," he said.' is direct speech.

During the Industrial Revolution, many factories and railroads were built.

inert *adjective* without power and unable to move. **inertia** *noun* lack of energy.

inevitable *adjective* sure to happen or impossible to stop. **inevitability** *noun*.

infamous *adjective* well known or famous for being bad. *An infamous thief.*

infant *noun* a very young child. **infancy** *noun* the time of being an infant.

infantry *noun* soldiers who fight on foot.

Soldiers in the infantry have to be in good shape, because they march long distances carrying heavy equipment.

infatuated *adjective* to have such a strong love for somebody that you cannot think sensibly about them. **infatuation** *noun*.

infect *verb* to fill with germs or to pass on a disease to somebody. *He infected the whole class with his cold.*

infection *noun* a disease caused by germs. *She has an eye infection.*

infectious *adjective* a disease or condition that can spread easily from one person to another. *Her enthusiasm is infectious.*

inferior *adjective* not so good or important in rank or quality. The opposite of inferior is superior. *An inferior bottle of wine.*

inferiority complex Somebody who has an inferiority complex always thinks that he or she is less important or less good than others.

infertile *adjective* 1 unable to produce babies. 2 Infertile land is of such poor quality that crops will not grow.

infested *adjective* full of pests such as insects or rats. *The chicken coop was infested with fleas.*

infinite *adjective* endless and without limits, so great that it cannot be measured or imagined. *I loved him for his infinite kindness towards animals.* **infinity** *noun*.

infinitive *adjective* the basic form of a verb, sometimes with 'to' in front of it. *To go, to dream, to plan, to talk, to visit.*

inflammable *adjective* catching fire easily.

inflate *verb* to make something expand by filling it with air or gas. *They inflated the balloons with a pump.*

Scuba divers often use inflatable rafts to take them out to dive sites.

inflation *noun* a rise in prices.

inflexible *adjective* unable to bend or change in any way. *Inflexible rules.*

inflict *verb* to make somebody suffer pain or something unpleasant.

influence *noun* 1 the power you have to make somebody do something or cause something to happen. 2 a person who has such power. *His uncle was a great influence on his decision to become an actor.* **influence** *verb*. **influential** *adjective*.

influenza or flu *noun* an infectious disease that gives you headaches, fever and aching muscles. *I was in bed for a week with the flu.*

inform *verb* to tell somebody about something. *Please keep me informed.*

informal *adjective* 1 friendly and relaxed, not following rules. *Informal clothes.* 2 used in ordinary conversation or writing. *'Hi' is an informal way of saying 'hello'.* **informality** *noun*.

information *noun* all the facts or knowledge about something. *Can you give me any information about the crash?*

information technology the use of computers to store, arrange and send out information.

informative *adjective* giving useful or helpful facts. *It's an informative program about endangered animals.*

ingenious *adjective* clever and imaginative. *An ingenious invention.* **ingenuity** *noun*.

Ingots are pieces of cast metal molded into a form useful for transport and storage.

SPELLING NOTE

The opposite word for 'inflate' is 'deflate', and the opposite word for 'inhale' is 'exhale'.

AMAZING FACT

Influenza is a very common disease and is not normally serious. But in 1918-19, a flu epidemic killed about 20 million people around the world.

Injections are required for travel to some countries.

---

ingot *noun* a lump of metal, usually in the shape of a brick. *The Queen was presented with a gold ingot.*

ingredient *noun* any one of a number of things that go into a mixture from which something is made, particularly in cooking. *Flour, eggs and milk are ingredients of pancake batter.*

inhabit *verb* to live in a place. *The island is not inhabited.*

inhabitant *noun* the people or animals that live in a place or country. *The inhabitants of the island speak a unique dialect.*

inhale *verb* to breathe in. *She inhaled the clean mountain air.*

inhaler *noun* a container that people who suffer from diseases such as asthma use to breathe in medicine. *The doctor gave him an inhaler to ease his breathing.*

inherit *verb* 1 to receive something such as money or property from somebody who has died. *She inherited the house from her aunt.* 2 to have the same qualities or characteristics as your parents or ancestors. *He has inherited his father's sense of humor!* **inheritance** *noun*.

inhuman *adjective* cruel, showing no kindness or pity. **inhumanity** *noun*.

initial *noun* (say in-ish-ul) the first letter of a word or name. *Robin Ashe's initials are R.A.* **initial** *adjective* first or at the beginning. *My initial reaction is good.*

initiative *noun* the ability to do things on your own and to lead the way. *Charlie showed a lot of initiative and got the job done quickly and well.*

inject *verb* to use a hollow needle to put liquid medicine into somebody's body. **injection** *noun*. *Billy didn't like having injections at the dentist.*

injure *verb* to hurt or damage a part of a person's or an animal's body. *She injured her arm when she fell.* **injury** *noun*.

ink *noun* a colored liquid used for writing with a pen or for printing.

Some people prefer to write with a fountain pen, even though it is less convenient.

inkling *noun* a slight idea, a hint. *She had no inkling I'd be at the party.*

inland *adjective* away from the sea and towards the middle of a country.

inn *noun* a small hotel, usually in the country.

inner *adjective* on the inside and near the middle. *The inner tube of my bike tire was completely worn out.*

innocent *adjective* 1 without blame or guilt. *The prisoner was innocent.* 2 harmless. *Innocent fun.* **innocence** *noun*.

innovation *noun* something that is completely new. A new invention or way of doing things.

innumerable *adjective* too many to be counted. *Innumerable stars in the sky.*

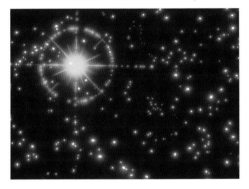

On a clear night, you can see innumerable stars in the sky.

inoculate *verb* to protect somebody from a disease by injecting them with a weak form of the disease. **inoculation** *noun*.

input *noun* information that you put into a computer. **input** *verb*.

inquest *noun* an official inquiry to find out why somebody suddenly died.

inquire *verb* to ask questions to find out about something. *Madge inquired about the times of trains.*

inquiry *noun* 1 a question. 2 a detailed and official investigation. *There was an inquiry into the cause of the fire.*

inquisitive *noun* eager to find out about things, always asking questions.

SPELLING NOTE

Note that 'inoculate' has only one 'n' and one 'l'. Also note that 'inquire' and 'inquiry' can be spelled 'enquire', 'enquiry'.

AMAZING FACT

Edward Jenner first inoculated a person in 1796. He injected a boy with cowpox as a vaccine against smallpox.

insanitary *adjective* unclean and likely to harm people's health by causing disease.

inscribe *verb* to write or carve words on to the hard surface of something.

inscription *noun* words written or carved on something.

insect *noun* a small animal with six legs, no backbone, and usually with wings. An insect has three parts to its body. Beetles, butterflies and flies are insects.

Butterflies are some of the world's most beautiful insects.

insecticide *noun* a poison that is used to kill insects that are pests.

insert *verb* to put something inside something else.

inside *noun* the interior and center part of something, near the middle. *The inside of my mouth is sore.* **inside** *preposition. The owl lives with its young family inside the hollow tree.* **inside** *adverb. Come inside a minute.* **inside out** the inside of a piece of clothing turned to the outside. The opposite of inside is outside.

insight *noun* having a clear understanding of something. *An insight into his behavior.*

insincere *adjective* not honest and pretending to have feelings about something. *He said he liked me but I knew he was insincere.*

insipid *adjective* without taste, dull. *An insipid bowl of soup.*

insist *verb* to demand and be very firm in asking or doing something. *He insisted on paying for lunch.* **insistent** *adjective*.

insolent *adjective* rude and insulting. *Insolent behavior.* **insolence** *noun*.

insoluble *adjective* 1 If something is insoluble, it will not dissolve. 2 A problem that is insoluble cannot be solved.

The molecules of an insoluble solid are joined together in a regular pattern.

insomnia *noun* sleeplessness or difficulty in going to sleep.

inspect *verb* to look at every part of something very carefully, to check. **inspection** *noun*.

inspire *verb* to influence somebody and encourage them to feel confident and enthusiastic about what they are doing. *The teacher inspired me to study harder.* **inspiration** *noun*. **inspiring** *adjective*.

install *verb* 1 to put something in a place ready to be used. *He installed a new heater.* 2 to give somebody an important position. *She was ceremonially installed as mayor.*

installment *noun* one of the parts into which something is divided. An episode. *An installment of the story was read every evening on the radio.* 2 one of a series of regular payments for something.

instant *noun* a very short time. *He paused for an instant.* **instant** *adjective* 1 happening right away. *An instant success.* 2 able to be prepared very quickly. *Instant soup.*

It's very convenient to have a mug of instant soup at lunchtime.

instead *adverb* in place of something or somebody. *Can I have milk instead of cream in my coffee?*

instinct *noun* behavior that is natural and does not have to be thought about or learnt. *Birds build their nests by instinct.* **instinctive** *adjective*. *Instinctive behavior.*

institute *noun* an organization that is established for a particular purpose. *A medical research institute.* **institute** *verb* to start something. *To institute reforms.*

institution *noun* 1 a large or important organization. *Hospitals, prisons, universities and other institutions.* 2 an established custom, habit or tradition. *Putting up decorations at Christmas is an institution.*

instruct *verb* 1 to teach or tell somebody how to do something. 2 to tell somebody what to do. *The teacher instructed the boys to wait until the bell rang.* **instruction** *noun*.

instructions *plural noun* directions or words that tell you how to do something. *Read the instructions carefully before connecting the computer.*

instructive *adjective* giving helpful information. *An instructive talk.*

AMAZING FACT

'Inspire' comes from a word that originally meant 'breathe in'.

SPELLING NOTE

Try not to confuse 'intense', meaning 'extreme' or 'very strong', as in 'intense heat' with 'intensive', meaning 'thorough' or 'concentrated', as in 'an intensive language course'.

---

instructor *noun* a person who instructs you to do something. *She's our yoga instructor.*

instrument *noun* 1 a device or tool you use to help you with your work. *Scientific instruments.* 2 A musical instrument is an object such as a piano or a guitar that you play to make music.

insulate *verb* to cover something with a material that will not let heat or electricity escape from it. *Electric wires are insulated with rubber or plastic.* **insulation** *noun*.

Safety demands that electrical wires should be fully insulated.

insult *verb* (say in-**sult**) to upset somebody by saying something rude to them or behaving in a bad way. **insult** *noun* (say **in**-sult). *It was an insult to my intelligence.*

insurance *noun* small sums of money (premiums) you pay regularly to an organization (an insurance company) that agrees to protect you and give you an amount of money to replace something of yours that has been stolen or damaged, or to pay medical bills if you injure yourself or become ill etc.

intact *adjective* not damaged, complete and not changed. *My feelings for her remain intact, despite the way she has behaved.*

intake *noun* 1 the number of people taken in. *A high intake of students.* 2 the process of taking something in. *The news was greeted by a sharp intake of breath.*

integrate *verb* 1 to combine people, often of different races, into one community. 2 to fit different parts together. **integration** *noun*.

integrity *noun* complete honesty and trustworthiness. *She's a woman of integrity.*

intelligent *adjective* clever and able to learn and understand things quickly and easily. **intelligence** *noun*.

Chimpanzees are intelligent creatures that can be taught many human skills.

intend *verb* to plan or have in mind to do something. *She intends to visit her sister.*

intense *adjective* 1 very strong or great. *Intense cold.* 2 very serious and with strong feelings. *He gets very intense about his work.* **intensity** *noun.*

intensive *adjective* 1 very thorough. *Intensive investigations.* 2 concentrated. *The patient is in intensive care.*

intention *noun* what you intend or plan to do. *Please state your intentions clearly.*

intentional *adjective* intended or done on purpose. *Intentional damage.*

inter- *prefix* among or between. *Interplanetary travel.*

interact *verb* to have an effect on one another. *All the chemicals in this experiment interact with one another.*

interaction *noun* the action or influence of people or things on one another.

interactive *adjective* (in computers) the exchange of information between a computer and the user.

intercept *verb* to stop somebody or something that is moving from one place to another. *He intercepted the ball in mid-air.*

The player cleverly intercepted the ball and passed it back to her own team.

interest *verb* to want to learn or find out more about something. **interest** *noun* 1 *He has a great interest in geology.* 2 extra money you pay to a bank etc. for money you have borrowed.

interested *adjective* wanting to find out or learn more about something.

interesting *adjective* If something is interesting you want to find out more about it. *Archaeology is a very interesting subject.*

interface *noun* in computing, a connection that allows two pieces of equipment to be operated together.

interfere *verb* to meddle or take part in something that has nothing to do with you. **interference** *noun.*

interior *noun* the inside part of something. **interior** *adjective. Interior design.*

interjection *noun* a word or phrase used to express surprise, pain etc. *'Ouch! It hurts.'*

The new plan of the house showed internal features, such as the staircase.

AMAZING FACT

Be careful not to confuse the two prefixes 'inter-' meaning 'between' and 'intra-' meaning 'within'. Think of the Internet, a system of connected computers around the world, and 'intranet' which is a system of connected computers, usually within a company.

DID YOU KNOW

'Interfere' was once used about horses and referred to when a horse struck its fetlock with the hoof of the opposite foot. It then came to mean 'to collide' and later 'to intervene'.

internal *adjective* relating to the inside of something or somebody. *The internal organs of the body.*

international *adjective* concerning several nations or countries. *An international peace-keeping force flew into the country.*

interpret *verb* 1 to translate or put the words of one language into another. 2 to decide or explain what something means. *He interpreted her nod as meaning 'yes'.* **interpretation** *noun.*

interpreter *noun* a person who translates from one language into another.

interrupt *verb* 1 to stop somebody while they are talking or doing something. *I'm reading, so don't interrupt me.* 2 to disturb or stop something happening for a short time. *Thunder interrupted the lesson.* **interruption** *noun.*

interval *noun* 1 a period of time between two dates or events. 2 a short break in a play or concert. **at intervals** happening sometimes but not constantly.

intervene *verb* to become involved in or join in something such as an argument to stop it happening. **intervention** *noun.*

intervening *adjective* the time between two events. *The intervening years.*

interview *noun* a meeting at which a person is asked questions to see if he or she is suitable for a job. A meeting at which things are discussed. **interview** *verb. He was interviewed for the job.*

intestines *plural noun* the long tube that food passes through after it has left our stomach.

The intestines are coiled inside the abdomen.

intimate *adjective* (say in-tim-at) 1 very friendly and close. *Intimate relations.* 2 personal and private. *Intimate details.*

I

intimidate *verb* to frighten somebody violently to make them do something you want, to threaten. **intimidation** *noun*.

intolerant *adjective* unable to put up with people with ideas or beliefs that are different from yours. **intolerance** *noun*.

intoxicated *adjective* having drunk too much alcohol. *Peter was intoxicated.*

intrepid *adjective* brave and bold, without fear. *Intrepid explorers.*

intricate *adjective* complicated and hard to follow, detailed. *An intricate pattern.*

intrigue *noun* (say **in**-treeg) a scheme or plot. *Intrigue was everywhere before the surprise party.*

intrigue *verb* (say in-**treeg**) to interest or fascinate somebody. *Animal behavior has always intrigued me.*

introduce *verb* 1 to make people known to one anotherfor the first time. *Can you introduce me?* 2 to bring in something or use it for the first time.

introduction *noun* 1 the act of introducing somebody or something. 2 a piece of writing at the beginning of a book telling you what it is about. 3 a first experience of something. *An introduction to the Internet.*

The introduction to the book described how fruits are formed.

intrude *verb* to enter somewhere or join in something when you are not wanted or have not been invited. To disturb. **intrusion** *noun*. **intrusive** *adjective*.

intruder *noun* somebody who intrudes or breaks in, such as a burglar.

intuition *noun* a feeling or understanding about something that you do not have to think about but cannot explain in a logical way. *His intuition told him that something was seriously wrong.*

The silk scarf was designed with an intricate pattern in gorgeous colors.

inundate *verb* 1 to flood. 2 to receive so much of something that you cannot cope with it, to overwhelm. *She was inundated with job offers.* **inundation** *noun*.

invade to send troops into another country or place to fight the people living there and to take control of it. **invasion** *noun*.

invalid *noun* (say **in**-val-id) a person who is ill or disabled.

invalid *adjective* (say in-**val**-id) something that is not legal and so cannot be used. *Your ticket is out of date and therefore invalid.*

invaluable *adjective* very valuable or priceless, very useful. *Learning to ride a bike is an invaluable experience.*

invent *verb* 1 to make something or think of something for the first time. *Who invented the computer?* 2 to make something up that is not true. *She invented an excuse so she wouldn't have to go to the dentist.*

invention *noun* something that has been invented. *A terrific new invention.*

inventive *adjective* able to think up new ideas, original. *Peter is very inventive.*

inventor *noun* a person who invents things.

invertebrate *noun* any animal without a backbone such as an insect, slug or worm.

The common garden worm is an invertebrate.

invest *verb* to put money into a bank or company in order to get more money back as a result. *We invested our savings in government bonds.*

investigate *verb* to try to find out all the facts about something, to examine carefully. *The police are investigating the boy's disappearance.* **investigation** *noun*.

invisible *adjective* something that cannot be seen. *Air is invisible.*

invitation *noun* written or spoken words asking you to come to something such as a party. *We made our own invitations.*

invite *verb* to ask somebody to come to something or to go somewhere. *He invited us to a Halloween party.*

inviting *adjective* tempting or attractive. *An inviting warm fire.*

invoice *noun* a document asking for payment for goods that have been sent or for work that has been done.

involve *verb* 1 to be necessary as a part of a job. *The job involves a lot of letter writing.* 2 to be interested in and concerned with. **involvement** *noun*.

IQ *abbreviation* intelligence quotient, a way of measuring a person's intelligence by asking special questions.

Iran *noun* a country in Southwest Asia.

Iranian *noun* a person who comes from Iran. **Iranian** *adjective. Iranian oil wells.*

Iraq *noun* a country in Southwest Asia.

Iraq is an Arab state at the top of the Persian Gulf. Its economy is built on reserves of oil.

irate *adjective* (say eye-rate) angry and complaining. *She wrote an irate letter to the editor.*

Ireland *noun* a country in Northwest Europe.

iris *noun* 1 a tall garden flower. 2 the colored part of your eye.

Irish *adjective* connected to or relating to Ireland and its people (the Irish). *It's a beautiful Irish song.*

iron *noun* 1 a heavy gray metal that is one of the chemical elements. 2 an electrical tool that heats up and which you use to smooth wrinkles out of clothes. **ironing** *noun.*

irony *noun* the use of words to say the very opposite of what they mean. *'It was nice of you to smash my best plate!'* **ironic** *adjective. It's ironic that I broke my leg after we'd come back down the trail.*

irregular *adjective* 1 not regular or usual. *He works irregular hours.* 2 not even or smooth.

irrigate *verb* to supply water for crops on dry land by means of ditches, pipes, canals etc. **irrigation** *noun.*

irritable *adjective* easily annoyed, in a bad mood. *Dad was in an irritable mood.*

irritate *verb* 1 to make somebody annoyed or impatient. 2 to make your skin feel sore or itchy. **irritation** *noun.*

Islam *noun* a religion that Muslims follow. It is based on the teachings of the prophet Muhammad. **Islamic** *adjective.*

The flag of Israel features the star of David on a white ground bordered with blue stripes.

AMAZING FACT

Be careful when you are writing 'it's' (a contraction of either 'it is' or 'it has') and 'its' (which means 'a characteristic of or something that belongs to it').

In 'it's' the apostrophe takes the place of the letters that are left out. for example, 'It's a nice day for a picnic.'

'Its' doesn't have an apostrophe: 'A robin built its nest in a tree in our back yard.'

An irrigation channel brought water to the parched fields.

Islamabad *noun* the capital of Pakistan.

island *noun* a piece of land surrounded by water. *She is buried on an island in the lake.*

isle *noun* an island, usually used as part of its name. *Isle of Skye.*

isobar *noun* a line on a weather map that connects places with the same or equal atmospheric pressure.

isolate *verb* to place something apart from others and by itself, to separate. *She had to be isolated because she had an infectious disease.* **isolation** *noun.*

Israel *noun* a country in the Middle East.

issue *noun* 1 an edition of a newspaper or magazine brought out at a particular time. *Today's issue has the latest news.* 2 something that is given out, a supply. 3 a problem or an important topic for discussion. *The issue of bullying.* **issue** *verb* to supply with. *The hikers were issued with special boots.* **take issue with** to disagree.

isthmus *noun* a narrow strip of land that joins two larger pieces of land.

IT *abbreviation* information technology, the use of computers to store and retrieve information.

Italian *noun* 1 a person who comes from Italy. 2 the language spoken in Italy. **Italian** *adjective. Italian opera.*

Italy *noun* a country in southern Europe.

itch *noun* an uncomfortable, tingling feeling on your skin that makes you want to scratch yourself. **itch** (itches, itching, itched) *verb. My mosquito bite itches.*

item *noun* a single thing on a list or in a group of other things. *An item of news.*

ivory *noun* the hard, smooth white material that the tusks of elephants and some other animals are made of.

Ivory Coast *noun* a country in Africa.

ivy *noun* a climbing evergreen plant with shiny, pointed leaves.

The Ivy League universities in the US are not so called becuse they are covered in ivy. They originally numbered 4 – written with the Roman numerals IV.

Jj

jab (jabs, jabbing, jabbed) *verb* to hit or stab with something pointed. **jab** *noun* a quick, short punch.

jack *noun* 1 a tool for lifting something heavy such as a car off the ground. 2 a picture playing card with a value between the ten and the queen.

jackal *noun* a wild animal of the dog family that feeds off the dead bodies of other animals. *Jackals come from Asia and Africa.*

jackass *noun* a male donkey.

jacket *noun* 1 a short coat that covers the top half of your body. 2 a covering for something. *A book jacket.*

jackknife *verb* when the trailer of a semi truck suddenly bends around towards the cab. *The truck jackknifed on the ice and blocked traffic in both directions.*

jackpot *noun* the biggest prize to be won in a game or a lottery.

jacuzzi *noun* a bathtub with underwater jets that make the water swirl.

jade *noun* a precious green stone used in making jewelery.

jaded *adjective* bored and tired and lacking in enthusiasm.

jagged *adjective* with many sharp, rough and uneven points. *We walked carefully along the jagged rocks.*

jaguar *noun* a South American wild cat with yellow and black spots like a leopard.

The jaguar turned and growled as it heard us approach.

jail *noun* a a prison where people are kept as a punishment for committing a crime.

Jakarta *noun* the capital of Indonesia.

jam *noun* 1 a sweet, sticky food made by boiling fruit and sugar together 2 a lot of vehicles or people crowded so closely together that they cannot move easily. *Sorry we're late, we got stuck in a traffic jam.* **in a jam** in a difficult situation.

SPELLING NOTE

The letter J developed from the letter I during the Middle Ages and was used to show an I at the beginning of a word. Later it became a symbol for the consonant J as in 'jewel' and 'jolly'.

jam (jams, jamming, jammed) *verb* 1 to get stuck or to make something get stuck so that it cannot move. *The door has jammed and I can't open it.* 2 to fill and press things tightly in a place. *Kevin jammed the bag into the trunk of the car.* **jam-packed** packed very tightly.

The Jamaican flag has a diagonal yellow cross bisecting a green and black ground.

Jamaica *noun* a country in the West Indies.

Jamaican *noun* a person who comes from Jamaica. **Jamaican** *adjective*. *Jamaican sugar.*

jangle *verb* to make a ringing noise like pieces of metal banging together. *The bracelets jangled as she raised her arms.*

January *noun* the first month of the year. January has 31 days.

Japan *noun* a country in East Asia.

Japanese *noun* 1 somebody who comes from Japan. 2 the language spoken in Japan. **Japanese** *adjective*. *Japanese gardens.*

Sumo wrestling is a very popular sport among the Japanese.

jar *noun* a glass container with a lid for storing food such as jam.

jar (jars, jarring, jarred) *verb* 1 to make an irritating noise that has an unpleasant effect on people. *The loud music jarred her nerves.* 2 to jolt or give a sudden shock.

jargon *noun* the special technical language used by a particular group of people. *Computer jargon.*

jaunt *noun* a trip or short journey made for pleasure. *A jaunt to the beach.*

jaunty *adjective* cheerful and carefree. *A jaunty walk.* **jauntiness** *noun*.

javelin *noun* a short, light spear thrown by hand, usually in athletic sports.

jaw *noun* one of two large bones in your mouth that hold your teeth. Your jaws move up and down when your speak and eat.

jazz *noun* a type of music with a very strong rhythm. *Their music is a jazz-reggae fusion.*

The javelin is one of the events in the Olympic Games.

jealous *adjective* unhappy because you want what somebody else has. **jealousy** *noun*. *Jealousy poisons the mind.*

jeans *noun* pants made from a strong cotton material called denim.

jeer *verb* to make fun of somebody in a rude, loud and unkind way, to mock.

jelly *noun* a clear, sticky, sweet food made from fruit or fruit juice. *My sister loves peanut butter and jelly sandwiches.*

jellyfish *noun* a sea animal without a backbone (invertebrate) that looks like a blob or a plastic bag floating on the surface.

Because of their transparent bodies, it is sometimes hard to spot jellyfish floating in the water. Some of them have stinging tentacles.

jeopardy *noun* (say jep-ur-dee) If somebody or something is in jeopardy they are in danger or somehow threatened.

jerk *verb* to move or pull something suddenly and quickly. **jerk** *noun*.

jersey (jerseys) *noun* a shirt worn as part of a sports uniform.

Jerusalem *noun* the capital of Israel.

jest *noun* a joke or something said or done for fun. **in jest** as a joke.

jester an entertainer at a royal court during the Middle Ages.

jet *noun* 1 a strong stream of liquid or gas forced under pressure. *The fountain threw up jets of water.* 2 an aircraft that is driven forward by a strong jet of air forced out of the back of the engine (a jet engine).

jet-lag *noun* great tiredness and a feeling of confusion that some people have after a plane trip across several time zones.

jetty *noun* a pier or landing stage where boats can moor and unload.

WORD HISTORY

The name 'jeans' comes from the name of the material they are made from: 'jenes' or 'geanes', the French names for the city of Genova where the cloth was first made.

The jesters danced and sang for the entertainment of the King and Queen.

Jew *noun* 1 a person of the Hebrew race described in the Old Testament of the Bible. 2 a person who follows the religion of Judaism. **Jewish** *adjective*.

jewel *noun* a beautiful and precious stone such as a ruby or emerald.

jewelry *noun* rings, bracelets, necklaces. earrings and other ornaments that people wear.

This gold necklace is part of a collection of jewelry that dates from the Bronze Age.

jiffy *noun* a very short time. *I'll be back in a jiffy.*

jig *noun* a lively folk dance. **jig** *verb*.

jigsaw *noun* a puzzle made up of pieces of cardboard or wood cut in different shapes that you fit together to form a picture.

jingle *noun* 1 the ringing sound made by small bells or keys knocking together. **jingle** *verb*. *She jingled the coins in her pocket.* 2 a simple but catchy tune or song used in radio and TV commercials.

jinx *noun* something that is thought to bring bad luck. *There is a jinx on this book.*

job *noun* 1 the work that somebody does regularly to earn money. 2 a task or a particular piece of work that has to be done. 3 a type of thing. *Our new camera is one of those digital jobs.* **good/nice job** to do something well. *Dad said I did a nice job on the lawn.*

jockey (jockeys) *noun* a person whose job it is to ride horses in races.

The jockey urged the horse on to win the race.

jodhpurs *plural noun* (say **jod**-purz) close-fitting pants that you wear for riding a horse. *Jodhpurs and riding boots.*

jog (jogs, jogging, jogged) *verb* 1 to run at a slow steady pace for exercise. 2 to push or shake something gently. *She jogged my arm and I spilled my pop.* **jog somebody's memory** to make somebody remember something.

join *verb* 1 to connect together. 2 to become a member of a club or organization. 3 to unite or come together. **join the club** something people say when they are in the same situation. *You got a D? Join the club!*

joint *noun* 1 a place where two things join and are fixed. 2 a place where two bones in your body are joined together, such as your elbow or knee. **joint** *adjective* shared by two or more people. *I can't take all the credit, it was a joint effort.*

The joints found in the human body are, from left to right, ball and socket, pivot, saddle and hinge.

joke *noun* something that you say or do that makes people laugh. **joke** *verb*. **beyond a joke** not at all funny but very serious.

joker *noun* 1 somebody who tells jokes. 2 an extra card in a pack of playing cards which in certain games may have any value.

jolly (jollier, jolliest) *adjective* happy, cheerful and full of fun.

jolt *verb* to move suddenly and roughly, to jerk. *The train jolted to a halt.*

Jordan *noun* a country in the Middle East.

The flag of Jordan has a red triangle with a white star on a black, white and green background.

Jordanian *noun* a person who comes from Jordan. **Jordanian** *adjective*. *Jordanian oil.*

jostle *verb* to shove or push and bump into people roughly.

jot (jots, jotting, jotted) *verb* to write down something quickly and briefly. *He jotted down a list of things he wanted.*

journal *noun* (say **jer**-nul) 1 a diary or daily record of things you have done etc. 2 a magazine, especially one that deals with a particular subject. *The Nursing Journal.*

journalese *noun* (say jer-nul-**eez**) a style of careless and far-fetched writing used in some newspapers and magazines.

journalism *noun* (say **jer**-nul-izum) the job of gathering news and writing articles for newspapers and magazines.

journalist *noun* (say **jer**-nul-ist) a person who writes or edits articles for a newspaper or magazine.

journey (journeys) *noun* (say **jer**-nee) the act of travelling from one place to another, a trip. **journey** *verb*.

joust *noun* (say **jow**-st) a sporting fight in the Middle Ages between two knights on horses, using long spears. **joust** *verb*.

WORD HISTORY

'Jubilee' comes from a Hebrew word 'yobel', meaning a ram's horn. The ram's horn was blown to proclaim a year of celebration, especially a celebration held every 50 years.

joy *noun* 1 a feeling of great happiness. 2 success or luck. The opposite of joy is sorrow.

joyride *noun* a ride in a stolen car, to experience danger. **joyrider** *noun*.

jubilee *noun* a celebration to commemorate an important event. **silver jubilee** a celebration of a 25th anniversary. **golden jubilee** a celebration of a 50th anniversary. **diamond jubilee** a celebration of a 60th anniversary.

Judaism *noun* the religion of the Jewish people. *He converted to Judaism.*

judge *noun* 1 a person who hears cases in a court of law and decides how a guilty person should be punished. 2 a person who decides who is the winner of a competition. 3 a person who forms an opinion about something. *She's a good judge of character.* **judgement** *noun*.

judo *noun* a Japanese sport of self-defence in which two people wrestle, using special movements, and try to throw each other to the ground.

jug *noun* a container with a handle and a lip part for pouring liquids.

juggle *verb* to keep throwing and catching a number of objects, such as balls, in the air without dropping them. *We learned to juggle at camp last summer. I'm pretty good at it now.* **juggler** *noun*.

juice *noun* (rhymes with loose) the liquid you can squeeze from fruit and vegetables. **juicy** *adjective*. *Mavis bit into a juicy orange.* **juiciness** *noun*.

juke-box *noun* a machine that plays music you select when you put coins into it.

Jousting only takes place in pageants and fairs these days.

July *noun* the seventh month of the year. July has 31 days.

jumble *verb* to mix things up so that they are an untidy mess. *She jumbled up the pieces of the jigsaw puzzle.* **jumble** *noun* a messy and mixed collection of things. *The floor of my closet is a jumble of clothes and shoes.*

jumbo *adjective* very large. **jumbo jet** a large passenger plane, a 747.

The jumbo jet took off with the 350 passengers aboard.

jump *verb* 1 to leap or throw your body up into the air. 2 to go over something by leaping. **jump** *noun* something you jump over. *The horse is coming to the last jump.* **jump at** to accept enthusiastically. *He jumped at the chance to go riding.*

jumper *noun* a dress without sleeves that you usually wear a blouse under.

jumpy (jumpier, jumpiest) *adjective* nervous. *My mistake made me feel jumpy.*

junction *noun* a place where railroad lines or roads join or cross over.

June *noun* the sixth month of the year. June has 30 days.

jungle *noun* a dense forest in a tropical country. *I spent a year exploring the jungle.*

WORD HISTORY

The name 'July' comes from the Latin word for this month. The month was named by the Romans in honor of the general and statesman Julius Caesar.

junior *adjective* 1 of lower rank or importance. *A junior executive.* 2 of or for younger people. *A junior dictionary.*

junk *noun* 1 things that are old and useless or worthless. 2 a Chinese sailing boat with a flat bottom.

Traditional junks can still be seen in modern Hong Kong harbor.

junk food *noun* food that is not good for you but may be quick and easy to prepare.

junkie *noun* a drug addict.

junk mail *noun* leaflets and advertisements that are sent to you in the mail and which you do not want.

junk shop *noun* a place that sells second-hand clothes etc.

jury *noun* a group of people who are chosen to hear a case in a court of law and decide whether an accused person is guilty or not.

just *adjective* fair and right, honest. *A just decision was eventually reached.*

just *adverb* 1 not long ago. *She just went home.* 2 only. *Just a minute!* 3 exactly. *This is just the right color.* 4 almost not. *There is just enough to eat.*

justice *noun* 1 treatment that is just, fair and right. 2 a country's system of laws and how they are operated by the law courts. 3 a judge. *A justice of the peace.*

justify (justifies, justifying, justified) *verb* to defend or to prove that something is just and fair. *How can you justify hitting the child?* **justification** *noun*.

jut (juts, jutting, jutted) *verb* to stick out farther than other things around it, to project *The balcony juts out from the side of the house.*

jute *noun* a fiber used to make rope and coarse cloth for sacks etc.

juvenile *adjective* 1 concerning young people. 2 childish and silly. *Juvenile behavior is inappropriate here.*

The toucan, the monkey and the chameleon are all creatures of the jungle.

Kk

Kabul *noun* the capital of Afghanistan.

kaleidoscope *noun* a tube that you turn as you look through it to see changing patterns of color made by mirrors and pieces of glass fitted at one end of it.

Kampala *noun* the capital of Uganda.

kangaroo *noun* a large Australian animal with strong back legs for jumping. The female has a pouch on her stomach in which she carries her baby, called a joey. Kangaroos belong to a group of pouched animals called marsupials.

A kangaroo with her baby in her pouch is a familiar sight to travelers in Australia.

karaoke *noun* (say ka-ree-ok-kee) a kind of entertainment from Japan in which people sing pop songs to recorded music and follow the words of the song on a screen.

karate *noun* a self-defence sport originating from Japan in which two people fight one another using special kicks and blows.

Kathmandu *noun* the capital of Nepal.

kayak *noun* (say **kye**-ak) a canoe covered in canvas, originally used by the Inuit people.

Kazakhstan *noun* a country in West Asia.

Kazakhstan exports oil, metals, chemicals, grain and wool.

kebab *noun* small pieces of meat or vegetable cooked on a skewer. *A chicken kebab.*

WORD HISTORY

The shape of the letter K comes from the ancient Egyptian symbol for an open hand. Its sound comes from 'kaph', a Semitic word for an open palm of a hand.

AMAZING FACT

Kangaroos, wallabies oppossums and other marsupials begin carrying their babies in their pouches before they are fully developed. The baby may stay inside its mother for only 11 days, it continues to develop in the pouch.

Kestrels live in Europe, Asia and Africa.

keel *noun* the long piece of steel that lies along the bottom of a ship's frame.

keen *adjective* 1 eager and interested. 2 sensitive and sharp. *A keen sense of smell.* 3 quick to understand things. *A keen mind.*

keep (keeps, keeping, kept) *verb* 1 to have something and not to give it to anybody. 2 to take care of something for somebody. *Can you keep a seat for me please?* 3 to remain. *Please keep still!* 4 to remain fresh or in a good condition. *Will this meat keep until Sunday?* 5 to look after and feed. *Mary keeps goats.* **keep** *noun* the food and money etc. a person needs to live. *He earns his keep by gardening.* **keep away** stay away. **keep down** *The food disagrees with her and she can't keep it down.* **keep on** to continue. **keep to** *Keep to the path all the way.* **keep up** *Keep up with your studies.*

keep the main tower in a castle.

keeper *noun* a person whose job it is to take care of animals in a zoo or who is responsible for the objects in a museum.

keg *noun* a small barrel.

kelp *noun* a kind of seaweed used as a fertilizer. *Sea otters eat kelp.*

kennel *noun* 1 a small shelter or hut for keeping a dog in. 2 **kennels** a place where dogs are bred or where dogs can be taken care of when their owners are away.

Kenya *noun* a country in Africa.

kept past tense of keep.

kerosene *noun* oil that is burned in a lamp or stove for light or heat.

kernel *noun* the edible middle part of a nut, inside the shell.

kestrel *noun* a small falcon. Kestrels kill and eat small animals.

ketchup *noun* a thick sauce, usually made from tomatoes.

kettle *noun* a container for boiling water in. Kettles have a lid, a handle and a narrow spout for pouring.

key *noun* 1 a shaped metal object that you turn to open a lock or to start an engine. 2 the buttons on typewriters and computers or the black and white bars on a piano or organ that you press with your fingers. 3 the answers to a problem or mystery. *The key to the crime.* 4 a set of musical notes in a scale based on one note. **key** *adjective* important. *A key witness.*

keyboard *noun* 1 the set of keys on a computer, piano etc. that you press when you use them. 2 an electronic musical instrument. *A keyboard player.*

This diagram shows what is inside the keyboard of your computer.

keyhole *noun* a hole in a lock where you put the key.

keystone *noun* the stone in the center of an arch. It holds the other stones in the arch in place. *A marble keystone.*

kg *abbreviation* kilogram.

khaki *noun* a very light brown color. *He's wearing khaki slacks.*

Khartoum *noun* the capital of Sudan.

kick *verb* to hit somebody or something with your foot. 2 to move your legs around with force. **kick** *noun* 1 *The pony gave Peter a hard kick.* 2 a thrill. *She gets a kick out of pop music.* **kick-off** the kick of a ball that starts a game. **kick out** to get rid of.

kid *noun* 1 a young goat. 2 a child.

kid *verb* to tease somebody by pretending that something is true. *It's not broken. I was just kidding.*

kidnap (kidnaps, kidnapping, kidnapped) *verb* to capture somebody and keep them prisoner until you get what you demand, e.g. money. **kidnapper** *noun*.

kidney (kidneys) *noun* Your kidneys are organs in your body that keep your blood clean by removing waste products and passing them out in the form of urine.

Kiev *noun* the capital of Ukraine.

Blood is cleansed in the kidneys and waste products leave the body in urine.

Cortex

Medulla

Blood vessels

Renal artery

Renal vein

WORD BUILDER

'Kilo' is a Greek word meaning a thousand. So a kilogram is a thousand grams, a kilowatt is a thousand watts and kilobyte is a thousand bytes.

AMAZING FACT

'Kindergarden' comes from the German words 'kind' (child) and 'garten' (garden) — so its original meaning was 'children's garden'.

Kigali *noun* the capital of Rwanda.

kill *verb* to end the life of a person or animal, to destroy something. **kill** *noun* 1 the act of killing. 2 the animal killed. *The tiger stood over its kill.*

killer *noun* a person or animal that kills.

kiln *noun* a very hot oven for baking pottery and bricks to make them hard.

Pottery is baked in a kiln.

kilogram *noun* a measure of weight equal to 1,000 grams. Also called a kilo. *A kilo of sugar.*

kilometer *noun* a measure of length equal to 1,000 meters.

kilt *noun* a knee-length pleated skirt made from plaid cloth, traditionally worn by Scottish men.

kimono *noun* a long loose robe with wide sleeves, traditionally worn by Japanese women.

The Japanese wear traditional dress to perform kabuki, their national dance theater.

kin *noun* (old-fashioned) your family and relations. **next of kin** your closest relation.

kind *adjective* helpful and friendly to people, gentle. *It was kind of you to visit me in the hospital.* **kindness** *noun*.

kind *noun* a group of things that are similar. A type or sort of something. *What kind of dog is this?* **kind of** something like. *An igloo is a kind of a house built of ice.*

kindle *verb* to set light to and start something burning.

kindergarten *noun* a class for very young children, usually five or six years old, that prepares them for school. *Miss Snyder was my kindergarten teacher.*

K

king *noun* 1 a male ruler of a country. Kings are not elected but inherit their position by succeeding the previous ruler. 2 a playing card with a picture of a king on it. 3 a chesspiece. When the king is taken the game is lost.

King Henry VIII of England had six wives, but he was not a reliable husband. He divorced two wives and had two others executed. One wife died a natural death and his last wife survived him.

kingdom *noun* 1 a country that is ruled by a king or queen. 2 a division of the natural world. *The animal kingdom.*

kingfisher *noun* a brightly colored bird with a dagger-like beak that it uses to catch fish from lakes and rivers. *We saw several different types of kingfishers on the early morning boat ride across the lake.*

Kingston *noun* the capital of Jamaica.

Kingstown *noun* the capital of St Vincent and the Grenadines.

Kinshasa *noun* the capital of the Democratic Republic of the Congo (formerly Zaire).

kiosk *noun* (say **kee**-osk) a small hut-like shop on the street where you can buy things like newspapers and tickets.

Kiribati *noun* a country of many islands in the Pacific Ocean.

kiss *verb* to touch somebody with your lips as a sign of love or friendship. **kiss** *noun. My dog gave me a sloppy kiss.*

kit *noun* 1 the clothes and equipment you need to do something. *We always keep a first-aid kit in the car.* 2 all the things you need to make something. *A model airplane kit.*

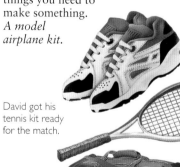

David got his tennis kit ready for the match.

AMAZING FACT

'Knickers' were originally called 'knickerbockers' after the pretended author of Washington Irving's 'History of New York', 1809.

---

kitchen *noun* a room in a house that is used for preparing and cooking food.

kite *noun* 1 a toy that you fly in the wind. It consists of a light frame covered in paper or cloth on the end of a long piece of string. 2 a bird of prey belonging to the hawk family.

kitten *noun* a very young cat. **kittenish** *adjective* behaving like a kitten, playful.

kitty *noun* a sum of money put in by several people for everybody in the group to use.

kiwi *noun* (say **kee**-wee) a New Zealand bird that cannot fly.

The kiwi is the national bird of New Zealand.

km *abbreviation* kilometer.

knack *noun* the ability to do something difficult with ease and skill.

knave *noun* (old-fashioned) a dishonest person.

knead *verb* to squeeze and stretch dough with your hands before baking. *I like making bread because kneading dough is very relaxing.*

knee *noun* the joint in the middle of your leg where it bends.

kneecap *noun* the movable bone in front of your knee.

The kneecap is also called the patella.

kneel *verb* to bend your knees and go down on them. *They knelt to pray.*

knew the past tense of know.

knickers *plural noun* short, loose pants that fit tightly at the knee.

knife (knives) *noun* a metal tool with a handle and a sharp blade that you use for cutting. **knife** *verb* to stab with a knife.

knight *noun* 1 in the Middle Ages a soldier who fought on horseback for his king or lord. 2 a man who has been given the title 'Sir' by the king or queen of Britain. 3 a chesspiece with a horse's head.

Knights used falcons for hunting.

knit (knits, knitting, knitted) *verb* 1 to make clothes by looping wool together with two long needles. 2 to join closely. *The broken bones will knit back together.*

knob *noun* a round handle on a door or drawer.

knock *verb* 1 to hit or strike something hard. *Is there somebody knocking at the door?* 2 to hit something so that it falls. *Sue knocked her mug off her desk.* **knock** *noun.*
knock out to hit somebody so hard they become unconscious.

knocker *noun* a hinged metal ring, knob or hammer on a door that you use for knocking. *He banged the door knocker.*

knot *noun* 1 a join or fastening made by tying pieces of string, rope or cloth together. 2 a hard, dark part in wood where a branch joined the tree. 3 a measure of speed for ships. 1 knot is about 1.85 kph.

knot (knots, knotting, knotted) *verb* to fasten something by tying its ends into a knot. *Fishermen's knots.*

These diagrams show how to tie a simple knot, for example in your shoelaces. Many more complicated knots are used by fishermen on their nets.

know (knows, knowing, knew, known) *verb* to have learned something or to have information about something and to have it in your mind. *Do you know how to speak French?* 2 to remember or to recognize somebody or something. *I know Maggy.*

WORD HISTORY
The word 'knight' comes from an Old English word 'cniht', meaning a boy servant or warrior.

DID YOU KNOW
The lord of a manor provided horses and armor for his knights. In time it became a great honor to be a knight, and knights formed an important part of the feudal system of the Middle Ages.

knowing *adjective* showing that you know something secret. *He knew she was lying and gave her a knowing look.*

knowledge *noun* the things that you know and understand, things that you learn by study. *A good knowledge of French.*

knowledgeable *adjective* smart and well-informed about a subject.

know-how *noun* practical knowledge and ability.

know-it-all *noun* somebody who thinks they know a lot about everything.

knuckle *noun* the bones at the joint of a finger. *I skinned my knuckles when I fell.*

koala *noun* an Australian animal that looks like a small bear. Koalas live in eucalyptus trees and feed on their leaves.

Koala bears sleep for 22 out of every 24 hours.

kookaburra *noun* an Australian bird of the kingfisher family that makes a loud laughing noise. *The kookaburra has a strange laugh.*

Koran or **Qu'ran** *noun* the holy book of Islam, the religion of the Muslims.

kosher *adjective* (say **koh**-shur) food that has been prepared in accordance with the laws of the Jewish religion.

kph *abbreviation* kilometers per hour.

Kuala Lumpur *noun* the capital of Malaysia.

Kuwait City *noun* the capital of Kuwait.

Kuwait *noun* a country in Southwest Asia.

Kuwait is a country that has grown rich because of its vast reserves of oil.

Kyrgyzstan *noun* a country in central Asia.

L1

lab *noun* a laboratory.

label *noun* a piece of paper, cloth or plastic that is attached to something and that gives information about it. **label** (labels, labelling, labelled) *verb* to put a label on something.

laboratory *noun* a room or building where scientists work.

laborious *adjective* difficult and needing a lot of hard work or effort. *Digging is a laborious job.*

labor *noun* 1 hard, physical or mental work. 2 the pain a woman feels when giving birth. 3 **Labor Day** a national holiday in the US and Canada on the first Monday in September. **labor** *verb* to work hard. **laborer** *noun* someone whose job involves physical work.

labyrinth *noun* a maze.

Labyrinths are sometimes built in large formal gardens.

lace *noun* 1 a delicate material made of fine threads woven into a pretty pattern with holes in it. 2 a long, thin cord that is threaded through holes and used, for example, to tie up a shoe or a boot. **lace** *verb. Lace up your skates tightly.*

lack *verb* to be without something that is needed or wanted. *She lacks the intelligence to be a good teacher.* **lack** *noun.*

lacquer *noun* (say **lack**-ur) a varnish or glossy paint.

lad *noun* a boy or young man.

ladder *noun* two long wooden or metal poles with cross-pieces called rungs used for climbing up or down. A set of steps.

ladle *noun* a large, deep spoon with a long handle used for lifting out liquids such as soup. *We covered our spaghetti with a big ladle of sauce.*

WORD HISTORY
The shape of the letter L comes from the ancient Egyptian symbol for a shepherd's crook. Its sound comes from 'lamed', a Semitic word for a shepherd's crook. The Greeks called the letter 'lambda'.

SPELLING NOTE
A word that sounds like 'lain' is 'lane'. Try not to confuse the two.

AMAZING FACT

Labyrinths are created by carefully planting hedges in an intricate pattern. When the plants are fully grown, they are taller than a person and so you cannot see which path to take. If you succeed in finding your way to the middle of the puzzle, there is usually a reward - a beautiful fountain or a peaceful place to sit.

lady *noun* 1 a woman, especially one with very good manners. 2 in Britain, the title of a noblewoman. *Sir John and Lady Brown.* **ladylike** *adjective. Ladylike behavior.*

ladybug *noun* a small oval flying beetle, usually with black spots on red wings. Ladybugs eat aphids and other harmful plant pests .

Ladybugs are the gardener's friend because they eat aphids.

lag (lags, lagging, lagged) *verb* to move or develop more slowly than others and so be unable to keep up. *Catch up! You're lagging behind everybody else.* **time lag** the time that passes between one event and another.

lagoon *noun* a seawater lake separated from the sea by sandbanks or rocks.

laid past tense of lay.

laid-back *adjective* (slang) relaxed and unworried. *A laid-back kind of guy.*

lain past participle of lie.

lair *noun* a den or hidden place where a wild animal sleeps.

lake *noun* a large area of fresh water with land all around it.

lamb *noun* 1 a young sheep. 2 the meat of a young sheep. *Roast lamb and mint sauce.* **lamb** *verb* to give birth (to lambs).

lame *adjective* 1 unable to walk properly because of an injured leg. *The pony is lame and walks with a limp.* **lameness** *noun.* 2 weak and not good enough. *That is such a lame excuse!* **lame duck** someone in an official position who does not have much power because their term is nearly finished.

lamp *noun* a device that gives light by burning electricity, gas, oil or a candle. *In the cabin on the river, we don't have electricity, we use kerosene lamps and candles to cook and to read.* **lamp-post** *noun* a tall post holding a street lamp. **lampshade** *noun* a cover placed over a lamp to soften its light.

lance *noun* a long spear once used by knights on horseback.

Knights tried to use their lances to knock their opponents out of their saddle.

land *noun* 1 all the dry surface of the Earth that is above the sea. 2 the ground used for farming, gardening, building etc. 3 a country or nation. **land** *verb* 1 to arrive on land from a ship. 2 to bring an aircraft down to the ground. *The plane landed at noon.* 3 to succeed in getting something. *He landed a really big contract yesterday.*

landing *noun* 1 a level area at the top of a flight of stairs. 2 bringing into ground or shore. *We made an emergency landing.*

landlady, landlord *noun* a person who rents a house or apartment to somebody.

landmark *noun* some building or object that you can see clearly from a distance. *The church steeple is a clear landmark.*

landscape *noun* a wide view or all that you can see from one place.

lane *noun* 1 a narrow country road. 2 one of the strips on a road that is wide enough for a single line of traffic. 3 a strip of track or water for a runner or swimmer.

language *noun* 1 all the words that we use to talk or write to one another. Human speech. 2 the system of words used in one or more countries. *Spanish is the language spoken in Spain and in most of South America.* 3 any other system of communicating. *Sign language.*

lanky *adjective* tall and thin.

lantern *noun* a container, often with glass sides, for holding a candle or oil lamp.

Laos *noun* a country in Southeast Asia.

The flag of Laos shows red and blue stripes and a white circle.

lap *noun* 1 the top, flat part of your legs when you are sitting down. 2 one trip around a track or the length of a pool.

lap (laps, lapping, lapped) *verb* An animal laps up water by flicking it into its mouth with its tongue.

The American presidents carved in the rock at Mount Rushmore in South Dakota are an instantly recognizable landmark.

La Paz *noun* the seat of government of Bolivia.

lapel *noun* the part below the collar of a jacket that folds back on the chest.

lapse *noun* 1 a small careless mistake. 2 a period of time that has passed.

laptop *noun* a small portable computer that you can use on your lap.

lard *noun* fat from pigs, used in cooking.

large *adjective* big in size, amount etc., not small. **largeness** *noun*. **at large** free after escaping. *The zoo's lion is still at large.*

largely *adverb* mostly.

lark *noun* a small brown bird that flies high in the sky and sings beautifully.

larva (larvae) *noun* an insect at its first stage of development after coming out of the egg and before becoming a pupa. A grub. A larva looks like a worm.

laser *noun* a device that produces a very narrow and powerful beam of light, used for cutting in surgery.

Precision cutting can be carried out with a laser.

lash *verb* 1 to hit violently, as with a whip. *The waves lashed against the rocks.* 2 to make rapid movements like a whip. *The cat lashed its tail in anger.* **lash** *noun* 1 a whip. 2 one of the small hairs growing around the eye (eyelash).

lasso *noun* (say lass-**oo**) a long rope with a loop or noose at one end, used to catch cattle and horses. **lasso** *verb*.

last *adjective* 1 coming after all the others. *The last horse in the race.* 2 the only one remaining. *The last piece of cake.* 3 most recent, just past. *Last night.* 4 previous or one before this one. *Her last job was very stressful.*

last *verb* 1 to continue. *The concert lasted four hours.* 2 to remain in good condition for some time. *These shoes are already worn out – they haven't lasted very long.*

late *adjective, adverb* 1 not early but after the usual or expected time. *She was an hour late for her appointment, but she always arrives late.* 2 near the end of a period of time. *They got home late last night.* 3 previous, recently dead. *The late owner.* **lateness** *noun*. **lately** *adverb* recently.

L

later *adverb* after some time.

lateral *adjective* concerned with the side, sideways. *Lateral movement.*

lathe *noun* a machine that holds and turns wood or metal while it is being shaped with a cutting tool.

lather *noun* the bubbles or foam you get when you mix soap or detergent in warm water. *This soap makes a good lather.*

Latin *noun* the language spoken by the ancient Romans.

latitude *noun* a position or distance measured in degrees on a map north or south of the equator.

The lines of latitude run horizontally around the globe.

latter *adjective* the second of two things, compared with the former, which is the first of two things.

Latvia *noun* a Baltic country in Europe.

laugh *verb* to make sounds that show that you are very happy or think something is funny. *We laughed at the joke.* **laugh** *noun. He has a really loud laugh.* **laughter** *noun. The sound of laughter shook the room.*

laughable *adjective* ridiculous and absurd.

launch *verb* 1 to send a boat or ship into the water. 2 to send a rocket into space. 3 to start something new or important. *They launched the company with a champagne party.* **launch** *noun.*

launchpad *noun* a place from which rockets are sent into space.

laundromat *noun* a place with washing-machines that people can pay to use to wash their dirty clothes.

laundry *noun* 1 a place where you can take clothes to be washed and ironed. 2 the clothes, sheets, towels etc. that need to be washed or that have been washed.

laurel *noun* a small tree or bush with shiny evergreen leaves.

lava *noun* the hot molten rock that flows from an erupting volcano.

lavatory *noun* a room with a toilet in it.

lavender *noun* 1 a small shrub with narrow leaves and sweet-smelling pale purple flowers. 2 a light purple color

lavish *adjective* generous and plentiful. *A lavish banquet.*

law *noun* 1 all the rules made by a government that everybody in a country must obey. 2 a general rule or principle that explains how something works. *Please review the law of gravity for the exam.*

lawful *adjective* allowed by law. *He was going about his lawful business.*

lawn *noun* an area around a house or building or in a park that is covered with grass.

lawn-mower *noun* a machine for cutting (mowing) grass.

lawyer *noun* a person whose job it is to advise people about the law and to represent them in a court of law.

lax *adjective* not strict, careless about observing rules etc. *Discipline in the school is too lax.*

lay past tense of lie (to rest).

lay (lays, laying, laid) *verb* 1 to put down. *He laid the map on the table.* 2 to put something in a particular position. *She laid her coat over the chair.* 3 (of a bird) to produce an egg.

lay *adjective* not formally trained in a particular subject. *He became a lay preacher in their church when they moved to the country.*

The launch of the rocket was an awesome sight.

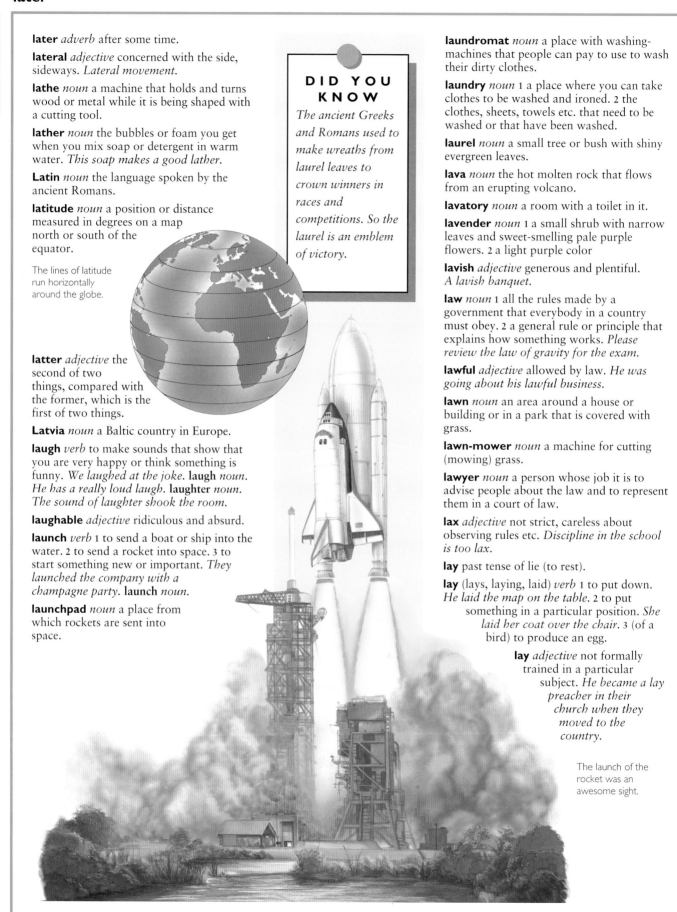

layaway *noun* a way of buying things by paying a small amount of money until the full amount is paid.

layout *noun* 1 the way text and pictures are arranged on a page. 2 the way things are arranged on a plan. *The layout of the new supermarket is really complicated.*

layer *noun* a thickness of something that lies between two other pieces of it or on top. *The cake was covered with a layer of icing.*

lazy (lazier, laziest) *adjective* not liking work, effort or exercise. *Cats are lazy and sleep a lot.* **laziness** *noun*. **lazily** *adverb*.

lead *noun* (rhymes with bed) 1 a soft, gray metal. 2 the substance in the middle of a pencil that makes a mark.

lead (leads, leading, led) *verb* (rhymes with need) 1 to go in front and show the way, to take in a certain direction. *Lead the way!* 2 to be in the first place. 3 to be in charge of other people. *The captain led her team bravely.* 4 to live a certain way of life. **lead** *noun* 1 the front position. 2 a piece of information or a clue that helps you to solve a crime etc. *We had some good leads.*

leader *noun* somebody who leads or who goes first.

leaf (leaves) *noun* 1 one of the flat, usually green, parts of a plant that grows from a stem or twig. 2 a page of a book.

The green leaves of summer provided a dappled shade for the picnickers.

leaflet *noun* a usually folded sheet of paper with information etc. printed on it.

The managers studied the architect's plan for the layout of the new supermarket.

AMAZING FACT

In green plants, leaves make food to nourish the plant. This process is called photosynthesis. The chlorophyll in the leaf uses a combination of carbon dioxide, water and light to make sugar. It then passes the sugar to the rest of the plant through tubes.

SPELLING NOTE

Do not confuse the past tense of 'lie' to rest ('I lay in bed thinking') with the verb 'lay' meaning 'put down'. ('When you've finished reading, lay the book on the table.')

Tom got a leather briefcase for his birthday.

leak *noun* a hole in a container or pipe through which liquid or gas can escape. **leak** *verb* 1 (of a gas or liquid) to escape through a hole or crack. *This pipe is leaking.* 2 to give away secret information.

lean *adjective* having little or no fat. *Lean meat.* **leanness** *noun*.

lean (leans, leaning, leaned or leant) *verb* 1 to bend towards something. *Tom leaned out of the window and waved to his friends.* 2 to rest against something for support. *Lean the ladder against the wall.*

leap (leaps, leaping, leapt or leaped) *verb* to jump up high or to jump over something. **leap** *noun*. **leap year** every fourth year in which February has 29 days instead of 28. Leap years have 366 days instead of 365.

learn (learns, learning, learned) *verb* to find out about something or how to do something. *Joe's learning to speak French.*

learned *adjective* A learned person has a lot of knowledge about something.

learning *noun* knowledge gained through studying. *His learning is phenomenal.*

lease *noun* an agreement between the owner of a property and a person renting it for a stated period of time. *They signed a 20-year lease on the house.*

leash *noun* a lead attached to a dog's collar so that you can take it for walks.

least *adjective* smallest or less than all the others. *This is the least expensive bike.* **at least** the minimum, but likely to be more. *It will cost at least $50 to get it fixed.*

leather *noun* the skin of animals used to make such things as shoes, purses and belts. **leathery** *adjective* tough like leather.

leave *verb* 1 to go away from somewhere. The opposite of leave is arrive. 2 to let something remain where it is. *She left her clothes all over the floor.* 3 to forget about something by not taking it with you. *I left my coat at home.* 4 what remains after the main part has been used or taken away. *Eight minus two leaves six.* 5 to pass on something to somebody after you die. *My uncle left me his gold watch.* **leave out** not to include or forget to put in.

leave *noun* 1 time away from a job. 2 permission to do something.

leaves plural of leaf. *The leaves are fantastic in the fall.*

Lebanon *noun* a country in the Middle East.

The flag of Lebanon has red and white stripes and a central symbol in green and gold.

lecture *noun* 1 a formal talk about a particular subject given to a class or audience. 2 a scolding or telling off. *The teacher gave him a lecture on how to behave.* **lecture** *verb*.

led past tense of lead. *The dog led the children out of danger.*

ledge *noun* a shelf-like space on a cliff, rock or wall. *The bird nested on the ledge.*

leek *noun* a long white vegetable with green leaves at one end. *Leek and potato soup.*

leer *verb* to look and smile at somebody in an evil way.

leeward *adjective* on the sheltered side, turned away from the wind.

left past tense of leave.

left *noun* You are reading these words from left to right. **left** *adjective*. *Close your left eye.*

left-overs *plural noun* food that has not been eaten after a meal. *I like eating left-overs.*

left-wing *adjective* in politics supporting socialism. The opposite of left-wing is right-wing.

leg *noun* 1 one of the parts of the body that animals and humans use for walking, running and standing on. 2 one of the parts that support a chair or other piece of furniture. **pull somebody's leg** to tease or make a fool of somebody by trying to make them believe something that is not true.

legal *adjective* 1 allowed by the law. *Fishing without a license is not legal.* 2 concerned with the law. *The legal system.* The opposite of legal is illegal.

legend *noun* an old, well-known story that may or may not be true. *The legend of Paul Bunyan.* **legendary** *adjective*.

legible *adjective* clear enough to be read easily. *The writing is very faded but it is just legible.* **legibility** *noun*.

Lemons grow in sunny countries around the Mediterranean Sea.

DID YOU KNOW
Native American legends are stories that explain things like how the Sun and Moon were created and where fire comes from.

This girl has her left leg forward and her left arm raised.

This diagram shows how the lens of the eye reverses an image on to the retina. The brain then interprets it, so that we see things the right way up.

legion *noun* a large division of the ancient Roman army (from three to six thousand soldiers).

legitimate *adjective* allowed by the law, lawful. **legitimacy** *noun*.

leisure *noun* free time when you can do what you want to and you do not have to work. **leisurely** *adjective*. *A leisurely life is the life for me.*

lemon *noun* a bright yellow, oval citrus fruit with a sour-tasting juice.

lemonade *noun* a drink made from the juice of lemons, water, sugar and ice.

lend (lends, lending, lent) *verb* to let somebody have something for a short time, before they give it back to you. *It was raining so I lent him my umbrella.* The opposite of lend is borrow.

length *noun* 1 how far it is from one end of something to the other horizontally. *A length of cloth.* 2 how long something lasts. *We were surprised at the length of her prison sentence.*

lengthen *verb* to make or become longer.

lengthy (lengthier, lengthiest) *adjective* long, lasting a long time.

lenient *adjective* not severe or strict. *A really lenient teacher.* **lenience** *noun*.

lens *noun* 1 a piece of curved glass or plastic used in a camera, a pair of glasses etc. that bends light and makes it go where it is needed. 2 a part of the eye that focuses light on to the retina.

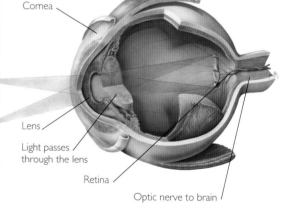

Cornea

Lens

Light passes through the lens

Retina

Optic nerve to brain

Lent *noun* in the Christian Church a period of 40 days fasting and penance before Easter. *Sarah gave up chocolate for Lent.*

lent the past tense of lend.

leopard
(say lep-urd) *noun* a large wild, spotted cat of Africa and Asia.

leper *noun* a person who has leprosy.

leprosy *noun* a disease of the skin and nerves which can lead to fingers and toes dropping off.

lesbian *noun* a woman who is sexually attracted to other women, a gay woman.

Lesotho *noun* a country in Africa.

-less *suffix* without. *Colorless, smokeless.*

less (lesser, least) *adjective* not so much. *Please make less noise.* **less** *adverb.* *You should eat less and sleep more.*

lessen *verb* to make or become smaller in size, importance etc.

lesson *noun* 1 a period of time when you are taught something by a teacher. 2 an experience that is a warning or example. *His accident was a lesson to him to be more careful in the future.*

let *verb* to allow. *He let me borrow his bike for most of the summer.* **let's** to suggest something. *Let's go swimming after school this afternoon.* **let off** 1 to set light to a firework or to fire a gun. 2 to allow somebody to go without punishing them. **letdown** disappointment. *The movie was a big letdown.* **let go** to set free.

lethal *adjective* able to cause death, deadly. *The venom of the puff adder is potentially lethal.*

letter *noun* 1 one of the signs we use to write words. 2 a written message we send to somebody.

Jamie wrote a letter to his cousins thanking them for the birthday present.

lettuce *noun* a plant with large green leaves that we eat in salads.

leukemia *noun* (say loo-kee-mee-uh) a serious cancer-like disease in which the blood produces too many white cells.

level *adjective* smooth and horizontal, not sloping. *A level surface.* **level** *adverb* equal or at the same height or distance.

lever *noun* 1 a strong bar that you use to lift something heavy by placing one end under the object and pushing down on the other end. 2 a long handle that you use to work a machine.

There is a saying: 'A leopard never changes its spots'. It means that you can't expect people to change their habits.

GRAMMAR NOTE
'Fewer' is the comparative of 'few', and means 'a smaller number of'. 'Less' is the comparative of 'little', and means 'a smaller quantity or amount'. 'Fewer' is used with countable nouns like 'tree', 'car' and 'house'. For example, 'There are fewer buildings in this part of town'. 'Less' is used with mass nouns like 'sugar,' 'gas' and 'sand'. 'This car uses less gas than the old one did.'

AMAZING FACT
Lichens are very simple plants. They don't have any true leaves, roots or flowers. They grow very slowly and are an ancient form of life. A small, hand-sized patch of lichen on a rock could be hundreds of years old.

liable *adjective* 1 legally responsible for something. *You are liable for damaging the machine.* 2 likely to. *In winter the lake is liable to freeze.*

liar *noun* a person who tells lies.

liberal *adjective* generous and tolerant. *A liberal attitude.*

liberate *verb* to set somebody or an animal free. **liberation** *noun.*

Liberia *noun* a country in Africa.

liberty *noun* freedom from control, slavery etc. **take liberties** to behave rudely and without respect.

librarian *noun* a person who is in charge of or who works in a library.

library (libraries) *noun* a room or building where a lot of books, records etc. are kept, usually for people to borrow. *Our public library has a reference room with six multimedia computers.*

Libreville *noun* the capital of Gabon.

Libya *noun* a country in Africa.

Libyan *noun* a person who comes from Libya. **Libyan** *adjective.* *The Libyan coast.*

lichen *noun* (say lie-kin) a flat, green or yellowish plant that grows in patches on rocks and tree trunks.

The Statue of Liberty in New York Harbor was a present to the US from the people of France.

When you see lichen growing on rocks, trees or buildings, it is a sign of relatively pure air.

lick *verb* 1 to touch something with the tongue. *The dog licked my hand.* 2 (informal) to defeat or overcome. *He is determined to lick the problem.* **lick** *noun.*

lid *noun* 1 a cover for a box, jar, pot etc. that you can remove or lift up. 2 the eyelid, the piece of skin that covers the eye.

The eyelid shields the eye from light and protects it against dust flying in the air.

Eyelid

lie (lies, lying, lied) *verb* to say something that you know is untrue. *She lied to the police about the theft.* **lie** *noun.* *It is dishonest to tell lies.*

lie (lies, lying, lay, lain) *verb* 1 to rest your body in a flat position. *She felt faint so she lay down.* 2 to remain. *The snow lay on the ground for weeks.* 3 to be located in a certain place. *The valley lies about a mile to the east of the farm.*

Liechtenstein *noun* a country in central Europe.

life *noun* 1 the time between a person's or an animal's birth and death when they are alive. 2 the ability of plants and animals to grow and develop, unlike such things as rocks, metals etc. 3 a way of living. *She leads a very exciting life.* 4 liveliness. *He is full of life.* **take somebody's life** to kill somebody.

lifebelt *noun* a ring or belt that floats and which a person holds on to or wears to prevent them sinking or drowning.

lifeboat *noun* a boat that rescues people who are shipwrecked or in danger at sea.

The lifeboat sped out to rescue the people who were sailing when the storm hit..

lifeguard *noun* a person who has been trained to help rescue swimmers in danger.

lifejacket *noun* an inflatable jacket that keeps you afloat in the water.

lifeless *adjective* 1 dead. *Her lifeless body.* 2 uninteresting. *Lifeless acting.*

lifelike *adjective* looking like a real person or animal. *A lifelike painting.*

lifestyle *noun* the way people live their lives, where they live and what their interests are.

SPELLING NOTE

Try not to confuse 'lightning' in 'thunder and lightning' (no 'e') with the present participle of 'lighten' (with an 'e') meaning 'to become brighter'.

lift *verb* 1 to pick something up and raise it to a higher place. *He lifted the child on to his knee.* 2 to rise. *The plane lifted into the air.* **to give someone a lift** to make someone feel happier. *Just seeing them gave me a lift.*

lift-off *noun* the launching of a rocket.

light (lights, lighting, lit or lighted) *verb* 1 to make something start burning. *Let's light the candles.* 2 to give light to a place. **light** *noun* 1 that which makes us able to see things. *The Sun gives us light.* 2 something that gives out light. **light** *adjective* 1 (of color) pale and not strong. *Light blue.* 2 full of bright light. *A light, airy room.*

The electric current flows through a thin coil of wire called a filament to light up the bulb.

light *adjective* 1 weighing little, not heavy. *As light as a feather.* 2 gentle or small in amount. *We ate a light meal.* 3 not too serious. *Light music on the radio.*

lighten *verb* 1 to become brighter or less dark. 2 to make something less heavy.

lighter *noun* a device for lighting cigarettes or a fire etc.

light-hearted *adjective* cheerful and without worry.

light year *noun* the distance in space that light travels in a year.

lighthouse *noun* a tower-like building near the ocean that sends out a very bright flashing light to guide ships or warn them off dangerous rocks.

All lighthouses used to be manned, with the lighthouse-keeper living there full-time. Nowadays, lighthouses are operated automatically and no one lives in them.

lighting *noun* artificial lights like candles and electric lights.

lightning *noun* a bright flash of electricity that lights up the sky during a thunderstorm.

like *verb* 1 to be fond of and to find somebody pleasant. 2 to enjoy something.

like *preposition* 1 nearly the same as or similar to, resembling. *He looks like his dad.* 2 in the same way as. *He roared like a lion.* 3 typical of or in the character of. *It's not like Laura to be early.* 4 for example, such as. *Indoor games like chess and ping pong are my favorites.*

likely (likelier, likeliest) *adverb* probable and expected to happen. *I think it's likely to rain, if not today, then tomorrow.*

likeness *noun* a resemblance. *There's a great likeness between the brothers.*

lilac *noun* a small tree or shrub with sweet-smelling purple or white flowers.

Lilongwe *noun* the capital of Malawi.

lily (lilies) *noun* a plant that grows from a bulb with white, yellow or red flowers.

Lima *noun* the capital of Peru.

limb *noun* an arm or leg of an animal or the branch of a tree.

lime *noun* 1 an oval, green citrus fruit similar to a lemon. 2 a substance obtained from limestone and used in making cement.

limerick *noun* a humorous poem in five lines. *An Irish limerick.*

limestone *noun* a kind of rock from which lime is obtained for making cement.

Stalactites and stalagmites form in limestone caves. Stalactites hang from the ceiling and stalagmites grow from the floor.

limit *noun* 1 a boundary or some point beyond which you should not go. *A 70 mph speed limit.* **limit** *verb* to prevent going beyond a certain limit or point, to restrict. *She limits herself to one cup of coffee.*

limp *adjective* drooping, soft and floppy.
limp *verb* to walk with difficulty and unevenly because you have an injury to your leg or foot. **limp** *noun.*

Waterlilies thrive in ponds. Their large waxy flowers and leaves float on the surface of the water.

DID YOU KNOW

This is a limerick:
'There was a young lady of Wilts,
Who walked up to Scotland on stilts;
When they said it is shocking
To show so much stocking,
She answered,
"Then what about kilts?"'

line *noun* 1 a long, thin mark on a surface. *She a drew straight line.* 2 a group of people, things or words in a row. *Wait in the line.* 3 a rope, string etc. with a special purpose. *A clothes line.* 4 a system of buses, trains or aircraft that travel regularly. 5 **lines** the words that actors have to say. **line** *verb.* *Noisy crowds lined the streets.*

line *verb* to sew material inside something. *I am going to line the jacket with blue silk.*

linen *noun* a strong cloth made from the fibers of the flax plant and used for sheets, tablecloths etc.

liner *noun* a large passenger ship or aircraft.

linger *verb* to dawdle, wait around, seeming unwilling to leave.

lining *noun* a layer of material to line the inside of something. *Most jackets have a lining, and in some, it's quilted, for warmth.*

linguist *noun* a person who studies languages and/or is good at learning and speaking them. *Some of the first studies of island cultures were done by linguists.*

link *noun* 1 a ring or loop in a chain. 2 a connection between two things. *The Eurotunnel is a link between England and France.* **link** *verb* to join up. *They linked arms.*

The links in a chain are extremely strong.

lion *noun* a large wild cat with light brown fur that lives in Africa and Asia. In some species, the male has a thick mane. Lions live in family groups called prides.

lioness *noun* a female lion.

The lioness was proudly guarding her cubs.

lip *noun* Your lips are the soft edges of your mouth. *My lips were chapped by the time we got home.*

lip-read *verb* (of a deaf person) to understand what somebody is saying by looking carefully at their lips while they are speaking. *Sally learned to lip-read.*

liquefy (liquefies, liquefying, liquefied) *verb* to make or become liquid.

liquid *noun* any substance that flows, such as water. Any substance that is not a gas or a solid. **liquid** *adjective*. **liquidize** *verb* to crush food like fruit and vegetables into a liquid in a liquidizer. **liquidizer** (*noun*).

Lisbon *noun* the capital of Portugal.

lisp *verb*, *noun* a speech problem in which the 's' sounds like a 'th'.

list *noun* a series of names or things written down . *Every Monday I make a 'to do' list for the week.* **list** *verb* to write things down on a list.

list *verb* (of a ship) to lean over to one side.

listen *verb* to pay attention to what you hear. **listener** *noun*.

lit past tense of light.

liter *noun* a measure of liquids equal to 1,000 milliliters.

literally *adverb* exactly as the words state. *He literally knocked me off my chair.*

literate *adjective* able to read and write.

literature *noun* 1 novels, plays and poetry that are especially good. 2 printed material on a particular subject.

Lithuania *noun* a Baltic country in Europe.

The flag of Lithuania has three stripes, yellow, green and red.

litter *noun* waste such as paper and bottles left lying around.

litter *noun* all the animals born to the same mother at the same time.

little *adjective* 1 small in size or quantity. 2 not much. *There's very little time left.*

live *verb* (rhymes with give) 1 to be alive, to have life. Plants and animals live. 2 to continue to stay alive. *The tortoise lived for 50 years.* 3 to have your home in some place. *My aunt lives in Iowa.*

live *adjective* (rhymes with dive) 1 not dead, but living. *There was a live rabbit under the bed.* 2 full of electricity. *This wire is live so be very careful.* 3 a performance on radio or television that is happening as you listen or watch.

SPELLING NOTE

Try not to confuse 'liquefy' or 'liquify', meaning 'to make something liquid' with 'liquidize', meaning 'to crush fruit etc. in a blender'.

Mom left the grocery list behind when she went to the supermarket.

AMAZING FACT

In order to survive, lizards have evolved in some very bizarre ways. Some lizards have adapted to their surroundings by becoming snake-like; their legs have become tiny, but movable flaps. The komodo dragon, which may grow to ten feet long, has well-developed limbs and is a good climber and swimmer.

livelihood *noun* the way a person earns money to live. *He earns a good livelihood from doing up old houses and selling them.*

lively *adjective* full of energy. *He has a very lively mind and is interesting company.*

liver *noun* 1 a large and important organ in your body that helps to clean your blood and helps to process food. 2 this organ from an animal used as food.

lives plural of life. *Do you think cats really have nine lives?*

livestock *noun* animals kept on a farm. *John keeps cattle and other livestock.*

living *adjective* alive not dead. **living** *noun* how a person earns money to live. *What do you do for a living?*

lizard *noun* a small reptile with a long scaly body, four legs and a tail. Most lizards live in warm countries.

This lizard has a collar that scares off its enemies.

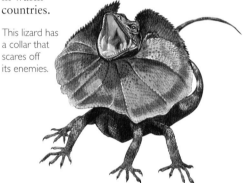

Ljubljana *noun* the capital of Slovenia.

llama *noun* a South American animal similar to a camel, but without a hump. *Llamas make good sheep guards, and one llama can guard over 100 animals.*

load *noun* something heavy that is carried. An amount of something to be carried. *A load of wood.* **load** *verb* 1 to put a load on to something that will carry it. *He loaded the wood on to the truck.* 2 to put bullets in a gun, a film into a camera or data into a computer. **loads of** a lot of something.

loaf (loaves) *noun* a large piece of bread baked in a shape. *A fresh loaf of bread.*

loan *noun* something that somebody lends you, usually money.

loathe *verb* (rhymes with clothe) to hate or to dislike something very much.

lob (lobs, lobbing, lobbed) *verb* to hit or throw something slowly or high in the air. **lob** *noun*.

lobby *noun* an entrance hall in a theater, hotel etc. *I met him for coffee in the lobby of the hotel.*

lobe *noun* the soft part of the ear that hangs down. *Her ear lobes were pierced several times, and she wore many earrings.*

lobster *noun* a shellfish or sea animal with a long body covered in a hard shell. It has ten legs including two large claws in front. Lobsters can be eaten.

Lobsters turn pink when boiled.

local *adjective* belonging to or affecting a particular area or place. *The local newspaper carried daily reports of our campaign.* **locally** *adverb*.

locality *noun* an area. *This is a very wealthy locality.*

locate *verb* 1 to find the exact position of. *Joe located the source of the river on the map.* 2 to be situated in a particular place. *The supermarket is located out of town, for the convenience of shoppers.*

loch *noun* a Scottish word for lake. *Loch Lomond is beautiful in the spring.*

lock *noun* 1 a device that fastens a door or lid and that you open and shut with a key. **lock** *verb* to fasten with a lock and key. 2 a section of a canal or river between gates that can be opened and shut to raise or lower ships by changing the level of the water. *The barge went through the lock.*

locust *noun* a large kind of grasshopper that travels in huge swarms and destroys crops. *A plague of locusts.*

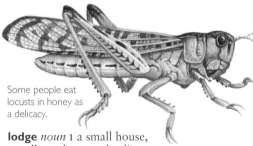

Some people eat locusts in honey as a delicacy.

lodge *noun* 1 a small house, usually at the gates leading to a large house. 2 a beaver's home. **lodge** *verb* 1 to live in rented rooms (lodgings). 2 to become firmly fixed in.

lodger *noun* somebody who pays to live in a room in another person's house.

loft *noun* a raised area in a barn or in a room. *I broke my leg jumping out of the loft onto the barn floor.*

log *noun* 1 a length of wood that has been cut from a branch of a felled tree. 2 a written record of the journey of a ship or aircraft. *The log book was fascinating.*

SPELLING NOTE

Some -logies
anthropology (the study of mankind)
astrology (the stars)
chronology (dates)
cosmology (universe)
dendrology (trees)
etymology (word origins)
meteorology (weather)
ornithology (birds)
pathology (diseases)
vexillology (flags)

logic *noun* the science of careful and correct reasoning. *I rely on logic, not imagination.*

logical *adjective* 1 following the rules of logic. 2 sensible and reasonable.

logo *noun* a symbol or lettering that represents a company or organization, an emblem or trademark. *The calendars were printed with the companies logo.*

-logy *suffix* the study of some subject. *Geology, anthropology, biology.*

loiter *verb* to stand around somewhere with nothing to do. *The woman loitering near that car looks suspicious.*

Lomé *noun* the capital of Togo.

London *noun* the capital of England and the United Kingdom.

lonely (lonelier, loneliest) *adjective* 1 unhappy at being alone. 2 far away and not often visited. *A lonely island off the coast of Alaska.*

long *adjective* 1 measuring far from one end to the other. The opposite of long is short. *The longest bridge in the world is in Japan.* 2 taking a lot of time. *It's a long flight from Los Angeles to Beijing.* 3 a certain amount of distance or time. *An hour-long flight.* **no longer** not any more.

long *verb* to want something very much. *She longed to go home.* **longing** *noun*. **longingly** *adverb*. *He looked longingly at the shiny bike.*

longitude *noun* the position of a place measured as a distance in degrees east or west of a line on a map that runs through Greenwich near London from the North and South Poles.

Lines of longitude run vertically around the globe.

look *verb* 1 to move your eyes to see something. 2 to seem or appear to be so. *Dick looks happy today.* **look after** to take care of somebody or something. **look for** to search. *Betty is looking for her skates.* **look forward to** to wait for something eagerly. *I'm really looking forward to getting out of the hospital.* **look into** to investigate. **look out** be careful. *Hey, look out! You almost stepped on that nail!* **look up to** to admire.

loom *noun* a machine for weaving thread into cloth.

Looms like this one are still used in some places.

loop *noun* a circular shape made in a rope or piece of string. **loop** *verb*. *He looped the rope around the post.*

loose *adjective* 1 not held firmly in place. *My loose tooth fell out.* 2 not attached or fastened. *The ponies were loose in the paddock all day.* 3 (of clothes) not fitting tightly, too big.

loosen *verb* to make or become loose. *His tie was too tight so he loosened it.*

loot *noun* goods and money that have been stolen. **loot** *verb*. *During the riots people looted shops and houses.*

lord *noun* 1 the title of a nobleman, bishop or male judge. 2 **Lord** the name given to God and Jesus. **lordly** *adjective*. *Lordly behavior is completely out of place here.*

lore *noun* stories or traditions that people learn from other people or that are passed down from older generations.

lorry *noun* a truck.

In Australia, lorries hauling several trucks are called road trains.

lot *noun* 1 large amount or number. 2 **lots** *Put lots of peanut butter on the bread.* 3 an article in an auction. 4 an area of land. *We play ball in a vacant lot down the street.*

lotion *noun* a liquid or cream that you put on your skin to clean, soften or protect it. *Suntan lotion.*

lottery *noun* a way of making money by selling a lot of tickets to try to win prizes.

loud *adjective* 1 making a large amount of sound, not quiet. 2 unpleasantly bright and colorful. *He was wearing a loud purple shirt.* **loudness** *noun*.

loudspeaker *noun* a piece of equipment in a radio, televison or stereo system etc. that turns electrical waves into sound. A device for making sounds louder.

When a sound signal from the amplifier passes through the metal coil, it makes the cone vibrate, producing sound.

lounge *noun* a public room in hotel or airport with comfortable chairs where you can relax. **lounge** *verb* to sit around in a lazy way doing nothing.

love *verb* to like somebody very much and want to be with them all the time. **lovable** *adjective* easy to love. **lover** *noun*.

lovely (lovelier, loveliest) *adjective* 1 beautiful to look at, listen to or touch. 2 very pleasant.

SPELLING NOTE

Try not to confuse 'loose', meaning 'set free', 'undo', and 'loosen', meaning 'to make less tight'.

lose (loses, losing, lost) *verb* 1 If you lose something, you do not have it any more and cannot find it. 2 to fail to win. *They lost the game.* 3 to go astray. *We lost our way.*

loser *noun* somebody who seems never to be successful. *He's a loser but he tries hard.*

loss *noun* something that has been lost and that you no longer have. *She was very upset by the loss of her precious bracelet.*

lost past tense of lose.

loving *adjective* showing love. *She gave him a loving smile.*

low *adjective* 1 not high but near the ground. 2 not loud. *He talked in a low voice so nobody could hear.* **the Low Countries** the Netherlands and Belgium.

low *verb* to moo or make a noise like a cow.

lower *verb* to move or let something down. *The soldiers lowered the flag.* The opposite of lower is raise.

loyal *adjective* always faithful and true to your friends. **loyalty** *noun*.

Luanda *noun* the capital of Angola.

lubricate *verb* to put oil or grease on parts of a machine so that they move easily and smoothly. **lubrication** *noun*.

lucid *noun* 1 easy to understand. *A lucid explanation.* 2 clear, not confused. *Despite the accident his mind was lucid.*

luck *noun* 1 something that happens to you by chance and that you have not planned or cannot control. *Winning a lottery is pure luck.* 2 something good but unexpected that happens to you. *It was luck, not skill!*

lucky (luckier, luckiest) *adjective* 1 something lucky happens by chance. *She was lucky to win the lottery.* 2 bringing good luck. *A lucky charm.*

ludicrous *adjective* (say **loo-dee-kruss**) very silly, absurd. *You look ludicrous in those clothes.*

luggage *noun* the suitcases and bags that travelers take with them.

lukewarm *adjective* 1 A liquid that is lukewarm is only just warm. 2 not enthusiastic. *The book received only lukewarm praise.*

lull *noun* a short period of quiet when little is happening. *There was a lull in the traffic noise.*

lull *verb* to soothe and make somebody relaxed and calm. *The gentle music lulled her to sleep.*

lullaby *noun* a gentle song that helps a child go to sleep. *Mom sang the baby a lullaby.*

lumber *noun* rough timber.

lumber *verb* to walk slowly in a heavy, clumsy way. **lumber with** to give somebody something they do not want. *Lizzie was lumbered with mowing the lawn.*

lumberjack *noun* a person who cuts down and saws up trees.

lump *noun* 1 a bump or swelling. *Luke has a lump on his knee.* 2 a small solid piece of something without shape. *A lump of clay.*

We had so much luggage that we had to pay extra.

WORD HISTORY

The formal word for the noon meal, 'luncheon', is really a long form of the original but less formal word 'lunch'.

Lumber has to be trimmed and planed into planks for building.

AMAZING FACT

The lynx has a much shorter tail than most of the other 'big cats'. It is a nocturnal animal that lives on rodents and young deer.

---

lunar *adjective* concerned with the Moon. *A lunar journey.* **lunar month** the time it takes for the Moon to orbit the Earth – 29 days.

lunatic *noun* somebody who is foolish or insane. **lunatic** *adjective*. *A lunatic idea.*

lunch *noun* a meal eaten in the middle of the day. **lunch** *verb*.

lung *noun* one the two organs inside your chest that you use for breathing. The lungs take in oxygen from the air and give out carbon dioxide.

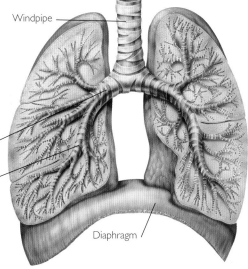

Windpipe

Bronchial tube

Bronchiole

The lungs are the organs of breathing.

Diaphragm

lunge *verb* to make a sudden thrust forward. *She lunged at the dog with a stick.* **lunge** *noun*.

lure *verb* to attract and tempt, to lead astray. *They were lured by the bright lights of the fairground.* **lure** *noun*.

lurk *verb* to wait around out of sight with a dishonest purpose, to prowl. *There is somebody lurking under the trees.*

Lusaka *noun* the capital of Zambia.

lush *adjective* growing thickly and healthily, fertile. *Lush vegetation.*

lust *noun* a very strong desire. *A lust for fame got him nowhere.*

lute *noun* an old-fashioned stringed musical instrument in the shape of half a pear.

Luxembourg *noun* a country in northwestern Europe, and its capital city.

luxury *noun* 1 something expensive that is very nice to have but that you do not really need. 2 great comfort and having a lot of expensive luxuries. *She grew up in luxury.* **luxurious** *adjective*. *A luxurious house.*

lynx *noun* a wild cat with a short tail and tufts of hair in its ears.

lyre *noun* a musical instrument like a small harp. *A gentle tune on the lyre.*

lyrics *plural noun* the words of a song. *I really like these lyrics.*

Mm

macabre *adjective* strangely frightening and gruesome. *A macabre film.*

macaroni *noun* tube-shaped pasta.

Macedonia *noun* a country in Southeast Europe. *Macedonian wine.*

machine *noun* a piece of equipment with moving parts that uses electricity or an engine to do a job or make work easier.

machinery *noun* 1 the parts of a machine. 2 machines. 3 an organized system of doing something. *The machinery of local government runs very slowly.*

macho *adjective* (say **match**-oh) (of a man) aggressively and exaggeratedly masculine. Strong and virile.

mad (madder, maddest) *adjective* 1 very angry. 2 wildly foolish, not sensible. *What a mad idea to run across a busy road.* 3 mentally ill, insane. **madness** *noun.*

Madagascar *noun* a country in the Indian Ocean off East Africa.

madam *noun* a formal and polite way of addressing a woman without using her name. *Can I help you, madam?*

madden *verb* to make somebody angry. *It maddens me when you bite your nails.*

made past tense of make.

Madrid *noun* the capital of Spain.

magazine *noun* a publication with a paper cover that usually comes out every week or month and which contains articles, photographs, stories etc.

maggot *noun* the larva or grub of the house-fly. Maggots look like small worms.

Maggots can be used to catch fish.

magic *noun* 1 in stories, a strange power that makes wonderful or impossible things happen. 2 clever tricks that look as though they happen by magic. *She pulled a pigeon out of the hat by magic.*

magical *adjective* 1 produced by magic. *The story is about a magical ring.* 2 strange and exciting. *It was a magical evening.*

magician *noun* (say maj-**ish**-un) a person who can do tricks or magic. *We had a magician at my little sister's birthday party.*

When the paperclips come within the magnet's magnetic field, they become magnetized too, and so attract other paperclips.

WORD HISTORY

The shape of the letter M comes from an Ancient Egyptian symbol for water. Its sound comes from 'mem', a Semitic word meaning 'water'.

magistrate *noun* a person who acts as a judge in a court of law that deals with less serious offences.

magnet *noun* a piece of metal that has the power to attract or make iron or steel move towards it. **magnetic** *adjective.* *A magnetic compass.* **magnetism** *noun.* **magnetize** *verb.*

magnificent *adjective* beautiful and very impressive. *A magnificent castle stood on the hill.* **magnificence** *noun.*

magnify (magnifies, magnifying, magnified) *verb* to make something seem larger than it really is by looking at it through a magnifying glass or microscope. *Astronomers use telescopes to magnify the stars.*

magnifying glass *noun* a special lens with a handle that makes objects look bigger than they really are.

mahogany *noun* a very hard, reddish-brown wood used in making furniture. *A mahogany table.*

maid *noun* a female servant.

maiden *noun* (old-fashioned) an unmarried young woman. **maiden name** a woman's last name before she marries. **maiden voyage** a ship's first voyage.

The maiden waited shyly for her knight to arrive.

mail *noun* 1 letters and parcels sent by post. **mail** *verb* to send by post. 2 a kind of armor made from small metal rings.

maim *verb* to injure somebody so badly that they are disabled for life.

main *adjective* the most important. *The main shopping area is near our house.*

mainframe *noun* a big, powerful computer that can be used by several people at once.

mainland *noun* the principal and largest mass of land without its islands.

maintain *verb* 1 to keep in good condition. *The county maintains all the parks.* 2 to support and take care of. 3 to state as true or as a belief. *She maintains that she is always right.* 4 to continue. *The schools have maintained high standards.*

maize *noun* a tall plant that produces cobs of sweetcorn, a cereal with large seeds.

majesty *noun* 1 impressive greatness, splendour. *The majesty of the mountains.* 2 **Your Majesty** the title people use when speaking to a king or queen. **majestic** *adjective.*

major *adjective* important, main. *The new principal made major changes.* **major** *noun* an officer in the army above a captain.

Maize is used as cattle fodder.

majority *noun* 1 more than half of a total. *The majority of people watch television every day.* 2 the number of votes by which somebody wins an election.

Majuro *noun* the capital of the Marshall Islands.

make (makes, making, made) *verb* 1 to put things together to produce something new, to create or build. 2 to prepare. 3 to cause or force something to happen. *The airplane made a forced landing.* 4 to add up or produce. *Three and six make nine.* 5 to earn or gain. *How much money does a waiter make?* **make** *noun* the maker's name or brand. *What make of car is this?* **make somebody's day** to make somebody feel happy all day long. *Hearing that song on the radio just made my day!*

make do *verb* to use something to replace what you really want. *You'll have to make do with this old wheelbarrow.*

make-up *noun* special colored creams and powders (cosmetics) that women and actors put on their faces. *She wears too much make-up.*

make up *verb* 1 to invent. *Make up a story about a monster.* 2 to become friends again after quarreling. 3 to put on make-up.

WORD HISTORY

'Malaria' comes from two Italian words, 'mal aria', meaning 'bad air'. People once thought the disease was caused by breathing the 'bad air' of marshy places.

AMAZING FACT

Mammals were the last major animal group to appear on Earth. During the period that dinosaurs lived, the only existing mammals were small rodents that looked like shrews.

The actress kept her make-up on the dressing table.

make-believe *verb* to pretend and imagine things. *Let's make-believe we are cowboys.*

makeshift *adjective* temporary and only meant to last until something better can be used. *Makeshift accommodation.*

mal- *prefix* bad or ill. *Malformed, malfunction, malnutrition.*

Malabo *noun* the capital of Equatorial Guinea.

malaria *noun* a tropical disease that is carried from person to person by the bite of a female mosquito.

Malawi *noun* a country in Africa.

Malaysia *noun* a country in Southeast Asia.

The Malaysian flag is red and white striped with a yellow Moon and Sun on a square blue ground.

Malaysian *noun* a person who comes from Malaysia. **Malaysian** *adjective. Malaysian rubber plantations.*

Maldives *plural noun* a country of many islands in the Indian Ocean.

Malé *noun* the capital of the Maldives.

male *noun, adjective* a human or animal belonging to the sex that does not produce babies or eggs. Boys and men are males. *A male horse is called a stallion.* The opposite of male is female.

Mali *noun* a country in Africa.

malicious *adjective* (say mal-**ish**-uss) unkind and wishing to see others hurt or unhappy, spiteful. *She has a very malicious tongue.* **malice** *noun.*

mall *noun* an enclosed shopping center.

mallard *noun* a kind of wild duck.

mallet *noun* a large wooden hammer.

malnutrition *noun* illness caused by eating too little food or the wrong kind of food.

malt *noun* dried barley that is used to make beer and whisky.

Malta *noun* a country in southern Europe.

Maltese *noun* 1 a person who comes from Malta. 2 the language of Malta. **Maltese** *adjective. The Maltese Cross.*

maltreat *verb* to treat a person or animal roughly or unkindly. *We should never maltreat our pets.*

mammal *noun* any animal of which the female feeds her young with milk from her own body. Humans, elephants and whales are mammals.

mammoth *noun* a kind of large hairy elephant that lived thousands of years ago during the Ice Age. Mammoths are now extinct.

Animals such as mammoths adapted to the Ice Age by growing thick woolly coats.

man *noun* 1 a fully grown male human. 2 humans in general. *When did man first appear on Earth?* **mankind** *noun. A giant step for mankind.*

manage *verb* 1 to control or be in charge of something. *Lucy manages the production department.* 2 to be able to do something, especially something difficult or awkward, to succeed. *She managed to solve the crossword.* **manager** *noun.* **management** *noun. Bad management.*

Managua *noun* the capital of Nicaragua.

Manama *noun* the capital of Bahrain.

mane *noun* the long thick hair on the neck of a horse or male lion.

manger *noun* a long narrow container in a barn or stable from which cattle and horses feed.

The baby Jesus was wrapped in swaddling clothes and laid in a manger.

mangle *verb* to damage something by crushing and twisting it out of shape.

manhood *noun* the state or condition of being a man.

mania *noun* a strong desire or enthusiasm for something. *He has a mania for snowboarding.*

maniac *noun* 1 a person suffering from a mental illness that makes them behave violently. 2 (informal) an over-enthusiastic person. *She drives like a maniac.*

Manila *noun* the capital of the Philippines.

mankind *noun* all people in general.

manner *noun* 1 the way in which something is done. *Let's do this in a professional manner.* 2 the way a person behaves or talks. *She has a very friendly manner.* 3 **manners** polite behaviour.

AMAZING FACT

The word 'marathon' comes from a long distance run made by a messenger from Marathon, Greece, to Athens in 490 BC to report a Greek victory in the battle at Marathon.

The map showed exactly where the treasure had been buried.

DID YOU KNOW

Some people object that the use of 'man', as in 'the origins of man' for people in general is sexist. You can get round the problem by using words such as 'person', 'people', or 'human'.

---

maneuvre *noun* (say man-oo-ver) a skillful or difficult movement or clever trick.

manor *noun* a large, important house in the country with land around it.

mansion *noun* a large, impressive house.

manslaughter *noun* killing somebody through carelessness but not with the intention of doing so.

mantelpiece *noun* a shelf above a fireplace.

manual *noun* a book with instructions on how to use or work something. **manual** *adjective* worked with the hands. *Manual controls, manual labour.*

manufacture *verb* to make things in large quantities by machine in a factory.

manure *noun* dung or animal waste used as a fertilizer to help produce better crops.

manuscript *noun* a handwritten or typed copy of a book etc. before it is printed.

Manx *adjective* relating to the Isle of Man. *Manx cats do not have tails.*

many *adjective, pronoun* a large number of people or things.

Maori (Maori or Maoris) *noun* (say mow-ree) the original people who lived in New Zealand.

map *noun* a drawing of an area, country etc. showing things like mountains, rivers, roads and towns. *A street map of Orlando.*

maple *noun* a tree with large leaves with five points. The maple leaf is the national emblem of Canada.

Maputo *noun* the capital of Mozambique.

marathon *noun* a race in which people run 26 miles (42 km).

marble *noun* 1 a very hard stone that can be polished to show its pattern or colour. 2 a small coloured glass ball used in children's games. *A game of marbles.*

march *verb* to walk with regular steps and arm movements in time with one another, like soldiers. **march** *noun* 1 a piece of music with a regular beat suitable for marching to. 2 a boundary. *The Welsh marches.*

March *noun* the third month of the year. March has 31 days.

mare *noun* a fully grown female horse. The opposite of a mare is a stallion.

margarine *noun* a soft yellow butter-like fat made mainly from vegetable oils.

margin *noun* the blank space or gap down the sides of a page.

marigold *noun* a plant of the daisy family with large orange or yellow flowers.

marine *adjective* to do with the sea. *Whales are marine mammals.* **Marine** *noun* someone who is in the Marine Corps..

My class visited the museum of marine life, where we saw many different sea creatures swimming in huge tanks.

mark *noun* 1 a stain or scratch on something. *There's a dirty mark on my shirt.* 2 a special sign on something. **mark** *verb* to check and correct a test or homework and give it a grade.

market *noun* a place where things are sold, usually from stalls in the open.

marmalade *noun* a jam made from oranges or some other citrus fruit and usually eaten at breakfast. *Orange marmalade.*

maroon *noun, adjective* dark reddish-brown. *Maroon socks.*

maroon *verb* to abandon or leave somebody alone in an isolated place such as a desert island.

marquee *noun* a very large sign on a theater that displays the name of the play or movie being shown.

They got married in a huge tent decorated to look like am Arabian palace.

marriage *noun* 1 a wedding ceremony. 2 the state of being married. *My sister got married last year.*

marrow *noun* 1 a long, large green vegetable like a huge cucumber. 2 a soft substance containing blood vessels in the hollow parts of bones.

marry (marries, marrying, married) *verb* 1 to take somebody as your husband or wife. *My uncle married an Australian.* 2 to carry out the ceremony of marriage.

WORD HISTORY

'Marmalade' is from a Portuguese word 'marmelada', named after the quince ('marmelo' in Portuguese), from which fruit the preserve was originally made.

AMAZING FACT

Newly-born marsupials are very small and have not finished developing when they crawl into their mother's pouch. The babies drink their mothers' milk inside the pouch and grow strong.

---

marsh *noun* an area of low-lying land that is always wet, a bog. *The house was always damp because it was so near the marsh.*

Marshall Islands *plural noun* a country of many islands in the Pacific Ocean.

marshmallow *noun* a soft, white sugary food. *We roasted marshmallows on the fire.*

marsupial *noun* an animal the female of which carries her young in a pouch on her stomach. Kangaroos are marsupials.

martial *adjective* to do with wars, battles, fighting, soldiers etc. *The band played marches and other kinds of martial music.* **martial arts** systems of self-defence such as karate, kendo and judo that come from China and Japan.

Martian *noun* an imaginary person from the planet Mars.

martin *noun* a bird with a forked tail similar to a swallow.

martyr *noun* somebody who chooses to suffer or be killed rather than give up their beliefs. **martyrdom** *noun*.

marvel (marvels, marveling, marveled) *verb* to be astonished or surprised. *I always marvel at how clever sheepdogs are.* **marvel** *noun. A computer is an electronic marvel.*

marvelous *adjective* excellent, very good.

mascara *noun* a coloring substance used on eyelashes to make them look longer or thicker. *Black mascara.*

mascot *noun* an animal or thing that people think brings good luck. *The team's mascot is a rabbit.*

masculine *adjective* concerned with men or typical of men, manly. **masculinity** *noun*. The opposite of masculine is feminine.

Maseru *noun* the capital of Lesotho.

mask *noun* a covering worn over the face to hide, disguise or protect it. **mask** *verb* to cover or disguise something.

This gold mask was found in Greece by the archeologist Heinrich Schliemann. He believed it to be the death mask of King Agamemnon of Troy.

mason *noun* a person who makes or builds things from stone.

masonry *noun* stonework.

M

mass *noun* 1 a large number or quantity. *The plant was covered in a mass of flowers.* 2 a large shapeless lump of something. 3 **the masses** the ordinary people. **mass** *verb* to gather into a group or mass. *The crowd massed on to the field.* **mass-media** ways of communicating through such things as newspapers, radio and television, from which most people get their news and information. **mass-produced** made by machines in great quantities.

mass *noun* the celebration of the Holy Communion service in Roman Catholic and some other Christian churches.

massacre *noun* (say **mass**-uh-ker) the brutal killing of a large number of people. **massacre** *verb*. *The troops stormed the castle and massacred all the prisoners.*

massage *verb* to rub and knead parts of a person's body to get rid of pain or stiffness and to help them relax. **massage** *noun*.

massive *adjective* huge in size and heavy. *A massive rock blocked the road.*

mast *noun* a pole that holds a flag or supports a ship's sails.

Tom the cabin boy climbed to the top of the mast and searched the horizon for sight of land.

master *noun* 1 the male owner of an animal. *The dog obeys its master.* 2 a man who controls other people. *He is master in his own house.* 3 a person who is very skilled at something. **master** *verb* 1 to learn something and become skilled in it. *She mastered Japanese in six months.* 2 to control or overcome. *He mastered his fear of flying and took off for the States.*

masterly *adjective* showing skill. *A truly masterly performance.*

masterpiece *noun* an outstandingly skillful work of art.

mastery *noun* 1 having complete control of something. *Mastery over his phobia.* 2 skill. *Mastery of the piano.*

mat *noun* 1 a small piece of material for covering a part of a floor. *Please wipe your feet on the mat.* 2 a small piece of material placed on a table to protect it from hot or wet plates, cups etc.

match *verb* to be like or equal to something, to go well together. *These two socks don't match.* **match** *noun* 1 an equal to. *At exams, she's no match for her sister.* 2 a game between two teams. *A tennis match between two champion players.*

GRAMMAR NOTE

Try not to confuse 'masterful', meaning 'showing authority' or 'overbearing' with 'masterly', which means 'showing skill'.

match *noun* a thin piece of wood with one end tipped with a material that ignites when you rub it against something rough.

mate *verb* (of animals) to come together to breed in order to produce offspring. **mate** *noun* one of the two animals brought together to breed.

material *noun* 1 a substance from which you can make other things. *Wood, glass, bricks and cement are some of the materials used in building houses.* 2 cloth for making clothes from.

Construction sites are full of different kinds of building materials.

maternal *adjective* relating to a mother or mothers, motherly. *Maternal feelings.* The opposite of maternal is paternal.

maternity *adjective* relating to a mother-to-be or birth. *A maternity ward.*

mathematics *plural noun* the study of the science of numbers, measurements, quantities and shapes. **mathematical** *adjective. I was given an extremely tricky mathematical problem.* **mathematician** *noun* an expert in mathematics.

maths *abbreviation* for mathematics.

matrimony *noun* marriage or the state of being married. **matrimonial** *adjective*.

matron *noun* 1 a person in a prison or school responsible for the women and children. 2 an older, married woman.

matter *verb* to be important. *These are grave matters and they should be treated seriously.*

matter *noun* 1 the substance or material from which all things are made. Matter can be a solid, a gas or a liquid. 2 a subject of interest. *Financial matters.* 3 a problem. *What's the matter with you today?*

mattress *noun* the thick oblong padding you put on a bed to lie on.

My father bought me a new mattress designed to help his bad back.

mature *adjective* 1 fully developed and adult, grown up. 2 ripe. **mature** *verb*. *Puppies mature into dogs.*

maul *verb* to injure somebody badly by attacking or handling them savagely.

Mauritania *noun* a country in Africa.

Mauritius *noun* a country in the Indian Ocean off East Africa.

mauve *noun, adjective* pale purple color.

maxim *noun* a general rule or wise piece of advice. *'Look before you leap' is an old maxim, and a wise one.*

maximum *noun* the greatest number or amount possible. *The box holds 50 matches at the maximum.* **maximum** *adjective.* *70 mph is the maximum speed on interstates.* The opposite of maximum is minimum.

May *noun* the fifth month of the year. May has 31 days.

maybe *adverb* perhaps, possibly. *Maybe we'll see you later.*

mayhem *noun* general chaos.

mayor *noun* a person in charge of the council or government of a town or city.

maze *noun* a system of complicated paths or lines to follow and which is difficult to find your way through. *The maze next to the palace is completely confusing.*

Mbabane *noun* the capital of Swaziland.

meadow *noun* a grassy field where animals can graze. *A meadow full of buttercups.*

meal *noun* the food that people eat at a particular time. Breakfast, lunch, tea and dinner are all meals.

mean *adjective* unwilling to give, not generous or kind. **meanness** *noun.*

mean (means, meaning, meant) *verb* 1 to intend or plan to do something. *I meant to telephone, but I forgot.* 2 to intend to show or express. *Red means danger.* **mean well** to intend to be helpful. *She is very slow, but she means well.* **by all means** certainly.

meaning *noun* 1 what something means. *Dictionaries tell us the meaning of words.* 2 the importance, purpose or intention of something. *What is the meaning of poetry?*

AMAZING FACT

The ancient Egyptians had a system of measurements that was based on the human body. The smallest unit, based on the hand, was a digit. Four digits made a palm. The distance between the little finger and thumb of an outstretched hand was called a span. A cubit was equal to 2 spans, 7 palms or the distance from fingertips to elbow.

Mazes like the one pictured take many years to mature.

Henry was awarded a medal for his achievements in athletics.

meaningful *adjective* full of significance, important. *A meaningful debate.*

meaningless *adjective* without any purpose. *His life seems meaningless.*

means *plural noun* 1 a method or way of doing something. *The prisoner found some means of escape.* 2 wealth. *A woman of substantial means.*

meantime *noun* the time between two things happening. *I'm going to the store, and in the meantime you can set the table.*

meanwhile *adverb* at the same time as. *The rain fell. Meanwhile, Megan slept.*

measles *noun* a mainly children's infectious disease causing a fever and a rash of small red spots on the skin.

measure *verb* to find out or to show how long, tall, wide or heavy something is. *Jim measured the length of his desk.* **measure** *noun* 1 a unit of measure. A meter is a measure of length. 2 an action or law. *The government took measures to reduce crime.*

Jane took a ruler to measure the space exactly.

measurement *noun* how much something measures. *What are the measurements of the room?*

meat *noun* the flesh of animals or birds that we eat.

mechanic *noun* a person who understands machines and is skilled at making or repairing them.

mechanical *adjective* 1 relating to machinery. 2 worked by machines. *A funny mechanical mouse.* 3 automatic and done without thought.

mechanism *noun* the system of the working parts of a machine.

medal *noun* a flat round piece of metal or plastic similar to a large coin with words or a symbol on it, which is given as a reward.

meddle *verb* to interfere in things when you have not been asked. **meddlesome** *adjective.* *He's turned into a meddlesome old man.*

media see mass-media.

medical *adjective* concerning doctors and their work in preventing and treating disease. **medical** *noun* a complete examination of your body by a doctor.

medicine *noun* 1 the tablets and liquid substances you swallow to try to treat and cure an illness. *The medicine tasted horrible.* 2 the science of treating illnesses.

medieval *adjective* relating to the Middle Ages, a period in European history that lasted between about AD 1100 and 1450.

meditate *verb* to think about something quietly and deeply. **meditation** *noun*.

meek *adjective* timid and patient and sometimes too obedient.

meet (meets, meeting, met) *verb* 1 to come face to face with somebody or something. 2 to come together by plan. *Let's meet at the library after supper.* 3 to join or come together from different places. *The place where two rivers meet is called a confluence.*

meeting *noun* a time and place planned for people to come together to discuss or contest something.

mega- *prefix* very big. *Megawatt.*

megabyte *noun* a unit of memory in a computer (about a million bytes).

megalith *noun* a very large stone put up in prehistoric times.

The megalith marked an ancient burial ground.

melancholy *noun, adjective* very sad or gloomy. *A melancholy tale.*

mellow *adjective* 1 (of fruit) sweet and juicy. 2 (of light) soft and golden. 3 (of people) older but pleasanter. **mellow** *verb*. *She has mellowed with age.*

melodious *adjective* nice to listen to. *A beautifully melodious voice.*

melody (melodies) *noun* a sweet, pleasing tune. *I played a lovely melody on the flute.*

melon *noun* a large round juicy fruit with a green or yellow skin and lots of seeds inside.

melt *verb* to change from a solid to a liquid by heating. *The ice-cream melted in the Sun.*

member *noun* somebody or something that belongs to a group, team, club, family etc. **membership** *noun*.

memorable *adjective* worth remembering, famous, easy to remember. *Their graduation memorable event.*

memorize *verb* to learn something so well that you can remember it word for word. *Actors have to memorize their lines.*

memory *noun* 1 the ability to remember things. *He has a good memory for telephone numbers.* 2 things that you can remember about the distant past. *Childhood memories.* 3 the part of a computer that stores and retrieves information.

Janice mended the rip in her skirt.

SPELLING NOTE

In British English we 'meet people'. The British may also 'meet with' opposition, disapproval or an accident. Americans 'meet with' people as well as with accidents etc.

AMAZING FACT

Because Mercury is so close to the Sun, it has a very short year. A year on Mercury is only 88 Earth days.

Mercury is also the name of a planet, the planet nearest to the Sun.

men *noun* the plural of man.

menace *noun* somebody or something that is a threat or danger and may cause damage. *Icy roads and bad visibility are a menace to drivers.*

mend *verb* to repair a tear or hole in a piece of clothing. *Mom mended my gymsuit over the weekend.*

menstruation *noun* blood that comes from a woman's womb about once a month. A period. **menstruate** *verb*.

mental *adjective* relating to the mind, done in the head. *Mental arithmetic.*

mention *verb* to make a casual or brief remark about something. *I think she did mention you would be out of town.* **mention** *noun*.

menu (menus) *noun* 1 a list of the dishes you can choose from in a restaurant. 2 a list of choices displayed on a computer screen. *If you get stuck in the program, just go back to the main menu and start again.*

merchandise *noun* goods for sale.

merchant *noun* a person who buys and sells large quantities of goods of a particular kind. *A coffee merchant.* **merchant navy** a nation's ships that carry goods.

merciful *adjective* willing to forgive somebody and not punish them.

merciless *adjective* cruel and showing no pity, ruthless.

mercury *noun* a silvery metal that is usually liquid. Mercury is used in thermometers.

mercy *noun* ready to show kindness and forgiveness to somebody who has done something wrong.

merely *adverb* simply, only. *She merely laughed when I fell down.* **mere** *adjective*. *Lucy is a mere child.*

merge *verb* to combine or blend together. *The two firms decided to merge.* **merger** *noun*.

merry (merrier, merriest) *adjective* 1 cheerful and happy. *Have a merry Christmas.* 2 (informal) very slightly drunk.

mesmerize *verb* to be so fascinated by something that you can think of nothing else. To be hypnotized.

mess *noun* not neat, with things lying everywhere, disorganized. *Your desk is such a mess!* **messy** *adjective.*

message *noun* information sent from one person or group to another. *Are there any telephone messages for me?*

met past tense of meet.

metal *noun* a hard material that goes soft and can be bent when heated. Metals are usually shiny and conduct heat well. Copper, gold, iron and silver are all metals.

metamorphosis *noun* the complete change in form that some animals go through as they develop. *The metamorphosis of a tadpole into a frog.*

metaphor *noun* an expression in which something or somebody is described as though they were something else. *She has a green thumb and he has a heart of gold.*

meteor *noun* a large piece of metal or rock that travels through space and normally burns up if it enters Earth's atmosphere.

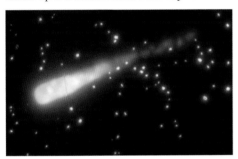

meteorite *noun* a meteor that has fallen to Earth from space.

meteorology *noun* the scientific study of the atmosphere and weather. **meteorologist** *noun* a person who forecasts the weather.

meter *noun* an instrument that measures how much electricity, gas, water etc. has been used. *He came to read the meter.*

meter *noun* a measure of length equal to 1,000 millimetres. **metric** *adjective* to do with the metre or metric system. **metric system** a system of weighing and measuring based on 10 and multiples of 10. Kilograms, liters and meters are all metric measures.

method *noun* a certain way of doing something, a system. *There are several methods for making coffee.*

methodical *adjective* in an orderly, well-organized way, according to plan.

metropolis *noun* a very large city.

Mexican *noun* a person who comes from Mexico. **Mexican** *adjective. A Mexican hat.*

Mexico City *noun* the capital of Mexico.

The meteor shower was spectacular, with up to six shooting stars lighting up the sky at once.

There are 12 hours between midnight and noon, so the hands of the clock move once around its face in that time.

Mexico *noun* a country in North America.

In Mexico 90 per cent of the population belongs to the Roman Catholic Church.

mice plural of mouse.

micro- *prefix* very small. *Microchip, microfilm, microsecond.*

microbe *noun* a living thing that is so tiny that it can be seen only through a microscope. *Swarming with microbes.*

microchip or **silicon chip** *noun* a tiny piece of silicon with electronic circuits printed on it, used in computers and other electronic equipment. *The microchip industry.*

Micronesia *noun* a country of many islands in the Pacific Ocean.

microphone *noun* an electrical instrument that is used to help record sound, or to make sounds louder than they really are.

microscope *noun* an instrument with lenses that makes tiny objects look much larger. *We looked at the ant under the microscope.*

microscopic *adjective* so tiny that it cannot be seen except through a microscope.

microwave *noun* an oven that cooks food very quickly by using energy in very short waves (electronic microwaves).

midday *noun* the middle of the day, 12 noon.

middle *noun, adjective* the part of something that is half-way or the same distance from its ends or its sides. *A cherry has a pit in the middle.* **middle age** the time of a person's life between about the ages of 40 and 60. **Middle Ages** a period in European history between about 1100 and 1450. **Middle East** an area at the eastern end of the Mediterranean Sea and including Egypt and Iran.

middle school a school for students 11-14.

midget *noun* an exceptionally short person.

midnight *noun* 12 o'clock in the middle of the night. **midnight** *adjective. A midnight feast.*

midwife *noun* a person whose job it is to help women at the birth of their babies.

migraine *noun* (say **my**-grane) a very severe, throbbing headache that makes you feel sick.

migration *noun* the movement from one place to another to live. **migrate** *verb*. *Geese migrate every winter*. **migratory** *adjective*.
migrant *noun* 1 a person who is moving or migrating from one country to another. 2 a bird that migrates each year.

mild *adjective* 1 gentle. *She has a mild nature*. 2 not too bad or severe. *A mild fever*. 3 (of weather) rather warm. *A mild winter*. 4 (of food or drink) not strong or too spicy. *A mild chili*.

mildew *noun* a grayish fungus that grows on plants or decaying matter.

mile *noun* a measure of distance equal to 1,760 yards or 1.6 km. **to be miles away** to daydream. *Sorry, I was miles away*.

militant *adjective* aggressive and ready to fight, very active in support of a cause.

military *adjective* relating to armed forces and warfare. *In some countries, all young men have to do military service*.

This scene shows what military life was like during the First World War.

milk *noun* 1 the white liquid that female mammals make in their bodies to feed their young. 2 the milk of cows and goats used as food for humans and to make things like cheese and butter. **milk** *verb* to take milk from a cow. **milky** *adjective*. **milk-tooth** one of the first, temporary teeth in young mammals. Milk teeth fall out and are replaced by teeth that should last you the rest of your life.

mill *noun* 1 a building with machinery for grinding grain into flour. 2 a factory. *A steel mill*. 3 a small grinding tool. *A pepper mill*.

millennium (millennia) *noun* a period of a thousand years.

milligram *noun* a very small measure of weight. There are 1,000 milligrams in a kilogram.

milliliter *noun* a very small liquid measure. There are 1,000 milliliters in a liter.

millipede *noun* a small worm-like creature with many pairs of legs.

WORD HISTORY

'Mile' comes from a Latin word for a thousand (as do 'millennium', 'milligram', 'millipede', etc). A mile was a Roman unit of length – 'mille passuum', or a thousand paces.

mime *noun* a kind of acting without words in which the actors use gestures and facial expressions. **mime** *verb*.

mimic (mimics, mimicking, mimicked) *verb* to imitate somebody's actions or speech, usually to amuse people. **mimic** *noun*. *He's a good mimic*.

minaret *noun* a tall tower near a mosque from the top of which the muezzin calls people to prayer.

A muezzin, a holy man, calls Muslims to prayer from the minaret on a mosque.

mince *verb* to chop food into tiny pieces. **mince** *Mince the onions finely and gently brown them before adding the spices*.

mincemeat *noun* finely chopped dried fruit and spices, used in making pies.

mind *noun* the part of you that thinks, feels, learns, understands and remembers. *He has a very fine mind*. Your intelligence. **make up your mind** to decide.

mind *verb* to care about or feel unhappy about something. *Do you mind if I turn on the TV?*

mindless *adjective* stupid and unthinking.

mine *noun* 1 an underground place where people dig to obtain such things as gold or diamonds. 2 a bomb buried under the ground or in the ocean. *The car was blown up by a mine*. **mine** *verb*. **minefield** *noun* an area covered with buried explosive mines, or a situation that is full of possible danger.

miner *noun* a person who works down a mine. *The miners voted to strike*.

mineral *noun* a natural substance such as coal, gold and salt, which is mined from the earth. **mineral** *adjective* of or containing minerals. *Mineral water*.

This beautiful blue-green mineral is Mexican selenite.

mingle *verb* to mix with or blend. *The police mingled with the crowd*.

mini- *prefix* smaller or shorter than normal.

miniature *adjective* very small. *A miniature railway*. **miniature** *noun* a small version of something much larger, such as a painting.

minimize *verb* 1 to make something seem unimportant. *She tried to minimize the problem.* 2 to make as small as possible.

minimum *noun* the smallest amount or number of something you can have. *You need a minimum of ten people for the trip.* **minimum** *adjective. The minimum cost will be $10.* The opposite of minimum is maximum.

mining *noun* the process or industry of extracting minerals from the earth. *The coal-mining industry.*

minister *noun* 1 a member of the clergy who holds services in a Protestant church. 2 the head of a government department. *The Minister of Health visited the medical school.*

ministry *noun* 1 the work of a clergyman. 2 a government department. *The Ministry of Agriculture.*

minnow *noun* a tiny fish found in lakes and rivers. *He used minnows for bait but he didn't catch a single fish.*

minor *adjective* small, unimportant, not serious. *A minor accident.* The opposite of minor is major. **minor** *noun* a young person who is under the age of 18.

minority *noun* 1 the smaller of two groups of people or things. *Only a minority voted against.* 2 a small number of people of one race, culture or religion living among a much larger group of people of a different race, culture or religion. The opposite of minority is majority.

Minsk *noun* the capital of Belarus.

mint *noun* 1 a plant whose leaves are used as a flavoring. 2 a place where coins are made.

minus *noun* a mathematical term or symbol (–) meaning subtraction or taking away. *Seven minus five equals two, or 7–5 = 2.*

minute *noun* (**min**-it) a period of time consisting of 60 seconds. There are 60 minutes in an hour.

minute (**my**-newt) *adjective* 1 very small, tiny. *A minute speck of dust.* 2 very detailed. *A minute examination.*

miracle *noun* an amazing and unexpected happening for which there is no explanation. *His escape from the blazing car was a miracle.* **miraculous** *adjective.*

A shoal of minnows flashed past as the children watched from the bridge.

mirage *noun* something that you imagine you see but that is not really there, an optical illusion. *The travelers saw a mirage of an oasis in the desert.*

mirror *noun* a piece of special glass, metal or plastic that reflects light and whatever is in front of it.

Mom kept a mirror on her make-up table for checking her make-up.

mis- *prefix* wrongly. *Misbehave, misjudge.*

misbehave *verb* to behave badly. **misbehavior** *noun.*

miscellaneous *adjective* a mixture or assortment of various things.

mischief *noun* annoying but harmless behavior. **mischievous** *adjective. A mischievous child.*

miser *noun* a very stingy person who likes to hoard money but who will not spend it. **miserly** *adjective.*

The miser spent a lot of time alone, enjoying counting his money.

misery *noun* a feeling of great unhappiness, wretchedness. *Natural disasters sometimes cause great hardship and misery.* **miserable** *adjective. Jane is miserable because she can't go to the concert with her friends.*

misfit *noun* somebody who does not belong to a group because they are in some way strange or different.

misfortune *noun* bad luck.

mishap *noun* an unfortunate accident.

mislay (mislays, mislaying, mislaid) *verb* to lose something for a short time because you have forgotten where you put it. *I seem to have mislaid my glasses.*

mislead *verb* to give somebody a false idea by making them believe something that is untrue. To deceive or give wrong information. **misleading** *adjective. This newspaper article is very misleading.*

miss *verb* 1 to fail to do something such as hitting or catching. *Peter threw me a ball but I missed it.* 2 to fail to be somewhere at the right time. *Matt missed the train by a minute.* 3 to be sad because somebody is no longer with you. *She missed her friend when he went to camp.*

Miss *noun* a title often put before the name of a girl or unmarried woman.

missile *noun* a weapon that is sent through the air and which explodes when it hits its target. *The missile hit the ammunition store.*

missing *adjective* 1 lost. *A missing dog.* 2 absent. *Two men are missing from the team.*

mission *noun* 2 an important job that somebody is sent somewhere to do. *The astronauts were sent on a mission to Mars.* 2 important work that somebody thinks they should do. *Her mission in life was to help the poor.*

missionary *noun* somebody who is sent to another country to tell the people about a religion. *The missionaries were eaten by tigers, or so the local people said.*

mist *noun* a low cloud of damp air that is difficult to see through.

mistake *noun* something that is wrong or incorrect, an error. *Can you see a spelling misstake?*

mistake (mistakes, mistaking, mistook) *verb* 1 to misunderstand or to make an error about something. *She mistook my instructions and went the wrong way.* 2 to confuse one person or thing for another. *I mistook you for your brother.*

mistaken *adjective* wrong and not correctly understood. *He has the mistaken belief that the Sun spins around the Earth.*

misty *adjective. Misty gray mornings.*

mistreat *verb* to treat in a bad, cruel or unfair way. **mistreatment** *noun.*

misunderstand (misunderstands, misunderstanding, misunderstood) *verb* not to understand the meaning of something correctly, to get the wrong idea.

misunderstanding *noun* 1 a wrong or false idea about the meaning of something. *There must be some misunderstanding.* 2 a quarrel or disagreement.

Steven put the ingredients for the cake in the mixer.

Their mission to the Moon was a milestone in the history of humankind.

WORD HISTORY

Mob comes from the Latin words 'mobile vulgus'. 'Vulgus' means 'masses' or 'crowd' and 'mobile' means 'moveable', 'fickle' or 'easily swayed'.

Mobile phones have become extremely popular in a very short time.

SPELLING NOTE

'Moccasin' is often misspelled. Note that it has two 'c's and only a single 's'.

mitten *noun* a kind of glove that has one part for the thumb and one part for four fingers. *We put on hats and mittens and went out to build a snowman.*

mix *verb* to combine or put different things together. **mixture** *noun. A cake mixture.* **mix-up** *noun* a confusion. *There's some mix-up in the dates.*

mixer *noun* a machine that you use to mix things together. *A cement mixer.*

mnemonic *noun* (say nem-on-ik) an aid, such as a rhyme, to help us remember facts.

moan *verb* 1 to make a low, unhappy sound because you are in pain or sad. 2 to grumble and complain. *He's always moaning about the weather.* **moan** *noun. A moan of grief.*

moat *noun* a deep, wide ditch, usually filled with water, around a castle. Moats helped to protect castles from attack.

mob *noun* a noisy, and often violent, crowd of angry people. **mob** *verb* to crowd around. *The fans mobbed the movie star.*

mobile *adjective* able to be moved about easily and quickly. *A mobile home.*

mobile phone *noun* a portable telephone that fits easily into a pocket or purse. Often shortened to mobile.

moccasin *noun* a soft leather shoe without a heel. Moccasins were first worn by Native Americans.

mock *verb* to make fun of somebody, often by copying them in a cruel and unpleasant way. *She mocked the way he stuttered.* **mock** *adjective* not real, imitation. *Mock diamonds.* **mockery** *noun.*

model *noun* 1 a small, to-scale copy of something. *A model of a castle.* 2 a good example. *He is a model of good behavior.* 3 a person whose job is to wear new clothes to show them off to people before they buy them. 4 a person who poses for an artist or photographer. 5 a style or particular version of a product. *This computer is the latest model.* **model** *verb.*

modem *noun* a device to send information between computers by telephone.

moderate *adjective* 1 not extreme, neither too big nor too small. 2 average.

modern *adjective* happening now, new and not old-fashioned. *Modern technology.*

modest *adjective* 1 quiet and not boastful. 2 not extreme or very large, moderate.

Mogadishu *noun* the capital of Somalia.

moist *adjective* a little wet, damp. **moisten** *verb* to make or become slightly wet.

moisture *noun* dampness. Tiny drops of water such as steam.

mold *verb* to model or shape something. **mold** *noun* a container into which a liquid is poured, which sets to make a solid shape.

mold *noun* a fungus found on stale food or damp things.

Moldova *noun* a country in eastern Europe.

The flag of Moldova has blue, yellow and red stripes with an eagle and crest in the centre.

mole *noun* a small brown spot that is slightly raised on the skin.

mole *noun* a small, dark gray, furry animal that digs tunnels under the ground with its strong front paws. Moles leave behind piles of soil called molehills. *Don't make a mountain out of a molehill.*

molecule *noun* the smallest amount of a substance that can exist on its own. A water molecule is made up of one atom of oxygen and two of hydrogen.

mollusc *noun* an animal with a soft body and no backbone such as a snail, slug or octopus.

A garden snail is a mollusc. It is like a slug with a shell on its back.

molten *adjective* heated, turned to liquid and melted. *Molten lava.*

moment *noun* a very short period of time. *Wait a moment.* **momentary** *adjective. A momentary pause.* **at the moment** now.

momentum *noun* the force gained by an object as it moves.

Monaco *noun* a country in southern Europe.

monarch *noun* (say **mon**-ark) a king or queen. **monarchy** *noun.*

AMAZING FACT

There are about 70,000 different types of molluscs. They range in size from a few millimeters to the giant squid, which may grow to be twelve meters.

Monkeys are extremely intelligent animals. Some types are becoming endangered due to hunting or destruction of habitat.

WORD BUILDER

The prefix 'mono' is a useful word builder, as in: 'monoplane' (an airplane with one set of wings), 'monorail' (a railway with carriages hanging from one rail), and 'monosyllable' (a word with one syllable).

---

monastery *noun* a group of buildings in which a community of monks lives and works, an abbey. **monastic** *adjective.*

money *noun* the coins and banknotes we use to buy things.

Mongolia *noun* a country in central Asia.

mongoose (mongooses) *noun* a small African or Asian animal with a long body that kills poisonous snakes.

mongrel *noun* a dog that is a mixture of different breeds. *Many mongrels make very good pets.*

monitor *noun* 1 a student who has been given special duties or responsibilities. 2 a computer screen. 3 an instrument, usually with a screen, that keeps a check on something and records any changes.

monk *noun* a member of a religious community of men who live, pray and work together in a building called a monastery.

monkey *noun* an animal with long arms and a long tail that climbs trees. Monkeys are primates and belong to the same group as apes and people. **monkey business** some mischievous or illegal activity. **monkey around with** to touch or play with something.

mono- *prefix* one or alone. *Monorail.*

monopoly *noun* having sole control of the manufacture or supply of a product or service. **monopolize** *verb* to control something completely.

monotonous *adjective* dull, boring and lacking any variety. *She has a monotonous voice.* **monotony** *noun.*

Monrovia *noun* the capital of Liberia.

monsoon *noun* a strong prevailing wind around the Indian Ocean that changes direction and brings rain.

monster *noun* 1 a terrifying but imaginary creature. 2 a cruel person. **monster** *adjective* very big or strange. **monstrous** *adjective.*

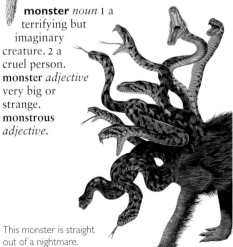

This monster is straight out of a nightmare.

Monte Carlo *noun* the capital of Monaco.

Montevideo *noun* the capital of Uruguay.

month *noun* a period of time and one of the twelve divisions of the year. **monthly** *adjective* happening once a month or every month. *A monthly magazine.* **calendar month** one of the twelve divisions of the year. From 1 March to 31 March is a calendar month. **lunar month** a period of about 29 days, the time it takes the Moon to orbit the Earth.

monument *noun* 1 an old and important building, statue etc. *Ancient monuments.* 2 a building or statue erected so that people will remember an important person or event. **monumental** *adjective*.

mood *noun* the way you feel or your state of mind at a particular time. *Winning the game put him in a good mood.* **moody** *adjective* bad-tempered or liable to change mood quickly for no apparent reason. **moodiness** *noun*.

moon *noun* 1 a natural satellite or small planet that orbits a larger planet. 2 **the Moon** the natural satellite that orbits the Earth once every four weeks (lunar month). The Moon is our closest neighbor in space.

As the Moon waxes and wanes, it passes through various phases.

moonlight *noun* the light from the Sun reflected by the Moon. *The moonlight shimmered in a silver stream across the lake.*

moor *verb* to tie up a boat so that it cannot drift away. **moorings** *noun*.

moose (plural moose) *noun* a large brown deer found in the forests of North America. The male has huge, flattened antlers. *We saw a moose on the road when we went to Vermont.*

The moose uses its antlers to fight off rivals for a mate.

mop *noun* an implement with soft material such as a sponge attached to a long handle, used for cleaning floors and dishes. **mop** (mops, mopping, mopped) *verb* to wipe with a mop or cloth. *He mopped his brow in the searing heat.*

WORD HISTORY

'Mosquito' comes from a Portuguese word that means 'little fly', originally from the Latin 'musca', 'fly'.

AMAZING FACT

'Moose' is a Native American word. Moose and elk are completely different animals – in the US and Canada, that is.

In Europe, the moose is actually called an 'elk', which is an old German name.

Tiles from Turkey are often patterned with intensely coloured mosaic designs.

mope *verb* to feel sad and sorry for yourself.

moral *adjective* relating to good behavior and what is right and wrong. *Euthanasia is a moral question.* **moral** *noun* a lesson or point made in a story about what is right and wrong. **morals** *plural noun* standards of behavior and beliefs in right and wrong.

morale *noun* (say mor-**al**) the spirit of hope, confidence and enthusiasm among members of a group or team. *After its win, the team's morale is very high.*

more *adjective, pronoun* bigger in number, size or amount. *She has more marbles than me.* **more** *adverb*. *Can you say it once more?*

morgue *noun* a mortuary or place where corpses are kept until they are buried or cremated.

Moroccan *noun* a person who comes from Morocco. **Moroccan** *adjective*. *A Moroccan mosque.* **Morocco** *noun* a country in Africa.

Morocco, in northern Africa, is a Muslim country with many mosques.

Moroni *noun* the capital of Comoros.

morning *noun* the part of the day from sunrise to noon.

morsel *noun* a very small piece of food.

mortal *adjective* 1 incapable of living for ever. All living things are mortal. 2 causing death. *A mortal illness.* **mortal** *noun* a human being.

mortgage *noun* (say **more**-gage) a loan of money from a bank that you use to buy a house. **mortgage** *verb* to transfer the ownership of your house or property to a bank in return for money they lend you.

mortuary *noun* a place where dead bodies are kept before they are buried or cremated.

mosaic *noun* (say moh-**zay**-ik) a picture or design made from small pieces of colored glass or stone set in concrete.

Moscow *noun* the capital of Russia.

Moslem another spelling for Muslim.

mosque *noun* a building in which Muslims worship. *They prayed in the mosque.*

mosquito *noun* (say moss-**kee**-toe) a small flying insect that bites animals and people and sucks their blood. Anopheles mosquitoes transmit the disease malaria.

moss (mosses) *noun* a small green plant that forms a soft covering on stones in damp places. **mossy** *adjective*.

most *noun*, *adjective* the largest in size, number or amount. *Most apples are green or red.* **most** *adverb*. *The most intelligent boy in the class.*

mostly *adverb* generally, mainly. *What you are saying is mostly nonsense.*

motel *noun* a hotel that caters for people traveling by car.

moth *noun* an insect like a butterfly that is usually seen flying at night.

The peppered moth camouflages itself against the bark of trees.

mother *noun* a female parent, the woman who gave birth to you. **mother** *verb* to look after like a mother. **motherly** *adjective*. **motherhood** *noun*. *Motherhood was her greatest joy.*

mother-in-law *noun* the mother of a person's husband or wife.

motion *noun* movement, the action of moving. *The motion of the coach sent him to sleep.* **motion** *verb* to signal or make a movement, usually with the hand.

motion picture *noun* a cinema film.

motionless *adjective* not moving.

motive *noun* a reason that causes somebody to do something. *What was the motive for the crime?*

motor *noun* an engine in a machine that uses fuel to make it work or move. **motor** *adjective* having to do with engines and vehicles.

motorcycle *noun* a two-wheeled vehicle with an engine.

motorist *noun* a person who drives a car. *A tax on motorists.*

motorcade *noun* a group of vehicles, often motorcycles, that travels surrounding an important person's car.

motorhome *noun* a large vehicle that hs facilities for eating and sleeping.

mottled *adjective* marked with patches of different color.

Moss formed on the shady side of the tree.

DID YOU KNOW

'Motel' is a good example of a hybrid or blend word. It is a blend of 'motor car' and 'hotel'. Other examples are 'brunch' ('breakfast' and 'lunch') and 'smog' ('smoke' and 'fog').

The mouse on a computer moves the cursor on the screen.

AMAZING FACT

'The Jazz Singer', starring Al Jolson, was the first 'talkie' – a motion picture that had sound.

---

motto *noun* a phrase that sums up what is important or a guiding principle.

mound *noun* 1 a small hill, a pile or heap. *A burial mound.*

mount *verb* 1 to climb on the back of a horse, pony etc. 2 to increase. *The cost of building is mounting.* 3 to fix something somewhere, for example in a frame so as to display it.

mount *noun* a mountain, usually as part of the name of a mountain. *Reaching the summit of Mount Everest is a dream for many mountaineers.*

mountain *noun* a very high and usually steep hill. *The city is surrounded by beautiful mountains.*

mountain bike *noun* a bicycle with sturdy, thick tires that can be ridden on rough terrain. *We were on mountain bikes so we took a shortcut over the hill.*

mourn *verb* to feel great sadness because somebody has died, to grieve. **mourning** *noun. They mourned the passing of their friends.*

mouse (mice) *noun* 1 a small furry animal with a long tail and sharp teeth. Mice are rodents. *There's a mouse living under the porch.* 2 a small device on your desk that you move on the surface with your hand to control the position of the cursor on a computer screen. *The mouse on this PC is really sticky.*

Roller

Ball

Wheel

moustache *noun* mustache. hair growing above a man's top lip.

mouth *noun* 1 the part of your face that opens when you speak and into which you put food. 2 the place where a river flows out to ocean. 3 the entrance to a cave etc.

mouthful (mouthfuls) *noun* the amount you put in your mouth at one time.

mouth-organ *noun* a small musical instrument that you play by moving it along your lips while blowing and sucking.

mouthpiece *noun* the part of a musical instrument, pipe etc. that you put in your mouth.

movable *adjective* able to be moved. *The hands of a clock are movable.*

move *verb* 1 to go from one position or place to another. *Don't move, I want to take your picture.* 2 to change your home. *We moved into a new house.* 3 to make you feel something deeply. *He was moved to tears by the sad film.*

movement *noun* 1 the act of moving. *She made a sudden movement.* 2 a group of people working together for a common cause. *The women's movement.* 3 a section into which some pieces of classical music are divided. *Most symphonies have a slow movement.*

movie *noun* a motion picture. *Let's go to the movies.*

moving *adjective* touching or moving the feelings. *It was a moving film about orphans.*

mow (mows, mowing, mowed, mown) *verb* (rhymes with go) to cut grass or hay with a machine called a **mower** or **lawnmower** *noun*. *Sid mowed the front lawn.*

Mozambique *noun* a country in Africa.

Mozambique lies on the east coast of Africa opposite the island of Madagascar.

mph *abbreviation* miles per hour.

Mr *abbreviation* mister (say **mist**-er) a title put before a man's name.

Mrs *abbreviation* mistress (say **miss**-iz) a polite title put before the name of a married woman. *Mrs Jones' maiden name was Henderson.*

Ms (say miz) a title that some people put before the name of woman, which does not show whether she is married or single.

much *adjective, adverb, pronoun* a large amount, a lot. *Did you see much?*

muck *noun* dirt, filth, mud. *Our boots were covered in sticky, black muck.*

mucus *noun* the liquid produced by your nose.

mud *noun* soft, wet earth. **muddy** *adjective*. *Take off your muddy boots, I just washed that floor!*

AMAZING FACT

In Ancient Egypt, it was not only humans who were mummified. Cats were also preserved.

WORD HISTORY

'Mummy' was originally an Arabic word 'mumiya' meaning 'an embalmed body'. 'Mum' was the Arabic word for the wax used in the process of preserving the corpse.

Mummies were stored in beautifully painted and decorated caskets.

---

muddle *noun* a thoroughly confused mess, a jumble. **muddle** *verb* 1 to mix things up in a confused way. 2 to confuse somebody or be confused.

mudguard *noun* a shield above a wheel on a vehicle that stops water and mud being splashed around.

muesli *noun* a food of mixed crushed cereals, nuts and dried fruit that people usually eat for breakfast.

muezzin *noun* a person who calls Muslims to prayer, usually from a minaret.

mug *noun* a tall cup with straight sides that you use without a saucer. *We had a mug of hot chocolate when we came in from skating.*

mug (mugs, mugging, mugged) *verb* to attack and rob somebody in the street. *Jane was mugged outside her apartment.* **mugger** *noun*.

mule *noun* an animal that is the offspring of a male donkey and a female horse or pony. *The mule carried us up the mountain.*

multi- *prefix* many. *Multi-colored.*

multi-media *adjective* involving the use of a mixture of different media such as TV, radio, video etc.

multiple *adjective* involving more than one, many. *She suffered multiple injuries in the accident.* **multiple** *noun* any number that can be divided exactly by another number. 20, 30 and 40 are multiples of 2, 5 and 10.

multiply (multiplies, multiplying, multiplied) *verb* to increase a number by adding the number to itself a given number of times. **multiplication** *noun*. The opposite of multiply is divide.

multitude *noun* a crowd, a large number of things. *I've a multitude of things to do.*

mumble *verb* to speak in a low, indistinct voice that is not easy to understand.

mummy (mummies) *noun* a dead body that has been preserved from decay by being rubbed with special oils and wrapped in cloths, especially in ancient Egypt.

mumps *noun* a painful infectious disease that makes your neck and the sides of your face swell.

munch *verb* to chew something in a noisy way. *The horse munched a crisp apple.*

mural *noun* a picture painted on a wall.

murder *verb* to kill somebody on purpose. **murder** *noun. The police are investigating three murders.* **murderous** *adjective.*

murderer *noun* a person who commits a murder. *The murderer was jailed for life.*

Muscat *noun* the capital of Oman.

muscle *noun* a part inside your body that stretches and relaxes to make different parts of your body move. *Tennis players need to have strong arm muscles.*

Thin tissue   Bundles of fibres

muse *verb* to think deeply about something.

museum *noun* (say meeyou-zee-um) a place where interesting or rare objects are kept on display for people to look at.

mushroom *noun* a fungus that looks like an umbrella. Some you can eat, but others are poisonous.

music *noun* 1 the pleasing mixture and pattern of sounds made by somebody singing or by musical instruments. 2 the written or printed signs and notes that represent musical sounds.

musical *adjective* 1 relating to music. *Musical instruments.* 2 good at making or understanding music. *She is very musical.* **musical** *noun* a play or film in which singing and dancing form an important part.

musician *noun* a composer of music, a person who plays a musical instrument well.

musket *noun* an old-fashioned kind of gun with a long barrel.

Muslim or **Moslem** *noun* a person who believes in Islam, the religion founded by the prophet Mohammed. **Muslim** *adjective.*

mussel *noun* a small shellfish with two black shells.

must *verb* that strengthens other verbs 1 to need to, to have to. *I must go to bed now.* 2 to be obliged to. *You must obey the rules.* 3 to be definitely or likely. *You must be happy to have won.*

mustard *noun* a hot-tasting yellow paste made from the seeds of the mustard plant and used to flavor food.

Each fibre is made of hundreds of strands called fibrils.

Muscles work in pairs. As one contracts or tightens, the other relaxes.

Muscle fibres are so small that 1 sq cm would contain a million of them.

SPELLING NOTE

Scholars and most Muslims prefer the spelling 'Muslim' to 'Moslem', although 'Moslem' is more widespread.

This is what mustard seeds look like under the microscope.

mute *adjective* 1 unable to speak. 2 silent, speechless. *They stared at one another in mute amazement.*

mutilate *verb* to damage somebody or something, usually by cutting off a part of it. *A mutilated body.*

mutiny *noun* a rebellion by sailors or soldiers against officers in charge. **mutiny** *verb.* **mutinous** *adjective. Mutinous troops.* **mutineer** *noun. The mutineers took over the ship and threw the captain overboard.*

mutter *verb* to speak in a very low angry voice that cannot be heard properly, to grumble. *Please don't mutter into your beard because I can't hear you.*

mutual 1 *adjective* shared by two or more people. In common. *We have mutual friends.* 2 done equally one to another. *Mutual respect.*

muzzle *noun* 1 the nose and mouth of an animal such as a dog or wolf. 2 straps put over an animal's muzzle to prevent it biting. *The dog wore a muzzle after it had bitten the mailman.* 3 the open end of a gun.

Myanmar *noun* a country in Southeast Asia, formerly called Burma.

mystery *noun* 1 something strange that has happened and which you cannot explain or understand, puzzling. *It's a complete mystery how he disappeared.* 2 a secret. **mysterious** *adjective. A mysterious castle.*

myth *noun* 1 an imaginary story from the distant past, usually about gods and heroes and how the world began. 2 a belief that is imagined and untrue. *It's a myth that spinach builds your muscles.* **mythical** *adjective. A mythical dragon got married to the princess in the fairytale.*

mythology *noun* a collection of myths. *Norse mythology.*

Greek mythology tells of the legend of the minotaur, a monster half-human and half-bull. The minotaur lived inside a maze and was eventually killed by the hero Theseus.

Nn

nag (nags, nagging, nagged) *verb* to annoy somebody by constantly complaining or trying to persuade them to do something. *Mom's always nagging me to clean my room.* **nag** *noun.*

A nail grows from the cuticle under the skin.

nail *noun* 1 the hard covering that protects the ends of your fingers and toes (fingernails, toenails). 2 a thin piece of metal with one end pointed and the other end flat that can be used for fastening pieces of wood etc. together. *She hammered a nail into the wall.* **nail** *verb. He nailed a notice on the door.*

Nairobi *noun* the capital of Kenya.

naked *adjective* with no clothes on, uncovered. **nakedness** *noun.*

name *noun* 1 a word by which a person, animal or place is known or called. *My cat's name is Archie.* 2 a reputation. *The bank has a very good name.* **name** *verb. They named their baby Billy.* **name after** to give somebody or something the same name as somebody else. *The city of Adelaide in Australia is named after Queen Adelaide.*

namesake *noun* somebody with the same name as you.

Namibia *noun* a country in Africa.

nanny *noun* a person who is trained to take care of young children in their own home.

nanny goat *noun* a female goat.

nap *noun* a short sleep.

nape *noun* the back of your neck.

napkin *noun* a square piece of cloth or paper that you put on your lap to protect your clothes or to wipe your hands or lips during a meal.

These are two deserts in Namibia, the Namib and the Kalahari.

Air is inhaled through the nasal passages, where it is warmed before it is taken into the chest.

narrate *verb* to tell a story or relate an account of something.

narrative *noun* a story or account of things that have happened.

narrator *noun* a person who tells a story or explains what is happening.

narrow *adjective* thin and not measuring very much from one side to the other. *The door is too narrow for the piano to go through.* **narrow** *verb. The road narrowed.* The opposite of narrow is wide.

narrow-minded *adjective* unwilling to understand or even consider ideas that are new or different.

nasal *adjective* relating to the nose. *The nasal passages.*

Nassau *noun* the capital of the Bahamas.

nasty (nastier, nastiest) *adjective* 1 unpleasant. *A nasty smell.* 2 unkind. 3 serious. *A nasty accident.*

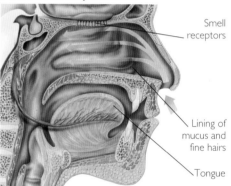

Smell receptors

Lining of mucus and fine hairs

Tongue

nation *noun* a country with all the people who live there under one government and often sharing the same language, customs etc. *The nations of the world.*

national *adjective* belonging to a nation. *National dress.* **national anthem** a country's official hymn or song. **national park** an area of countryside under the care and ownership of the nation.

nationalism *noun* great pride in the culture, history and success of your own country.

nationalist *noun* 1 person who is very proud of their country. 2 a person who wants their country to be independent. *Scottish nationalist.*

nationality *noun* belonging to a particular nation. *He is of Russian nationality.*

nationalize *verb* to put a privately owned company under state control. **nationalization** *noun.* The opposite of nationalize is privatize.

native *noun* 1 one of the first inhabitants of a country. *Native American.* 2 a person who was born in a particular place. *She's a native of Miami.* **native** *adjective. What is your native language?*

Native American *noun* a member of the original race of people who lived in North America (often incorrectly called American Indians).

nativity *noun* the birth of Jesus Christ.

NATO *abbreviation* North Atlantic Treaty Organization. A group of North American and European countries that give military support to each other.

natural *adjective*
1 relating to or concerned with nature. *Earthquakes are natural disasters.*
2 made by nature and not by humans. *The natural beauty of the mountains.*
3 ordinary and not surprising. *It's natural to laugh if you are amused.*

naturalist *noun* somebody who studies wildlife. *A naturalist in the field.*

nature *noun* (say **nay-chur**) 1 everything in the world around us not made by people, such as plants, animals, oceans, mountains etc. 2 characteristics that make up what a person or animal is really like. Personality. *He has a forgiving nature.*

naughty (naughtier, naughtiest) *adjective* badly behaved, mischievous. **naughtiness** *noun*. **naughtily** *adverb*.

nautical *adjective* relating to ships, sailing and the sea. *A nautical map.*

naval *adjective* relating to the navy or ships of war. *The battle of Trafalgar was fought at sea – it was a naval battle.*

navel *noun* the small round hollow in your stomach where your umbilical cord was attached when you were born. Belly-button.

navigate *verb* to steer a ship or to pilot an aircraft in the right direction with the help of maps and special instruments. **navigation** *noun*.

navigator *noun* somebody who navigates or directs the movement of a ship or aircraft.

navy *noun* the warships and sailors that help defend a country at sea.

navy blue *noun, adjective* very dark blue.

N'Djamena *noun* the capital of Chad.

Some tribes of Native Americans lived in conical tents called tepees.

AMAZING FACT

Native Americans came to the Americas from Asia via Siberia and Alaska about 30,000 years ago. Tribes settled in various places and developed distinct languages and cultures. Many states retain their Native American names: Wisconsin means 'grassy place', Ohio is 'fine river' and Michigan means 'great water'.

The compass, sextant and map are three tools of navigation.

---

n.b. *abbreviation* Latin words 'nota bene', meaning 'note well'.

near *preposition, adjective, adverb* 1 not far away, close to. *We live near the park.* 2 closely related. **near** *verb*. *As the boat neared the rocks it slowed down.*

nearby *adjective* not far away. *We stayed in a nearby town.*

nearly *adverb* almost but not quite. *He's nearly as tall as his father.*

neat *adjective* 1 very clean and tidy. *A neat pile of clothes.* 2 well done. *She has extremely neat handwriting.*

necessary *adjective* what must be done or is needed, essential and very important. *The climb is dangerous so please take all necessary precautions.*

neck *noun* the narrow part of a person or animal that joins the head to the body.

necklace *noun* a piece of jewelry that you wear around your neck.

nectar *noun* sweet juice that bees collect from flowers to make honey.

nectarine *noun* a fruit similar to a peach but with a smooth skin.

need *verb* 1 to want something that is a necessity. *We all need air to live.* 2 to have to do something. *I need to take the dog to the vet.* **need** *noun*. *You don't need to hurry.*

needle *noun* 1 a thin piece of steel with a sharp point at one end and a hole (or eye) for thread at the other end that is used for sewing. 2 a long thin pointed stick made of plastic or steel that is used for knitting. 3 an instrument with a long thin part used for giving injections. 4 a moving pointer on a meter. 5 the narrow pointed leaf of a coniferous tree. *Those Christmas trees are beautiful but you wind up with needles all over the place.*

needless *adjective* unnecessary. *Needless to say, you are welcome here anytime.*

needlework *noun* sewing and embroidery.

negative *adjective* 1 meaning 'no'. 'I will not come' and 'I'll never go' are negative answers. 2 a number less than zero. The opposite of negative is positive. **negative** *noun* 1 a photographic film showing dark areas as light and light areas as dark, used to make prints. 2 (in electricity) the opposite charge to positive.

neglect *verb* to fail to take care of or give enough attention to. *The lawn is overgrown and wild because he neglected to weed it.* **neglect** *noun*. *The house fell into neglect.*

negotiate *verb* to discuss something in order to come to an understanding or agreement, to bargain. **negotiation** *noun*. *The dispute was settled by negotiation.*

neigh *noun* the sound that a horse makes.
neigh *verb*. *The horse neighed happily.*

neighbor *noun* (say nay-bor) somebody who lives near or next door to you.

neighborhood *noun* the area surrounding where you live.

neighboring *adjective* next to one another. *Italy and France are neighboring countries.*

neighborly *adjective* friendly and helpful like a good neighbor.

neither *adjective, pronoun* not either, not one and not the other. *Neither answer is right.* **neither** *conjunction. I neither like him nor dislike him.*

neon *noun* a chemical gas. Neon is sometimes used in glass tubes to make them glow orange-red when electricity is passed through (neon light).

Nepal *noun* a Himalayan country in South Asia.

nephew *noun* the son of your brother or sister. *My nephew Tim.*

nerve *noun* 1 a long thin fiber in your body that carries messages and feelings between your brain and body so that your body can feel and move. 2 calm bravery. *You need a lot of nerve to be a paraglider.*

nervous *adjective* 1 relating to the nerves. *The nervous system.* 2 timid and easily frightened. *A nervous horse.*
nervousness *noun*.

Nerves carry information and instructions to and from the brain and from one part of the brain to another.

nest *noun* a home built by birds, some insects and some animals in which to lay eggs, give birth and raise their young. **nest** *verb. Swallows are nesting in the stable.*

nestle *verb* to curl up close together. *The kittens nestled together in the hay.*

net *noun* 1 a material made of knotted string or rope with a regular pattern of holes between the threads. 2 net material used as a fishing net, tennis net, hairnet etc.

netball *noun* a game in which two teams of seven players try to score goals by throwing a ball through a high net at each end of a court. *May was captian of the netball team.*

Netherlands *noun* a country in northwestern Europe, sometimes called Holland.

The flag of the Netherlands has horizontal red, white and blue stripes.

GRAMMAR NOTE

'Neither' is always followed by a singular verb, as in 'neither Jim nor Jane is clever' (not 'are clever'). And remember that you should always use 'neither... nor', as in 'neither you nor I' and never 'neither you or I'.

AMAZING FACT

Most species of newts lay 200–400 eggs at a time but some, such as the rough-skinned newt of North America, lay just one egg at a time.

nettle *noun* (or stinging nettle) a wild plant with leaves covered with hairs that sting you if you touch them.

network *noun* 1 a widespread organization. *The telecommunications network.* 2 an arrangement looking like a pattern of criss-crossing lines. *A network of underground tunnels.* 3 a system of linked computers that share a storage system.

neuter *adjective* (say **new**-ter) neither male nor female, with no sexual organs or with the sexual organs removed.

neutral *noun* 1 not taking sides or having strong feelings for or against in, for example, a disagreement or war. *A neutral country.* 2 (of colours) not too strong. *Gray is a neutral colour.*

neutron *noun* one of the particles that make up the nucleus of an atom but carry no electrical charge.

never *adverb* not ever, at no time in the past or in the future. *I will never let you go.*

new *adjective* 1 just made, built, bought, not used, fresh. *I got a new bike for my birthday.* 2 not known, seen or done before. *A new way of doing things.* 3 different, changed. *We have a new science teacher.* The opposite of new is old.

New Delhi *noun* the capital of India.

news *noun* information about events that have recently happened.

newsletter *noun* a short, written news report about a club, organization, etc.

newspaper *noun* printed sheets of folded paper containing news reports, articles, photographs, advertisements etc. and published daily or weekly.

newt *noun* an animal with short legs and a long tail that lives on land but lays its eggs in water. Newts are amphibians.

Newts are commonly found in ponds and damp places.

New Year *noun* the beginning of a year, starting on January 1.

New Zealand *noun* a country in Australasia.

New Zealander *noun* a person who comes from New Zealand. **New Zealand** *adjective. New Zealand lamb.*

next *adjective* 1 the nearest. *She lives next door.* 2 the one immediately after. *I'll catch the next train.* **next** *adverb. What happens next?*

Niamey *noun* the capital of Niger.

nib *noun* the point at the end of a pen that touches the paper as you write.

nibble *verb* to eat something by biting very small bits of it.

Nicaragua *noun* a country in Central America.

nice *adjective* pleasant and kind. *What a nice girl she is.*

nickel *noun* 1 a silver-colored metal that is mixed with other metals to make coins. 2 a US 5 cent coin.

nickname *noun* a special name that people call you instead of your real name.

Nicosia *noun* the capital of Cyprus.

niece *noun* the daughter of your brother or sister. *I love my niece.*

Niger *noun* a country in Africa.

Nigeria *noun* a country in Africa.

Nigerian *noun* a person who comes from Nigeria. **Nigerian** *adjective. Nigerian gold mines are very productive.*

night *noun* the time when it is dark, between sunset and sunrise. The opposite of night is day.

nightfall *noun* the end of the day and the beginning of the night.

nightingale *noun* a small brown European bird whose singing is heard at night.

nightly *adjective, adverb* taking place at night or every night. *The news is broadcast nightly at 9 o'clock.*

nightmare *noun* 1 a terrifying dream. 2 a frightening experience or situation. *Trying to avoid the gunfire was a nightmare.*

nil *noun* nothing. 0. *Our chances of winning the game are almost nil.*

nimble *adjective* able to move quickly and easily, active.

nip (nip, nipping, nipped) *verb* to give a small sharp bite, to pinch. *The dog nipped my sister on the ankle.* **nip something in the bud** to stop something befoe it can become a problem.

nipple *noun* the small part that sticks out on each of a person's breasts and from which a baby sucks milk from its mother.

nitrogen *noun* a colorless, tasteless gas that makes up over three-quarters of the Earth's atmosphere and the air we breathe.

WORD BUILDER

The sense of a word with the prefix 'non-' is usually easy to work out, if the meaning of the main or root word is clear. Here are examples: 'non-alcoholic', 'non-believer', 'non-existent', 'non-fiction', and 'non-stop'.

At night time you can see the Moon shining and the stars twinkling in the sky.

The first inhabitants of America were nomads who walked there from Siberia.

AMAZING FACT

There are still many nomadic peoples in Africa and Asia such as the Bedouin tribes of North Africa and the Middle East and the Maasai of Kenya.

noble *adjective* 1 aristocratic, important and of high social rank. *The Bourbons are a noble French family.* 2 honest and of a good and generous nature. **nobility** *noun.* **nobleman, noblewoman** *noun.*

nobody *pronoun* not one person. *There's nobody at home.* **nobody** *noun* an unimportant person. *She's a nobody.*

nocturnal *adjective* concerned with or active during the night. *Nocturnal animals.*

Bats are nocturnal creatures.

nod (nods, nodding, nodded) *verb* to bend your head up and down, perhaps as a sign of agreement or to say yes. **nod off** to half fall asleep by letting your head droop.

noise *noun* sound, usually one that is harsh, loud and unwanted. *Cats make a terrible yowling noise.* **noisily** *adverb.* The opposite of noise is silence.

noisy (noisier, noisiest) *adjective* making a lot of unpleasant noise, full of noise. *Noisy streets.*

nomad *noun* a member of a group of people without a permanent home who travel from place to place with their herds looking for pasture. **nomadic** *adjective. A nomadic way of life.*

nominate *verb* to propose that somebody would be the right person to do a job and should be a candidate in an election. To put forward somebody's name. *I nominate Tom as president of the club.* **nomination** *noun.*

non- *prefix* not, without. *Non-alcoholic drink is recommended for drivers.*

none *pronoun* not one, not any. *You've eaten all the cookies and there are none left!*

nonfiction *noun* books about real events rather than novels, poetry, plays etc.

nonsense *noun* 1 foolish words that are meaningless. *You're talking utter nonsense.* 2 silly behavior. *I'll stand no nonsense.*

nonstop *adjective* going on without stopping. *A nonstop flight to San Francisco.*

noodles *plural noun* long thin pieces of pasta used in soups etc.

noon *noun* midday, 12 o'clock in the middle of the day.

noose *noun* a loop in a rope that tightens as one end of the rope is pulled.

nor *conjunction* and not (used with neither). *I like neither spinach nor cabbage.*

normal *adjective* ordinary, as expected, usual. *She's a perfectly normal child.* **normality** *noun.*

north *noun* If you face the direction of the Sun as it rises in the morning, north is on your left. The opposite of north is south.

North America *noun* one of the Earth's seven continents.

North Korea *noun* a country in East Asia, officially called the Democratic People's Republic of Korea.

northern *adjective* in the north or of the north. *The lakes of northern Italy are beautiful in spring.*

Northern Ireland *noun* a country that is part of the United Kingdom.

North Pole *noun* the most northerly point on Earth. The north end of the Earth's axis.

northward *adjective, adverb* towards the north. *The troops marched northward.*

Norway *noun* a Scandinavian country in Europe.

Norwegian *noun* 1 a person who comes from Norway. 2 the language spoken in Norway. **Norwegian** *adjective. Norwegian fjords were created by glaciers.*

nose *noun* the part sticking out in the middle of your face that you use for breathing and smelling. **pay through the nose** pay too much.

nostalgia *noun* a feeling of sadness for the past and the happy times you had.

nostril *noun* one of the two holes at the end of your nose.

notable *adjective* famous or important. *Notable Mexican painters.*

notch *noun* a small cut in the shape of a V.

note *verb* 1 to write something down as a reminder. *He noted down my telephone number.* 2 to call attention to something, to notice. *Note the delicate shape of this vase.*

The magnetic needle of a compass always points to the north.

GRAMMAR NOTE

Where you put 'not' can change the meaning of a sentence. 'He is trying not to win,' is different from 'He is not trying to win.'

We always pin our holiday postcards to the noticeboard.

SPELLING NOTE

'Nought' or 'naught'? 'Naught' means 'nothing', as in the phrase: 'It came to naught.' 'Nought' is used for the figure 0 or zero.

note *noun* 1 a short letter. *We wrote thank-you notes to everyone who sent flowers.* 2 a few words you write down as a reminder of something. *He made a note of my address.* 3 a single musical sound or a symbol representing the sound.

These notes, composed long ago, are the beginning of a popular piece of music.

notebook *noun* a small book in which to write notes. *He scribbled in his notebook.*

noted *adjective* well-known.

nothing *pronoun* no thing, not any thing. *She says she has nothing to wear!*

notice *noun* 1 a written message or announcement that is put in a public place so everybody can read it. *The notice on the wall says: Private.* 2 warning. *The water may be cut off without notice.* **hand in your notice** to tell your employer that you intend to leave your job. *I had to give three months notice.*

notice *verb* to become aware of, to see or hear. *She noticed a big crack in the wall.*

noticeable *adjective* easily seen or noticed. *There's been a noticeable improvement in your handwriting.*

noticeboard *noun* a piece wood or cork etc. to which notices can be attached, usually with drawing pins.

notify (notifies, notifying, notified) *verb* to tell somebody formally about something. *You should notify the post office when you move.* **notification** *noun.*

notion *noun* a general idea, vague belief or strange idea. *What put that notion into your head?*

notorious *adjective* well known for being bad or unpleasant, infamous.

Nouakchott *noun* the capital of Mauritania.

nought *noun* (say nawt) the figure 0.

novel *noun* a long written story about imaginary people and events.

novel *adjective* new but different and original. *A novel design.*

novelty *noun* something new, unusual and different. *Gifts and novelties.*

November *noun* the eleventh month of the year. November has 30 days.

novice *noun* 1 a beginner without any experience. 2 a person who is training to be a monk or nun.

now *adverb* 1 the present time. *I am busy now.* 2 immediately and with no delay. *Do it right now, please!*

nowadays *adverb* at this present time. *Few people wear hats nowadays.*

nozzle *noun* the narrow part at the end of a pipe, tube or hose through which a gas, liquid or powder is forced out.

nuclear *adjective* to do with the nucleus, especially that of an atom, and the power created by splitting its nucleus. *Nuclear energy, nuclear missile, nuclear reactor.*

nucleus (nuclei) *noun* the central part or core of something such as an atom or a living cell.

The nucleus is found at the centre of an atom. Negatively charged electrons whirl around it.

nude *adjective* naked, not wearing clothes. **nude** *noun* a person not wearing clothes. **nudity** *noun*.

nudge *verb* to gently poke or push somebody with your elbow.

nugget *noun* a rough lump of precious metal. *A gold nugget.*

nuisance *noun* somebody or something that is annoying. *My little brother is always making a nuisance of himself.*

numb *adjective* unable to feel anything. *My fingers are numb with cold.*

Nuku'alofa *noun* the capital of Tonga.

number *noun* 1 a word or numeral we use for counting. One, two, three. 1, 2, 3. 2 a quantity or amount. *She has a large number of CDs.* **number** *verb* 1 count. *The flock numbered 500 sheep.* 2 to put a number on. *The pages are numbered.*

numeral *noun* a symbol or group of symbols you use to write a number. 5, 10, 12 are Arabic numerals and V, X, X11 and C are Roman numerals.

numerate *adjective* able to understand numbers and do calculations. **numeracy** *noun*. *Literacy and numeracy.*

AMAZING FACT

November comes from a Latin word meaning 'ninth' because it was the ninth month of the Roman calendar.

AMAZING FACT

The system of writing numbers that we now use, Arabic numerals, actually originated in India. Most Arabian countries use completely different symbols to represent numbers.

Nutritious foods include fruit, vegetables, wholemeal bread, fish, cheese and eggs.

---

numerical *adjective* concerning numbers. *Numerical order.*

numerous *adjective* many. *He made numerous visits to the hospital.* The opposite of numerous is few.

numismatics *plural noun* the study of coins and medals.

nun *noun* a member of a religious community of women who live, pray and work together in a building called a convent or an abbey.

nurse *noun* a person who has been trained to look after ill, injured or old people, especially in hospital. **nurse** *verb*. *Ned nursed his dad when he was ill.*

nursery *noun* 1 a place where young children can go to play during the day while their parents are away. 2 a child's bedroom and playroom in a home. 3 a place where plants are grown to be sold.

nursery rhyme *noun* a short, simple poem that children like to recite.

nut *noun* 1 a fruit with a hard shell and a soft, seed (nut) inside that you can eat. *Brazil nut, hazelnut, walnut.* 2 a piece of metal with a hole through it for screwing on to a bolt. Nuts and bolts are used for holding pieces of metal etc. together. **go nuts** (slang) suddenly to become very angry. *She went absolutely nuts when I broke the mirror.*

nutcracker *noun* an instrument for cracking the shells of nuts.

nutritious *noun* nourishing and good for you as food. *We try to serve three nutritious meals every day.*

nutty *adjective* 1 tasting of nuts or filled with nuts. *A nutty fruitcake.* 2 (slang) foolish. *Our science teacher is like the nutty professor.*

nylon *noun* a strong artificial fiber made of chemicals used in making clothes, ropes, brushes etc. *Nylon stockings.*

Oo

oak *noun* a large deciduous tree with hard wood. The nut of an oak tree is called an acorn. *'Mighty oaks from small acorns grow' is a saying that means major accomplishments may have humble origins.*

oar *noun* a long pole with a flat part at the end (the blade), used for rowing a boat.

oasis (oases) *noun* an area in a desert where there is water and where plants grow. *At last we arrived at the oasis, where we ate dates and drank mint tea.*

oath *noun* a serious promise to tell the truth, be faithful etc. *I swore an oath on the Bible to tell the truth.*

oatmeal *noun* oats that have been ground to make porridge etc.

oats *plural noun* a type of cereal grain, used as food. *Porridge oats.*

obedient *adjective* obeying, willing to do what you are told to do. *The children were brought up to be very obedient.*

obese *adjective* (say oh-**beez**) very fat. **obesity** *noun.*

obey *verb* to do what somebody asks or tells you to do. *A sheepdog always obeys commands.* **obedience** *noun.*

obituary *noun* an announcement of somebody's death, usually in a newspaper and with a short account of the person's life and achievements.

object *noun* (say ob-ject) 1 a non-living thing that you can see and touch. 2 the purpose or thing you are trying to achieve, aim. *The object of the meeting is to choose a new team.* 3 in grammar, the person or thing towards which the action of a verb is directed. *'Flower' is the object in the sentence 'John picked a flower.'*

WORD HISTORY

The shape of the letter O comes from an ancient Egyptian symbol for the eye. Its sound comes from 'ayin', a Semitic word for the eye. The Greeks called it 'omicron'.

Porridge is a favourite breakfast food in Scotland, where oats grow well.

Firemen worked among the rubble of the town that had been all but obliterated by the bombing.

Ann clapped loudly when the oboe solo ended.

AMAZING FACT

'Obscure' comes from a Latin word meaning 'dark'.

object *verb* (say ob-**ject**) to say that you dislike or disapprove of something. *He objected to the woman's rude behavior.*

objectionable *adjective* disagreeable. *What an objectionable man!*

objective *noun* the aim or goal you are trying to achieve. **objective** *adjective* based on facts and not influenced by feelings, opinions or prejudice. *She wrote a completely objective report on the causes of the famine in the Sudan.*

obligation *noun* something that you have to do, a duty. **obligatory** *adjective. Answering these questions is obligatory.*

oblige *verb* 1 to make somebody do something, to force or compel. *She was obliged to leave the room.* 2 to help or do a favor for somebody. *Please oblige me by closing the door.*

obliging *adjective* willing to help others. *A very obliging young man gave me his seat.*

oblique *adjective* 1 sloping. 2 indirect. *The question seemed rather oblique to me.*

obliterate *verb* to destroy something completely. *Bombs obliterated the town.*

oblong *noun* a shape with four sides with two parallel long sides and two parallel short sides.

obnoxious *adjective* very unpleasant. *An obnoxious smell wafted out of the school dustbins.*

oboe *noun* a woodwind instrument.

obscene *adjective* (say ob-**seen**) indecent and sexually offensive. *I will not tolerate obscene behavior.* **obscenity** *noun.*

obscure *adjective* 1 not well known. *An obscure book by Dickens.* 2 not clear or easy to see or understand. *An obscure problem.* **obscurity** *noun.* **obscure** *verb. The pillar obscured my view of the stage.*

observatory *noun* a building with large telescopes for observing the stars, planets and the skies.

From an observatory astronomers watch the night sky and record sightings of the planets.

observe *verb* 1 to watch somebody or something carefully. 2 to see and notice something. 3 to obey something such as a law or custom. *Jews observe the festival of Hanukkah in December.* 4 to remark. *Tim observed that the post was late.* **observant** *adjective* quick at observing things. **observation** *noun*.

obsolete *adjective* out of date and no longer used. *This computer is obsolete.*

obstacle *noun* something that blocks the way and makes it difficult for you to do something. A hindrance.

obstinate *adjective* refusing to obey or do what somebody wants, stubborn. *An obstinate child.* **obstinacy** *noun*.

obtain *verb* to get something by buying, taking, being given etc. **obtainable** *adjective*. *Tickets are obtainable in the foyer.*

obtuse angle *noun* an angle between 90 and 180 degrees. An obtuse angle is greater than a right angle.

An obtuse angle is bigger than a right angle.

obverse *noun* the side of a coin showing the head or principal design. The opposite of obverse (heads) is reverse (tails).

obvious *adjective* easy to see and understand, clear. *It's obvious to me that she's broken her finger.*

occasion *noun* a particular time when something happens. *Weddings and birthdays are important occasions.*

SPELLING NOTE

'Occurred', 'occurrence' and 'occurring' are frequently misspelled. Note the 'cc', the 'rr' and the '-ence' (not '-ance').

Some of the world's earliest sea journeys took place across the Pacific Ocean.

The octopus is a favorite food of the Greeks. It can be fried gently in olive oil until tender, and served with tomatoes and garlic.

AMAZING FACT

The main defence of the octopus is its ability to squirt a cloud of ink around itself so that it can escape unseen.

occasional *adjective* happening sometimes but not regularly.

occupation *noun* 1 the work a person does for a living, a job. 2 a hobby or something you like doing in your spare time. 3 the invasion and taking control of a town or country by an army. *The German occupation of France during World War II.*

occupy (occupies, occupying, occupied) *verb* 1 to live in. *Who occupies the house next door?* 2 to keep busy. 3 to invade and capture an enemy town, country etc. **occupant, occupier** *noun*.

occur (occurs, occurring, occurred) *verb* to happen. *Thunder storms occur mainly in summer.* **occur to** to suddenly think about something. **occurrence** *noun*.

ocean *noun* any of the great masses of salt water that surround the continents.

o'clock *adverb* 'of the clock', an expression we use when telling the time.

octagon *noun* a flat shape with eight sides. **octagonal** *adjective*.

octave *noun* in music, the eight notes of any scale.

October *noun* the tenth month of the year. October has 31 days.

octopus (octopuses) *noun* a sea creature with a round body and eight tentacles.

odd *adjective* 1 strange, not ordinary. 2 of numbers, not even and not divisible by two. Three, five and 37 are odd numbers. 3 one of a pair and not matching. *An odd sock.* 4 different. *Odd jobs.* 5 **odds** chances or probability of something happening (especially in gambling). **odd one out** the one that is different.

ode *noun* a poem, often addressed to somebody or to something.

odious *adjective* very unpleasant.

odor *noun* a strong smell, often an unpleasant one.

odorless *adjective* without smell.

offend *verb* 1 to upset a person's feelings. 2 to do wrong or commit a crime. **offence** *noun. Drunken driving is a serious offence.* **offensive** *adjective. Offensive behavior.*

offhand *adjective* 1 unthinking and casual, rude. *An offhand manner.* 2 impromptu and without preparation. *I can't tell you the answer offhand.*

offer *verb* 1 to say that you are willing to do something. 2 to ask somebody if they would like something. To hold out. *She offered him a glass of juice.* 3 to say how much you are willing to give for something. *Harry offered her $100 for the clock.* **offer** *noun.*

office *noun* 1 a place where people work and where a business is run. Offices usually contain desks, telephones, computers etc. 2 an important position. *The office of mayor.*

The new office was ready for the company secretary to move into.

officer *noun* 1 a senior person in the armed forces or police who is in charge of other people. 2 a policeman or policewoman.

official *adjective* coming from or done by people in authority. *An official inquiry.* **official** *noun* a person with a position of authority. *Government officials.*

offspring *noun* the children or young of humans and animals.

often *adverb* frequently, again and again. *We often go swimming in the evening.*

ogre *noun* a frightening and cruel giant in fairy stories.

oil *noun* different kinds of smooth, thick liquids that do not mix with water and which burn easily. You can use oil as a fuel for heating and cooking and for making machines run smoothly. **oil** *verb.*

ointment *noun* a cream that you put on your skin to heal cuts and scratches.

OK or **okay** *adjective, adverb* all right.

old *adjective* 1 having lived, existed, or lasted for a long time. 2 having lived for a certain amount of time. *Owen is 11 years old.* 3 belonging to an earlier time. *My old geography teacher.* 4 worn out and no longer new. *Old clothes.* The opposites of old are young and new.

SPELLING NOTE

Try not to confuse 'official', meaning 'authorized' with 'officious', meaning 'meddling' or 'bossy'. So we can talk about 'the official opening of a library' and 'an officious librarian'.

old-fashioned *adjective* out of date, belonging to the past.

olive *noun* a small black or green oval fruit that can be crushed to produce olive oil used in cooking. Olive trees grow in Mediterranean countries.

Olympic Games *plural noun* international competitions in sports held in a different country every four years.

Oman *noun* a country in the Middle East.

Oman lies on the Arabian Sea and exports fish as well as petroleum.

omelette *noun* a food made by beating eggs together and frying them, often with a filling.

omen *noun* a sign or warning of good or evil in the future. *Seeing the shooting star was a good omen.*

ominous *adjective* suggesting that something bad is about to happen, threatening. *Those dark clouds look very ominous to me.*

omit (omits, omitting, omitted) *verb* 1 to leave something out. *Your name has been omitted from the list.* 2 to fail to do something. *She omitted some important details.* **omission** *noun.*

omnivore *noun* an animal that eats both plants and flesh. **omnivorous** *adjective.*

once *adverb* 1 at one time in the past. 2 happening one time only. *She comes here once a day.* **once** *conjunction* when. *Once you understand it, you'll never forget it.*

onion *noun* a strong-tasting, rounded bulb eaten as a vegetable.

Sometimes chopping onions makes your eyes water.

on-line *adjective* a service etc. with a direct connection to and interaction with a computer. *On-line shopping is a reality for many homes.*

onlooker *noun* somebody watching something happen without taking part, a spectator. *The onlookers cheered.*

only *adverb* 1 no more than. *It'll only take me a minute to get ready.* 2 just. *She only wants to play for an hour.* **only** *adjective* no others of the same kind. *This is the only watch I have.* **only** *conjunction* but. *I'd love to come, only I can't.* **only child** a child with no brothers or sisters.

ooze *verb* to flow slowly through a narrow opening. *Mud oozed under the door.*

opaque *adjective* If something is opaque, you cannot see through it and it does not let light through.

open *adjective* 1 not shut so people or things can go through, not covered. 2 ready for business. *The shop is open.* 3 honest. *She was very open about her doubts.* **open** *verb* 1 to make open or no longer shut, to become open and no longer shut. *Omar opened the door and let the cat in.* 2 to begin. *The story opens during the Civil War.*

opening *noun* 1 a space. *An opening in the fence.* 2 the beginning of something. *The official opening of the library is next week.* 3 an opportunity. *An opening into the music business would be a dream come true.*

opera *noun* a play with music in which the words are sung. **operatic** *adjective.*

operate *verb* 1 to make something work. *Can you operate this machine?* 2 to cut a part of somebody's body to heal a disease or repair an injury. *The surgeon had to operate on Lyn's broken ankle.* **operation** *noun.*

opinion *noun* what you think or believe about something. *What is your opinion of the Canadian team?*

opinionated *adjective* stubbornly believing that your opinions are right.

opossum *noun* a small tree-dwelling American marsupial.

The opossum has strong feet and claws for climbing trees.

Opera becomes much more interesting when you understand the story.

The trains were traveling in opposite directions.

AMAZING FACT

The opossum is North America's only marsupial. It climbs trees and uses its tail to hold on.

When opossums are in danger, they pretend to be dead. When someone acts as though they have been hurt but haven't, we say they are 'playing possum'.

opponent *noun* somebody who is against you in a contest or fight etc. *Sam outwitted his opponents in the debate.*

In chess, it is important to try and predict what your opponent's moves will be.

opportunity *noun* a good time to do something. *Now is your opportunity to study German.*

oppose *verb* to be against and try to prevent something. *The town opposed the building of a new mall.* **opposition** *noun.*

opposite *noun* something that is completely different in every way from another thing. *Happy is the opposite of sad.* **opposite** *adjective* 1 different. *They drove in opposite directions.* 2 facing, on the other side. *They stood on opposite sides of the street.*

oppress *verb* to govern or treat people harshly and unjustly. **oppression** *noun. Albania suffered years of oppression.* **oppressor** *noun.*

opt *verb* to choose. *We opted to go skiing.* **option** *noun. I have two options, to go or to stay.* **opt out** to decide not to take part.

optical *adjective* relating to the eyes and eyesight. *An optical illusion.*

optician *noun* a person who sells glasses and who is trained to test people's eyesight.

optimism *noun* the belief that only the best will happen and all will end successfully. **optimist** *noun. She is always a cheerful optimist.* **optimistic** *adjective. The opposite of optimistic is pessimistic.*

optional *adjective* not compulsory, that you can choose or not choose.

oral *adjective* relating to the mouth. *Oral hygiene.* 2 spoken not written. *An oral test.*

O

orang-utan *noun* a large Indonesian ape with shaggy reddish fur and long arms.

orange *noun* 1 a round juicy fruit with a reddish-yellow skin (peel). 2 the color of this fruit. **orange** *adjective*.

orator *noun* a skilled public speaker.

orbit *noun* an imaginary path followed by an object such as a spacecraft or planet as it moves around a planet or star. **orbit** *verb*. *The Moon orbits Earth once a month.*

orchard *noun* a piece of land on which a lot of fruit trees are grown.

organ *noun* a part inside the body that does a particular job. The heart, kidneys, liver and lungs are organs.

organ *noun* a musical instrument with a keyboard and pipes of different length through which air is pumped to produce sounds. *Rousing chords from the organ.*

organic *adjective* grown without using chemicals or pesticides. *Organic farming.*

organism *noun* any living animal or plant.

orchestra *noun* (say or-kess-trah) a large group of people who perform music together, playing different instruments. **orchestral** *adjective*.

orchid *noun* (say or-kid) one of many varieties of plant that usually has brightly colored, strangely shaped flowers.

ordeal *noun* a difficult, unpleasant or dangerous experience.

order *noun* 1 a command given by somebody in control telling people what to do. *The officer gave his orders.* 2 a sequence or a way things are arranged. *Alphabetical order.* 3 neatly arranged, organized. *He put his papers in order.* **order** *verb* 1 to tell somebody firmly to do something. 2 (in a restaurant) to ask for something to be brought to you, to ask for something to be obtained. *We ordered pie and ice-cream.* **out of order** not working, broken.

ordinary *adjective* not special or interesting. Usual. *A very ordinary sort of guy.*

ore *noun* rock or earth containing metal that can be extracted.

Copper, a reddish-gold metal, is extracted from copper ore.

We used to love helping with the apple-picking in Grandma's orchard.

WORD HISTORY

The orchestra in ancient Greek theaters was a 'dancing place', where dancers and musicians performed in an area between the stage and the audience. Much later the musicians who played there themselves became known as the orchestra.

organization *noun* 1 a group of people working together, a club, business etc. 2 the act of organizing something so it runs smoothly. *The organization of the conference.*

organize *verb* 1 to plan and prepare something in an orderly way. 2 to put things in order. **organizer** *noun*.

oriental *adjective* relating to countries of the Far East such as China, India and Japan.

origami *noun* the Japanese art of folding paper into beautiful shapes.

Kylie made a beautiful origami swan.

origin *noun* 1 the start or source of something and why it began. *What is the origin of Halloween?* 2 ancestry or where somebody or something came from. *She's of Jamaican origin.*

original *adjective* 1 the first of its kind to exist or to be made. *The original palace was burned down.* 2 not an imitation. *Original paintings.* 3 different and imaginative. *An original design.*

originate *verb* to start to exist, to have origins. *Cricket originated in England.*

ornament *noun* a small, pretty object that you wear or put on a shelf or table as a decoration. *Get the Christmas tree ornaments out.* **ornamental** *adjective. Ornamental gardens.*

This ornament is a Chinese ginger jar.

ornithology *noun* the scientific study of birds. **ornithologist** *noun.*

orphan *noun* a child whose parents are both dead. *Orphans of the war.*

orphanage *noun* a place where orphans are taken care of. *Romanian orphanages.*

orthodontist *noun* a dentist who specializes in straightening and adjusting irregular or crooked teeth.

orthodox *adjective* what is accepted and generally thought to be right by most people. Believing in traditional ideas. *She has very orthodox views.* **orthodoxy** *noun.*

oscillate *noun* to swing backwards and forwards like a pendulum. **oscillation** *noun.*

Oslo *noun* the capital of Norway.

ostrich *noun* a very large bird with long legs and a long neck. Ostriches can run very fast but cannot fly. They come from Africa.

Ostriches are now being farmed in some countries for their meat, which tastes a little like venison.

other *adjective*
1 different, not the same as. *The other way is shorter.*
2 opposite. *On the other side of the road.* **other** (others) *pronoun* the rest, more. *Jim's here, but where are the others?*

otherwise *conjunction* or else. *Eat your food, otherwise it will get cold.* 2 except for that. *It was cold, otherwise we had a good time.* **otherwise** *adverb* differently. *He's naughty and cannot behave otherwise.*

ought *verb* must, should.

Ottawa *noun* the capital of Canada.

The outback is strangely still and peaceful.

AMAZING FACT

The ostrich is the world's largest living bird. It cannot fly but is the fastest creature on two legs and is capable of running 45 mph. Ostrich eggs are the largest laid by any bird – one is equivalent to about 40 hen's eggs.

otter *noun* a small animal with brown fur that lives near rivers and eats fish. Otters have webbed feet to help them swim.

Ouagadougou *noun* the capital of Burkina Faso.

ounce *noun* a measure of weight equal to 28.3 grams. There are 16 ounces in a pound. *This caviar is sold by the ounce.*

out- *prefix* 1 surpassing, more. *Outclassed.* 2 external, outside. *Outhouse.* 3 longer, beyond. *Outlive.*

outback *noun* the huge unpopulated inland areas of Australia.

outbreak *noun* a sudden appearance or start of something. *An outbreak of flu.*

outcome *noun* the result. *What's the outcome of the competition?*

outdoor *adjective* in the open air. *Outdoor activities.* **outdoors** *adverb, noun. In summer we eat outdoors.* The opposite of outdoors is indoors.

outer space *noun* everything beyond the Earth's atmosphere. The universe.

This is a spiral galaxy way beyond planet Earth in outer space.

outfit *noun* a set of clothes, especially for a particular occasion. *Masie wanted a new outfit for the wedding.*

outgrow (outgrows, outgrowing, outgrew, outgrown) *verb* to grow too large or too old for something. *He has outgrown his shoes.*

outing *noun* a day-trip or short journey somewhere for pleasure.

outlaw *noun* a criminal who has not been caught and is hiding. **outlaw** *verb* to make something illegal.

outline *noun* 1 a line around the edge of something that shows its shape. *Mike drew the outline of the building.* 2 the main points rather than a detailed description of something. *An outline of the play's plot.* **outline** *verb. She outlined her plans.*

outlook *noun* 1 a view. *A room with a fine outlook.* 2 a person's general attitude or way of looking at things. *Jennie has a cheerful outlook on life.* 3 what is likely to happen. *The weather outlook is good.*

output *noun* 1 the amount of something produced in a factory, by a person etc. 2 data produced by a computer.

outrage *noun* a feeling of anger about a shocking or violent act. **outrageous** *adjective* shocking. *Outrageous behavior.*

outright *adjective* complete, absolute. *She's the outright winner.* **outright** *adverb* instantly. *I told him the bad news outright.*

outset *noun* the beginning. *I knew from the outset she'd win.*

outside *noun* the exterior or outer part of something, the surface of something farthest from the middle. **outside** *adjective, adverb, preposition. The outside lane of the freeway.* The opposite of outside is inside.

outskirts *plural noun* the parts around the outer edges of a town.

outspoken *adjective* saying clearly and strongly what you think even if you offend people. *An outspoken critic of the system.*

outstanding *adjective* 1 excellent. *An outstanding performance.* 2 not paid. *An outstanding bill.*

This is a very basic outline.

WORD BUILDER

Dozens of new words have been made (and can be made) with the prefix 'over–'. Here are a few: 'over-anxious', 'over-boil', 'over-charge', 'overcook', 'overeat', 'overload' and 'over-optimistic'.

We were warm and snug sitting by the fire, but outside it was raining.

outwit (outwits, outwitting, outwitted) *verb* to be too clever for somebody.

oval *noun* egg-shaped. **oval** *adjective. Rugby balls and footballs are oval.*

It was the first time they had played with an oval ball.

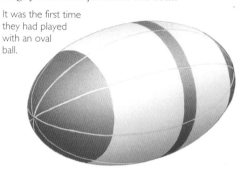

oven *noun* the box-like part of a stove in which you roast or bake food.

over *preposition* 1 above, higher. *She hung the picture over her bed.* 2 across. *The dog jumped over the stream.* 3 more than. *She's got over a dozen pairs of shoes.* 4 on top of. *He laid blankets over the bed.*

over *adverb* 1 ended. *The ordeal is over.* 2 down from being upright. *I fell over.* 3 upside down. *Flip the pancake over.* 4 not used, remaining. *Any cake left over?* **over and over again** many, many times.

over- *prefix* 1 excessive. *Overconfident.* 2 above, in a higher position. *Overlord.* 3 movement or position above. *Overhang.* 4 extra. *Overcoat.*

overalls *plural noun* heavy cotton pants with a bibthat covers your chest and two straps that go over your shoulders.

overboard *adverb* over a ship's side and into the water. *He jumped overboard to rescue the child.* **go overboard** to become too enthusiastic about something.

overcast *adjective* (of the sky) cloudy. *The sky was overcast and it looked like rain.*

overcome (overcomes, overcoming, overcame, overcome) *verb* 1 to conquer or defeat, to get the better of. *She has overcome her fear of flying.* 2 to be affected by very strong emotions. *He was overcome with sadness when he heard the news.*

overdue *adjective* behind time, late. *The plane is overdue.*

overflow *verb* to spill or run over the edges of a container. *The river overflowed its banks and flooded the meadow.*

overhaul *verb* to examine something carefully to see if it needs repairing. **overhaul** *noun. She gave her bike a complete overhaul.*

overhead *adjective, adverb* above you. *Put your hand luggage in the overhead compartment.*

overheads *plural noun* all the regular costs involved in running a business such as lighting, heating, insurance and advertising.

overhear (overhears, overhearing, overheard) *verb* to hear accidentally what people are saying when they do not know you are listening.

overlap (overlaps, overlapping, overlapped) *verb* to partly cover or lie across something else. *Roof shingles overlap.*

These roof shingles overlap so that rain won't get through.

overlook *verb* 1 to fail to see or do something, to not notice. *You have overlooked how much it will cost!* 2 to forgive and not punish somebody. *I'll overlook your mistake.* 3 to have a view above something. *Your rooms are at the front of the hotel and overlook the square.*

overrated *adjective* not as good as most people say. *An overrated film.*

overrun (overruns, overrunning, overran) *verb* 1 to spread over; to swarm. *The kitchen was overrun with cockroaches.* 2 to go beyond the time allowed. *The TV program overran by ten minutes.*

overseas *adjective, adverb* abroad, across the sea. *Overseas visitors.*

overtake (overtakes, overtaking, overtook, overtaken) *verb* to develop or increase more than someone else. *He overtook the others.*

New and faster race cars are overtaking traditional designs.

overthrow (overthrows, overthrowing, overthrew, overthrown) *verb* to defeat or cause something to fall. *The French revolution overthrew the monarchy.* **overthrow** *noun*.

overtime *noun* extra time spent working outside normal working hours.

overture *noun* a short piece of music at the start of a ballet etc. that sets the mood.

WORD HISTORY

'Ozone' comes from the Greek word for 'to smell', 'ozein'. The name was first given to the gas by the German chemist C.F. Schönbein in 1840 because of its extraordinary smell.

overturn *verb* to fall over or cause something to fall over so that it is upside down. *The semi crashed and overturned.*

overwhelm *verb* 1 to defeat completely, to crush. 2 to cover completely. *The waves overwhelmed the boat and we all bailed frantically.* 3 to put too great a load on. *Kate was overwhelmed with work and decided to take a break in Italy.*

owe *verb* to have to pay or give something to somebody, especially money that is borrowed. *I owe you $16 for the tickets.*

owl *noun* a bird of prey with a flat face and large eyes that hunts for small animals such as mice at night. *A wise old owl.*

Owls often nest in hollow trees. They fly slowly and almost silently, very close to the ground, so they can spot their prey in the dark without being heard.

own *verb* to have something that belongs to you, to possess. *Who owns this skateboard?* **own** *adjective* belonging only to you. *Meg has her own computer.* **owner** *noun.* **on your own** by yourself and without help, alone. *He cooked the meal all on his own.*

ox (oxen) *noun* a bull that is used in some countries for pulling carts, ploughs etc.

oxygen *noun* a colorless, tasteless gas that makes up about a fifth of the Earth's atmosphere. All life on Earth needs oxygen to live. *Astronauts need to take a supply of oxygen with them into outer space.*

oyster *noun* an edible sea creature that lives inside two shells (a bivalve). Some oysters produce a pearl inside their shell. *David loves oysters and all other shellfish.*

ozone *noun* a gas that is a form of oxygen with three atoms instead of two.

ozone-friendly *adjective* not harmful to the layer of ozone around the Earth. *An ozone-friendly aerosol.*

ozone layer *noun* a layer or belt of ozone high in the atmosphere that protects the Earth by absorbing harmful rays from the Sun. *The ozone layer is becoming depleted, and as a result, many more people who don't wear protective cream in the sun are contracting skin cancer.*

Pp

pace *noun* 1 walking or running speed, or the speed at which something happens. *Work at your own pace.* 2 a single step when walking or running. *She took three paces forwards.* **keep pace with** to go forward at the same rate. *He kept pace with the latest developments.* **pace** *verb* 1 to walk with regular steps. 2 to set the speed, especially for a runner in a race.

pacemaker *noun* 1 a person who sets the speed that others in a race try to keep up with. 2 a machine that is used to keep a weak heart beating.

pacifist *noun* a person who believes that all wars are wrong and who refuses to fight.

pacify (pacifies, pacifying, pacified) *verb* to make calm or quiet.

pack *verb* 1 to put things into a box, bag or case for carrying, storing or moving them. 2 to crowd together, to fit into a space. *The theater was packed with children.* 3 When you pack something in something, you wrap it up to protect it. *The bowl was packed in bubble wrap but it cracked anyway.* **pack in** to do a lot of things in a short time. *We packed in a lot of sightseeing while we were in Mexico City.* **pack off** to send somebody away. *He got packed off to boarding school when he was seven.* **send somebody packing** to make somebody leave, especially a person you don't want to be with. **pack up** to pack your belongings. *Let's pack up and get going, otherwise we're going to miss the plane.*

Jane wrapped the china in newspaper and packed it carefully in the box.

pack *noun* 1 a number of things wrapped or tied together for carrying. *He carried food in a pack on his back.* 2 a group of wild animals, especially wolves or dogs. 3 a group of unpleasant people or a number of bad things. *A pack of lies.* 4 a group of Cub Scouts or Brownies. 5 a complete set of cards. 6 a packet of things. *Alan bought a pack of cigarettes.*

WORD HISTORY

The shape of the letter P comes from the ancient Egyptian symbol for mouse. The sound comes from 'P', a Semitic word for mouse.

DID YOU KNOW

An artificial pacemaker that helps to keep a person's heart beating is operated by a tiny battery. It replaces a small section of the natural heart muscle, which we also call the pacemaker, that regulates our heartbeat.

package *noun* 1 a number of things packed together, a parcel. 2 an offer that includes a number of things. **package** *verb*. *Juice is packaged in cartons.*

package tour *noun* a complete vacation at a fixed price, including travel, accommodation and food. *We went on a package tour of Egypt.*

pack rat *noun* someone who collects or keeps lots of unnecessary things.

pact *noun* an agreement. *The two countries signed a trading pact.*

pad *noun* 1 anything filled with soft material used to protect, clean or stuff something. *Skaters wear knee pads.* 2 a number of sheets of paper fixed together at the top or the side that can be torn out. *A writing pad.* 3 the place where a helicopter or rocket takes off. 4 the soft part of an animal's paw. **pad** (pads, padding, padded) *verb* to put a pad in or on something. *The jacket has padded shoulders.*

It's a good idea to wear protective padding on your knees and elbows while rollerblading.

padding *noun* soft material on or inside something to make it soft.

paddle *noun* a short pole with a flat blade on one or both ends for moving a small boat in water. **paddle** *verb* to move a boat through water. *They paddled really hard in their canoes.*

paddock *noun* a field near a house or stables where horses are kept.

paddy field *noun* a field where rice is grown. *The paddy fields of China.*

padlock *noun* a lock that can be put on and taken off, for use on a door, box or locker. **padlock** *verb*. *He padlocked the footlocker.*

pagan (say **pay**-gun) *adjective*, *noun* not believing in the main religions of the world but in many gods.

page *noun* a piece of paper in a book, newspaper or magazine.

page *noun* 1 a young person who works in a government office, usually as a temporary, summer job. *My older brother spent the summer working as a page on Capital Hill in Washington.* 2 a boy who attends a bride at a wedding.

page *verb* to call the name of a person, especially in a hotel or hospital. *Can you page Mr Smith?*

pageant *noun* 1 a show, usually outdoors, about the history of a place and its people. 2 a contest, usually for women, in which their beauty and personalities are judged.

pager *noun* a radio device with a bleeper to alert somebody or pass a message.

pagoda *noun* a temple, especially Buddhist or Hindu, shaped like a tower.

Many of the pagodas of southeast Asia have beautiful gilded roofs.

paid *verb* past tense of pay.

pail *noun* a bucket. *A pail of milk.*

pain *noun* 1 an unpleasant feeling of hurt when you are injured or ill. 2 a feeling of unhappiness when something upsetting happens. **pain** *verb*. *It pains me to see you unhappy.* **take pains** to make an effort. *She takes great pains with her homework.* **a pain in the neck** an annoying person. **painful** *adjective*. **painless** *adjective* not causing pain. *A painless operation.*

painkiller *noun* medicine that lessens or stops pain.

painstaking *noun* careful and thorough. *A painstaking investigation.*

paint *noun* 1 a colored liquid or other substance that can be put on a surface. 2 **paints** a set of tubes or cakes of paint, usually in a box, for painting pictures. **paint** *verb* 1 to put paint on something. *He painted the chair black.* 2 to make a picture with paint.

Hannah knocked over the can of paint, and it spilled all over the floor.

painter *noun* 1 a person who paints artistic pictures. *A portrait painter.* 2.a person whose job is painting and decorating houses or rooms

painting *noun* a painted picture.

pair *noun* 1 two things, usually used together. *A pair of shoes.* 2 two people. 3 an object made up of two parts. *A pair of scissors.* **pair** *verb* to form a pair.

WORD HISTORY

The first palace was on the Palatium, the Palatine hill in Rome, where the house of the Roman emperor was situated. The Palatine was one of the seven hills on which ancient Rome was built.

AMAZING FACT

Pandas' natural habitat are the forests of Eastern Asia. There are two types of panda. The red panda is about the size of a house cat and has a bushy tail. The giant panda looks like a black and white bear. They aren't bears, though, their closest relatives are raccoons!

pajamas *plural noun* a loose top and pants worn for sleeping in.

Pakistan *noun* a country in South Asia.

palace *noun* a large house which is the home of a king or queen or other important person. **palatial** *adjective* like a palace.

palate *noun* 1 the top of the mouth. 2 a person's sense of taste.

pale *adjective* 1 having little color. You look pale when your face is almost white or lighter than usual. *She went pale when she heard the bad news.* 2 light, not bright in color. *In the pale light of dawn.*

palette *noun* a board, with a hole for the thumb, on which an artist mixes colours.

Palikir *noun* the capital of Micronesia.

palindrome *noun* a word or phrase that reads the same backwards or forwards. 'Deed' is a palindrome.

palisade *noun* a fence made of pointed iron or wooden poles.

pallid *adjective* unhealthily pale.

palm *noun* the inner part of the hand between the fingers and the wrist. **palm** *verb* to steal something by picking it up and hiding it in your palm. **palm off** to trick someone into buying or taking something.

palm *noun* a tree that grows in hot countries with large leaves at the top and no branches. *Swaying coconut palms.*

pampas *noun* treeless grassy plains in South America. *Herding cattle on the pampas.*

pamper *verb* to treat too kindly or do too much for somebody.

pamphlet *noun* a small booklet that gives information about something.

pan *noun* 1 a metal container with a handle for cooking. 2 the bowl of a lavatory.

The flag of Panama has red, blue and white squares and blue and red stars.

Panama *noun* a country in central America.

Panama City *noun* the capital of Panama.

pancake *noun* a thin flat cake made of flour, eggs and milk (called batter) and fried on both sides.

pancreas *noun* a gland near the stomach that produces chemicals to help digestion.

panda *noun* a large bear-like animal with black and white fur that lives in Chinese bamboo forests. Also called a giant panda.

pane *noun* a piece of glass in a window.

panel *noun* 1 a flat piece of wood or other material that is part of a door or larger object. 2 a group of people chosen to discuss or decide something. *An advisory panel.* 3 a piece of material different in color or fabric that is put in a dress. **paneled** *adjective. A paneled room.* **paneling** *noun.*

pang *noun* a sudden strong feeling. *A pang of sadness.*

panic *noun* a sudden uncontrollable fear. *She was in a panic when she lost her bag.* **panic** (panics, panicking, panicked) *verb* to suddenly become afraid and do things without thinking carefully.

panic-stricken *adjective* afraid, filled with terror. *The panic-stricken burglar fled.*

panorama *noun* a complete view of a wide area. *A panorama of fields spread below.*

pansy (pansies) *noun* a small garden flower.

pant *verb* to breathe quickly with your mouth open, usually after running or when you're hot. *The dog panted.*

panther *noun* a wild animal of the cat family, usually black.

panties *noun* underpants worn by girls.

pantomime *verb* acting out something in a play or a game using actions, not words.

pantry (pantries) *noun* a small room in a house, where food is kept.

pants *plural noun* 1 trousers. 2 underpants.

papacy (say **pay**-puh-see) *noun* the power of the Pope or the position of Pope.

papal (say **pay**-pul) *adjective* to do with the Pope. *A papal decree.*

paparazzi *plural noun* photographers who follow famous people to take pictures.

paper *noun* 1 material made in thin sheets from wood or cloth for writing, printing or drawing on or for wrapping and covering things. 2 a newspaper. 3 a piece of writing done as part of a class. *My term paper is due next week and I haven't even started it yet!* 4 **papers** documents showing who a person or thing is. **paper** *verb* to put wallpaper on a wall. *We want to paper the den.*

paperback *noun* a book with a soft cover.

Papua New Guinea has a population of four million people.

The name 'pansy' came originally from the French word for thought, 'pensée'.

There was a wonderful parachute display.

SPELLING NOTE

Note that the words to do with the Pope, 'papacy' and 'papal', are spelt with an 'a' (not 'popacy' or 'popal'!). The origin of all the words is the Latin 'papa', meaning bishop, from the Greek 'papas', meaning father.

papoose *noun* a bag on a frame for carrying a baby on a person's back.

Papua New Guinea *noun* a country in Australasia, forming part of the island of New Guinea.

par *noun* 1 an average or normal amount, degree or condition. When something is on a par with something else, both are equally good or equally bad. 2 in golf, the number of strokes an average player should take on one hole.

parable *noun* a simple story with a moral point. *Parables from the Bible.*

parachute *noun* a device attached to a person or thing to make them fall slowly when dropped from a plane. **parachutist** *noun.*

parade *noun* 1 a procession or gathering of people or things for the purpose of being looked at or to celebrate a special event. *An Easter parade.* 2 soldiers marching together for inspection or for a ceremony. **parade** *verb* 1 to march in procession in order to be looked at by other people. *The winners paraded triumphantly around the stadium.* 2 to show something off in order to impress.

paradise *noun* 1 a place or situation where everything is perfect. *The island is a tropical paradise.* 2 A place that has everything that you want or need to do a particular activity. 3 heaven.

paradox (paradoxes) *noun* 1 a statement that seems wrong or impossible, but has some truth in it. 2 two facts or ideas that are opposite to what is generally believed to be true. **paradoxical** *adjective.*

paraffin *noun* a soft white substance used for making candles.

paragliding *noun* cross-country gliding using a parachute shaped like wings.

paragraph *noun* a section of a piece of writing consisting of a number of sentences on a subject. A paragraph starts on a new line. *Please write two paragraphs.*

Paraguay *noun* a country in South America.

parakeet *noun* a small parrot.

parallel *adjective* lines that are at the same distance from each other are parallel. *The road runs parallel to the railroad.*

parallel *noun* 1 a line parallel to another. 2 something similar to something else, or a comparison that shows likeness. *She is without parallel.*

parallelogram *noun* a four-sided figure with opposite sides parallel.

paralyze *verb* 1 to make some or all of the body's muscles unfeeling and unable to move. *A stroke paralysed his left arm.* 2 to make somebody or something unable to act, move or work properly. *Paralysed with fear.* **paralysis** *noun.*

Paramaribo *noun* the capital of Suriname.

parapet *noun* a low wall at the edge of a bridge or roof.

paraplegic *noun* (say par-uh-**plee**-jick) a person whose lower body, including both legs, is paralysed. **paraplegic** *adjective.* **paraplegia** *noun.*

parasite *noun* a plant or animal that lives on or in another and gets food from it. **parasitic** *adjective.*

Ticks are parastites that live on sheep. They can also infest humans, dogs and cats.

parasol *noun* an umbrella used as a sunshade. *A dainty parasol.*

parcel *noun* 1 a package, something wrapped up so it can be sent by mail or carried. 2 a piece of land that is part of a larger area.

parchment *noun* a kind of thick yellowish paper. In ancient times parchment was made from the skin of sheep or goats and used for writing on.

pardon *noun* forgiveness. *I beg your pardon.* **pardon** *verb* to forgive or excuse a person. **pardonable** *adjective.*

parent *noun* Your parents are your father and mother. **parental** (say puh-**rent**-ul) *adjective. Parental care.*

parenthesis (parentheses) *noun* (say puh-ren-thi-sis) one of the two signs ( ) used to who that something (extra information) is being inserted into a sentence.

Paris *noun* the capital of France.

DID YOU KNOW

The term 'parrot-fashion' came about because people sometimes teach parrots to 'talk', or repeat the sounds they make. Today, many people feel it is wrong to keep birds in cages. In the wild, parrots have a harsh, screaming voice. They use their short, hooked bill to open nuts and feed on fruits and seeds.

AMAZING FACT

There are both animal and plant parasites.

Animal parasites such as fleas and ticks, live on birds and mammals and suck blood.

Plant parasites, such as fungus, take nourishment from plants by twining around or growing into the host.

Mistletoe, traditionally used as a decoration at Christmas time, is a parasite that lives off trees.

parish (parishes) *noun* 1 the area that is served by a church. 2 The people who belong to that church. **parishoner** *noun.*

park *noun* 1 a public garden or place, usually in a town. 2 the large private garden of a country house.

park *verb* to leave a car or other vehicle somewhere for a time. *I parked the car in the parking lot.*

parliament *noun* an institution made up of a group of people who are elected and make a country's laws. **parliamentary** *adjective.*

parlor *noun* 1 a store or business. *A beauty parlor.* 2(old-fashioned) a sitting room. *The piano is in the parlor.*

parody (parodies) *noun* a piece of writing or music that makes fun of somebody else's style by copying it.

parrot *noun* a tropical bird with bright feathers and a hooked beak.

Conservationists are working to stop the illegal export of parrots from their native homes. Many parrots die in transit.

parrot-fashion *adjective* mechanical, without understanding. *She repeated everything parrot-fashion.*

parsley *noun* a plant with green leaves, used to add flavor to food.

Parsley has a very high vitamin C content.

parsnip *noun* a white or yellowish root vegetable.

parson *noun* a member of the clergy.

part *noun* 1 any piece or portion of a whole, anything that belongs to something bigger. *The afternoon is the best part of the day.* 2 an important piece of a machine or other apparatus. *You can order spare parts for the bike.* 3 a line in your hair made by dividing it with a comb. 4 a person's role in a play or film. *She played the part of the witch.* 5 any of several equal amounts in something. *This mixture is two parts milk to one part cream.* 6 a share in doing something. *It was a shrewd move on her part.* **for the most part** mostly. **play a part in** to have an important effect on what happens. **take part** to participate in an activity.

part *verb* to separate or divide, to leave each other. *Let's part friends.* **part with** to give away. *I won't part with my dog.*

partial *adjective* 1 not complete. *A partial success.* 2 supporting one person or side, more than the other, especially in a way that is unfair. 3 liking something very much. *I'm very partial to chocolate.* **partiality** *noun.*

participate *verb* to take part in something or have a share in an event. **participation** *noun. Your participation is appreciated.*

particle *noun* a very small piece or amount. *Food particles.*

particular *adjective* 1 relating to one and not any other. *This particular car is faster than the others.* 2 special. *She takes particular care of her hair.* 3 difficult to please, fussy. **particularly** *adverb.*

particular *noun* 1 a detail. *He is right in every particular.* 2 **particulars** facts or details, especially about events. *Fill in your particulars.* **in particular** especially.

parting *noun (formal)* a occasion when people leave each other. *Parting is such sweet sorrow.*

partition *noun* 1 a thin wall that divides a room. 2 division into two or more parts. **partition** *verb* to divide into two or more parts. *A partition divides these rooms.*

partner *noun* one of two people who do things together or share the same activity. *My tennis partner.* **partner** *verb.* **partnership** *noun.*

Her tennis partner was very good at volleying.

part of speech *noun* one of the classes of words in grammar. Nouns, verbs and adjectives are parts of speech.

partridge *noun* a bird with brown feathers. Partridges are shot for sport and food.

A partition in a room creates a feeling of privacy.

GRAMMAR NOTE

The passive voice is used when: 1 *the subject is unknown 'The phone booth was vandalized.'* 2 *the subject is not important 'Oranges are grown in Florida.* 3 *the subject does not want to be mentioned 'A decision was made.'*

DID YOU KNOW

The common or gray partridge was introduced to North America from Europe and western Asia. Partridges eat mainly plant food such as seeds and young shoots.

part-time *adjective, adverb* during a part of a day or week. *She works part-time.* The opposite of part-time is full-time.

party (parties) *noun* 1 a gathering of people who come together to enjoy themselves. *We gave a birthday party for my sister.* 2 a political organization. *The Democratic Party.* 3 a group of people who work or travel together. *A party of tourists.* 4 a person who is taking part in a lawsuit. *The guilty party has to pay the costs.* **be party to** to be responsible for something. *I was party to the decision.* **party** *verb* to go to parties.

pass (passes, passing, passed) *verb* 1 to move past something or somebody. 2 to get or go through or between. *No one is allowed to pass this line.* 3 to go by, or spend time. *Three months passed before she heard from him.* 4 to give something to another person. *Can you pass me the jam?* 5 to do well and be successful, especially in an exam. *She passed her driver's test.* 6 to accept or agree, especially a law. *The law was passed by Congress.* 7 in sports to kick, throw or hit, especially a ball, to somebody in your team. **pass on** to tell something to another person. **pass out** to faint.

pass (passes) *noun* 1 a way between two mountains. 2 a successful result in an exam or test. 3 kicking, throwing or hitting a ball to somebody in your team. 4 a document or ticket that allows you to do something, especially go into a place. **make a pass** to try to make somebody interested in you, usually in an unwelcome approach. *The boss made a pass at me.*

passenger *noun* a person who is driven in a car or is traveling by public transportation.

The passenger enjoyed a comfortable ride.

passer-by (passers-by) *noun* a person who happens to pass a place. *A few passers-by saw the accident.*

passion *noun* a very strong attraction or strong feeling about somebody or something. *She has developed a passion for painting.* **passionate** *adjective.*

passive *adjective* 1 not active, showing no feeling or interest in what is said or done to you. 2 in grammar, the passive voice is a form of a verb that describes what happens or will happen to somebody or something. 'The car was driven by me' is passive. 'I drove the car' is active. **passive** *noun.*

Passover *noun* a Jewish festival in memory of the freeing of the Jews from Egypt.

passport *noun* an official document that has to be shown when entering or leaving a country.

Passports are usually the property of the government that issues them, not the actual passport holder.

password *noun* a secret word or phrase that you have to know to show that you are a friend or to gain access to something.

past *adjective* 1 referring to the time before now. *In the past few hours.* The verbs 'went', 'called' and 'wrote' are in the past tense. **past** *adverb, preposition* 1 up to and beyond a point. *The bus drove past.* 2 after. *It's ten past four.* **be past it** to be no longer able to do things, because you are too old. **past** *noun* the time before the present.

pasta *noun* an Italian food made of a mixture of flour, eggs and water. Spaghetti, macaroni and noodles are all forms of pasta. *Pasta with parmesan cheese.*

paste *noun* 1 a soft mixture used for sticking things together. 2 food, especially fish or meat, made into a soft mixture that can be spread on bread. 3 hard shiny glass used for making imitation jewellery. **paste** *verb* to stick something using paste. *I was busy pasting clippings into my scrap-book.*

pastel *noun* 1 a colored chalk. 2 a picture drawn with colored chalk. *He loves working in pastels.* 3 a light color.

pasteurize *verb* to remove bacteria from milk by heating and then cooling it.

pastry (pastries) *noun* 1 a mixture of flour, fat and water rolled out and baked in the oven. 2 something made of pastry.

pasture *noun* land covered with grass, suitable for grazing animals such as cattle or sheep. *Lush pasture.*

SPELLING NOTE

Take care not to confuse 'past' with 'passed'. 'Past' is an adjective, adverb or preposition, as in: 'We walked past the school.' 'Passed' is the past tense of the verb to pass, as in: 'A week passed before we received the letter.' 'Past' can also be a noun: 'That's all in the past.'

Pasta may be colored with spinach, tomato or beet.

AMAZING FACT

Italian words for pasta, such as spaghetti, macaroni, linguini and tagliatelli, are all plural forms. The plurals end in 'i'.

This is also true of other Italian plural nouns such as graffiti and paparazzi.

pasty (say **pay**-stee) (pastier, pastiest) *adjective* looking pale and unhealthy. *When Dave got out of the hospital he looked terrible, big bags under his eyes and a pasty face.*

pat (pats, patting, patted) *verb* to tap lightly with your fingers on something flat. *He patted the dog.* **pat** *noun* 1 a friendly pat. 2 a light sound. 3 a small piece of butter or something else soft. **pat on the back** praise for doing well. **know something off pat** to be prepared for something and have a ready answer. *He had the answer off pat.*

patch (patches) *noun* 1 a small piece of material to put over a hole or damaged place. *She put a patch on her jeans.* 2 a pad worn to protect an eye that has been hurt. 3 a small piece of ground. *A vegetable patch.* 4 a small area of something or a part that is different from the space around it. *Patches of fog.* **A bad patch** is a period of bad luck. **patchy** *adjective*. **patch** *verb* to put a patch on something. *Can you patch these shorts for me, please?* **patch up** 1 to repair something roughly. 2 to end a quarrel. *They tried to patch things up, but it hasn't worked.*

Aunt Mary kindly sewed a patch on my trousers.

patent *noun* the official right given to an inventor to make or sell their invention and stop others from copying it. **patent** *verb* to get a patent for an invention. **patent** *adjective* 1 protected by a patent. 2 obvious. *It was a patent lie.* **patent leather** leather that has a shiny surface.

paternal *adjective* like or relating to a father. *Paternal feelings.*

path *noun* 1 a strip of ground for people to walk on or made by people walking over it. *We followed the path through the woods.* 2 a line along which somebody or something moves. *The path to success.*

pathetic *adjective* sad, weak or helpless. *What a pathetic joke!* **pathetically** *adverb*.

patient *adjective* able to wait calmly without getting annoyed. *Please be patient, I'll be as quick as I can.* **patience** *noun*.

patient *noun* a person who has medical treatment from a doctor or hospital.

patio *noun* a paved area next to a house.

patriot *noun* a person who loves and supports his or her country. **patriotic** *adjective*. **patriotism** *noun*.

patrol (patrols, patrolling, patrolled) *verb* to go at regular times over an area or a building to make sure that there is no trouble. *Soldiers patrolled the border.* **patrol** *noun* 1 the time of patrolling. *A soldier on patrol.* 2 a person, group of soldiers or vehicles patrolling an area.

patron (say **pay**-trun) 1 somebody important who gives money to or takes an interest in a person, especially an artist. 2 a person who uses a store regularly.

patronize *verb* 1 to act towards others in a superior way, as if more important. *She has no right to patronize me.* 2 to support and give money to artists.

patron saint *noun* the protecting saint of a person or place. Saint Christopher is the patron saint of travelers.

patter *verb* to make light tapping sounds. **patter** *noun* 1 a number of quick, light tapping sounds. *The patter of children's little feet.* 2 the fast talk of a salesperson or an entertainer.

pattern *noun* 1 an arrangement of lines, shapes or colors, especially a design that is repeated. 2 a particular way in which something is done or happens. *A behavior pattern.* 3 The shape of something to be copied. *A dress pattern.*

pauper *noun* a very poor person.

pause *noun* 1 a moment of silence. 2 a break from doing something. **pause** *verb* to stop for a short while.

pave *verb* to put flat stones or bricks on a path or an area. **pave the way** to make something more likely to happen. *Their meeting paved the way to an agreement.*

pavement *noun* a path at the side of the street for people to walk on.

paviion *noun* 1 a building next to a sports field for the use of players and spectators. 2 an ornamental building used for dances, concerts or exhibitions.

paw *noun* an animal's foot. **paw** *verb* to feel or touch with a hand or foot.

pawn *noun* 1 the smallest and least valuable playing piece in chess. 2 an unimportant person used by others to their own advantage. *He was a pawn in their game.*

Carrie spread out the dress pattern to see how much material she would need.

The peacock spread out its tail feathers and ruffled them in the sunshine.

pawn *verb* to leave something, especially valuable articles, with a pawnbroker as a security for money borrowed. *He pawned his guitar to buy some food.*

pawnbroker *noun* a person who lends money to people in exchange for articles which they leave as security.

pay (pays, paying, paid) *verb* 1 to give money for goods bought or work done. *I paid fifteen dollars for his old bike.* 2 to settle a bill or debt. *I'll pay!* 3 to give somebody an advantage, to be worth the trouble or cost. *It doesn't pay to cheat.* 4 to give or say something to a person, especially in certain phrases. *He paid her a compliment.* **pay back** to give back the money that you owe. **pay somebody back** to make somebody suffer for what they did to you. **pay up** to pay fully, to give all the money you owe. **pay** *noun* money received for work.

payee *noun* a person to whom money is paid or should be paid, especially by check.

payment *noun* 1 paying money or being paid. *When can we expect payment?* 2 an amount of money paid to somebody.

PC *abbreviation* 1 personal computer. 2 politically correct.

PE *abbreviation* physical education, sports and exercises taught at school.

pea *noun* the small round green seed growing inside a pod, eaten as a vegetable.

peace *noun* 1 a time when there is no war between countries, no trouble, quarreling or fighting among people. 2 calm and quietness. *Leave us in peace.* **make peace** to end a quarrel. **peaceful** *adjective*.

peach *noun* a round juicy fruit with soft yellowish-red skin and a large pit.

peacock *noun* a large male bird with long colorful tail feathers that it can spread out like a fan.

peahen *noun* a the female of the peacock.

peak *noun* 1 the pointed top of a mountain. 2 the highest level or most successful part of something. *She has reached the peak of her career.* **peak** *verb* to reach its highest point or level of success.

peanut *noun* a small edible nut that has a soft shell.

peanut butter *noun* roasted peanuts crushed into a paste and eaten as a spread on bread.

pear *noun* the hard, juicy fruit of the pear tree. *Pear and apple pie.*

pearl *noun* 1 a hard, round, shiny white object that grows inside the shell of an oyster and is a valuable jewel. *My aunt gave me her pearl necklace.* 2 something that looks like a pearl or is a copy of a pearl. **pearly** *adjective*.

They found a pearl inside the oyster.

peasant *noun* a person who works on a farm or owns a small piece of land.

peat *noun* rotted plant material found under the ground. Peat is used for burning instead of coal or to improve soil and make plants grow better.

pebble *noun* a smooth round stone.

pecan *noun* a long nut with a smooth shell.

peck *verb* 1 to hit, tap or bite with the beak. *The bird pecked a hole in the apple.* 2 to kiss quickly and lightly. **peck** *noun* 1 a quick hit or tap with the beak. 2 a quick kiss.

peculiar *adjective* 1 strange, unusual, often in an unpleasant way. *He gave me a peculiar look.* 2 relating to a particular thing or person only. **peculiarity** *noun*.

pedal *noun* a bar which is pushed or pressed with the foot to make a bicycle move or work a car or machine. **pedal** (pedals, pedalling, pedalled) *verb* to work something by using pedals. *He had to pedal hard to get up the hill.*

pedant *noun* a person who is very strict about unimportant rules and pays too much attention to detail. **pedantic** *adjective*.

pedestal *noun* the base on which a statue or pillar stands.

pedestrian *noun* a person walking, especially in a town. **pedestrian** *adjective* 1 for people walking. 2 dull, uninspired. *A very pedestrian plot.*

pediatrician (say pee-dee-uh-**tri**-shun) *noun* a doctor who specializes in children's illnesses. **pediatric** *adjective*.

pedigree *noun* a list showing the families from which a person or animal has come, especially to show the quality of an animal. *A dog with a fine pedigree.* **pedigree** *adjective*. *A pedigree cat.*

The pedigree dalmatian was in perfect condition and won first prize at the show.

peek *noun* a quick look. **peek** *verb*. *He peeked round the corner.*

peel *noun* the skin of oranges, apples, potatoes and other fruit and vegetables. **peel** *verb* 1 to take the skin off fruit and vegetables. 2 to come off in layers, strips or flakes. *The paint is peeling.*

peep *verb* 1 to look quickly, often secretly. 2 to look through an opening. 3 to begin to show. *The ticket peeped out of his pocket.* *noun* 1 a quick look. 2 a high, weak sound.

peer *verb* to look very hard or closely, usually because something is difficult to see.

peer *noun* a person who is the same age or has the same rank.

peer group *noun* a group of people of the same age.

peevish *adjective* bad-tempered.

peg *noun* 1 a piece of wood, metal or plastic used to fasten things. *Every time we go camping we seem to lose at least one tent peg.* 2 a hook or knob for hanging things on. **peg** (pegs, pegging, pegged) *verb* 1 to fix with pegs. 2 to keep prices or wages unchanged.

pelican *noun* a large water bird with a long beak and a pouch for storing fish.

Pelicans can be seen in the Florida Keys.

pellet *noun* a small ball of metal, paper or other material.

pelt *noun* the furry hide of an animal. *verb* to hit or throw something at someone.

pelvis *noun* the round bony frame with the hip bones at the lower end of the spine.

The hip bones are called the pelvis.

pen *noun* an instrument for writing with ink. *A fountain pen.*

pen *noun* a small place, an enclosure, for farm animals or pets. **pen** (pens, penning, penned) *verb* to shut into a small place. *The chickens were penned in for the night.*

penal (say **peen**-ul) *adjective* connected with the punishment of criminals. *The penal system is undergoing reform.*

penalize *verb* to punish.

penalty *noun* 1 punishment. 2 a point or a chance to score a goal, especially in rugby or hockey, because an opponent has committed a foul.

pencil *noun* a wooden instrument for writing or drawing, with a thin stick of lead or colored material inside it. **pencil** (pencils, pencilling, pencilled) *verb* to write or draw with a pencil.

pendulum *noun* a weight hanging from a rod so it can swing from side to side. Some clocks have a pendulum.

penetrate *verb* to force or manage to find a way into something. *A strange smell penetrated the room.* **penetration** *noun.* **penetrating** *adjective. The lawyers asked some penetrating questions.*

penguin *noun* a black and white bird that lives in the Antarctic and cannot fly.

penicillin *noun* an antibiotic used in medicine to destroy bacteria.

peninsula *noun* a piece of land that is almost surrounded by water. *Italy is a peninsula.* **peninsular** *adjective.*

penis (penises) *noun* the part of the body a man or male animal uses for urinating and for reproducing.

DID YOU KNOW

Penguins are flightless birds, but they are extremely good swimmers and divers. They are also able to leap up out of the water onto ice or land - at a height of up to two meters. The male penguin 'babysits' the single egg that a female penguin lays by rolling it up onto his feet to get it off the ice. He then keeps it warm for about two months until it hatches.

The pendulum on a grandfather clock is what makes the comforting 'tick-tock' sound.

AMAZING FACT

Penguins are flightless birds, but they are extremely good swimmers and divers.

penknife *noun* a small knife with a blade that folds into the handle.

pen-name *noun* the name a writer uses in books instead of his or her own name. A pseudonym. *She writes under a pen-name.*

penniless *adjective* having no money, very poor. *They were penniless orphans.*

penny (pennies) *noun* a US coin worth one hundredth of a dollar, a cent. **a penny/every penny** any or all of your money. *I refuse to spend a single penny on that!*

penpal *noun* a friend, especially somebody from a foreign country, you write letters to and receive letters from. Email penpals are called keypals.

pension *noun* a sum of money paid regularly by the government or a firm to a retired or disabled person.

pentathlon *noun* an athletic competition made up of five different events.

penthouse *noun* a flat or apartment on the roof or top floor of a tall building. They always stay in the penthouse suite when they come to town.

people *plural noun* 1 two or more persons. *Only three people came.* 2 all the men, women and children of a particular place, class or group. *Young people.*

pepper *noun* 1 a hot-tasting powder made from peppercorns and used for making food spicy. 2 a hollow green, red or yellow vegetable.

Peppercorns are spread out in the Sun to dry before they are used to flavor food.

peppermint *noun* 1 a mint grown for its strong flavouring. 2 candy that tastes of peppermint.

per *preposition* for each. *Ten kilometers per hour.* **per annum** for each year. *She earns $20,000 per annum.* **per cent** in each hundred. *Ten per cent (10%).*

perceive *verb* to notice or see something.

percentage *noun* an amount stated as part of a whole or as a share of one hundred parts. *A large percentage of students pass their exams every year.*

perception *noun* the ability to notice, an understanding.

perceptive *adjective* quick to notice and understand. *A very perceptive guess.*

perch *noun* 1 a branch or other place a bird rests on. 2 a high position taken up by a person. **perch** *verb* to be on something high. *The house perched on top of the cliff.*

percussion *noun* 1 the striking together of two hard things. 2 musical instruments that are hit together, especially drums and cymbals.

The cymbals are a popular but rare percussion instrument nowadays.

perennial *adjective* lasting for a long time or for many years. **perennial** *noun* a plant that lives for many years.

perfect *adjective* 1 excellent, without fault. 2 complete. *A perfect stranger.* **perfectly** *adverb. I feel perfectly at home here.*

perform *verb* 1 to do something, especially something difficult. 2 to act in a play or do something in front of an audience. **performer** *noun.*

performance *noun* 1 doing something in front of an audience. *Samantha went to the first performance of the new play.* 2 an action performed.

perfume *noun* 1 a fragrant liquid people put on to smell nice. 2 a nice smell.

perhaps *adverb* it may be, possibly. *Perhaps we'll win the game.*

perimeter *noun* the border or outer edge around something. *We walked all round the perimeter of the grounds.*

period *noun* 1 the punctuation mark (.) used to show the end of a sentnece. 2 a length or portion of time. *For a short period. Sunny periods.* 3 a woman's monthly flow of blood. **period** *adjective* made at an earlier time in history.

periodic *adjective* happening at regular intervals. *I make periodic visits to the site.*

The perimeter of the court was marked with a white line.

> **DID YOU KNOW**
>
> *Periscopes are sometimes used at sporting events or other occasions where there are crowds, so that people can see over the heads of others. They work by reflecting the light across mirrors.*

> **DID YOU KNOW**
>
> *Sometimes the word 'period' is used at the end of a spoken sentence, meaning 'and that's all there is to it.' For example, "You are not going to the party, in fact, you're not going out, period."*

periodical *noun* a magazine that comes out at regular intervals, for example monthly. **periodical** *adjective.*

periscope *noun* a tube with mirrors and lenses through which somebody in a submarine can see things above the water.

The submarine's periscope appeared above the surface of the sea.

perish *verb* 1 to die or become destroyed. 2 to rot or fall to pieces. *Soft fruit perishes quickly.* **perishable** *adjective.*

perk *noun* an advantage.

perk up *verb* to become or make somebody more cheerful. *She perked up after lunch.*

permanent *adjective* lasting for ever, not expected to change. *My permanent address.* **permanently** *adverb.*

permissible *adjective* allowed by the rules.

permission *noun* the right to do something, the act of allowing something. *The teacher gave us permission to leave early.*

permissive *adjective* allowing too much personal freedom.

permit (say per-mit) (permits, permitting, permitted) *verb* to allow or make something possible. **permit** (say per-mit) *noun* an official document stating that somebody is allowed to do something or go somewhere.

perpendicular *adjective* a line is perpendicular to another line if they form a right (90°)angle. *Perpendicular lines.*

perpetrate *verb* to be guilty of something, to do something wrong. **perpetrator** *noun. We caught the perpetrator of the crime.*

perpetual *adjective* never ending or changing. *The perpetual noise of the traffic.* **perpetually** *adverb.*

perpetuate *verb* to preserve from being forgotten. *Let us perpetuate his memory.*

persecute *verb* to continually treat a person or group of people cruelly, especially because of their beliefs. **persecution** *noun.*

persevere *verb* to go on doing something and not give up. **perseverance** *noun.*

persist *verb* 1 to continue in spite of warning. *If he persists in breaking the rules, he will be expelled.* 2 to continue to exist. *If your headaches persist, take these pills.* **persistent** *adjective.* **persistently** *adverb.* **persistence** *noun.*

person *noun* 1 a human being. *It's too much work for one person.* 2 in grammar, any of the three forms of pronouns or verbs that show who is speaking. **in person** bodily. *I can't come in person, but I'll send my brother to pick up the prize.*

personal *adjective* 1 belonging, concerning or done by a particular person. *I want your personal opinion.* 2 concerning a person's private life. *There's no need to be personal.* **personally** *adverb. Don't take it personally.*

personal computer *noun* a computer used by a single person, especially at home.

personality (personalities) *noun* 1 the character or nature of a person. *He has a weak personality.* 2 a famous person. *A well-known television personality.*

personal stereo *noun* a small cassette player or radio with headphones.

personnel *noun* the people employed in a business. *The personnel are very friendly.*

perspective *noun* 1 the art of drawing so that things in the background look further away than things in the foreground. *The house is in perspective.* 2 a particular way of thinking about something. *What happened put everything in perspective.*

perspire *verb* to sweat. **perspiration** *noun.*

persuade *verb* to make somebody do or believe something. *We persuaded him to buy a new bike.* **persuasion** *noun.* **persuasive** *adjective. A persuasive salesman.*

perturb *verb* to worry. *The news about the accident perturbed him greatly.*

Peru *noun* a country in South America.

Peruvian *adjective* of Peru. *Peruvian people speak Spanish.* **Peruvian** *noun.*

perverse *adjective* continuing to do something wrong or in a different way from what is wanted. *How perverse of you to like exams.* **perversely** *adverb.* **perversity** *noun.*

pervert (say per-vert) *noun* a person whose behavior, especially sexual behavior, is not normal or is disgusting. **pervert** (say puh-vert) *verb* to turn away from what is right or what it used to be. *He perverted the course of justice.* **perversion** *noun.*

pessimism *noun* thinking that whatever happens will be bad. **pessimist** *noun.* **pessimistic** *adjective.*

The line of the trees in this photograph show perspective.

GRAMMAR NOTE

'Phenomena' is sometimes used mistakenly as a singular. Remember that 'phenomena' is the plural of 'phenomenon'. 'The growth in popularity of mobile phones is a remarkable phenomenon.'

pester *verb* to annoy somebody continually, especially by asking questions or wanting something.

pet *noun* 1 an animal kept in the home as a companion. *Cats are my favorite pets.* 2 a person who is a favorite. *The teacher's pet.* **pet** (pets, petting, petted) *verb* to treat or touch with special love.

petal *noun* one of the bright colored parts that form a flower.

petrify (petrifies, petrifying, petrified) *verb* 1 to make somebody extremely frightened. *The strange noises petrified him.* 2 to turn into stone. *A petrified forest.*

petrol *noun* a liquid made from oil and used as a fuel for engines.

This lily has pink petals.

petty (pettier, pettiest) *adjective* unimportant. *Petty squabbles.*

pew *noun* a long wooden bench in a church. *He sat on the pew and prayed.*

phantom *noun* a ghost.

pharaoh (say fair-oh) *noun* a king of ancient Egypt.

Tutankhamun was one of the most famous pharaohs of ancient Egypt.

pharmacy (pharmacies) *noun* 1 a drug store, where medicines are sold. 2 the making or giving out of medicine. **pharmacist** *noun.*

phase *noun* a stage of development. **phase** *verb* to happen or make something happen in stages. *We can phase payment over three years, if it would make it easier for you.*

pheasant *noun* a long-tailed bird that is hunted for food. *A pheasant shoot.*

phenomenal *adjective* unusual, amazing. *He's got phenomenal strength for his age.*

phenomenon (phenomena) *noun* an unusual fact, event or thing. *Summer snow is an almost unknown phenomenon.*

philately (say fil-at-il-ee) *noun* stamp-collecting. **philatelist** *noun.*

-phile *suffix* indicating a person or thing that has a liking for something. *Francophiles like France and everything French.*

Philippines *noun* a country of many islands in Southeast Asia.

The flag of the Philippines is blue, red and white with a design of the Sun and stars.

philistine (say fil-ist-ine) *noun* a person who does not like or want to understand art and beautiful things.

philology *noun* the study of the development of language. **philologist** *noun*.

philosopher *noun* a person who studies or teaches philosophy.

philosophy *noun* 1 the study of the meaning of life and how people should live. 2 the ideas and beliefs that a philosopher has, or your own rules for living your life. *The philosophy of the ancient Greeks.* **philosophical** *adjective*.

Phnom Penh *noun* the capital of Cambodia.

phobia (say foh-bee-uh) *noun* a great fear of something. *He's got a phobia about spiders.*

phone *noun* a telephone. **on the phone** speaking to somebody by phone. **phone** *verb* to telephone. *Please phone home.*

phone-in *noun* a program on radio or television in which people call up and take part. *I took part in a phone-in about pets.*

photo *noun* a photograph.

photocopier *noun* a machine that can quickly copy documents and other papers by photographing them.

photocopy (photocopies) *noun* a photographic copy of a document or page made by a photocopier. **photocopy** (photocopies, photocopying, photocopied) *verb. Can you photocopy this page?*

photogenic *adjective* looking nice in photographs. *She is very photogenic, and will probably be a model when she is old enough to work.*

The photographer told the guests to smile for the camera.

Old-fashioned phones had a dial instead of push-buttons.

photograph *noun* a picture made with a camera and a film sensitive to light. **photograph** *verb* to use a camera to take a photograph. **photography** *noun*. **photographic** *adjective*.

photographer *noun* somebody who takes photographs. *A wedding photographer.*

photosynthesis *noun* the process by which green plants make food in their leaves, using the Sun's energy, carbon dioxide and water.

phrase *noun* a group of words used together, that form part of a sentence. 'In the park' is a phrase in 'We went for a walk in the park.' **phrase** *verb* to express something in words. *A well-phrased letter.*

physical *adjective* 1 connected with a person's body, not their mind. *Physical exercise.* 2 of things that can be touched and seen. *The physical world.* 3 connected with physics. **physically** *adverb*.

physician *noun* a doctor.

physics (say fiz-iks) *noun* the study of forces such as heat, light, sound, electricity and gravity. *She's good at physics and maths.*

physiotherapy (say fiz-ee-o-the-ruh-pee) *noun* treatment by means of exercise, massage, light and heat. **physiotherapist** *noun. The injured player was treated by the physiotherapist.*

physique (say fiz-eek) *noun* the shape and size of a person's body, especially a man's.

piano *noun* a large musical instrument that is played by the pianist's fingers pressing down on black and white keys. **pianist** *noun*.

Christine has a grand piano in her living room, but rarely gets time to play it.

piccolo *noun* a small flute that plays high notes. *A piccolo solo.*

pick *verb* 1 to pull or break off part of a plant, especially a flower or fruit. *We picked some strawberries.* 2 to choose carefully. *He always picks the best.* 3 to remove unwanted things or pull bits off something. 4 to take up. *Birds picking at the grain.* **pick a lock** to open a lock without a key. **pick a fight** to provoke a fight or an argument with somebody. **pick somebody's pocket** to steal from somebody. **pick on** to unfairly criticize or treat someone in an unfair way. **pick out** to choose something from a group. **pick up** 1 to lift or take up. 2 to take someone or something from a place. 3 to take somebody as a passenger. *They picked up a hitch-hiker.* 4 to get better. *His health is picking up.* 5 to learn or hear something. *I picked up some Italian in Florence.*

pick *noun* 1 choice. *Take your pick.* 2 the best of many. *You can have the pick of the bunch.*

pick *noun* 1 a pickax. 2 a plectrum.

pickax *noun* a pointed tool with a long handle used for breaking up rocks or hard ground.

A geologist needs a pickaxe to get samples of rocks for analysis.

pickle *noun* cucmbers preserved in water, salt and vinegar. **pickle** *verb* to preserve food in water, salt and vinegar. **be in a pickle** to be in a difficult situation.

pickpocket *noun* a thief who steals things from people's pockets.

picnic *noun* a meal eaten out of doors, at the beach or in a field. **picnic** (picnics, picnicking, picnicked) *verb* to have a picnic. **picnicker** *noun*.

The picnic hamper was packed full of good things to eat and drink.

pictorial *adjective* with pictures.

DID YOU KNOW

Wild pigs, or boars, were probably first kept by people in Asia about 5,000 years ago. They were used for clearing vegetation and for their meat, which we now call pork and bacon.

Pigs are extremely intelligent creatures.

picture *noun* 1 a painting, drawing or photograph of somebody or something. 2 a movie at a theater or on television. 3 an idea or impression. *She had quite a different picture of the house in her mind.* 4 a perfect example or a description of an event. *The baby is a picture of health.* **go to the pictures** to go to the cinema to see a film. **get the picture** to understand a situation somebody is telling you about. **put somebody in the picture** to tell somebody about a situation they need to know about. **picture** *verb* to imagine something.

picturesque *adjective* attractive and interesting. *A picturesque mountain village.*

pie *noun* a pastry case filled with fruit, meat, fish or vegetables, baked in a pan.

piece *noun* 1 a part or bit of something. *A piece of cake.* 2 one single thing, object or example. *A piece of paper.* 3 something written or composed, especially an article or a play. *A piece of music.* 4 a counter or any object used when playing a board game. *A chess piece.* **piece together** to make something by putting pieces together. *We tried to piece together the facts.*

pier *noun* 1 a bridge-like structure built out into the sea, used as a landing-stage or for people to walk along. 2 a pillar for supporting a bridge or roof.

pierce *verb* to make a hole with something sharp or pointed. *She had her ears pierced when she was just a baby.* **piercing** *adjective* sharp in an unpleasant way. *A piercing scream.*

pig *noun* 1 a pink or black fat animal with a snout, usually kept on farms for its meat. 2 a dirty or greedy person.

pigeon *noun* a gray bird with a fat body.

pigeon-hole *noun* a small open box or one of many compartments on a wall for papers and messages. *He left the letter in my pigeon-hole, so I could pick it up later.*

piglet *noun* a young pig.

pigment *noun* a substance that gives a particular color to things. *The red pigment of blood.* **pigmentation** *noun*.

pigsty (pigsties) *noun* 1 a hut for pigs. 2 a dirty room or home.

pile *noun* 1 a number of things lying on top of each other. 2 a large quantity of things or amount of money. **pile** *verb* to put things in or on a pile. **pile in** to come or get into a place in a large group. **pile out** to leave a place in a large group.

We leave newspapers in a pile on the porch for recycling.

pile *noun* a heavy wooden, metal or stone post that is hammered into the ground as a support for a bridge or building. *A pile-driving machine.*

pilfer *verb* to steal small amounts or things that are not valuable. *She used to pilfer from my purse.* **pilferage** *noun.*

pilgrim *noun* somebody who travels to a holy place for religious reasons.

pilgrimage *noun* a journey made by pilgrims to visit a holy place.

pill *noun* 1 a tablet of medicine. 2 a tablet taken by women, so they do not become pregnant.

pillar *noun* 1 a tall upright stone or wooden post that supports a building. 2 something that looks like a pillar. *A pillar of smoke.* 3 an important member of a group of people. *He's a pillar of society.*

pillow *noun* a cushion for resting your head on, especially in bed.

pillowcase *noun* a cover for a pillow.

pilot *noun* 1 a person trained to fly an aircraft. 2 a person who steers a ship in and out of port. **pilot** *verb* 1 to act as a pilot of an aircraft or a ship. 2 to guide carefully.

pilot *noun* a test to find out if something will work. *It's the pilot for the series.*

pimple *noun* a small spot on the skin. **pimply** *adjective. A pimply complexion.*

WORD HISTORY

The pineapple probably got its name because the fruit looks like a large pine cone. It is thought that pineapples originated in Brazil. Christopher Columbus and his crew were probably the first Europeans to taste the fruit.

They set off on a pilgrimage across the desert.

DID YOU KNOW

There are two cups or sixteen ounces in a pint, two pints in a quart and two quarts or four pints in a gallon.

---

pin *noun* 1 a metal needle with a sharp point and a round head for fastening pieces of cloth or paper together. 2 a short pointed piece of metal or wood for fixing or marking something. **pin** (pins, pinning, pinned) *verb* 1 to fasten with a pin or pins. *She pinned a flower to her dress.* 2 to hold or keep in a particular position, to make unable to move. *She was pinned under the wrecked car.* 3 to fix. *I'm pinning all my hopes on getting the job.*

pincers *plural noun* 1 an instrument used for gripping things or pulling things out. 2 the claws of a crab or lobster.

pinch *verb* 1 to squeeze somebody's skin using your thumb and first finger. *It hurt when he pinched my arm.* 2 to be too tight. *My shoes are too small, they pinch.* 3 to steal. *Don't pinch my candy.* **pinch** (pinches) *noun* 1 an amount that can be held between thumb and first finger. *A pinch of salt.* 2 a squeeze, usually a painful one. 3 suffering or stress, especially caused by not having enough money to buy things. *We are feeling the pinch, now that I have lost my job.* **in a pinch** if absolutely necessary.

pine *noun* an evergreen tree with leaves that look like needles.

pine *verb* to become weak and sad because of wanting something very much. *The dog is pining for his master.*

The seeds of the pine tree are inside the pine cone.

pineapple *noun* a large tropical fruit with spiny leaves, a thick skin and sweet, yellow juicy flesh.

pink *adjective* pale red. You can mix pink by adding a lot of white to red.

pinpoint *verb* to find or discover exactly what or where something is. *Can you pinpoint the problem?*

pins and needles *noun* a strange tingly feeling that you get when part of your body has 'fallen asleep' or become numb and the feeling returns to the area.

pint *noun* a measure for liquids. *The oil was a little low so we added a pint.*

pioneer *noun* the first person to go to a place or do or study something new. **pioneer** *verb* to help to develop something. *He pioneered the solar car.*

pious *adjective* very religious.

pipe *noun* 1 a long hollow metal or plastic tube through which water or gas can flow. 2 an object used for smoking tobacco. 3 a tube-like musical instrument, played by blowing. **pipe** *verb* 1 to carry liquid or gas through a pipe. 2 to send music or other sound through a loudspeaker. 3 to play music on a pipe. 4 to add a strip of decoration (called piping), especially to cloth. **pipe down** to be quiet.

pipeline *noun* pipes, often underground, for carrying oil, water or gas a long way. **in the pipeline** being planned or on the way. *Plans for a shorter school day are in the pipeline.*

piranha *noun* a small, fierce, meat-eating fish from South America.

pirate *noun* 1 a sailor who attacks and robs other ships. 2 somebody who copies or broadcasts somebody else's work, like books, video tapes or cassettes, without permission. *Pirate radio stations do not pay for the music they play.* **pirate** *verb* to copy or broadcast somebody else's work without permission. **piracy** *noun*.

pit *noun* 1 a deep hole. 2 a coal mine. 3 a hard fruit seed. 4(usually plural, pits) a place at the side of the racing track where racing cars are repaired and refueled. *The Ferrari came into the pits.* **pit** (pits, pitting, pitted) *verb* to make a hole in something. *The road was pitted with holes.* **pit against somebody** to set or match a person against another in a competition. *We were pitted against the club champions.*

pitch (pitches) *noun* 1 a throw of the ball for the batter to hit in baseball. 2 the highness or lowness of a sound. *Her voice dropped to a lower pitch.* 3 the degree or strength of something. *A pitch of excitement.* **pitch** *verb* 1 to set up, especially a tent or camp. 2 to throw or fling something. 3 to fall suddenly or heavily. *I tripped and pitched forward.* 4 to give a particular feeling to something, to set a level. *Her stories are pitched so that even the youngest children can easily understand them.* **pitch in** to join in an activity, to get working or eating.

pitch-dark *adjective* very dark.

A little of the white pith can be seen on the inside of this strip of lemon peel.

AMAZING FACT

Piranhas are not large fish, measuring not more than about 12 inches in length, but they travel in very large schools. Despite their bloodthirsty reputation, carnivorous piranhas feed mainly on fish, seeds and fruit.

Piranhas have sharp teeth.

Pizzas are often topped with tomatoes, anchovies and olives.

DID YOU KNOW

There were many pirates, or buccaneers, around the Caribbean Sea in the second half of the 17th century. The word pirate comes from the Greek 'peirates', meaning 'an attacker'.

---

pitfall *noun* an unexpected difficulty.

pith *noun* 1 the white substance under the peel of oranges, lemons and other citrus fruit. 2 the soft white substance in the stems of certain plants and trees.

pitiful *adjective* sad and weak, making you feel pity. *A pitiful story.*

pitiless *adjective* showing no feeling or pity. *The boss is pitiless, he makes us pay for every error.*

pity *noun* 1 feeling sorry for somebody who is suffering or unhappy. *Don't help me out of pity.* 2 a state of disappointment. *It's a pity you can't come to the party tonight.* **take pity on** to feel sorry for somebody and help them. **pity** (pities, pitying, pitied) *verb* to feel sorry for somebody.

pivot *noun* 1 a point or pin on which something turns. 2 the most important thing, which everything depends on. **pivot** *verb* to turn round as if on a pivot. **pivotal** *adjective*. *His mother has a pivotal influence on him.*

pizza *noun* a round piece of bread dough baked with a mixture of tomatoes, cheese and other food on top.

placard *noun* a large poster or notice. *The demonstrators carried placards with slogans on them.*

place *noun* 1 a particular position where something belongs or should be. *I put the books back in place.* 2 any point like a building, an area, a country or a town. *This is the place where we used to live.* 3 a seat. *He saved me a place.* 4 a house or home. *Come round to my place after school.* 5 a particular point in a story or book or part of it. *I lost my place because my bookmark fell out.* 6 a position in a group, race or competition. *First place.* 7 somebody's role in relation to other people or things. *It's not my place to tell him off.* 8 a point in a series of things, especially in an explanation. *In the first place I don't want to come, and in the second place I haven't been invited.* **all over the place** everywhere. **in place** in the proper position, suitable. **out of place** not in the proper position, unsuitable. **in place of** instead of. **take place** to happen. *When did the meetinhg take place?*

place *verb* 1 to put something in a particular place. 2 to say that somebody has achieved a particular position or put somebody in a particular position. *This places him in a difficult position.* 3 When you place an order, you order goods from a firm.

placid *adjective* calm, not easily made angry or upset. *She has a placid nature.*

plague *noun* 1 a dangerous illness that spreads quickly and kills many people. 2 a large number of unpleasant things. *A plague of rats.* **plague** (plagues, plaguing, plagued) *verb* to annoy or trouble all the time. *The child plagued me with questions.*

plaice (plaice) *noun* (say place) a flat sea-fish used for food.

plaid *noun* (say plad) a cloth with a pattern of squares and lines. *A plaid shirt.*

plain *adjective* 1 simple, not decorated, patterned or flavored. Not complicated. *I prefer plain food.* 2 easy to see, hear or understand. *It was plain he didn't like her.* 3 honest and open, especially about feelings or opinions. 4 not beautiful or handsome. **plainly** *adverb.* **plainness** *noun.*

plain *noun* a large flat area of land.

plait (say plat) *verb* to braid, to twist three or more strands, especially hair or rope, under and over one another into one thick length. **plait** *noun* a braid, a length of hair or rope that has been plaited.

plan *noun* 1 an outline or drawing showing all the parts of something. *We were looking at the plans for the new house.* 2 an arrangement for carrying out something that is to be done or used in the future. *We have made plans for our trip.* 3 a map of a town or district. **plan** (plans, planning, planned) *verb* to make a plan for something.

plane *noun* 1 an airplane. 2 a flat surface. 3 a tool with a sharp blade for making wood smooth by shaving small pieces off its surface. **plane** *verb* to smooth wood with a plane. *Peter planed down all the doors.*

plane *noun* a tall tree with big leaves.

DID YOU KNOW
Nine planets orbit the Sun. From nearest the Sun: Mercury, Venus, Earth, Mars, Jupiter, Saturn, Uranus, Neptune and Pluto.

The procession of people prayed to be spared from the plague.

AMAZING FACT
The nursery rhyme, 'Ring-a-ring-a-roses' originates from the time of the plague in the 1300s when herbs and fragrant flowers were thought be protection against the disease.

Workers on a plantation, harvesting sugar cane.

WORD HISTORY
Plaster of Paris was first made from gypsum in the Montmartre district of Paris in the 15th century. It is called the same in French: 'plâtre de Paris'.

planet *noun* any of the large bodies in space that travel around the Sun, such as Earth, Venus and Mars. **planetary** *adjective.*

The planet's rings appear to be solid.

plank *noun* a long, usually heavy, flat piece of wood. *Two men carried the plank.*

plankton *noun* tiny plants and animals that live in water and are food for many fish.

plant *noun* 1 a living thing that grows in the earth and has leaves and roots. Plants need water and light. 2 a factory. 3 a thing, especially stolen goods, hidden on somebody to make that person look guilty. *The drugs were a plant by the police.* **plant** *verb* 1 to put something in the ground to grow. 2 to fix firmly or place in a position. *She planted herself in the chair next to mine.* 3 to hide something or somebody secretly in order to wrongly accuse an innocent person. *He planted the stolen bike in his friend's garage.*

plantation *noun* 1 a large piece of land, especially in hot countries, on which crops like tea, sugar or cotton are grown. 2 a large group of trees planted especially for wood.

plaque (say plak) *noun* 1 a flat metal or stone plate fixed to a wall in memory of a famous person or event. *The plaque was unveiled.* 2 a substance that forms on teeth and gums and in which bacteria can live.

plaster *noun* 1 a mixture of lime, water and sand which hardens when dry and is used for covering walls and ceilings. 2 a white paste (called plaster of Paris) that dries quickly and is used for making molds or for casts around broken bones. **plaster** *verb* 1 to cover with plaster. 2 to cover something thickly, usually too thickly. *They plastered stickers all over the window.*

plastic *noun* a man-made material that can easily be formed into various shapes. Plastic is light and does not break easily. **plastic** *adjective* made of plastic.

plastic surgery *noun* medical operations to repair and replace damaged skin or injured and deformed parts of the body or to change a person's appearance.

plate *noun* 1 a flat dish from which food is eaten or served. *A dinner plate.* 2 a flat sheet of metal, glass or other hard material. 3 a small piece of metal with a person's name on it. 4 metal articles, dishes, bowls and cutlery with a thin covering of gold or silver. 5 a picture or photograph usually printed on special paper in a book. 6 a piece of plastic with false teeth on, shaped to fit inside a person's mouth. **plate** *verb* to cover metal objects with a thin layer of gold, silver or tin. *The spoons are silver plated.*

plateau (plateaux) *noun* (say platt-**oh**, platt-**ohz**) a flat area of land high above sea-level.

The high plateau was lit up with brilliant reds and purples in the setting sun.

platform *noun* 1 a flat raised structure, often made of wood, which people stand on when they make speeches or give a performance. 2 the area in a train station where people wait for or get off a train. 3 a statement of what a political party intends to do. 4 the type of operating system that a computer uses.

platinum *noun* a very valuable metal used for making jewellery.

platypus (platypuses) *noun* an Australian animal with a beak like a duck.

play *verb* 1 to take part in a sport, a game or other pleasant amusement. 2 to make music with a musical instrument, perform a musical work or operate a tape-recorder or cassette player. *She plays CDs all the time.* 3 to act in a play or film. *He played a king in the school play.* 4 to behave in a certain way. *She played it very cool when offered the job.* **play along** to pretend to agree with somebody. **play up** to emphasize an aspect of something in order to give a good impression. *I suggest that you play up the fact that you have plenty of experience.*

The platypus has a beak for feeding underwater and strong webbed feet for digging.

play *noun* 1 a story performed in a theater, on TV or on the radio. A piece of writing to be performed. *He has written a new play.* 2 playing. *Children learn through play.* **in/out of play** when the ball is/is not in a position where it is allowed to be played by the rules of the game. **come into play** to begin to be used. *The new rules are coming into play from Wednesday.*

player *noun* a person who plays a game.

playground *noun* a place where children can play. *We used to play kickball in the playground after lunch.*

playing card *noun* one of a set of cards used to play games. *We always take a pack of playing cards on holiday.*

plea *noun* 1 a strong request. *A plea for help.* 2 an excuse. *The accused entered a plea of insanity.* 3 a statement made by the accused in court stating whether they are guilty or not guilty.

plead *verb* 1 to make a strong request. *He pleaded with the teacher to give him another chance.* 2 to state in court whether one is guilty or not guilty. 3 to offer an excuse.

pleasant *adjective* nice, enjoyable. *We spent a pleasant day together.* A pleasant person is friendly and polite. **pleasantness** *noun.*

please *verb* 1 used when politely asking somebody to do something or asking for something. *Please pass the salt.* 2 to give satisfaction, make a somebody happy. *He always tries to please his parents.* **please yourself** to do what you want. **as you please** as you think best. *I'll do as I please.*

pleasure *noun* 1 a feeling of satisfaction, happiness and enjoyment. 2 something that is enjoyable and pleases you.

pleat *noun* a flattened fold in cloth. **pleat** *verb* to make folds. **pleated** *adjective. Our basic uniform is a plain blouse and a pleated skirt.*

The skirt had a kick pleat in the back of it.

plectrum *noun* a pick, a small piece of plastic, wood or metal, held in the hand and used for playing the guitar.

pledge *noun* 1 a serious promise or agreement. *The Pledge of Allegiance .* 2 something given as a sign of friendship or love. 3 a person who is becoming a member of a sorority or a fraternity. **pledge** *verb* 1 to make a serious promise. 2 to make a serious promise to give something. *The company pledged $6,000 to cancer research.*

plenty *pronoun, noun* enough, as much or more than is needed. *We've got plenty of time before the next train.* **plenty** *adverb* more than enough. *There's plenty of room in the trunk.*

pliers *plural noun* a gripping tool for holding or pulling out things. *He used a pair of pliers to pull out the nail.*

plight *noun* a difficult situation.

plod (plods, plodding, plodded) *verb* 1 to walk slowly with a heavy step. 2 to work slowly and without much interest.

plot *noun* 1 a small piece of ground. *A vegetable plot.* 2 a secret plan. *The police uncovered a plot to shoot the president.* 3 the story in a film or novel. *The director changed the plot.* **plot** (plots, plotting, plotted) *verb* 1 to make a secret plan. 2 to mark the position or course, especially of a ship or plane, on a map.

plow *noun* a farming tool with sharp blades for turning the soil over before seeds are planted. **plow** *verb* to turn over the soil with a plow. *To plow a field.* **plow through** to make your way through, usually with difficulty. *He plowed through all the books.* **plow back** to put money back into a business.

These are needle-nose pliers.

GRAMMAR NOTE

The plural of most English nouns is formed by adding an s at the end. But there are exceptions. Nouns ending in '–y' usually change to '–ies': 'sty', 'sties'. Some nouns that end in '–o' change to '–oes': 'hero', 'heroes'; but 'photo', 'photos'. Some nouns ending in '–f' change to '–ves': 'half', 'halves'; but 'roof', 'roofs'. Some nouns have irregular plurals, and these are given in their entries.

plum *noun* 1 a soft juicy fruit with a pit in the middle. 2 a dark reddish-blue color. 3 something very good. *He's got a plum job in the new company.*

plumber *noun* a person whose job is to fit and repair water pipes. **plumbing** *noun*.

plump *adjective* slightly fat, round. **plumpness** *noun*.

plunder *verb* to rob, especially in a war. *The soldiers plundered the town.* **plunder** *noun*. **plunderer** *noun*.

plunge *verb* 1 to suddenly fall or jump downwards or forwards. *He plunged into the water.* 2 to push quickly and forcefully. *The murderer plunged the knife into his victim's back.* 3 to fall steeply. *Prices have plunged to rock bottom.* **plunge** *noun* a dive. **take the plunge** to decide to do something risky or difficult.

plural *noun* a word that expresses more than one. *Cats is the plural of cat.* **plural** *adjective.* *Pliers is a plural noun.*

plus *preposition* 1 showing that one number is added to another, often written as a plus sign (+). *Three plus three, or 3 + 3.* 2 with the addition of. *She lost her job plus the company car.* **plus** *noun* 1 a plus sign (+). 2 an advantage. *Knowing lots of languages is a definite plus.*

plutocrat *noun* a person who is powerful because he or she is very rich.

The man in front drives the team of oxen that pull the plow, while the man behind steadies it and keeps the furrow straight.

pluck *verb* 1 to pull feathers off. *The cook plucked a chicken.* 2 to pull out, especially something unwanted. *She plucks her eyebrows.* 3 to pick a flower or fruit. 4 to pull and let go the strings of a stringed instrument. **pluck up courage** to overcome fear to do something. **pluck** *noun* courage.

plug *noun* 1 a plastic object with metal pins that fit into a socket to connect wires to the electricity supply. 2 a piece of rubber, wood or other material to block up a hole. *She pulled the plug out of the sink to let the water out.* 3 a piece of publicity praising a product. *His new song got a plug on TV.* **plug** (plugs, plugging, plugged) *verb* 1 to block up a hole. 2 to advertise something by frequently mentioning it.

AMAZING FACT

'p.m.' is an abbreviation of a Latin phrase – 'p' stands for 'post' meaning after and 'm' stands for 'meridiem' meaning noon or midday.

ply *noun* 1 a thickness of wood or cloth. *Three-ply wood has three layers.* 2 a thickness of wool, thread or rope measured in strands.

ply (plies, plying, plied) *verb* 1 to go regularly from one place to another. *The ferry plies the route between the mainland and the island.* 2 to use a tool or weapon. 3 to keep a person supplied, especially with food or questions. 4 to do a particular kind of work regularly. *They plied their trade by night.*

p.m. *abbreviation* written after a number and used to show the time after noon. *Stores close at 5.00 p.m.*

pneumatic *adjective* worked or filled with compressed air. *A pneumatic drill.*

pneumonia *noun* an illness with inflammation of one or both lungs.

poach *verb* to cook an egg, fish or fruit in boiling water or other liquid, sometimes in a special pan. *Poached plums.*

poach *verb* 1 to catch or shoot animals, fish or birds without permission from somebody else's land. *He was caught poaching rabbits.* 2 to take or use unfairly somebody else's ideas or belongings. *The tennis club has poached our best players.* **poacher** *noun*.

pocket *noun* 1 a small bag-shaped part of an article of clothing. 2 a small area. *Pocket of cloud.* **out of (the) pockets of** the money that belongs to someone. *The trial was paid for out of the pockets of American taxpayers.* **pocket** *verb* 1 to put something into a pocket. 2 to steal something. **pocket** *adjective* small enough to fit into a pocket. *A pocket calculator.*

People rely on pocket calculators more and more.

poem *noun* a piece of writing with lines that often rhyme.

poet *noun* a person who writes poems. **poetic** *adjective.* **poetry** *noun* poems. *A book of poetry.*

pogrom *noun* a planned killing often for racial or religious reasons.

point *noun* 1 a sharp end. *The point of a pencil.* 2 a small dot. *A decimal point.* 3 something that shows an important idea, particular fact or a position from which something is seen. *The point is, he can't act.* 4 a particular place or time. *At that point in the trip I just wanted to go to sleep.* 5 a mark on a scale. *The boiling-point of water.* 6 a score in some games or competitions. *They beat us by three points.* 7 a detail or quality of something or somebody. *He has his good points.* 8 a purpose, use. *There is no point in shampooing the carpet before the party.* 9 an electrical socket. *A power point.* 10 (usually plural, points) a junction of railroad tracks for changing a train from one line to another. **up to a point** to a certain degree. *I agree with him up to a point.* **beside the point** of little importance. **come to the point** to give the necessary facts. **point of view** a way of looking at something.

In many cultures it is not polite to point at people.

point *verb* 1 to direct or aim. *He pointed the water pistol at his friend.* 2 to show a direction or where something is, especially by holding out a finger. *The sign pointed in the other direction.* 3 to show that something is likely to happen. *Everything points to a war.* 4 to fill in the spaces between the bricks with cement. **point out** to draw attention to something. *She pointed out a mistake.*

point-blank *adjective, adverb* 1 aimed or said very directly or rudely. *She told him point-blank that she didn't like him.* 2 from a very close distance. *At point-blank range.*

pointed *adjective* 1 with a point at one end. 2 said or done in an unfriendly, critical way. *The teacher made a few pointed comments about homework being handed in late.*

pointless *adjective* with no purpose. *A pointless question.*

poison *noun* a substance that harms or kills animals or plants. **poison** *verb* 1 to put poison in or on something. To kill with poison. *The air is being poisoned by car fumes.* 2 to spoil something or influence somebody in a harmful way. *He poisoned her mind against her friend.* **poisonous** *adjective. A poisonous snake.*

poke *verb* 1 to push or jab, usually with something sharp. *She poked him in the ribs.* 2 to stick out or push through. *She poked her head through the door.* **poke** *noun.* **poke around** to search. *He was poking around in the house.* **poke fun at** to make jokes against, have a laugh at. **buy a pig in a poke** to buy something without seeing it and find afterwards that it is useless.

pokey (pokier, pokiest) *adjective* too small. *A pokey room.*

Poland *noun* a country in central Europe.

polar *adjective* near the North or South Pole.

polar bear *noun* a white bear that lives near the North Pole.

pole *noun* a long, round, usually thin stick or post. *One of the tent poles is missing.*

pole *noun* 1 either of the two ends of the earth's axis. The point as far north as the North Pole or as far south as the South Pole. 2 either of the ends of a magnet. 3 either of the two points of an electric battery. *The positive pole, the negative pole.* **be poles apart** to have completely different opinions on a subject.

WORD HISTORY

Long ago market traders would try to trick customers by putting a cat in a bag and claiming that it was a pig. Those who failed to check properly would buy 'a pig in a poke' – actually a cat! The 'poke' came from Old French for 'pouch', or 'bag'.

Poland is famous for its shipyards and its sausages.

police *noun* the men and women whose job and duty is to catch criminals and protect people and property. **police** *verb* to keep order by using the police. *Boxing matches are heavily policed.*

police force *noun* an organized group of police. *He joined the police force when he graduated.*

policeman *noun* a male member of a police force. *The policemen flagged him down.*

police officer *noun* a male or female member of a police force.

policewoman *noun* a female member of a police force.

policy (policies) *noun* a plan of action or statement of aims. *It's hospital policy.*

policy *noun* a document that shows the agreement made with an insurance company. *A life insurance policy.* **policyholder** *noun*.

polish *verb* to make things smooth and shiny by rubbing. **polish off** to finish quickly, especially food or work. **polish up** to make something better, improve it. *I must polish up my French.* **polish** *noun* 1 a substance, like wax, for polishing. 2 a shining surface. 3 elegance and good behavior.

Polish *noun* the language spoken in Poland. **Polish** *adjective*. *Polish sausages.*

polite *adjective* having good manners. **politely** *adverb*. *The children thanked their grandmother politely.* **politeness** *noun*.

political *adjective* concerning the government of a country. *A political party.*

politics *noun* the ways in which a country is governed, political affairs. **politician** *noun*.

polka *noun* a dance for couples or the music to which it is danced.

poll *noun* (say pole) 1 voting in an election. 2 a questioning of people chosen by chance to find out the general opinion about something, an opinion poll. **poll** *verb* 1 to receive a stated number of votes at an election. 2 to vote at an election.

pollen *noun* a fine yellow powder on the male part of the flower that fertilizes other flowers to produce seeds. Bees carry pollen from one flower to another.

The hummingbird gets pollen on its beak as it sucks nectar from the flower.

pollinate *verb* to fertilize with pollen. **pollination** *noun*.

pollute *verb* to make dirty and dangerous to live in or use. *Many of our rivers have been polluted.*

pollution *noun* 1 polluting the water, air or atmosphere. 2 substances that pollute. *There's too much pollution on our beaches.*

poly- *prefix* many. Polyatomic means having many atoms.

polygon *noun* a shape with many sides.

This is an irregular polygon.

polymath *noun* somebody who has knowledge in many fields of learning.

polythene *noun* a very light plastic material for making plastic bags and packaging.

polyunsaturated *adjective* containing fats that are healthier and more easily digested. *Polyunsaturated margarine is made from vegetable fats.*

pompous *adjective* full of self-importance. **pomposity** *noun*.

pond *noun* a very small lake.

ponder *verb* to think deeply and carefully.

ponderous *adjective* 1 slow and clumsy. *His movements were very ponderous.* 2 dull and serious. *He speaks in a ponderous way.* **ponderously** *adverb*.

pony (ponies) *noun* a small horse.

Sophie had always wanted a white pony of her own.

poodle *noun* a dog with curly hair.

pool *noun* 1 a small amount of water or other liquid. *A pool of blood spread across the floor.* 2 a swimming pool.

pool *noun* 1 an amount of money used by gamblers. 2 a common supply of workers or goods that can be shared by a number of people. *Our firm has a pool car that we all use.* 3 an American billiard game. **pool** *verb* to share. *We pooled our money and rented a villa in Spain for the summer.*

poor *adjective* 1 having very little money. 2 not good, of low quality or small in quantity. *She's in poor health.* 3 needing help or sympathy. *The poor little boy was crying.* **poorly** *adverb* badly. *Most foreign. The stage was poorly lit.*

pop *adjective* popular. *A pop singer.* **pop** *noun* popular music.

pop *noun* 1 a short explosive sound. *The cork came out with a pop.* 2 a fizzy drink. **pop** *verb* 1 to make a bursting sound. *The balloon went pop.* 2 If you pop something somewhere, you put it there quickly. *She popped a mint in the child's mouth.* 3 to cook popcorn. *Come over and we'll pop some corn and watch a video.* **pop in on** to make a short visit. **pop out** If something pops out of something, it suddenly comes out. *Her eyes almost popped out when she saw that she had the winning numbers.* **pop up** to spring up or to appear unexpectedly.

popcorn *noun* grains of maize heated until they burst open and look like little balls.

Popcorn is a popular snack at the movies.

Pope *noun* the head of the Roman Catholic Church.

poppy (poppies) *noun* a plant with big flowers.

Poppies grow on the fields of Flanders, in Belgium, where so many soldiers fell during World War I.

popular *adjective* 1 liked, enjoyed or admired by many people. *Katie is a very popular name.* 2 of or for the general public. *The popular press pays too much attention to gossip.* **popularity** *noun*.

If attacked, the porcupine runs backwards at its enemy, driving in its sharp spines.

populate *verb* to live in, inhabit. *We live in a heavily populated area.*

population *noun* the people living in a place, especially a country or town. *The population of India is expanding rapidly.*

porcelain *noun* a hard shiny material, used for making cups, plates and other articles, which is produced by baking clay. China.

porch *noun* a roofed entrance to a building.

porcupine *noun* a small animal with long spines over its back and sides.

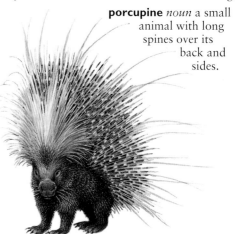

pork *noun* meat from pigs.

porpoise *noun* a large sea animal similar to a dolphin.

porridge *noun* soft food made from oats cooked in water and milk.

port 1 a harbor where goods are loaded and unloaded. 2 a town with a harbor. 3 the left side of a ship when you are facing towards the front of it.

port *noun* a strong sweet red Portuguese wine. *Fine ruby port.*

portable *adjective* able to be carried. *A portable television.*

Port-au-Prince *noun* the capital of Haiti.

portcullis *noun* a framework of pointed bars above the entrance in old castles that could be lowered as a protection against attack. *Let down the portcullis!*

porter *noun* 1 a person who is employed in a building like a hotel or hospital to stand at the entrance and open doors. 2 a person employed to carry people's luggage at a train station, an airport or in a hotel.

Port Louis *noun* the capital of Mauritius.

Port Moresby *noun* the capital of Papua New Guinea.

Port of Spain *noun* the capital of Trinidad and Tobago.

Porto Novo *noun* the capital of Benin.

portrait *noun* a painted picture, drawing or photograph of somebody.

portray *verb* 1 to make a picture of somebody or something. 2 to describe in words. 3 to play the part of a character in a film or play.

Portugal *noun* a country in Southwest Europe.

Portuguese *noun* the language spoken in Portugal and Brazil. Portuguese *adjective*. *The Portuguese flag.*

Port Vila *noun* the capital of Vanuatu.

pose 1 a particular position in or for a photograph or painting. *He sat in an unnatural pose.* 2 a way of behaving in order to impress or deceive people. **pose** *verb* 1 to sit or stand in a pose for a photograph or painting. *It was a very formal portrait requiring them to pose, unmoving, for long stretches of time.* 2 to pretend. *The spy was posing as a car mechanic.* 3 to bring into being, to cause. *Lack of money is posing too many problems.* **poser** *noun*.

The Japanese woman adopted a traditional pose for the photograph.

position *noun* 1 the place where something is or stands. *The house is in a sunny position.* 2 the way of sitting or standing. *He slept in an uncomfortable position.* 3 a situation or condition. *You've put me in an awkward position.* 4 a job. 5 a particular place in a group. 6 an opinion. **position** *verb* to put somebody or something into position. *I positioned the table by the door.*

positive *adjective* 1 sure, certain, having no doubt about something. *I am positive that I have seen you before.* 2 practical, helpful. *Let me give you some positive advice.* 3 agreeing, saying yes. *I got a positive reply to my request.* 4 real, noticeable. *It was a positive delight to see the children playing so happily together.* 5 greater than zero. *A positive number. The positive sign is +.* 6 If a medical test is positive, it shows that something, usually a disease, is present. **positively** *adverb* 1 definitely, really being the case. 2 without doubt. *The food was positively horrible.*

possess *verb* 1 to have or own. *I wish he possessed some of his brother's charm.* 2 to influence somebody's behavior or thinking. *What possessed you to drive so fast?*

possession *noun* 1 ownership, possessing. *How did the papers come into your possession?* 2 the things you possess or own. *He left all his possessions to his best friend.*

possessive *adjective* 1 wanting to keep things for yourself. *My brother is very possessive about his bike.* 2 in grammar, a possessive word shows ownership. 'My' and 'their' are possessive adjectives. **possessiveness** *noun*.

possible *adjective* able to happen, be done or that may be true. *Please come as soon as possible.* **possibility** *noun*. **possibly** *adverb*.

post *noun* 1 an upright bar of wood, metal or concrete fixed into the ground, especially as a support. *A lamp post.* 2 the starting or finishing point in a race. 3 a job. 4 a special place on duty, especially on guard.

post *verb* 1 to put up a public notice on a wall or bulletin board or on the Internet. *We posted news about the project on our school's website.* 2 to send somebody to a particular place to work or on duty or guard. *Guards were posted.* **postal** *adjective*. **keep somebody posted** to keep somebody informed.

post- *prefix* later than. *A post-war building.*

postage *noun* the amount of money charge for sending a letter or package by mail.

postal service *noun* the national service for carrying mail from one place to another.

postcard *noun* a card for sending a message without an envelope.

We sent a postcard from the beach.

poster *noun* a large picture or notice that is stuck to a wall or noticeboard.

posthumous *adjective* printed or happening after a person's death. **posthumously** *adverb*. *Posthumously awarded a medal.*

post-mortem *noun* an examination of a dead body to find the cause of death.

post office *noun* the place that deals with the mail and postal business.

postpone *verb* to fix a later date or move to a later time. *The game was postponed because of rain.* **postponement** *noun*.

P

pot *noun* a round container for cooking or keeping things in. **go to pot** to be ruined, especially from lack of care. **take pot luck** to take whatever is offered or available. **pot** (pots, potting, potted) *verb* 1 to put into a pot, especially food for preserving or plants. 2 to hit a ball into one of the pockets in snooker or pool.

potato *noun* a round vegetable with brown or red skin that grows underground.

potential *adjective* capable of happening or being used. Not yet developed, but able to come into existence. *This film is a potential success.* **potential** *noun. The boy shows lots of potential.* **potentially** *adverb.*

potholing *noun* the sport of exploring underground caves. **pothole** *noun.* **potholer** *noun. The potholer called for help.*

pottery *noun* 1 pots, plates and other objects that are made from clay and then baked in an oven. 2 a place where pottery is made. **potter** *noun.*

Classical Greek pottery is often decorated with designs of red and black showing scenes of life in ancient Greece.

potty *noun* a pot used by little children as a toilet. *The baby is being potty-trained.*

pouch (pouches) *noun* a small bag or anything shaped like a bag.

poultry *noun* farm birds like chickens and ducks that are kept for eggs and meat. *We passed a poutry farm on our way out of town.*

pounce *verb* to leap or swoop down quickly, especially in order to get something. *The cat pounced on the mouse as it crept out from behind the porch.*

pound *noun* a unit of weight equal to 454 grams or 16 ounces. *Let's buy a pound of cheese and a loaf of bread for the picnic.*

pound *noun* a place where stray animals and illegally parked cars are taken and kept until collected by the owner.

pound *verb* 1 to hit something loudly and repeatedly. *I can feel my heart pounding.* 2 to crush into a powder or paste.

This is a nuclear power station.

pour *verb* 1 to flow or make liquid or another substance flow. *He poured me a drink.* 2 to rain. *It's been pouring all day.* 3 to come or go quickly and in large amounts. *Fan mail has been pouring in.* **pour out** to tell freely and with feeling, especially a story or your troubles. *She poured out all her worries.*

poverty *noun* the state of being very poor. *They live in poverty.*

powder *noun* any substance that has been crushed or rubbed to dust. *Talcum powder.* **powder** *verb* to put powder on. *She powdered her nose.* **powdered** *adjective* in the form of powder. *Powdered milk.* **powdery** *adjective* like powder.

power *noun* 1 the ability to do something or have a certain effect. *He did everything in his power to help.* 2 force, physical strength. *The power of the waves threw the boat on to the beach.* 3 energy, the force that makes things work. *Electric power.* 4 authority, the right to do something. *The power of the press.* 5 a person or organization that has great influence. *The US is a world power.* **in power** having the right to govern. **powerful** *adjective.* **powerless** *adjective* without energy or influence.

practicable *adjective* that can be done.

practical *adjective* 1 good at doing or making things. Clever at dealing with difficulties, sensible. 2 useful, convenient, good for a particular purpose. *A plastic tablecloth is very practical, you can just wipe it clean.* 3 concerned with action and practice, rather than just ideas. A practical lesson is a lesson in which you make things or do experiments. *She didn't get the job because she had no practical experience.* **practicality** *noun.*

practical joke *noun* a funny trick played on a person.

practically *adverb* 1 in a practical way. 2 almost. *He practically walked into her.*

practice *noun* 1 something done regularly or as an exercise. *We have football practice twice a week.* 2 doing something, knowledge of a skill. *In practice this arrangement will never work.* 3 the business of a doctor or lawyer. **out of practice** no longer very good, because of lack of practice.

practice *verb* 1 to do something often in order to be good or get better at it. *I'm practicing this piece on my guitar for the concert.* 2 to take part in an activity, do something actively. *People are allowed to practice any religion in this country.* 3 to work as a doctor or lawyer.

The soccer team practices every day after school.

pragmatic *adjective* dealing with things in a practical way, a way which is best under the actual conditions. **pragmatist** *noun*.

Prague *noun* the capital of the Czech Republic.

Praia *noun* the capital of Cape Verde.

prairie *noun* flat grassland in North America. *Wheat prairies.*

The pioneers traveled across the prairies of the US.

praise *verb* to say that somebody or something is very good. *He praised her courage.* **praise** *noun* words that praise somebody or something.

prattle *noun* meaningless childish talk. **prattle** *verb*. *She prattled on about the clothes she wants to buy.*

prawn *noun* a small shellfish like a shrimp.

pray *verb* to speak to god or gods. *She prayed for strength.*

prayer *noun* 1 the activity of praying. 2 the words used in praying. A set form of words used during a religious service.

praying mantis *noun* an insect.

pre- *prefix* before a particular time. *A pre-war building.*

preach (preaches, preaching, preached) *verb* to give a talk, especially a moral or religious talk or sermon. *Come on! You're the one who's always preaching fairness.* **preacher** *noun*.

precaution *noun* something done in order to avoid a possible known danger or trouble. **precautionary** *adjective*. *We took precautionary measures and put up a fence.*

AMAZING FACT

If you add a word or part of a word (called a prefix) to the beginning of a root word, you can form a new word. The word 'prefix' itself comes from 'pre–' ('before') and 'fix' ('fasten').

DID YOU KNOW

The name 'praying manits' meaning 'diviner' was given to this insect by the Ancient Greeks because they thought it had supernatutal powers. the female often eats the male after mating.

precede *verb* to come or go in front.

precinct (say pree-sinkt) *noun* 1 a part of a city with its own police force and government officials. 2 the area around a cathedral or university, often enclosed by walls.

precious *adjective* 1 very valuable. 2 much loved by somebody. *My dolls are very precious to me.* **precious little/few** very little or very few.

precipice *noun* a very steep side of a rock, mountain or cliff. **precipitous** *adjective*. *A precipitous mountain path.*

Karen got ready to rappel down the precipice.

precipitation *noun* 1 the amount of rain or snow that falls. 2 being too hurried, unwise haste. **precipitate** *verb*.

precise *adjective* exact, clear. *He gave a precise description of the accident.* **precision** *noun*. **precisely** *adverb*. *At precisely that moment he appeared at the door.*

precocious (say prik-oh-shus) *adjective* seeming older, having developed earlier than is normal in mind or body. *He is a precocious little boy, he talks like an adult.*

predecessor (say pree-dis-ess-er) *noun* somebody who has had a job before another person, or something that was used before something else. *The new principal is much better than his predecessor.*

predict *verb* to say what will or might happen, to forecast. **prediction** *noun*. *My prediction is that the idea will be very successful.* **predictable** *adjective*. *A predictable mistake.*

prefabricated *adjective* made in parts in a factory. *Prefabricated buildings are fitted together on site.* **prefabricate** *verb*.

preface *noun* an introduction to a book or speech. *The preface is by a famous writer.*

prefer (prefers, preferring, preferred) *verb* to like one person or thing better than another. *I prefer coffee to tea.* **preference** *noun*. *What is your preference?*

prefix (prefixes) *noun* a word or group of letters in front of a word to make a new word. The prefix 'un-' before 'load' makes the word 'unload'.

pregnant *adjective* When a woman or female animal is pregnant, a baby develops inside her body. **pregnancy** *noun*.

prehistoric *adjective* of the time before history was written down. *Dinosaurs were prehistoric animals.*

Scientists think that prehistoric animals such as the dinosaur were wiped out when the Earth suffered a dramatic climate change, killing the vegetation on which they fed.

prejudice *noun* an unfair opinion or dislike of somebody or something, not based on knowledge or experience. *They were accused of racial prejudice and brought to trial.* **prejudiced** *adjective*.

premature *adjective* done or happening earlier than usual or expected. *A premature baby may need to be put in an incubator.*

premiere *noun* the first showing or performance of a movie or play.

premises *plural noun* a building and its grounds. *Residential premises.*

preoccupied *adjective* thinking a lot about something and therefore not giving attention to other matters. *She is so preoccupied with plans for her wedding that she can't work.* **preoccupation** *noun*.

prepare *verb* to get or make ready. **prepared** *adjective* 1 got ready in advance. 2 willing. *I'm not prepared to help you.*

preposition *noun* in grammar, a word or group of words used with a noun or pronoun to show its connection with another word such as place, position or time. In 'the woman on the stage', 'on' is a preposition.

prescribe *verb* 1 to advise what medicine or treatment a patient should have. *The doctor prescribed antibiotics.* 2 to state what must be done. **prescription** *noun*. *I have a prescription for this medicine.*

DID YOU KNOW
The youngest ever President of the United States was the 26th president, Theodore Roosevelt (1858–1919), who was 42 when he entered office; he was President from 1901 to 1909.

present *noun* (say **pre**-zunt) something given, a gift. *Christmas presents.* **present** *verb* (say pree-**zent**) 1 to give something formally, especially something like a prize. *They presented her with a bouquet of flowers.* 2 to introduce somebody to an important person or introduce a television or radio program. *Professor Bird presented the documentary.* 3 to put on a play or show. 4 to offer, show or be the cause of. *He loves sailing because it presents such a challenge.* **presentation** *noun*.

We open our Christmas presents first thing on Christmas morning.

present *noun* (say **pre**-zunt) the time that is taking place now or the things that are happening at the moment. *Try to live in the present, not the past.* **at present** now.

present *adjective* (say **pre**-zunt) 1 there, in this or that place. *Is a defendant present?* 2 existing now. *The present government.* 3 being talked or written about now. *We'll make an exception in the present case.* **presence** *noun*. *I don't talk about it in her presence.* **presently** *adverb*.

president *noun* 1 the leader of a country. *The President of the United States.* 2 a person who has a high position in an organization such as a club, a college or a company. *The president of our golf club.* **presidency** *noun*. **presidential** *adjective*.

Nelson Mandela cast a vote for the ANC in South Africa's first free election. He became the first black president of his nation.

press *verb* 1 to push hard against something or push one thing against another. *You have to press harder to make it work.* 2 to squeeze or flatten. To press flowers in a book. 3 to iron. *Can you press my jacket?* 4 to persuade somebody to do something or make demands. *She's always pressing us to stay longer.* **press on** to go on doing something. **pressed for** If you are pressed for time, you are in a hurry. If you are pressed for money, you do not have enough money at the moment. *I am pressed for time and money.*

press (presses) *noun* 1 the action of pushing against something. *At the press of a button.* 2 a device or machine for pressing. *A flower press.* 3 newspapers, magazines and journalists. *He was interviewed by the press.* 4 a business for printing and making books and magazines. 5 a machine for printing books and magazines. *A printing press.*

The newspapers rolled off the printing presses.

press conference *noun* an interview with journalists. *He held a press conference.*

pressure *noun* 1 the action of pressing. 2 the force with which something presses. *The water pressure is very low.* 3 a feeling of being forced to do something, a strain. *She was under pressure to do well at school.* **put pressure on somebody** to force somebody to do something. *They put pressure on her to leave the country.* **pressure** *verb* to forcefully make somebody do something. *They pressured me into going to college.* **pressurize** *verb*.

presume *verb* to think that something is the case or true. *An accused person is presumed innocent until proved guilty.* **presumption** *noun*.

pretend *verb* to act in a way as if something is true or real, although in fact it is not, either as a game or to deceive people. *He's snoring, pretending to be asleep.* **pretence** *noun. He doesn't really like the job, it's all a pretence.*

Pretoria *noun* the seat of government of South Africa.

pretty (prettier, prettiest) *adjective* nice, attractive. *A pretty girl.* **prettily** *adverb.* **prettiness** *noun.*

She's a pretty girl with pierced ears.

pretty *adverb* quite or rather. *It was pretty hot.* **pretty much** very nearly, almost.

We went up into the mountains to observe the birds of prey.

prevailing *adjective* most common or general, especially of a custom or belief. *The prevailing wind is a westerly.*

prevent *verb* 1 to stop somebody from doing something. 2 to make sure something does not happen. *How can we prevent war?* **prevention** *noun. Crime prevention.* **preventive** *adjective. Preventive medicine.*

previous *adjective* happening or being earlier in time or before the one you are talking about. *In my previous job.* **previously** *adverb. They previously lived in Germany.*

prey (say pray) *noun* 1 an animal that is hunted and eaten by other animals. *The lion pounced on its prey.* 2 a helpless person, a victim. **bird of prey** a bird that hunts and eats animals or other birds. **prey on** *verb* 1 to hunt for food. 2 to attack and steal from people. 3 to trouble you greatly, to make you worry about something. *The journey is preying on my mind.*

price *noun* 1 an amount of money for which something is bought or sold. *We have to fix a price.* 2 what you must do in order to get what you want. *He paid the price of becoming rich and famous.* **price** *verb* 1 to fix the price of something. 2 to mark goods in a shop with a price. *I've priced the salsa at $2.00 a jar.*

priceless *adjective* worth a lot of money, very valuable. *A priceless painting.*

prick *verb* 1 to make a small hole in something. *I pricked my finger with a needle.* 2 to hurt somebody with a pin or something sharp, or feel a sharp pain on the skin. *The thorns pricked me.* **prick** *noun* 1 a small hole. 2 a sharp pain.

prickle *noun* 1 a small sharp point that sticks out from a plant or an animal. *The prickles of a cactus.* 2 a feeling that something is pricking you. **prickle** *verb* to have or give a pricking feeling. *Wool makes my skin prickle.* **prickly** *adjective. Prickly holly leaves.*

pride *noun* 1 a feeling of delight and pleasure in what you or people you know have done. *She showed him her certificate with pride.* 2 something that makes you feel proud. *The children are her pride and joy.* 3 too high an opinion of yourself, especially because of wealth or position. 4 self-respect. *He swallowed his pride and said sorry.* **pride yourself on** to be proud of. *She prides herself on never having missed a class.*

priest *noun* 1 a member of the Christian clergy, a clergyman. 2 a specially trained person who performs religious ceremonies. **priestess** *noun*.

prim (primmer, primmest) *adjective* very correct and easily shocked by anything rude.

primary *adjective* extremely important, main. *A peace agreement is our primary aim.* **primarily** *adverb*.

primary color *noun* The primary colors are red, yellow and blue. All other colors can made up by mixing them in different ways.

Primary colors can be mixed to form all the other colors of the spectrum.

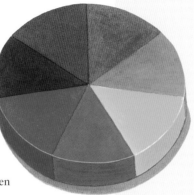

primary school *noun* elementary school, a school for children between 5 and 11 years old.

prime *adjective* 1 most important. *Computers are of prime importance in all businesses, hospitals and schools.* 2 of the very best quality, best. *Early evening is the prime time for advertising on television.* **prime minister** the head of a government. **prime number** a number that can be divided only by itself and the number 1. 3, 7 and 11 are prime numbers.

prime *noun* the best or most successful stage of something. *He is past his prime.*

prime *verb* 1 to give somebody information beforehand so that they are prepared, especially for difficulties. *She had primed him before the interview, so he could answer all the questions.* 2 to cover a surface, especially wood, with a coat of paint or oil to prepare it for painting. 3 to get a machine ready for use.

primitive *adjective* 1 belonging to a society of people who lived at an earlier time. *Primitive man made tools from sharp stone and animal bones.* 2 simple or old-fashioned. *This cottage is too primitive for me, it has no indoor plumbing.*

primrose *noun* an early-flowering wild plant that has flowers of various colors.

prince *noun* a man or boy in a royal family, especially the son of a king or queen.

princess *noun* 1 a woman or girl in a royal family, especially the daughter of a king or queen. 2 the wife of a prince.

principal *adjective* most important.

principal *noun* 1 the head of a school or college. 2 money lent or put into a business on which interest is paid.

AMAZING FACT

An easy way to remember how to spell 'principal' is to think of the principal as your pal or friend!

SPELLING NOTE

As an adjective, 'principal' is spelt '-pal'. As a noun, 'principal' is the spelling for the head of a school or an amount of money. A 'principle' (with '-ple') is a rule.

We followed the tire prints and discovered the stolen car.

Light passing through a prism is split into all the colors of the rainbow.

---

principle *noun* 1 a general rule about how something should be done or how it works. *The principles of grammar.* 2 a rule for behavior. *It was against his principles.* **in principle** in general. *In principle I agree with you.* **on principle** because of your personal beliefs. *I'm against war on principle.*

print *verb* 1 to produce words or pictures on paper with a machine or shapes covered with ink. To make books, magazines and pictures in this way. *How many copies of this dictionary were printed?* 2 to write words without joining the letters, usually in capitals. *Please print your name and then sign here.* 3 to press a mark on to a surface or make a pattern on cloth. *The pattern has been printed on to the scarf by hand.* 4 to make a photograph from a negative film. **print** *noun* 1 the printed letters and numbers on a page. *The print is too small to read without glasses.* 2 a mark made on a surface showing the shape of the thing pressed on it. *The tires left prints in the sand.* 3 a printed picture, photograph or pattern. **in print** 1 printed in a book, magazine or newspaper. *Don't believe everything you see in print.* 2 If a book is in print, it is still available and can be bought. **printing** *noun*.

printer *noun* 1 a person or firm that prints books, newspapers and other printed material. 2 a machine connected to a computer that prints out what you have written or any other information.

print-out *noun* information from a computer printed on a piece of paper.

prior *preposition, adjective* earlier or more important than something else. *They had already decided prior to the event.*

prior *noun* a monk who is the head of a religious house, called a priory.

priority *noun* something considered more important than other things. *We must do that as a priority.*

prism (say **priz**-um) *noun* 1 a solid shape with a flat base and parallel upright edges. 2 a three-sided block, usually made of glass, that breaks up light into the colors of the rainbow.

prison *noun* a building where criminals are kept locked up as a punishment. *The thief was sent to prison for three years.*

The prison had tall gates with a window to check a visitor's identity.

prisoner *noun* a person kept in prison as a punishment. 2 a person or animal who has been captured and is kept locked up.

privacy *noun* being private, away from others and able to do things without other people seeing you.

private *adjective* 1 for one person or a small group of people, not public, not shared with others, personal. *A house with a private swimming pool.* 2 secret or kept secret. *He has some private information about the president.* 3 personal, rather than to do with work or business. *He never talks about his private life at work.* 4 quiet, sheltered. Somebody who is a private person is shy and does not like to share their feelings with other people. 5 independent, not owned by the state. *Private hospitals and private schools are not paid for by the government.* **in private** without other people listening or hearing, away from others. *Could we have a talk in private?*

privileged *adjective* having an advantage that most other people do not have. *She came from a privileged background.* **privilege** *noun. It was a privilege to be able to work with such a famous director.*

prize *noun* something of value given to the winner of a game, competition or particular good work. **prize** *verb* to value highly. *Italian tomatoes are prized for their taste.*

The first prize for excellence at school went to Jennifer Jones.

pro *noun* a professional. *He turned pro when he was just eighteen.*

pro- *prefix* for somebody or something, in favor of. *He is very pro-Italian.* **pro and con** for and against.

WORD HISTORY

Originally a privilege was a 'law affecting an individual', from the Latin 'privilegium'. This word itself came from two other Latin words: 'privus', meaning 'private', and 'legis', meaning 'law'.

probably *adverb* very likely. *I'll probably see you tomorrow.* **probable** *adjective. He is the probable winner.*

probation *noun* 1 a period of time during which somebody's abilities at work are tested before they are finally given the job. 2 a system of letting a criminal go free if he behaves well. Somebody on probation is supervised by an official, a probation officer, for a period of time.

probe *noun* 1 a long thin metal instrument used by doctors to search inside the body. 2 an object used for exploring space. **probe** *verb* to search or explore.

problem *noun* something difficult, a question for which an answer is needed. **problematic, problematical** *adjective.*

proboscis (say pro-**boss**-iss) *noun* 1 the long part of an insect's mouth. 2 an elephant's trunk.

The elephant's trunk is technically called a proboscis.

procedure *noun* a way of doing something, especially in a correct way.

proceed *verb* 1 to continue with an action, often after stopping. 2 to go forward in a particular direction.

proceedings *plural noun* 1 a series of happenings. 2 a lawsuit.

process (processes) *noun* (say **proh**-sess) 1 a series of actions for doing or achieving something. *Packing the car was a slow process.* 2 a series of things that happen naturally. *Chemical processes.* 3 an action in law. **process** *verb* 1 to treat food and other materials using a particular process. *To process (develop) a film.* 2 to produce information by putting it through a process. *It will take a week for us to process the applications.*

procession *noun* a group of people or vehicles moving forward, following each other. *A funeral procession.*

proclaim *verb* to make officially known. **proclamation** *noun.*

prod (prods, prodding, prodded) *verb* 1 to push with your finger or something pointed. 2 to get or remind somebody to act. *You have to prod him into action.* **prod** *noun.*

prodigal *adjective* wasteful, especially of money. *The prodigal son.*

produce *verb* 1 to make, grow or create. *The Sun produces heat.* 2 to show, bring out to be seen. *He produced a ticket to prove he had paid.* 3 to cause to happen. *Good soil will produce good vegetables.* 4 to organize a film, play, record or program. *The film was directed and produced by the same person.* **produce** *noun* things produced, especially things grown. **producer** *noun*.

product *noun* 1 something produced, especially something manufactured. *Cleaning products.* 2 the result of thought or conditions. 3 in math, the number obtained by multiplying two or more numbers.

production *noun* 1 the process of producing, making or growing things in large quantities. 2 something produced, a play, opera or show.

productive *adjective* producing a lot of things, especially in large amounts. *We had a very productive meeting.*

profession *noun* a job that needs special training. *Teaching always has been a poorly paid profession.*

Science is a serious profession.

professional *adjective* 1 of a particular profession. 2 doing work as a job for payment. *You can earn a lot of money as a professional golfer.* 3 showing the skill of a professional, competent. **professional** *noun*. *He is a true professional.* **professionally** *adverb*.

program [1] *noun* a set of instructions for a computer to carry out. **program** (programs, programming, programmed) *verb*. *Can you program a computer to answers questions?* **programmer** *noun*.

program [2] *noun* 1 a fixed plan of events, activities or a list of duties. *What is on the program today?* 2 a booklet or list that gives information about what you have come to see or take part in. *A theater program.* 3 a performance, talk or show on radio or television. *A new music program.* **program** *verb*. *Do you know how to program the VCR?*

The theater program explained the history of the production.

progress (say **pro**-gress) *noun* 1 forward movement, the process of gradually getting nearer to something. *We made slow progress up the hill.* 2 development or improvement. *You are making good progress in your work.* **in progress** happening now. *When we arrived, the game was already in progress.* **progress** *verb* (say pro-**gress**) to make progress.

progressive *adjective* 1 moving forward or happening gradually over a period of time. *The progressive closure of the coal industry.* 2 having modern ideas how things should be done. *Most progressive schools are against wearing uniform.*

prohibit *verb* to say that something must not be done, to ban. **prohibition** *noun*.

project *noun* (say **proj**-ekt) 1 a plan. 2 a study of a subject by a student. *Our class is doing a project on Asian music.* **project** *verb* (say pruh-**jekt**) 1 to stick out above a surface or edge. 2 to make a light or picture from a film appear on a surface. *The pictures were projected on to a screen.* 3 to throw or send through the air with force. *Missiles were projected into space.* 4 to plan. *The minister's projected visit to Spain has been cancelled.* **projection** *noun*.

projector *noun* a machine for showing films or slides on a screen or wall.

We bought a projector so we could see our safari slides.

prolong *verb* to make longer or make something last longer. *Let's not prolong this silly argument.*

prominent *adjective* 1 important, well known. *The Ritz is full of prominent people.* 2 standing out, noticeable. *His eyes are the most prominent part of his face.* **prominently** *adverb*. **prominence** *noun*.

promise *noun* 1 a statement that you make to somebody to say that you will do or give them something. *She always keeps her promises.* 2 expectation or hope of success. *The singer shows great promise.* **promise** *verb*. *He promised to buy her a new bike.*

promising *adjective* likely to be successful.

promote *verb* 1 to give somebody a more important job or higher rank. 2 to bring to notice, especially to increase sales or somebody's popularity. *The company is promoting a new shampoo on television.* **promotion** *noun*. **promoter** *noun*.

prompt *adjective* without delay, punctual. *A prompt reply.* **promptly** *adverb.* *He arrived promptly at 9 o'clock.*

prompt *verb* 1 to make you decide to do something. *Poor results prompted the manager to change the team.* 2 to remind an actor or speaker of the next words when they have been forgotten.

prone *adjective* lying face downwards. **be prone to** be likely to do or have something. *He is prone to bad moods.*

prong *noun* a spike of a fork.

The fork has three prongs.

pronoun *noun* in grammar, a word that is used in place of a noun that has already been or will be mentioned. He, she, it, her, them are pronouns.

pronounce *verb* 1 to make the sound of a letter or word. In the word 'gnaw' the 'g' is not pronounced. 2 to declare formally. He was pronounced dead. **pronunciation** *noun.* *His French pronunciation is very good.*

proof *noun* 1 a thing or fact that shows that something is true. *He has no proof that the car belongs to him.* 2 a trial copy of something printed, made for checking before other copies are printed.

proof *suffix* showing that something cannot be damaged or gives protection against something harmful. *A waterproof jacket. A foolproof plan.*

prop *noun* 1 a support used to keep something up. 2 (usually plural, props) the furniture and other objects used in a play or film. **prop** (props, propping, propped) *verb* to support or keep in position by putting something under or against. *She propped the door open with a shoe.* **prop somebody up** to help and give support to somebody.

The plastic knife was often used as a prop during theater productions.

propaganda *noun* information, often false information, given to influence people. *The extremists put out a lot of propaganda.*

DID YOU KNOW

Propellers work by thrusting a vehicle forwards. A ship's propeller is connected to a shaft, which is turned by the engine. As it turns, the propeller pushes water backwards, and this thrusts the ship forwards.

All religions have prophets, or people who have developed ideas about life and existence.

SPELLING NOTE

Note that the noun from 'pronounce' is spelt 'pronunciation': the middle part is spelt – and pronounced! 'Nun' rather than 'noun'.

propel (propels, propelling, propelled) *verb* to push or drive forward.

propeller *noun* blades fixed to a bar which spin round and make an aircraft or ship go.

proper *adjective* 1 suitable, correct, right for the situation. *Everything was in its proper place.* 2 respectable. *Proper behavior.* 3 great, real. . **properly** *adverb.* *She doesn't eat properly, all she has for lunch is bag of chips.*

prophecy (prophecies) *noun* telling something that will happen in the future.

prophet *noun* 1 a person who is believed to be chosen by God to teach a religion to the people. *Muslims are followers of the Prophet Muhammad.* 2 somebody who makes prophecies.

proposal *noun* 1 a plan or suggestion. 2 an offer of marriage.

propose *verb* 1 to suggest an idea or plan. 2 to ask somebody to marry you. *Tom proposed to Emma.*

prosecute *verb* to accuse somebody of a crime and try and prove it in a court of law. *He was prosecuted for burglary.* **prosecution** *noun* 1 the action of prosecuting somebody. 2 the lawyers who try to prove that the accused person is guilty.

prospect (say **pross**-pekt) *noun* 1 a possibility or hope. *What are the prospects of getting a job?* 2 a wide view.

prospect (say pruh-**spekt**) *verb* to search in the ground, especially for gold, silver or oil. **prospector** *noun.*

prosper *verb* to be successful or rich.

prosperity *noun* success and riches. **prosperous** *adjective.*

prostitute *noun* a person who offers sex for payment. **prostitution** *noun.*

prostrate *adjective* lying face downwards flat on the ground.

protect *verb* to keep safe from harm, danger or enemies. *Vitamin C helps protect against flu.* **protection** *noun. As a protection against the cold.* **protector** *noun.*

protective *adjective* 1 giving protection. 2 wishing to protect. *She is very protective of her children.*

protein *noun* a body-building substance found in all living things. Protein is in foods such as meat, eggs, beans and milk.

protest (say **pro**-test) *noun* an act of saying or showing that you do not agree with something. *There were many protests against experiments on animals.* **protest** (say pruh-**test**) *verb* 1 *The students protested against the war.* 2 to state firmly. *He protested his innocence.* **protester** *noun*.

protestant *noun* a member of the Christian church which separated from the Catholic church in the sixteenth century.

proton *noun* a very small piece of matter, an atomic particle, that has a positive electric charge.

prototype *noun* the first model of something, from which others have been developed or are copied.

proud *adjective* 1 feeling pleased about something good that you or somebody else has done. *We are all very proud of you for being so brave.* 2 having self-respect or having too high an opinion of yourself. *She is too proud to say sorry.* **proudly** *adverb*. *She proudly showed us her son's medal.*

prove *verb* 1 to show that something is true. *Can you prove that all the doors were locked?* 2 to turn out or to be found to be as expected. *He proved to be a bad loser.*

proverb *noun* a short well-known saying, usually giving a general truth. 'Too many cooks spoil the broth' is a proverb. **proverbial** *adjective*. *The proverbial ill wind blows no one any good.*

provide *verb* 1 to give things that are needed or useful. *The campsite provides laundry facilities.* 2 to state arrangements or make special arrangements that must be fulfilled. **provider** *noun*.

provided, providing *conjunction* on the condition that. *I'll loan you some money provided you promise to pay me back.*

Ottawa is the capital of Canada. Its metropolitan area lies astride the borders of the provinces of Ontario and Quebec.

The prototype of a new car may be extremely expensive to build because the production facilities for mass manufacturing the car don't exist.

---

province 1 a part of a country, a state. *Newfoundland is a province of Canada.* 2 (usually plural, the provinces) all the country outside the capital. 3 special knowledge or learning somebody has or is responsible for. *I'm in computing, but games consoles are outside my province.* **provincial** *adjective*.

provoke *verb* 1 to make somebody angry, usually on purpose. *That dog bites if provoked.* 2 to cause or force an action. *The boy's rudeness provoked a fight.* **provoking** *adjective* annoying. **provocation** *noun*. **provocative** *adjective*.

prow *noun* the front part of a boat.

prowess *noun* great ability or skill.

prowl *verb* to move about quietly, trying not to be seen or heard. **prowl** *noun*. An animal on the prowl is looking for food. **prowler** *noun*.

prune *noun* a dried plum.

Prunes are delicious with cream or custard.

prune *verb* to cut off or shorten branches of a tree or bush.

psalm *noun* (say sahm) a religious song from the Bible. The Book of Psalms is part of the Old Testament. *They read the 23rd Psalm at the memorial service.*

pseudonym *noun* a false name used by a writer. *He writes crime novels under the pseudonym John Smith.*

psychiatry *noun* (say sigh-**kie**-uh-tree) the study and treatment of mental illness. **psychiatric** (say sigh-key-**ah**-trik) *adjective*. **psychiatrist** *noun*.

psychology *noun* the study of the human mind and how it works. **psychological** *adjective*. *He has some serious psychological problems.* **psychologist** *noun*.

pub *noun* a bar that may also serve food.

puberty *noun* (say **pew**-buh-tee) the time in a young person's life when they physically develop into an adult.

pubic *adjective* (say **pew**-bic) relating to the area around the sexual organs.

public *adjective* belonging to, for, connected with or known by everyone. Not private. *Public transport.* **public** *noun* all the people. *The castle is open to the public.* **in public** with other people there. *People sometimes say different things in public than they say in private.*

public school *noun* a free local school that is paid for by the government.

publish *verb* 1 to have books, magazines, newspapers and other material printed and sold. *Her first book was published last spring.* 2 to make known to the public. *They published news of her death the day she died.* **publisher** *noun.*

pudding *noun* a sweet, thick, creamy food made with flour, fat, eggs and other ingredients. *I love vanilla pudding.*

puddle *noun* a small pool of liquid, especially rainwater on the ground. *My little brother stops to play in every puddle.*

puerile (say pew-er-I'll) *adjective* childish.

puffin *noun* a sea-bird with a brightly colored beak.

Puffins feed on fish from the ocean

pull *verb* 1 to use force to make something come towards or after you. *He pulled the chair up to the table.* 2 to drive, move a vehicle. *The car pulled out of the driveway.* 3 to attract interest or support. *Their concerts always pull big crowds.* 4 to injure. *He pulled a muscle in the race.* **pull apart** to separate by using force. **pull down** 1 to make something lower. *Pull the blind down if the sun bothers you.* 2 to destroy a building, usually to build a new one. **pull in** 1 to drive a car somewhere and stop. *We pulled in at the gas station.* 2 to arrive at a station. *The bus from Toledo has just pulled in.* **pull off** 1 to take clothes off quickly. *He pulled off his boots.* 2 to succeed in a difficult situation. *He managed to pull the trick off.* **pull out** 1 to take something out. *The dentist pulled out a tooth.* 2 to move or drive out of a place. *The train pulled out of the station.* 3 When you pull out of an agreement, you get out of it. **pull through** to recover from a serious illness or accident. *She was very badly injured in the accident, but fortunately she pulled through.* **pull yourself together** to control your feelings and behave in a sensible way.

A pulley is an essential mechanism on any crane.

WORD HISTORY
You might think that the name of the drink 'punch' came from its power or zing. In fact, it has nothing to do with this. The origin is the Sanskrit word 'panca', meaning five. The number refers to the five ingredients that traditionally went into punch: wine, water, sugar, spice and fruit juice.

pulley *noun* a wheel over which a rope or chain is moved, used for lifting heavy things.

pulp *noun* 1 the soft inner part of a fruit or vegetable. 2 a soft mass of other material. *Wood pulp.* 3 cheap books and magazines. **pulp** *verb* to crush.

pulpit *noun* a small platform for the preacher in a church.

pulse *noun* 1 the regular beating of blood as it is pumped through the body by the heart. You can feel your pulse when you touch your wrists. 2 the regular beat or throbbing of music. **pulse** *verb* to beat or shake with strong, regular movements.

pulverize *verb* 1 to crush into or become fine powder. 2 to destroy. *The town was pulverized by shelling.*

puma (say pew-muh) *noun* a large brown wild cat of the western US, also called a cougar or mountain lion.

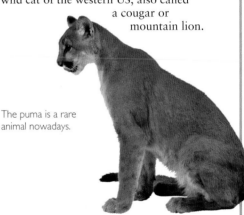

The puma is a rare animal nowadays.

pump *noun* a machine with a tube for forcing liquid, air or gas into or out of something. *A gas pump.* **pump** *verb* 1 to force liquid or air into or from something with a pump. *Her heart was pumping fast. I must pump up my tires.* 2 to get information, usually by asking questions. *He pumped me about my new job.* 3 to force something into somebody or something. *They have pumped a lot of money into the business.*

pumpkin *noun* a large round fruit with a hard orange skin. People hollow out pumpkins to make lanterns at Halloween.

pun *noun* an amusing use of words that have the same sound but different meanings.

punch *verb* 1 to hit hard with a fist. *He punched him in the stomach.* 2 to make a hole in something. **punch** (punches) *noun* 1 a hit with a fist. *The boxer had to take a lot of punches.* 2 a tool for making holes, especially in paper or leather. 3 a drink made of fruit juice and sometimes alcohol.

P

punchline *noun* the last few words in a joke that make it funny. *My mother loves telling jokes but she usually forgets the punchline.*

punctual *adjective* doing things at the right or fixed time. *He is always punctual, never even a minute late.* **punctually** *adverb.*

punctuate *verb* 1 to put full stops, commas and other punctuation marks in text. 2 to interrupt from time to time, especially a speech. **punctuation** *noun.*

puncture *noun* a small hole made by a sharp object. **puncture** *verb* to make or get a puncture.

Peter drove into the field and punctured his tire on a huge thorn.

punish *verb* to make somebody suffer because they have done something wrong. **punishment** *noun. Punishment ranges from a fine to a jail sentence, depending on the seriousness of the offense.* **punishable** *adjective. In some countries murder is still punishable by the death penalty.*

Punjabi *noun* the language of the Punjab, an area in north-western India and Pakistan. **Punjabi** *adjective. The Punjabi people.*

punt *verb* to kick a ball by dropping it from the hands on to the foot. **punt** *noun.*

puny *adjective* very small, thin or weak. *He's just a puny little kid, don't be afraid of him.*

pupa (pupae) *noun* (say **pew**-puh) the stage in an insect's life between the larval and adult stages. *The pupa of a butterfly is called chrysalis.*

The pupa was due to hatch in a few days.

pupil *noun* somebody, usually a child, who is being taught.

pupil *noun* the small, round black opening in the middle of the colored part of the eye. *Her pupils dilated.*

puppet *noun* 1 a doll you can move by pulling strings that are fixed to it, or by putting your hand inside its body (called a glove puppet). 2 somebody whose actions are controlled by others. *He is the politicians' puppet.*

W O R D H I S T O R Y

What's the connection between somebody being taught and the middle of the eye? They are both called 'pupils', but why? They actually come from the same Latin words, 'pupillus' or 'pupilla', meaning little boy or girl. A pupil in school is a boy or girl. The word came to refer to the eye because of the tiny reflection you get of yourself when you look closely into someone else's eye – you see a tiny boy or girl!

---

puppy (puppies) *noun* a young dog.

The puppies looked identical.

purchase *verb* to buy. **purchase** *noun* 1 something bought. *Most of her purchases were clothes.* 2 buying. *Do you remember the date of purchase?* 3 a firm hold for pulling or stopping something from slipping. *His hands lost their purchase and he fell into the precipice.*

pure *adjective* 1 not mixed with anything else, clean and clear. 2 complete, total. *The hotel is pure luxury.* **purity** *noun.*

purge *verb* to get rid of unwanted people or feelings. *I'll purge this town of crime.*

purple *adjective, noun* reddish-blue.

purpose *noun* 1 a plan, a reason for doing something. *What is the purpose of this meeting?* 2 a feeling of having an aim, willpower. *Teaching has given her a sense of purpose.* **on purpose** intentionally, not by accident. *She bumped into him on purpose.*

purr *verb* to make a low sound like a cat when it is pleased. **purr** *noun.*

purse *noun* a bag used to carry money and personal things.

purse *verb* to draw your lips together into a rounded shape. *She pursed her lips in distaste at the horrible smell.*

pus *noun* (say puhss) a thick yellowish liquid that comes out of an infected wound or other part of the body.

push *verb* 1 to press using force in order to make something or somebody move away or to a different position. *He pushed the window up.* 2 to make your way through something by using force. *Don't push in front of me.* 3 to force somebody to do something or force something on people. *The advertisers are pushing a new drink.* 4 to try to sell something illegal. *They've been accused of pushing drugs.* **push ahead** to carry out. *We are pushing ahead with the new building.* **push around** to make someone who is weaker or less important do something. *Stop pushing him around, pick on somebody your own size.* **push for** to try to get. *We're pushing for a better computer in the library.* **push in** to come into a line in front of other people. **push on** to continue to travel or work. **push** (pushes) *noun* 1 the action of pushing. 2 drive or energy.

pushy *adjective* unpleasantly eager to get things done so as to make yourself noticed.

pussyfoot *verb* to act very cautiously.

put (puts, putting, put) *verb* 1 to move, place, lay or fix something or somebody in a certain place or position. *Put your bike in the garage.* 2 to cause something or somebody to be in a particular state. *The news put her in a good mood.* 3 to express something in words or write something down. *She put it very well.* 4 to give money for something, or time or energy to something. *They only put $800 into the business.* **put across** to describe or explain something to somebody. **put away** to put something into a place where it is usually kept. **put something off** not to do something until later. **put somebody off** to make somebody dislike something or lose interest. *The smell puts me off fish.* **put on** 1 to make a light or piece of equipment work. *We put another CD on.* 2 *He put on his clothes.* 3 to pretend to be something or behave in an unnatural way. *She only puts on that shy voice.* 4 to add more to something. *She has put on weight.* **put out** 1 to stop a candle or fire from burning, to stop a light shining. 2 to make something known. *They put out a warning.* 3 to place things that are needed somewhere ready to be used. *I put out a clean shirt for you.* 4 to annoy or upset. *I was put out when everybody laughed at me.* **put up** 1 to build. *We put up a new fence.* 2 to give somebody a place to sleep. *We can put up your friends.* 3 to raise or unfold. *She put up her hand.* 4 to fix. *To put up a poster.* 5 to provide. *Who is putting up the money for the event?* 6 to increase. *Prices have been put up.* **put up to** If you put somebody up to something you tell them to do something foolish. **put up with** to tolerate something or somebody.

putrid (say **pew**-trid) *adjective* rotting and smelling bad. *Putrid vegetation.*

putter *verb* to spend time doing things in a relaxed way. *Dad is puttering around in the garage.*

putty *noun* a soft paste used to fix glass into window frames or fill holes.

puzzle *noun* 1 a game or toy. *We did a jigsaw puzzle when I was in the hospital.* 2 a difficult question, problem or something that is hard to understand. *Why she wants to go there is a puzzle to me.* **puzzle** (puzzles, puzzling, puzzled) *verb* to make somebody feel confused because they do not understand. *The whole conflict puzzles me.* **puzzle over** to think hard about something confusing. **puzzlement** *noun*.

There is a crossword puzzle in the paper every day.

pylon *noun* a tall metal structure used for holding wires that carry electricity over long distances. *Electricity pylons.*

Pyongyang *noun* the capital of North Korea.

pyramid *noun* 1 a shape with a flat base and three or four sloping sides that come to a point at the top. 2 an ancient Egyptian stone building over the tombs of the kings and queens of Egypt in a pyramid shape.

pyrotechnics *noun* 1 the art of making fireworks. 2 a fireworks display.

The Ancient Egyptians built huge pyramids that cost thousands of lives.

python *noun* a large snake that kills by winding its body round animals and squeezing them.

Q

Qatar *noun* a country in the Middle East.

quack *verb* to make the harsh sound that a duck makes. **quack** *noun*.

quadrangle *noun* 1 a four-sided shape. 2 a four-sided area or courtyard with buildings all around it.

quadrant *noun* 1 a quarter of a circle. 2 an instrument for measuring vertical angles.

quadri- *prefix* four.

quadrilateral *noun* a flat shape with four straight sides.

quadruped *noun* any animal with four legs.

quadruple *verb* to multiply by four. *My wages have quadrupled in the last ten years.* **quadruple** *noun*.

quadruplet *noun* one of four babies born at the same time to the same mother (quad for short). *The quadruplets were doing fine.*

quagmire *noun* a very soft, marshy area of land. *I got bogged down in a quagmire.*

quail *verb* to show fear by trembling.

quail *noun* a small, plump bird related to the partridge, often shot as game.

Quail eggs are very popular as appetizers.

quaint *adjective* attractively unusual and old-fashioned. Charming. *A quaint cottage.* **quaintness** *noun*.

quake *verb* to shake, to tremble. *Quentin quaked with fear at the sight of the ghost.*

qualification *noun* your skills or the training you have had that make you suitable to do a certain job.

qualify (qualifies, qualifying, qualified) *verb* 1 to be suitable for a job, especially by passing a test or exam to reach a certain standard. *Karen has qualified as a vet.* 2 to obtain enough points to go on to the next part of a competition etc. 3 to limit. To make a remark less strong. *He qualified his remark that all his pupils are lazy and said only some are lazy.*

WORD HISTORY

The shape of the letter Q comes from an ancient Egyptian symbol for monkey. The sound probably came from 'qoph', a Semitic word for monkey. The Greeks called it 'koppa'.

AMAZING FACT

Qatar is an 'emirate' or nation that is ruled by a monarch called an 'emir'. Oil was discovered in Qatar in the 1940s.

AMAZING FACT

The biggest quarry in the world is in Utah. It is the Bingham Copper Mine. It is approximately 770 meters deep.

---

quality *noun* 1 how good or bad something is. *The sound quality is very poor.* 2 what somebody or something is like. Good characteristics. *His best quality is his cheerfulness.*

qualm *noun* a feeling of unease or doubt.

quandary *noun* uncertainty. *I'm in a quandary – should I go or should I stay?*

quantity *noun* an amount or number of things. *A large quantity of fodder.* **in quantity** in large amounts.

quantum leap *noun* a dramatic advance. *A quantum leap in space research.*

quarantine *noun* a period when a person or an animal that may be carrying a disease is kept away from others to prevent the disease from spreading.

quarrel (quarrels, quarreling, quarreled) *verb* to have an angry argument or disagreement with somebody. To stop being friendly. **quarrel** *noun*. **quarrelsome** *adjective*. *Quarrelsome children.*

quarry *noun* 1 a place where sand or stone is dug out of the ground for building etc. **quarry** *verb*. 2 an animal that is being hunted. Prey.

quart *noun* a measure of liquid equal to 2 pints or .95 litres.

quarter *noun* 1 one of four equal parts into which something can be divided. A fourth. 2 a 25-cent US and Canadian coin. 3 three months. 4 a district of a city. *My parents used to live in the Latin Quarter in New Orleans.* 5 **quarters** a place to stay. *Officers' living quarters.* **quarterly** *adjective* happening every three months. *A quarterly magazine.*

The green square is a quarter of the size of the purple square.

quartet *noun* 1 a group of four singers or players. 2 a piece of music written for four musicians.

quartz *noun* a crystal-like mineral used in electronic equipment.

quasi- *prefix* almost or seeming to be. *Quasi-official, quasi-scientific.*

quaver *verb* to speak in a trembling voice because of fear or nervousness. **quaver** *noun*. *There was a quaver in her voice.*

quay *noun* (say key) a place in a harbor for boats to load and unload.

The fishing boats bobbed on the water by the quay.

queasy (queasier, queasiest) *adjective* a feeling that you are going to be sick. **queasiness** *noun*.

queen *noun* 1 a female ruler of a country or the wife of a king. A monarch. Queens are not elected but either inherit their position by succeeding the previous ruler or marrying a king. 2 a playing card with the picture of a queen on it. 3 a chesspiece that can move in any direction. **queen mother** the widowed mother of a reigning king or queen.

queer *adjective* strange, unusual.

quell *verb* to prevent by squashing. *The police quelled the riots.*

quench *verb* 1 to drink enough to satisfy your thirst. 2 to put out a fire.

query *noun* a question, a doubt. **query** (queries, querying, queries) *verb*.

quest *noun* a thorough search.

question *noun* 1 what you ask when you want to find out about something. 2 a problem. *The question of finance.* **question** *verb. The police questioned her for hours.*

question mark *noun* a punctuation mark (?) that is put at the end of a question.

questionnaire *noun* a list of questions to be answered by a number of people as part of a report etc.

queue *noun* (sounds like cue) 1 braid of hair worn hanging down the back. 2 (in Britain) a waiting line of people or vehicles. **queue** *verb.*

quibble *noun* a small, unimportant point not really worth arguing about. *Don't quibble!*

quiche *noun* (say key-sh) a pastry tart with a filling of beaten egg, cheese, ham etc.

quick *adjective* 1 moving rapidly, fast. 2 done in a short time. *A quick and tasty snack.* 3 fast to understand, lively. *She's got a very quick abd lively mind.* **quickness** *noun*.

quicksand *noun* dangerously wet sand into which you can sink if you walk on it.

In British English, the word queue is used to mean a line of people.

The quintet played some lively music at the dance.

> **GRAMMAR NOTE**
>
> *Be careful how you use 'quite', because this little word can mean 'very' or 'sort of'. 'This cake is quite good' could mean fairly good but not very good. But there is no doubt about 'This cake is quite excellent'. So it might be quite a good idea to avoid using 'quite', if it's going to cause offence.*

quicksilver *noun* the liquid metal mercury.

quid pro quo *noun* something that a person does or gives in exchange for something else.

quiet *adjective* 1 without much noise. Silent. 2 calm or without movement. *We were looking forward to a quiet vacation at the coast.* **quietness** *noun*.

quill *noun* 1 one of the sharp spines on a hedgehog or porcupine. 2 a long, strong feather used as a pen.

quilt *noun* a light bed covering filled with warm soft material.

quintet *noun* 1 a group of five singers or players. 2 a piece of music written for five musicians. *A string quintet.*

quintuplet *noun* one of five babies born at the same time to the same mother (quint for short). *The quintuplets were a surprise.*

quip *noun* a witty and often cutting remark.

quit (quits, quitting, quitted or quit) *verb* 1 to give up or stop doing something. *She quit smoking.* 2 to go away.

quite *adverb* 1 totally. *I'm quite sure you are right.* 2 to some extent, rather. *It was quite a good meal.*

Quito *noun* the capital of Ecuador.

quiver *verb* to shake slightly but quickly. *Her lip quivered and she started to cry.*

quiver *noun* a long container for arrows.

quiz *noun* a game in which people are asked questions to test their knowledge. *Sue got all the answers right and won the quiz.*

quota *noun* a share of something.

quotation *noun* a person's words repeated exactly by somebody else, a passage from a play or book for example.

quotation marks *plural noun* the punctuation marks ("") used before and after words somebody has said or to highlight words.

quote *verb* 1 to repeat words that were first said or spoken by somebody else. *He quoted some lines from Shakespeare.* 2 to give a price.

Qu'ran another spelling for Koran.

R

Rr

Rabat *noun* the capital of Morocco.

rabbi *noun* a Jewish religious leader and teacher. *The rabbi prayed in the synagogue.*

rabbit *noun* a small furry animal with long ears that lives in a hole (called a burrow) in the ground.

rabble *noun* a crowd of noisy people.

rabies *noun* a disease passed on by a bite that makes people and animals go mad and die. *He was bitten by a fox and got rabies.*

raccoon *noun* a small furry North American animal with a long tail.

race *noun* a contest to see who is the fastest. **race** *verb* 1 to take part in a race. *I'll race you to the end of the road and back again.* 2 to go very quickly.

As they came around the bend into the last lap of the race, Tom moved into the lead.

race *noun* a group of people with the same ancestors and history, or a division of people with a type of body or color of skin. The human race. Race relations are the relationships between people of different races who live in the same country.

racial *adjective* relating to people's race. **racially** *adverb*. *Racially different.*

racist *noun* a person who does not like people from other races because he thinks his own race is the best. **racist** *adjective*. *Racist remarks.* **racism** *noun*.

rack *noun* 1 a framework with bars, pegs or shelves for holding things or hanging things on. *A coat rack.* 2 a shelf for luggage in a train or bus. 3 an instrument used in the Middle Ages for torturing people by stretching them. **rack** *verb* to hurt a lot. *He left his family for another woman and was racked with guilt.* **rack your brain** to try hard to think of something.

racket *noun* a paddle with strings across it for playing tennis, squash or badminton.

SPELLING NOTE

Be careful about the difference between the adjectives 'racial', which refers to race, and 'racist', which refers to racism and so is offensive.

SPELLING NOTE

The word 'radar' is an acronym, which means that is made up of the initial letters of other words. It comes from 'radio detection' and 'ranging'. The system was developed during the 1930s.

racket *noun* 1 a loud noise. 2 a dishonest way of making money, a swindle.

racoon *noun* see raccoon.

radar *noun* a way of finding the position or speed of objects that cannot be seen by using radio signals that show on a screen. *The plane was last seen on radar.*

radiant *adjective* 1 sending out light or heat. *The radiant Sun.* 2 looking very happy. *She looked radiant on her wedding day.*

radiate *verb* to send out light, heat or happiness. **radiation** *noun*. *Exposure to radiation can cause serious illness and even death.* **radiate from** to spread out from a central point in many directions.

radiator *noun* 1 an apparatus, usually connected to a heating system, used for heating buildings. 2 a device that keeps a car's engine cool.

radio (radios) *noun* 1 a method of sending or receiving sound through the air by means of electrical waves. 2 a piece of equipment, a radio set, for listening to radio programs. 3 broadcasting of programs. *She works in radio.* **radio** *verb*. *The ship radioed for help.*

radioactive *adjective* Something is radioactive if it has atoms that break up and send out radiation in the form of rays that can be harmful to living things. *After the reactor accident there was radioactive dust in the air.* **radioactivity** *noun*.

radish *noun* a small red vegetable that is eaten raw.

radius *noun* 1 the distance, a straight line, from the center of a circle to its outside edge. A circle's radius is half its diameter. 2 the distance from a particular central point where something happens or exists. *All citizens living within a three-mile radius of the town center are entitled to free bus travel.*

The radius of the circle is shown by the green line from the center to the circumference.

raft *noun* 1 logs tied together and used as a boat. 2 an inflatable rubber boat. *The raft saved Jane's life.*

rag *noun* 1 a small, usually torn piece of cloth. *Get some rags from the house and you can help me wash the car.* 2 a badly written newspaper. **rag** (rags, ragging, ragged) *verb* to make fun of, tease.

rage *noun* 1 a strong uncontrollable anger. 2 the latest fashion. *Snowboarding is all the rage.* **rage** *verb* 1 to be very angry. 2 to be very violent. *The storm raged all night.*

raid *noun* 1 a sudden attack on an enemy. 2 an unexpected visit by the police. **raid** *verb* to make a raid. *The police raided the promoter's office.* **raider** *noun*.

rail *noun* 1 a fixed bar to hang things on or hold on to, or forming part of a fence. *Put the towel on the rail.* 2 one of a pair of metal bars that a train runs on. **by rail** in a train.

railing *noun* (usually plural, railings) a fence made from metal bars. *The child got his head stuck in the railings.*

railroad *noun* 1 the track or route between two places on which trains run. 2 a system of rail transport and the organization operating that system.

rain *noun* drops of water that fall from clouds. **rain** *verb* 1 to fall as rain. *It's raining.* 2 to fall like rain. *Tears rained down her cheeks.*

rainbow *noun* an arch of colors that you can sometimes see in the sky when the Sun shines through rain.

Some people say that a crock of gold is buried at the rainbow's end.

raincoat *noun* a waterproof coat that is worn in the rain. *Put on your raincoat, because it's pouring outside.*

rainfall *noun* the amount of rain that falls in a place in a certain time. *The Atacama Desert in Chile has the lowest rainfall of any place on Earth.*

rainforest *noun* a tropical forest with tall trees in which it rains a lot.

The world's rainforests are home to many species of plants and animals that may hold the key to health cures of the future.

raise *verb* 1 to move to a higher position. *Raise the flag.* 2 to increase in amount or level. *To raise prices.* 3 to manage to get something together. *The school raised $100 for charity.* 4 to bring up a child, breed animals. 5 to bring up for discussion or attention. *I'm sorry to have to raise the question of money.* 6 to make appear. *It raised doubts in my mind.* **raise** *noun* an increase in salary. *They offered me a raise if I would stay in my job, but I didn't accept.*

rake *noun* a gardening tool with a row of metal teeth attached to a long handle. **rake** *verb* to collect or make smooth with a rake. *He raked the leaves into a pile.* **rake up** 1 to collect. 2 to talk about something unpleasant that should be forgotten. *She kept raking up the past until it drove him out of his mind with guilt.*

rally (rallies) *noun* 1 a large public meeting in support of something. *A peace rally.* 2 a car or cycling competition. 3 a series of shots players exchange in tennis or badminton. **rally** (rallies, rallying, rallied) *verb* 1 to come together in support of something. *My friends rallied round and helped me when I was ill.* 2 to become stronger again, recover.

ram *noun* a male sheep. *The ram with the curly horns can be quite aggressive.*

ram *noun* a device for pushing something. **ram** (rams, ramming, rammed) *verb* to push with great force. *He rammed the post hard into the ground.*

RAM *abbreviation* random-access memory. The amount of memory in a computer that is available and stored directly.

Ramadan *noun* the ninth month of the Muslim year, when no food or drink may be taken between sunrise and sunset. *They sat in the market place waiting for the Sun to go down, so they could eat a bowl of soup.*

ramble *noun* a long walk, often in the country. **ramble** *verb* 1 to go for a ramble. 2 to talk or write in a confused way. *My grandmother often rambles and says strange things.* **rambler** *noun*. **ramble on** to talk for a long time without sticking to the subject.

ramp *noun* a slope used instead of a step or stairs. *She pushed the wheelchair up the ramp.*

rampart *noun* a wide bank of earth built to protect a fort or city.

ramshackle *adjective* badly made and needing repair. *A ramshackle old shed.*

ran *verb* past tense of run.

ranch (ranches) *noun* a cattle-farm in North or South America. **rancher** *noun*.

rancid *adjective* tasting or smelling unpleasant, especially fatty food. *The smell of rancid butter makes me feel sick.*

random *adjective* made or done without any plan. *A random selection of CDs.* **at random** without any plan or pattern. *He asked us questions at random.*

rang *verb* past tense of ring.

range *noun* 1 a connected series of hills or mountains. 2 the distance at which you can see or hear or that a gun can shoot. *Within range, out of range.* 3 a number of different things of the same kind. *We sell a wide range of gardening tools.* 4 the limits that can be measured between two points, the distance between which things vary. *The age range is from 20 to 30.* 5 grassy land in North America for grazing or hunting. 6 an area for shooting practice. 7 a stove for cooking. **range** *verb* 1 to reach from one limit to another, to vary within limits. *Sizes range from small to extra large.* 2 to place or arrange. 3 to wander.

ranger *noun* somebody who takes care of a park or forest. *A forest ranger.*

Rangoon *noun* the capital of Myanmar.

rank *noun* 1 a position or grade in an organization. *He holds the rank of general.* 2 a line of people or things. *A taxi rank.* **rank** *verb* to put or be in a position on a scale. *I rank him as one of the best of the new breed of American writers.*

Jeff herded that cattle on his uncle's ranch.

DID YOU KNOW

The city of Rangoon is also sometimes called Yangon. And the country of which it is capital has the official name Myanmar, but is often called by its old name of Burma. Rangoon became the capital in 1886, and was badly damaged in World War II when it was occupied by the Japanese. A famous golden temple in Rangoon, called the Shwe Dagon Pagoda, is Myanmar's holiest Buddhist shrine.

The distant mountain range was covered in snow.

ransack *verb* 1 to search a place thoroughly, usually leaving it in a mess. *The police ransacked the building in their search for clues.* 2 to search and rob a place.

ransom *noun* a sum of money that has to be paid to free a kidnapped person. **hold to ransom** to keep somebody as a prisoner until money is paid for them to be set free. **ransom** *verb* to set somebody free in exchange for a ransom.

rap *noun* 1 the sound of a quick hit or knock against something. 2 blame or punishment. *I'm always taking the rap.* 3 rhymes with a backing of rock music. **rap** *verb* 1 to hit something quickly and lightly. *He rapped on the door.* 2 to speak in rhymes with a rock music backing.

rape *verb* to perform intercourse against someone's will. **rape** *noun*. **rapist** *noun*.

rapid *adjective* quick. **rapidly** *adverb*. *The town is growing rapidly.*

rapier *noun* a thin, light sword.

rare *adjective* 1 uncommon, not often found or happening. *A rare plant.* 2 lightly cooked. *I like my steak rare.* **rarely** *adverb* not often. *We rarely eat dessert.* **rarity** *noun*.

Pandas are now quite rare, because the clearance of bamboo forests has deprived them of their major food source.

rash *adjective* acting foolishly without thinking first. *Don't make rash promises.* **rashly** *adverb*. **rashness** *noun*.

rash (rashes) *noun* an outbreak of small red spots on the skin, caused by an illness or allergy. *An itchy heat rash.*

raspberry (raspberries) *noun* a small soft red fruit that grows on bushes.

raspy *adjective* rough or hoarse sounding.

rat *noun* 1 an animal with a long tail that looks like a large mouse. 2 a nasty, untrustworthy person.

Rats are rodents that can carry disease in the wild, though some people love them as pets.

rate *noun* 1 speed. *We were traveling at a steady rate.* 2 an amount, value, cost or speed measured by comparing it to some other amount. *The unemployment rate.* 3 a charge. *The **going rate** for babysitting.* **at any rate** in any case. **at this rate** if things go on in the same way as now. *He'll never find a job at this rate.* **rate** *verb* to consider, to put a value on something. *How do you rate my chances of passing the test?*

rather *adverb* 1 to a slight extent or to a large extent. *It's rather cold today.* 2 more willingly, in preference. *I would rather not say.* 3 more exactly. *I went to bed late last night – or rather, early this morning.* 4 to a greater degree. *I'm looking for something practical rather than fashionable.*

ratio (say **ray-shee-oh**) *noun* the relationship between two numbers or amounts which shows how much greater one is than the other. *If there are ten applicants for every five jobs, the ratio of applicants to jobs is two to one.*

ration *noun* a fixed amount allowed to one person. *I've eaten my ration of chocolate for this week.* **ration** *verb* 1 to limit somebody to a ration. 2 to limit something. *During the hot weather water was rationed.*

rational *adjective* 1 sensible. *There must be a rational explanation.* 2 able to think, make decisions and judgements. *She's usually a very rational person.* **rationally** *adverb.* **rationality** *noun.*

rat-race *noun* a competitive struggle for success or power.

rattle *noun* 1 short, sharp sounds. 2 a baby's toy that makes a rattling sound. **rattle** *verb* 1 to make short, sharp sounds. *The windows rattled in the wind.* 2 to make somebody nervous. *She gets rattled if you ask her too many questions.* **rattle off** to say something quickly without thinking. *She rattled off the answers automatically.* **rattle on** to continue to talk quickly and without thinking.

rattlesnake *noun* a poisonous American snake that makes a rattling noise with its tail. *He was bitten by a rattlesnake.*

raucous (say **raw-kus**) *adjective* loud and unpleasant, especially of voices. *There was a lot of raucous shouting.*

rave *verb* 1 to talk wildly and in an uncontrolled way. *He had a high temperature and was raving all night.* 2 to talk or write enthusiastically about something. **rave** *noun.*

rave *noun* a dancing party, usually at night.

WORD HISTORY

The adjective 'ravenous' has nothing to do with the bird called a raven. 'Ravenous' comes from Latin and old French words meaning 'on the prowl for prey', presumably because the prowling person or animal is very hungry.

SPELLING NOTE

The prefix 're–' is usually spelt with a hyphen before a word that begins with an 'e', such as 're-enact', or if it could be confused with another word (to re-form means to form again, to reform is to make or become better).

A number of hard rings at the end of the rattlesnake's tail make a rattling noise when shaken together.

raven *noun* a large black bird. **raven** *adjective* glossy black. *Raven hair.*

ravenous *adjective* very hungry.

ravine *noun* a very deep, narrow valley.

raw *adjective* 1 not cooked. 2 in the natural state, not treated. *Raw materials.* 3 untrained, new to the job. 4 without skin. *Her fingers were rubbed raw.* 5 cold and wet, especially of weather. **rawness** *noun.*

raw deal *noun* unfair treatment.

ray *noun* 1 a beam of heat, light or energy. *The rays of the Sun.* 2 a small amount. *A ray of hope.* 3 one of a number of lines radiating out from the centre of something.

razor *noun* an instrument used for shaving hair from the skin.

re- *prefix* again. *He remarried last year.*

reach *verb* 1 to arrive at, to get to. *When did the news reach you?* 2 to stretch out a hand to get or touch something. *Can you reach the box on the top shelf?* **reach** (reaches) *noun* 1 the distance that you can reach. *Put the bottle out of her reach.* 2 the length of an arm. *Sebastian has a very long reach.* 3 a straight stretch of a river between two bends.

She reached up to the top of the cabinet where she hid the children's presents.

react *verb* to behave in a particular way because of something, to behave differently as a result. *How did your boss react when he heard about the strike?* **reaction** *noun.* 1 an effect produced by an earlier action. 2 a change in one chemical substance caused by another. *A chemical reaction.*

reactionary *adjective* against changes in society. **reactionary** *noun.*

reactor *noun* a machine used to produce nuclear energy.

read (reads, reading, read) *verb* (say **red**) 1 to look at and understand or say out loud something written or printed. *He plays lots of instruments, but he can't read music.* 2 to judge how somebody feels. *I can read her mind.* 3 to say. *The sign reads 'Exit'.* 4 to show, register. *The thermometer reads 35 degrees.* **read up** to find out about something by reading about it. **readable** *adjective* interesting and easy to read. **reader** *noun.* **reading** *noun. The children in her class have learned to really love reading.*

ready (readier, readiest) *adjective*
1 prepared, able to be used or do something. *Lunch is ready.* 2 willing to do something. 3 about to do something. *She was ready to cry.* 4 quick and prepared. 5 easily reached. *Have your tickets ready.* **readiness** *noun*.

real *adjective* actually existing, not imaginary or artificial. *Real pearls.*

real estate *noun* 1 property such as houses and land 2 the business of buying and selling real estate. **real estate** *adjective*

realistic *adjective* 1 practical, based on actual facts. 2 like people or things in real life. **realism** *noun*.

It was not very realistic of him to want a sports car when he had a family of five.

reality (realities) *noun* something real, the truth. **in reality** in actual fact.

realize *verb* 1 to understand, to become aware of something. *I never realized that she was your mother.* 2 to make a hope or plan happen. *He realized his dreams of becoming an actor.* 3 to get money by selling something. **realization** *noun*.

really *adverb* 1 truly, without doubt. *It's really hot today.* 2 used for showing interest, doubt or surprise. *"Our school is going to be on the news tonight." "Oh, really?"*

realm *noun* (say relm) 1 a kingdom. 2 an area of thought or knowledge. *Fairies exist only in the realm of fantasy.*

reap *verb* 1 to cut down and gather. *We reaped the harvest.* 2 to gain as a result of something done. *One day she'll reap the benefit of all that hard work.*

rear *noun* the back part. *We were at the rear of the crowd when it happened.* **rear** *adjective. The rear wheel.*

rear *verb* 1 to bring up a child or animal. 2 to lift up, or rise upright on its back legs. *The snake suddenly reared its head.*

SPELLING NOTE

Note the spelling of 'receipt', 'receive' and 'receiver': it's 'ei', not 'ie'. An easy way to remember this is the saying 'I before E except after C,' but there are exceptions to the rule, such as 'weird'.

The summer was very hot that year and everyone reaped a good harvest.

reason *noun* 1 a cause of an event, an explanation for an action. *What's the reason for the strike?* 2 the ability to think and make judgements, common sense. *He won't listen to reason.* **with reason** rightly. **reason** *verb* 1 to think carefully and decide. 2 to argue in order to persuade somebody to do something. *It was impossible to reason with the kidnappers.*

reasonable *adjective* 1 sensible. 2 fair, not too much. *An extremely reasonable price.* **reasonably** *adverb*.

rebel (rebels, rebelling, rebelled) *verb* (say rib-el) to fight or protest against anybody in power. *They rebelled against the government.* **rebel** *noun* (say reb-ul) somebody who rebels. *The rebels stormed the castle and killed the king.* **rebellious** *adjective*. **rebellion** *noun* fighting or opposition to anybody in power.

rebuke *verb* to criticize someone for doing something wrong. *His boss rebuked him for not wearing a tie.* **rebuke** *noun*.

recall *verb* 1 to remember. 2 to ask somebody to come back. **recall** *noun*.

recede *verb* 1 to move back or further away. *His hair is receding and he will soon go completely bald.* 2 to become less clear.

As we took off in the helicopter, the farm receded into the distance.

receipt *noun* (say ris-eet) 1 a piece of paper that states that money or goods have been received. *I will need a receipt for the payment.* 2 the act of receiving. *He rang the school on receipt of the letter.*

receive *verb* 1 to get or take something given or sent to you. *The news was received with horror.* 2 to suffer. *She received nasty injuries to the spine.* 3 to welcome a visitor. *We were very well received.*

receiver *noun* 1 the part of a telephone you speak into. *Pick up the receiver and dial this number.* 2 a person who receives something, especially stolen goods. 3 the part of a radio or television set that receives broadcasts. 4 a person officially appointed to take charge of a bankrupt business.

The satellite beamed the television program to a receiver near Michael's house.

recent *adjective* having happened only a short time ago. *A recent discovery.* **recently** *adverb.* *I was at college until recently.*

reception *noun* 1 the way somebody or something is received, a welcome. *His new book got a very good reception.* 2 an office or place in a hotel or large organization where appointments, reservations and enquiries can be made. 3 a formal party. 4 the quality of receiving sounds or pictures from radio or television.

recess (recesses) *noun* 1 a period of time when work or business is stopped. *The judge announced a recess.* 2 a space in the wall of a room. *Let's put shelves in the recess.* 3 the part of the school day when children at school are allowed to go out and play.

recession *noun* 1 a decline in wealth and economic success. *The government is doing its best to avoid recession.* 2 receding.

recipe *noun* instructions on how to make a particular dish, or something else. *We tried out a new recipe for enchiladas.*

The recipe for winter vegetable soup called for lots of carrots and onions.

recital *noun* 1 a musical performance. *A piano recital.* 2 a detailed account.

recite *verb* to say something learned out loud. *She recited the poem in class.*

reckless *adjective* not caring about danger.

reckon *verb* 1 to guess or suppose. *I reckon business could double in the next year.* 2 to add up. **reckon with** *phrasal verb* something that needs to be taken seriously. *The new defense is a force to be reckoned with.*

reclaim *verb* 1 to get something back that was taken away from you. 2 to make land ready for use again. *These fields were all reclaimed from the sea.*

recline *verb* to lean or lie back.

recognizable *adjective* easy to identify or recognize. *An easily recognizable style.*

recognize *verb* 1 to know what something is or who somebody is. 2 to be willing to agree, to see clearly. 3 to accept as real, welcome or lawful. *The new government was not recognized by the people.* **recognition** *noun.*

recollect *verb* to remember.

recommend *verb* to say that somebody or something would be good or useful for a particular job. *I can recommend a good carpenter.* **recommendation** *noun.*

record *noun* (say rek-ord) 1 information, especially facts, either written down or stored on a computer. *She keeps a record of how much she spends.* 2 a disk on which sound, especially music, is stored. 3 the best yet done, especially in sport, or the most amazing achievement. *He broke the world record for 400 meters.* 4 facts known about the past or somebody's past life. *This airline has a good safety record.* **for the record** to be reported. **off the record** not to be written down or made known. **record** *verb* (say rik-ord) 1 to put something down in writing or on a computer. 2 to store sound or television pictures on disc or tape. *We recorded the program, so we can watch it tomorrow.* **recording** *noun.*

The recording came out on CD and on tape.

recover *verb* 1 to become well again. *She is recovering from a very serious illness.* 2 to get something back after it is lost or taken away. **recovery** *noun.*

recruit *noun* a new member of an army, group or society. **recruit** *verb* to get new members. *Lots of people were recruited to put up tents in the field.*

rectangle *noun* a shape with four straight sides and four right angles. **rectangular** *adjective.* *A rectangular dish.*

recuperate *verb* to get better and become strong again after an illness.

recur (recurs, recurring, recurred) *verb* to happen again, either once or many times. *A recurring dream.* **recurrence** *noun.*

recycle *verb* to treat things that have already been used so that they can be used again. *To recycle newspapers and bottles.* **recyclable** *adjective.* *Some aluminum drinks cans are recyclable.*

red *noun* the color of blood. **red** *adjective*. *Red wine*. **see red** to become very angry. **in the red** to have spent more money than you have, to be in debt. **red herring** something that takes people's attention away from what is important.

redundant *adjective* no longer needed because there is no work or something is no longer used. *The workers were all made redundant when the firm closed down*. **redundancy** *noun*.

refectory (refectories) *noun* the dining hall in a monastery or university.

The monks ate every day in the refectory.

refer (refers, referring, referred) *verb* 1 to speak about or mention. 2 to go to for information. *We were not allowed to refer to a dictionary in the exam.* 3 to send somebody or something, especially a problem, to somebody else for action. *He was referred to a specialist.*

reference *noun* 1 mentioning something. *There were a number of references to the trial in the paper.* 2 referring to somebody or something for information. A note that tells you where information can be found. *I use my computer for quick reference.* 3 a statement, usually a letter, about a person's character. *His former teacher gave him a good reference.* **with reference to** regarding.

reference book *noun* a book for looking things up in. *Dictionaries, encyclopedias and other reference books.*

referendum *noun* a vote in which all the people in a country or area can decide on a particular political question.

refine *verb* 1 to make substances pure by taking out unwanted substances. *Refined sugar.* 2 to make more cultured. *Refined behavior can sometimes be unfriendly.*

refinery (refineries) *noun* a factory where substances such as oil or sugar are refined.

reflection *noun* 1 the sending back of light, heat or sound from a surface. 2 an image of something in a mirror or shiny surface. *She looked at her reflection in the lake.* 3 a deep thought. *Reflections on old age.* 4 Something that makes a bad impression. *Gangs are a sad reflection on society.* 5 being the result of something. *His meanness is a reflection of his upbringing.* **on reflection** after thinking about something. **reflect** *verb*.

reform *verb* to make or become better. *He reformed completely after the accident.* **reform** *noun Prison reforms.*

refrain *verb* to hold yourself back from doing something. *I refrained from saying what I really thought.*

refrain *noun* part of a song that is repeated at the end of each verse.

refreshing *adjective* 1 pleasing and interesting, different from what you are used to. *It was refreshing to meet such helpful people.* 2 giving strength. *A refreshing week of exercise and fresh air.* **refresh** *verb*.

refreshments *plural noun* light food or drink. *Refreshments are served.*

refrigerator *noun* a large machine in which food and drinks are kept cool.

refuge *noun* a place that gives shelter and protection from trouble or danger. *The explorers found a refuge from the cold.*

refugee *noun* a person who has been forced to leave home, usually his or her country, because of war or disaster. *Refugees poured across the border after the earthquake.*

The refugees walked many miles looking for shelter.

refuse *verb* (say ri-**fewz**) to say 'no' to something, to not do or accept something. *She refused my offer of help.* **refusal** *noun*.

refuse *noun, formal* (say **ref**-yooss) waste material, trash. *There is a weekly refuse collection.*

regal *adjective* (say **ree**-gul) suitable for a king or queen, splendid.

regatta *noun* a meeting for boat races.

region *noun* a large area, especially of land. *Forest regions.* **in the region of** about.

register *noun* 1 a list of things or names. *A register of births, deaths and marriages is kept at City Hall.* 2 the range of a voice or musical instrument. **register** *verb* 1 to list something in a register. 2 to show on a scale, record. *The thermometer registered 35 degrees.* 3 to make something clear, usually a feeling or an opinion. 4 to send a letter or package by registered mail. 5 to enroll in a school, college or course.

regret (regrets, regretting, regretted) *verb* to feel sorry about something you have done or not done. *She regretted her mistakes.* **regret** *noun*. **regrettable** *adjective*. **regretful** *adjective*.

regular *adjective* 1 happening, coming or doing something again and again at certain times. *Regular meals.* 2 evenly arranged or shaped, not varying. *Regular, white, shining teeth.* 3 normal, standard or proper. *That's not the regular procedure.* 4 A regular verb is a verb that follows the common pattern. The verb 'write' is not a regular verb. **regularly** *adverb.* **regularity** *noun.*

rehearse *verb* to practise something, especially a play, speech or music, before a performance. **rehearsal** *noun.*

reign *verb* (say rain) 1 to rule a country as a king or queen. 2 to exist. *Silence reigned.* **reign** *noun. During the reign of Queen Elizabeth.*

The coin was issued to commemorate the long reign of the king and queen.

rein *noun* a strap for guiding a horse. *Don't let go of the reins!*

reindeer (reindeer) *noun* a deer with large antlers that lives in the coldest parts of the world. *The people of Lapland herd reindeer.*

reinforce *verb* to make stronger. *Reinforced concrete is strengthened with metal bars.* **reinforcement** *noun.*

reject *verb* 1 to not accept a person or thing. *The machine rejects bent coins.* 2 to throw away or send back as not good enough. *The oranges were rotten and had to be rejected.* **rejection** *noun.*

rejoice *verb* to feel or show great happiness. *Rejoice and be merry!*

relapse *verb* to fall back into a worse state, to return to a previous condition, usually after having been better. **relapse** *noun.*

relate *verb* 1 to see or show a connection, to compare one thing with another. *It is difficult to relate these two results.* 2 to tell a story. 3 to get along with. *He cannot relate to children, not even his own.*

relation *noun* 1 a member of your family. 2 a connection. *There is no relation between her health and her results at school.* **relations** the dealings between people or groups. *Business relations with Germany.*

All the relations gathered together for the family reunion.

relationship *noun* 1 how people and things are connected. *The relationship between light and heat.* 2 a family connection. *What is your brother's relationship to her?* 3 a friendship or the way people or groups behave towards each other. *She has never had a lasting relationship.*

relative *noun* a person who is related to another, a relation. *My aunt is my only living relative.*

relative *adjective* 1 compared to each other or to something else. 2 connected with. **relatively** *adverb. Relatively well off.*

relax *verb* 1 to become less stiff, tight or strict. *He relaxed his grip.* 2 to be more calm and rest. *After work I like to relax.*

relay *noun* 1 a relay race. 2 a fresh group taking over from a tired one. *We worked all through the night in relays.* 3 a piece of equipment that receives messages by telephone, television or radio and passes them on to another place. **relay** *verb* to pass on a message or broadcast.

relay race *noun* a team race in which each member runs part of the whole distance.

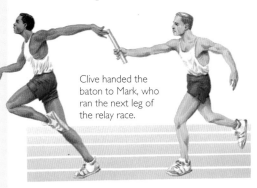

Clive handed the baton to Mark, who ran the next leg of the relay race.

release *verb* 1 to set free. *He was released from prison.* 2 to let your grip go. 3 to allow to be shown or published. *His new single will be released on Monday and shoot to the top of the charts.* **release** *noun* 1 being released or something released. 2 a new movie, record or piece of news that has come out. 3 a handle, button or other device that can be pressed to unfasten something.

relent *verb* to become less stern. *She relented after hearing the explanation.*

relentless *adjective* continued, strong or determined. *His questions were relentless.*

relic *noun* 1 something that was used or made a long time ago. *The relics found at the site gave them an idea of the culture.* 2 something that belonged to a saint and is usually kept in a church.

relief *noun* 1 a lessening or ending of pain, worry or boredom. *The medicine gave relief.* 2 help for people in trouble, especially food, money and clothes. *Famine relief.* 3 a raised shape of a surface.

relieve *verb* 1 to lessen pain, trouble or boredom. 2 to take over a duty from somebody else. *To relieve the guard.* **relieve of** to help someone by carrying something heavy or doing something difficult.

religion *noun* a belief in god or many gods. **religious** *adjective.* *A religious text.*

reluctant *adjective* unwilling. **reluctantly** *adverb.* *He reluctantly agreed to help.*

rely (relies, relying, relied) *verb* to depend on something happening or trust somebody or something. *She has always relied on her parents for help.* **reliance** *noun.*

remain *verb* 1 to be left behind after other parts have gone. *Two of the guests remained.* 2 to continue to be the same, to stay unchanged. *He remained silent.* **it remains to be seen** we will know later on.

remainder *noun* the rest, the part that is left over. *She paid $10 and promised to give me the remainder next week.*

remains *plural noun* 1 parts that are left after everything else has gone. *They found some remains of Greek pottery.* 2 a dead body.

The mummified remains were found in a clay pit.

remark *noun* something said. *He made some embarrassing remarks about her new glasses.* **remark** *verb.*

remarkable *adjective* worth speaking about, impressive. **remarkably** *adverb.* *She did remarkably well in the exam.*

remember *verb* 1 to keep in the mind. *I'll always remember the first time we met.* 2 to call back into mind, especially after having forgotten it for a while. **remembrance** *noun.*

remind *verb* to tell or make somebody remember something. *She reminds me of my mother.* **reminder** *noun.*

remnant *noun* 1 a small part of something left over. *We ate up the remnants of the meal.* 2 a small piece of material.

remorse *noun* a feeling of guilt about something you have done wrong. **remorseful** *adjective.* *Gary felt very remorseful.*

remove *verb* to take something away, off or out. *How can I remove this stain?* **removal** *noun.* *The removal of the troops.*

SPELLING NOTE

Note the spelling of relieve. It has 'i' before 'e' and not 'e' before 'i'.

WORD HISTORY

Rent comes from the Latin word 'reddere', 'to give', so it means something given or paid.

AMAZING FACT

The saying 'Opposites attract' refers to people who have different personalities, rather than magnets, which is where the saying comes from.

renew *verb* 1 to replace something old with something new of the same kind. *Passports have to be renewed every ten years.* 2 to begin or make again. *After meeting up again we renewed our friendship.* 3 to put new strength into something, to make as good as new again. **renewal** *noun.*

renowned *adjective* famous, well known for something good. *A renowned playwright.* **renown** *noun.*

rent *noun* the amount of money paid for the use of something, especially an apartment, house, car, etc. that belongs to somebody else. **rent** *verb.* *We rented a car at the airport.* **rent out** to allow something to be used in return for rent.

repair *verb* to mend or put something right that has broken or gone wrong. **repair** *noun.* *I left the car for repairs.*

The vase was impossible to repair, because a big chunk had been knocked out of it and lost.

repay (repays, repaying, repaid) *verb* to give back, especially money. *He repaid her kindness with insults.* **repayment** *noun.*

repeat *verb* to say or do the same thing again. **repeat** *noun.*

repel (repels, repelling, repelled) *verb* 1 to drive back. *The army repelled the attack.* 2 to find something horrible or disgusting. *The sight of blood repels him.* **repellent** *adjective, noun.* *Put on lots of insect repellent.*

Like poles of a magnet repel each other, opposite poles attract each other.

replace *verb* to put something back in its place or take the place of somebody or something else. *She broke one of my best cups but replaced it next day with a new one.*

replica *noun* a copy, especially of a painting. *This is only a cheap replica of the original statue in the British Museum.*

reply (replies) *noun* something said or written as an answer to somebody. *I rang Jane's doorbell, but there was no reply.* **in reply** as an answer. **reply** (replies, replying, replied) *verb* to give an answer.

report *verb* 1 to tell or give information about something. *They reported the accident to the police.* 2 to make a complaint against somebody. *The teacher reported the boy to the principal.* 3 to let somebody know that you are there. *We have to report to the manager every morning.* **report** *noun* 1 a written or spoken account of an event. 2 the sound of an explosion. **report card** *noun* a written account of a student's grades.

reporter *noun* somebody who writes or broadcasts news reports.

Reporters often take notes during an interview even though they may record it too.

represent *verb* 1 to be a picture, sign or example of something. To show or mean. *Love is often represented by a heart.* 2 to act for another person, especially as a lawyer or leader of a group. *We chose Gregory to represent our class.* **representation** *noun*.

representative *noun* somebody chosen to represent others. *Sales representatives often spend a lot of time driving between appointments.* **representative** *adjective* being an example of what others are like. *This painting is representative of the artist's work.*

repress *verb* to hold back or control. *Steve could hardly repress a grin.* **repression** *noun*.

reprieve *noun* an order to delay or cancel the punishment of a prisoner, especially one who was to die. *She won a last-minute reprieve.* **reprieve** *verb*. *The prisoner was reprieved and set free at last.*

reprimand *verb* to tell somebody officially that they should not have done a particular thing. **reprimand** *noun*. *The superintendent gave him a severe reprimand.*

reproduce *verb* 1 to make a copy of something. To cause something to be seen or heard again. *This painting has been reproduced in many books.* 2 to produce young. *Dinosaurs reproduced by laying eggs.* **reproduction** *noun*.

reptile *noun* an animal with scaly skin whose blood changes temperature according to the temperature around it. Snakes, lizards and crocodiles are all reptiles.

republic *noun* a country with an elected president at the head, rather than a king or queen. **republican** *noun*.

DID YOU KNOW

Reptiles are cold-blooded, which means that they need lots of sunshine to warm them up. Reptiles live in all warm parts of the world, and they usually lay eggs which are soft and leathery. Dinosaurs were reptiles, though some scientists think that they may have been warm-blooded creatures. The word reptile comes from the Latin repere, 'to crawl': reptiles are 'crawling animals'.

In summer they used to go sailing on the reservoir.

AMAZING FACT

The first republics in history were Ancient Greece and Ancient Rome. They were considered republics even though many of the people were slaves.

repugnant *adjective* horrible and disgusting. *A repugnant smell.*

repulsive *adjective* horrible. *Some people find eating snails repulsive.* **repulsion** *noun*.

reputation *noun* people's opinion of how good somebody or something is. If you live up to your reputation, you behave in the way people expect you to.

request *noun* asking for something or the thing asked for. *My next request is an early song by Mozart with words by Schiller.* **request** *verb* to ask politely.

require *verb* 1 to need. 2 to demand, make somebody do something. *Students are required to bring their own dictionaries.* **requirement** *noun*.

rescue *verb* to save from danger, to set free. *The fireman rescued the child from the burning house.* **rescue** *noun*. **rescuer** *noun*.

research (researches) *noun* a study of a subject to find out facts and information. **research** *verb*. *He is researching the feeding habits of monkeys.* **researcher** *noun*.

resemble *verb* to be like or similar. *She resembles her younger sister – they have the same nose.* **resemblance** *noun*.

reservation *noun* 1 an arrangement to keep something for somebody for later use. *Hotel reservations.* 2 doubt in your mind. *I've got reservations about this plan.* 3 a piece of land kept for a special purpose.

reserve *verb* to keep or order something for somebody. *We reserved two rooms in the hotel.* **reserve** *noun* 1 something kept for later use. *Reserves of food.* 2 an extra player who may replace another player before or during a game. 3 a piece of land for a special purpose. *A nature reserve.* 4 not showing your feelings. **reserved** *adjective*. *She is very reserved, which is why I don't like her.*

reservoir (say rez-uh-vwar) *noun* a place where water is stored.

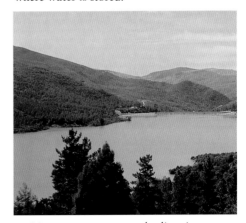

resident *noun* a person who lives in a particular place. *Parking is for residents only.* **resident** *adjective*. *The resident doctor.*

resign *verb* to give up your job or post. *He disagreed with the committee and resigned.* **resign yourself** to accept and put up with something without complaint. *She resigned herself to a very boring evening at the office dinner.* **resignation** *noun.*

resist *verb* to fight back against something or not allow yourself to do something. *I can't resist another piece of cake.* **resistance** *noun.* **resistant** *adjective.*

resolution *noun* 1 being firm. 2 something you make up your mind to do. *My New Year's resolution is to learn to play the guitar.* 3 a decision taken at a meeting by a vote. 4 solving problems.

resolve *verb* 1 to decide. *She resolved to work harder.* 2 to solve a problem or clear up a difficulty.

resort *noun* a vacation place. *Davos is a famous skiing resort.*

The family visited a resort in the mountains that was famous for its good skiing facilities.

resort *verb* to turn to, especially something bad. *When he lost his money he resorted to crime and broke into the office safe.*

resourceful *adjective* good at finding ways of doing things.

resources *plural noun* possessions such as wealth or goods. *Oil is one of the country's main resources.*

respect *noun* 1 a high opinion or admiration of somebody. *She has great respect for his work.* 2 If you show respect to somebody, you are polite. 3 a detail or particular point. *She's like her mother in every respect.* **with respect to** relating to. *With respect to your order, please find the invoice enclosed.* **respect** *verb.*

respond *verb* to reply or react to something. **response** *noun.* *He made no response to the question.*

responsibility (responsibilities) *noun* 1 the duty of having to deal with something and making decisions. Being responsible. *If you borrow my bike, it's your responsibility to lock it up.* 2 a duty, something for which you are responsible. *Parents have a lot of responsibilities.*

The result was a resounding win for the team from Athens.

responsible *adjective* 1 having the duty of taking care of somebody or something, having to take the blame if things go wrong. *She is responsible for keeping her room clean.* 2 trustworthy. **be responsible for** to be the cause of. *Who is responsible for the damage?* **responsibly** *adverb.*

rest *noun* 1 not doing anything active. Quiet or sleep. 2 a support. **rest** *verb* 1 to take or have a rest. *She never rests for a second.* 2 to support or be supported. *Now rest your head on your knees.* **rest assured** to be certain. **restful** *adjective.* **restless** *adjective.*

Alan rested in bed after a day at the zoo.

rest *noun* the part that is left, the others. *Take what you want and throw the rest away or give it to charity.*

restaurant *noun* a place where you can buy and eat meals.

restore *verb* 1 to give back, especially something stolen or lost. 2 to put or bring back as before. *The old church has been restored.* **restoration** *noun.*

restrain *verb* to hold back from doing something, to control. *I had to restrain myself from hitting him.* **restraint** *noun.*

restrict *verb* to keep within a limit. *She restricts herself to two cups of coffee a day.* **restriction** *noun.*

result *noun* 1 something that happens because of an event or activity. An effect. *You get good results with this washing detergent.* 2 the final score of a game, competition or race. 3 the answer to a sum. *Each time I add up the numbers I get a different result.* **result** *verb* to happen as an effect.

resume *verb* to begin again. *Talks resumed yesterday.* **resumption** *noun.*

résumé *noun* a summary of someone's work and educational history.

resurrect *verb* to bring back into use. *I resurrected the old piano.* **resurrection** *noun. The resurrection of some old ideas.*

resuscitate *verb* to revive a person so they become conscious again. **resuscitation** *noun.*

retail *verb* to sell goods. *The camera retails at $150.* **retail** *noun* selling goods to the public. **retailer** *noun.*

retain *verb* to keep or continue to have. *Frozen vegetables retain most of their nutritional value.*

retina *noun* the area at the back of the eye that is sensitive to light. *He has a damaged retina.*

retire *verb* 1 to give up work, especially when you are old. *My father retired at 60.* 2 to leave a place or room. 3 to go to bed. **retirement** *noun.*

Grandfather is really enjoying his retirement.

retreat *verb* to go away or move back, especially when forced to do so. *After a three-day battle the enemy retreated.* **retreat** *noun* 1 the act of retreating. 2 a quiet, restful place. *A weekend retreat in the country.*

return *verb* 1 to come or go back. *He returned from his vacation yesterday.* 2 to give, put or send back. *She returned the book I lent her.* **return** *noun* 1 the act of returning or returning something. 2 profit on an investment of money. **in return** in exchange. *I gave him my stamp collection in return for a computer game.*

reunion *noun* a meeting of old friends or family members who have not seen each other for some time. *At the school reunion, Clarrie met up with a lot of her old friends.*

reveal *verb* 1 to uncover something so it can be seen. *Her dress revealed a tattoo on her shoulder.* 2 to make known. *To reveal a secret.* **revelation** *noun.*

revenge *noun* hurting in return for having been hurt. *In revenge for her betrayal he refused to return her things.* **revenge** *verb.*

revenue *noun* the money that an organization receives from people, especially money paid as tax to the government.

reverse *adjective* opposite in position or order. *The reverse side of the paper has all the answers on it.*

Marie put the car into reverse and backed into the parking place.

WORD HISTORY

'Retina' comes from the Latin 'rete', meaning 'net'. Perhaps early doctors saw it as a sort of net at the back of the eye that caught light. If so, they were right in a way. The retina actually contains light-sensitive cells that send signals along the optic nerve to the brain. There are two kinds of cells: rods are sensitive to light and dark, and cones are more sensitive to color.

The people won a massive victory in the French Revolution.

reverse *noun* 1 the exact opposite. *She always does the reverse from what you expect.* 2 the back. 3 a gear in which you drive a car backwards. **in reverse** in the opposite way from what usually happens. **reverse** *verb* 1 to go backwards. *Always check the mirrors before you reverse out of the driveway.* 2 to change to the opposite or change round. *Roles are often reversed, with men taking care of the children and women going out to work.*

review *noun* 1 a critical opinion in a newspaper, magazine or on radio or television about a book, film, concert or play. *He writes film reviews.* 2 an inspection or examination. *Hospital practices have been under review.* **review** *verb.*

revise *verb* 1 to improve a piece of writing. 2 to change or correct something. *He's been so helpful I'll have to revise my opinion of him.* **revision** *noun. The wording of the bill has undergone extensive revision.*

revive *verb* to come back to life or strength again. To bring back. *A quick shower will revive me.* **revival** *noun.*

revolt *verb* 1 to fight against something. *The army revolted against the dictator.* 2 to be disgusted. **revolting** *adjective. A revolting banana skin was in the wastepaper basket.*

revolt *noun* a fight to change a system.

revolution *noun* 1 a rebellion, especially one overthrowing a political system. 2 complete change in ways of doing things or methods. *The green revolution.* 3 one complete turn of a wheel. **revolutionary** *adjective.* **revolutionize** *verb.*

revolve *verb* to turn or keep turning round.

revolver *noun* a small gun that does not have to be reloaded after each shot.

reward *noun* 1 something given in return for something good or useful you have done. 2 an amount of money given to somebody who helps the police. **reward** *verb. The boy was rewarded for his bravery with a medal.*

rewarding *adjective* giving you satisfaction. *Teaching can be a rewarding job.*

Reykjavik *noun* the capital of Iceland.

rheumatism (say roo-muh-tizum) *noun* an illness that makes joints or muscles stiff and painful. **rheumatic** *adjective.*

rhino (rhinos) *noun* a rhinoceros.

rhinoceros (rhinoceroses) *noun* a large animal from Africa or Asia with one or two horns on its nose.

The rhinoceros is endangered because poachers value its horn.

rhyme *noun* 1 a similar sound at the ends of words or lines in poetry, as in 'say' and 'day' and 'school' and 'fool'. 2 a word that rhymes with another. 3 a short piece of writing with rhymes. **rhyme** *verb.*

ribbon *noun* 1 a long strip of material for tying things together or used as a decoration. *She tied her hair with a red ribbon.* 2 a narrow strip of inked material that is put into a typewriter. *A typewriter ribbon.*

rice *noun* white or brown grains that are cooked and eaten.

The rice terraces at Luzon in the Philippines were carved out of the rock thousands of years ago.

rich *adjective* 1 having a lot of money or possessions. *A country rich in oil.* 2 containing a lot of goodness or quality of sound or color. *Rich soil is good for growing things.* 3 containing a lot of cream, oil, sugar or eggs. *Rich food.* 4 expensive, luxurious. **riches** *plural noun.* **richly** *adverb.* **richness** *noun.*

rickety *adjective* not made strongly, likely to break. *The old chairs were very rickety.*

riddle *noun* a difficult question to which you must guess the answer.

DID YOU KNOW

Rhymes can be either masculine or feminine. A masculine rhyme is one in which the two words have the same sounds in their final stressed syllables, such as 'betray' and 'delay'. In a feminine rhyme, the words' same sounds are in stressed syllables before other unstressed syllables, such 'joviality' and 'morality', or 'stocking' and 'shocking'.

AMAZING FACT

The word 'rhinoceros' comes from the Greek word for nose – rhino. When people have plastic surgery on their nose, it is called 'rhinoplasty'.

riddle *verb* to make holes in somebody or something, to make full of holes. *He riddled the target with bullets.* **riddled with** full of. *Your essay is riddled with mistakes.*

ride (rides, riding, rode, ridden) *verb* 1 to sit on a horse, bicycle or motorcycle and go along on it. 2 to travel in a car, bus or train. 3 to float on something. *The boat rode the waves.* **rider** *noun.* **ride up** to move up the body. **ride** *noun* a journey on an animal, a bike or in a vehicle. **take for a ride** to cheat somebody.

ridicule *noun* unkind or unfair laughter intended to make someone or something look or seem stupid.

ridiculous *adjective* silly. *She wore a ridiculous hat to the wedding.*

rifle *noun* a gun with a long barrel, fired from the shoulder.

rifle *verb* to search through and possibly steal things. *They rifled through my desk.*

rig *noun* 1 a large structure that is used for drilling for oil or gas. 2 the way a ship's sails and masts are arranged. **rig** (rigs, rigging, rigged) *verb* 1 to fit out a ship with ropes and sails. 2 to arrange an event dishonestly in order to get certain results. *The race was rigged.* **rig up** to put something together quickly out of materials that are handy. *The scouts rigged up a tent for the night.*

Oil rigs are lit up at night to warn ships of their presence.

Riga *noun* the capital of Latvia.

rigging *noun* the ropes and sails of a ship.

right *adjective* 1 of or belonging to the right-hand side. *In England cars drive on the left.* 2 correct, true. *Is that the right time?* 3 morally good, just. *Giving her the money back was the right thing to do.* 4 most suitable or healthy. *She is the right person for the job.* **right** *adverb* 1 towards the right-hand side. 2 directly, straight. *He stood right in front of me.* 3 properly, correctly. 4 immediately. *Get in this house right now.* 5 expressing agreement. *Right, I'll see you tomorrow afternoon.* **right angle** an angle of 90 degrees.

right-wing conservative.

right *noun* 1 the right-hand side, part or direction. *Keep to the right.* 2 a political party or group of people with conservative views. 3 morally good actions. *The difference between right and wrong.* 4 something you are allowed to do or have, a claim. *I know my rights.* **right of way** a right to go before other vehicles. **right** *verb* 1 to make something return to its usual position. *The boat righted itself.* 2 to make something right. *To right a wrong.*

rigid *adjective* 1 stiff, not bending. 2 strict. *The army has rigid discipline.*

rim *noun* the edge of a cup, plate, wheel or other round object.

rind *noun* the tough outer skin of fruit, cheese or bacon. *Orange rind.*

Orange rind is finely chopped and added to marmalade.

ring *noun* 1 a circle or something the shape of a circle. *Smoke rings.* 2 a small circle of metal worn on the finger. *A wedding ring.* 3 a space with seats around it where a circus performs or a boxing or wrestling match takes place. 4 a group of people who are doing something illegal. **ring** *verb* to put a ring around something. *The woods were ringed by search parties.*

ring (rings, rang, ringing, rung) *verb* 1 to make or cause the sound of a bell. *The telephone is ringing.* 2 to be filled with sound. *It was so loud, my ears were ringing.* **ring true/false** to sound true or untrue. **ring** *noun* the action or sound of ringing. **ring up** to add up a bill on a cash register. *She forgot to ring up the blouse.*

rink *noun* a place for skating.

For her birthday, Jemma took her friends ice-skating at the local rink.

rinse *verb* to wash something with clean water and without soap. *She rinsed the plates.* **rinse** *noun* 1 rinsing with clean water. 2 a special liquid for coloring the hair.

SPELLING NOTE

Riddles were originally clever puzzles that people had to solve. They occur in many myths and legends, with gods and rulers 'talking in riddles'. Now they tend to be more like jokes, such as "'Railroad crossing without any cars,' can you spell it without any R's?"(Answer: 'i-t')

WORD HISTORY

A rival was originally a person using the same stream as another, from the Latin 'rivus', meaning stream. Perhaps in places where there was a water shortage, the two rivals competed with each other for use of the stream. Strangely, the word river is thought to come from the Latin 'ripa', meaning bank.

riot *noun* violent or noisy behavior by a number of people, usually in a public place. **riot** *verb* to take part in a riot.

rip (rips, ripping, ripped) *verb* 1 to tear quickly. *She ripped her jeans on the barbed wire.* 2 to remove quickly. *He ripped the letter out of her hand.* **rip** *noun.* **rip off** to cheat by asking for too much money.

rip-off *noun* a fraud or swindle.

ripe *adjective* 1 ready to be picked and eaten. 2 ready, fit for something. *The country is ripe for change.* **ripen** *verb.* *The bananas will ripen soon.*

ripple *noun* a small wave or small waves. *Ripples on the pond.* **ripple** *verb* to make ripples or move in ripples.

I threw a stone in the pond and watched the ripples grow.

rise (rises, rising, rose, risen) *verb* 1 to go up, get higher. *The water is rising.* 2 to come up. *The Sun rises in the east.* 3 to get up from a lying, sitting or kneeling position, to get out of bed. *He rises early.* 4 to get stronger. *The child's voice rose to a scream.* 5 to come up to the surface. 6 to show above the surroundings as a tall shape. *The tower rose above the rooftops.* **rise from the dead** to come back to life. **rise up** to fight against somebody in power. *The people rose up against the dictator.* **rise** *noun* 1 a small hill or upward slope. 2 an increase, such as a rise in prices or the temperature. 3 the act of growing more powerful. *The rise and fall of the Roman Empire.* **give rise to** to lead to, especially something bad.

risk *noun* a danger of something bad happening. A chance of a loss. *There's a risk of showers.* **risk** *verb* to take a chance. *I don't want to risk losing my place in the line.* **risky** *adjective.* *Gambling is a risky business, but Peter enjoys it.*

ritual *noun* a series of actions that people regularly carry out in certain situations. *Family rituals.*

rival *noun* somebody who competes with you. **rival** *verb* to be as good as somebody or something else. *Nobody else's cooking can rival his mother's.* **rivalry** *noun.* *A great rivalry between two brothers caused big problems for the family.*

river *noun* a large stream of fresh water. *The Mississippi River is the longest river in the US.*

rivet *noun* a short nail with a flat head used for holding pieces of metal together. **rivet** *verb* 1 to fasten with rivets. 2 to attract or hold somebody's attention. *She watched the film, riveted to the screen.* **riveting** *adjective. He gave a riveting performance.*

Riyadh *noun* the capital of Saudi Arabia.

road *noun* 1 a specially made way between places for traffic to travel on. 2 a method or way. *The road to success is often very bumpy.* **on the road** travelling.

roam *verb* to wander around.

roar *noun* a loud, deep noise like the sound a lion makes. *The roar of traffic.* **roar** *verb* 1 to make a loud, deep sound like a lion or thunder. 2 to say or shout something loudly. *She roared with laughter.* **a roaring success** something very successful. **to do a roaring trade** to sell a lot of something.

roast *verb* 1 to cook meat or vegetables in the oven or over a hot fire. 2 to get very hot. *I've been roasting in the Sun all day.* **roast** *noun.* **roast** *adjective* roasted. *Roast meat.*

rob (robs, robbing, robbed) *verb* 1 to take what belongs to somebody else, usually by force. *The thieves robbed the safe.* 2 to take away. *She was robbed of a real opportunity.* **robber** *noun.* **robbery** *noun.*

robe *noun* a loose coat that you wear over your pajamas.

robin *noun* a small bird with a red breast.

robot *noun* a machine programmed to do things automatically. *Cars are put together by robots in factories.* **robotic** *adjective.*

This robot is used in car manufacture.

robust *adjective* strong. *A plan for a more robust economic structure was presented.*

rock *noun* 1 the hard stony part that is part of the earth's crust. 2 a large stone that sticks up above the ground or out of the ocean. *We climbed up a rock and then jumped off it.* **rocky** *adjective.*

rock *verb* 1 to move backwards and forwards or from side to side. *She rocked the baby in her arms.* 2 to shock or shake. *The news of his death rocked the world.* **rock** *noun* 1 a rocking movement. 2 music with a strong beat, rock music.

rock-bottom *adjective* at the lowest point. *Everything was sold at rock-bottom prices.*

SPELLING NOTE

Be careful about the spellings of 'roll' and 'role'. A roll is something that is rolled up, including the round shape of bread. The actor's part or somebody's position is spelt 'role', as in 'role-play' or 'role model'. This word comes from French, and is sometimes still spelled in the French way with a circumflex accent, 'rôle'.

rocket *noun* 1 a machine in the shape of a long tube that flies by burning gases and is used to send up missiles or spacecraft. 2 a kind of firework. **rocket** *verb* to move up quickly. *The song rocketed to Number One in the charts.* **rocket through** to move through a place very quickly.

rocking-chair *noun* a chair in which you can rock backwards and forwards.

The rocking chair stood by the fire in Grandma's house.

rod *noun* 1 a long thin stick. 2 a stick with a line for fishing.

rode *verb* past tense of ride.

rodent *noun* an animal that has sharp front teeth for gnawing. Rats, mice and squirrels are all rodents.

rodeo (rodeos) *noun* (say **roh**-dee-oh) a show at which cowboys ride wild horses and catch cattle with ropes.

rogue *noun* a dishonest person.

role *noun* 1 an actor's part in a play, film or musical. 2 somebody's position in a particular situation. *She didn't like the role of leader, but accepted it gracefully.*

role-play *noun* an exercise in which people play the part of a character.

roll *verb* 1 to move along turning over and over. 2 to make something into the shape of a ball or tube. 3 to move along on wheels or as if on wheels. *The years rolled by.* 4 to make flat by pressing. *To roll pastry.* 5 to make a deep sound. *Thunder rolled.* 6 to move from side to side. *The barrels rolled back and forth on the deck.* **roll over** to face the other way by turning over. **roll up** to roll something into a tube or ball. **roll a window up** to close a car window. *He forgot to roll the windows up before we went through the car wash.* **roll** *noun* 1 something rolled into a tube. 2 bread in a round shape for one person. 3 a rolling movement. 4 a rolling sound. 5 an official list of people's names.

rollerblades *plural noun* boots fitted with small wheels in a line for roller-skating. **rollerblading** *noun.*

roller-skate *verb* to move over a surface wearing roller-skates. **roller-skate** *noun* a shoe fitted with wheels. **roller-skating** *noun.*

ROM *abbreviation* read-only memory. ROM is the memory a computer uses which cannot be changed.

Roman Catholic *noun* a member of the Roman Catholic Church, which has the Pope at its head. Roman Catholics believe in the Christian religion. **Roman Catholic** *adjective*.

Romania *noun* a country in eastern Europe.

Romanian *noun* 1 the language of Romania. 2 a person who comes from Romania. **Romanian** *adjective*. *The Romanian flag.*

The Romanian flag has blue, yellow and red vertical stripes.

romantic *adjective* having feelings about love and beauty, seeing things in an unreal way. Romantic novels and films are about love and usually have a happy ending. **romantic** *noun*. **romantically** *adverb*. **romance** *noun*.

Rome *noun* the capital of Italy.

roof *noun* 1 the covering on top of a building, tent, car or bus. 2 the upper part of the inside of the mouth.

rook *noun* 1 a black crow. 2 a chess piece, also called a castle.

rookie *noun* an inexperienced person who has just started to do a job or play a sport.

room *noun* 1 a part in a house or other building that has its own walls, floor, ceiling and door. 2 space. **roomy** *adjective* spacious.

rooster *noun* a male chicken.

root *noun* 1 the part of a plant that grows under the ground. 2 the part of a tooth or hair beneath the skin. 3 the cause or basis of something. *The root of the problem.* 4 in mathematics, a number in relation to the number it makes when multiplied by itself. *The square root of 9 is 3.*

root *verb* 1 to grow roots. *Ivy roots very quickly.* 2 to search through things. *Pigs root around for food.* **rooted to the spot** unable to move.

The tree's roots spread far down into the earth and draw moisture up the trunk and into the branches and leaves.

The Earth rotates on its axis as it moves around the Sun.

rope *noun* a strong thick string. **know the ropes** to know how something should be done. **rope** *verb* tie together with a rope. **rope in** to persuade somebody to help you with an activity. **rope off** to separate an area with ropes, usually to keep people away from it. *The accident area was roped off.*

rose *noun* 1 a sweet-smelling flower with a thorny stem that grows on a bush. 2 a pink color.

rose *verb* past tense of rise.

Roseau *noun* the capital of Dominica.

rosemary *noun* a bush with evergreen leaves that are used in cooking.

Rosh Hashanah *noun* a festival marking the Jewish New Year.

rosy *adjective* 1 pink 2 . something positive or promising. *She painted a rosy picture of life at the boarding school.*

rot (rots, rotting, rotted) *verb* to go bad, to decay. *The apples were rotting in the box.* **rot** *noun* the process of decay. **rotten** *adjective*. 1 *Rotten apples.* 2 bad, unpleasant.

rota *noun* (say roh-tuh) a list of people who take turns doing a particular job.

rotate *verb* 1 to move round a fixed point. *A wheel rotates.* 2 to take turns or come round in regular order. *We rotate the babysitting.* **rotation** *noun*. *The Earth's rotation is a mystery to me.*

rotor *noun* a part of a machine that rotates, especially the rotating blades of a helicopter.

rouble *noun* Russian money.

rough *adjective* 1 uneven, not smooth or polished. *Rough skin.* 2 not calm, gentle or polite, using force. *Rough manners.* 3 not exact, without detail. *A rough description.* **roughly** *adverb*. **roughness** *noun*.

rough *verb* If you **rough somebody up**, you physically hit them. **rough it** to live in an uncomfortable way. *We're going to spend the weekend at the festival, roughing it in a tent.* **rough out** to make a quick drawing or plan of something. **rough** *noun* 1 the long grass on a golf course. 2 a piece of writing or a drawing without much detail, not finished.

round *adjective* 1 shaped like a circle or ball. 2 complete. 3 going and returning. *A round trip ticket to Toronto costs just a few dollars more than a one-way.* **roundness** *noun.* **in round numbers** estimated or not exactly, but to the nearest 10, 100, 1000, etc.

round *adverb* all year round *The skating rink at the Civic Center is open all year round.*

round *preposition* 1 in a circle. 2 on all the sides of. 3 in every direction or everywhere. 4 in the neighborhood. **round the clock** all the time. *Paul made us work round the clock.*

round *noun* 1 something round. 2 a regular trip to a number of houses. *I have a paper round so I have to get up early every morning.* 3 a share given out to everyone. *This round of drinks is on me!* 4 one stage in a negotiation, game or competition. *This round of peace talks looks very promising.* 5 a bullet or bullets from a gun. 6 in golf, playing all the holes once. in boxing or wrestling, one period of the match.

roundabout *adjective* not in the shortest or most direct way. *He told us in a roundabout way that he was leaving.*

rout *verb* to defeat heavily in a battle, election or other contest. **rout** *noun.*

route *noun* the way you take to get to a place. *Our route across Colorado took us through some of the most beautiful country in the state.*

routine *noun* (say roo-**teen**) the usual way of doing things. *Getting up late upsets my routine.* **routine** *adjective.* *A routine job.*

rove *verb* to roam.

row *noun* (rhymes with go) a line of people or things. *A row of trees.*

row *verb* (rhymes with go) to move a boat through the water with oars. **rower** *noun.* **rowing** *noun.*

row boat *noun* a small boat with oars.

rowdy (rowdier, rowdiest) *adjective* behaving in a rough and noisy manner. *The kids in that family are all rowdy.*

The meeting was held at a round table, where all the participants were equal.

Rubies are gemstones valued for their beautiful red color.

royal *adjective* belonging to or connected with a king or queen. **royally** *adjective.*

royalty (royalties) *noun* 1 people of the royal family. 2 part of the price of a book that is paid to the writer for each copy sold.

rub (rubs, rubbing, rubbed) *verb* to move something backwards and forwards or round and round against something else. *Rub some cream on it to make it better.* **rub off on** to have affect someone or something. *Her enthusiastic attitude rubbed off on the whole team.*

rubber *noun* an elastic substance that keeps out water, made from the juice of some tropical trees. *Rubber gloves.* **rubbery** *adjective.*

rubbish *noun* 1 unwanted things to be thrown away, trash. 2 nonsense, foolish talk.

rubble *noun* broken stones or bricks. *Fill the hole with rubble.*

ruby (rubies) *noun* a red precious stone. **ruby** *adjective. Dorothy clicked the heels of the ruby slippers.*

rudder *noun* a piece of metal or wood at the back of a boat or plane, used for steering.

rude *adjective* 1 impolite. *It's rude to laugh.* 2 vulgar. *Rude jokes.* 3 unexpected and unpleasant. *A rude awakening.* 4 very simple and roughly made. *A rude attempt at art.* **rudeness** *noun.* *Her rudeness is appalling.*

rug *noun* 1 a mat, smaller than a carpet. 2 a thick blanket.

rugby *noun* a game similar to football. *Tim loves playing rugby.*

rugged *adjective* 1 craggy and rocky. *The rugged landscape around the lakes is exciting.* 2 rough and strong. *He's got a handsome but very rugged face.*

ruin *noun* 1 destruction. *Procrastination will be the ruin of her.* 2 the state of no longer having any money. 3 part or parts of a building still standing after the rest has been destroyed. *The ruins of a castle.* **ruin** *verb* 1 to destroy or harm. 2 to lose all your money.

The castle ruins provided a fascinating introduction to the archaeology lesson.

rule *noun* 1 an order or a law that says what is allowed or not allowed. Instructions on how things are to be done. *The rules of grammar.* 2 power to govern or control. *Under British rule.* **as a rule** usually. **rule** *verb* 1 to govern or control. 2 to decide. *The judge ruled that he must pay a fine.* 3 to make a straight line with a ruler. *Ruled paper.* **rule out** to decide that something is impossible.

ruler *noun* 1 a person who rules. 2 a long, flat piece of wood, metal or plastic with straight edges that are marked with inches and/or centimeters, used for measuring things or drawing straight lines.

rum *noun* an alcoholic drink made from sugar cane.

rumble *verb* to make a low rolling sound. *My stomach is rumbling.* **rumble** *noun.*

rumor *noun* talk, especially false information, spread from one person to another. **rumor** *verb* to say as a rumor.

rump *noun* the back part (buttocks) of an animal. *Rump steak.*

run (runs, running, ran, run) *verb* 1 to move quickly on your legs. 2 to take part in a race. *He runs for our school.* 3 to go, travel or drive somebody somewhere. *The bus runs every hour.* 4 to flow. *Shall I run you a bath?* 5 to move quickly. *A strange thought ran through her mind.* 6 to work, operate. *He left the car running.* 7 to organize, control or own. *He runs a store.* 8 to stretch or continue. *The road runs through the forest.* 9 to continue to go on for a period of time. *The play ran for a week.* **run away** to leave suddenly. **run behind** to be late ending or starting. **run into** 1 to hit a person or thing while driving. 2 to happen to meet or come across. *She ran into an old friend.* **run out** to have used up everything and have nothing left. *We ran out of money.* **run over** to hit somebody when driving. *He ran over his neighbor.*

rung *noun* a bar in a ladder. *My foot was on the bottom rung when I fell off the ladder and broke my arm.*

rung *verb* past tense of ring.

runner *noun* 1 a person who runs, especially in a race. 2 a thin wooden or metal strip on which something slides or moves. *We waxed the runners of the sled.* 3 a messenger. 4 a long strip of carpet.

Anna was a good runner who trained every day.

DID YOU KNOW

From 1922 to 1991 Russia was part of the USSR (Union of Soviet Socialist Republics) or Soviet Union, which was the biggest country in the world. When the Soviet Union broke up into separate republics, the Russian Federation, or Russia, remained the world's largest country. Its area covers more than 17 million square kilometers, much larger than the continent of Europe.

DID YOU KNOW

Rugby, or rugby football, was first played at Rugby School in Warwickshire, England, which is where the name comes from.

runner-up *noun* somebody who finishes second in a race or competition.

runway *noun* the long strip of hard surface on which planes take off and land.

rural *adjective* of or like the countryside, far away from the city.

rush *verb* 1 to hurry, act quickly. *Don't rush me, I have to think about it.* 2 to move quickly. *He was rushed to the hospital.* 3 to get through, over or into something by pushing forward. **rush** (rushes) *noun* 1 hurry or hurried activity. 2 a sudden interest or demand for something. *A rush for tickets.*

rush hour *noun* the busy part of the day when most people are traveling to or from work.

Russia *noun* a country in eastern Europe and Asia.

Russian *noun* 1 the language of Russia. 2 a person who comes from Russia. **Russian** *adjective.* *A Russian church.*

Russia is a vast country that spans eight time zones.

rust *noun* a reddish-brown substance that forms on iron when it becomes damp. **rust** *verb.* *The bike will rust if you leave it out in the rain.* **rusty** *adjective.*

An old rusty can was all that Tom caught when he went fishing.

rustic *adjective* connected with the country, rough and simple. *Rustic furniture.*

rut *noun* 1 a deep, narrow track made in the ground by wheels. 2 a fixed way of thinking or doing things which is difficult to get out of. *The only way to get out of this rut is to leave home and start a new life.*

ruthless *adjective* showing no pity, cruel. *They believe you have to be ruthless in business.* **ruthlessness** *noun.*

Rwanda *noun* a country in Africa.

rye *noun* a grass grown in cold countries, and the grain of that plant which is used for making flour. *Rye bread.*

Ss

sabbath *noun* a weekly day of rest, Saturday for Jews, Sunday for most Christians.

sabotage *noun* secretly carried-out damage, usually to machines or buildings as a protest, to weaken an enemy or ruin a plan. **sabotage** *verb. The bridge had been sabotaged by enemy troops.*

sachet *noun* (say **sash**-ay) a small closed plastic or paper bag for holding something.

sack *noun* a large bag made of strong material. *A sack of potatoes.*

sacred (say **say**-krid) *adjective* connected with religion, holy.

sacrifice *noun* 1 giving something to a god as an offering. 2 giving up something you like or value for the good of something else. **sacrifice** *verb* to offer or give up something as a sacrifice. *He sacrificed his job to look after his sick parents.* **sacrificial** *adjective. A sacrificial lamb.*

sad (sadder, saddest) *adjective* unhappy, showing or causing sorrow. **sadly** *adverb.* **sadness** *noun. Tears of great sadness spilled down her cheeks.*

saddle *noun* a seat on a horse or bicycle for a rider to sit on. **saddle** *verb* to put a saddle on a horse or other animal.

safe *adjective* out of danger or free from risk or harm. *Have a safe flight.* **safely** *adverb. They arrived home safely.*

safe *noun* a strong box or cupboard with special locks for keeping money or valuable things in. *Put your jewels in the safe in the room and change the combination.*

Marcia kept her jewels locked in the hotel's safe.

safeguard *noun* a protection against something unwanted. *She eats a lot of fruit as a safeguard against catching colds and the flu.* **safeguard** *verb* to protect.

---

safety *noun* being safe, freedom from danger or harm.

safety belt *noun* 1 a strap attached to the seat in a car or plane worn by travelers. 2 a belt for fastening to something solid worn by somebody working high up or in a dangerous position.

safety pin *noun* a metal pin for fastening things together.

sag (sags, sagging, sagged) *verb* to hang down loosely or in the middle, usually because of weight. **sag** *noun.*

saga *noun* (say **sah**-guh) a long story. *A family saga is my favorite entertainment.*

sage *noun* a plant used as a herb.

sage *adjective* wise. **sage** *noun* a wise person. *Three sages came on camels.*

said *verb* past tense of say.

sail *noun* 1 a large piece of cloth attached to the mast of a ship to catch the wind and make the ship move. **set sail** to leave a port. 2 the blade of a windmill. **sail** *verb* 1 to travel across the water, to be able to control a sailing boat. 2 to move quickly and easily. *She sailed through the exam.* 3 to begin a voyage. *Our ship sails tomorrow.*

Jonanthan took a course in navigation so he could sail long distances across the sea.

sailboard *noun* the board used for windsurfing. *He bought a new sailboard.*

sailing boat *noun* a boat driven by sails.

sailor *noun* 1 somebody who can sail a boat. 2 a member of a navy, somebody who works on a ship.

saint *noun* a holy person or a very kind and patient person. **saintly** *adjective.*

sake *noun* for the sake of somebody or something, for the good of somebody or for the purpose of something. *For heaven's sake, stop arguing with each other.*

salad *noun* 1 a mixture of uncooked vegetables, such as lettuce, cucumber and tomatoes, eaten cold.

salad dressing *noun* a sauce for putting on salads. *Salad dressing with garlic and herbs.*

salary (salaries) *noun* fixed pay, usually monthly, earned by somebody for work.

sale *noun* 1 the selling of goods for money. 2 a special time when goods are sold in stores at lower prices. **on sale** if something is on sale, it can be bought in the stores. **for sale** offered to be sold. *The house is for sale.*

saliva *noun* the watery liquid that naturally forms in the mouth.

salmon (salmon) *noun* (say sam-un) a large fish with pink flesh eaten as food.

Salmon swim upstream in spring to spawn.

salt *noun* a white substance found in seawater, used for making food taste better or for preserving it. Salt crystals. **rub salt into somebody's wounds** to make somebody's pain even worse. **salt** *verb* to put salt in or on food. **salty** *adjective*.

salute *verb* 1 to greet somebody. Soldiers salute by raising their right hand to their forehead. 2 to show respect or admiration. *We salute the enormous efforts you have made.* **salute** *noun. A salute to freedom.*

salvage *verb* to save from something that has been destroyed, so it can be used again. **salvage** *noun.*

salvation *noun* 1 being saved from sin, the saving of the soul, especially in the Christian religion. 2 something that stops loss or damage. *The charity is their salvation.*

same *adjective* 1 not different, exactly alike. *She wore the same dress as me.* 2 not changed. *She still works at the same place.* 3 a particular one or one already mentioned. *I saw a flash and at the same moment the car crashed into a tree.* **same** *adverb* in the same way. *I don't feel the same about tests now.* **sameness** *noun.*

sample *noun* a small quantity that shows what something or what the rest is like. *A free sample of washing detergent.* **sample** *verb* to test a part of something.

Diane took samples of curtain material home to try them against her walls.

WORD HISTORY
The sandwich is named after the 4th Earl of Sandwich, John Montagu (1718–92), who was so addicted to gambling that he never wanted to leave the gaming table. So when the Earl needed something to eat, a servant would bring him some cold beef, which he liked to have between two slices of bread. This snack soon came to be known as a sandwich.

SPELLING NOTE
Santa Claus is the legendary Saint Nicholas, the patron saint of children. Nicholas was a bishop who lived in Asia Minor, present-day Turkey, over 1600 years ago. Stories about Nicholas giving gold to poor children led to the legend of Father Christmas bringing gifts to all children.

San'a *noun* the capital of Yemen.

sanction *noun* 1 permission given to do something. 2 actions taken by countries against a country that is breaking international laws. A punishment ordered when a law or rule is broken. *The sanctions included a total trade ban.* **sanction** *verb* to allow something to be done. *The minister sanctioned the sale of the pictures.*

sanctuary (sanctuaries) *noun* 1 a holy place, especially in a church or temple. 2 a place of safety. 3 a place where animals or birds are protected. *A bird sanctuary.*

sand *noun* a mass of finely crushed stones as on beaches and in deserts. **sandy** *adjective* 1 full of sand. *A sandy beach.* 2 yellowish-red. *Sandy hair.*

sand *verb* to smooth or clean a surface by rubbing sandpaper over it.

sandal *noun* a shoe with straps over the foot, worn in summer.

sandpaper *noun* paper with sand stuck to it, used for smoothing surfaces. **sandpaper** *verb. Please sandpaper the woodwork.*

sandwich *noun* two slices of bread with a filling between. **sandwich** *verb* to put something between two others. *The bag was sandwiched between two big suitcases.*

Trudy packed the sandwiches for the picnic.

sane *adjective* 1 able to think normally, not mentally ill or mad. 2 sensible. **sanity** *noun.*

sang *verb* past tense of sing.

sanitary *adjective* 1 concerning the treatment of waste for the protection of public health. *In the Middle Age sanitary conditions were very poor.* 2 clean, free from dirt or infection.

San José *noun* the capital of Costa Rica.

sank *verb* past tense of sink.

San Marino *noun* a country in southern Europe. Its capital is also called San Marino.

San Salvador *noun* the capital of El Salvador.

Santa Claus *noun* another name for Father Christmas. Small children are told that Santa Claus comes in a sleigh to bring presents to them at Christmas.

Santiago *noun* the capital of Chile.

Santo Domingo *noun* the capital of the Dominican Republic.

São Tomé *noun* the capital of São Tomé and Príncipe.

São Tomé and Príncipe *noun* a country in the Gulf of Guinea off West Africa.

sap *noun* the watery liquid in plants and trees. *The sap rises in the spring.*

sap (saps, sapping, sapped) *verb* to weaken somebody's strength or confidence, especially over a period of time.

sapling *noun* a young tree.

sapphire *noun* a bright blue precious stone.

Sarajevo *noun* the capital of Bosnia-Herzegovina.

sarcasm *noun* amusing, often hurtful things said to mock or upset somebody's feelings, usually by saying the opposite of what is really thought. **sarcastic** *adjective. Your sarcastic tone of voice.* **sarcastically** *adverb.*

sardine *noun* a small seafish. *There's a can of sardines in the cabinet.*

sari (saris) *noun* a long piece of material wrapped around the body, usually worn by Indian women.

Madhur wore a red silk sari embroidered with gold thread.

sat *verb* past tense of sit.

Satan *noun* the devil, an evil power. **satanic** *adjective.*

satellite *noun* 1 a heavenly body like a small planet, or a man-made object like a spacecraft, moving around a larger planet. The Moon is a satellite of the Earth. *A weather satellite was sent into space.* 2 a person or country taking orders from another more powerful one.

satellite dish *noun* a dish for receiving signals from a space satellite.

satin *noun* a shiny cloth, usually made from silk. *Kate dressed up in satin pantaloons.*

satire *noun* amusing writing used to show how foolish or bad people or their ideas are.

satisfy (satisfies, satisfying, satisfied) *verb* 1 to give enough of what is wanted to make somebody pleased. *Nothing satisfies her, she is always complaining.* 2 to be enough or good enough for what is needed. *One bowl of soup is not enough to satisfy my hunger.* 3 to make somebody free from doubt, to convince. *I had satisfied myself that everybody had gone.* **satisfaction** *noun.* **satisfactory** *adjective* good enough. **satisfying** *adjective* pleasing.

Saudi Arabia is one of the world's richest countries, due to its vast reserves of oil.

WORD HISTORY

Both 'sardine' and 'satin' come from place names. The small fish were originally caught off the coast of the Italian island of Sardinia, and they have been called sardines since the 15th century. The silky fabric called satin comes originally from China. The Arabs called the fabric 'zaytuni', which was their name for the Chinese port of Qingjiang.

saturate *verb* 1 to make very wet. 2 to fill completely so that no more can be held. *The handkerchief was saturated with perfume.* **saturation** *noun.*

Saturday *noun* the seventh and last day of the week. Saturday comes after Friday and before Sunday.

saucepan *noun* a metal cooking pot with a lid and a handle.

saucer *noun* a small dish on which a cup stands. *A cup and saucer.*

Saudi *noun* a person from Saudi Arabia. **Saudi** *adjective. A Saudi prince.*

Saudi Arabia *noun* a country in Southwest Asia.

sauna *noun* 1 a hot steam bath. 2 a room or place where you have a sauna.

saunter *verb* to walk in a slow, casual way.

sausage *noun* chopped-up meat in a thin casing that looks like a tube. *He had sausage, bacon and eggs for breakfast.*

savage *adjective* wild, uncontrollable or cruel. *The boy was bitten by a savage dog and had to have stitches.* **savagely** *adverb.* **savage** *noun* a cruel, wild or primitive person.

savannah *noun* a grassy plain with few trees. *The African savannah.*

save *verb* 1 to make somebody or something free from danger. *He saved my life.* 2 to keep something, especially money, for later use. *He has saved enough to buy a new bike.* 3 to make something unnecessary for somebody, so they don't have to do it. *Using a computer saves time.* 4 to stop a player from scoring. **save** *noun.*

savings *plural noun* money saved, especially in a bank. *My savings are under the bed.*

saw *verb* past tense of see.

saw *noun* a tool with a blade with sharp teeth along one edge for cutting wood or metal. *He gave me the saw to cut the wood into lengths.*

Arnold took the saw from the shed and prepared to cut the dead branch from the tree.

say (says, saying, said) *verb* 1 to speak words, using your voice to express something. 2 to give an opinion or thought in words or writing. *He said how nice everybody was to him on his trip to India.* **say** *noun* the power of acting or deciding. *She had no say in the matter.* **have your say** to have a chance to say what you think.

saying *noun* a sentence people often say that makes a wise statement.

scab *noun* 1 a dry crust, mainly of dried blood, which forms over a cut or wound. 2 somebody who does not join a strike.

scaffolding *noun* a framework of metal poles and boards put up around a building for workers to stand on while building or repairing a house.

scald *verb* 1 to burn yourself with hot liquid or steam. 2 to clean pans or instruments with boiling water or steam. **scald** *noun* a skin burn from hot liquid or steam. **scalding** *adjective. Scalding hot water.*

scale *noun* 1 a small, flat piece of hard skin that covers the skin of fish and reptiles. 2 a hard layer that forms at the bottom of a kettle, in pipes or on teeth. **scale** *verb* 1 to remove the scales, especially from fish. 2 to remove from a surface in thin pieces.

scale *noun* 1 a set of numbers, marks or degrees for measuring. *A ruler with a metric scale.* 2 a set of numbers comparing measurements on a map or model with the measurements in the real world. *The model is to scale.* 3 a size or importance in relation to other things. *The party is going to be on a grand scale.* 4 a set of musical notes arranged in order going upward or downward. *She practices the scales on the piano every day.* **scale** *verb* 1 to climb up. *The thief scaled the wall.* 2 to make a copy of something according to a certain scale. **scale down** to make something smaller in size or amount than it used to be.

scales *plural noun* a weighing machine. *Bathroom scales.*

scalp *noun* 1 the skin under the hair on the head. 2 a piece of skin and hair that was taken as a mark of victory when somebody was scalped. **scalp** *verb* to cut the scalp off a dead enemy.

The blood dries in the air to form a hard crust called a scab.

A scan can detect tumors growing inside the brain.

scamper *verb* to run quickly with small, short steps. *Ned scampered up the tree.*

scan (scans, scanning, scanned) *verb* 1 to look closely and carefully, to examine. *Mother scanned our faces to see if anything was wrong.* 2 to look at something quickly without reading it properly or to search through information, especially on a computer. 3 to use special equipment to examine a person or pass an electronic beam over an area in search of something. 4 to count the pattern of beats in each line of poetry. **scan** *noun.*

scandal *noun* 1 careless talk, gossip that shocks. *The tabloid newspapers love a bit of scandal.* 2 action that shocks or makes people angry. **scandalous** *adjective.*

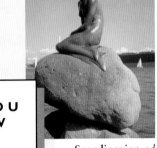

Scandinavia *noun* a region covering the countries of northern Europe – Denmark, Finland, Iceland, Norway and Sweden.

The Little Mermaid sits on a rock on the harbor at Copenhagen, Denmark. She is Scandinavia's best-loved sculpture.

Scandinavian *noun* a person from Scandinavia. **Scandinavian** *adjective. Scandinavian languages.*

scanner *noun* 1 a device for putting pictures into a computer. 2 a machine used in hospitals for examining a person by moving a beam of light or X-rays over them.

scanty (scantier, scantiest) *adjective* very small, hardly big enough. **scantily** *adverb. Helen and Sarah were scantily dressed.*

scar *noun* a mark on the skin which is left after a wound or burn has healed. **scar** (scars, scarring, scarred) *verb* to mark with a scar or scars.

scarce *adjective* not enough compared with what is wanted, difficult to find. *Fruit is scarce in winter.* **scarcity** *noun. There is a scarcity of good humor in the office.*

scarcely *adverb* hardly, only just.

scare *noun* a sudden fear, alarm. **scare** *verb* to frighten or make you frightened, to become afraid. *I'm scared of the dark.* **scare away** to frighten somebody so that they go away. **scary** *adjective*.

scarecrow *noun* a figure dressed in old clothes that is put up in a field to frighten birds away.

The scarecrow was dressed in the farmer's old clothes.

scarf (scarves) *noun* a piece of cloth worn around the neck or head.

scarlet *adjective*, *noun* bright red.

scarper *verb* to run away.

scatter *verb* to throw or go in different directions. *He scattered his toys about and made a terrible mess.*

scatty (scattier, scattiest) *adjective* being a little crazy or forgetful.

scavenge *verb* to look through trash for food or other things. *The old man scavenges in garbage cans for food.* **scavenger** *noun* 1 somebody who scavenges. 2 a bird or animal that feeds on waste and decaying flesh.

scene *noun* 1 one of the parts of a play, film or book. 2 the background for a play. *There were only three scene changes.* 3 the place where an event or action happens or an area of activity. *The scene of the crime.* 4 a showing of anger. *He made a scene in the restaurant when I arrived late.* 5 a view. *She paints mountain scenes.* **behind the scenes** secretly. **set the scene** to prepare in order to understand what is going to happen next.

scenery (sceneries) *noun* 1 the landscape and everything natural around you. *When we reached the mountains, the scenery suddenly changed for the better.* 2 things used on a theater stage, like the furniture and painted backgrounds.

Nick and Daphne like walking in the mountains because the air is clear and the scenery is breathtaking.

WORD HISTORY

The word 'sceptic' comes from the Greek 'skepsis', meaning speculation. The original Sceptics were ancient Greek philosophers who thought it was impossible to know things definitely. This philosophy began with Pyrrhon of Elis (c. 365–c.270 BC), who was influenced by some of the thinkers he met on his travels to India.

scent *noun* 1 a pleasant smell. *The scent of violets.* 2 a liquid perfume you put on your skin to smell nice. 3 a smell left by an animal that other animals can follow. **scent** *verb* 1 to smell. *The dog scented a fox.* 2 to feel that something is going to happen, to detect. *I scent trouble.* 3 to put scent on something or fill with scent. *The air was scented with flowers and full of the buzz of insects.*

sceptic (say **skep-tik**) *noun* somebody who does not believe things. **sceptical** *adjective* *I'm sceptical about our chances of winning.*

schedule (say **sked-yool**) *noun* a plan that gives a list of events and times for doing things. **on schedule** on time. **behind schedule** not on time. **schedule** *verb* to put into a plan or timetable. *A scheduled flight to Paris.*

scheme *noun* a plan of action or an arrangement. *I like your color scheme better than your furniture.* **scheme** *verb* to make clever, secret plans. **schemer** *noun*.

scholar *noun* 1 a person who studies an academic subject and knows a lot about it. 2 a student who receives money (a scholarship) to study at a school or university.

school *noun* 1 a place for teaching children. 2 the time when teaching is done and you are at school. 3 all the teachers and students in a school. 4 a place for the study of a particular subject, especially a college or university department. 5 a group of people who think the same or have the same methods of work. 6 a group of dolphins or fish. **school** *verb* to train. **schooling** *noun*.

science *noun* the study of nature, natural things and the testing of natural laws. If you study science you might do chemistry, physics or biology. Psychology is a social science. **scientific** *adjective*. *Microscopes and thermometers are scientific instruments.*

scientist *noun* somebody who studies science or works in one of the sciences.

Jane trained as a scientist, then got a job as a lab technician.

scissors *plural noun* a tool with two sharp blades for cutting.

scoff *verb* to speak in a mocking way about somebody or something. *The other scientists scoffed at his unorthodox methods.*

scold *verb* to tell somebody off, to speak angrily. *She scolded the children.*

scone *noun* (say skohn rhyming with bone) a small flat English cake usually eaten with butter.

scoop *noun* 1 a deep round spoon for dishing out soft food such as ice-cream. 2 a shovel-shaped spoon for picking up grain, flour or sugar. *A flour scoop.* 3 the amount a scoop holds. 4 an exciting news story reported by a newspaper before any other newspapers. 5 a successful piece of business, usually a large profit made from acting faster than others. **scoop** *verb* 1 to lift something or make a hole as if with a scoop. *She scooped out a hole in the sand.* 2 to pick something up with a scoop or spoon. *I scooped out some ice-cream.*

scooter *noun* 1 a kind of small motorcycle. 2 a child's vehicle with a long handle and two small wheels attached to a board.

scope *noun* 1 an opportunity, a chance for action. *I wish there was more scope for doing more music in the new schedule.* 2 a range, a whole area of action.

scorch *verb* to burn something so it goes slightly brown. *The grass was scorched by the hot Sun.* **scorching** *adjective* very hot.

score *noun* 1 the number of points, goals or runs made in a game. 2 a written copy of a piece of music for the performers, showing what each one has to play. 3 a piece of music for a film or play. 4 twenty. *Two score and ten is 50.* When you get scores of something, you get a large number. *Scores of complaints.* 5 a reason or point. *He won't let us down, you can trust him on that score.* **score** *verb* 1 to win points in a game or competition, to get a goal, try or run in sport. 2 to keep a record of scores. 3 to gain or win success or an advantage. *She is only interested in scoring points over her sister at parties.* 4 to mark or cut lines with a sharp instrument. *Score the card to make it easier to fold.* 5 to write out a musical score. **scorer** *noun. The scorer of most goals gets a medal and a certificate.*

scorn *noun* the feeling that somebody or something is worthless, contempt. **scorn** *verb* to show scorn. *She admires the rich and scorns the poor.* **scornful** *adjective. She is scornful about boys.* **scornfully** *adverb.*

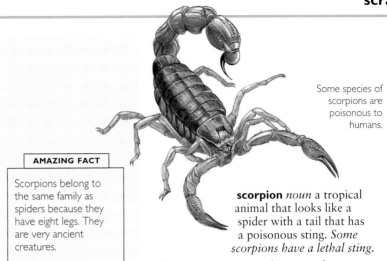

Some species of scorpions are poisonous to humans.

AMAZING FACT

Scorpions belong to the same family as spiders because they have eight legs. They are very ancient creatures.

Scooters are popular again in some countries.

DID YOU KNOW

The first language of Scotland was Gaelic, which was introduced by Celts from Ireland about 1400 years ago. This became the native tongue of the Highlands and Islands of northern and western Scotland. English was introduced into these areas when it started being used in schools in the mid-18th century, but Gaelic is still spoken in the region today.

scorpion *noun* a tropical animal that looks like a spider with a tail that has a poisonous sting. *Some scorpions have a lethal sting.*

Scot *noun* a person who comes from Scotland.

Scotland *noun* a country that is part of the United Kingdom.

Scots *noun* a dialect of the English language spoken in Scotland. **Scots** *adjective. A Scots writer from Glasgow.*

Scottish *adjective* from or belonging to Scotland. *The Scottish team.*

scour *verb* to clean something by rubbing it with rough material. *She scoured the pans.*

scour *verb* to search everywhere. *She scoured the papers for information.*

scout *noun* 1 somebody sent out to get information or look for talented sportsmen. 2 a member of the Scout Association. **scout** *verb* to go about looking for somebody or something. *We scouted around for a good hotel, but without any luck.*

scowl *noun* an angry expression on the face. **scowl** *verb* to frown to show anger. *He didn't say anything, he just scowled at me.*

scrap *noun* 1 a small piece, especially something unwanted or a small amount. *A scrap of paper.* Scraps are pieces of food that are usually thrown away. 2 waste material, especially metal. *Scrap metal.* **scrap** (scraps, scrapping, scrapped) *verb* to throw something unwanted away or cancel a plan or an idea.

After the accident, Gerry's car was totalled and he to sold it as scrap.

scrap heap *noun* a pile of waste, unwanted things and ideas. *That plan might as well go on the scrap heap, it'll never work.*

scrape *verb* 1 to remove something by pulling or pushing a knife or other object over it. *He scraped the mud from his boots.* 2 to make something clean or smooth by pulling a knife or something rough over it. *She scraped the carrots before boiling them.* 3 to rub roughly or damage by rubbing. *He scraped his knee.* 4 to get or pass something with difficulty. *She scraped through the exam.* **scrape by** to get just enough food or money to stay alive. **scrape** *noun* 1 a scraping movement or sound. 2 damage or hurt caused by scraping. 3 a difficult position, usually caused by yourself. *She got into a scrape for not doing her homework.*

scraper *noun* a tool for scraping.

scratch *verb* 1 to rub, cut or mark with something sharp or rough. *The cat scratched me.* 2 to rub the skin to stop itching. 3 to withdraw from a race or competition before it starts. **scratch** *noun* 1 a mark, cut or injury made by scratching. 2 the action or sound of scratching. *The dog scratches all day long.* **scratchy** *adjective.* **start from scratch** to start from the beginning. **be up to scratch** to be good enough.

scrawl *verb* to write messily. *He scrawled a message on the pad.* **scrawl** *noun.*

scrawny (scrawnier, scrawniest) *adjective* thin and bony. *A scrawny pigeon.*

scream *noun* 1 a loud cry or noise, usually because of pain or fear. *I could hear screams of laughter.* 2 somebody or something very funny. *You'd like her, she's a scream.* **scream** *verb* to make a scream.

screen *noun* 1 a flat surface on which television pictures, films or photographs are shown. *A computer screen.* 2 an upright frame, usually made to fold, used to divide a room or other area. 3 something that gives protection or hides. **screen** *verb* 1 to shelter, hide, protect or divide something or somebody. *The trees screened her from view.* 2 to show a film on television or in the cinema. 3 to examine or look carefully at somebody's ability or health. **screen off** to make part of a room into a separate area.

If you stare at the screen on your computer all day, you may risk eyestrain or headaches.

I bought Bob a set of screwdrivers to thank him for fixing my washing machine.

A scroll is like a book on one long sheet of paper. The reader unrolls and rolls it as he or she reads.

WORD HISTORY

'Scuba' comes from the first letters of the words 'self-contained underwater breathing apparatus'.

AMAZING FACT

Word meaning changes as our lifestyles change. For example, the meaning of 'scroll' has changed since computers have become such an important part of our lives. It still has the original meaning of a roll of paper but it also means to move up or down a screen to view more information.

screw *noun* 1 a metal pin with spiral grooves round it used for fastening or holding things together. 2 a turning movement or something that twists like a screw. *He gave it another screw to make sure it was tight.* 3 a propeller on a ship or plane. 4 slang for a prison guard.

screwdriver *noun* a tool for turning screws.

scribble *verb* 1 to write quickly and messily. 2 to make meaningless marks or rough drawings. **scribble** *noun. I can't read her scribble.*

script *noun* 1 a written form of a play, film or talk. *He writes scripts for television programs.* 2 handwriting. 3 a particular system of writing. *Arabic script.*

scripture *noun* sacred writing.

scroll *noun* 1 a long roll of paper or other material with writing on it. 2 a spiral design.verb

scrotum (say **skroh**-tum) *noun* the bag of skin that holds the testicles.

scrounge *verb* to get something, usually money or food, by asking for it without paying or working for it. **scrounger** *noun.*

scrub (scrubs, scrubbing, scrubbed) *verb* 1 to clean by rubbing hard, usually with a brush. *She scrubbed the floor.* 2 to cancel. *The game was scrubbed.* **scrub** *noun.*

scrub *noun* low-growing bushes and trees or land covered with them.

scruffy (scruffier, scruffiest) *adjective* dirty and messy. **scruffiness** *noun.*

scrum, scrummage *noun* 1 a group of rugby players from both teams pushing against each other to get the ball. 2 a crowd pushing against each other.

scuba *noun* a container of air under pressure which a diver carries on his back and uses for breathing while swimming under water.

scuba-diving *noun* swimming underwater using a scuba tank.

sculpt *verb* to carve or model shapes in clay, wood or metal. **sculpture** *noun* the art of making shapes in wood, clay or metal or the shape made in this way. **sculptor** *noun* an artist who makes sculptures.

scum *noun* 1 a covering of dirt on top of water or other liquid. 2 worthless people.

scurf *noun* bits of dry, dead skin in the hair.

scurvy *noun* a disease caused by not eating enough fruit and vegetables with vitamin C.

scythe *noun* a tool with a long curving blade on a long handle for cutting grass.

sea *noun* 1 salty water that covers most of the Earth's surface. 2 a particular area of the sea surrounded by land. *The North Sea.* 3 a large number. *A sea of daffodils.* **by the sea** at the seaside. **at sea** 1 on the sea. 2 confused. *She was completely at sea.*

seagull *noun* a seabird.

Seagulls eat worms on land and fish at sea.

sea horse *noun* a very small upright fish with a head that looks like a horse.

seal *noun* a large sea-animal without legs but big flippers that eats fish and lives both on land and in the sea.

seal *noun* 1 something stuck to a letter or container that must be broken before opening. *The seal on the package was damaged.* 2 a piece of wax or lead stamped with a design or fixed to documents to show that they are official. 3 the metal tool with the design or a small decorative sticker for sealing a letter or document. 4 something made to close an opening to stop gas, air or liquid getting out. **seal** *verb* 1 to close something tightly. *To seal an envelope.* 2 to put a seal on something. 3 to stop something up or close an opening. *He sealed the cracks with mud.* 4 to make something certain. *We sealed the agreement by shaking hands.* **seal off** to close tightly to stop somebody or something from getting in or out. *The police sealed off the street around the accident.*

sea level *noun* the height of the sea halfway between high and low tide, used for measuring height on land and depth at sea. *1,000 meters above sea level.*

sea lion *noun* a kind of large seal.

seam *noun* 1 a line of stitches that joins two pieces of cloth together or a line where two edges meet. 2 a long layer of coal or another mineral in the ground.

SPELLING NOTE

When it is used with names, 'sea' is written with a capital 's': 'the North Sea'. The biggest sea in the world is the South China Sea, which is part of the Pacific Ocean. The next three biggest are the Caribbean Sea, the Mediterranean Sea and the Bering Sea.

AMAZING FACT

Seahorses swim by moving a fin located in the middle of their backs. They are strange, delicate-looking creatures – and their behavior is unusual, too. The males, not the females, take care of the eggs until they hatch by keeping them in a pouch on their belly.

search *verb* 1 to look carefully through a place to try to find something. *She searched for her purse.* 2 to examine somebody's clothing for something hidden. *They were searched by the police.* **search** *noun*.

seasick *adjective* feeling sick when travelling in a ship. **seasickness** *noun*.

seaside *noun* a place at the edge of the sea, especially one where people go for their holiday. *Let's take a trip to the seaside.*

The children loved the seaside.

season *noun* 1 one of four periods of time each year. The four seasons are spring, summer, fall (autumn) and winter. 2 the time of year when something usually happens. *The football season.* **in season** available and ready for eating. *Peaches are in season.* **out of season** 1 not available. 2 not busy. *We usually go to Venice out of season, when it is easy to find a cheap hotel.*

| Winter | Spring | Summer | Fall or Autumn | Winter |

As the seasons change, so the leaves bud, open, flourish, dry and eventually drop.

season *verb* 1 to add salt, pepper or other spices to food to give it a special taste. 2 to leave wood to dry so it can be used. **seasoning** *noun* salt, pepper and spices used to season food.

season ticket *noun* a ticket that can be used whenever you like during a fixed period of time.

seat *noun* 1 a place for sitting on or the part you sit on. *I prefer to sit in the back seat.* 2 a place an official member holds. *A seat on the committee.* 3 a place where something is. *Rochester is the county seat.* **take a back seat** to leave decisions to others. **seat** *verb* 1 to have enough seats for. *The stadium seats 50,000 people.* 2 to sit down.

seat belt *noun* a belt fixed to the seat of a car or plane which you fasten around you for safety. *Fasten your seat belts ready for take-off, please.*

seaweed *noun* a plant that grows in the ocean.

seaworthy *adjective* in good condition and fit for a sea voyage. **seaworthiness** *noun*.

second *adjective* 1 next in order after the first. *February is the second month of the year.* 2 another or extra. *Many families have a second car.* **second** *adverb*.

second *noun* 1 a length of time. There are 60 seconds in a minute. 2 a very short time, a moment. *Wait a second.* 3 a person or thing that is second. *I was the second to arrive.* 4 a thing that is not the best. Seconds are goods that are sold cheaply, usually because they are of lower quality. **second** *verb* to help or speak in support of somebody. *I seconded her proposal.*

second-hand *adjective* owned by somebody else before. *We bought a second-hand car.*

second-rate *adjective* of poor quality.

secret *adjective* 1 not told or shown to anybody else, not known by everybody. *We made a secret plan to leave before midnight.* **secret** *noun* something secret. **secrecy** *noun* the habit of keeping secrets. **secretive** *adjective*. *Secretive whisperings.*

Philip confided his most secret thoughts to his diary.

secretary (secretaries) *noun* 1 somebody whose job it is to deal with letters, telephone calls and arranging meetings and other business affairs. 2 a government official. *The Secretary of State.*

sect *noun* a small group of people who have the same religious or political beliefs.

section *noun* 1 a part of something larger. *Picture books go in the children's section.* 2 one of a number of equal parts that can be put together. 3 a cross-section. *This a section through an apple.* **sectional** *adjective*.

secular *adjective* not religious.

secure *adjective* 1 safe, well protected against danger. *Secure locks and windows.* 2 firmly fixed or certain not to be lost. *She has a secure job.* 3 not worried, happy. *Small children need to feel secure with their parents.* **secure** *verb* 1 to make something safe from harm or attack. 2 to get, usually after having made an effort. *We managed to secure two tickets for the concert.* 3 to fix firmly in position. *The shelf was secured to the wall.* **securely** *adverb*. **security** *noun*.

AMAZING FACT

The difference between 'to see' and 'to look' is attention, like the difference between 'hear' and 'listen'. In other words, you can see something, then decide to pay attention and look at it.

WORD HISTORY

The word 'secret' comes from the Latin 'secretus', meaning 'separate' or 'hidden'. 'Secretary' comes from the same source, because it originally referred to a person who was entrusted with a secret.

AMAZING FACT

Plants use a variety of methods to scatter or spread their seeds. Some seeds, such as those from the maple tree, have wings that carry them on the wind. Others, like the acorns produced by oak trees, are stored or eaten by animals. Some seeds have tiny hooks that stick to the fur of animals, allowing them to 'hitch a ride'.

When a seed germinates, it sends up a shoot and sends down a root. It needs water, warmth and light to do this.

sedative *noun* a drug that calms you or helps you go to sleep.

sediment *noun* solid material that sinks to the bottom of a liquid.

Sediment was heaped at the side of the pond.

seduce *verb* to tempt or persuade somebody to do something they might not normally do. *The sales seduced me into buying myself new clothes.* **seductive** *adjective*. **seduction** *noun*.

see (sees, seeing, saw, seen) *verb* 1 to use your eyes, to look at something. 2 to visit or meet. *He has to see the doctor.* 3 to understand. *I see what you mean.* 4 to watch a film or play. 5 to make sure something is done. *I'll see that dinner is ready.* 6 to imagine or tell what might happen. *I can't see him giving the money back.* 7 to go with somebody, to accompany. *Can you see her home?* 8 to learn something, usually by reading about it. *I see that your team has been promoted.* **see you!** goodbye! **see about** to make arrangements for something to be done. *My brother will see about the tent.* **we'll see about that** perhaps. **see off** to go to the airport or station with somebody who is going on a trip to say goodbye. **see through** 1 to see the truth about somebody or something, not to be fooled. *He made all sorts of promises, but I saw through him.* 2 to support or help until the end. **see to** to take care of, to deal with something.

seed *noun* 1 the small hard part of a plant from which a new plant grows. 2 one of the players named as the best before the start of a competition. *The top seeds don't play against each other in the early rounds.* **seed** *verb* 1 to plant or grow seeds. 2 to place players, especially tennis players, in order of likelihood of winning.

seedling *noun* a young plant raised from seed. *The seedlings are in the greenhouse.*

seedy (seedier, seediest) *adjective* looking poor, run-down or uncared for. *He lives in a seedy part of town.*

seek (seeks, seeking, sought) *verb* to search for, to try to get or find.

seem *verb* to appear to be, to give the impression of being something. *It seemed like a good idea at the time.* **seemingly** *adverb*.

seen *verb* past tense of see.

seep *verb* to flow slowly through a small opening. *The water seeped slowly away.*

see-saw *noun* a teeter-totter, a plank balanced in the middle for children to sit on at each end, so that when one end goes down the other goes up. **see-saw** *verb* to move backwards and forwards or up and down.

seethe *verb* 1 to be very angry, excited, or upset about something. *She was seething with rage.* 2 to bubble as if boiling.

segment *noun* a part marked or cut off from other parts. *Split the oranges into segments.*

Annette divided the orange into segments and offered one to each of the triplets.

segregate *verb* to put somebody or something apart from the rest. *It is wrong to segregate people by the color of their skin.* **segregation** *noun*. *Religious segregation causes wars.*

seismic *adjective* of earthquakes or sudden shakings of the ground. *There is a lot of seismic activity in the area.*

seismology *noun* the study of earthquakes. **seismologist** *noun*.

seize *verb* 1 to take hold of suddenly and forcefully or to take control of. *Panic seized us.* 2 to take by force, to arrest or capture somebody. *The goods were seized by the police.* 3 to take and use something, especially a chance or an idea. **seize up** to become unable to move. *My back seized up after the tennis match.*

seldom *adverb* not often.

select *verb* to choose somebody or something. **selection** *noun*.

self (selves) *noun* somebody's personality or nature. *She is her old self again.*

self- *prefix* done by or to yourself.

Luke and Hannah enjoyed choosing their own food at the self-service restaurant.

self-centered *adjective* interested only in yourself. *A very self-centred child.*

self-confidence *noun* a feeling of power or confidence to do things successfully. **self-confident** *adjective*.

self-conscious *adjective* embarrassed and nervous because you know or think people are looking at you. *I'm too self-conscious to be a good actor.*

self-contained *adjective* complete in itself. *The apartment is a self-contained unit.*

self-control *noun* control over your feelings. **self-controlled** *adjective*. *He is very self-controlled and never loses his temper.*

self-defence *noun* the use or skill of defending yourself.

James always excelled himself in his self-defence class.

self-employed *adjective* working for yourself and not for an employer. **self-employment** *noun*.

self-explanatory *adjective* clear and needing no explanation.

self-important *adjective* having a high opinion of yourself. **self-importance** *noun*.

self-respect *noun* a feeling of pride in your own ability and respect for yourself.

self-sacrifice *noun* giving up what you want, so others can have it.

self-satisfied *adjective* very pleased with yourself. **self-satisfaction** *noun*.

self-service *adjective* a system in stores, restaurants or gas stations where you serve yourself and pay a cashier.

self-sufficient *adjective* able to make or produce everything that is needed without outside help. A self-sufficient country does not have to buy goods from other countries. *The country has enough raw materials to be entirely self-sufficient.* **self-sufficiency** *noun*.

selfish *adjective* thinking mainly of yourself and what you want. **selfishness** *noun*. **selfishly** *adverb*.

sell (sells, selling, sold) *verb* to give something in exchange for money. **sell out** 1 to sell everything so there is nothing left. *They have sold out of sunglasses.* 2 to agree secretly to work for the other side, to betray. **sell up** to sell everything you have. *I'll sell up and leave.* **seller** *noun*.

semen *noun* (say **seem**-un) the fluid produced by the male sex organs that carries sperm for fertilizing.

semi- *prefix* half or partly. *A semi passed us and honked its air horn.*

semicircle *noun* one half of a circle. **semicircular** *adjective*.

semicolon *noun* a punctuation mark (;) used in writing that separates different parts of a sentence.

senate *noun* 1 the upper house or council in the government of some countries, for example in the USA, France and Australia. 2 the highest council of state in ancient Rome.

senator *noun* a member of a senate.

send (sends, sending, sent) *verb* 1 to make somebody or something go or be taken somewhere. 2 to make something move quickly in a direction. *The explosion sent glass flying everywhere.* 3 to cause somebody to feel in a particular way. **send for** to ask somebody to come or order something. *They sent for an ambulance and it arrived within a few minutes.* **send up** to make something go up. *The coffee shortage has sent the prices up.*

Senegal *noun* a country in Africa.

The flag of Senegal has green, yellow and red strips, with a star in the center.

senile *adjective* mentally confused because of old age. **senility** *noun*.

senior *adjective* 1 older in age. 2 higher in rank. 3 A senior citizen. **seniority** *noun*.

Fresh produce is sold at the Farmers' Market every Saturday.

During the mating season a warthog's sense of smell becomes highly developed.

sensation *noun* 1 a feeling, especially of heat or pain. 2 a state of excitement. *The new film created a sensation.* 3 a general feeling in the mind that cannot be described. *It gave me a strange sensation to see the house I lived in as a child.*

sensational *adjective* exciting or shocking.

sense *noun* 1 any of the five senses, the ability to see, hear, smell, touch and taste. 2 the ability to make good judgements, be sensible. *He should have shown a little more sense.* 3 a meaning or explanation. *This word has many senses.* 4 an awareness of something. *She has a great sense of humor!* **make sense** to have a clear meaning. **make sense of** to understand. *Can you make sense of his letter?* **sense** *verb* to become aware of something. *He sensed danger.*

sensibility *noun* sensitiveness.

sensible *adjective* able to make good decisions, wise. *It was not very sensible to leave without a map.*

sensitive *adjective* 1 easily hurt in your feelings or offended. 2 quick to feel the effect of something, easily affected by something. *My eyes are very sensitive to bright light.* 3 being aware of other people's feelings or problems. 4 measuring exactly or showing very small changes. *A very sensitive scale.* **sensitivity** *noun*.

sensual *adjective* enjoyable or giving pleasure to your body. *Eating and drinking were sensual pleasures in ancient Rome.* **sensuality** *noun*.

sent *verb* past tense of send.

sentence *noun* 1 a group of words that form a statement, question or command. When you write a sentence, you start with a capital letter and end with a period. 2 a punishment for a criminal who is found guilty in court. *He received the death sentence.* **sentence** *verb* to give a punishment to somebody in court.

sentiment *noun* 1 an opinion or judgement based on your feelings or thoughts. *We did not agree with the writer's sentiments.* 2 a tender feeling like love, happiness or sadness or memories of the past.

sentimental *adjective* having or showing romantic feelings, usually not reasonable or practical ones. Sentimental songs are about love, sadness or childhood memories. *She keeps her old teddy for sentimental reasons.* **sentimentality** *noun*.

sentry (sentries) *noun* a soldier keeping watch. *The sentry fell asleep on duty.*

A sentry in traditional dress stands on duty outside the Vatican in Rome.

Seoul *noun* the capital of South Korea.

sepal *noun* any of the leaves forming the calyx of a bud.

separate (say **sep**-rut) *adjective* 1 divided, not joined to anything, not shared with another. *She cut it into two separate parts.* 2 different. *He gave her three separate reasons for not going.*

separate (say **sep**-uh-rate) *verb* 1 to keep apart, to be or become divided. *A wall separates our gardens.* 2 to stop living together. *My parents separated when I was eight.* **separation** *noun* 1 separating or being separated. 2 a time of being or living apart.

September *noun* the ninth month of the year. September has 30 days.

septic *adjective* infected with poison. *The wound has turned septic.*

sepulcher *noun* a tomb. *The king was buried in a sepulchre.*

sequel *noun* 1 a book or film that continues the story of an earlier one. 2 an event or situation that follows something else that happened before.

sequence *noun* 1 a number of things that come one after another. 2 the order in which things are arranged. *Don't mix up the tickets, they have to be kept in sequence.* 3 a part of a film when something particular happens. *In the opening sequence the hero changes into a monster.*

This sequence of diagrams shows step-by-step instructions for making a gift bag.

DID YOU KNOW

Seoul has been an important settlement since the 11th century. During the Korean War (1950–53) the city was badly damaged and changed hands four times. The city now has a population of more than 10 million.

serene *adjective* calm and peaceful.

sergeant (say **sar**-junt) *noun* 1 an officer in the army or air force who ranks above corporal. 2 an officer in the police force who has this rank.

serial *noun* a story with a number of separate parts. **serialize** *verb*. *The book has been serialized on television.*

series (series) *noun* a number of things coming one after another or in order. *A series of books on outer space.*

serious *adjective* 1 thoughtful, not cheerful, joking or funny. If something is serious, it is important and has to be thought about carefully. 2 not slight, causing worry. *A serious illness.* **seriously** *adverb*. **seriousness** *noun*.

sermon *noun* 1 a speech given in church. 2 a lecture or telling-off.

serpent *noun* a snake.

A serpent is a symbol of temptation.

servant *noun* somebody who works for another person, usually in their house.

serve *verb* 1 to work for somebody, an organization or your country. 2 to provide with something necessary or be suitable for something. *That old raincoat has served me well.* 3 to help customers in a shop or restaurant. *A very nice waitress served us.* 4 to give or offer food to people. *Strawberries are usually served with cream.* 5 to spend a time in prison. *He has already served three years of his sentence.* 6 to begin a game of tennis by hitting the ball. **it serves you right** it is your own fault. **serve** *noun* serving, as in tennis. *He has a good serve.* **server** *noun*.

service *noun* 1 something that helps people or provides what the public need. *The train service is poor.* 2 a job done for somebody. *You might need the services of a lawyer.* 3 the serving of customers in a shop or restaurant. *The food is good, but the service is slow.* 4 the repairing of cars and other machines. *I took the car in for a service.* 5 a set of plates and dishes. *A tea service.* 6 a religious ceremony. *Morning service.* 7 serving in tennis. **service** *verb* to check or repair a car or other machine. *They routinely serviced the aircraft between flights.*

session *noun* 1 a formal meeting of an organization. *The court is in session.* 2 a meeting or a time used for an activity.

set (sets, setting, set) *verb* 1 to put or place in a position. *The story is set in the mountains.* 2 to fix something. *He set a price for the house.* 3 to cause somebody or something to be in a condition. *They set the house on fire.* 4 to prepare something for use or to start doing something. *To set the table.* 5 to go hard. *Wait for the glue to set.* 6 to give yourself or somebody work or a task. 7 to go down. *The Sun was setting as we arrived at the lake.* **set about** to start doing something. *He doesn't know how to set about getting a job.* **set back** 1 to place something at a distance behind something. *The house is set back from the road.* 2 to delay or make late. *The rain has set back the final.* 3 to cost somebody a lot of money. *How much did the car set you back?* **set off** 1 to begin a journey. 2 to make something begin or happen. *Don't set her off crying.* 3 to cause an explosion. *He set off the rocket.* **set out** 1 to present or make something known. *He set out the rules.* 2 to start a journey. **set to** to begin to do something. **set up** 1 to place in position. *We still have to set up the telescope.* 2 to arrange. *He set up a meeting.* 3 to start, establish. *They set up a new school in the village.*

set *noun* 1 a group of people or things that go together. *A set of screwdrivers.* 2 a radio or TV receiver. 3 the place where a play or film is acted. 4 a group of six or more games that make up part of a tennis match.

setback *noun* something that makes your position less good than it was before.

The chess set was carved out of black and white wood.

settee *noun (old-fashioned)* a small sofa. *The children hid behind the settee when they played hide and seek.*

setting *noun* 1 the surrounding or place in which something is or happens. *A dark forest is the perfect setting for a fairy tale.* 2 the positions in which the controls of a machine are set. *The dishwasher has three settings – hot, cold and economy.*

settle *verb* 1 to decide or fix something. *They have finally settled their quarrel.* 2 to become quiet or make calm, to rest. *The medicine will settle your stomach.* 3 to stay in a place or job, to stop being restless. *He traveled the world and finally settled in Canada.* 4 to sink in liquid or come down and cover something. *The snow is settling.* 5 to pay a bill or money owed. **settle down** 1 to become quiet or calm. 2 to start living a quiet life. *He got married and settled down.* 3 to sit down and concentrate on something.

GRAMMAR NOTE

Watch out for sexism in your writing. Many people now object to the use of 'he' and 'his' when what is really meant is 'he or she' and 'his or hers'. One way round this is to use 'they' or 'their': 'If a student is unsure how to register, they should ask their tutor.' You can also easily avoid male-sounding words, for example by using 'the human race' or 'humans' for 'mankind', etc.

---

settlement *noun* 1 a place people have gone to and built homes in, setting up a community. *There was a settlement near the river.* 2 an agreement or decision between two sides. 3 payment of a debt.

The settlement was made up of conical houses with roofs of straw.

settler *noun* a person who goes to live in a new country.

sever *verb* to break or cut. *He severed all links with his family.*

several *adjective, pronoun* some things or people, usually a fairly small number, not many more than two.

sew (sews, sewing, sewed, sewn) *verb* (say soe) to join pieces of material together or make or mend clothing with a needle and thread or a sewing-machine.

sewage (say soo-ij) *noun* waste material from houses people live and work in which flows through sewers.

sewer (say soo-uh) *noun* a large pipe under the ground that carries sewage away.

sewing machine *noun* a machine for sewing things.

Anita made all her children's clothes on the sewing machine.

sex (sexes) *noun* 1 the condition of being either male or female, gender. *It is difficult to tell what sex the bird is.* 2 the two groups, male and female, into which people and animals are divided. *The opposite sex.* 3 sexual activity by which people and animals produce young and all the activities connected with this act. **sexy** *adjective.*

sexism *noun* the belief that one sex is not as good as the other, especially that women are less able than men.

sexist *adjective* showing sexism. *It's simply sexist to say that women are bad drivers.* **sexist** *noun.*

sexual *adjective* 1 being male or female. *The sexual differences between boys and girls.* 2 connected with sex as male and female activity and the wish for it. 3 connected with the process by which people and animals produce young. **sexually** *adverb*. **sexuality** *noun*.

Seychelles *noun* a country in the Indian Ocean off West Africa.

The Seychelles has a flag of unfurling colors, blue, orange, red, white and green.

shade *noun* 1 darkness under or next to an object, made when something blocks out the Sun. *We sat in the shade of a tree.* 2 Something that keeps out light. *The lamp needs a new shade.* 3 the different forms of a color. How light or dark a color is. *Many shades of blue.* 4 a little bit. *There was a shade of fear in his voice.* 5. a slight difference. *A word with many shades of meaning.* **shade** *verb* 1 to protect something from bright light. *He shaded his eyes with his hand.* 2 to make part of a drawing darker. *She shaded in the background with a pencil.*

shadow *noun* 1 a dark shape on a surface made when something stands between a light and the surface. *I saw his shadow on the wall.* 2 a dark area. *She has shadows under her eyes.* 3 a darkness in a place due to no light reaching it. *The valley is in shadow.* 4 a form not as real as it used to be. *She is just a shadow of her former self.* 5 a little bit. *A shadow of doubt.* **shadow** *verb* 1 to follow somebody secretly. *The detective shadowed the man on his journey through the town.* 2 to make a shadow on something.

shady (shadier, shadiest) *adjective* 1 giving shade. 2 dishonest. *Shady dealings.*

shaft *noun* 1 a long thin pole or handle. *The shaft of an arrow.* 2 a beam of light coming through an opening. 3 a deep, narrow hole.

shaggy (shaggier, shaggiest) *adjective* untidy and rough hair or fur. *A shaggy beard.*

shake (shakes, shaking, shook, shaken) *verb* 1 to move quickly backwards and forwards or up and down. *He shook the pears from the tree.* 2 to shock or upset. *She was shaken by the bad news.* 3 to tremble. *They were shaking with laughter.* **shake hands** to hold somebody's right hand when meeting or saying goodbye to them. **shake your head** to move your head from side to side to say 'no'. **shake** *noun* 1 the action of shaking. 2 a drink. *Milk shake.* **shaky** (shakier, shakiest) *adjective* weak, not very good or unsafe. **shakiness** *noun*.

The shallow part of the river provided an easy crossing for the buffalo.

WORD HISTORY

The word 'shambles', which is plural but usually treated as if it were singular, comes from the Old English 'sceamul', which meant a stall or stool. Stalls were used by butchers to set out their meat for sale, and the word 'shamble' came to mean a slaughterhouse. Presumably the stalls must often have been scattered around a room or street, leading to the modern meaning of a shambles.

These building blocks are made of many different shapes.

shallot *noun* a small onion.

shallow *adjective* 1 not deep. *A shallow river.* 2 not showing much thought, not very serious. *She lives a shallow life.*

sham *noun* something false pretending to be real. *Her friendliness is just a sham.* **sham** (shams, shamming, shammed) *verb*. *She shammed interest.* **sham** *adjective*.

shamble *verb* to walk dragging your feet.

shambles *plural noun* a place or scene of disorder, a mess. *After the party the whole house was a shambles.*

shame *noun* 1 a feeling of guilt or embarrassment. *He had a deep sense of shame after the incident.* 2 feeling sorry about something. *It's a shame you can't come.* **shame** *verb* to feel shame or make somebody feel ashamed. **shameful** *adjective*.

shampoo *noun* 1 a special liquid for washing hair. 2 a liquid for cleaning a car or carpet. **shampoo** *verb* to wash or clean with shampoo. *Please shampoo your hair.*

shape *noun* 1 the outer form of something, an outline. *A square and a circle are shapes.* 2 condition. *She looks in good shape.* **take shape** to develop. **shape** *verb* 1 to make something into a particular shape. *The cake was shaped like a heart.* 2 to develop in a particular way. *Being bullied at school shaped her whole life.*

share *noun* 1 a part belonging, given or done by a person. *He does his share of the housework.* 2 one of the equal parts into which the ownership of a company is divided. *He owns shares in the telephone company.* **share** *verb* 1 to have or use something with others. *She shares a house.* 2 to give a portion of something to others, to divide. *They shared the money between them.*

shark *noun* a large fish with sharp teeth.

Contrary to popular belief, most sharks will not kill humans.

sharp *adjective* 1 with a fine cutting edge or point. *A sharp knife.* 2 clearly seen. *A sharp outline.* 3 quick in thinking, seeing or hearing, quickly aware of things. 4 having a quick change in direction or steep and sudden. *A sharp curve.* 5 severe and sudden, firm. *A sharp frost.* 6 sudden and loud. *A sharp cry of pain.* 7 sour, fresh in taste. *Those berries are too sharp for me, even with sugar sprinkled over them.* 8 a sharp note in music is higher than the normal pitch. **sharply** *adverb.* **sharpness** *noun.*

sharp *adverb* 1 immediately. *Turn sharp left at the church.* 2 exactly, punctually. *We arrived at 3 o'clock sharp.*

shatter *verb* 1 to suddenly break into small pieces. *A stone shattered the windshield.* 2 to destroy or upset. *My hopes were shattered.*

shave *verb* 1 to cut hair off the skin with a razor. 2 to cut or scrape thin pieces off something. *You'll have to shave some wood off the bottom to make the door shut.* **shave** *noun. He needs a good shave.* **a close shave** a near accident or disaster. **shaver** *noun.*

shawl *noun* a piece of material worn around the head or shoulders or wrapped around a baby. *Wrap the baby warmly in the shawl.*

shear (shears, shearing, sheared, shorn) *verb* to cut off hair or wool from sheep.

Sheep are still sheared by hand.

DID YOU KNOW
The Arabic word 'sheikh' is a term of respect and courtesy, dating from pre-Islamic times, that means 'old man'.

WORD BUILDING
The word 'shepherd' is a contraction, or shortening, of the words 'sheep herd', meaning a person who herds sheep.

shears *plural noun* a tool that looks like a large pair of scissors for cutting hedges and long grass. *Shears for shearing sheep.*

shed *noun* a small building for storing things. *A bike shed.*

shed (sheds, shedding, shed) *verb* 1 to flow out or let something fall. *She shed many tears.* 2 to get rid of or give off. *Snakes shed their skin as they grow.*

sheep (sheep) *noun* a farm animal with thick woolly fur. *A flock of sheep.*

sheepish *adjective* embarrassed, usually because you have done something silly. *He gave her a sheepish look.*

sheet *noun* 1 a large piece of cloth, usually cotton, put on a bed. 2 a piece of paper. 3 a large, flat, thin piece of glass, metal or wood. 4 a wide stretch of something thin. *The road was a sheet of ice.*

sheikh (say shake) *noun* an Arab chief or prince. *The sheikh gave the queen a ruby.*

shelf (shelves) *noun* 1 a flat board fixed against a wall or in a cabinet for putting things on. 2 a piece of rock on a mountain that sticks out like a shelf.

shell *noun* 1 the hard outer covering of an animal, egg, fruit, nut or seed. 2 the walls of a building or ship. 3 a metal case filled with explosives for firing from a large gun. **shell** *verb* 1 to take something out of a shell. *She was shelling peas.* 2 to fire explosive shells. *The town was shelled during the attack.*

Karen made a beautiful collection of shells from the beach.

shelter *noun* 1 something that gives protection, usually a small building or covered place. *A bus shelter.* 2 protection or being kept safe. *They found shelter under a tree.* **shelter** *verb* 1 to protect somebody or something from harm. *They sheltered an escaped prisoner.* 2 to take shelter.

shepherd *noun* a person who looks after sheep. *The shepherds watched their flocks.*

shield *noun* 1 a large piece of metal, wood or leather which soldiers used to carry to protect their body. 2 a badge shaped like a shield. 3 a protection, or protective cover. *Sun lotion acts as a shield against the Sun.* **shield** *verb* to protect.

shift *verb* to move from one place to another, to change direction. *She shifted in her seat.* **shift** *noun* 1 a change of position or direction. *A shift in the wind.* 2 the time for which a worker or a group of workers works. *A late shift.* 3 a straight dress.

shifty (shiftier, shiftiest) *adjective* dishonest, not to be trusted.

shilling *noun* 1 a British coin used until 1971 which was worth 12 old pence. 2 an amount of money in some other countries.

shimmer *verb* to shine with a soft light.

shin *noun* the front of the leg between the knee and the ankle.

Getting kicked in the shins can be very painful.

shin

shine *verb* to polish, make bright by rubbing. **shine** *noun* polishing.

shine (shines, shining, shone) *verb* 1 to give off light, to be bright. *The Sun is shining.* 2 to direct light at something. *Can you shine the flashlight on the wall?* 3 to be excellent. *He is good at sports, but he really shines at tennis.* **shine** *noun* a brightness or polish.

shiny (shinier, shiniest) *adjective* looking bright or polished.

ship *noun* a large boat for carrying people or goods.

ship (ships, shipping, shipped) *verb* to take or send goods by ship.

shipshape *adjective* neat and organized.

shipwreck *noun* 1 the loss of a ship at sea. 2 a ship that has been wrecked. **shipwreck** *verb* to lose a ship at sea. *They were shipwrecked on a desert island.*

WORD HISTORY

A 'shoal' of fish is the same as a 'school' of fish. The word 'shoal' probably comes from the Middle Dutch word 'schole' meaning 'school'.

WORD HISTORY

The verb 'to shirk' probably comes originally from the German noun 'Schurke', meaning rogue or scoundrel. 'Only a scoundrel shirks the doing the dishes!'

Terrifying high seas resulted in a shipwreck in which the crew and passengers were drowned.

shipyard *noun* a place where ships are built.

shirk *verb* to try to get out of doing a job. *He is always shirking the yard work.*

shirt *noun* a piece of clothing for the top half of the body, worn with trousers or a skirt. *He was wearing a satin shirt.*

shiver *verb* to tremble, especially with cold or fear. **shiver** *noun*. **shivery** *adjective*. *She has a temperature and feels shivery.*

shoal *noun* a group of fish swimming together. *A shoal of zebrafish surrounded the boat as soon as we threw the bread in the water.*

shock *noun* 1 a strong unpleasant feeling of surprise or fear. *It was a shock to hear that he had died.* 2 a movement from something being hit, an explosion or a crash. *We could feel the shock of the bridge crashing.* 3 the effects of electricity passing through the body, an electric shock. *I got a shock when I touched the wire.* **shock** *verb* to surprise or upset somebody, to make somebody feel shocked. *I was shocked by his rudeness.*

shocking *adjective* very bad or wrong. *A shocking waste of money.*

shoddy (shoddier, shoddiest) *adjective* badly made or done. *Lynne produced truly shoddy work.* **shoddiness** *noun*.

shoe *noun* 1 a covering you wear on your feet, usually made of leather with a hard sole. 2 a horseshoe. **shoe** *verb* to attach a horseshoe to a horse's hooves.

shoelace *noun* a strip of material like a piece of string for tying up shoes.

shone *verb* past tense of shine.

shoo *verb* to make somebody, usually an animal, go away by saying 'shoo' and waving your arms.

shook *verb* past tense of shake.

shoot (shoots, shooting, shot) *verb* 1 to fire a gun or an arrow. 2 to kill or injure somebody by shooting. 3 to kick or throw a ball at a goal or a basket. 4 to move or send quickly in a direction, to move over or through something. *The pain shot up his arm.* 5 to put out new growth or shoots from a stem. 6 to photograph a scene in a film. **shoot** *noun* 1 a young growth of a plant. 2 shooting of a film or still photographs for an advertisement or book.

shop *noun* a small store where a certain type of goods are sold. **shop** (shops, shopping, shopped) *verb* to buy things in a shop. **shopper** *noun*. **shopping** *noun*. *Let's go shopping after school.*

shoplifter *noun* somebody who steals things from stores. **shoplifting** *noun*.

shore *noun* the land along the edge of a large body of water. *We live on the North Shore.*

short *adjective* 1 not long, little in distance or length. Having or taking only a little time. If somebody is short, he is not tall. 2 not enough of something. *We are short of money.* 3 rude, usually because you are angry or impatient with somebody. If somebody has a short temper, they get angry easily. 4 Short pastry is made with a lot of fat and is very crumbly. **for short/ short for** abbreviated. *My name is William, Will for short.* **shortness** *noun*. **short** *adverb* suddenly. *He stopped short at the edge of the cliff.* **short** *noun* a short film.

shortage *noun* lack of something, not having enough. *There is a terrible food shortage in Sudan.*

shortcoming *noun* a fault or defect.

shorten *verb* to make or become short.

shorthand *noun* a way of writing that uses special signs or shorter forms for words and phrases, so something can be written down as fast as somebody is saying it.

shortly *adverb* 1 soon, in a little time. 2 in a few words. 3 in a cross way, not politely.

shorts *plural noun* short pants.

short-sighted *adjective* 1 not considering the long-term effects of something. 2 not able to see things far away without glasses.

shot *verb* past tense of shoot.

shoulder *noun* the two parts of the body between the neck and the top of the arms. *He put the backpack over his shoulder.* **shoulder** *verb* 1 to take on something, especially a problem or responsibility. 2 to push with the shoulder. *He shouldered his way through the crowd.*

shout *noun* a loud call or cry. **shout** *verb* to cry or call loudly.

shove *verb* to push roughly. **shove** *noun*.

shovel *noun* a tool used for digging or lifting and moving sand, soil, snow and other things. **shovel** (shovels, shoveling, shoveled) *verb* 1 to move, lift and work with a shovel. *He shoveled the snow off the driveway.* 2 to push a lot of something quickly into a place. *Don't shovel the food into your mouth!*

AMAZING FACT

A West German man, Hans-Gunter Winkler, has won a record number of show-jumping events. He has the Men's World Championship twice, the European Championship and has won five Olympic gold medals,

There was a wonderful flower show in the park.

AMAZING FACT

The phrase, 'a parting shot', which means to say or do something as you leave, was originally 'a Parthian shot'.

The Parthians were an ancient kingdom in Western Asia. As the Parthian troops retreated, they customarily fired a final shot at the enemy.

Dean used the shovel to move the huge pile of gravel.

show (shows, showing, showed, shown) *verb* 1 to allow or offer to be seen. 2 to be seen easily, to be noticeable. *Any marks show on white.* 3 to demonstrate, or make somebody understand something. *He showed me how to use the computer.* 4 to point to a mark or number. 5 to guide. *The waitress showed us to our seats.* 6 to prove or make something clear. *Her grades show that she has really worked hard this year.* 7 to act towards somebody in a certain way. *He shows no pity for the homeless.* **show off** to show something to impress people. **show up** 1 to arrive at a place. *Only a few people showed up at the party.* 2 to be seen clearly, be noticeable. **show** *noun* 1 a public showing, a collection of things to be looked at. 2 a performance in a theater, on television or in a club. 3 a way of behaving. If something is for show, it is only done to make a good impression. **on show** to be seen by the public. *His paintings are on show at the gallery.* **showy** *adjective* too noticeable, gaudy. *The decor was showy and obviously expensive, without being attractive.*

show business *noun* the business of entertainment. If you are in show business, you work in television, films or the theater.

shower *noun* 1 a short rainfall. 2 a fall of many small things arriving at the same time. *She was covered in a shower of blossom.* 3 a device, usually in the bathroom, for washing yourself that sprays water. 4 a wash under a shower. 4 a party for a woman getting married or having a baby. **showery** *adjective*. **shower** *verb* 1 to give someone things. 2 to have a shower.

Peter had a relaxing shower after work.

showjumping *noun* the sport of riding a horse over fences and barriers.

shown *verb* past tense of show.

shred *noun* 1 a small piece torn or cut off something. 2 a very small amount. *There is not a shred of truth in what he says.* **shred** (shreds, shredding, shredded) *verb* to cut or tear into shreds.

shrewd *adjective* having common sense, clever. *She is a very shrewd businesswoman.*

shriek *noun* a sudden loud, wild cry. *A shriek of laughter.* **shriek** *verb*.

shrill *adjective* high-sounding and painful to the ear. *A shrill voice.*

shrimp *noun* a small shellfish with a long legs and a tail like a fan.

shrine *noun* a holy place where people pray. *They left offerings at the shrine.*

The Temple of Angkor Wat become a Buddhist shrine in the 1500s.

shrink (shrinks, shrinking, shrank, shrunk) *verb* 1 to become smaller in size. *The sweater has shrunk in the wash.* 2 to move back, usually in fear. 3 to avoid doing something because it is not pleasant. **shrinkage** *noun*.

shrivel (shrivels, shriveling, shriveled) *verb* to become dry and wrinkled.

shrub *noun* a small bush.

shrug (shrugs, shrugging, shrugged) *verb* to raise your shoulders to show that you don't know or don't care. **shrug** *noun*.

shudder *verb* to tremble with fear, cold or horror. **shudder** *noun*.

shuffle *verb* 1 to walk by dragging your feet. 2 to mix up the order of a pack of playing cards before beginning a game. **shuffle** *noun*.

These cards haven't been shuffled yet.

WORD HISTORY

The word 'shrewd' used to have a much more negative meaning than it does today. At first it meant 'wicked' or 'cruel'. Then it came to mean 'strict' or 'harsh', before taking on a sly slant.

WORD HISTORY

The original Siamese twins, Chang and Eng (1811–74), were joined at the hip. They were called Siamese because they were born in Siam, which is now called Thailand. Since that time many pairs of Siamese twins have been successfully separated.

shun (shuns, shunning, shunned) *verb* to avoid. *I was hurt when he shunned me.*

shut (shuts, shutting, shut) *verb* 1 to move into a covered, blocked or folded-together position, to close. 2 to close for a period of time or stop business. **shut down** to stop business or work. *The factory has shut down.* **shut in** to leave or lock in a room. *He shut himself in his room to work.* **shut up** 1 to make a place safe before leaving. 2 to stop talking or stop somebody from talking.

shutter *noun* 1 a cover fitted on the outside of a window that can be opened or shut to keep out the light. *Please close the shutters.* 2 the part in a camera that opens to let in light when a photograph is taken.

The light is regulated by the shutter. It travels through the lens and on to the film inside the camera.

Shutter

shuttle *noun* 1 a train, bus or aircraft that makes regular journeys between two places. *There is a shuttle service between the sports ground and the campus.* 2 a pointed instrument used in weaving by which a thread is carried between other threads. 3 a spacecraft used to make a number of journeys into outer space, a space shuttle. **shuttle** *verb* to move or send backwards and forwards.

shy *adjective* nervous and uncomfortable when with others. *He is too shy to speak up.* **shyly** *adverb*. **shyness** *noun*.

shy (shies, shying, shied) *verb* to move away suddenly. *The horse shied at the sound of the police siren.*

Siamese twins *plural noun* twins who are born with their bodies joined together. *The Siamese twins were successfully separated and grew up happily.*

sibling *noun* a brother or sister.

sick *adjective* 1 ill, not well. 2 likely to vomit or throw up food. *Going on a boat always makes me feel sick.* 3 angry or fed up. *I'm sick of housework.* 4 making fun of misfortune or illness. *He told some sick jokes.* **sickly** *adjective*.

sickness *noun* 1 illness or bad health. 2 a disease. 3 feeling sick, vomiting.

S

side *noun* 1 a surface of something that is not the top or the bottom. 2 one of the two surfaces of something flat. *Please write on both sides of the paper.* 3 the two halves of an area which could be divided by a line in the middle, the right or the left part of your body, or a place next to somebody or something. *I've got a pain in my left side.* 4 an edge or border. *Our friends live on the other side of town.* 5 an upright surface of a building or mountain. 6 a particular position in a discussion, or a group which holds a particular position. *Which side is he on?* 7 a team. **on the side** as a sideline. *She sells flowers on the side.* **side by side** next to one another. **to be on the safe side** to be careful and prepared in case something happens. **side** *verb* to take somebody's side. *My mother always sides with my brother.*

side effect *noun* an effect in addition to the intended one. *This drug can have extremely unpleasant side effects.*

siege *noun* an operation, usually by an army, surrounding a place to force it to give in by stopping food reaching the people in it. *The town was under siege for months.*

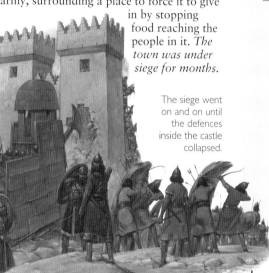

The siege went on and on until the defences inside the castle collapsed.

Sierra Leone *noun* a country in Africa.

siesta (say see-est-uh) *noun* a rest or nap in the afternoon.

sieve (say siv) *noun* a tool, mainly used in the kitchen, made of wire or plastic net on a metal ring for liquid or soft parts to pass through and large lumps to be left in the net. **sieve** *verb* to put something through a sieve.

sift *verb* 1 to put something through a sieve. 2 to examine something carefully. *He sifted through his papers to find the letter.*

sigh *verb* to let out a deep breath with a sound as a sign of tiredness, sadness or gladness. **sigh** *noun* the act or sound of sighing. *She breathed a sigh of relief when the job finally came to an end.*

The skull and crossbones flag was originally the sign of pirates.

sight *noun* 1 the ability to see. 2 the act of seeing something or something seen or worth seeing. *We went to see the sights of Florence.* 3 something that looks very bad or laughable to look at. *Her hair looks a real sight.* 4 the distance within which things can be seen. *She doesn't let the children out of her sight.* 5 a part of a telescope or gun you look through to help you aim. **in sight** likely to happen very soon. *A cure is in sight.* **catch sight of** to see for a moment. **know somebody by sight** to recognize somebody without ever having spoken to them or knowing their name. **sight** *verb* to see something for the first time by coming near. *After a month at sea they sighted land.*

sightseer *noun* a tourist visiting interesting places. **sightsee** *verb*. **sightseeing** *noun*.

sign *noun* 1 a mark or shape that has a particular meaning. *A dove is a sign of peace.* 2 a movement of the body showing a particular meaning. *Putting your finger to your lips is a sign to be quiet.* 3 a board or notice that gives a warning or piece of information. *A road sign.* 4 something that shows that something exists or is happening. *A temperature is the first sign of the flu.* **sign** *verb* 1 to make a movement as a sign to somebody. 2 to write your name on a document or form as a sign of agreement. *We signed the contract.*

sign language *noun* a way of talking, usually to deaf people, by using hand movements.

signal *noun* 1 a sound or action that warns, gives a message or causes something else to happen. *Smoke signals.* 2 a piece of equipment, usually with colored lights, at an intersection or a railroad crossing that tells traffic whether to stop or go . 3 a sound or picture sent by radio or TV. **signal** (signals, signaling, signaled) *verb* 1 to make a signal to somebody. 2 to show an intention by using a signal. *He signaled right, but went left.* 3 to be a sign of something.

The signal turned red just as we got to the corner.

signature *noun* a person's name written by himself or herself, usually at the end of a letter or document.

significant *adjective* meaningful or important. *Significant considerations.*

Sikh (say seek) *noun* a member of an Indian religious group.

silence *noun* 1 the absence of sound, extreme quietness. 2 not speaking, making a noise, answering questions or mentioning a particular thing. **silence** *verb* to stop somebody or something from speaking or making a noise.

silent *adjective* not speaking, totally quiet.

silhouette (say sil-oo-ett) *noun* 1 an outline of a dark shape against a light background. 2 an outline drawing filled in with black or cut out of black paper. **silhouette** *verb*. *The church was sharply silhouetted against the sky.*

The church stood out in dramatic silhouette against the night sky.

silk *noun* a soft, fine cloth made from the fine thread produced by silkworms. *A luxurious silk scarf.*

silkworm *noun* a type of caterpillar that produces a silk covering for its body (cocoon) which is used to make silk.

sill *noun* a flat shelf at the bottom of a window. *A plant on the window sill.*

silly (sillier, silliest) *adjective* foolish. *It was such a silly question.*

silt *noun* fine sand or mud that is carried along by a river. **silt up** to fill or become blocked with silt.

silver *noun* 1 a valuable soft metal used for making ornaments, jewelry and coins. 2 the color of silver. 3 coins and things made from silver, especially cutlery and dishes. *She always polishes her silver so it sparkles.* 4 a silver medal, given as the second prize. **silver** *adjective* 1 made of silver. 2 like the color of silver. *Silver paint.*

silver wedding *noun* the 25th anniversary of a wedding.

simile (say **sim**-il-ee) *noun* a comparison of one thing with another, being similar to somebody or something else.

simmer *verb* to cook very gently, just below boiling point. *Simmer the rice for ten minutes, then stir in the beans.*

simper *verb* to smile in a silly way. **simper** *noun*. *I can't stand the way she simpers when the boss asks her to do something.*

WORD HISTORY

The word 'silhouette' was named after Etienne de Silhouette (1709–67), a finance minister of France, but we are not sure why. Silhouette proposed taxing rich people very heavily, and it could be that this is why his name was applied to a thin, minimal drawing. Or perhaps it was simply that Silhouette himself drew such outlines as a hobby.

GRAMMAR NOTE

In a simile two things are compared in order to point out a feature they share. A simile contains the words 'as' or 'like'. For example: 'as blind as a bat'.

---

simple *adjective* 1 easy to understand or do, not difficult. *Give me a simple explanation of how it works.* 2 uncomplicated, without much decoration. Ordinary or plain. *Simple food tastes best.* 3 with nothing added. *The simple truth is, she hopeless at the guitar.* 4 without much intelligence or easily fooled. *He's a bit simple.* **simplicity** *noun*.

simplify (simplifies, simplifying, simplified) *verb* to make something easy to understand. **simplification** *noun*.

sin *noun* 1 the breaking of a religious law or something that should not be done. *Stealing is a sin.* **sin** (sins, sinning, sinned) *verb* to break a religious law or do something that is believed to be very bad. **sinner** *noun*.

since *conjunction, preposition, adverb* 1 from that time until now. *I haven't seen her since they moved.* 2 during or at a time after a particular time or event in the past. *He used to play tennis regularly, but has since given up.* 3 because, used to state a reason for doing or not doing something. *Since you say you are too tired, we won't go for a walk along the beach.*

sincere *adjective* honest, not false. **sincerely** *adverb*. *I sincerely hope that they will believe what he tells them.* 'Sincerely' is written at the end of a letter before your signature. **sincerity** *noun*.

sing (sings, singing, sang, sung) *verb* to make musical sounds with the voice, usually by saying words that fit a tune. *Can you hear the birds singing?* 2 to make a buzzing or ringing sound. **singer** *noun*.

Singapore *noun* a city and country in Southeast Asia.

The flag of Singapore has a red stripe with a white Moon and stars, and a white stripe beneath.

singe (say sinj) *verb* to burn slightly.

single *adjective* 1 only one, not more. 2 not married. 3 for or by one person. *She reserved a single room at the hotel.* 4 considered by itself, separate. *He repeated every single word I said.* **singly** *adverb*. **single** *noun* 1 a small record with one song on each side or a CD with just one song on it. *I liked their new single but the album was disappointing.* 2 a single person or thing.

single-handed *adjective* without help.

singular *noun* a word that expresses one person or thing. **singular** *adjective*.

sinister *adjective* evil or harmful. *The empty house was a sinister place.*

sink *noun* a basin with faucets in the kitchen, the bathroom or the utility room.

sink (sinks, sinking, sank, sunk) *verb* 1 to go down below the surface of water. *The ship sank to the bottom of the sea.* 2 to go or fall down. *She sank to the ground.* 3 to get smaller or less. *Prices are sinking.* 4 to become weaker. *His voice sank to a whisper.* 5 to become depressed. *Her heart sank.* 6 to put money or work into something. *My brother has sunk all his savings into a new car.* 7 to make something hard or sharp go deeply into something. *She sank her teeth into the apple.* **sink in** to be or become understood. *I hope my warning has really sunk in.*

sinus *noun* a space in the bones of the face just behind the nose. *If you have a cold, your sinuses often get blocked.*

sip *verb* to drink taking in small mouthfuls at a time. **sip** *noun. She took a sip of tea.*

sir *noun* 1 You say 'sir' when you speak politely to a man. It is mainly used by young people to older people, or by staff in stores or restaurants. 2 used at the beginning of a formal letter to a man. *Dear Sir.* 3 a title given to a knight or baronet.

siren *noun* 1 a device that makes a long, loud warning sound. Police cars and fire engines have sirens. 2 a dangerously beautiful woman.

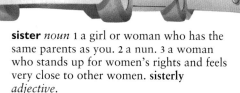

The police cars went into the chase, sirens blaring.

sister *noun* 1 a girl or woman who has the same parents as you. 2 a nun. 3 a woman who stands up for women's rights and feels very close to other women. **sisterly** *adjective.*

sister-in-law (sisters-in-law) *noun* the sister of a person's husband or wife.

sit (sits, sitting, sat) *verb* 1 to be in a position with the upper body upright and the bottom resting on something. 2 to rest on a surface, especially when talking about a bird or animal. *The bird was sitting on a branch.* 3 to meet and work together. *The zoning committee sits once a month.* 4 to be in a place. **sit around** to do nothing for a long time. **sit back** to relax and not do anything while things are happening. **sit tight** to stay in the same place or situation without taking any action. *Sit tight and wait until it's over.*

site *noun* a place where something was or is happening. *A construction site.*

The medical students studied anatomy by looking at a skeleton.

situation *noun* what is happening in a particular place at a particular time or the things that are happening to you. *The situation in Africa looks very bad. What would you do in my situation? Alex will fill you in on the current situation and then we can discuss the next step.*

size *noun* 1 how big or small something is. *The dog had eyes the size of saucers.* 2 a set of measurements, especially for clothes and shoes. *What size does he take?* **size** *verb* to arrange people or things according to their size. **size up** to form an opinion of a person or thing, to decide how to act after thinking about a situation. *It took me a little while to size up the situation.*

sizzle *verb* to make a crackling or hissing sound like the sound made when you fry food. *The bacon sizzled in the pan.*

skate *noun* a boot with a steel blade (ice-skate) or wheels (roller-skate) attached to the sole for skating. **skate** *verb* to move around on ice wearing ice-skates (or on a hard surface wearing roller-skates). *We skated across the frozen lake.*

skate *noun* a large, flat seafish.

skateboard *noun* a board with small wheels at each end for a person to ride on for fun. **skateboarding** *noun.*

skeleton *noun* 1 the framework of bones in a human or animal body. 2 something forming a framework or an outline. *The metal skeleton of the building went up quickly.* **a skeleton in the cupboard** something of which you are afraid or ashamed.

skeleton key *noun* a master key that opens a number of different locks.

sketch (sketches) *noun* 1 a quickly made drawing. *He made a sketch of the castle.* 2 a short description of something. 3 a short, funny piece of writing or acting. **sketch** *verb* 1 to draw something quickly. 2 to give a short description of something with few details. **sketchy** *adjective. A sketchy plan.*

ski *noun* one of a pair of long flat pieces of wood, metal or plastic that are fastened to a ski boot for skiing on the snow. **ski** (skis, skiing, skied) *verb* to move on snow wearing skis. *We're going to Aspen to ski this year.* **skier** *noun.*

skid (skids, skidding, skidded) *verb* to move sideways out of control on wheels. *The car skidded on the icy road.* **skid** *noun.*

skill *noun* the knowledge or ability to do something well. **skillful** *adjective*. *She is a very skillful painter*. **skillfully** *adverb*. **skilled** *adjective*. *A skilled job*.

skim (skims, skimming, skimmed) *verb* 1 to remove cream or other unwanted things from the surface of a liquid. *Skim the cream off the milk*. 2 to read something quickly. *He skimmed the newspaper*. 3 to move quickly along or just above something. *The plane skimmed the treetops, then landed*.

skin *noun* 1 the outer covering of the body. *Fur coats are made from animal skins*. 2 the outer covering of some fruit and vegetables. *He slipped on a banana skin and broke his ankle*. 3 a thin layer that forms on liquid when it gets cool. **skin** (skins, skinning, skinned) *verb* to take the skin off something. *I skinned my knee*.

This cross-section through the skin shows how hairs grow and perspiration reaches the surface.

skinny (skinnier, skinniest) *adjective* very thin. *A skinny little boy*.

skin tight *adjective* fitting tightly against the body.

skip (skips, skipping, skipped) *verb* 1 to jump or hop along lightly. *The children skipped around the garden*. 2 to jump up and down over a rope (jump rope). 3 to leave something out in order to go on to another subject. *I read the book but skipped the boring parts*. 4 to not do something you usually do. *I skipped lunch*. **skip** *noun*.

skipper *noun* a person in charge of a ship.

skirt *noun* a piece of clothing for women or girls that hangs down from the waist. **skirt** *verb* 1 to go around the edge of something. *The old road skirts the town*. 2 to avoid dealing with something. *She tried to skirt the issue because she was embarrassed*.

skit *noun* a short (usually funny) piece of acting. *We did a skit for the talent show*.

Skopje *noun* the capital of Macedonia.

skull *noun* the bones of the head that enclose the brain.

skunk *noun* a small North American black and white animal that gives out a bad smell if it is frightened.

sky (skies) *noun* the space above the Earth that you see when you are outside and look up. *You can see the Moon in the sky*.

skyscraper *noun* a very tall building.

Skyscrapers were originally built so that many people could live in a small area.

slab *noun* a thick flat piece. *A slab of cement*.

slack *adjective* 1 not pulled tight, especially a rope or wire. 2 not firm, weak. *The rules are very slack*. 3 not busy or working hard. *Business is slack*. **slackness** *noun*. **slack** *verb* to not work enough, to be lazy.

slacks *noun*. a pair of pants.

slam (slams, slamming, slammed) *verb* 1 to shut loudly. *Don't slam the door!* 2 to push or put down quickly and with force. *He slammed on the brakes*.

slander *noun* an untrue spoken statement about somebody which damages a person's reputation. **slander** *verb* to harm somebody by making a false statement.

slang *noun* words and expressions used in informal conversation. 'Dough' and 'bread' are slang words for money.

slap (slaps, slapping, slapped) *verb* 1 to hit somebody or something with the palm of your hand. *She slapped his face*. 2 to put roughly or carelessly. *He slapped paint on the walls*. 3 to put down with force. *He slapped the book on the table*. **slap** *noun*.

slapdash *adjective* careless.

slate *noun* 1 a dark gray rock that splits easily into thin layers. 2 a piece of slate used for covering roofs. 3 a small board made of slate which was used for writing on with chalk. **slate** *verb* to criticize severely or attack. *The papers slated his new film*.

The teacher wrote a sum on the slate.

slaughter *verb* 1 to kill animals for food. 2 to kill cruelly, especially many people. **slaughter** *noun*.

slave *noun* somebody who is owned by another and has to work for that person without getting paid. **slave** *verb* to work very hard, like a slave. *I slaved away cleaning the house all Sunday.* **slavery** *noun*.

slay (slays, slaying, slew, slain) *verb* to kill.

sleazy (sleazier, sleaziest) *adjective* dirty and poor-looking. **sleaze** *noun*. **sleaziness** *noun*.

sled *noun* a vehicle for sliding across snow and ice on metal blades. **sled** *verb* to go on a sled.

sleek *adjective* smooth and shiny, especially hair or fur. *A sleek black cat.*

sleep *noun* a rest state of the body when the eyes are closed and the mind is not conscious, a period of sleep. *Most people need about eight hours sleep.* **sleep** (sleeps, sleeping, slept) *verb* to be asleep, to have a sleep. **sleepy** *adjective*. **sleepiness** *noun*.

sleeper *noun* 1 a person who sleeps. *I'm a very light sleeper, so any noise will wake me up.* 2 one of a row of heavy beams supporting a railroad track. 3 a bed on a train. *I reserved a sleeper to Rome.*

sleeping bag *noun* a warm bag made of thick material in which you can sleep, usually when camping.

sleet *noun* a mixture of rain and snow, frozen rain. **sleet** *verb*. *It's sleeting.*

sleeve *noun* 1 the part of a piece of clothing that covers the arm. 2 a stiff envelope for a record or a stiff case for a book.

slender *adjective* thin, slim.

sleuth (say slooth) *noun* a detective.

slice *noun* 1 a thin piece cut from something. 2 a part or share of something. **slice** *verb* 1 to cut into slices. 2 to cut off a slice. 3 to cut through something.

slick *adjective* 1 well-made and good-looking, but not meaningful. *The show was too slick.* 2 clever, but not honest. *A slick salesman.* 3 quick and smooth.

slick *noun* a thin sheet of oil floating on water. *The oil slick damaged the shore.*

Arthur wanted to sleep under the stars, but he didn't realize that his sleeping bag would get damp in the dew.

slide (slides, sliding, slid) *verb* 1 to move smoothly over or on something. *She slid the door open.* 2 to move quietly and quickly, usually in order to go unnoticed. **slide** *noun* 1 the action of sliding. 2 a structure with a slope for sliding down, usually for children in a playground. 3 a small piece of film in a frame that you can look at on a screen or through a viewer to see it bigger. *A slide show.* 4 a glass plate on which something is put to be looked at under a microscope.

We checked each slide under the microscope.

slight *adjective* 1 small and thin. 2 small and not important. *A slight problem.* **slightly** *adverb*. **slightness** *noun*.

slight *verb* to treat somebody without respect. **slight** *noun*.

slim (slimmer, slimmest) *adjective* 1 thin, not fat. 2 small. *There is still a slim chance that we'll tickets for the concert.*

slime *noun* thick, sticky liquid, usually unpleasant. *The snail left a trail of slime.* **slimy** *adjective*. **sliminess** *noun*.

sling *noun* 1 a piece of material tied round the neck to support a broken arm. 2 a loop or an object made of ropes and straps for carrying or lifting things. *She carries her baby in a sling.* **sling shot** a strap for throwing stones, like a catapult. **sling** (slings, slinging, slung) *verb* 1 to throw carelessly. *He slung his bag in the ditch.* 2 to throw with force. *They were slinging stones.* 3 to attach or hold in a sling.

A broken arm supported in a sling helps the healing process

slip (slips, slipping, slipped) *verb* 1 to slide and almost fall because you have lost your balance. 2 to move, go or put something quickly and smoothly, especially without being noticed. *The girl slipped out of the room.* 3 to put on or take off, especially clothes. 4 to get away, escape or be forgotten. *His birthday slipped my mind.* 5 to get worse or fall in quality. **slip up** to make a mistake. **slip** *noun* 1 the act of slipping. 2 a slight mistake. 3 a small piece of paper. 4 a piece of clothing without sleeves that women wear under a dress. **give somebody the slip** to escape from somebody.

slipper *noun* a soft shoe worn indoors.

slippery *adjective* difficult to hold or stand on because of being wet or very smooth.

slipshod *adjective* careless.

slip-up *noun* a slight mistake.

slit *noun* a narrow cut or opening. **slit** (slits, slitting, slit) *verb* to cut or make a slit in.

slog (slogs, slogging, slogged) *verb* 1 to do hard dull work without stopping. 2 to walk in difficult terrain, etc. *They slogged through the mud to the base camp.*

slogan *noun* a short phrase that is easy to remember, mainly used to advertise something. *A catchy slogan.*

slope *noun* 1 a piece of ground that goes up or down. 2 a slanting line or direction. **slope** *verb* to have a slope or to lean to the right or the left. **slope off** to go off quietly, usually in order to avoid work.

slot *noun* a slit, groove or channel. **slot** *verb* to put into a slot.

slot machine *noun* a machine that you put money in to gamble.

slouch *verb* to move with shoulders and head drooping down. **slouch** *noun*.

Slovakia *noun* a country in eastern Europe.

The flag of Slovakia has white, blue and red stripes, and a crest.

Slovenia *noun* a country in Southeast Europe.

slovenly *adjective* careless and untidy. *Their slovenly appearance made a bad impression.*

slow *adjective* 1 taking a long time or too long, not quick. 2 showing a time that is earlier than the correct time. *My watch is five minutes slow.* 3 not able to understand things quickly, not very active. **slow** *verb* to make or become slower. **slowly** *adverb*. **slowness** *noun*.

slow motion *noun* movement that is much slower than in real life, especially as shown in a film or on television. *They showed the touchdown again in slow motion.*

The slopes at Whistler are challenging for the novice.

DID YOU KNOW

Slovakia was part of Hungary until 1918, when it became part of Czechoslovakia. It has been an independent republic since 1993.

GRAMMAR NOTE

People often use 'slow' as an adverb in spoken English: 'Drive/eat slower.' In formal writing, it is better to use 'slowly' as the correct adverb: 'Drive/eat more slowly.'

slug *noun* a small slow-moving animal like a snail without a shell.

sluggish *adjective* slow-moving.

slum *noun* an area of a town that is poor, with dirty streets and bad living conditions.

slumber *noun* sleep. **slumber** *verb*.

slur (slurs, slurring, slurred) *verb* 1 to say words unclearly so they are difficult to understand. 2 to say unfair or bad things. **slur** *noun* 1 a slurring way of speaking. 2 unfair or bad remarks that could damage a person's reputation. *His comments were a slur on my character.*

sly (slyer, slyest, or slier, sliest are also used) *adjective* cunning and not honest, keeping things secret. *A sly fox tricked the red hen.* **on the sly** secretly.

smack *verb* 1 to hit with the hand. 2 to open and close your lips noisily. 3 to put, throw or hit something so it makes a loud noise. **smack** *noun*. **smack** *adverb*. *He drove smack into the wall, fortunately no one was hurt.*

smack *noun* a particular taste. *This smacks of lemon.* **smack** *verb* to have a trace of. *She smacks of money.*

smack *noun* a sailing boat used for fishing.

small *adjective* not big, little in size, weight or importance. **smallness** *noun*.

small change *noun* coins.

small-minded *adjective* thinking in a small way, unwilling to change your mind or listen to others. The opposite of small-minded is broad-minded.

small talk *noun* conversation about unimportant things. *We made small talk.*

smart *adjective* 1 neat and elegant looking. 2 clever. 3 stylish and fashionable. 4 sharp and quick. *They marched by at a smart pace.* **smartly** *adverb*. **smartness** *noun*.

smart *verb* 1 to feel a stinging pain. *My eyes are smarting.* 2 to feel upset, especially about something unkind said or done to you.

smash (smashes) *noun* 1 the action or sound of something breaking to pieces. 2 a car crash. 3 a very successful show or film, a smash hit. 4 a disaster in business. 5 a hard stroke, especially in tennis. **smash** *verb* 1 to break noisily into many pieces. 2 to go, drive, hit or throw with great force. 3 to destroy or ruin.

Alison accidentally smashed the vase.

smear *verb* to spread a soft substance.

smell *noun* 1 the ability the nose has to smell things. *Dogs have a strong sense of smell.* 2 something in things that has an effect on the nose, something you can smell. *A smell of gas.* 3 smelling something. **smell** (smells, smelling, smelled) *verb* 1 to use your nose to discover a smell. *Ooh! Smell this cheese!* 2 to have or give out a smell. If you say something smells, it has a bad smell. 3 to have a feeling or notice. *She smelled trouble.* **smelly** *adjective*.

smile *noun* an expression on the face with the corners of the mouth turned up that shows happiness or friendliness. **smile** *verb* to give a smile.

The photographer said, "Now smile!".

smirk *noun* an unpleasant smile. **smirk** *verb* to give a smirk.

smoke *noun* 1 gas and small bits of solid material that are seen in the air when something burns. *Smoke from the chimney.* 2 smoking a cigarette or pipe. *He likes a smoke.* **smoke** *verb* 1 to give out smoke. *The volcano is smoking.* 2 to have a cigarette, cigar or pipe in your mouth and suck in the smoke and blow it out again. 3 the habit of smoking. *Do you smoke?* 4 to preserve meat or fish by hanging it in smoke. **smoky** *adjective*. **smoker** *noun*.

smolder *verb* 1 to burn slowly without a flame. 2 to have strong feelings without showing them. *She smoldered with hatred.*

smooth *adjective* 1 having an even surface without lumps or holes, not rough. 2 calm and comfortable without sudden bumps. *A smooth ride.* 3 free from lumps, evenly mixed. 4 very polite, almost too pleasant. *I don't trust Gary, he's really too smooth.* 5 pleasant tasting, not sour or bitter. 6 not harsh. *A smooth voice.* **smooth** *verb* to make smooth. **smooth something over** to make a difficulty seem less serious.

smother *verb* 1 to die from not having enough air, or to kill by covering somebody's mouth so they cannot breathe. 2 to put a fire out by covering it with something. *He smothered the flames with a blanket.* 3 to cover thickly. *The cake was smothered in cream.* 4 to control or hold something back. *She tried to smother a yawn, but he saw she was bored.*

smudge *noun* a dirty mark, usually made by rubbing something. **smudge** *verb* to make a smudge on something or become messy.

The smugglers lured a boat on to the rocks with flashing lights by night. The next day, after the ship was wrecked, they brought the treasure ashore.

The snake coiled and hissed dangerously.

smug *adjective* being too pleased with yourself and what you can do. *He had a smug look on his face when he got his prize.*

smuggle *verb* to take something secretly into a country or place. *It is against the law to smuggle drugs.* **smuggler** *noun*. **smuggling** *noun*. *Smuggling is illegal.*

snack *noun* a small, quick meal, especially one eaten between main meals. **snack** *verb*.

snag *noun* 1 a problem or difficulty. 2 a sharp part that sticks out and may catch you in passing. **snag** *verb* to get caught on and tear.

snail *noun* a small animal with a slimy body and a shell on its back. **at a snail's pace** very slowly. *Mom walks at a snail's pace.*

snake *noun* a long thin reptile with no legs and a fork-shaped tongue. Some snakes are poisonous. *A snake slithered out of the tree.*

snap *noun* 1 the action or sound of snapping. *The trap closed with a snap.* 2 a photograph taken quickly, a snapshot. 3 a cookie. *Ginger snaps.* 4 a metal fastener (usualy for clothes) that has two parts that snap together. **snap** (snaps, snapping, snapped) *verb* 1 to break with a sharp cracking noise. *His patience finally snapped.* 2 to make a sharp sound like something breaking. 3 to bite or catch something with the teeth. *The dog snapped at her ankle.* 4 to say something quickly and in an angry way. 5 to move or shut quickly into a position with a sharp sound. 6 to take a photograph. *She snap a shot of us at the beach.* **snap at** to take or get something quickly. *We snapped at the chance of spending a week in the sun.* **snap up** to buy something quickly because it is a bargain. *Kate snapped it up in the sales.*

snap *adjective* done immediately. *A snap decision may sometimes be regretted.*

snare *noun* a trap for catching birds or small animals. **snare** *verb. He snared a rabbit and ate it for his dinner.*

snarl *verb* to growl angrily or speak in an angry voice. **snarl** *noun.*

snarl *noun* a tangle in wool or a tangled-up situation. *Traffic snarls.*

sneak *verb* 1 to move quietly and secretly, trying not to be seen or heard. 2 to take something somewhere secretly. *He sneaked his pet mouse into school.*

sneak *noun* a person who tells others secretly that somebody else had done something bad, a tell-tale. **sneaky** *adjective.* **sneakily** *adverb.*

sneaker *noun* a canvas shoe with a rubber sole.

sneeze *noun* a sudden outburst of air through the nose and mouth. **sneeze** *verb. I felt a tickle in my nose and had to sneeze.*

snide *adjective* intending to hurt your feelings by being nasty, especially in a pretended funny way, about something that is important to you. *She made some snide remarks about my friends.*

sniff *verb* 1 to make a sound by breathing in air through your nose. 2 to smell something. *The dog sniffed the ground.* **sniff** *noun.* **sniffer** *noun.*

snigger *verb* to laugh quietly and in a disrespectful way, especially at something rude. **snigger** *noun.*

snip (snips, snipping, snipped) *verb* to cut with scissors or shears in short quick cuts. *She snipped at my hair.*

snip *noun.* 1 an act of snipping. 2 a bargain. *I had to buy it, it was a real snip.*

snivel (snivels, sniveling, sniveled) *verb* to speak or cry in a sniffing and whining way.

snob *noun* somebody who admires people with money, power and a higher social class. **snobbish** *adjective.* **snobbery** *noun.*

snooker *noun* a game played on a special table in which you hit a white ball with a long stick (cue) and get points each time you knock a colored ball into a pocket at the side of the table.

snooze *noun* a short nap. **snooze** *verb.*

snore *verb* to breathe noisily while asleep. *Peter claims not to snore, but he makes a funny sawing noise while asleep.* **snore** *noun. We could hear their snores next door.*

snorkel *noun* a tube through which you can breathe when you swim under water. **snorkeling** *noun. We went snorkeling on the coral reef in the Florida Keys.*

Each snowflake has an individual pattern never to be repeated.

snort *verb* to make a rough noise by breathing out through the nose. **snort** *noun.*

snout *noun* an animal's long nose. *A pig's snout is ideal for rootling in the ground.*

snow *noun* frozen white bits of water (flakes) that fall from the sky in cold weather and cover the ground. **snow** *verb.*

snowball *noun* snow pressed into a hard ball, for throwing.

snowflake *noun* a tiny and unique piece of snow.

snowman *noun* a shape of a person made of snow. *The children built a snowman.*

snug *adjective* 1 cosy, warm and comfortable. *I love being snug in bed, especially when there's a storm.* 2 fitting very closely or tightly. **snugly** *adverb.*

snuggle *verb* to move into a comfortable position, especially close to another person. *The little boy snuggled up to his mother.*

so *adverb* 1 very, to such an extent. *He is so smart.* 2 in this or that way. *He was wrong and she told him so.* 3 also. *My brother has blue eyes and so has my sister.* 4 when agreeing with something that has been said. *'I didn't manage to tidy up my room.' 'So I see.'* **so** *conjunction* that is why, for that reason. *I missed the bus, so I was late.* **so far** up to now. **or so** about that number. *We've been here for a week or so.* **and so on/forth** and other things like this. *They brought their pens, paints, and so forth.* **so long!** goodbye! **so as to** in order to. *She asked us to come, so as to get to know us.* **so what?** I don't care, it's not important.

soak *verb* to make or become completely wet. *We were completely soaked.* **soak up** to take in liquid. **soak** *noun.*

The car splashed through a puddle and completely soaked Elizabeth, who was just jumping out of the way.

so-and-so *noun* 1 a certain somebody or something that doesn't need to be specified. *She told me to do so-and-so.* 2 a rude or annoying person. *The principal is a real old so-and-so.*

soap *noun* 1 a product used with water for washing and cleaning. *A bar of soap.* 2 a soap opera. **soap** *verb*.

soap opera *noun* a light television or radio serial, usually about the daily life of a group of people. *An Australian soap opera.*

soar *verb* 1 to fly or go up in the air. 2 to rise, increase quickly. *Prices are soaring.*

The eagle soared through the mountain air, watching out for prey.

sob (sobs, sobbing, sobbed) *verb* to cry in gasps. *Linda sobbed all night.* **sob** *noun*.

sober *adjective* 1 not drunk. 2 serious and thoughtful, not silly. 3 dull, not bright. *Sober colors.* **soberly** *adverb*. **sober up** to stop being drunk.

soccer *noun* a game in which two teams of eleven players try to kick a round ball into their opponents' goal.

social *adjective* 1 liking to be with other people, friendly. *It was a the social event of the year.* 2 of somebody's position in society or of relations between people. *Social workers are supposed to help people.* 3 living together by nature. *Social animals live in groups.* **socially** *adverb*.

socialism *noun* a political system in which business and industry are controlled by the government with every person getting an equal share of the state's money. **socialist** *noun, adjective*.

society (societies) *noun* 1 a large group of people in a country who have a particular way of life. *In ancient Greek society women did not have an important role.* 2 a group of people with the same interests.

sock *noun* a piece of clothing that covers your foot. *A pair of socks.*

sock *verb* (slang) to punch.

socket *noun* 1 a device usually in a wall into which you put a plug to make an electrical connection. 2 a hollow opening into which something fits.

sofa *noun* a couch, a soft seat with a back for two or three people to sit on.

Sofia *noun* the capital of Bulgaria.

soft *adjective* 1 not hard, firm. *A soft bed.* 2 smooth to the touch, not rough. *Babies have soft skin.* 3 gentle, not loud or bright. Calm. *Her soft voice.* 4 kind and caring. *A soft heart.* **softly** *adverb*. **softness** *noun*.

soft drink *noun* a drink that is not alcoholic. *Lemonade is a soft drink.*

soften *verb* 1 to make or become soft. 2 to become kinder. 3 to make something less terrible or strong. *He tried to soften the shock by telling some amusing stories.*

software *noun* programs for computers.

soggy (soggier, soggiest) *adjective* unpleasantly wet and heavy. *Soggy ground.*

soil *noun* the earth on which plants and trees grow. *The soil here is very sandy.*

soil *verb* to make or become dirty.

solar *adjective* of or from the Sun. If you heat a building with solar power, you make use of the power of the Sun.

solar system *noun* the Sun and all the planets going around it.

sold *verb* past tense of sell.

soldier *noun* a member of an army.

sole *noun* 1 the bottom of the foot, especially the part you walk or stand on. 2 the flat bottom part of a shoe. 3 a flat fish. **sole** *verb* to put a sole on a shoe.

sole *adjective* being or belonging to only one. *He is the sole survivor.* **solely** *adverb* only. *She acted solely for herself.*

solemn *adjective* 1 serious, not cheerful. 2 formal, in a sincere way. *He made a solemn promise.* **solemnly** *adverb*.

solicitor *noun* a lawyer who gives legal advice to his clients and prepares legal documents. *A solicitor in criminal law.*

solid *adjective* 1 filled up inside, not hollow, with no spaces or gaps. *Solid gold.* 2 not liquid or gas, having a shape. *When milk freezes it turns solid.* 3 of good quality, strong and not flimsy, reliable. *A solid house.* 4 showing complete agreement. 5 continuous, without a break. *I slept for six solid hours.* **solidly** *adverb*. **solidity** *noun*.

solid *noun* 1 something that is solid. *The baby is on solids now.* 2 a solid figure in geometry with length, width and height.

solitary *adjective* 1 alone, without a companion. *A solitary walk.* 2 spending a lot of time alone, lonely. *Bears are solitary animals.* 3 single. *I can't think of a solitary reason for moving.*

solo *noun* a piece or passage performed by one person alone. **solo** *adjective.* **solo** *adverb.* *He flew solo for the first time.*

soloist *noun* a person who plays a piece of music or sings a song alone. **solo** *noun.*

Solomon Islands *noun* a country of many islands in the Pacific Ocean.

solution *noun* 1 an answer to a question or problem. 2 a liquid in which something has been dissolved. *Bathe the cut knee in a solution of salt and water.*

solve *verb* to find the answer to a problem or puzzle. *Try and solve this riddle.*

Somalia *noun* a country in Africa.

somber *adjective* dark and gloomy, or serious and sad. *Somber music filled the chapel.*

some *adjective* 1 a small number or amount, a few. 2 somebody or something that is not named. *Some guy asked me the way to town.* 3 a fairly large number or amount. *She had been dead for some years before we knew about it.* 4 about. *The river is some 10 m deep.* **some** *pronoun* a certain amount, number or part of something. *Some wore red, others pink.*

somebody, someone *pronoun* some person, but not a particular person. *Somebody/someone told me that you were moving house, and now I know it's true.*

somersault *noun* a jump or move in which you bring your legs over your head. **somersault** *verb.* *He somersaulted across the lawn.*

something *pronoun* a thing that is unknown, some thing. *May I have something to drink?* **something like** rather like or about. *She got something like $50 for her old bike.* **something to do with** connected with. *The party is something to do with her birthday.*

sometime *adverb* at one point in time. *I'll see her sometime next week.*

sometimes *adverb* from time to time, not always. *She sometimes walks to school.*

somewhere *adverb* in or to a place, but not a known one. *She lives somewhere in Ohio.*

son *noun* the male child of a man or woman. *Their son is called Peter.*

son-in-law (sons-in-law) *noun* a daughter's husband. *Their son-in-law is a lawyer.*

song *noun* 1 a piece of music with words for singing. 2 singing. 3 the sound of a bird. **song and dance** a big fuss about nothing. **for a song** very cheaply.

sonic *adjective* of the speed of sound or sound waves. *A sonic boom.*

sonnet *noun* a poem with 14 lines.

soon *adverb* 1 in a very short time from now. 2 early. *The sooner the better.* **as soon as** 1 quickly. *As soon as possible.* 2 at the moment when. *As soon as I get paid.* **as soon** readily or willingly. *I'd just as soon go home.* **sooner or later** at some time, certainly. *Sooner or later she'll have to get busy and start studying.*

soot *noun* black powder left from burning or carried in the air in smoke. *The chimney is blocked with soot.* **sooty** *adjective.*

soothe *verb* to make less angry or less painful. **soothing** *adjective.* *A soothing medicine will do your throat good.*

sophisticated *adjective* 1 used to fashionable and elegant ways, not simple. 2 complicated, with many parts. *A highly sophisticated machine.* **sophistication** *noun.*

soppy *adjective* foolishly sentimental.

sorcerer *noun* a man who does magic with the help of evil spirits. *The sorcerer's apprentice.* **sorceress** *noun.* **sorcery** *noun.*

The sorcerer consulted a magic book to find the right spell.

sore *adjective* 1 painful or aching. *A sore throat.* 2 upset or angry. *She is still feeling sore about not being invited.* 3 serious, causing worry. *In sore need.* A sore point is something you do not want to talk about because it upsets you. **soreness** *noun.*

sore *noun* 1 a painful place on the body where the skin is infected. 2 a painful memory or subject.

sorry (sorrier, sorriest) *adjective* 1 feeling sadness or pity for somebody, expressing regret. *I'm sorry your dog died.* 2 feeling disappointed with yourself for doing or not having done something, usually said as an apology. *I'm sorry I laughed.* 3 used as a polite way to say that you did not hear or that you do not agree with something. *Sorry, what was the name?* 4 in a bad way, not good. *The house is in a sorry state.*

sort *noun* 1 a particular group of people or things that are the same in certain ways, a kind or type. *I don't like this sort of music.* 2 a person. *He is not the complaining sort.* **out of sorts** slightly ill or annoyed. **sort of** a little, in some way. *Her hair is sort of blond.*

sort *verb* to put things in order or arrange in groups according to their kind. *I spent all day sorting my books.* **sort out** to tidy, deal with or put in order. *She tried to sort out their quarrel, but they remained enemies.*

soul *noun* 1 the part of a person that is believed to live on after the body has died. 2 a person's thoughts and feelings. *That man has no soul, he is hard and unfeeling.* 3 anybody. *She didn't know a soul at the party.* 4 a style of pop music.

soulless *adjective* 1 without feeling or care for others. 2 dull.

sound *noun* 1 something you hear or that can be heard. When you turn the sound down on a television, you make it less loud. 2 an idea or impression from something read or heard. *I don't like the sound of your plans.* **sound** *verb* 1 to make a sound or cause something to make a sound. *The siren sounded a warning.* 2 to say what noise something makes or is. *The rustling of the leaves sounded ghostly.* 3 to seem. *She sounds happy.* **sound out** to find out what somebody thinks or will do.

sound *adjective* 1 healthy, in good condition. 2 reliable and sensible. *Sound advice.* 3 deep or strong. **soundly** *adverb. Our team was soundly beaten in the first five minutes.* **sound asleep** deeply asleep.

soundproof *adjective* able to stop all sound from getting in or out. *A soundproof room.*

South on the compass is opposite to north (opposite to the magnetic North Pole).

This is how an echo forms in a cave. Sound waves travel to the end wall, then bounce back. The bounce is the echo.

soundtrack *noun* speech and music that go with a film. *I have the soundtrack on CD.*

soup *noun* a liquid food you drink or eat with a spoon. *A nourishing soup.*

sour *adjective* 1 tasting sharp. *Lemons are sour.* 2 not fresh, gone bad. *The milk is sour.* 3 bad-tempered, unfriendly. *She gave me a sour look.* **sour** *verb* to become unpleasant or less friendly.

source *noun* a place where something starts. *The source of the river is in the hills.*

south *noun* the direction of one of the four main points of the compass. South is to the right of a person facing the rising Sun. **south** *adjective, adverb* towards, from or in the south. *The south wind is warm.*

South Africa *noun* a country in Africa.

South America *noun* one of the Earth's seven continents.

South Korea *noun* a country in East Asia, officially called the Republic of Korea.

southerly (say suth-uh-lee) *adjective* in or towards the south. *We drove in a southerly direction until we came to the coast.*

souvenir (say soo-vun-eer) *noun* something you buy or keep to remind you of a holiday or another event. *A souvenir of Blackpool.*

sovereign (say sov-rin) *noun* 1 a king or queen who rules a country. 2 an old British gold coin. **sovereign** *adjective* 1 independent, not under the control of another country. 2 having the highest power in a country.

sow (sows, sowing, sowed, sown) *verb* (rhymes with go) to plant seeds into the ground that will grow into plants.

sow *noun* (rhymes with cow) a female pig.

soya *noun* a plant that can be made into flour, oil, butter or other food.

soya bean *noun* the seed of soya.

spa *noun* a place with a spring of mineral water where people come to cure illnesses.

space *noun* 1 an empty area in a place. *The desk takes up too much space.* 2 the whole area outside the Earth where the stars and other planets move. 3 an empty area or gap in something. *A parking space.* 4 a period of time. *Within the space of a month.* **space** *verb* to arrange things with gaps between them.

spacecraft *noun* a vehicle for travelling in space. *The spacecraft was in orbit.*

space shuttle *noun* a reusable spacecraft that can travel into space and back a number of times. *The space shuttle was launched.*

spacesuit *noun* a suit for wearing in space with its own air supply.

spade *noun* a tool with a blade and a handle for digging.

spade *noun* a playing card with a picture of a black heart-shaped leaf with a short stem. *The ace of spades.*

spaghetti *noun* long, thin sticks of pasta that you boil before eating.

Spain *noun* a country in Southwest Europe.

span *noun* 1 a period in time from beginning to end, or the length of time over which something exists. *During a ten-year span at the factory he was never late.* 2 the length of something from one end to the other. *The wing span of a glider.* 3 the distance from the tip of the thumb to the tip of the little finger when the hand is spread. 4 the part between two supports of an arch or a bridge. **span** (spans, spanning, spanned) *verb* 1 to last for a length of time or reach across. 2 to form an arch or bridge over.

Spanish *noun* 1 the language spoken in Spain, Mexico and other South American countries. 2 the people of Spain. **Spanish** *adjective. Spanish flamenco dancing.*

spank *verb* to slap on the bottom.

spar *verb* to practice boxing or martial arts with someone.

spare *adjective* 1 kept for use when needed. *She left a spare key with her neighbor.* 2 free or not being used. *Have you got any spare cash?* 3 thin. *A spare figure.* **spare time** time when you are not busy. **spare** *noun* a spare part for a machine or engine.

spare *verb* 1 not to harm or kill somebody or something, to keep from harming. *Take all I have but spare the children.* 2 to find enough money or time to give to somebody or for a purpose. *Can you spare me a minute?* 3 to keep from using or spending. *No expense was spared.* **enough to spare** more than enough.

sparing *adjective* using or giving very little.

spark *noun* 1 a small bit of burning material that flies up from a fire. 2 a flash of light produced by electricity. 3 a small bit. *A spark of interest.* **spark** *verb* to give out sparks. **spark off** to lead to or be the cause of something. *The discussion sparked off a bitter quarrel between the two families.*

sparkle *verb* 1 to shine with a lot of small flashes of light. 2 to bubble. *Sparkling wine.* 3 to be lively, bright and witty.

sparrow *noun* a small brown bird.

sparse *adjective* small in number or amount, not crowded. *His sparse white hair.* **sparsely** *adverb. Sparsely populated.*

spawn *noun* the eggs of fish, frogs and some other water animals. **spawn** *verb* 1 to lay spawn. 2 to produce something, especially in large numbers. *The latest fashion show has spawned new ideas.*

Our pond was full of frogspawn. We waited eagerly for the tadpoles to hatch.

speak (speaks, speaking, spoke, spoken) *verb* 1 to say things using your voice, to talk. 2 to know and be able to talk a language. *She speaks French.* 3 to give a speech. *He spoke for an hour.* **speak out** to speak freely about something, especially in favour or against it. **speak up** to speak more loudly.

speaker *noun* 1 somebody making a speech. 2 somebody who speaks a language. *English speakers.* 3 a piece of equipment on a radio or cassette player through which the sound comes, a loudspeaker.

spear *noun* a weapon with a long pole and sharp point for throwing or stabbing. **spear** *verb* to make a hole in or catch with a spear or something pointed. *She speared the meat with a fork and stuffed it in her mouth.*

Spears are used for hunting animals for meat.

special *adjective* 1 not usual, better or more important than others. *I'm doing it as a special favor.* 2 for a particular person or thing. *Astronauts wear special suits in space.* **specially** *adverb* 1 more than usual, especially. *It is specially you.* 2 for a special purpose. *A school specially for deaf students.*

specialist *noun* a person who has special skills or knowledge in a particular subject, an expert. *A heart specialist is a doctor who treats heart diseases.*

speciality (specialities) *noun* 1 a particular work or study. *Her speciality is French.* 2 fine or best product. *The chef's soup is the speciality of the house.*

specialize *verb* to study one subject or know about one thing so you are an expert in it. *His father specializes in racing bikes.*

species (species) *noun* (say **spee**-sheez) a group of animals or plants that are of the same kind and are the same in all important ways. *This species has become very rare.*

specify (specifies, specifying, specified) *verb* to describe or name something exactly. **specification** *noun. Please give me the exact specifications for the project.*

specimen *noun* 1 a typical thing or example. 2 one piece or a small amount of something that shows what the whole is like. *The doctor took a specimen of blood.*

speck *noun* a small spot.

spectacle *noun* 1 a big show or public performance. 2 a strange or silly sight. *Don't make a spectacle of yourself.*

spectacles *plural noun* a pair of glasses.

spectacular *adjective* grand, impressive. *A spectacular view of the mountains.*

spectator *noun* a person who watches something, especially sport.

spectrum (spectra) *noun* 1 the band of colors as seen in the rainbow. 2 a range of different kinds of things, ideas or opinions.

The spectrum contains all the colors of the rainbow.

speech (speeches) *noun* 1 the act or power of speaking. 2 words spoken to a group of people, a talk. *The minister made a speech.*

speed *noun* 1 how quickly something moves, travels or happens. *I was amazed at the speed of his serve.* 2 fastness or swiftness. **at speed** fast. **speed** (speeds, speeding, sped) *verb* 1 to go quickly. *He sped past us.* 2 to go too fast. *He was stopped by the police for speeding.* **speed up** (speeded up) to make something go or happen faster.

speed limit *noun* the fastest speed you are allowed to drive by law.

spell *noun* 1 a period of time. *It rained for a short spell.* 2 a quick period of activity or illness. *A spell in the hospital.*

spell *noun* words or an attraction that are supposed to have magical powers. *The witch cast a spell on him.*

spell (spells, spelling, spelt) *verb* 1 to put letters of the alphabet in the right order to make a word or words. *Her name is spelt R-o-s-y.* 2 to mean. *Her silence usually spells trouble.* **speller** *noun.*

The Sphinx stands at Giza, near the Nile in Egypt.

spelling *noun* the way a word or words are spelled.

spend (spends, spending, spent) *verb* 1 to give money to pay for something. 2 to pass or use up time. *I spent all day reading.* **spender** *noun. A big spender.*

sperm (sperm or sperms) *noun* the male cell that fertilizes a female egg to produce new life.

sphere *noun* 1 a round shape like a ball. 2 a particular area of interest or activity. *The sphere of politics.* **spherical** *adjective.*

sphinx (sphinxes) *noun* an ancient Egyptian stone statue with the body of a lion and a man's head. *The sphinx asked me a riddle.*

spice *noun* powder or seeds from a plant used to give a taste to food. **spicy** *adjective.*

spider *noun* a small creature with eight legs that spins webs in which it catches other insects. **spidery** *adjective* long and thin. *Spidery handwriting.*

A tarantula is a spider that has hairs on its body and legs which contain an irritant.

spike *noun* 1 a long pointed piece of metal. *The spikes on the fence.* 2 a piece of metal with a sharp point fixed to the bottom of some shoes, especially running shoes. **spike** *verb* 1 to put spikes in or on something. 2 to catch or pierce with a spike.

spill (spills, spilling, spilt or spilled) *verb* 1 to pour out, especially over the edge of a container. *I spilled some milk.* 2 to come out in large numbers. *People spilled out of the stadium.* **spill** *noun.*

spin (spins, spinning, spun) *verb* 1 to make thread by twisting together fibres. 2 When spiders spin, they make a web out of thread from their bodies. 3 to turn around fast or make something go round and round. *My head is spinning.* **spin a yarn** to tell a story. **spin out** to make something last longer. **spin** *noun* 1 the movement of going around and around. 2 a short ride in a car or other vehicle. *A spin in the country would be very pleasant on a sunny afternoon.*

spinach *noun* a vegetable with large green leaves. *Spinach is good for you.*

spindly (spindlier, spindliest) *adjective* long, thin and weak-looking. *Spindly legs.*

spine *noun* 1 the row of bones down the middle of your back, the backbone. 2 a sharp point like a thorn on an animal's body or on a plant. 3 the stiff back part of a book to which the pages and covers are fastened. The title of the book is usually printed on the spine.

Spine

When you are making a photocopy, please don't break the spine of my book.

spire *noun* the pointed part on top of a church or tower.

spirit *noun* 1 a person's mind, the part that is connected with thoughts and feelings. *She was in good spirits.* 2 a supernatural being, a ghost. 3 liveliness and energy, effort shown. *He keeps the team spirit going.* 4 what something really means, not what it actually says. *Making her pay for her food would be against the spirit of our agreement.* 5 a strong alcoholic drink. Whisky and brandy are spirits. **spirit** *verb* If you spirit somebody or something away, you take them quickly and secretly to another place.

spit (spits, spitting, spat) *verb* 1 to force liquid out of your mouth. 2 to rain lightly. **spit out** 1 *She ate a grape and spat out the seeds.* 2 to say something quickly and angrily. *She spat out his name.* **spit** *noun* the watery liquid that is produced in the mouth, saliva. **spitting image** an exact likeness. *She is the spitting image of her mother.*

spit *noun* 1 a thin, pointed metal rod for cooking meat over a fire. 2 a point of land sticking out into the sea.

Barry roasted the meat for the barbecue on a spit.

spite *noun* a wish to hurt or annoy somebody. *She said it out of spite.* **spite** *verb.* **in spite of** despite.

WORD HISTORY

The term 'spitting image' was originally 'spit and image', from the phrase 'the very spit of', which meant the exact likeness. Perhaps this was because everyone's spit looks exactly the same?

spiteful *adjective* being nasty about people you do not like. *A spiteful remark.*

splash *verb* 1 to hit water or throw liquid about so it flies up in drops and makes a noise. If you splash somebody, you make them wet. *We splashed through the waves.* 2 to fall or hit in small noisy drops. *Rain splashed on the window.* 3 to throw liquid on something. *He splashed his face with water.* **splash** (splashes) *noun* 1 the sound made when something hits water. 2 a small amount of liquid that has been spilt. *There is a splash of paint on your skirt.* 3 a bright color or effect. *A yellow dress with a splash of red.*

splendid *adjective* 1 beautiful and impressive to look at. 2 great.

splendor *noun* impressive beauty. *The utter splendor of the throne room.*

splinter *noun* a small, sharp piece of wood or other hard material that has broken off a bigger piece. *I'm trying to get this glass splinter out of my finger.* **splinter** *verb* to break into splinters.

Karen got a splinter of glass stuck in her finger.

split (splits, splitting, split) *verb* 1 to break, tear or crack. *This wood splits easily.* 2 to divide into parts or share. *The children were split into groups.* **split the difference** to agree on a price which is halfway between the two amounts. **split up** to separate. *We split up and went separate ways.* **split** *noun* 1 a cut or break made by splitting. 2 the splitting or dividing of something. 3 a division between different things. 4 a dish made from cut-up fruit and ice-cream. *A banana split.*

spoil (spoils, spoiling, spoiled or spoilt) *verb* 1 to ruin or damage something so it is no longer any good. *The rain spoiled our weekend.* 2 to harm somebody so they become very selfish by giving them everything they want. *Some parents spoil their children.* 3 to treat very well or too well. *I spoilt myself with an ice-cream.* **spoils** *plural noun* stolen goods, especially those taken in war.

spoilsport *noun* somebody who stops others from having fun and wants to spoil their enjoyment of things.

spoke *verb* past tense of speak.

spoke *noun* each of the bars or wire rods that go from the rim of a wheel to the centre. *Bicycle spokes.*

sponge *noun* 1 a small sea animal with a body full of holes. 2 a piece of the body of the sea animal or soft rubber or plastic with holes in for washing or padding things. 3 a soft cake. **spongy** *adjective*. **sponge** *verb* 1 to wash or wipe with a sponge. 2 to live by getting money or things free from people without giving anything in return. *He sponges off his friends.* **sponger** *noun*.

sponsor *noun* a person or business who gives money or help to a person, team or event, usually in return for advertising a product. **sponsor** *verb* to be a sponsor for somebody or something. *We are sponsoring the school football team.*

spook *noun* a ghost. **spooky** *adjective*. *A spooky old house.*

spool *noun* a round holder or roll for winding something on. *A spool of thread.*

spoon *noun* an object with a long handle and a shallow bowl used for eating or stirring food. **spoon** *verb* to lift or take with a spoon. *She spooned soup into bowls.*

spoonerism *noun* an exchange of the first letters of a pair of words, usually with a funny result. 'You have hissed the mystery lesson,' is a spoonerism.

spoonful *noun* the amount a spoon can hold. *Two spoonfuls of sugar.*

sport *noun* 1 an activity, competition or game, usually done outdoors. 2 somebody who is kind, cheerful and does not mind losing or being teased. *He is a very good sport.* **sport** *verb* to have or wear something. *He was sporting a bright blue tie.*

spot *noun* 1 a small round mark or a dirty mark. *A blue dress with red spots.* 2 a particular place. *This is the spot where the accident happened.* 3 a short appearance. *A spot on TV.* 4 a drop. *Spots of rain.* to put someone **on the spot** If you put somebody on the spot, you make them give an answer or make a decision without preparation. **in a tight spot** in difficulty. **spot** (spots, spotting, spotted) *verb* 1 to notice, pick out. *Can you spot the mistake?* 2 to rain lightly. 3 to mark with spots. **spotted** *adjective*. *A spotted scarf.* **spotty** *adjective*. not consistent. *The performance was spotty.*

spotless *adjective* very clean. *Her house is always absolutely spotless.*

The spooky old house on the hill was always lit up at night, though no one had lived there for years.

spout *noun* 1 the tube or pipe-like opening for pouring liquid from a kettle, jug or pot. 2 a stream of liquid going upwards with great force. **spout** *verb* 1 to stream out with great force. 2 to say a lot in a boring way. *He spouted boring facts all evening.*

This teapot has an elegantly curved spout.

sprain *verb* to damage a joint by twisting or bending it. *He sprained his ankle jumping into the swimming pool.* **sprain** *noun*.

sprawl *verb* 1 to sit or lie with your arms and legs spread out. *He sprawled on the couch.* 2 to spread over a large area. *The town sprawls across the valley.*

spray *verb* to scatter small drops of liquid on or over something. *She sprayed the room with air freshener.* **spray** *noun* 1 small drops of liquid sent through the air, either blown by the wind or from a special container. *Sea spray.* 2 a special container with liquid in it for spraying. *Hair spray.*

spray *noun* a number of flowers or leaves on a stem or branch.

We ordered a spray of spring flowers to be sent to Sally's bedside.

spread (spreads, spreading, spread) *verb* 1 to open something out so that all of it can be seen, to stretch out. *The bird spread its wings and flew away.* 2 to cover a large area or time. *The rainforest spreads for thousands of kilometers.* 3 to cover something with something. 4 to make or become more widely known or have a wide effect. *The fire spread to the next village and engulfed the huts in flames.* 5 to share or divide evenly. *We spread the work over a period of three years.* **spread** *noun* 1 the act or action of spreading. *The spread of Aids is increasing, especially in Africa.* 2 the distance or time of spreading. 3 a big meal with lots of food and drink. *Claire put on a magnificent spread for Thanksgiving.* 4 a soft food, paste that can be spread with a knife. *Cheese spread.* 5 a number of things, ideas or interests.

spring *noun* 1 the season of the year between winter and summer. 2 a coil of wire that goes back to its normal shape after it is pressed. *One of the springs in the mattress has gone.* 3 a place where water comes up from the ground. *A mountain spring.* 4 being able to stretch and go back to a normal shape. *There is no spring in the sofa.*
spring (springs, springing, sprang, sprung) *verb* 1 to move quickly and suddenly. 2 to come into being, appear or be the result of. *Her unhappiness springs from her wish to be famous.* 3 to make something happen or known suddenly and unexpectedly. *We sprang a surprise birthday party on him.*

sprinkle *verb* to scatter small drops or tiny pieces on something. *They sprinkled sand on the icy path.*

sprint *verb* to run at full speed for a short distance. sprint *noun* 1 running very fast. *He made a sprint for the bus.* 2 a short race. **sprinter** *noun.*

sprout *noun* 1 a new growth on a plant. 2 a vegetable like a small cabbage. *Brussels sprouts.* **sprout** *verb* to grow or come out.

spruce *adjective* very neat, clean and smart looking.
spruce *verb* to make yourself look neat. *He spruced himself up to meet his girlfriend's parents.*

spruce *noun* a kind of evergreen tree.

We have a spruce tree in our front yard that we decorate at Christmas.

spud *noun* (slang) potato.

spun *verb* past tense of spin.

spurn *verb* to refuse with anger or pride. *He spurned her offer of help.*

spurt *verb* 1 to flow out suddenly, to gush out. *Blood spurted from the wound.* 2 to run faster, increase speed suddenly. *She spurted towards the finishing line.* spurt *noun* 1 a sudden spurting. 2 a sudden increase of effort or speed.

spy (spies) *noun* somebody who finds out secret information about other people or countries. **spy** (spies, spying, spied) *verb* 1 to work as a spy to get information. 2 to watch secretly. *He spies on his neighbors.* 3 to notice. *I spied a mint in your purse.*

squabble *verb* to quarrel about something unimportant. **squabble** *noun. I hope you have made it up after your squabble.*

A square has four equal sides.

The farmer grew his best crops of squash in years.

squalid *adjective* dirty and messy. **squalor** *noun. She lives in squalor.*

squander *verb* to spend money or time foolishly and wastefully. *She squandered her savings and now she regrets it.*

square *adjective* 1 having the shape of a square with four equal sides and four right angles. 2 forming a right angle. 3 fair, honest. *He wasn't square with me.* 4 even in points, equal or settled. *I've paid up and now we are square.* 5 having an area equal to that of a square with sides of the length stated or being the length from a corner in both directions. *The room has an area of 3 square meters.* **a square meal** a good meal that fills you. **a square number** any number that is the square of another number. 4 is a square number (4 = 2 x 2). **square root** a number that equals another number when it is multiplied by itself. 2 is the square root of 4 (2 x 2 = 4).

square *noun* 1 a shape with four sides that are all the same length and four corners at right angles. 2 a place surrounded by buildings that is the shape of a square. *We went skating in Washington Square.* 3 a number equal to another number when it is multiplied by itself. 16 is the square of 4. (16 = 4 x 4). **square** *verb* 1 to make something square, give a square shape to something, or mark squares on something. 2 to multiply a number by itself. 6 squared is 36. 3 to pay or settle something. *He has to square his account first.* 4 to match or fit a particular explanation or situation. *His story does not square with the facts.*

squash (squashes) *noun* 1 a game played with rackets and a small rubber ball that is hit against the walls of an indoor court. 2 a vegetable *Acorn squash.* 3 a crowd of people in a small place. **squash** *verb* 1 to press something so it goes into a flat shape, to crush. *The grapes got squashed at the bottom of the bag.* 2 to press into a small place. *We all squashed on to the bus.* 3 to defeat or make somebody lose heart.

squat (squats, squatting, squatted) *verb* 1 to sit on your heels, to crouch. 2 to live in an empty building without being allowed to or paying rent. **squat** *noun. We lived in a squat for a year.* **squatter** *noun.*

squat *adjective* short and fat.

squeak *verb* to make a short, very high, loud sound. *Mice squeak.* **squeak** *noun*. **squeaky** *adjective*. *Squeaky floorboards.*

squeal *verb* 1 to make a long, very high sound or cry. 2 to report a criminal to the police. **squeal** *noun*. *A squeal of brakes.*

squeamish *adjective* easily upset or made sick, especially if something looks unpleasant. *She is very squeamish and can't stand the sight of blood.*

squeeze *verb* 1 to press from two sides. *He squeezed his finger in the door.* 2 to press to get liquid out of something. *To squeeze an orange.* 3 to manage to get through or into something. *She squeezed herself into her jeans.* **squeeze** *noun*.

squid *noun* a sea creature with a long soft body, eight arms and two long tentacles.

The Greeks love to eat squid cut into rings and deep-fried in batter.

squint *verb* to look with your eyes almost closed. *She squinted in the bright sunlight.*

squirrel *noun* a small furry animal with a long bushy tail that climbs trees and eats nuts. *Squirrels store acorns in the fall so that they will have food during the winter.*

squirt *verb* to force or come out in a thin stream of liquid. *She squirted the water pistol at me.* **squirt** *noun*.

Sri Lanka *noun* a country in South Asia, formerly called Ceylon.

St *abbreviation* 1 street. 2 saint.

St George's *noun* the capital of Grenada.

St John's *noun* the capital of Antigua and Barbuda.

St Kitts and Nevis *noun* a country in the West Indies.

St Lucia *noun* a country in the West Indies.

St Vincent and the Grenadines *noun* a country in the West Indies.

stab (stabs, stabbing, stabbed) *verb* to strike or pierce with something pointed. *The thief stabbed the policeman with a knife.* **stab** *noun* 1 the act of stabbing. 2 a wound made by something pointed. 3 a sudden painful feeling. *A piercing stab of guilt.* 4 If you have a stab at something, you try something and hope to be successful. *I had a stab at the exam questions, but I didn't do very well.*

SPELLING NOTE

Most people use 'stadiums' as the plural of the sports ground, but 'stadia' can also be used. Most of the original Latin words ending in '–um' have '–a' as their plural.

DID YOU KNOW

Sri Lanka is an island in the Indian Ocean off the southern tip of India. It had a highly developed civilization as early as the 5th century BC.

stable *noun* a building in which horses are kept. *There are two horses in the stable.*

stable *adjective* firmly fixed in a position, not likely to fall or change. *A stable relationship.* **stability** *noun*.

stadium (stadiums or stadia) *noun* a sports ground. *A baseball stadium.*

Every seat in the stadium was booked for the big game.

staff *noun* 1 the people who work for an organization, for example an office or a store. 2 a strong stick. **staff** *verb* to provide workers, supply with staff. *The restaurant is staffed with excellent cooks.*

stag *noun* a male deer.

stage *noun* 1 a period, point or part in a development or journey. *We divided the hike into three easy stages.* 2 the platform on which plays and musicals are performed. 3 acting in theatres. *A stage production.* If you are on stage, you are acting. **stage** *verb* 1 to put on a play or perform a show. 2 to organize. *The students staged a protest.*

stagger *verb* 1 to walk or move unsteadily. *The drunk staggered across the street.* 2 to surprise. *I was staggered that he had left the country.* 3 to arrange things so that they do not happen at the same time. *We staggered our vacations, so that someone was always there to mind the store.*

stain *noun* 1 a mark that is difficult to remove. 2 a liquid used for darkening or staining wood. 3 a mark of shame or guilt. **stain** *verb* 1 to make a stain on something. *The grape juice has stained my fingers.* 2 to color with a special liquid. *We stained the chairs red.*

stained glass *noun* glass made up of pieces of different colors fitted together and used for windows and other objects.

The stained glass in the church was old and very valuable.

stainless steel *noun* metal made from steel that does not rust or stain.

stair *noun* one of a number of steps. The stairs are a set of steps which go from one floor to another.

staircase *noun* a set of stairs inside a house.

stalactite *noun* a downward-pointing spike of limestone hanging like an icicle from a cave roof.

stalagmite *noun* an upward-pointing spike of limestone standing like a pillar on the floor of a cave.

stale *adjective* not fresh. **staleness** *noun*.

stalemate *noun* a situation in which neither side can win. *We had reached stalemate in our discussions.*

stalk *noun* a stem of a plant or fruit.

stalk *verb* 1 to walk in a stiff, angry or proud way. 2 to follow an animal or person quietly in order to hunt or catch them. **stalker** *noun*.

stall *noun* 1 a small cubicle or other enclosed area for washing or going to the toilet. 2 a place for an animal in a barn or stable. *Cattle in their stalls.* 3 the point at which an engine stops. *The pilot put the plane into a controlled stall.* **stall** *verb* to stop suddenly or make an engine stop. *The car stalled at the intersection.*

stall *verb* to not give a clear answer or not do something in order to get more time, to delay. *I'll try and stall them for a while.*

stallion *noun* a male horse, especially kept for breeding. *A beautiful white stallion.*

stamen *noun* the male part of a flower that produces pollen.

stamina *noun* the strength of body or mental energy needed to do tiring things for a long time.

stammer *verb* to repeat sounds of the same word when speaking, to speak with pauses. **stammer** *noun*.

stamp *noun* 1 a small piece of gummed paper with a design on it that is stuck on an envelope before mailing to show that postage has been paid. 2 a small pad with a design or letters on one side which is pressed on to a surface. 3 the mark made by using a stamp. 4 a mark or sign typical for something. *His songs bear the stamp of poverty.* **stamp** *verb* 1 to lift your foot and put it down hard on the ground. *The little boy stamped his foot and cried.* 2 to walk noisily and with heavy footsteps. 3 to put a postage stamp on a letter or package. 4 to press a design or letters on something.

SPELLING NOTE

'Stalactite' comes from an ancient Greek word for 'dripping', and 'stalagmite' from the Greek 'stalagma', 'drop'. Both types of rock formation are formed by dripping, trickling water containing dissolved limestone.

AMAZING FACT

Stamp collecting is also called 'philately' and the person who collects stamps is known as a 'philatelist'.

Paul collected lots of different stamps and stuck them in an album.

---

stand (stands, standing, stood) *verb* 1 to be on your feet in an upright position. 2 to put or be in an upright position. 3 to remain or stay the same. *My invitation still stands.* 4 to put up with or endure. *I can't stand him.* 5 to pay for. *Let me stand you a drink.* **stand between** to be an obstacle. *Only two unresolved issues stand in the way of the agreement.* **it stands to reason** it makes sense or is likely to happen. *It stands to reason she'll fail the exam if she never does any work.* **stand by** to be ready to help or take action. *Ambulances were standing by at the race.* **stand for** 1 to represent or mean. *UN stands for United Nations.* 2 to put up with, to allow. *She doesn't stand for any nonsense.* **stand out** 1 to be easily seen and clear. *Red stands out well.* 2 to be outstanding. *He stands out as a real artist.* **stand up** 1 to get up. 2 to be accepted as true. *His story won't stand up in court.* 3 to defend. *You must learn to stand up for yourself.* 4 If you stand somebody up, you don't meet them as arranged. **stand up to** 1 to resist attack. 2 to stay in good condition. *The carpet stood up to constant use.*

stand *noun* 1 a piece of furniture for putting things on or in. *A music stand.* 2 a stall or kiosk for selling things. *A lemonade stand.* 3 a position against or in favor. *She took a stand against animal experiments.* 4 a place in court from which to give testimony. *She was nervous as she took the stand.*

standard *adjective* 1 of the usual or accepted kind. *The standard rules of good behavior.* 2 most widely used or best of its kind. *The standard book on grammar.*

standard *noun* 1 how good something is. *The standard of spelling is very high.* 2 something used for measuring or judging the quality of something. *Different countries use different standards.* 3 a flag of an important person or family. *The royal standard.*

stanza *noun* a verse of poetry.

staple *adjective* regular or main. *Rice is the staple food of India.*

Potatoes are the staple food in Ireland.

staple *noun* 1 a small piece of wire used for holding pieces of paper together. Staples are pushed through the paper with a stapler. 2 a U-shaped nail. **staple** *verb* to fasten papers together with a stapler. **stapler** *noun*.

star *noun* 1 a large ball of burning gas in space, a heavenly body. 2 a shape, an object or a mark with points sticking out round it. If a hotel has five stars, it means that it is extremely good. 3 a famous actor, sports player or performer. *A movie star.* **star** (stars, starring, starred) *verb* 1 to have an important part in a play or film. 2 to mark with a star shape. **starry** *adjective*.

starch (starches) *noun* 1 a white substance in food. There is starch in bread, rice and pasta. 2 a white substance for stiffening clothes, especially clothes made of cotton. **starch** *verb* to stiffen with starch.

stare *verb* to look at somebody or something hard or for a long time. *Don't stare at me, it makes me blush.*

starfish (starfish or starfishes) *noun* a sea animal with five arms that has a star shape.

starling *noun* a small, dark speckled bird.

start *verb* 1 to come into being or to begin, especially something you were not doing before. *She started laughing.* 2 to take place, to begin. *His music started a new craze.* 3 to set out on a career. *She started as a secretary.* 4 to jerk or move suddenly, usually because you are surprised or frightened. *A sudden noise makes me start.* **start** *noun* 1 the place of starting, the beginning of an activity. *Let's make an early start.* 2 a sudden uncontrolled movement. *She woke up with a start.* **a head start** an advantage or an amount of time somebody has over somebody else. *We had an hour's head start.* **make a fresh start** to start again from the beginning.

startle *verb* to make somebody jump or be surprised. *The noise startled him.*

starve *verb* 1 to suffer or die from not having any food to eat. To make somebody die from hunger. *Thousands starved to death during the drought.* 2 to be very hungry. *When's lunch, I'm starving.* 3 When you are starved of something, you lack that particular thing and need it very much. *The children were starved of love.* **starvation** *noun*. **starving** *adjective*.

state *noun* 1 a condition which somebody or something is in. *His state of health.* 2 the government of a country or a country. *Italy is a European state.* 3 part of a large country. *The state of Texas.*

DID YOU KNOW

An ancient Greek scientist called Thales discovered static electricity over 2,500 years ago, when he rubbed a piece of amber with a cloth.

Starfish cling to the rocks with suckers under their arms.

SPELLING NOTE

Be careful not to mix up the spelling of the adjective 'stationary' (not moving) and the noun 'stationery' (writing materials). Both come from the Latin for 'standing', which came to refer to a shopkeeper as opposed to a 'moving' pedlar.

state *verb* to express something in words, especially in a formal way. *The police stated that the charges had been dropped.*

statement *noun* 1 something you state, facts and information given in a written or spoken declaration. *I don't believe the politician's statement.* 2 a printed document showing amounts of money paid in, taken out or owed, usually sent out by your bank. *I get a monthly bank statement.*

static *adjective* not moving or changing.

static electricity *noun* electricity that builds up or is present in certain things like your hair or a carpet.

station *noun* 1 a place where trains or buses stop for people to get on and off. *Where is the train station?* 2 a building for a particular service. *A police station.* 3 a company that sends out radio or television program. *The new radio station plays dance music all day.* **station** *verb* to put people or things in a certain place for a particular purpose.

stationary *adjective* not moving. *The bus was stationary when the accident happened.*

stationery *noun* materials for writing, such as paper, envelopes, pens and pencils.

Jennifer was in charge of the office stationery cupboard.

statistics *plural noun* information shown in numbers that can be compared. *The statistics seem to show that grad point averages have been getting better every year.* **statistical** *adjective*.

statue *noun* a model of a person or animal in stone, wood or metal. *The statue of the Venus de Milo has no arms.*

stay *verb* 1 to remain in the same place or condition. *The weather stayed warm.* 2 to live at a place as a visitor. *She is staying with her brother in Dallas.* 3 to last out. *The horse stayed the course.* **stay put** to remain in one place. **stay on** to remain in a place or for an extra spell of time. *He stayed on as assistant pro.* **stay up** to go to bed after your normal bed time.

stay *noun* 1 a short time spent somewhere. 2 a delay or postponement. *The judge ordered a stay of execution.*

steady (steadier, steadiest) *adjective* 1 not moving, firm. *He is not very steady on his legs.* 2 not changing, regular. *She has now found a steady job.*

steak *noun* a thick slice of meat (especially beef) or fish.

steal (steals, stealing, stole, stolen) *verb* 1 to take something that belongs to somebody else without any right. *He stole some money.* 2 to move quietly and secretly. *She stole out of the room.*

steam *noun* 1 the hot mist that is produced when water is boiled. *The steam from a boiling kettle.* 2 the power from steam used to drive machines. *A steam engine.* 3 energy. If you run out of steam, you have no more energy. **steam** *verb* 1 to give out steam. 2 to cook in steam, not water. *Do you want to steam the fish?* 3 to travel by steam power. *The ship steamed out of the harbor.*

steel *noun* a very strong hard metal used for making knives and tools.

steep *adjective* 1 rising or falling sharply. *A steep slope.* 2 expensive. *$100 for his old bike is a bit steep.*

steeple *noun* a tall pointed church tower.

steeplechase *noun* a race across country with hedges, fences and ditches.

steer *verb* 1 to control a car, boat or ship so it goes in the direction you want it to go. 2 to guide. *He steered me towards the door.*

steering wheel *noun* the wheel in a car or truck that the driver holds and turns to steer with. *He gripped the steering wheel.*

AMAZING FACT

Steam fills 1700 times as much space as the water that it has been boiled from. If you compress steam into a small container, it pushes against the sides. If there is a place or thing that the steam can move, such as a piston, the steam will force the piston outward. When the steam cools, it turns back into water, takes less space, and the piston returns to its original position. Early steam engines used this principle to power pumps to pump water out of mines.

The glorious days of the steam train are long gone, and rail travel is now less exciting but much cleaner.

WORD HISTORY

The steeplechase gets its name from early races when a local church with a tall steeple was used as a landmark, probably the finish. Steeplechase races using horses can be traced back to 18th-century fox hunting.

---

stem *noun* 1 the long central part of a plant above the ground. 2 the thin part of a plant that has leaves or flowers on it. 3 the thin part of a wine glass or bowl that looks like a stem. **stem** (stems, stemming, stemmed) *verb* to stop something flowing or spreading. *The nurse tried to stem the flow of blood.* **stem from** to have as its origin, to come from. *Her fear of dogs stems from being bitten as a child.*

She cut the stem of the flower near the base and put it in water.

Stem

stench (stenches) *noun* a very nasty smell.

stencil *noun* a piece of paper, metal or plastic with a design or letters cut out of it, used for making designs or letters on something. **stencil** (stencils, stenciling, stenciled) *verb*.

step *noun* 1 the movement made when lifting a foot and putting it down in a different place. *He takes very big steps.* 2 the sound made when walking. *She could hear steps coming towards her.* 3 a short distance. *The beach is just a few steps from the house.* 4 a flat surface on which you put your foot when you walk up or down, a stair. 5 one of a series of actions that are done to get a certain result, or one of a series of stages. *What is the next step?* 6 a movement of the feet in dancing. If you are in step, you are moving your feet forward at the same time as your partner or others walking. If you are out of step, you are not in agreement with the others. **step by step** doing one thing at the time, slowly. **take steps to do something** to get a result. **watch your step!** be careful! **step** (steps, stepping, stepped) *verb* to walk. *She stepped into the house.* **step in** to become involved in order to help. *Her mother stepped in and sorted out her problems.* **step up** to increase in size or speed. *We must step up production.*

We have a small stepladder in the kitchen and a big one in the garage.

stepchild (stepchildren) *noun* a child of a husband's or wife's earlier marriage. **stepbrother** *noun*. **stepsister** *noun*.

stepfather *noun* your stepfather is the man who has married your mother after your real father has died or your parents have divorced. **stepmother** *noun*.

steppe *noun* a large area of grassland without trees, especially in Russia.

stereo *adjective* stereophonic, giving out sound or sound coming from two different places. *Stereo equipment*. **stereo** *noun* 1 a stereo sound or recording. 2 a stereo record/CD player.

stereotype *noun* a fixed idea or typical example of somebody or something. *He is small and thin and does not fit the stereotype of a boxer*. **stereotype** *verb*.

stern *adjective* strict. **sternly** *adverb*. *He looked at her sternly*.

stern *noun* the back end of a ship.

stethoscope *noun* a medical instrument that a doctor uses to listen to somebody's heartbeat. *The stethoscope felt cold*.

stew *verb* to cook slowly in liquid. **stew** *noun* a meal with meat and vegetables cooked in liquid.

stick *noun* 1 a long thin piece of wood, a branch broken from a tree. 2 a piece of wood specially made for leaning on when walking. *A walking stick*. 3 any long thin piece of something. *A stick of celery*. **get the wrong end of the stick** to misunderstand something. **stick** (sticks, sticking, stuck) *verb* 1 to push something pointed into something. *She stuck a tack into the bulletin board*. 2 to fix one thing to another thing with glue or another sticky substance. *Don't forget to stick a stamp on the envelope*. 3 to become fixed, unable to move. *I'm stuck*. 4 to not give up, to keep on doing something. 5 to stay. *We must stick together*. 6 to put. *Stick your bags in the corner*. **stick at** to continue to work hard at something. *If she sticks at the job, she'll do well*. **stick to** 1 If you stick to somebody, you are loyal to that person and support him. 2 If you stick to something, you refuse to change. *We are sticking to our plan*. **sticky** *adjective*. **stickiness** *noun*.

We crossed the stile and walked towards the distant hills.

Dr Smith listened to Peggy's heart through his stethoscope.

stiff *adjective* 1 not bending or moving easily. *Stiff cardboard*. 2 firm, not runny. *Beat the cream until it is stiff*. 3 not friendly, formal. *The new teacher is very stiff with the children*. 4 difficult. *A stiff test*. 5 strong. *A stiff drink*. **stiffness** *noun*.

stile *noun* a step used to climb over a fence or gate. *Let me help you over the stile*.

still *adjective* 1 not moving. 2 silent. 3 not fizzy. *Still water*. **still** *adverb* 1 up to now or up to that moment. *Is he still waiting?* 2 even. *More amazing still, she never spoke again*. 3 nevertheless, in spite of what has been said. *The children were very naughty – still, she shouldn't have hit them*. 4 even so. *He is not the most brilliant member of the team, but he still deserves to play*.

still *noun* 1 quietness with no activity. *In the still of the night*. 2 a still photograph taken from a cinema film. 3 an apparatus for making alcoholic spirits.

stimulate *verb* to make more active or interested in something. *Sunlight stimulates growth*. **stimulation** *noun*.

sting *noun* 1 the sharp pointed part of some insects such as bees, or on some plants such as nettles, that can prick and hurt. 2 a sharp pain or wound caused by a sting. **sting** (stings, stinging, stung) *verb* 1 to prick with a sting. 2 to feel a strong pain or to feel hurt. *His eyes were stinging from the smoke*. 3 to take too much money from somebody. *They stung us for ten dollars*.

stink *noun* 1 a nasty smell. 2 a big fuss, usually made by complaining. **stink** (stinks, stinking, stank or stunk) *verb* 1 to smell very badly. *The locker room stinks*. 2 to be very unpleasant or bad. *The plan stinks*.

The skunk was responsible for the terrible stink.

stir (stirs, stirring, stirred) *verb* 1 to mix something by moving it around with a spoon. 2 to move. *She is fast asleep and hasn't stirred.* 3 to excite or be touched by something. *The news stirred him into action.* **stir up** cause trouble between others, especially by telling stories. *She loves stirring things up.* **stir** *noun* 1 the action of stirring. 2 excitement, shock. *The discovery caused quite a stir.*

stir-fry (stir-fries, stir-frying, stir-fried) *verb* to cook small pieces of meat and vegetables quickly by stirring them in a wok or frying pan. **stir-fry** *noun.*

stirrup *noun* a metal loop on a horse's saddle for the rider's foot.

stock *noun* 1 the supply of goods or other things to be sold or used. *A large stock of food.* 2 a group of farm animals used for breeding or kept for their meat. 3 your ancestors or original family, or a type of animal or plant. *Many Americans are of European stock.* 4 a liquid made from vegetables or meat used in cooking. *Chicken stock.* 5 shares in the ownership of a business company. **take stock** to think about something before deciding what to do next. **stock** *verb* 1 to keep goods in stock. 2 to fill or supply a place with food or other thing.

stock exchange *noun* a place where shares are bought and sold.

Stockholm *noun* the capital of Sweden.

stodgy (stodgier, stodgiest) *adjective* 1 heavy, sticky and filling, especially food. *Stodgy rice.* 2 dull and uninteresting.

stole *verb* past tense of steal.

stole *noun* a long piece of material worn around the shoulders.

stomach *noun* 1 an organ in the body where food is digested. 2 the front part of the body below the waist. 3 the ability or the willingness to put up with something **stomach** *I just didn't have the stomach for more violence. verb* to put up with, usually something unpleasant.

Bill sat on the stool to play the guitar.

Many people called 'dealers' work at the stock exchange. Their job is to buy and sell shares.

stone *noun* 1 very hard material found in the ground, rock. 2 a small piece of rock. *He threw a stone at the window.* 3 a jewel. *A precious stone.* 4 something that forms in a person's kidneys or gallbladder. *A kidney stone.* **stone** *verb* 1 to throw stones at somebody. *They stoned the traitor to death.* 2 to take the stones out of fruit. **stony** *adjective.*

stone *adverb* completely cold, deaf, etc.. *The food was stone cold by the time the guests arrived.*

stoned *adjective* under the influence of drugs.

stood *verb* past tense of stand.

stool *noun* a seat with legs but without arms or a back. *A milking stool.*

stoop *verb* 1 to stand or walk with your shoulders bent forward. 2 to lower or allow yourself to do something. *I wouldn't stoop to thanking that woman.* **stoop** *noun.*

stop (stops, stopping, stopped) *verb* 1 to come to an end or put an end to an activity or movement. To finish moving, to not continue working. *My watch has stopped.* 2 to prevent somebody from doing something or something from happening. *How can I stop him from smoking?* 3 to stay, especially for a short visit. *She stopped by for a visit.* 4 to fill a hole, to close. 5 to block. 6 to prevent money from being paid. *She stopped the check.* **stop** *noun* 1 the moment something stops, a pause, an end. 2 a place where buses stop. 3 a knob or lever that changes the level of the notes (pitch) and controls the pipes on an organ.

stopwatch *noun* a watch that can be started and stopped and is used for timing things such as races.

storage *noun* the keeping of things in a special place. *We put our furniture in storage when we went overseas.*

store *noun* 1 a place where things are sold, a shop, especially a larger one. 2 a supply of something that is kept for later use. **in store** 1 kept ready for later use. 2 about to happen. *There are lots of adventures in store for you.* **store** *verb* to keep things until they are needed. *The wood is stored in the shed.*

stork *noun* a tall bird with a long beak and long legs. *We saw a stork nest on safari.*

storm *noun* 1 a very strong wind, usually with rain, thunder or snow. 2 an excited or angry show of feeling. *A storm of protest.* **storm** *verb* 1 to attack or force your way into a place. *The soldiers stormed the stronghold.* 2 to show anger by moving around or shouting loudly and angrily. *He stormed out of the room.* **stormy** *adjective*.

story (stories) *noun* 1 a description of real or made-up events. 2 a lie. *He is always telling stories.* 3 a floor or level of a building. *It's a four-story building.*

stout *adjective* 1 thick and strong. *Stout climbing boots.* 2 rather fat. *He is short and stout.* 3 firm. *A stout supporter of the club.*

stove *noun* a device for heating a room or cooking on. *A hot stove.*

straddle *verb* to sit or stand across something, with one leg on each side. *To straddle a horse.*

The stove roared indoors, keeping us warm while the wind rattled at the windows.

straggle *verb* 1 to grow in an untidy way. *Ivy straggled over the wall.* 2 to move forward slowly behind others. **straggler** *noun*. **straggly** *adjective*. *Straggly hair.*

straight *adjective* 1 going in the same direction, not bent or curved. *Straight hair.* 2 upright. *The picture is not straight.* 3 neat. 4 honest. *A straight answer.* If you keep a straight face, you look serious and try not to laugh. **straight** *adverb* 1 in a straight line. 2 directly, without stopping. *Go straight home.* **straight away** immediately. **go straight** to leave a life of crime and live an honest life.

straighten *verb* to make something straight or become straight.

straightforward *adjective* 1 easy to understand or do. *The installation instructions are quite straightforward.* 2 honest. *He is a very straightforward person.*

strain *verb* 1 to stretch tightly, usually by pulling. 2 to make a great effort. *She strained her ears to hear.* 3 to damage a part of your body. *I've strained a muscle.* 4 to pour something through a strainer to remove liquid. *He strained the peas.* **strain** *noun* 1 the condition or force of being stretched. *The cable broke under the strain.* 2 a state of worry or tension. Something that tests you or uses up strength. *Looking after children is a great strain.* 3 an injury to a muscle. 4 a tune. *The strains of a song wafted up to where she sat on the deck.*

We use a tea strainer because we don't like leaves floating in our tea.

DID YOU KNOW

The layer of atmosphere just above the Earth's surface, where we live, is called the troposphere; then comes the stratosphere; then the mesosphere, thermosphere, and finally the exosphere.

The rocket took off and climbed steeply until it reached the stratosphere.

strain *noun* 1 a type of plant or animal. *A new strain of beans.* 2 a quality that develops, or a characteristic. *There has always been a strain of recklessness in my family.*

strainer *noun* an instrument for straining solids from liquids.

strange *adjective* unusual or surprising, not known or seen before. **strangely** *adverb*. *Strangely, it seems that she did not leave at her usual time.*

stranger *noun* 1 somebody you don't know. 2 somebody who is in a place he doesn't know. *I'm a stranger in this town.*

strangle *verb* to kill by pressing on the throat of an animal or to stop the flow of nutrients to a plant. **strangulation** *noun*.

strap *noun* a strip of leather or other material used for fastening. **strap** (straps, strapping, strapped) *verb* to fasten with a strap or straps. *He strapped the child into the car seat.* **be strapped on** fastened. *Make sure your backpack is strapped on tightly.*

strategy (strategies) *noun* 1 a particular plan to achieve something. *He worked out a clever strategy to get more money.* 2 the planning of the movements of armies in war. *A military strategy.*

stratosphere *noun* the outer part of the air which surrounds the earth, between about 10 and 50 km above the earth's surface.

straw *noun* 1 dried stalks of grain. 2 a thin tube of paper or plastic used for drinking through. *Drinking straws.* **the last straw** the last or latest in a row of unpleasant events. *After a terrible day at the office, losing my purse was the last straw.*

strawberry (strawberries) *noun* a soft and juicy red fruit.

stray *verb* 1 to wander away from somewhere you are supposed to be. 2 to move away from a subject, to not concentrate. *During study hall his thoughts strayed to football.* **stray** *adjective* without a home or not in its usual place. *Stray animals need loving homes.*

streak *noun* 1 a long stripe or mark that is different from what is around it. *He has a few gray streaks in his hair.* 2 a quality of character, a trace. *That boy has a streak of cruelty.* **streak** *verb* 1 to move very quickly. 2 to mark with streaks. 3 to run in a public place with no clothes on. **streaker** *noun*. *There was a streaker at the football game.*

stream *noun* 1 a flow of water smaller than a river. 2 a flow of people or things. *A long stream of cars.* **stream** *verb* 1 to flow. *Tears streamed down her face.* 2 to move like a stream or float in the air. *The sun streamed in through the window.*

streamer *noun* a long ribbon or strip of colored paper.

Streamers hung from the ceiling at David's party.

streamlined *adjective* smooth and regular in shape, able to move easily through air or water. Racing cars and powerboats are streamlined. **streamline** *verb*.

street *noun* a road with buildings along the side in a town or village. *The street where I live.* on the **streets** in the active part of a city.

streetwise *adjective* used to the ways of modern city life. *If you're not streetwise in this town, you'll get mugged or ripped off.*

strength *noun* 1 the quality of being strong. *Superman has enough strength to lift a truck.* 2 something that gives power. *Translation is her biggest strength.*

strengthen *verb* to make or become stronger. *Defeat strengthened our resolve.*

strenuous *adjective* using or needing great effort. *I had a very strenuous day at work.*

stress (stresses) *noun* 1 worries caused by difficulties in life. *She has been under a lot of stress because of her father's illness.* 2 saying a word or part of a word more strongly than another. In the word 'bookstore', the stress is put on 'book'. 3 the force of weight or pressure on something. *The heavy traffic puts stress on the bridge.* **stress** *verb* to give importance to something. *He stressed the need for peace.* **stressful** *adjective*.

The patient was put on a stretcher and taken by ambulance to the hospital.

stretch *verb* 1 to become wider or longer. If you pull a rubber band it stretches. 2 to spread out or extend over a distance or period of time. *The forest stretches from the mountains to the sea.* 3 to straighten your body to full length. To push out your arms to reach something. 4 to reach, be long enough. 5 If a job stretches you, you have to work very hard at it. **stretch** (stretches) *noun* 1 stretching or being stretched. *The cat got up and had a good stretch.* 2 an area of land or water, or a period of time. *He was given a long stretch in prison.* **stretchy** *adjective*. *Stretchy material.*

stretcher *noun* a long piece of cloth between two poles, or something similar, on which a sick or injured person can be carried lying down. *The injured player was carried off on a stretcher.*

strict *adjective* 1 firm, making people do what you want. *Our teacher is very strict about punctuality.* 2 exact, complete. *The strict truth.* **strictness** *noun*.

stride (strides, striding, strode, stridden) *verb* to walk with long steps. *She strode across the lawn to meet him.* **stride** *noun* 1 a long step in walking. 2 If you make great strides, you do much better.

strife *noun* trouble between people.

strike (strikes, striking, struck) *verb* 1 to hit somebody or something. *He was struck by lightning.* 2 to stop working for a time, usually to get more money or because you are angry about something. 3 to suddenly happen or come to mind. *It struck me that we should have visited him.* 4 to sound. *The clock struck eight.* 5 to find something in a place. *They struck oil in the desert.* 6 to seem. *She strikes me as very intelligent.* 7 If you are struck by something, you are very impressed by it. *He was struck by her beauty.* 8 to light or produce a flame. *He struck a match.* **strike lucky** to have good luck. **strike out** to be unsuccessful at something. **strike up** 1 to begin a friendship. 2 to begin to play music of to talk. *I was amazed when she suddenly struck up a conversation.* **strike** *noun* 1 a time when no work is done. *The train drivers are on strike.* 2 a hit. 3 an air attack. 4 finding oil or gold.

string *noun* 1 a thin piece of cord for tying things. 2 nylon or wire in a guitar or other stringed instrument for making sounds. The strings are the stringed instruments in an orchestra. 3 a line or number of things. *A string of accidents.* **string** (strings, stringing, strung) *verb* 1 to put a string or strings on something. *To string a tennis racket.* 2 to thread on a string or hang something on a string. *Flags were strung across the street.* **highly strung** somebody who is easily excited or hurt in feelings.

strip (strips, stripping, stripped) *verb* 1 to take a covering off something. *We stripped the paint off the wood.* 2 to undress. *He stripped off his shirt.* 3 to take somebody's belongings away from them. *He was stripped of his rights.* **strip** *noun* 1 a long narrow piece of material or land. 2 a comic strip. **stripper** *noun*.

stripe *noun* 1 a long line of color among other colors. 2 a band of cloth sewn on to a soldier's or policeman's uniform to show his rank. **stripy** *adjective*. **striped** *adjective*.

The stripes on her uniform indicated a high rank.

strobe lighting *noun* a light that goes on and off very quickly.

stroke *noun* 1 a hit or blow. *He cut off the giant's head with a single stroke of his sword.* 2 a movement or action with your arms, especially in sports like golf or tennis. *She swims with strong strokes.* 3 a line made by the movement of a pen or brush. *Brush strokes.* 4 the sound made by a clock striking. *He arrived on the stroke of three.* 5 a sudden illness that often makes people unable to move parts of their body. **a stroke of luck** being very lucky.

stroke *verb* to move your hand slowly and gently over something. *She stroked the dear old cat.* **stroke** *noun*.

stroll *verb* to walk slowly and in a relaxed way. **stroll** *noun*. *A stroll in the park.*

strong *adjective* 1 having great power, especially of the body. *He is very strong and can lift heavy weights.* 2 feeling confident and sure, not easily frightened or upset. *She has a very strong will.* 3 not easily broken. 4 having a great effect or taste, not weak. *A strong smell of gas.* 5 having a certain number of people. *Our club is a hundred strong.* **strongly** *adverb*. **strong** *adverb*. *She is old but still going strong.*

The Taj Mahal is one of the world's most beautiful structures.

This watch is studded with diamonds.

stronghold *noun* 1 a fortified place. 2 a place where many people do or believe the same. *This town is a rightwing stronghold.*

struck *verb* past tense of strike.

structure *noun* 1 an arrangement of parts, something built. *The bridge is an interesting structure.* 2 the way in which parts are put together or in which something is made. *The structure of a sentence.* **structure** *verb* to arrange or organize. **structural** *adjective*.

struggle *noun* a hard fight. **struggle** *verb* 1 to twist, kick and fight to get free. *She struggled against her attacker.* 2 to make a great effort, fight hard to do something difficult. *He struggles with his homework.*

strum (strums, strumming, strummed) *verb* to play the guitar by moving your fingers up and down the strings.

strut (struts, strutting, strutted) *verb* to walk in a proud way, usually with your head held high and chest out.

stub (stubs, stubbing, stubbed) *verb* to hurt your toe by hitting it against something.

stub *noun* 1 a short end left when something has been used. *The stub of a pencil.* 2 the part of a check or ticket that you keep.

stubble *noun* short stiff pieces of something growing, especially a short beard after shaving.

stubborn *adjective* having a strong will. If you are stubborn, you do what you want.

stuck *verb* past tense of stick.

stud *noun* 1 a small piece of metal like a nail with a large head used as a decoration. *A belt with silver studs.* 2 a kind of fastener, used instead of a button, usually two parts that are pressed together. **stud** (studs, studding, studded) *verb* to decorate with studs. *A watch studded with diamonds.*

stud *noun* 1 horses kept for breeding. 2 the place where horses are kept for breeding.

student *noun* somebody who is studying or training, especially at a college or university.

studio *noun* 1 a room where a painter or photographer works. 2 a room where film, radio or television programs are made.

study (studies, studying, studied) *verb* 1 to spend time learning about a particular subject. 2 to look at something carefully. *He studied her face for a long time.* **study** (studies) *noun* 1 the activity of studying a subject. 2 a subject you study or a piece of writing on a subject. *He made a study of Greek philosophy.* 3 a drawing or painting planned as part of a larger picture. *A study of a rose.* 4 a room used for reading, writing and studying.

stuff *noun* 1 things or personal things. *Take your stuff up to your room.* 2 material of which something is made. *Try this, it's good stuff for a cold.* **stuff** *verb* 1 to fill something. *She stuffed the cushion with feathers.* 2 to push something quickly and carelessly somewhere. *He stuffed the card in his pocket.* 3 to eat a lot. *I stuffed myself with cookies.*

stuffing *noun* 1 material used to fill something. 2 cut-up food put into meat or vegetables. *Turkey with chestnut stuffing.*

stumble *verb* 1 to trip and almost fall over. 2 to stop or make a mistake while reading or speaking. *He stumbled over a difficult word.*

stun (stuns, stunned, stunning) *verb* 1 to make somebody unconscious by hitting them on the head. 2 to shock. *He was stunned by the news of her death.*

stung *verb* past tense of sting.

stunning *adjective* brilliant, beautiful.

stunt *noun* a dangerous and risky act that somebody does in a film or in order to draw attention. *Most actors don't do their own stunts, they hire a stuntman.*

stuntman *noun* somebody who does stunts in a film so the actor does not have to take any risks.

We went into the sty to see Beryl's new litter of pigs.

WORD HISTORY

The word 'style' comes from the Latin 'stilus', meaning a pen. It came to have the wider meaning of 'the manner of writing with a pen', which gave rise to the present senses of style.

The stuffing was poking out of the teddy bear's foot.

The stuntman drove up the ramp and over the roofs of several other cars.

stupid *adjective* foolish, not clever or intelligent. **stupidity** *noun* being stupid.

sturdy (sturdier, sturdiest) *adjective* strong, not easily broken. *A sturdy chair.* **sturdily** *adverb*. *Sturdily built.* **sturdiness** *noun*.

stutter *verb* to find it difficult to say the first sound of a word, to stammer. **stutter** *noun*. *He stuttered because he was nervous.*

sty (sties) *noun* a place where pigs are kept.

sty or **stye** (sties or styes) *noun* a red swelling on the edge of the eyelid.

style *noun* 1 a kind or sort. *This is a new style of house.* 2 the way something is written, spoken or performed. *The essay was written in an interesting style.* 3 a superior quality or elegance. *They live in grand style.* 4 a kind of fashion or design. *The latest styles in shoes.* 5 part of a flower involved in pollination. **style** *verb* to design or make in a particular style. **stylish** *adjective* showing superior quality, elegant, fashionable. *Stylish clothes.*

sub- *prefix* 1 below, under. *Submarine.* 2 subordinate, secondary. *Subsection.*

subconscious *adjective* of thoughts and feelings which you are not completely conscious or aware of. **subconsciously** *adverb*. **subconscious** *noun*.

subdue (subdues, subduing, subdued) *verb* 1 to overcome or bring under control. *He managed to subdue his emotions.* 2 to soften. *The restaurant had subdued lighting.*

subject (say **sub-djikt**) *noun* 1 somebody or something being talked or written about. 2 something studied. *What's your favorite subject this semester?* 3 in grammar, the word or phrase that does the action of a verb. In the sentence 'The flower is red,' 'flower' is the subject. **change the subject** to talk about something different.

subject (say sub-djikt) *adjective* 1 having to follow or obey something. *We are all subject to the laws of the land.* 2 liable or prone to. *She is subject to colds.* 3 dependent on. *The plan is subject to approval.*

subject (say sub-djekt) *verb* 1 to make somebody experience something. *They subjected him to torture.* 2 to bring under control. **subjection** *noun.*

subjective *adjective* depending on your own taste and opinions.

sublime *adjective* grand or extreme. *Mozart's music is sublime.*

submarine *noun* a ship that can travel under water. **submarine** *adjective.* *A submarine cable.*

submit (submits, submitting, submitted) *verb* 1 to give way. *They had to submit to defeat.* 2 to put forward for consideration. *She submitted her plans to the committee.* **submission** *noun.*

subscribe *verb* 1 to pay regularly for something. *He subscribes to several magazines.* 2 to agree. *I don't subscribe to that theory.* **subscriber** *noun.* **subscription** *noun. Please pay your subscription.*

subside *verb* 1 to sink lower. *The floods finally subsided.* 2 to become less strong. *Her fear subsided.* **subsidence** *noun.*

substance *noun* 1 matter. *Chemical substances.* 2 the main part. *The panel agreed with the substance of the report, but questioned some details.*

substitute *noun* a person or thing that takes the place of another. *They put on a substitute in the second half and he scored.* **substitute** *verb* to use in place of another. **substitution** *noun.*

subtle (say sut-ul) *adjective* 1 small and hard to grasp. *A subtle difference between the two.* 2 delicate. *A very subtle taste.* 3 clever. *A subtle argument.* **subtlety** *noun.*

subtract *verb* to take away, deduct. *Subtract 5 from 8.* **subtraction** *noun.*

suburb *noun* a housing district at the edge of a town. **suburban** *adjective.* **suburbia** *noun* the suburbs. *They live in suburbia.*

subway *noun* an underground railroad.

They explored the ocean depths by submarine.

succeed *verb* 1 to do well. *The plan was good and succeeded.* 2 to come next. *Who will succeed the current chairman?*

success *noun* 1 doing well, achieving an aim. 2 somebody or something that does well. *The play is a real success on Broadway.* **successful** *adjective.*

succession *noun* 1 a series of people or things. *They met with a succession of defeats.* 2 following in order. 3 coming next, especially to the throne. **in succession** one after another.

succulent *adjective* 1 juicy. *A succulent steak.* 2 fleshy. *Succulent plants.*

such *adjective* 1 of this kind. *Such people are to be avoided.* 2 so great. *I had such a fright!* **such-and-such** particular but not specified. *He promises to come at such-and-such a time but is always late.* **such as** of the same kind as. *Big cats such as tigers and lions.* **suchlike** of such a kind. *Ghosts and ghouls and suchlike.*

suck *verb* 1 to take liquid into the mouth by using your lip and tongue muscles. *She sucked the juice from an orange.* 2 to squeeze something in your mouth. *He still sucks his thumb.* 3 to pull. *The boat was sucked into the whirlpool.* **suck up to** to flatter somebody to gain their favor. *He's always sucking up to the teachers.*

sucker *noun* 1 something that sticks to a surface by suction. 2 a person who is easily deceived. *He thinks I am a sucker.*

Sucre *noun* the legal capital of Bolivia.

Sudan *noun* a country in Africa.

Sudan has the biggest sugar factory in Africa, and the third largest in the world.

Sudanese *noun* the people of Sudan. **Sudanese** *adjective. His second wife is Sudanese.*

sudden *adjective* happening unexpectedly or without warning. *A sudden storm broke and lightning flashed.* **all of a sudden** suddenly. **suddenly** *adverb.*

suds *plural noun* froth on soapy water.

sue (sues, suing, sued) *verb* (say soo) to take legal action against somebody. *He sued his employer for damages.*

suede *noun* (say swade) soft leather with a velvety surface. *Blue suede shoes.*

suffer *verb* 1 to feel or experience something bad. *Before the operation he was suffering badly.* 2 to put up with. *He does not suffer fools gladly.* **sufferer** *noun.* **suffering** *noun.*

sufficient *adjective* enough. **sufficiently** *adverb*. **sufficiency** *noun*.

suffix *noun* letters added to the end of a word to make another word. In the word 'forgetful', 'ful' is a suffix.

suffocate *verb* 1 to make it difficult or impossible for somebody to breathe. *The fumes almost suffocated her.* 2 to suffer or die because you can't breathe. **suffocation** *noun*. *Auntie died of suffocation.*

sugar *noun* a sweet food obtained from the juices of various plants, especially sugar cane and sugar beet. **sugar** *verb* to sweeten, especially with sugar. **sugary** *adjective*.

suggest *verb* 1 to put forward as a possibility. *She suggested a different plan.* 2 to bring into the mind. *The color white suggests peace.*

suggestion *noun* 1 a plan or idea. 2 an act of suggesting. 3 a small amount. *A slight suggestion of an accent.* 4 putting beliefs into somebody's mind.

suicide *noun* 1 killing yourself deliberately. *He committed suicide.* 2 somebody who commits suicide. **suicidal** *adjective*.

suit *noun* 1 matching jacket and pants for men, or jacket and skirt for women. 2 special clothes, such as a spacesuit or swimsuit. 3 one of the four sets of cards in a pack (hearts, clubs, diamonds or spades). 4 a lawsuit.

suit *verb* 1 to go well with, or look good on. *That jacket suits you.* 2 to be suitable or convenient. *Friday doesn't suit me at all.* 3 to adapt. *He suited his style to the audience.* **suit yourself** to do as you want to.

suitable *adjective* right for the purpose, appropriate. *Make sure you wear suitable clothes.* **suitability** *noun*.

suitcase *noun* a case used to hold clothes and other things when traveling. *I packed my suitcase and drove to the airport.*

sulk *verb* to be in a bad mood and show this by being silent. *She hated the party and sulked all evening.* **sulk** *noun*. **sulky** *adjective*. *A sulky pout.*

sullen *adjective* 1 silent and bad-tempered. *She gave me sullen looks.* 2 dark and gloomy. *A sullen sky.* **sullenness** *noun*.

sultan *noun* a Muslim ruler.

sultana *noun* 1 a seedless raisin. 2 the mother, wife or daughter of a sultan.

sum *noun* 1 a total. The sum of 4 and 3 is 7. 2 a problem in arithmetic. 3 an amount of money. **sum** *verb* to find a total. **sum up** 1 to summarize, especially at the end of a talk. *The judge summed up the case at the end of the hearing.* 2 to form a judgement. *He summed her up very quickly.*

summarize *verb* to make a summary of. *He summarized the agreement in a few words.* **summarizer** *noun*.

summary *noun* a short account giving the main points. *A quick summary of events.*

summary *adjective* 1 brief. 2 without delay or mercy. *Summary justice.*

summer *noun* the warm season between spring and fall. **summery** *adjective*.

summit *noun* 1 the top of a mountain. 2 the highest point. *He was at the summit of his career.* 3 a meeting between heads of government. *The leaders attended a summit meeting.*

summon *verb* 1 to call to appear. *He was summoned to court as a witness.* 2 to call upon. *She summoned him to help her.* **summon up** to build up, gather. *He summoned up all his energy.*

summons *noun* an official order to appear in a law court.

Sun *noun* 1 the star which the Earth travels around and from which it receives light and warmth. *It's dangerous to look directly at the Sun.* 2 light and warmth from the Sun. *She loves sitting in the sun.* **Sun** (suns, sunning, sunned) *verb* to be in the Sun. *The cat was sunning itself on the terrace.*

The surface of the sun is a phenomenal 6,000 degrees Centigrade and would melt absolutely anything.

sunburn *noun* reddening of the skin caused by too much sun. **sunburn** *verb* to suffer from sunburn. *She was badly sunburned.*

Sunday *noun* the first day of the week, after Saturday and before Monday.

sundial *noun* an instrument that shows the time by a shadow on a dial.

sunflower *noun* a very tall plant with a large round flower.

sung *verb* past tense of sing.

sunglasses *plural noun* dark glasses that protect the eyes from strong sunlight.

sunk *verb* past tense of sink.

sunlight *noun* light from the Sun.

sunny (sunnier, sunniest) *adjective* 1 bright with sunlight. *A sunny room.* 2 cheerful. *She gave me a sunny smile.*

sunrise *noun* the rising of the Sun at dawn.

We sat on the beach and watched the sunrise.

sunset *noun* the setting of the sun.

sunshine *noun* light from the Sun. *We sat in the sunshine and did our knitting.*

suntan *noun* browning of the skin from exposure to the sun. **suntan** *verb*.

super *adjective* exceptional, brilliant.

super- *prefix* 1 above or beyond. *Superstructure.* 2 extra large or good. *Supertankers are the biggest ships.*

superb *adjective* excellent. *A superb wine.*

superficial *adjective* not very deep. *A superficial wound.* **superficiality** *noun*.

superfluous *adjective* more than enough.

superintend *verb* to supervise and inspect. **superintendent** *noun*.

superior *adjective* 1 in a higher position. *A superior officer.* 2 better than average. *Superior quality.* **superior** *noun*. *She is my superior.* **superiority** *noun*.

superlative *adjective* 1 of the highest quality. 2 in grammar, the highest degree of an adjective. Bravest is the superlative form of brave. **superlative** *noun*.

supermarket *noun* a large self-service store that sells food and other goods. *We buy all our groceries from the supermarket.*

Penny looked at the sundial and saw that it was already half past two.

GRAMMAR NOTE

The superlatives of short words add '–est' on to the end: 'oldest', 'youngest', 'tallest'. Longer words use 'most' in front: 'most beautiful', 'most cowardly'. Don't use '–est' and 'most' with the same word.

The bridge was supported by a metal framework on concrete pillars.

AMAZING FACT

Superstitions vary from culture to culture. In the US, black cats are considered bad luck, but in the UK, good luck cards often have a black cat on them! Black cats crossing your path are supposed to be bad luck in both places.

supernatural *adjective* magical or mystical. *He thought there were supernatural forces at work.* **supernatural** *noun*.

supersede (say soup-uh-seed) *verb* to take the place of somebody or something.

supersonic *adjective* faster than the speed of sound. *Concorde is a supersonic aircraft.*

superstition *noun* a personal belief in the special effects of something. Most superstitions are not based on scientific fact. **superstitious** *adjective*. *He is very superstitious and won't walk under ladders.*

supervise *verb* to oversee actions or work. *The foreman's job is to supervise the workers.* **supervision** *noun*. **supervisor** *noun*. **supervisory** *adjective*.

supper *noun* an evening meal. *Mom called when supper was ready.*

supple *adjective* easily bent, flexible. *Athletes have to be supple.* **suppleness** *noun*.

supplement *noun* 1 an added part. *She takes vitamin supplements to add to her diet.* 2 a separate section, especially a color magazine. *The Sunday supplement.* 3 an extra charge. **supplementary** *adjective*.

supply *verb* to provide something that is needed. **supply** (supplies) *noun* 1 providing what is needed. 2 a stock. *A large supply of tires.* 3 (plural supplies) provisions and equipment. *The explorers took enough supplies for three months.* **in short supply** scarce. **supplier** *noun*.

supply and demand *noun* a relationship between the amount of something that is required and its availability

support *verb* 1 to carry the weight of something. *This wall supports the whole house.* 2 to provide with things needed. *He has a family to support.* 3 show the truth of something. *The evidence supports her statement.* 4 to speak in favor. *Most speakers supported the resolution.* **support** *noun*. **supporter** *noun*.

suppose *verb* to assume or think. *I suppose they'll come back.* **be supposed to** to be expected or required to do something. *You were supposed to be there by nine.*

suppress *verb* 1 to prevent from being seen or known. *She tried to suppress a yawn.* 2 to put out of your mind. *She tried to suppress her fear.* **suppression** *noun*.

supreme *adjective* highest in rank, most important. *The case went to the Supreme Court.* **supremacy** *noun*.

surcharge *noun* an extra charge. **surcharge** *verb*. *The travel agency added a surcharge to my bill.*

sure *adjective* 1 convinced. *I'm sure he's telling the truth.* 2 certain. *She is sure to go.* 3 reliable, definite. *A sure way to find out.* **sure** *adverb* certainly. **for sure** without doubt. **sure enough** certainly. **be sure** not fail to do something. *Be sure to lock up before you leave.*

surely *adverb* 1 certainly. *Slowly but surely.* 2 according to reason. *Surely that can't be right?* 3 safely. *The goat picked its way surely up the cliff.*

surf *noun* foam made by the sea breaking near the shore. **surf** *verb* to ride the surf on a board. **surfing** *noun*. **surfer** *noun*.

surface *noun* 1 the outside of a solid body. *We have to dust every surface.* 2 the top of a liquid or of the ground. *The diver swam to the surface.* 3 outward appearance. *On the surface everything was quiet.* **surface** *verb* 1 to make a surface. 2 to rise to the surface. *The submarine surfaced slowly.* 3 to come to light. *The missing papers have suddenly surfaced.*

surgeon *noun* a doctor who performs medical operations.

surgery *noun* medical treatment involving an operation. *The surgery was complicated and the operation lasted five hours.*

surgical *adjective* relating to medical surgery. *Surgical instruments have to be totally sterile.*

Suriname *noun* a country in South America.

surly *adjective* bad-tempered and unfriendly. *He had a surly look about him.*

surplus *noun* an extra amount left over when requirements have been met. **surplus** *adjective*. *These items are surplus to government requirements.*

The flag of Suriname has green, white and red stripes with a yellow star.

surprise *noun* an unexpected event. *Promotion came as a surprise to her.* **surprise** *verb* 1 to catch by surprise. 2 to shock. *I'm surprised at you!* 3 to take by surprise. *He surprised her taking another piece of chocolate cake out of the fridge.* **surprising** *adjective*. **surprisingly** *adverb*.

surrender *verb* 1 to give up. *The army surrendered after the heavy defeat.* 2 to hand over. **surrender** *noun*.

Dedicated surfers travel all over the world to ride the waves. Some of the best surfing beaches are in Australia and in Hawaii.

WORD HISTORY

The word 'surly' has changed its meaning over the years. It originally meant 'sir-like', in the sense of lordly or masterful, and was spelt 'sirly'. This changed to meaning haughty (misusing a lordly position perhaps), then fell to the present meaning of bad-tempered and unfriendly.

The trapeze artist seemed to be suspended in mid-air as she leapt from one bar to another.

surround *verb* to be all around or enclose. *Trees surround the house.* **surround** *noun* an area or border surrounding something.

surroundings *plural noun* things around somebody or something. *She quickly got used to her new surroundings.*

survey *verb* (say ser-**vay**) 1 to take a general look. *He surveyed the situation.* 2 to examine the condition of something. *They had the area surveyed.* **survey** *noun* (say **ser**-vay) 1 a general view. *The book gave a historical survey.* 2 an examination of property. 3 a report or plan of an examination of an area. **surveyor** *noun*.

survive *verb* 1 to continue to live or exist. *They were lucky to survive the earthquake.* 2 to live longer than someone. *He was survived by his wife and two children.* **survival** *noun*. **survivor** *noun*.

suspect *verb* (say suh-**spekt**) 1 to be inclined to believe. *The police suspect murder.* 2 to doubt somebody's innocence. *They suspect him of drug-dealing.* **suspect** *noun* (say **suh**-spekt) a suspected person. **suspect** *adjective* (say **suh**-spekt) not to be trusted.

suspend *verb* 1 to hang up. 2 to put off. *The game was suspended due to bad weather.* 3 to keep away from school. *They were suspended for bad behavior.*

suspenders *plural noun* two straps that attach to your pants and go over your shoulders to keep your pants up.

suspense *noun* anxious or exciting uncertainty. *The film was full of suspense.* **keep in suspense** to make somebody wait for important information. *Don't keep me in suspense – have I passed?*

suspension *noun* 1 the act of suspending or being suspended. 2 springs and other devices that support a vehicle on its axles and give a comfortable ride.

suspension bridge *noun* a bridge with a roadway suspended from cables.

suspicion *noun* 1 feeling inclined to believe or doubt something. *His suspicions were confirmed when she was arrested.* 2 a slight trace. **above suspicion** too good to be suspected. **under suspicion** suspected. **suspicious** *adjective*. *She disappeared under very suspicious circumstances.*

S

Suva *noun* the capital of Fiji.

swagger *verb* to walk or behave in an arrogant way. *The dictator swaggered into the room.* **swagger** *noun.*

swallow *verb* 1 to cause to pass down the throat. *Chew your food well before you swallow it.* 2 to accept something too easily. *I made up an excuse and he swallowed it.* 3 to overcome. *He swallowed his pride and apologized.* **swallow** *noun.*

swallow *noun* an insect-eating bird with a forked tail. *Swallows flew high above the trees.*

Swallows migrate long distances..

swam *verb* past tense of swim.

swamp *noun* waterlogged land, a bog or marsh. **swamp** *verb* to overwhelm, flood. *The radio station was swamped with letters of complaint.* **swampy** *adjective.*

swan *noun* a large, white waterbird with a long neck. *Black swans are unusual.*

swank *adjective* fashionable or expensive. *They stayed in a swank hotel on the Upper East Side.*

swap *verb* to exchange one thing for another. *They swapped sandwiches.* **swap** *noun.*

swat (swats, swatting, swatted) *verb* to hit with a sharp blow. *He swatted the fly with a newspaper, but missed.*

sway *verb* 1 to lean in one direction and then another. 2 to be uncertain. 3 to control or rule over. *He swayed the crowd with his speech.* **sway** *noun* 1 a swaying motion. 2 influence or rule. *Common sense held sway.*

Swaziland *noun* a country in Africa.

swear (swears, swore, sworn) *verb* 1 to promise something faithfully. *He swore that he would never return.* 2 to make somebody promise something. *He swore them to secrecy.* 3 to use vulgar language. *He was sent off for swearing at the referee.* 4 to have great belief in something. *She swears by acupuncture.* **swear to** to be certain. *I couldn't swear to it.* **swearer** *noun.*

sweat *noun* 1 moisture that is given off by the body through the skin. 2 a sweating condition. *I broke into a sweat right away.* **sweat** *verb* to give off sweat, to perspire. **sweat it out** put up with a difficulty to the end. **sweaty** (sweatier, sweatiest) *adjective.*

The flag of Swaziland has spears and shields against a striped blue, yellow and red background.

sweater *noun* a piece of warm, knitted clothing for the top half of your body.

Sweden *noun* a Scandinavian country in Europe.

Swedish *noun* 1 the language spoken in Sweden. 2 the people of Sweden. **Swedish** *adjective. The Swedish national anthem.*

sweep (sweeps, sweeping, swept) *verb* 1 to clean dust or dirt with a brush. *He swept the floor.* 2 to remove quickly. *The floods swept away the bridge.* 3 to go quickly. *She swept out of the room.* 4 to cover quickly. *The trend swept the country.* **sweep** *noun* 1 an act of sweeping. 2 an expanse of land. 3 a search or attack. **sweeper** *noun.*

sweeping *adjective* wide-ranging. *They made sweeping changes to the rules.*

sweet *adjective* 1 tasting sugary, not bitter. 2 very pleasant. *Sweet memories.* 3 charming or kind. *When I knew her she was a sweet little girl.* **sweetness** *noun.* **sweetness** *noun.* **sweeten** *verb.*

Tom has a sweet tooth and enjoys cakes, milkshakes and fruit.

sweet pea *noun* a climbing plant with sweet-smelling flowers.

swell (swells, swelled, swollen) *verb* to grow larger, to expand. *He swelled with pride.* **swell** *noun* 1 the process of swelling. 2 the rise and fall of the sea's surface.

swelling *noun* a part of the body that has swollen. *There was a swelling on his neck.*

sweltering *adjective* uncomfortably hot.

swept *verb* past tense of sweep.

swerve *verb* to change direction suddenly. **swerve** *noun. She swerved to avoid the car and jumped the curb.*

swift *adjective* quick. *We had a very swift response to the application.* **swiftly** *adverb.* **swiftness** *noun.*

swift *noun* a small bird with long wings, similar to a swallow.

swill *verb* to drink a lot of something. *They swilled champagne at the reception.* **swill** *noun* sloppy food for pigs.

swim (swims, swimming, swam, swum) *verb* 1 to move through the water. 2 to cover by swimming. *We swam two lengths of the pool.* 3 to float on the surface. 4 to feel dizzy. *My head was swimming.* **swim** *noun. We went for a quick swim.* **swimmer** *noun.* **swimming pool** *noun* an indoor or outdoor pool for swimming.

swindle *verb* to cheat a person. *He swindled her out of her savings.* **swindle** *noun.* **swindler** *noun. A notorious swindler.*

swing (swings, swinging, swung) *verb* 1 to move to and fro or in a curve. *The door swung open.* 2 to change from one opinion or mood to another. *Popular opinion is swinging away from the government.* **swing** *noun* 1 a swinging movement. 2 a seat hanging from ropes or chains, for swinging on. 3 the amount by which opinions change from one side to another. *A big swing against the chairman.* 4 a kind of jazz music. **in full swing** fully active. *A party in full swing.*

swirl (say swurl) *verb* to move round quickly in circles. **swirl** *noun.* **swirly** *adjective. Swirly patterns on her dress.*

Swiss *noun* the people of Switzerland. **Swiss** *adjective. A Swiss watch.*

switch *noun* 1 a device for turning something on and off. 2 a change. **switch** *verb* 1 to turn on or off. *Don't forget to switch off the lights.* 2 to change. *They switched seats.*

Switzerland *noun* a country in southern Europe.

swivel (swivels, swiveling, swiveled) *verb* to turn round. *I swiveled in amazement.*

swoop *verb* to come down with a rush. *The eagle swooped on its prey.* **swoop** *noun.*

sword *noun* (say sord) a weapon with a long metal blade and a handle.

swordfish *noun* a large seafish with a long upper jaw that looks like a sword.

swum *verb* past tense of swim.

swung *verb* past tense of swing.

syllable *noun* a part of a word with one sound. 'Dog' has one syllable, 'tiger' and 'giraffe' have two syllables, and 'gorilla' has three syllables.

syllabus *noun* the program or outline of a course of study. *The chemistry syllabus.*

symbol *noun* a mark or sign used to represent something. *The dove is a universal symbol of peace.* **symbolic** *adjective.* **symbolically** *adverb.*

symbolize *verb* to be a symbol.

symmetrical *adjective* able to be divided into two halves that are exactly the same. A butterfly shape is symmetrical. **symmetry** *noun. Beautiful symmetry.*

Every Friday night they went to the synagogue to pray.

A swordfish has a razor-sharp upper jaw that looks like a sword.

sympathy *noun* 1 the understanding and sharing of another person's feelings or opinions. 2 feeling pity and sadness for somebody. **sympathetic** *adjective.*

symphony *noun* a long piece of music for an orchestra, usually in three or four parts (called movements). **symphonic** *adjective.*

symptom *noun* 1 a sign that an illness exists. *The symptoms of pneumonia.* 2 a sign of something. *These are symptoms of social unrest.* **symptomatic** *adjective.*

synagogue (say sin-uh-gog) *noun* the building where Jewish people worship.

synonym (say sin-uh-nim) *noun* a word that means the same or nearly the same as another. 'Small' and 'little' are synonyms. **synonymous** (say sin-on-im-us) *adjective.* 'Shut' is synonymous with 'close'.

syntax (say sin-tax) *noun* in grammar, the way words are arranged to form sentences.

synthesizer *noun* an electronic musical instrument with a keyboard that can make a wide range of different sounds.

synthetic *adjective* artificially made, not natural. *Nylon is a synthetic material.*

Syria *noun* a country in Southwest Asia.

Syrian *noun* the people of Syria. **Syrian** *adjective. Her husband is Syrian.*

The syringe was filled with plasma.

syringe *noun* a device for injecting liquids into the body, also called a hypodermic needle.

syrup *noun* a thick sweet liquid. *On Sundays we have pancakes with maple syrup.* **syrupy** *adjective. This fruit juice is so sweet, it's syrupy.*

system *noun* 1 a group of connected parts that work together as a whole. *A new computer system.* 2 an organized set of methods. **get something out of your system** get rid of something. **systematic** *adjective.*

T

Tt

tab *noun* a small piece of paper or metal attached to something that you can hold or pull. *Pull the tab to open the carton.*

table *noun* 1 a piece of furniture with a flat top supported by one or more legs. 2 a list of facts or figures, especially arranged in columns. **multiplication tables** a list of numbers multiplied. **tablecloth** a cloth for covering a table. **tablespoon** a large spoon used for serving food. **tablespoonful** the amount that a tablespoon can hold.

tablet *noun* 1 a small, usually round, solid piece of medicine that you swallow, a pill. 2 a small flat piece of soap.

table tennis *noun* ping pong. a game for two or four people who use paddles to hit a small ball over a net on a large table.

tabloid *noun* a small-sized newspaper with lots of photographs and short news stories.

taboo *noun* something that is forbidden or generally disapproved of by custom or tradition. *Cannibalism is a taboo among most people.* **taboo** *adjective.*

tack *noun* 1 a short, sharp nail with a large flat head. 2 the saddle, reins, bridle etc. needed to ride a horse, saddlery.

tack *verb* 1 to use tacks or small nails to fasten something. 2 to sew something roughly with long stitches before sewing it neatly. 3 to sail into the wind on a sideways or zigzag course.

These are all pieces of tack.

tackle *verb* 1 to try to deal with a problem or difficulty. *He tackled the problems one at a time.* 2 to try to get a ball from another player or bring a player to the ground in games such as football. **tackle** *noun.*

tackle *noun* all the things you need for doing something. *Fishing tackle.*

tacky *adjective* 1 sticky. *The paint is still tacky.* 2 (slang) vulgar, in bad taste.

Tajikistan used to be part of the Soviet Union, but gained independence in 1991.

tact *noun* skill in not upsetting people, especially when a situation is difficult. **tactful** *adjective.* **tactless** *adjective.*

tactics *plural noun* the way of organizing or planning things to the best advantage so as to win a game, battle etc. or to achieve what you want. **tactical** *adjective.*

tadpole *noun* a tiny black creature with a long tail that lives in water and that will grow into a frog, toad or newt.

tag *noun* 1 a small paper, cloth or plastic label. *I sewed a name tag on to his collar.* 2 a children's chasing game.

tail *noun* 1 the long part that sticks out of the back of an animal, bird or fish. 2 a part that sticks out at the back of something. *The tail of an aircraft.* 3 **tails** the side of the coin that does not have a head (heads and tails). **tail** *verb* to follow closely.

tail gate *verb* to drive too closely to the care in front of you.

tailor *noun* a person whose business is to make clothes, especially men's suits.

Taipei *noun* the capital of Taiwan.

Taiwan *noun* a country in East Asia.

Tajikistan *noun* a country in central Asia.

take (takes, taking, took, taken) *verb* 1 to reach out for something and to hold or grasp it. 2 to move or lead to another place. *He took the dishes to the sink.* 3 to remove. *Who has taken my ruler?* 4 to perform an action, to do. *I'm going to take a bath.* 5 to photograph. *She took my picture.* 6 to swallow. *Take three tablets a day.* 7 to accept. *Take my advice.* 8 to need or require. *It takes half an hour to get to the airport.* 9 to travel by. *Take the bus.* 10 seize or capture. *The troops took the town.* 11 to choose. *Take whichever one you like.* **take after** to look or behave like. *He takes after his father.* **take away** 1 to subtract. 2 to remove. **take down** 1 to remove something that is hanging. *They took down the decorations.* 2 to write down. *He took down some notes.* **take in** 1 to deceive. *She took me in with her sad story.* 2 to understand. *I didn't take in all you said.* **take off** 1 to remove clothes. 2 (of an aircraft) to leave the ground. **take on** 1 to start to employ somebody. 2 to challenge somebody. **take out** 1 to remove from a place. 2 to invite somebody somewhere. **take over** to take control of. **take place** to happen. *Our wedding took place under the stars.*

talc (talcum powder) *noun* a soft, scented powder that you sprinkle on your body after a bath.

tale *noun* 1 a story. *A fairy tale.* 2 an untrue or gossipy story, a lie.

talent *noun* great skill or natural ability to do something really well.

talk *verb* to speak, to use words to express feelings ideas etc., to discuss. **talk** *noun* 1 a conversation. 2 a short, informal lecture. **talk down to** to speak to somebody condescendingly as if to a child. **talking to** a telling-off or reprimand.

talkative *adjective* fond of talking a lot. *Are girls more talkative than boys?*

tall *adjective* high or of more than average height. *He's a tall man.* 2 having a certain height. Henry is 6 feet tall. **tall story** a story that is hard to believe.

Tallinn *noun* the capital of Estonia.

talon *noun* a hooked claw of a bird of prey.

tambourine *noun* a small drum with metal discs around the edge that you shake or tap with your fingers.

Tambourines are an old type of musical instrument.

tame *adjective*. A tame animal or bird is not wild and is not afraid of human beings. **tame** *verb*.

tamper *verb* to interfere or meddle with something without permission. *She tampered with the lock and now it's broken.*

tan *noun* 1 light brown. 2 (suntan) light brown skin caused by its being exposed to the Sun. **tan** *verb*.

tandem *noun* a bicycle with two seats, one behind the other.

tandoori *noun* an Indian way of cooking food in a clay oven. *We had tandoori chicken at the Indian restaurant.*

tangerine *noun* 1 a fruit like a small orange with a loose skin. 2 the color of a tangerine.

tangle *verb* to twist things such as hairs, wires, rope or string together. **tangle** *noun*. *Our kitten attacked my mom's knitting basket and left a big tangle of wool.*

tank *noun* 1 a large container for storing a liquid or gas. 2 a heavy military vehicle armed with guns.

tanker *noun* a large ship or truck used for carrying liquids such as oil.

WORD HISTORY

The word 'tank' was coined during World War I as a secret code name for the newly invented military vehicle. The name was kept when the vehicles eventually went into battle.

WORD HISTORY

Tangerines are named after the Moroccan port of Tangier, from where the fruit was originally imported to Europe.

tantrum *noun* a sudden attack of bad temper. *Brian threw a tantrum at school.*

Tanzania *noun* a country in Africa.

Tanzanian *noun* a person who comes from Tanzania. **Tanzanian** *adjective*. *Kilimanjaro is the most famous Tanzanian mountain.*

Taoiseach *noun* (Say tee-shak) the prime minister of the Republic of Ireland.

tap *noun* 1 the of hitting someone or something lightly 2 a tool to let liquid out of a barrel. 3 a small electronic device that is installed in a telephone so that you can listen to other people's calls. *A phone tap.* 4 the British word for 'faucet'.

In Britain, people say 'tap' instead of 'faucet'.

tap (taps, tapping, tapped) *verb* 1 to knock gently but repeatedly. *A twig tapped against the window.* 2 to install a device so that you can take water, information etc. *Her phone was tapped because she was a spy.*

tape *noun* 1 a strip of cloth, paper, plastic etc. used to tie up parcels. *Masking tape.* 2 a long strip of magnetic material on which sound and pictures can be recorded, usually in a plastic box or cassette.

tape *verb* to record sound on an audio tape or images on a video tape.

tape measure *noun* a metal or cloth strip marked in centimeters or inches for measuring. *Did you bring a tape measure?*

tape recorder *noun* an instrument for recording sound on tape and for playing back sound. **tape-record** *verb*.

taper *verb* to become narrower towards the end. *The road begins to taper at the corner.*

tapestry *noun* a heavy cloth with pictures or designs woven into it and which is hung on a wall.

The tanks went into action and blocked the bridge.

tapir *noun* a large Central or South American animal with a long snout that looks a bit like a pig.

tar *noun* a thick, black sticky substance that is made from wood and coal. **tar** (tars, tarring, tarred) *verb. He tarred the roof to make it waterproof.*

tarantula *noun* a large, hairy poisonous spider. *There was a tarantula in the road.*

Tarawa *noun* the capital of Kiribati.

target *noun* 1 a mark that you aim at and try to hit. *He shot an arrow at the target.* 2 aim or purpose that you are trying to achieve. *Production targets are high.*

tariff *noun* 1 a list of prices, especially for hotel rooms and meals. 2 a tax to be paid on exports and imports.

tarmac *noun* asphalt, a mixture of tar and crushed stones, used to make road surfaces.

tarragon *noun* a plant whose leaves are used to flavor food.

tart *noun* a pie with no crust on top. *A strawberry tart.* **tart** *adjective* sharp or sour to taste.

tartan *noun* plaid, a Scottish woollen cloth.

Tashkent *noun* the capital of Uzbekistan.

task *noun* a job or piece of work that must be done, a duty. *A time-consuming task.*

taste *noun* 1 the sense you use to tell the flavor of food and drink. 2 the particular flavor of food: sweet, sour, salty or bitter. 3 a sense of knowing what is beautiful or good. **tasteful** *adjective.* **taste** *verb.*

There are about 10,000 microscopic taste buds sunk in the surface of the tongue.

tasteless *adjective* 1 without flavor. 2 unattractive and showing poor taste. *Tasteless furniture.*

tasty *adjective* having a pleasant taste.

tattoo *noun* 1 a permanent colored pattern on somebody's skin. 2 a military display of music, marching etc. usually held at night.

taught past tense of teach.

taunt *verb* to tease somebody and say hurtful things in order to make them angry. **taunt** *noun. She taunted him about the size of his nose, which really was enormous.*

taut *adjective* stretched or pulled tight so that it is firm. **tauten** *verb.*

AMAZING FACT

Tapirs live mainly in forests and eat vegetation such as leaves, buds and fruit. They are nocturnal creatures and most species are very shy.

WORD HISTORY

Our word 'tea' comes from 'tíe', the word used in Amoy Chinese. The Dutch borrowed the word and renamed it 'thee'. It was then absorbed into other European languages e.g. 'tea' (English) and 'te' (Italian).

---

tautology *noun* the use of a word that repeats the meaning of a word that has already been used. 'A four-sided square', 'free gifts' and 'a new innovation' are all examples of tautology.

tavern *noun* an old-fashioned word for an inn or bar.

tawny *noun* a light, brownish-yellow color. **tawny** *adjective.*

tax (taxes) *noun* an amount of money that people and businesses have to pay to the government to help pay for public services. **tax** *verb. The government taxes our income far too much.* **taxation** *noun.*

taxi (taxis) *noun* a car with a driver that you can hire, usually in towns and cities. *We took a taxi to the airport.*

taxi (taxies, taxiing, taxied) *verb* of an aircraft, to travel along the runway before takeoff or after landing.

Tbilisi *noun* the capital of Georgia.

tea *noun* 1 a drink made by pouring hot water on the dried leaves of a tea plant. 2 dried leaves or flowers used to make a hot drink.

Tea bushes grow in China, Africa, India and Sri Lanka. The leaves are picked and dried before being exported.

teach (teaches, teaching, taught) *verb* 1 to tell somebody about a subject and to help them learn about it, to educate. 2 to show somebody how to do something. *Jane taught me how to skate.*

teacher *noun* a person who teaches, especially at a school.

This picture is the stereotype of an old-fashioned teacher.

team *noun* a group of people who work together or who play on the same side in a game. *Our team won the game.*

tear *noun* (rhymes with near) one of the drops of salty liquid that comes from your eyes when you cry. **tearful** *adjective.*

tear (tears, tearing, tore, torn) *verb* (rhymes with fair) 1 to pull something apart, to rip. 2 to make a hole in something. *Tina tore her skirt on a nail.* 3 to pull something violently. *Vic tore the poster off the wall.* **tear** *noun.* 4 to move quickly. *The dog tore across the field and jumped over the fence.*

tease *verb* to annoy somebody by making fun of them for your own amusement.

teaspoon *noun* a small spoon. **teaspoonful** the amount that a teaspoon can hold.

teat *noun* 1 the nipple or soft pointed part on a female mammal through which her babies suck milk. 2 a piece of rubber or plastic on a feeding bottle through which a baby can suck milk etc.

technical *adjective* 1 concerned with science and machines and how they work. *Technical experts.* 2 concerned with a particular specialized subject. *Technical jargon is very boring.*

technique *noun* (say tek-**neek**) a special way of doing something skilfully.

technology *noun* the study of technical ideas and the practical use of science in industry. **technological** *adjective.*

teddy-bear (teddy) *noun* a soft toy bear.

tedious *adjective* boring because it is dull and long.

teenager *noun* a person between the ages of 13 and 19. **teenage** *adjective.*

teeth *plural* of tooth.

Each person has two natural sets of teeth during their life. The first 20 are called milk teeth, the second 32 are adult teeth.

teetotaler *noun* somebody who never drinks alcohol. **teetotal** *adjective. Many Muslims are teetotal.*

Tegucigalpa *noun* the capital of Honduras.

Tehran *noun* the capital of Iran.

telecommunications *plural noun* the technology of sending information over long distances by radio, telephone, television, etc.

telephone *noun* an instrument that uses electrical current traveling along wires, or radio waves, to allow you to speak to somebody over long distances. **telephone** or **phone** *verb. Please phone me tonight.*

Television signals are picked up by the receiver's TV aerial, demodulated and amplified to work the picture tube and loudspeaker of the TV set.

DID YOU KNOW

Teddy bear is named after 'Teddy' the pet name of Theodore Roosevelt, the US president (1858–1919), who was well known as a bear hunter.

This is Pashupatinath temple near Kathmandu in Nepal. Hindus are taken here to be cremated on the funeral pyres next to the Bagmati River.

telescope *noun* a tube-shape instrument with lenses that you look through with one eye to make distant objects appear bigger and nearer.

television *noun* a box-shaped instrument that receives program that have been broadcast and shows them on a screen as moving pictures with sound.

Screen

Electron beam / Electron gun

telex *noun* a system of sending written messages by means of teleprinters.

tell (tells, telling, told) *verb* 1 to pass on information etc. by speaking. 2 to know or recognize. *Can you tell what this is?* 3 to order. *Terry told us to be there on time.* **tell off** to scold. **telling-off** *noun.*

telling *adjective* meaningful and striking. *A telling argument.*

temper *noun* the tendency to become angry quickly. *She has a bad temper.* **lose your temper** to become angry.

temperament *noun* your personality or the way you usually feel and behave. *She has a very calm temperament.*

temperamental *adjective* prone to sudden changes of mood, excitable.

temperature *noun* 1 a measure of how hot something is. *The temperature has dropped to below freezing.* 2 a fever. *Take your temperature with this thermometer.*

tempest *noun* a violent storm with strong winds. **tempestuous** *adjective. A tempestuous sea.*

temple *noun* 1 a building in which people of some religions worship. 2 the flat part on either side of your head between your ear and forehead.

tempo *noun* the speed at which music is played.

tempt

tempt *verb* to try to persuade somebody to want to do something they would not normally do, to entice. *He tried to tempt me to cheat in the exam.* **temptation** *noun*.

tempting *adjective* attractive. *That swimming pool looks very tempting.*

tenant *noun* a person who rents from somebody the place he or she lives in.

tend *verb* to happen often or usually, to be inclined to. *It tends to be cold at night.* **tendency** *noun*. *A tendency to eat too much.*

tend *verb* to look after a person or animal.

tender *adjective* 1 sore to touch, painful. *The bruise feels very tender.* 2 easy to chew, not tough. *Tender meat.* 3 loving and gentle, kind. *A tender smile.* 4 delicate. *Tender seedlings.* **tenderness** *noun*.

tendon *noun* a strong cord-like tissue joining muscles to bones.

Muscle

Bone

Tendon

A tendon is like a tough rope that joins a muscle to a bone.

tennis *noun* a game played on a specially marked tennis court by two or four people using rackets to hit a ball to each other over a net.

tenor *adjective*, *noun* the highest normal singing voice for a man.

tense *adjective* 1 showing excitement, stress or nervousness. 2 stiff and tightly stretched, taut. **tension** *noun*. **tense** *verb*. *She tensed her muscles for the fight.*

tense *noun* a form of a verb that shows when something happens (present tense), happened (past tense) or will happen (future tense).

tent *noun* a shelter made from a waterproof material such as canvas or nylon stretched and supported over poles and held down by ropes.

tentacle *noun* one of the long, snake-like limbs of animals such as octopuses and squid.

A squid has eight tentacles.

SPELLING NOTE

The plural of some English words of Latin origin can be variable. For example, the plural of 'terminus' is usually 'termini' (but it can be 'terminuses').

WORD HISTORY

'Tennis' comes from a French word 'tenez' meaning 'hold' or 'take', which a player called out to his opponent to attract their attention.

A terrapin can sometimes be kept in an aquarium as a pet.

tepee *noun* a cone-shaped tent made of animal skins or tree bark, first used by Native Americans.

tepid *adjective* only slightly warm.

term *noun* 1 a length of time. *The term of office is three years.* 2 a word or name for something. *ROM is a computer term.* **terms** plural *noun* agreed conditions. *Terms of employment.* **term** *verb* to name. **to be on good terms with somebody** to get along with or to like somebody.

terminal *noun* 1 a building where people begin or end a trip. *Planes for Australia depart from terminal four.* 2 a computer monitor linked to a network. **terminal** *adjective* (of an illness) incurable and liable to cause death.

terminate *verb* to stop, to come to an end.

terminus *noun* a station at the end of a railroad line or bus route.

terrace *noun* 1 a level area cut out of sloping ground, often used to grow crops. 2 a flat area next to a building where people can sit.

terrapin *noun* a small, North American turtle. *Terrapins live in fresh water.*

terrestrial *adjective* 1 relating to the Earth rather than to space. *Terrestrial television.* 2 living on land and not in the air or in water. *Terrestrial animals.*

terrible *adjective* 1 dreadful, causing fear or hardship. 2 bad. *It's a terrible film.*

terrier *noun* one of several breeds of small dogs. *A fox terrier yaps a lot.*

terrific *adjective*. 1 very good, wonderful. 2 very large in size or intensity. *A terrific bang.*

terrify (terrifies, terrifying, terrified) *verb* to make somebody very frightened. *My dog is terrified of thunder.*

territory *noun* 1 an area of land, especially land controlled by a government. 2 an area of land where an animal lives and defends.

terror *noun* great fear.

terrorism *noun* the use of violence and threats to obtain demands. **terrorist** *noun*. *Terrorists planted bombs along the route.*

test *verb* to try out something, to check to see if something works. *An eye test.* **test** *noun* 1 a set of questions or actions that a person has to answer or perform to find out how much they know or can do. **test tube** *noun* a thin glass container that is closed at one end, used in laboratories to do tests.

tether *verb* to tie an animal by a rope to a post so that it cannot move far or escape. **tether** *noun.* **at the end of your tether** to run out of patience.

testicle *noun* one of two glands in a man's scrotum that produce sperm.

text *noun* the printed words in a book or newspaper. *The text is a little blurred.*

textbook *noun* a book containing information about a particular subject, especially used in schools and colleges.

textile *noun* woven cloth. **textile** *adjective.* *The textile industry.*

Tartan is a textile that is woven in Scotland.

texture *noun* the way something feels when you touch it, e.g. rough or smooth.

Thai *noun* a person who comes from Thailand. **Thai** *adjective.* *Thai silk.*

Thailand *noun* a country in Southeast Asia.

thank *verb* to express gratitude for something that someone has given you or done for you. **thanks** *noun* a word we use to say how pleased we are for what somebody has done for us.

thankful *adjective* feeling glad or grateful.

Thanksgiving *noun* a holiday celebrated in the fall in the US and Canada. Many people eat turkey on this day and give thanks for what they have.

thatch (thatches) *noun* layers of reeds or straw used in roofs.

Thatched houses need to be insured for lots of money because of the risk of fire.

WORD HISTORY

'Thesaurus' was originally a Greek word meaning 'treasury' and has been used since the 19th century to describe a treasury of information and knowledge or a treasury of words.

There are often thermometers in art galleries and museums.

thaw *verb* to change from being frozen solid to a liquid through warming, to melt. *The ice on the pond is thawing.*

theater *noun* a building where you go to watch movies or to see plays performed on a stage. **theatrical** *adjective* connected with plays or acting. *A theatrical family.*

theft *noun* stealing.

theme *noun* 1 the principal subject. *The theme of the book is poverty.* 2 (in music) the main melody.

theme park *noun* a park with different activities and attractions all based on one particular subject or idea.

theme song *noun* a tune that is often repeated in a film or musical.

theology *noun* the study of God and religion. **theologian** *noun* a person who studies theology. **theological** *adjective.*

theory *noun* 1 an unproved idea put forward to explain something. 2 the rules and principles of a subject rather than the actual practice. *In theory it should work – in practice it doesn't seem to!*

therapeutic *adjective* being good for the health and the treatment of illnesses.

therapy *noun* a treatment for an illness without the use of surgery or drugs. **therapist** *noun.* *I need a therapist.*

therm *noun* a measurement of heat.

thermal *adjective* relating to heat, using heat. *Thermal energy.*

thermometer *noun* an instrument for measuring temperature in degrees Celsius or Fahrenheit.

thermostat *noun* a device that automatically switches off furnaces, irons etc. when the temperature is hot enough.

thesaurus (thesauruses) *noun* a book that lists together words with similar meanings. *In my thesaurus the words 'glow', 'gleam', 'glitter', 'sparkle' and 'flash' are listed under the headword 'shine'.*

thick *adjective* 1 measuring a long way between two sides. Wide, not thin or slender. 2 measuring a certain amount between two sides. *The wood block is 2 inches thick.* 3 dense and closely packed. *Thick, blond hair.* 4 a liquid that does not have much water in it and does not flow freely. *I ordered a super thick chocolate malt.* **thickness** *noun.* **thicken** *verb.* The opposite of thick is thin.

thief (thieves) *noun* a person who steals things. *The thief ran off with my purse.*

thigh *noun* (rhymes with high) the top part of your leg above your knee.

thimble *noun* a small metal or plastic covering for the tip of your finger to prevent you pricking it when sewing.

Thimphu *noun* the capital of Bhutan.

thin (thinner, thinnest) *adjective* 1 measuring a short distance between two sides. Narrow, not thick. The opposite is thick. 2 having very little fat, slender. The opposite is fat.

thing *noun* 1 an unnamed object that you see or touch. 2 **things** belongings. *Have you packed your things for the trip?* **it's a good thing** it's lucky. *It's a good thing you brought an umbrella – it's pouring!*

think (thinks, thinking, thought) *verb* 1 to use your mind. 2 to believe, to have an opinion or idea. 3 to remember. 4 to plan or intend. *We're thinking about taking karate.* 5 to admire. *I think a lot of you.* **think up** to invent. **think twice about something** to consider whether to do something or not.

third *adjective* the next after the second. **third** *noun* one of three equal parts that make up a whole. **third rate** *adjective* of poor quality. **The Third World** the less industrialized, developing countries of the world.

thirst *noun* 1 feeling the need to drink. 2 a strong wish for something. *a thirst for adventure.* **thirsty** *adjective*.

Thirteen Colonies *noun* the first British Colonies in the US that declared independence in 1776.

thistle *noun* a prickly wild plant with purple flowers.

thorax *noun* 1 the middle section of an insect's body that carries the wings and legs. 2 the chest of a human.

All insects have a thorax and an abdomen.

Thorax

Abdomen

Sting

thorn *noun* a sharp point that grows on a plant such as a rose.

thorough *adjective* (say thur-oh) 1 done well and carefully. *A thorough search.* 2 complete. *A thorough success.* **thoroughness** *noun*.

AMAZING FACT

Some people believe that we can communicate by thought alone. This is called 'telepathy'.

DID YOU KNOW

The original Thirteen Colonies stretched all the way from Maine in the north to Georgia in the south. Virginia, the oldest, was founded in 1607.

---

thought past tense of think. **thought** *noun* an idea, something that you think.

thoughtful *adjective* 1 thinking quietly and carefully. 2 considerate and thinking about others. *It was very thoughtful of you to buy me flowers.*

thoughtless *adjective* inconsiderate and not thinking about other people's feelings. *That was a thoughtless thing to say, I'm sorry.*

thread *noun* a long thin piece of twisted cotton, silk etc. used for sewing or weaving. **thread** *verb* to put thread through a hole (eye) of needle to sew.

threadbare *adjective* (of clothes) worn thin.

She matched the thread with the color of her dress.

threat *noun* 1 a warning that something unpleasant may happen. 2 a possible cause of future harm, a danger. *A threat of drought hung over the country.*

threaten *verb* to warn that you may do something unpleasant or harm somebody. *Mat threatened to hit me.*

three-dimensional *adjective* having depth as well as height and width, solid.

thresh *verb* to beat grain from stalks of corn. *We threshed the grain at harvest.*

threw past tense of throw.

thrifty (thriftier, thriftiest) *adjective* not wasteful, careful about spending money etc. **thrift** *noun*.

thrill *noun* a feeling of great excitement and enjoyment. **thrill** *verb*.

thriller *noun* a book, play or film with an exciting story. **thrilling** *adjective* very exciting.

They all screamed because the rollercoaster ride was such a thrill.

thrive *verb* to be healthy and successful. *A thriving business.*

throat *noun* the front part of your neck. The tube from inside your mouth that takes food and drink to your stomach and air to your lungs. *He has a sore throat.*

throb (throbs, throbbing, throbbed) *verb* to beat strongly and rapidly. *My heart throbbed with terror.*

throne *noun* a special seat for a king or queen. *The king sat on the throne.*

through *preposition, adverb* (say throo) 1 from one side to the other. *The train went through the tunnel.* 2 among or between. *We walked through the crowd.* 3 by means of, because of. *We heard about it through word of mouth.*

throughout *preposition* 1 in all parts. *Throughout the world.* 2 from the beginning to the end, during. *Throughout the night.*

throw (throws, throwing, threw, thrown) *verb* to make something go through the air, to hurl or fling. *Tracy threw the ball to me but I missed it. The horse threw the rider twice.* **throw away** 1 to get rid of something you do not want. *Oh, no! I threw the receipt away by mistake.* 2 to waste something or miss a chance to do something. This is a great opportunity, don't throw it away. **throw together** to put something together quickly. **throw up** (slang) to vomit.

thrush *noun* a small brown bird with a speckled breast that sings beautifully.

The Wood thrush is native to Washington, D.C..

thrust *verb* to push suddenly and with force, to shove. *Doug thrust the clothes into the bag.* **thrust** *noun.*

thud *noun* a low, dull sound made, for example, by something heavy hitting the ground. **thud** *verb.*

thumb *noun* the short, thick finger at the side of your hand. **thumb a ride** to hitch-hike. **thumbs down** showing that you do not approve. **thumbs up** showing that you approve. *Our plan got the thumbs up.*

thump *noun* the dull heavy sound made by punching somebody.

thunder *noun* the rumbling noise you hear after a flash of lightning. **thunder** *verb* to make the dull, continuous noise of thunder.

thunderstorm *noun* a storm with thunder, lightning and heavy rain.

thunderstruck *adjective* amazed.

thwart *verb* to hinder somebody doing what they planned. *He thwarted my plan.*

thyme *noun* an herb, a plant whose leaves are used for flavoring food.

tiara *noun* a small, jeweled crown worn by women. *A golden tiara.*

The princess wore her most beautiful tiara to the ball.

tick *noun* 1 a small mark (✔) used to show that something is correct or to mark in a list. 2 a small, regular sound. *The tick of a clock.* 3 a small creature with eight legs that sucks the blood of animals. **tick** *verb. She ticked off our names as we got on the bus.*

ticket *noun* 1 a small printed piece of paper that shows that you have paid for something such as a train or bus fare or for a seat in a theater etc. 2 A piece of paper that requires a payment from a driver who has committed a parking or speeding offence.

tickle *verb* to touch somebody very lightly in a place that makes them laugh or giggle. *He tickled the baby's tummy.* **tickle** *noun.*

ticklish *adjective* easily tickled.

tidal wave *noun* an exceptionally huge wave caused by an earthquake.

A tidal wave is sometimes called a tsunami. It can cause enormous damage and great loss of life.

DID YOU KNOW

The word 'tide' originally meant 'time'. The meaning of the modern word came about because of the rising and falling of the ocean at regular times of the day.

tide *noun* the regular rising and falling movement of the ocean as it comes into the land and goes away from the land. Tides are caused by the pull of the Moon and Sun on the Earth. *We went out in the boat at high tide.*

tidy (tidier, tidiest) *adjective* neat and with everything in its proper place. **tidy** *verb.* **tidiness** *noun.*

tie *noun* a narrow piece of cloth that is worn around the neck under a shirt collar and knotted at the throat.

tie (ties, tying, tied) *verb* 1 to fasten something with rope, string etc. *She tied her shoelaces.* 2 to score an equal number of points in a contest. *They tied for second place.* **tie** *noun. The score was a tie.*

tier (rhymes with near) *noun* two or more layers, two or more raised rows of seats etc. one above the other.

tiger *noun* a large wild cat from Asia that has an orange coat with black stripes.

tight *adjective* 1 very closely fitting. *These jeans are too tight.* 2 firmly fixed so that it will not move. *The lid is so tight I can't open the jar.* 3 fully and firmly stretched. 4 having little room to spare. *It's a tight schedule.*

tightrope *noun* a tightly stretched rope along which acrobats walk.

tights *plural noun* a piece of clothing made of thick colored material that fits tightly over your feet, legs and hips and worn mainly by women. *The ballet dancers wore matching leotards and tights.*

tile *noun* a flat piece of hard material used for covering floors, roofs and walls. **tile** *verb. Dad tiled the bathroom.*

till *conjunction, preposition* until, up to a certain time. *Wait till I get home.*

till *noun* a cash register, a box or container for money in a business.

till *verb* to plow and cultivate land.

tilt *verb* to slope or lean so that one side is higher than the other.

SPELLING NOTE

'Tinsel' comes from a French word, 'étinceller', which means sparkle.

The pattern of stripes on a tiger's skin is unique. No two tigers have quite the same pattern.

SPELLING NOTE

Both 'till' and 'until' are interchangeable, meaning 'up to the time that' or 'as far as'. For example: "I will stay until you get back." And: "Go straight ahead till you come to a stoplight."

Tiles can be used to decorate many rooms in the house.

timber *noun* wood ready for building or making furniture etc.

time *noun* 1 the passing of years, months, weeks, days, hours etc. 2 a particular moment. *What time does the plane take off?* 3 how long something takes or a period in which you do something. **time** *verb* to measure how long something takes. **from time to time** occasionally. **in time** in step with the music. **once upon a time** some time long ago. **on time** not late.

times *preposition* multiplied by. *Four times four is 16.*

timetable *noun* schedule, a list showing the times of classes at school or the times when trains, planes etc. depart and arrive.

timid *adjective* lacking courage and easily frightened, shy. **timidity** *noun*.

tin *noun* a soft, silvery-white metal. usually mixed with other metals or forming a coat on other metals. *My dad made a 'telephone' out of two tin cans and a piece of string.*

These days, most cans are made of aluminum or other metals besides tin.

tinge *noun* a slight coloring. *White paint with a tinge of blue.*

tingle *verb* to have a slight stinging or tickling feeling. **tingle** *noun*.

tinker *verb* to fiddle with or make small changes to something with the idea of repairing or improving it.

tinkle *noun* a ringing sound like a small bell. **tinkle** *verb*.

tinsel *noun* strips of glittering material used for decorations.

tint *noun* a light, delicate shade of a color. **tinted** *adjective. Tinted glasses.*

tiny (tinier, tiniest) *adjective* very small. *A tiny insect fell into his beer.*

tip *noun* 1 the end of something long and thin. *Touch the tip of your nose.* 2 a small gift of money you give, for example, to a waiter or taxi driver. 3 a useful piece of advice. *He gave me a few tips on how to draw faces.*

tip (tips, tipping, tipped) *verb* 1 to knock over something so that the contents spill out, to empty. *He tipped over the milk bottle.* 2 to give somebody a small gift of money for helping you.

tipsy *adjective* very slightly drunk.

tiptoe *verb* to walk on your toes so that you make very little noise.

Simon tiptoed past his baby brother's crib but the baby woke up anyway.

Tirana *noun* the capital of Albania.

tire *noun* the rubber covering over the wheel or a car, bicycle, etc. *verb* 1 to become tired or make somebody tired. 2 to become bored with something. **tired** *adjective*.

tiresome *adjective* irritating, annoying.

tissue *noun* 1 the cells that make up a particular part of an animal or plant. *Leaf tissue*. 2 **tissue paper** very soft, thin paper used for wiping, wrapping etc.

tit-for-tat *adjective* something bad that is done to someone in response to something similar. *The saying 'an eye for an eye' is an example of a tit-for-tat attitude.*

title *noun* 1 the name of a book, film, piece of music etc. 2 a word like Dr, Mrs, Ms., Mr. or Senator put before a person's name to show marital status, position, etc.

titter *verb* to laugh in a silly, nervous way, to giggle. **titter** *noun*.

toad *noun* an amphibian like a frog with a rough, warty skin.

Toads like to live in moist places. They feed on insects.

toadstool *noun* an umbrella-shaped fungus similar to a mushroom, but nearly always poisonous. *The elf sat on a toadstool.*

toast *noun* a slice of bread that has been heated under a grill until it has turned crisp and brown. *Toast and peanut butter.*

toast *verb* to hold up your glass and wish for the success or happiness of somebody. **toast** *noun*. *We drank a toast to the bride.*

AMAZING FACT

Tokyo is one of the biggest cities in the world. Many people work there, but most of them live outside of the city. Some people have to spend over 4 hours a day traveling to and from work.

WORD HISTORY

'Tire' comes from the word 'attire' (clothing), because it was thought of as the clothing of a wheel. And the fitting of tires to wheels was once known as shoeing.

---

tobacco *noun* the cut and dried leaves of the tobacco plant which people smoke as cigars and cigarettes or in pipes.

toboggan *noun* a sled without runners. **toboggan** *verb*.

today *adverb, noun* 1 this very day. 2 the present time, nowadays. *People travel more by plane today than they used to.*

toddler *noun* a child who is just learning to walk. *Toddlers are a real handful.*

toe *noun* 1 one of the five parts at the end of your foot. 2 the front part of a shoe, sock etc. that fits over your toes. **on your toes** ready and alert. **toe the line** to do as you are told. *Imran expected his staff to toe the line.*

toffee *noun* a sticky, brown candy made from sugar and butter.

toga *noun* a loose flowing garment worn by men in ancient Rome.

together *adverb* 1 with another. *She stuck the two pieces together.* 2 at the same time as another. *They arrived home together.*

Togo *noun* a country in Africa.

The flag of Togo has a ground of yellow and green stripes and a white star on a red square.

toilet *noun* a bowl for getting rid of waste from the body.

token *noun* 1 a piece of metal, shaped like a coin, that you use instead of money in certain machines. *A subway token.* 2 a small sign or symbol of something. *A token of love.*

Tokyo *noun* the capital of Japan.

told past tense of tell.

tolerate *verb* to put up with or allow something to happen, to endure. *How can you tolerate living in such a mess!* **tolerable** *adjective*. **tolerance** *noun*. **tolerant** *adjective*.

tomahawk *noun* a war hatchet once used by Native Americans.

tomato (tomatoes) *noun* a round, sweet fruit eaten raw in salads and much used in cooking. *Tomato and cheese pizza.*

tomb *noun* a place where a body is buried. A grave. **tombstone** a stone with writing on it marking where a person is buried.

tomorrow *adverb, noun* 1 the day after today. 2 the future. *Tomorrow's children.*

ton *noun* a unit of weight equal to 2,000 pounds. *This dictionary weighs a ton!*

tone *noun* 1 the quality of a sound or the way something is said. *The piano has a mellow tone.* 2 a shade of color. 3 muscle tone. **tone** *verb*.

Tonga *noun* a country of many islands in the Pacific Ocean.

tongue *noun* the, moveable part of your mouth that you use for speaking and for tasting things. **tongue-twister** something that is difficult to say.

Different parts of the tongue are sensitive to different tastes.

Bitter tastes
Sour tastes
Salty tastes
Sweet tastes

tonic *noun* a medicine or something else that makes you feel better or stronger.

tonight *adverb, noun* this night of this day.

tonsils *plural noun* two soft lumps of flesh at the back of your throat. They may swell and become sore in an illness called tonsilitis. *When I had my tonsils out, all I could eat was ice-cream.*

too *adverb* 1 as well, also. *I can sing too.* 2 more than enough or than is needed. *There are too many knives in this drawer.*

took past tense of take.

tool *noun* a hand-held instrument or implement such as a hammer or drill that you use to do a particular job.

tooth (teeth) *noun* 1 one of the hard white bony parts inside your mouth that you use for biting and chewing. 2 one of the pointed parts of a comb or saw.

toothache *noun* severe pain in a tooth. *I had a really bad toothache.*

toothbrush *noun* a brush for cleaning teeth.

top *noun* 1 the highest part of something; the summit. *The top of the mountain.* 2 a covering, a lid. *Put the top back on the toothpaste.* 3 a piece of clothing that a woman or a girl wears on the upper part of her body. 4 a cone-shaped toy that spins on a point. **top** *adjective* the highest or best. *A top football player.* The opposite of top is bottom. **top** (tops, topping, topped) *verb.* **top dog** *noun* a leader or winner. **top heavy** *adjective* heavier at the top than at the bottom and so likely to topple over. **top secret** information that is very secret.

TONGUE TWISTERS

If Peter Piper picked a peck of pickled peppers, how many pickled peppers did Peter Piper pick?

She sells sea shells by the seashore.

SPELLING NOTE

Try not to confuse 'to', 'too', and 'two'. 'Two days is too long to wait. Do you think so too?'

A tooth is coated in enamel. Inside it are blood vessels and nerves.

topaz *noun* a semi-precious stone of varying colors.

topic *noun* a subject to talk about or write about. *A fascinating topic.*

topical *adjective* relating to important or interesting things happening now.

topography *noun* the study and description of the landscape's features such as the position of its mountains, roads, towns etc.

topple *verb* to overbalance and fall because it is too heavy at the top.

topsy-turvy *adjective* upside-down and in a state of confusion.

Torah *noun* a scroll used in synagogues on which are written the first five books of the Old Testament – Genesis, Exodus, Leviticus, Numbers and Deuteronomy known as the Pentateuch.

torch *noun* a pole with burning material at one end that gives light, sometimes used as a symbol. *The Oympics officially begin when the torch is lit.*

tore past tense of tear.

torment *verb* (say tor-**ment**) to tease and be deliberately cruel to somebody or an animal. **torment** *noun* (say **tor**-ment).

tornado (tornadoes) *noun* a violent storm with strong winds that spin at high speeds causing great damage.

The tornado ripped through the town leaving a trail of destruction.

AMAZING FACT

Tornados or 'twisters' can reach speeds of up to 300 miles per hour.

torrent *noun* 1 a violent rushing stream. 2 a flood or heavy downpour of rain. **torrential** *adjective. Torrential rain.*

torso (torsos) *noun* the main part of a body but excluding the head and limbs.

tortoise *noun* (say **tor**-tuss) a slow-moving land reptile with a hard shell.

The tortoise won its race against the hare.

torture *verb* to make somebody suffer extremely cruel physical or mental pain, often to force them to confess something. **torture** *noun. He was cruelly tortured.*

toss *verb* 1 to throw something carelessly into the air. 2 to move up and down and from side to side. *The boat tossed on the sea.* 3 to cover a food with another food. *Toss the salad just before you eat it.*

total *noun* the amount when everything is added together. **total** *adjective* complete. *A total success.*

totem pole *noun* a large pole carved or painted with traditional symbols of Native American families.

Magical creatures are carved on this totem pole. It was made by skilled craftspeople in Canada.

totter *verb* to walk in an unsteady way.

toucan *noun* a brightly colored South American bird with a huge beak.

touch *verb* 1 to feel something with your hand or with some other part of your body. 2 to come into contact and be so close to something that there is no space in between. 3 to move the feelings. *I was touched by your kind letter.* **touch** *noun* one of the five senses, the ability to feel. **in touch** in communication. **out of touch** not in communication.

touchdown *noun* In football, the action of taking the ball into the opponents end zone.

touching *adjective* causing a deep feeling of pity, sorrow etc. *A touching love story.*

touchy *adjective* easily offended or annoyed. *Beth seemed very touchy.*

tough *adjective* (say tuff) 1 strong and very hard to damage or break. 2 able to put up with hardships or difficulties. *Arctic explorers need to be tough.* 3 difficult. *A tough exam.* 4 hard to chew. *Tough meat.* 5 strict. *The government is tough on crime.* **toughen** *verb.* **toughness** *noun.*

toupee *noun* a false piece of hair worn to cover a bald part of the head.

tour *noun* 1 a journey on which you visit many different places. 2 a short trip around one place. **tour** *verb.*

tourist *noun* a person who visits different places for pleasure.

tournament *noun* a sports competition or contest in which the skills of the players are tested.

tousled *adjective* (of hair) untidy.

tow *verb* to pull or drag something behind. *The tractor towed the car out of the mud.*

toward *preposition* 1 in the direction of *Toward the beach.* 2 regarding. *My feelings toward you.* 3 as a contribution. *Everyone gave $12 toward the cost.*

towel *noun* a piece of thick, absorbent cloth or paper for drying things.

tower *noun* a tall, narrow building or part of building. **tower** *verb* to rise very high. *The chimney towered over the factory.* **towering** *adjective.*

Paris's most famous landmark is the tower designed by Gustave Eiffel.

town *noun* a place with a lot of houses and other buildings such as schools, shops, factories and offices.

town hall *noun* the building housing the local public offices.

toxic *adjective* poisonous. *Toxic waste.*

toy *noun* a thing for a child to play with. **toy** *verb* to play with or consider something not too seriously. *Ted toyed with the idea of becoming a policeman.*

trace *verb* 1 to copy a design etc. by placing a thin piece of half-transparent paper over it and drawing over the lines of the design etc. 2 to search and find where somebody is. *The police traced her to a hotel in Bolder.* **trace** *noun* a small mark or amount.

track

track *noun* 1 a series of marks left on the ground by an animal, person or vehicle. 2 a path. 3 a railroad line. 4 a course for horses, runners, cars etc. 5 one of the pieces of music on a CD or tape recording. **off the beaten track** remote or not visited by lots of tourists. **keep (or lose) track of** to know where somebody is, what is going on etc.

tract *noun* 1 a wide area of land. *Huge tracts of desert.* 2 a leaflet.

tractor *noun* a strong vehicle used on farms to pull plows and other machinery.

Tractor cabs are air-conditioned for comfort in the heat of the summer.

trade *noun* 1 the business of buying and selling goods. 2 an occupation or job that requires a special skill, a craft. *Paul's a plumber by trade.* **trade** *verb* to buy and sell, to exchange.

trade in *noun* a car, boat or other vehicle or piece of equipment that you give to cover part of the cost of a new one. *Dad got our car there because they accept trade-ins.*

tradition *noun* customs, beliefs and habits that people hand down from one generation to another. **traditional** *adjective*. *A very traditional folk song.*

traffic *noun* vehicles traveling along the road at the same time.

traffic jam *noun* traffic that has come to a standstill.

It is very frustrating to get stuck in a traffic jam behind a slow truck.

traffic light *noun* a traffic signal.

tragedy *noun* 1 a very sad event, a terrible disaster. 2 a play about sad events and with an unhappy ending. **tragic** *adjective*. *Two children were killed in the tragic accident.*

trail *noun* 1 marks left behind by a person or animal as they move through a place. *A trail of footprints in the snow.* 2 a track or path through open countrysde or forest.

WORD HISTORY

Streetcars or trams were originally sleds or trucks that were pulled along. The word was then used for the wooden or iron track along which the tram was pulled. The later passenger vehicles were called tramcars – 'trams' for short.

trail *verb* 1 to follow a trail of somebody or something. *I am on your trail.* 2 to drag or be dragged along the ground.

trailer *noun* 1 a vehicle for carrying things that is towed by a car or lorry. *The car pulled a boat on a trailer.* 2 an advertisement for a film that shows short extracts from it.

train *noun* 1 a railway engine with a set of carriages or trucks. 2 a series of ideas or events. *You broke my train of thought.*

train *verb* 1 to learn the skills you need to do something. 2 to teach an animal or person how to do something. 3 to practise and exercise for a sport.

trainee *noun* someone who is being trained for a job. *The new trainees are really eager and dedicated.*

trainer *noun* a person who trains or teaches somebody or an animal to compete in a sport. *A horse trainer.*

traitor *noun* a person who is disloyal and betrays friends or country.

tram *noun* streetcar, a large vehicle like a bus but which runs on rails in the road and is driven by electricity.

tramp *verb* to walk a long way slowly and steadily. **tramp** *noun* a person without a home who travels from place to place on foot.

trample *verb* to walk heavily on something and crush it.

tranquil *adjective* (say **tran**-kwill) calm and quiet. **tranquility** *noun*. *The tranquility of the valley was relaxing.*

tranquilizer *noun* a medicine that is given to somebody to make them feel calm and peaceful. **tranquilize** *verb*.

trans- *prefix* across or beyond. *Transatlantic telephone calls.*

transfer (transfers, transferring, transferred) *verb* (say tranz-**fur**) to move somebody or something from one place to another. *She transferred her affection to another man.*

transfer *noun* (say **tranz**-fur) 1 the act of moving a person or thing from one place to another. 2 a design or picture on a small piece of paper that can be transferred and stuck to another surface by rubbing or heating. *A transfer of a teddy bear.*

344

transform *verb* to make a complete change in form or nature. *We transformed the garage into an office.* **transformation** *noun*.

transfusion *noun* injecting blood into a person who has lost a lot of blood in an accident. *He needed a blood transfusion.*

transistor *noun* 1 an electronic device that controls the flow of electricity in radios and television sets. 2 a small portable radio that uses a transistor.

translate *verb* to change words from one language into another. **translator** *noun*. **translation** *noun*.

transmit (transmits, transmitting, transmitted) *verb* 1 to pass something on from one place or person to another. *How are diseases transmitted?* 2 to send out a radio or television program over the air. **transmission** *noun*.

transparency *noun* a photograph that lets light through so that you can project it on to a screen.

transparent *adjective* able to be seen through. *Clear water is transparent.*

The cocktail glass is transparent, and so is the drink. You can see the olive on the stick inside it.

transplant *verb* 1 to move a plant growing in one place to another place. 2 to perform a surgical operation to put a part of one person's body into the body of another person. **transplant** *noun*. *A heart transplant.*

transport *verb* to carry people or goods from one place to another.

transportation *noun* cars, buses, trains and planes or any other way of traveling.

trap *noun* a device for catching birds and animals. **trap** *verb* 1 to catch an animal using a trap. 2 to catch a person by a trick. *They trapped her into admitting guilt.*

trapeze *noun* a bar hanging from two ropes used by acrobats and gymnasts to swing from and perform skillful movements.

trash *noun* garbage.

DID YOU KNOW

You can see through transparent substances because they let all the light that hits them go through.

Transluscent substances let only some light through. Substances that don't let any light through are called 'opaque'.

AMAZING FACT

The first successful human heart transplant operation was performed in South Africa by Dr Cristiaan Barnard in 1967.

travel (travels, traveling, traveled) *verb* to journey or move from one place to another. *Sound travels fast.* **travel** *noun*. *Air travel.*

traveler *noun* 1 a person who travels regularly. 2 a person who travels from place to place in a mobile home or van.

trawl *verb* to fish with a wide net called a trawl. *Rod trawled the deep ocean for fish.*

trawler *noun* a fishing boat that pulls a large net called a trawl behind it.

tray *noun* a flat object with a rim around the edge for carrying things such as food and drinks.

treachery *noun* disloyalty, the betrayal of people who trust you. **treacherous** *adjective* 1 disloyal. 2 dangerous. *Treacherous rocks.*

tread (treading, trod, trodden) *verb* to walk or to put your foot down on something, to trample. *Don't tread on me!* **tread** *noun* 1 the top part of a ladder or stairs you put your foot on. 2 the raised pattern of ridges on a car tire or on the sole of a shoe.

treason *noun* the betrayal of your country, especially by giving away secrets to the enemy in wartime. **treasonable** *adjective*. *A treasonable crime.*

treasure *noun* 1 a store of gold, jewels and other precious things. 2 a precious object such as a painting. **treasure** *verb* to value something very much or to take care of something because it is important to you.

treasurer *noun* a person who keeps track of the money of a club etc.

The treasure Sally found in the attic consisted of beautiful jewels and valuable gold coins.

treat *verb* 1 to behave towards somebody in a particular way. *She treats me like a servant.* 2 to give medical care to a person or animal. *The doctor is treating her for eczema.* **treatment** *noun*. **treat** *noun* a special gift like a visit or a meal. *Staying with them was a real treat!*

treaty *noun* a formal agreement between two or more countries. *An arms treaty.*

treble *adjective, adverb* the upper key of the range of musical notes. *The treble clef sign looks like a backwards 'S' with a line through it.*

treble *noun* a boy with a high singing voice.

tree *noun* a tall plant that has a long, thick wooden stem called a trunk and branches and leaves. *My kite got stuck in a tree.*

Trees are the lungs of the world, as they take in carbon dioxide and give out oxygen.

AMAZING FACT

Trees are the largest of all plants. Some grow to over 100 meters high.

---

trek *noun* a long journey, usually on foot and in a remote area. **trek** *verb*.

trellis *noun* a fence or framework of wooden strips for plants to climb up.

tremble *verb* to shake all over because you are frightened, cold or excited.

tremendous *adjective* 1 very big. *A tremendous crowd.* 2 very good. *We had a tremendous time.*

trench *noun* a long, thin ditch or channel dug in the earth. *Trench warfare.*

trend *noun* the general direction in which things seem to be changing and becoming different. *A trend for smaller families.* **set a trend** to start a fashion.

trespass *verb* to go on somebody's land without their permission. **tresspasser** *noun*.

tri- *prefix* meaning three or three times. *Tricycle, triangle, trilogy, tripod, tripartite.*

trial *noun* 1 the period of time when a prisoner is in a law court and when the lawyers, jury and judge try to decide whether or not he or she has done wrong and is guilty. 2 a test of something to see how well it works.

triangle *noun* 1 a flat shape with three straight sides and three corners. 2 a triangular musical instrument that makes a bell-like sound when you hit it. **triangular** *adjective*.

A triangle has three sides.

DID YOU KNOW

English spelling does not allow triples of the same letter, so where a compound word contains three of the same letters consecutively a hyphen is inserted, as in bell-like and cross-section.

The Masai people of Kenya are a tribe of cattle herders. They wear bright red cloth and beaded collars.

tribe *noun* a group of families descended from the same ancestors who live together and who have the same traditions, language etc. **tribal** *adjective*. *Tribal chief.*

tributary *noun* a stream that flows into a river or another stream.

trick *noun* 1 something you do to cheat somebody or to make a fool of somebody. 2 some clever or skillful thing that you have learned to do to entertain people. *Card tricks.* 3 a practical joke. **trick** *verb* to deceive or make a fool of somebody.

trickle *verb* to flow slowly like a very small stream. *Tears trickled down his cheeks.* **trickle** *noun*. *A trickle of water.*

tricky *adjective* difficult to deal with. *A tricky situation.*

tricolor *noun* a flag with three bands of different colors such as the French and Irish flags.

tricycle *noun* a cycle with three wheels.

tried past tense of try.

trifle *noun* 1 a sweet made of sponge cake and fruit covered in jelly, custard and cream. 2 something that is of no importance. **trifling** *adjective*.

trigger *noun* the small lever you pull with a finger to fire a gun.

trilogy *noun* a group of three novels, plays, operas etc. that go together and make a related series by having the same people or themes in common.

trim (trims, trimming, trimmed) *verb* 1 to cut the edges or ends off something to make it neat, to clip. *He trimmed her hair.* 2 to decorate a piece of clothing. **trim** *adjective* having a good shape. *He has a trim figure.*

Trinidad and Tobago *noun* a country in the West Indies.

The flag of Trinidad and Tobago has a diagonal black and white stripe on a red ground.

trinity *noun* 1 a group of three. 2 the Trinity in Christianity, the Father, the Son and the Holy Spirit as one God.

trio *noun* a group of three singers or players, a piece of music written for three musicians. *A folk trio.*

trip (trips, tripping, tripped) *verb* 1 to catch your foot in something and stumble or fall over. 2 to move with quick, light steps. *She tripped along the path as happy as could be.* **trip up** to make a mistake.

trip *noun* 1 a short return journey or visit. *A trip to Paris.* 2 (slang) a dream-like experience caused by drugs.

tripe *noun* 1 the stomach lining of such animals as cows and pigs which is cooked and eaten. 2 worthless nonsense. *Don't talk such tripe.*

triple *adjective* three times as great or many. 2 consisting of three parts. **triple** *verb.* *The tree has tripled in height in one month.*

triplet *noun* one of three babies born at the same time to the same mother.

tripod *noun* (say **try**-pod) a three-legged support for a camera etc.

Tripoli *noun* the capital of Libya.

triumph *noun* (say **try**-umf) a great success or achievement, a victory. **triumph** *verb.* *He triumphed over evil.* **triumphant** *adjective.*

trivial *adjective* of very little importance. *A trivial problem.*

troll *noun* an ugly, mischievous creature in fairy tales from Scandinavia.

Trolls are favorite storybook creatures for children in Norway, Sweden and Denmark.

trolley *noun* an electric passenger vehicle that moves along the street on metal tracks.

trombone *noun* a large, brass musical instrument that you blow through and move a slide to change the note.

This tropical rainforest can be found in the equatorial region of South America.

WORD HISTORY

'Truant' once meant a beggar. In the 16th century it took on the meaning of a pupil absent without leave from school. It originally comes from a Welsh word 'truan', meaning 'wretched'.

AMAZING FACT

Trinidad and Tobago is one country made up of two islands in the West Indies.

troops *plural noun* a group of soldiers. **troop** *verb* to move together as a crowd. *The fans trooped into the stadium.*

trophy *noun* (say **trow**-fee) an award or prize such as a silver cup given to somebody who wins a game or competition.

tropic *noun* 1 one of the two lines of latitude running around the Earth at about 23 degrees north and south of the equator and known as the Tropic of Cancer and the Tropic of Capricorn. 2 **tropics** *plural noun* the very warm regions between the Tropic of Cancer and the Tropic of Capricorn. **tropical** *noun. Tropical rain forests.*

trot *noun* one of the four paces of a horse, between a walk and a canter. **trot** (trots, trotting, trotted) *verb* 1 of a horse, to run but not to canter or to gallop. 2 of humans, to move quickly. *Trot along now.*

trouble *noun* a difficult, unpleasant or worrying situation, a problem. **trouble** *verb* 1 to cause worry, concern or distress. 2 to make an effort to do something, to bother. *She didn't trouble to ask if she could help.*

troublesome *adjective* causing problems or worries, annoying. *A troublesome wasp.*

trough *noun* 1 a long, narrow container for food and water for animals. 2 in weather forecasting, an area of low pressure between areas of high pressure.

trousers *plural noun* pants or slacks, a piece of clothing covering your body from your waist to your ankles with a separate part for each leg.

trout (trout) *noun* a silvery-brown freshwater fish of the salmon family that can be eaten. *Trout with almonds.*

trowel *noun* 1 a small spade-like hand tool with a short handle used for garden work. 2 a flat hand tool used to spread plaster etc. *Lay it on with a trowel.*

truant *noun* a student who stays away from school without permission or a good excuse.

truce *noun* a short period when two sides in a war etc. agree to stop fighting.

truck *noun* a motor vehicle that can carry heavy loads. *My uncle lives on a farm and drives a pick-up truck.*

trudge *verb* to walk slowly with tired, heavy steps. **trudge** *noun.*

true *noun* 1 what really happened. 2 not invented or guessed at but real and accurate. 3 loyal and trustworthy. *A true friend.*

trumpet *noun* a brass musical instrument that makes sounds when you blow into it.

trunk *noun* 1 the long stem of a tree from which the branches grow. 2 The part of a car for putting luggage, etc. in. 3 a large container with a hinged lid and a handle for carrying or storing things such as clothes. 4 the main part of your body but not including your limbs, neck and head, the torso. 5 an elephant's long nose.

trunks *plural noun* shorts worn by men and boys for swimming.

The best event at the county fair was the tug o' war.

trust *verb* to believe that somebody is honest, reliable and truthful and that they will do nothing to harm you, to depend on. **trustworthy** *adjective*. **trustworthiness** *noun*.

truth *noun* what is real, accurate and correct, what has actually happened. *Are you telling me the truth?* **truthful** *adjective*. **truthfulness** *noun*.

try (tries, trying, tried) *verb* 1 to attempt to do something. *I don't think I can do it but I'll try.* 2 to test something by using it to see what it is like. *Try this ice-cream and see if you like it.* 3 to judge somebody in a court of law. **try** *noun* 1 an attempt. 2 in rugby, a way of scoring by putting the ball down on the ground over the opponents' goal line. **trying** *adjective* exhausting and irritating. *A trying child.*

tsar *noun* (say zar) in former times, a Russian king or emperor. His wife was called a tsarina. Also spelt czar, czarina.

T-shirt a kind of shirt or undershirt with short sleeves and no collar.

tub *noun* a round, wide and usually open container.

tuba *noun* a large brass musical instrument that makes deep sounds when you blow into it.

tubby *adjective* short, round and rather fat.

tube *noun* 1 a long, hollow metal, plastic or rubber cylinder, a pipe. 2 a long container. *A tube of toothpaste.* **tubular** *adjective*.

tuber *noun* the roundish swollen part of the underground stem of some plants. Potatoes are tubers.

tuck *verb* to fold under or push the loose end of something into a place to make it look tidy. *He tucked his shirt into his pants.* **tuck in** *verb* to put someone to bed. *I tuck my sister in and read her a story.*

tuft *noun* a bunch or clump of hair, feathers, grass etc.

WORD HISTORY

'Tsar' is sometimes spelled 'Czar'. It is a Russian word derived from the Latin, 'Caesar'. The German equivalent is 'kaiser'.

WORD HISTORY

'Turban' comes from the Portuguese 'turbante', which in turn comes from a Persian word for this headdress.

I joined the school band to play the tuba.

tug or tugboat *noun* a small powerful boat that tows ships in and out of port.

tug o' war *noun* a contest between two teams who pull on opposite ends of a long rope to test their strength.

tulip *noun* a plant with brightly colored flowers that grows from a bulb in the spring. *The tulips of Amsterdam.*

tumble *verb* to fall down suddenly or to fall and roll over. *Tim tumbled down the stairs.*

tumbler *noun* a drinking glass.

tummy *noun* (slang) the stomach.

tumor *noun* a lump or growth on the body made of diseased or abnormal cells.

tuna *noun* a large sea fish, used for food.

tundra *noun* the vast treeless plains of the Arctic that remain frozen all year.

tune *noun* a sequence of musical notes in a pattern that is pleasant to listen to and often easy to remember. **tune** *verb* 1 to adjust a musical instrument so that it plays the correct notes. 2 to adjust a radio so that it receives the program you want. **tuneful** *adjective*. **change your tune** to change the way you think.

tunic *noun* 1 a tight-fitting jacket, often worn as part of a uniform. 2 a loose, sleeveless garment without a collar.

Tunis *noun* the capital of Tunisia.

Tunisia *noun* a country in Africa.

Tunisian *noun* a person who comes from Tunisia. **Tunisian** *adjective*. *The Tunisian coast is extremely beautiful.*

tunnel *noun* a long underground passage for a railway etc. **tunnel** (tunnels, tunnelling, tunnelled) *verb* to dig a tunnel.

turban *noun* a headdress worn by various people consisting of a long piece of cloth wound around the head.

turbine *noun* an engine that works by water, steam, or hot air etc. pushing round the curved blades on a wheel.

Wind turbines produce a clean, renewable source of electricity.

turbojet *noun* an aircraft driven by a turbine.

turf *noun* 1 short, thick grass. 2 a piece of earth with grass growing from it, cut from the ground.

turkey *noun* a large bird that is reared for its meat.

Turkey *noun* a country partly in Europe and mostly in Asia.

Turkish *noun* 1 a person who comes from Turkey. 2 the language of Turkey. **Turkish** *adjective. Turkish architecture.*

Turkmenistan *noun* a country in West Asia.

turmoil *noun* a state of great confusion and unrest.

turn *verb* 1 to go around or move around a central point, to revolve or twist. *Turn the handle.* 2 to move and change direction. *He turned to look at me.* 3 to move so as to make the topside become the bottom side. *He turned the mattress.* 4 to change or to become different. *The frog turned into a prince.* 5 to adjust a switch, tap etc. *Turn the lights off.* **turn** *noun.* **do somebody a good turn** to help somebody. **turn down** 1 to refuse. 2 to make quieter. **turn up** 1 to arrive. 2 to make louder. *Please turn up the sound.*

turnip *noun* a round, white root vegetable.

turnstile *noun* a revolving gate that lets people walk through one at a time.

turquoise *noun* a greenish-blue semi-precious stone. The color of the stone.

turret *noun* a small tower on a castle or the side of a building.

turtle *noun* a large reptile covered with a shell like a tortoise that lives in the sea.

Turkey is famous for its richly patterned carpets.

Sabon

'Sabon' is the name of the type used in this book.

Turtles swim ashore to lay their eggs in the sand on the beach.

tusk *noun* one of a pair of long, curved, pointed teeth that sticks out of the mouth of elephants, walruses and wild boar.

tutor *noun* a teacher who gives classes to one person at a time or to very small groups of people. *My math tutor is very helpful.*

tutu *noun* the very short, stiff skirt worn by female ballet dancers.

Tuvalu *noun* a country of islands in the Pacific Ocean.

TV *abbreviation* television.

AMAZING FACT

The female turtle buries her eggs in the sand. When the eggs of the turtle hatch, the hatchlings have to dig their way up to the surface.

tweed *noun* a strong woollen cloth, often made of several colors.

tweezers *plural noun* a small tool with two prongs for lifting things or for pulling out hairs etc., pincers.

twice *adverb* two times.

twiddle *verb* to turn something round and round in a purposeless way. *He kept twiddling with the radio knobs.* **twiddle your thumbs** to have nothing to do.

twig *noun* a thin, tiny branch of a tree.

twilight *noun* the time of day when it is getting dark, between sunset and night.

twin *noun* one of two babies born at the same time to the same mother.

twine *noun* very strong string made by twisting threads together.

twinge *noun* a sudden, short pain. *A twinge of rheumatism.*

twinkle *verb* to sparkle with little unsteady flashes of light. *Stars twinkle in the sky.* **twinkle** *noun. He has a twinkle in his eye!*

twirl *verb* to turn or spin something quickly round and round.

twist *verb* 1 to turn. *To open the box you must twist the knob.* 2 wind something around something else. *She twisted her hair around her finger.* 4 to bend and turn in different directions. *The road twisted around the mountain.* 4 to bend something so as to damage it. *She twisted her wrist.* **twist** *noun.* **round the twist** mad.

tycoon *noun* a rich, powerful business person or industrialist. *A newspaper tycoon.*

type *noun* 1 the different designs of letters used in printing. 2 a kind or sort. *Apples and pears are two types of fruit.*

type *verb* to write something by pressing the keys of a typewriter or computer.

typewriter *noun* a machine with keys that you press to print letters and figures on a piece of paper.

typhoid *noun* (say tie-foid) a very dangerous infectious disease in which the intestines become inflamed.

typhoon *noun* (say tie-foon) a tropical storm with violent winds.

typical *adjective* 1 the most usual or characteristic of its kind. *They bought a typical New England house with a big porch and a backyard full of trees.* 2 what you would expect. *It's typical of you to be late, I'm afraid.*

tyrant *noun* a cruel, unjust and unkind ruler. **tyranny** *noun.* **tyrannical** *adjective. The country's economy collapsed under the tyrannical dictator.*

Uu

udder *noun* the bag-like part of a cow, sheep etc. that hangs down between its back legs and from which milk is taken.

UFO *abbreviation* unidentified flying object. *Ted likes films about UFOs.*

Uganda *noun* a country in Africa.

Ugandan *noun* a person who comes from Uganda. **Ugandan** *adjective. Ugandan exports include avocados.*

ugly (uglier, ugliest) *adjective* unattractive and not beautiful to look at. **ugliness** *noun.*

UHF *abbreviation* ultra high frequency.

Ukraine *noun* a country in eastern Europe.

Ukrainian *noun* a person who comes from the Ukraine. **Ukrainian** *adjective. Ukrainian Easter eggs are like works of art.*

Ulan Bator *noun* the capital of Mongolia.

ulcer *noun* (say **ull**-sur) a sore on your skin or in your body. *A stomach ulcer.*

ultimate *adjective* final, last. *Our ultimate wish is to win.*

ultimatum *noun* a final offer or warning.

ultra- *prefix* beyond. *Ultra high frequency.*

ultraviolet light *noun* light that is beyond the visible spectrum at its violet end and which causes your skin to tan.

umbilical cord *noun* the tube that connects the body of a mother and child until the child is born.

The unborn baby receives nourishment from its mother through the umbilical cord.

umbrella *noun* something that you hold over your head to keep you dry when it rains. The umbrella's frame is covered with a round piece of material and connected to a long handle. An umbrella folds up when you are not using it.

umpire *noun* a person who watches a game and makes sure that the rules are followed.

UN *abbreviation* United Nations.

The flag of the United Nations is a symbol of world peace and harmony.

un- *prefix* 1 not, opposite. *Uncomfortable.* 2 the opposite of an action. *Unfasten.*

unaccustomed *adjective* not used to doing something. *He is unaccustomed to work.*

unanimous *adjective* (say you-**nan**-im-us) of the same opinion, agreed by everybody. *A unanimous decision.* **unanimity** *noun.*

unassuming *adjective* modest and not showing off. *An unassuming young man.*

unaware *adjective* not knowing that something exists or is happening.

unbalanced *adjective* 1 lacking balance, unfair. *An unbalanced account of what happened.* 2 slightly mad. *She became rather unbalanced after the accident.*

unbecoming *adjective* not suitable.

unbiased *adjective* not favoring one side or the other, fair. *An unbiased opinion.*

uncanny *adjective* strange, weird and unnatural. *An uncanny silence.*

uncle *noun* the brother of your mother or your father or the husband of your aunt.

unconscious *adjective* 1 not conscious, in a kind of sleep and not knowing what is happening. 2 not being aware of something. *I was unconscious of the difficulties you were in until yesterday.*

uncooperative *adjective* making no attempt to help or do things for others.

uncouth *adjective* coarse and rough in behavior and speech, rude.

undaunted *adjective* not discouraged or put off doing something despite setbacks and difficulties. *Her grandmother's criticism left her undaunted.*

undeniable *adjective* so certainly true that you cannot disagree.

under- *prefix* 1 below, beneath. *Underground.* 2 less than or not enough. *Underdeveloped.* 3 lower in rank. *Undersecretary, understudy.*

undercarriage *noun* the landing gear of an aircraft, including the wheels.

undercover *adjective* secret. *Undercover activities were common during the war.*

underdog *noun* in a game or contest, an unfortunate person or team that is unlikely to win. *I always want the underdog to win.*

undergo (undergoes, undergoing, underwent, undergone) *verb* to experience, endure or suffer something. *The town has undergone many changes in recent years.*

undergraduate *noun* a student in the first four years of college . *Her major as an undergraduate was biology but she went on to do a Master's in nutrition.*

underground *adjective* 1 beneath the ground or surface of the Earth. *Underground passages.* 2 acting in secret. *An underground group.*

WORD BUILDER

Here are some words with the 'under-' prefix. You can easily work out what they mean: 'underclothes', 'undercook', 'underemployed', 'underfeed'.

understanding *noun* 1 having a knowledge of something and knowing what it means or how it works, intelligence. *He has no understanding of machinery.* 2 sympathy and knowledge of a person. *There's a deep understanding between them.* 3 an agreement. *Maybe we can come to an understanding about who does what.*
understanding *adjective* tolerant and kind.

understudy *noun* an actor who learns the lines of the actor who usually plays a part and who takes over that part in an emergency. *The understudy was a great hit.*

undertake (undertakes, undertaking, undertook, undertaken) *verb* to agree or promise to do something and to be responsible for it. **undertaking** *noun.*

undertaker *noun* a person whose job it is to prepare dead bodies for burial or cremation and arrange funerals.

underwear *noun* clothes that you wear under your other clothes next to your skin.

underworld *noun* 1 all the criminals and their activities in a city. 2 the place in myths where the spirits of dead people go.

undergrowth *noun* bushes and plants that grow near the ground under trees in woods and forests. *He hid in the undergrowth.*

underhand *adjective* secret and dishonest, deceitful. *An underhand plot.*

underline *verb* 1 to draw a line under words to make them stand out. 2 to stress the importance of something *The accident underlines the need to be more careful.*

undermine *verb* to weaken or slowly destroy something. *The cold, damp climate is undermining her health.*

understand (understands, understanding, understood) *verb* 1 to know what something means, how it works or why it happens. 2 to know somebody or something well. *I just don't understand how she can be so cruel.* 3 to believe something to be true because you have been told. *I understand that you got married in secret.*

Moles spend most of their time underground. Because they are used to living in the darkness, their eyesight is very poor.

Marcus undid his shoelaces, took off his shoes and put on his slippers.

undo (undoes, undoing, undid, undone) *verb* 1 to unfasten, untie, unwrap something that was fixed or tied. *She undid her shoelaces.* 2 to do away with or reverse something that has been done. *Try to undo the damage your remarks have done.*

undoubted *adjective* accepted as true, certain. *An undoubted success.*

undress *verb* to take your clothes off.

undue *adjective* excessive, more than necessary. *Undue noise.*

U

undying *adjective* never dying or fading. *They swore undying love.*

unearth *verb* to dig up or find something after searching for it, to discover. *He unearthed some old photos in a trunk.*

unearthly *adjective* 1 strange and terrifying, like nothing on Earth. *An unearthly sound of howling.* 2 absurdly unreasonable. *She telephoned at some unearthly hour.*

uneasy *adjective* anxious, not settled. *I feel uneasy around dogs.* **uneasiness** *noun.*

uneven *adjective.* 1 not smooth or flat. 2 not equally matched, one-sided. *An uneven contest.* 3 (of a number) odd and leaving a remainder of one when divided by two. *Five is an uneven number.*

unfailing *adjective* never failing or weakening, continuous, endless. *You can count on my unfailing loyalty.*

unfeeling *adjective* severe and hard-hearted.

unfit *adjective* 1 unhealthy, in poor physical condition. 2 unsuitable and not good enough. *This food is unfit to eat.*

unfold *verb* 1 to spread out by opening. *He unfolded the blanket.* 2 to reveal or gradually to make something clear. *The story unfolded gradually.*

unfurl *verb* to unroll, spread out and display something that has been wrapped up. *The soldier unfurled the flag.*

unforeseen *adjective* not expected. *Due to unforeseen circumstances, I cannot come.*

unfounded *adjective* not based on fact. *Unfounded rumors.*

ungainly *adjective* clumsy and ungraceful.

unicorn *noun* an animal in stories that looks like a white horse with a long, spiralled horn on its forehead.

Legend says that if a maiden falls asleep with the head of a unicorn in her lap, she will dream of the man she is to marry.

The track through the hills was very uneven, making our progress slow and difficult.

uniform *noun* special distinctive clothes worn by members of a particular group or organization. Nurses, firefighters and soldiers wear uniforms. **uniform** *adjective* not changing, always the same. *The concrete blocks are of uniform size and color.*

unify *verb* to make several things come together to form a whole to share a common purpose. *The various Italian states unified to make modern Italy.*

unintelligible *adjective* very difficult to understand. *Your writing is unintelligible.*

uninterested *adjective* showing no interest or enthusiasm. *I told him about the game but he seemed quite uninterested.*

union *noun* 1 A labor union is an organized group of workers who discuss with managers any problems affecting all the workers. 2 the act of joining things together, something united.

unique *adjective* (say yoo-**neek**) 1 being the only one of its kind and different from anybody or anything else. *His style of painting is unique.* 2 very unusual. **uniqueness** *noun.*

unisex *adjective* designed for or capable of being used by both men and women. *A unisex hairdresser.*

unison *noun* in unison all together.

unit *noun* 1 a single, complete thing that is part of a whole. 2 a group working together. *The physiotherapy unit.* 3 an amount that is used as a standard weight or measurement. *A liter is a unit of liquid measurement.*

unite *verb* to join together to form one thing or to do something together, to combine. **unity** *noun.*

United Arab Emirates *noun* a country in The Middle East.

United Kingdom *noun* a country in Northwest Europe, made up of England, Scotland, Wales and Northern Ireland.

United States of America *noun* a country in North America.

Alaska (top left on the map) belongs to the United States of America.

universal *adjective* relating to and including everybody and everything.

universe *noun* (say **yoo**-ni-verse) the whole of everything that exists, including the Earth, Sun, Moon, planets and all the stars in space. *The end of the universe.*

university *noun* a place of higher education where people go after they have left school to study for a degree or do research.

unkempt *adjective* messy and not well looked after. *An unkempt beard.*

unleaded *adjective* (of gasoline) containing no lead. *This car runs on unleaded gas.*

unless *conjunction* if not. Except when. *I will go unless you stop talking.*

unlucky *adjective* 1 having bad luck and with bad things happening to you. 2 causing bad luck. *Some people believe it is unlucky to walk under ladders.*

unmistakable *adjective* distinct and not possible to be mistaken for somebody or something else. *His handwriting is quite unmistakable. An unmistakable style.*

UN *abbreviation* United Nations.

unravel (unravels, unraveling, unraveled) *verb* to undo knots or untie woven, knitted or tangled threads. *My sleeve is already starting to unravel.* 2 to solve a mystery or difficult problem.

The cat unraveled my knitting. I had to roll the wool back up into a ball.

unreasonable *adjective* 1 not sensible. *An unreasonable fear of spiders.* 2 too much, excessive. *Unreasonable demands.*

unreliable *adjective* not to be trusted or depended on. *Dad's old car is unreliable.*

unrest *noun* 1 discontent. 2 restlessness. Disturbance and riots. *There was profound unrest across the country.*

unruly *adjective* badly behaved, hard to control or rule. *An unruly child.*

unscathed *adjective* not harmed or damaged. *The horses escaped the stable fire unscathed and lived to see another day.*

unscrupulous *adjective* not caring whether something is right or wrong, having no principles. *An unscrupulous employer.*

unseemly *adjective* not suitable for the time and place. *Her laughter at the funeral was really quite unseemly.*

unsettle *verb* to make or become unstable and anxious, to disturb. *Thunder unsettles our dogs and cats.*

GRAMMAR NOTE

We use 'an' instead of 'a' before words that start with a vowel **sound***.*
So say and write 'a uniform' or 'a used car' but say or write 'an unusual vase' or 'an umbrella'.

unsightly *adjective* unpleasant to look at, ugly. *An unsightly building blocks the view.*

unsound *adjective* 1 not in a good condition, unhealthy. *The upstairs floors are unsound.* 2 not based on fact. *I thought her theory was very unsound.*

unstable *adjective* 1 liable to change suddenly. *She's very moody and unstable.* 2 not steady, wobbly. *The table is unsteady.*

unsuitable *adjective* not right or fitting for a particular purpose. *Slippers are unsuitable for playing football.*

untidy (untidier, untidiest) *adjective* messy and with nothing in its proper place. *Adrian's office is always untidy!*

Shelby left her bedroom in an untidy mess.

untie (unties, untying, untied) *verb* to undo or loosen the knots of something that was tied. *She untied the bows in her hair.*

until *conjunction, preposition* up to the time of or when. *She stayed up until long past midnight to see the end of the movie.*

untold *adjective* too much or too many to calculate. *Locusts do untold damage to some crops.*

unusual *adjective* strange, rare and unexpected. *An unusual necklace.*

This very unusual vase will create lots of interest at the antiques fair.

unwelcome *adjective* not wanted. *An unwelcome visitor.*

unwieldy *noun* bulky, clumsy and difficult to hold, manage or move.

unwitting *adjective* 1 not knowing and not intended. *An unwitting error.*

unworthy *adjective* not deserving. *Such a ridiculous story is unworthy of attention.* 2 out of character and below standards expected. *It's unworthy of you to tell lies.*

unwrap (unwraps, unwrapping, unwrapped) *verb* to remove the covering or wrapping off something such as a package.

It takes a lot longer to wrap presents than it does to unwrap them.

up *adverb, preposition* 1 to a higher level, amount etc. *Jack went up the hill.* 2 to a sitting or standing position. *Please stand up.* 3 completely, so that it is finished. *She ate up all the ice-cream.* 4 out of bed. *She gets up early.* 5 along. *I walked up the path* 6 into pieces. *He tore up the letter.* **ups and downs** good times and bad times. **up and coming** on the way to being successful.

upbeat *adjective* happy and ever hopeful.

upbringing *noun* the way that a child is brought up and told how to behave.

update *verb* to add all the latest information and make more modern. *The files are constantly updated.*

upheaval *noun* a great change causing a lot of worry. *Moving is a huge upheaval.*

uphill *adverb* going up a slope or hill. *We walked uphill.* The opposite is downhill. **uphill** *adjective* difficult and needing a lot of effort. *An uphill struggle to survive.*

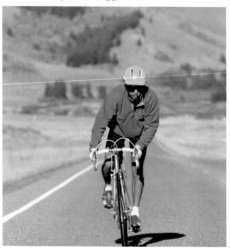

Adam cycled slowly uphill, thinking of the chocolate he would eat when he reached the top.

AMAZING FACT

The word 'urchin' comes from an ancient word meaning hedgehog.

uphold (upholds, upholding, upheld) *verb* to give support to or defend an action or cause. *The umpire upheld the referee's decision, and was booed.*

upholstery *noun* the springs, padding, covering and cushions of chairs and sofas. *Leather upholstery.* **upholster** *verb.*

upkeep *noun* the cost of keeping something in a good condition. *What's the yearly upkeep of your car?*

upon *preposition* on, on top of.

upper *adjective* above, in a higher position. *the upper part of your body.*

upright *adjective, adverb* 1 in a vertical position. *Upright posts.* 2 good and honest. *An upright person.*

uprising *noun* a rebellion or revolt against people in authority.

uproar *noun* noisy and angry or excited confusion, a disturbance.

uproot *verb* to pull a plant out of the ground by its roots.

upset (upsets, upsetting, upset) *verb* 1 to overturn or knock something over by accident. *The cat upset the creamer.* 2 to make somebody feel worried or unhappy. *You've upset your mother by being so rude.* **upset** *adjective* feeling unsettled or sick. *I don't eat seafood because it always gives me an upset tummy/stomach.*

upside-down *adjective* 1 with the top facing down and the bottom facing up. 2 utter disorder. *She turned the house upside-down looking for her watch.*

He hung upside-down on the bar until all the blood rushed to his head.

upstairs *adjective, adverb* situated on or going to a higher floor. *He walked upstairs.* The opposite is downstairs.

uptight *adjective* 1 (slang) nervous, angry, irritated. 2 prim and conventional.

up-to-date *adjective* modern, containing all the very latest information etc. *An up-to-date map.* The opposite is out-of-date.

urchin *noun* a poor, shabbily dressed, mischievous child.

Urdu *noun* one of the official languages of Pakistan, also widely spoken in India.

urge *verb* to encourage and try to make somebody do something, to plead. *He urged her to try a little harder.* **urge** *noun* a strong desire to do something, an impulse. *She had a sudden urge to go for a walk.*

urgent *adjective* very important and needing to be dealt with at once. *An urgent phone call.* **urgency** *noun*.

urine *noun* the clear, yellowish fluid waste passed from the bodies of animals and humans from the bladder. **urinate** *verb* to pass urine from the body.

urn *noun* 1 an ornamental vase or a container for a dead person's ashes. 2 a large container for holding hot drinks. *A tea urn.*

Uruguay *noun* a country in South America.

Uruguay is famous for its pampas grasslands, its fine herds of beef cattle and the cowboys called gauchos.

Uruguayan *noun* a person from Uruguay. **Uruguayan** *adjective*. *Uruguayan pasturelands.*

USA *abbreviation* United States of America.

usage *noun* 1 a way of using, treatment. *The video has been damaged through rough usage.* 2 the usual or customary way of doing or saying things. *British English usage is to say 'bonnet' for 'hood', 'pavement' for 'sidewalk', and 'lift' for 'elevator'.*

use *verb* (say **yoo**-zz) 1 to make something do a job. *She used scissors to cut the cloth.* 2 to consume or take. *Don't use all the hot water.* **use** *noun* (rhymes with juice) 1 the act of using or being in use. *The photocopier is in constant use.* 2 the purpose for using something. *This tool has many uses.*

used *adjective* not new, already owned by somebody. *Some used cars can be real bargains but others can turn out to be extremely expensive in the long run.*

WORD HISTORY

'Utopia' comes from a Latin word for 'no place' and was the title of a book by Sir Thomas More (1477–1536) describing an ideal land where everything is shared by everyone and where everyone is educated.

used to *verb* 1 accustomed to. *He isn't used to so much exercise.* 2 something that once happened often or that was once true. *We used to swim every afternoon.*

useful *adjective* helpful, having a purpose. *Useful tips on removing stains.* **usefulness** *noun*. *Gary's usefulness was very limited.*

useless *adjective* 1 of little or no help, having no effect. *It's useless asking him the way.* 2 (slang) very bad. *I'm useless in the kitchen.* **uselessness** *noun*.

user *noun* a person who uses something. *A rehabilitation centre for drug users.*

user-friendly *adjective* designed to be easy to use and understand. *It's a very user-friendly program.*

usual *adjective* happening often or most of the time, normal and everyday. *She got home at the usual time.* **usually** *adverb*. *We usually go shopping on Saturday.*

utensil *noun* a tool or container, especially one used everyday in the home. *Cooking utensils.*

Cooking is easier when you have the right utensils.

uterus *noun* the womb in which a baby develops.

utmost *adjective* 1 the greatest possible. *It's a matter of the utmost importance.* 2 farthest. *The utmost ends of the Earth.*

utopia *noun* an imaginary place where everything is perfect, a paradise. **utopian** *adjective*. *Sarah leads a utopian existence.*

utter *verb* to speak or make a sound with your mouth. *He uttered a squeal of delight.*

utterly *adverb* completely. *An utterly stupid thing to do.* **utter** *adjective*. *An utter idiot.*

U-turn *noun* 1 a U-shaped turn that a vehicle makes to go back the way it came. 2 a reversal of plans.

Uzbekistan *noun* a country in West Asia.

Uzbekistan was a member of the Soviet Union. It became independent in 1991.

Roy did not trust the used car salesman.

Vv

vacant *adjective* empty, unoccupied and not in use. *There's a vacant lot next door.*
vacancy *noun* a bed or room that is available in a motel or hotel. *Do you have any vacancies?* **vacate** *verb*.

vacation *noun* a time that is spent not working or at school.

vaccinate *verb* (say **vak**-sin-ate) to inject somebody to protect them from a disease such as measles. **vaccination** *noun*.

vaccine *noun* (say **vak**-seen) a medicine made from the germs of a disease given to people to protect them from the disease.

vacuum *noun* space that is empty of all gas. **vacuum** *verb* to clean with a vacuum-cleaner.

vacuum-cleaner *noun* an electrical machine that sucks up dust from carpets etc.

The first ever vacuum-cleaner was designed to blow the dust away rather than to suck it up.

Vaduz *noun* the capital of Liechtenstein.

vagina *noun* a passage in a woman's body that leads to the womb.

vague *noun* (say vayg) not clear or definite. *I could just see a vague shape in the twilight, but I couldn't identify who it was.*

vain *adjective* 1 too interested in your appearance or what you can do, too proud. 2 useless or unsuccessful, meaningless. *A vain attempt.* **in vain** without success.

valentine *noun* 1 a card you send to somebody you love on 14 February – Saint Valentine's Day. 2 the person to whom you send the card. *Be my valentine.*

valiant *adjective* brave.

valid *adjective* acceptable, legally acceptable. *A valid ticket.* **validity** *noun*.

DID YOU KNOW

There are stories and legends about vampires in many different countries. Some stories say that the way to protect yourself against a vampire is to carry a cross or some garlic. They also say that you cannot see the reflection of a vampire in a mirror.

WORD HISTORY

Vandals were Germanic people who invaded Gaul, Spain and Rome in the fourth and fifth centuries, destroying beautiful cities, churches and palaces as they went. Any destructive people became known as vandals after the word was first used during the French Revolution.

Valletta *noun* the capital of Malta.

valley (valleys) *noun* low land between hills, sometimes with a river flowing through it.

valuable *adjective* 1 precious and worth a lot of money. **valuables** *plural noun*. 2 useful, helpful. *Valuable advice.*

value *noun* 1 the amount of money that something is worth or that it can be sold for, price. *What is the value of this diamond?* 2 the importance or usefulness of somebody or something. **value** *verb*. *I value our friendship.*

valve *noun* a device on a tube, pipe etc. that controls the flow of a gas or liquid. You pump air into a tire through a valve.

vampire *noun* in stories, a corpse that leaves its grave at night to suck people's blood.

Count Dracula was the creation of Bram Stoker, a 19th century Irish novelist.

van *noun* a small enclosed truck for carrying goods.

vandal *noun* a person who deliberately and for no good reason smashes and ruins things. **vandalize** *verb*. **vandalism** *noun*.

vane *noun* **weather vane** a pointer that moves with the direction of the wind and so shows which way the wind is blowing.

vanilla *noun* a sweet flavouring for ice cream, cakes etc. made from the pod of a tropical kind of orchid.

vanish *verb* to disappear, to become invisible. *The bus vanished into the mist.*

vanity *noun* being too proud of what you look like or of what you can do. Conceit.

Vanuatu *noun* a country of islands in the Pacific Ocean.

Eighty islands make up the Pacific nation of Vanuatu. Some are coral islands with reefs and brilliant blue lagoons.

vapor *noun* a gas produced by heating a liquid or solid form of the substance. Steam is water vapor.

variable *adjective* changing or varying a lot, not stable. *The weather has been variable.*

variation *noun* 1 varying. 2 something that has changed. 3 differences.

varied *adjective* different kinds of.

variety *noun* a collection or number of different things or kinds. *There are many varieties of sheep.*

Anthony had a variety of gold and silver coins in his collection.

various *adjective* of different sorts, several. *Victor had various jobs after he left school.*

varnish *noun* a shiny, transparent liquid that you paint on to wood to protect it and to make it look glossy.

vary (varies, varying, varied) *verb* 1 to alter, to change constantly. *The weather varies from day to day.* 2 to make different. *I try to vary the menu from one day to the next.*

vase *noun* an ornamental container or jar for flowers.

vast *adjective* very wide, immense. *The vast rainforests of the Amazon.*

vastly *adverb* very greatly.

vat *noun* a large container or tub for storing liquid. *A vat of wine.*

Vatican City *noun* an independent city and state within the city of Rome, Italy.

vault *noun* 1 a strong room in which to store valuable things. *The vault has a time lock on it.* 2 an arched roof.

Down in the vaults the air was very cold and damp.

vault *verb* to jump over something using a pole. **vault** *noun*.

DID YOU KNOW

The word 'veal' comes from the French word for calf, 'veau'. After the Norman Conquest of the British Isles (1066) the French word for some animals was used for the name of the meat, so we get beef (from the French 'boeuf'), pork (from 'porc'), mutton (from 'mouton') and veal.

AMAZING FACT

Vatican City is the world's smallest independent country. It is tiny, about the size of a small farm, and stands on a hill in northwest Rome. Only about 750 people live there, yet it has its own flag, railroad and radio station and issues its own stamps.

VCR *abbreviation* video cassette recorder.

VDU *abbreviation* visual display unit.

veal *noun* the meat of a calf used as food.

veer *verb* to turn suddenly and change direction, to swerve.

vegan *noun* a vegetarian who does not use or eat any animal products.

vegetable *noun* a plant that is grown to be eaten. Carrots and peas are vegetables. **vegetable** *adjective*. *Vegetable curry.*

Fresh vegetables are a good source of vitamins and minerals.

vegetarian *noun* somebody who does not eat meat, only vegetables and sometimes dairy foods and fish.

vegetation *noun* plant life. *Rainforests have lush vegetation.*

vehicle *noun* a machine such as a car, bus or truck that transports people and goods from one place to another on land.

veil *noun* a very fine piece of material worn by some women to cover their face or head.

vein *noun* (rhymes with pain) 1 one of the tubes inside your body through which blood flows back to your heart. 2 one of the fine lines on a leaf or insect wing.

velocity *noun* speed, particularly speed at which something travels in one direction.

velvet *noun* a material with a soft thick pile. *I wore a red velvet dress to the play.*

Venezuela *noun* a country in South America.

Venezuelan *noun* a person who comes from Venezuela. **Venezuelan** *adjective*. *Venezuelan oil wells.*

venison *noun* the meat from deer, used as food. *Vension was served at the banquet.*

venom *noun* poison produced by some snakes and spiders. **venomous** *adjective*.

ventilate *verb* to let fresh air move freely through a place. *A well-ventilated bathroom.* **ventilation** *noun*.

ventriloquist *noun* a person who entertains by making their voice seem to come not from their mouth but from a dummy or from another place.

venture *verb* to risk doing something. *'Nothing ventured, nothing gained.'* **venture** *noun. A risky business venture.*

veranda *noun* porch, a platform around the outside of a house, usually with a roof.

verb *noun* a word or words in a sentence that describes what somebody or something is doing etc. In the sentence 'The dog is eating its bone,' 'is eating' is the verb.

verbose *adjective* using too many words. 'At this point in time' is a verbose way of saying 'now'.

verdict *noun* the decision of the judge and jury at the end of a trial in a law court saying whether the accused is guilty or not guilty. *The jury returned a verdict of guilty.*

verge *noun* to be **on the verge of** doing something means about to do it. **verge** *verb.* to be close to an extreme *His behavior verges on rudeness.*

verify (verifies, verifying, verified) *verb* to prove by showing the truth of something.

vermin *noun* any animal, bird or insect that transmits disease or damages food crops.

The old house was infested with vermin.

verse *noun* 1 a part of a poem consisting of a group of lines. 2 poetry and having rhythm and sometimes rhyme.

version *noun* 1 one form or a changed type of something. *A new version of the song.* 2 one person's description. *Mary gave her version of the accident.*

versus *preposition* a Latin word meaning against, often shortened to v. *The Miami Dolphins versus The Minnesota Vikings.*

vertebra (vertebrae) *noun* any one of the bones that make up the spine.

vertebrate *noun* any animal with a backbone. *Humans are vertebrates.*

vertical *adjective* upright, straight up. *The telegraph posts should be vertical.* The opposite is horizontal.

vessel *noun* 1 a ship or boat. 2 a container for liquids. *A drinking vessel.*

WORD HISTORY

The ancient Greeks believed that ventriloquism was the work of demons and thought the voice came from the abdomen. The word comes from the Latin 'venter' (belly) and 'loqui' meaning 'to speak'.

The train traveled across the viaduct.

WORD HISTORY

'Vermin' comes from a Latin word meaning 'worm'. It was later used to describe any unwanted animals.

AMAZING FACT

There are seven main groups of vertebrates: mammals, birds, reptiles, amphibians, fish, sharks, skates and, the simplest group, lampreys.

vet or **veterinary surgeon** *noun* a person who is trained to treat sick animals, an animal doctor.

veto *noun* the ability not to allow something to happen. **veto** *verb. The general vetoed the decision.*

vex (vexes, vexing, vexed) *verb* to annoy or worry somebody.

via *preposition* (say vee-ah) by way of. *We fly to Nairobi via Rome.*

viable *adjective* likely to be successful, workable. *Building a bridge across the Atlantic is simply not viable.*

viaduct *noun* (say **vye**-a-dukt) a long, arched bridge that carries a road or railway across a valley.

vibrate *verb* to shake to and fro rapidly. *The walls vibrate when the subway goes by.* **vibration** *noun.*

vicar *noun* a clergyman in charge of a parish in the Anglican Church.

vicarage *noun* the house where a vicar lives.

vice *noun* very bad, immoral or criminal behavior. A bad habit.

vice *noun* a device that grips things firmly while you are working on them.

Paul had a new vice clamped to his work bench.

vice- *prefix* in place of. Next in rank to. *Vice-president.*

vice-versa *adverb* the same is true either way or the other way round. *When he wants to eat, she doesn't want to eat and vice versa.*

vicinity *noun* (say viss-**in**-it-ee) the surrounding or nearby area.

vicious *adjective* violent, cruel.

victim *noun* a person who has been attacked, injured, robbed or killed.

victimize *verb* to deliberately choose somebody to treat unfairly or cruelly.

victor *noun* the winner in a competition, battle etc. *The victor was given a medal.*

Victoria *noun* the capital of Seychelles.

victory *noun* success in a battle, contest etc. A win. **victorious** *adjective*.

video *noun* 1 a machine (video cassette recorder) that records television programs so that you can watch them at another time. 2 a tape (videotape contained within a videocassette) used to record a television program.

vie (vies, vying, vied) *verb* to compete.

Vienna *noun* the capital of Austria.

Vientiane *noun* the capital of Laos.

Vietnam *noun* a country in Southeast Asia.

Vietnamese *noun* a person who comes from Vietnam. **Vietnamese** *adjective*. *Vietnamese ricefields.*

vigorous *adjective* physically energetic, enthusiastic, strong. *A vigorous walk in the Black Forest.* **vigor** *noun*.

Vikings *plural noun* seafarers from Scandinavia who invaded many parts of Europe between the 8th and 11th centuries. **Viking** *adjective*. *Viking ships.*

The Vikings sailed for thousands of miles across the icy northern oceans in small wooden boats that were completely open to the elements.

DID YOU KNOW

The first European to reach the Americas was probably a Viking from Iceland called Leif Ericsson around the year AD 1000.

The Sonoma Valley in California is famous for its vineyards.

vile *adjective* disgusting and very unpleasant, horrible. *What is that vile smell?*

villa *noun* a big country house.

village *noun* 1 a very small town. 2 the people who live in a village. *The whole village came to the meeting.*

villain *noun* 1 a person who breaks the law on purpose. 2 a wicked person, especially in a film, novel etc. *The villain of the story was a cruel king.* **villainy** *noun*.

Vilnius *noun* the capital of Lithuania.

vine *noun* a climbing plant on which grapes grow. *A vine clambered up the terrace.*

vinegar *noun* a sharp-tasting liquid made from wine or malt and used to flavor food.

vineyard *noun* (say **vin**-yard) a place where grapes are grown for making wine. *My parents visited a vineyard in France.*

vintage *adjective* 1 (of wine) a very good example of a particular year. 2 (of cars) made between 1919 and 1930. 3 of high and enduring quality.

V

viola *noun* a stringed musical instrument that is slightly larger than a violin and with a lower sound. *The beautiful mellow sound of the viola reached my ears.*

The viola is an important part of the string section of an orchestra.

violent *adjective* 1 using a lot of physical force to frighten, hurt or even kill. 2 sudden, strong and rough. *A violent storm blew up over the dark Sargasso Sea.* **violence** *noun. I don't like violence on television or at the movies.*

violet *noun* 1 a small plant with purplish flowers and a sweet smell. *Come, buy my lovely violets!* 2 the purplish color of a violet. **violet** *adjective.*

violin *noun* a musical instrument with four strings stretched across a wooden frame. *Hilary was learning to play the violin.*

viper *noun* a European poisonous snake, an adder. *Ian was bitten by a viper.*

virgin *noun* a person who has never had sexual intercourse. *Queen Elizabeth I remained a virgin.* **virginity** *noun.*

virtual *adjective* 1 in practice, but not in name. *His wife was the virtual governor.* 2 almost but not completely; not actually said. *The virtual collapse of law and order.* **virtual reality** an impression of a real environment in which you can interact, created by a computer.

virtue *noun* a particular good quality, goodness. *Kindness and honesty are virtues.*

virus *noun* 1 a microscopically tiny organism or living thing, smaller than bacteria, that can carry or cause disease. *A flu virus.* 2 a computer program that can damage or destroy data in a computer.

We looked at the virus under the microscope.

AMAZING FACT

New computer viruses are developed every day. A virus might send just a harmless joke or a cryptic message to your screen – or it could do serious damage.

W O R D H I S T O R Y

The word 'vitamin' is taken from the Latin word 'vita' meaning 'life' and the chemical 'amine'. The word was invented by the chemist Casimir Funk in 1913.

viscount *noun* (say vie-count) the title of a nobleman. *We invited the viscount and the viscountess to lunch, but unfortunately, they had another engagement.*

viscountess *noun* (say vie-count-ess) the wife of a viscount. *The viscountess wore blue at her sister's wedding.*

visible *adjective* capable of being seen. *From the top of a bus the whole street is visible.*
visibility *noun* how clearly you can see. *On foggy days visibility is poor.*

vision *noun* 1 sight, your ability to see. 2 what you can see or imagine in a dream. 3 great power of imagination and ability to plan. *His vision is that everybody should own their own home.*

visit *verb* 1 to go to see somebody or a place. 2 to stay somewhere for a short time. **visit** *noun.* **visitor** *noun.*

visual *adjective* relating to seeing and sight. *Computers display information on a visual display unit.*

visualize *verb* to form a picture in your mind, to imagine. *Can you visualize the awful situation Jane put me into?*

vital *adjective* essential to life, very important. *Air and water are vital to all living creatures.*

vitality *adjective* full of life and energy.

vitamin *noun* any one of several substances in food that we need to stay healthy. *Terry takes a vitamin supplement with her breakfast.*

vivid *adjective* bright and clear. *Vivid colors are the ones I like best.*

vivisection *noun* the use of living animals in scientific experiments.

vixen *noun* a female fox. The male is called a dog. The young are called cubs.

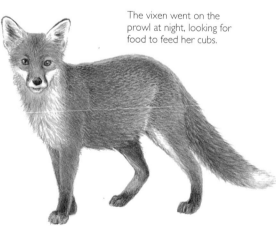

The vixen went on the prowl at night, looking for food to feed her cubs.

viz *adverb* namely.

vocabulary *noun* all the words somebody knows in a language. *His vocabulary in Spanish is about 1,000 words.*

vocal *adjective* 1 relating to the voice. *Vocal cords.* 2 speaking out freely and loudly. *He is very vocal about his beliefs.*

vocation *noun* a calling or very strong feeling that you want to do a particular job. *Dan had a vocation to become a teacher.* 2 a profession or occupation, a career.

vodka *noun* a colorless, strong alcoholic drink. *Penny likes vodka and tomato juice.*

vogue *noun* a fashion.

voice *noun* the sound produced by your vocal cords when you speak or sing, the power to speak.

void *noun* emptiness, a huge space with nothing in it. **void** *adjective* having no legal effect. *Null and void.*

volcano (volcanoes) *noun* a mountain with a crater (hole) on top through which molten lava from below the Earth's crust erupts from time to time. **volcanic** *adjective.*

WORD HISTORY

'Vodka' is a Russian word meaning 'little water'. Other Russian words that have come into the English language include 'steppe', 'tundra' and 'samovar'.

AMAZING FACT

Volcanoes have caused enormous damage throughout history. One of the most famous of volcanoes, Vesuvius, destroyed the city of Pompeii in AD 79.

volume *noun* 1 the amount of space that something takes up or contains. *The volume of water in the lake.* 2 one of a set of books. *A 20-volume encyclopedia.* 3 the loudness of sound. *Turn up the volume so I can hear.*

voluntary *adjective* done willingly and not because you have been forced. *She made a voluntary statement.* 2 done without payment. *She does voluntary work for charity.* **volunteer** *noun.*

vomit *verb* to bring food back from your stomach through your mouth.

vote *verb* to choose from a group the person or thing you prefer by raising your hand or marking a piece of paper. **vote** *noun. Each candidate got three votes.*

vow *verb* to make a very serious promise, to pledge. *He vowed to improve conditions for all the residents.* **vow** *noun.*

vowel *noun* a letter that is not a consonant – a,e,i,o and u and sometimes y.

voyage *noun* a long ocean journey.

vulgar *adjective* rude, offensive, coarse. **vulgarity** *noun. The teacher put a stop to vulgarity in the playground.*

vulnerable *adjective* easily harmed because unprotected, weak. *Old people are particularly vulnerable during the cold winter months.* **vulnerability** *noun.*

vulture *noun* a large bird of prey that feeds mostly on carrion (dead animals). *The vulture swooped out of the sky and landed on the sheep's carcass.*

When a volcano erupts, igneous rocks are formed from magma, which may solidify beneath or on the Earth's surface. Magma reaches the surface through vents, which are holes in the ground.

wad *noun* a thick lump of soft material, a tight bundle or pile of paper. *A wad of dollar bills was thrust into my hand.*

waddle *verb* to walk in a clumsy way with short steps like a duck.

wade *verb* to walk through water or mud. To move slowly and with difficulty.

wafer *noun* a very thin crisp cookie.

waffle *noun* a light crisp cake made of batter with a pattern of little squares on it. *Waffles are very popular in our house.*

waffle *verb* to have trouble making a decision.

wag (wags, wagging, wagged) *verb* to move quickly from side to side or up and down. *The dog wagged its tail as soon as it saw us.*

wage (wages, waging, waged) *verb* to begin and ccontinue to do something for a period of time. *The police are waging war on car theft.*

wages *plural noun* the money you earn for the work you do.

wagon *noun* 1 a four-wheeled cart pulled by a horse. 2 a small cart with four wheels that children play with. *We pulled the kids around the neighborhood in a red wagon.*

Early settlers traveled west in covered wagons pulled by mules, oxen and sometimes horses.

wail *noun* a long, sad cry. **wail** *verb*. *The wind wailed in the trees.*

waist *noun* the narrow, middle part of your body above your hips.

waistband *noun* the part of a skirt or a pair of pants that goes around your waist.

wait *verb* to stay where you are until something happens or someone arrives, to pause. *We waited 15 minutes for the bus to the airport.*

waiter *noun* a man or a woman (also waitress) who brings food and drinks to you in a restaurant.

wake (waking, woke, woken) *verb* 1 to stop being asleep. 2 to rouse somebody from sleep. **wake** *noun* (especially in Ireland) a group of people who stay with a dead body to mourn on the night before it is buried.

Wales *noun* a country that is part of the United Kingdom.

walk *verb* to move along on your feet. **walk** *noun. A walk in the hills.* **walker** *noun*. **walk off with** to take something without asking. **walk-over** an easy victory in a competition.

wall *noun* a structure made of bricks or stones surrounding a piece of land. The side of a building or room. **walled** *adjective. A walled garden.* **up the wall** crazy. *The noise is driving me up the wall.*

wallaby *noun* a small kind of kangaroo.

Wallabies are marsupials. The female wallaby carries her baby in a pouch.

wallet *noun* a small, folding case or purse for keeping money and credit cards.

wallflower *noun* 1 a sweet-smelling plant with red or orange flowers. 2 somebody whom no one ever seems to want to dance with.

wallow *verb* 1 to roll and splash around in water or mud. 2 to enjoy something to excess. *She wallowed in everybody's praise.*

walnut *noun* the edible nut of the walnut tree. Walnut wood is used for furniture.

walrus *noun* a large sea animal similar to a seal with two long tusks.

waltz *noun* a graceful dance for two people with three beats to a bar.

wan *adjective* pale and tired-looking.

wand *noun* a stick that magicians and fairies use to perform magic.

wander *verb* to move slowly from one place to another without going in any particular direction, to roam. **wanderer** *noun*.

wane *verb* to become smaller, to lose power. *The Moon is waning tonight.* The opposite is to wax.

want *verb* to desire something or to wish to do something. *I want to go home.*

war *noun* 1 armed fighting between countries or groups of people. A long period of fighting. 2 a struggle or campaign. *The war against poverty is global.*

Shortly after the tanks landed on the beach, the soldiers charged ahead to fight the war.

ward *noun* 1 a part of a hospital with beds where patients stay. *Mom's in the maternity ward.* 2 a ward of court is a child who is under the protection of a court or an adult guardian. 3 a part into which a town is divided for voting.

-ward, *suffix* in the particular direction of. *Homewards, southward.*

warden *noun* somebody who is in charge of a prison. *The new warden is much more reasonable than the last one was.*

wardrobe *noun* the clothes that someone owns.

warehouse *noun* a building for storing goods.

The farmer used his barn as a warehouse for fertilizer.

warfare *noun* the state of fighting wars.

warlike *adjective* hostile and prepared for war. *The soldiers had a warlike manner.*

warm *adjective* 1 slightly hot but not too hot. 2 friendly and enthusiastic. *A warm smile.* **warm** *verb.* *Can you warm the plates?* **warmth** *noun.* *The warmth of the Sun is doing my old bones a lot of good.*

warn *verb* 1 to tell somebody about a possible danger in the future. 2 to advise. *He warned me to go carefully.* **warning** *noun* a notice or statement that warns.

AMAZING FACT

The 'DC' in Washington DC stands for District of Columbia. The city of Washington covers the entire District. The site was chosen by George Washington in 1790 and planned by the French engineer Pierre L'Enfant.

DID YOU KNOW

Wasps, like bees and some other insects that are poisonous or have stings, are brightly colored.
Their bright colors are a warning to birds and other animals to leave them alone or take the risk of being stung!

---

warp *verb* to become twisted or misshapen through damp or heat. *The heat of the fire has warped the table.*

warren *noun* a network of underground burrows or passages in which rabbits live.

warrior *noun* a great fighting soldier.

Warsaw *noun* the capital of Poland.

warship *noun* a ship armed with guns for use in war.

wart *noun* a hard lump on your skin. **warty** *adjective.* *He has warty hands.*

was past tense of be.

wash *verb* 1 to clean with water, soap etc. *Wash your hands.* 2 to flow over or against something. 3 to carry away by flowing water. *The rain washed the mud away.*

washing *noun* clothes that need washing or that have been washed.

The washing dried quickly in the warm sunshine.

washing-machine *noun* a machine that washes clothes.

washed-up *adjective* someone who was once famous or successful but is no longer is said to be washed up.

Washington DC *noun* the capital of the United States of America.

wasp *noun* a yellow and black striped insect that can sting.

waste *noun* 1 things that you throw away because they are broken, worn or you do not need them any more, rubbish. 2 not using things in a careful way. *It's a waste to throw away food.* **waste** *verb* to use more of something than you need or to throw something away that could be used. **waste** *adjective. Waste paper.*

wasteful *adjective* extravagant, using more than is needed. **wastefulness** *noun.*

waste basket *noun* a basket or container for garbage.

watch *verb* 1 to look at for some time. *Watch how I do this.* 2 to notice and be careful about something. *Watch how you cross the road.* 3 to keep guard or take care of somebody or something. *Watch the soup – don't let it boil over.* **watchdog** *noun* a dog that guards property **watch out!** be careful.

watch *noun* a small clock that you usually wear on your wrist.

watchful *adjective* always noticing what is happening, alert. **watchfulness** *noun*.

water *noun* a clear liquid that falls as rain and that all living things drink to survive. Water is found in oceans, rivers and lakes. Water is made of two gases – oxygen and hydrogen. **water** *verb* 1 to pour water on. 2 to produce tears in the eyes or saliva in the mouth. 3 to dilute.

watercolor *noun* a painting done with watercolors, paints you mix with water.

waterfall *noun* water from a stream or river flowing down over a cliff or big rock to the ground below.

water-lily *noun* a plant with flat, floating leaves that grows in water.

watermill *noun* a mill – a tall building for grinding grain – with machinery powered by water. *The watermill on the River Floss.*

The wheel on the mill is turned by the running water. The energy is used to turn stones inside the mill to grind grain into flour.

water-polo *noun* a ball game played in a swimming pool by two teams of seven players. *Water-polo is great exercise.*

waterproof *adjective* not letting water through. *A waterproof coat.*

water-skiing *noun* a sport of skimming over the water on skis, towed by a rope attached to a motorboat.

watertight *adjective* closed so tightly that water cannot get through.

watery *adjective* full of water or containing too much water. *Watery soup.*

watt *noun* a unit of electricity.

wave *noun* 1 a moving curved line or ridge on the surface of water, especially the sea. 2 a curl or curved piece of hair. 3 the vibrating way in which energy such as heat, light, sound and radio travels. 4 the act of moving your hand up and down to attract attention, say goodbye etc.

wave *verb* 1 to move your hand up and down to say 'hello' or 'goodbye'. 2 to move something quickly to and fro, to flutter. *The flag waves in the wind.*

All the different colors of light have different wavelengths. The longest waves we can see are red.

WORD HISTORY

Watt, the unit of electricity, is named after James Watt, a Scottish inventor who developed the steam engine.

wavelength *noun* 1 the size of a radio wave to transmit a program. 2 the distance between electrical, radio or sound waves.

wax *noun* 1 a solid substance made from fat or oil that becomes soft and sticky when you heat it. Wax is used to make things like candles and furniture polish. 2 a similar substance produced by bees (beeswax). 3 a wax-like substance found in your ears.

wax *verb* to grow bigger. *The Moon waxes and then it wanes (grows smaller).*

way (ways) *noun* 1 an opening, a passage. *Don't block the way.* 2 a road or path that you should follow, a route. *Is this the way home?* 3 a direction. *Look the other way.* 4 a distance that you travel. *It's a long way to the mall from here.* 5 a state or condition. *He's in a bad way.* 6 means or method of doing something. *Is this the right way to mix paints?* 7 manner. *In a clumsy way.* 8 **ways** customs. The typical behavior of somebody. **by the way** incidentally. **in the way** blocking the place you want to go.

-ways *suffix* in the direction of. *sideways.*

weak *adjective* having little strength or power, easily broken. **weakness** *noun*.

weaken *verb* to make or become weak.

wealth *noun* 1 a lot of money and possessions, great riches. 2 a large amount. *A wealth of detail.* **wealthy** *adjective* rich.

weapon *noun* some device such as a gun, dagger or sword with which to fight.

The magnificent dagger in its scabbard was one of the prize weapons in the museum's collection.

wear (wears, wearing, wore, worn) *verb* 1 to be dressed in, to have on your body. *Do you wear glasses?* 2 to become damaged through use. *I wore a hole in the knee.* **wear** *noun*. *Men's wear.* **wear down** to weaken a person's resistance. *She wore him down with her nagging.* **wear off** to fade away or to become less. *The pain is wearing off.* **wear out** 1 to become damaged and useless. 2 to feel tired.

wearing *adjective* tiring, exhausting.

weary (wearier, weariest) *adjective* very tired. *You must be weary after your long journey.* **weariness** *noun*.

weather *noun* the condition of the atmosphere at a particular time or place: warm, cold, windy or rainy. *The game was called off because of the weather.*

weather forecast *noun* a report on what the weather is expected to be like in the near future. *The weather forecast is good.*

weathervane *noun* a pointer that moves with the wind and so shows which way the wind is blowing.

weave (weaves, weaving, woven, woven) *verb* 1 to make cloth by using a machine called a loom that passes threads over and under other threads. 2 to make baskets etc. by plaiting cane etc. 3 (past tense wove or weaved) to move in and out between people or things. *He wove through the traffic on his bike.*

web *noun* **cobweb** a fine sticky net of threads spun by a spider to catch insects.

webbed *adjective* having the toes joined by pieces of skin. *Ducks and geese have webbed feet to help them swim better.*

wedding *noun* the marriage service.

we'd *abbreviation* we had.

wedge *noun* 1 a piece of wood that is thick at one end and thin and pointed at the other, used to stop things such as doors from moving. 2 something in the shape of a wedge. *A wedge of cheese.* **wedge** *verb*. *She wedged the door open.*

wee *adjective* very small.

weed *noun* a wild plant that grows where it is not wanted. **weed** *verb* to remove weeds.

weedy *adjective* 1 full of weeds. 2 weak and thin. *A weedy person.*

week *noun* a period of time from Monday to the following Sunday. There are seven days in a week and 52 weeks in a year. **weekly** *noun*. *A weekly magazine.*

weekend *noun* Saturday and Sunday.

weep (weeps, weeping, wept) *verb* to cry. *She wept when she read the sad story.*

There were two sets of weights, one to weigh cooking ingredients, the other for heavier things.

Dewdrops glisten on this spider's web.

weigh *verb* 1 to place something on scales to find out how heavy it is. 2 to have a certain weight. *Dave weighs more than he used to.*

weight *noun* 1 how heavy somebody or something is. 2 a unit of weight or a piece of metal of a certain weight.

weird *adjective* very strange, unusual.

welcome *verb* to greet somebody in a way that shows that you are very pleased to see them. **welcome** *noun, interjection. Welcome home!* **welcoming** *adjective*.

weld *verb* to join two pieces of metal together by melting the ends and pressing and hammering them together. **welder** *noun*.

welfare *noun* 1 A person's welfare is their general wellbeing, health, happiness and prosperity. 2 money or help a person in need gets from the state.

well *noun* a very deep hole in the ground from which you can get water or oil from far beneath the Earth.

well *adjective* in good health, in good order. *I'm very well thank you.* **well** *adverb* 1 in a good or correct way. *Victoria plays tennis well.* 2 thoroughly. *I washed the car very well.* 3 also. *Two bags of chips and a coke as well.* **well** *interjection. Well, I hope you had a nice time.*

we'll *abbreviation* we shall or we will.

Wellington *noun* the capital of New Zealand.

wellingtons or wellington boots *plural noun* rubber or plastic boots up to your knees that keep your feet and legs dry.

John kept his wellingtons by the door so he could go straight out into the barnyard in the morning.

well-off *adjective* wealthy. *We are well-off.*

Welsh *noun* the language of Wales. **the Welsh** the people of Wales. **Welsh** *adjective. Welsh sheep are very hardy.*

went past tense of go.

wept past tense of weep.

were past tense of (plural) be.

we're short for we are.

weren't short for were not.

werewolf *noun* in stories and folklore, a man who sometimes turns into a wolf, usually at full moon.

A werewolf.

west *noun* the direction in which the Sun sets. The opposite direction is east. **west** *adjective, adverb. They travelled west.*

western *adjective* relating to the west, of the west. *Western Europe.* **western** *noun* a book or film about life in the 19th century in the western USA and involving gunfights and cowboys.

Western Samoa *noun* a country of islands in the Pacific Ocean.

West Indian *noun* a person from the West Indies. **West Indian** *adjective. The story is set on a West Indian island.*

West Indies *plural noun* a series of islands that separate the Caribbean Sea from the Atlantic Ocean.

wet (wetter, wettest) *adjective* covered with or full of water or some other liquid. 2 rainy. *The weekend was very wet.* **wet** (wets, wetting, wet or wetted) *verb* to make something wet. The opposite is dry.

we've short for we have.

whale *noun* a very large sea mammal that looks like a fish. Whales need air to breathe.

Wheat is the world's second largest crop after rice.

SPELLING NOTE

The following words sound similar and should not be confused: 'we're' and 'weir' (a small dam across a river), 'we've' and 'weave', 'whale' and 'wail' (a long, sad cry), 'wheel' and 'we'll', 'where' and 'ware', 'whine' and 'wine'.

Whales feed on tiny sea creatures called krill, which they sieve through the baleen, plates of fringed material growing from the upper jaw.

wharf (wharfs or wharves) *noun* platform or landing place where ships dock to be loaded or unloaded.

wheat *noun* a cereal crop from whose grain flour is made.

wheel *noun* a circular object or disc that rotates around an axle and that is used to move a vehicle or help make machinery work. **wheel** *verb. She wheeled the cart down the aisle.*

wheelbarrow *noun* a small handcart with one wheel at the front and two legs and two handles at the back.

wheelchair *noun* a chair with large wheels for somebody who cannot walk easily.

when *adverb, conjunction* 1 at what time. *When does the bus arrive?* 2 at the time that. *I'll change my clothes when I get home.*

whenever *adverb, conjunction* when, at every time, at any time. *Come whenever you like, as long as you bring me a present.*

where *adverb* 1 in what place. *Where's the dog?* 2 to what place. *Where did you go last weekend?* 3 from what place. *Where did you find those shoes?* **where** *conjunction* at or in what place. *He went over to the window where there was more light.*

whiff *noun* a sudden, slight scent of something. *A whiff of honeysuckle.*

whim *noun* a sudden, and often silly, desire or thought. *On a sudden whim, Richard bought two tickets for Paris and gave one to Sarah.*

whimper *verb* to make a quiet, crying noise because of pain. **whimper** *noun. The puppy gave a frightened whimper.*

whine *verb* 1 to complain about something in a miserable, irritating voice. *If you don't stop whining you'll have to stay home!* 2 to make a long, high-pitched sound because you are in sad or in pain.

whip *noun* a strip of leather or a cord attached to a stick, used for hitting animals. **whip** (whips, whipping, whipped) *verb* 1 to hit with a whip. 2 to whisk or beat eggs etc. until they are stiff. 3 to move very quickly. *The actress whipped off her clothes.*

whirl *verb* to move round and round quickly. **whirl** *noun*. *A whirl of activity.*

whirlpool *noun* a current of water that turns round and round rapidly.

A whirlpool can be extremely dangerous.

whirlwind *noun* a strong wind that spins as it travels over land and sea.

whisk *noun* a kitchen implement made of wire for beating air into eggs, cream etc. **whisk** verb. *The chef whisked the sauce.*

whisker *noun* 1 a long, stiff hair growing around the mouth of an animal such as a cat or dog. 2 hair growing on a man's face.

whiskey *noun* an alcoholic drink made from barley, rye or other grains *Whiskey and water.*

whisper *verb* to speak very quietly using only your breath without vibrating your vocal cords. **whisper** *noun*.

whistle *noun* 1 the shrill noise you can make when you blow through your lips. 2 a device you blow to make a sound like a whistle. **whistle** *verb*. *He whistled a happy tune.*

white *noun* 1 the color of milk or new snow. 2 the liquid in an egg around the yoke. 3 (often White) a person belonging to a race with light-colored skin. **white** *adjective*. **whiten** *verb*. **white lie** a small lie told in order to avoid hurting somebody's feelings. *It was just a little white lie.*

whizz kid *noun* a very bright and successful young person. *Dean is a real whizz kid.*

whizz (whizzes, whizzing, whizzed) *verb* to move very quickly with a rushing noise. *The racing cars whizzed past.*

WHO *abbreviation* World Health Organization.

GRAMMAR NOTE

Try not to confuse 'who's' and 'whose'. 'Who's' is an abbreviation of 'who has' or 'who is', as in 'Who's eaten all the cake?' 'Whose' means 'of whom' or 'of which', as in 'The man whose mother is a singer.' It also means 'of whom' in questions, as in 'Whose book is this?'

WORD HISTORY

'Whiskey' comes from Gaelic words meaning 'water of life'. Gaelic is the original language of Scotland.

To 'blow the whistle' on someone means to reveal that they are doing something wrong.

AMAZING FACT

Words like WHO are acronyms, words made up of the first letter of each of the words in a title. Other acronyms are NATO, North Atlantic Treaty Organization and SCUBA, self-contained underwater breathing apparatus.

---

whole *adjective* the complete and total amount of something. *She ate a whole box of candy.* **whole** *noun*. *Two halves make a whole.*

wholesale *noun* 1 the sale of goods in large quantities or amounts by a wholesaler to shops (retailers) who then sell to the public. 2 on a big scale. *Wholesale slaughter.*

wholesome *adjective* good for you. *Wholesome soup.*

whooping cough *noun* an infectious disease that makes you cough a lot and make a terrible noise as you breathe in.

who's short for who is.

why *adverb* for what reason.

wick *noun* the twisted thread in a candle or oil lamp which you light.

Wick

Wicks have to be kept trimmed so that the lamp doesn't smoke when it is lit .

wicked *noun* very bad, evil and cruel. **wickedness** *noun*.

wicket *noun* a curved wire or hoop used in the game of croquet.

wide *adjective* 1 measuring a long way from one side to the other, broad. *Interstates are very wide roads.* 2 measuring a certain distance. *The pool is 10 m wide.* 3 including a large area or variety. *Wide experience.* The opposite of wide is narrow.

widespread *adjective* happening over a wide area or among many people. *Widespread flooding.*

widow *noun* a woman whose husband has died. *The widow sobbed beside the grave.*

widower *noun* a man whose wife has died.

width *noun* how much something measures from one side to the other. *What is the width of the door?*

wield *verb* 1 to hold and use with the hands. *He wielded an axe.* 2 to exercise power. *Dictators wield complete power.*

wife (wives) *noun* the woman that a man marries. *The sultan had 20 wives.*

wig *noun* a false covering of hair that fits on a bald head or over somebody's own hair.

wigwam *noun* a dome-shaped tent made from animal skins by Native Americans.

wild *adjective* 1 natural and not cultivated or tamed by people. *A wild flower.* 2 uncontrolled, angry. *A wild storm.*

wilderness *noun* a wild, uncultivated area where nobody lives. A desert.

wildlife *noun* wild animals and plants in their natural habitats.

will *noun* 1 an ability to make firm decisions, determination. *A will to win.* 2 what somebody wants. *The will of the people.* 3 a written document listing who is to have your belongings and money after your death. *I changed my will.*

willing *adjective* happy to do whatever is needed. **willingness** *noun. Eva always shows a great willingness to help.*

willow *noun* a tree with long thin, hanging branches that grows near water.

The weeping willow is a graceful tree to plant beside a pond.

willowy *adjective* tall and graceful like a willow tree. *A willowy young girl.*

wilt *verb* to become weak and droop and shrivel like a plant without water.

wily (wilier, wiliest) *adjective* cunning and full of artful tricks.

wimp *noun* a man who is weak, feeble and lacking courage. *Poor Rob is a real wimp.*

win (wins, winning, won) *verb* 1 to come first in a contest. 2 to obtain something through luck. *He won the lottery.* **win** *noun.*

wince *verb* to jerk and make your face look twisted because of pain or fear.

winch *noun* a machine with a rope around a turning part for lifting things.

wind (winds, winding, wound) *verb* (rhymes with kind) 1 to bend and twist. 2 to roll or wrap around. 3 to tighten a clock spring. **wind up** 1 to end in a place or situation. 2 to end an activity. *It's late, let's wind this up and go home.*

wind *noun* (rhymes with pinned) 1 a strong moving current of air. **windy** *adjective. A windy day.* 2 gases in the stomach that make you feel uncomfortable.

winded *adjective* out of breath through heavy exercise.

Windhoek *noun* the capital of Namibia.

wind instrument *noun* a musical instrument that you play by blowing into it. *Clarinets, and flutes are wind instruments.*

windmill *noun* a mill – a tall building for pumping water, grinding grain etc. – with machines powered by wind blowing a set of arm-like sails.

Some windmills are still working, others have been turned into museums or homes.

window *noun* a hole covered with glass in a wall or roof of a building that lets in light and air.

windpipe *noun* a tube leading from your mouth to your lungs that carries air to your lungs. *A fishbone got stuck in her windpipe.*

windshield *noun* the window at the front of a car, truck etc. .

windsurf *verb* to ride over waves on a special board with a sail. **windsurfer** *noun.*

wine *noun* an alcoholic drink made from grapes or sometimes other plants.

wing *noun* 1 one of the parts of a bird, bat or insect used for flying. 2 one of the parts sticking out of the side of an aircraft that is used for flying. 3 a part of a building that extends from the main part. *The east wing.* 4 part of a stage unseen by the audience. 5 a division within a political party.

Birds evolved the power of flight millions of years ago. Humans have tried and failed to fly, like birds, with wings.

wingspan *noun* the length across the wings of a bird, insect or a bird.

wink *verb* 1 to open and close one eye quickly. 2 (of light) to flash on and off. **wink** *noun. He gave me a wink to show that he was only joking.*

DID YOU KNOW

The British use different words for many parts of a car (automobile). Instead of saying 'windshield' they say 'windscreen', they say 'bumpers' not 'fenders', and 'gear lever' instead of 'gear shift', 'bonnet' not 'hood' and 'boot' rather than 'trunk'.

AMAZING FACT

In Greek mythology, Icarus tried to escape imprisonment by fastening wings made of wax and feathers to his shoulders. Icarus flew so close to the Sun that the wax melted and he fell to his death.

winner *noun* a person, animal or vehicle that wins a race, contest etc.

winning *adjective* charming. *Will has a winning smile, but he doesn't fool me!*

winnings *plural noun* money that has been won. *She frittered all her winnings away.*

winter *noun* the season of the year between fall and spring. **wintry** *adjective*.

wipe *verb* to rub something with your hand or a cloth in order to clean or dry it. **wiper** *noun* a windshield wiper.

wire *noun* a thin length of metal that can easily be twisted, used especially to carry electricity and for fencing. **wire** *verb* to put in wires to carry electricity. *The house was wired last year.* **wire** *adjective*. *Wire fencing.*

wireless *noun* an old-fashioned word for radio. *Let's listen to the wireless tonight.*

wisdom *noun* being wise and having great understanding and judgement. **wisdom tooth** *noun* a tooth that sometimes grows at the back of your jaw after the other teeth have stopped growing.

wise *adjective* sensible and having a great understanding and experience of something, knowing the right action or decision.

-wise *suffix* 1 acting like somebody or something. In the direction of. *Clockwise.* 2 with reference to something. *Health-wise, I'm fine, and so is your father.*

wish *verb* 1 to want or to desire something. 2 to say that you hope something will happen. *I wish you well.* **wish** *noun* a strong desire for something. *A wish to travel.*

wishbone *noun* the V-shaped bone in the breast of birds.

wit *noun* 1 common sense, the ability to think clearly. 2 skill in saying things in a clever and funny way. 3 a clever and amusing person. *He's a great wit.* **witty** *adjective*. *What a witty writer!* **at your wits' end** not knowing how to solve a serious and worrying problem.

-witted *suffix* having a particular kind of ability. *Quick-witted.*

witch *noun* a woman in fairy stories who can perform magic.

witchcraft *noun* magic used by witches.

The witch said a magic spell over the toad and turned it into a prince.

SPELLING NOTE

Are you a pronunciation wizard? Try these: 'bough', 'bought' 'tough' 'cough', 'enough', 'plough', 'through', 'though', 'thought', 'thorough'.

witchdoctor *noun* a person who is believed to have magic powers to cure illnesses.

withdraw (withdraws, withdrawing, withdrew, withdrawn) *verb* 1 to take back or take away, to remove. *She withdrew $100 from her bank account.* 2 to go away from. *After the war the troops withdrew.* **withdrawal** *noun.* **withdrawn** *adjective*. 1 remote. 2 unable to communicate. *She's unhappy and withdrawn.*

wither *verb* to dry up, droop and die, to shrivel. *Flowers wither without water.*

Sue forgot to put fresh water in the vase and the flowers began to wither.

within *preposition* inside, not beyond. *They were within a mile of home.*

withhold (withhold, withholding, withheld) *verb* to hold on to and refuse to give something, to keep back. *He withheld the evidence from the court.*

without *preposition* not having, in the absence of. *He made it without any help.*

witness *noun* a person who has seen something important happen and so can describe what happened to others, especially to the police or in a law court. **witness** *verb*.

wives the plural of wife.

wizard *noun* 1 a man in fairy stories who can perform magic. 2 an expert at something. *A computer wizard.*

wobble *verb* to move in an unsteady way from side to side, to shake a little. **wobbly** *adjective*. *A wobbly table.*

woe *noun* great sorrow, misery. **woeful** *adjective*. *A woeful look.*

woke past tense of wake.

wolf (wolves) *noun* a wild animal of the dog family that hunts in a packs. **wolf** *verb* to eat greedily.

The wolf is one of the ancestors of the domestic dog.

woman (women) *noun* a grown-up female human. *A truly beautiful woman.*

womb *noun* a part inside a woman or any female mammal where her young develop before being born.

wombat *noun* a small burrowing Australian marsupial related to the koala.

In Australia, there are signs by the road telling you to beware of wombats.

won past tense of win.

wonder *verb* 1 to ask yourself something, to want to know about. *I wonder what day it is.* 2 to be surprised or astounded. **wonder** *noun* 1 a feeling of surprise and amazement. 2 something so impressive that it causes a feeling of amazement.

wonderful *adjective* 1 very pleasing, excellent. *What a wonderful day.* 2 marvelous and very impressive. *Computer technology is a wonderful achievement.*

wonky *adjective* unsteady and liable to collapse. *This chair is a little wonky.*

wood *noun* the substance that trees are made of. Furniture is usually made of wood and so is paper. 2 **woods** a place where there are a lot trees growing closely together. **woody** *adjective. Woody carrots.*

wooded *adjective* covered with trees. *A wooded mountainside.*

wooden *adjective* made of wood.

woodpecker *noun* one of a family of birds that have a strong pointed beak for drilling holes in trees to find insects to eat.

woodwind *noun* a group of musical instruments that you play by blowing through a mouthpiece and into a hollow tube. *The flute and clarinet are woodwind instruments.*

woodwork *noun* (the making of) things made of wood.

woodworm *noun* the larva of a beetle that makes holes in wood by feeding on it.

wool *noun* the thick hair of sheep and goats used for knitting and making cloth, the yarn made from wool.

AMAZING FACT

Wombats and other marsupials such as wallabies, opposums and kangaroos, carry their young in a pouch on their stomach where they continue their development. Australia has only marsupial mammals.

SPELLING NOTE

Try not to confuse 'wander' and 'wonder'. 'Wander' means 'to move about without trying to reach anywhere in particular'. 'Wonder' means 'something exciting, strange or marvellous'. As a verb it can also mean 'to think about' or 'to feel surprise'.

The clarinet is a woodwind instrument.

AMAZING FACT

Not all woodwind instruments are made of wood. Saxophones and most flutes are made of metal, while recorders are sometimes made of plastic.

---

woolly *adjective* made of wool. *A woolly hat keeps his head warm in winter.*

word *noun* a group of letters that mean something. We speak or write words to communicate. **give your word** to promise. **keep your word** to keep your promise. **in a word** to sum up. **word for word** each word exactly as said or written. **have words with** to quarrel.

word processor *noun* a computer with a keyboard and screen that is used to type letters, write articles, store information etc.

wore past tense of wear.

work *noun* 1 the job that somebody does to earn money. 2 the energy you use to do or make something. *Hard work.* 3 something you have made or done. *Works of art.* **work** *verb* 1 to do a job. 2 to use effort to do work. 3 to operate or make something go. *Can you work this machine?* **work out** to calculate and solve. *Work out a problem.* **have your work cut out** to have a difficult task to do.

workable *adjective* able to be done successfully. *A workable plan.*

worker *noun* somebody who works or who does a particular job. *Factory workers.*

works *plural noun* 1 all the writing or painting done by a writer or artist. 2 *the works.* everything.

workshop *noun* a place where things are made or repaired.

world *noun* 1 the universe and space with all the stars and planets. 2 the Earth and everything on it. 3 everyhing to do with a particular subject or

The world looks very fragile when viewed from outer space.

activity. *The world of music.* **the New World** America.

worldly *adjective* knowing a lot about people and society.

worm *noun* a long, thin legless anima!.

worn past tense of wear.

worn-out *adjective* 1 too old and no longer in a good condition. 2 exhausted.

worry (worries, worrying, worried) *verb* 1 to be uneasy and think something bad may happen. *She worried about leaving her dog alone all day.* 2 to bother somebody.

worse *adjective* less good or well. *The weather was bad yesterday but it's worse today.*

worship (worships, worshipping, worshipped) *verb* 1 to show respect for God or gods, especially in a church or temple. **worshipper** *noun*. 2 to love somebody very much.

worst *adjective, adverb* least good or well, most bad. Worst is the opposite of best.

worth *noun, adjective* 1 the value of something or somebody. 2 good or useful. *This job is worth doing well.*

Only an experienced jeweler is able to tell how much this jewelry is really worth.

worthless *adjective* having no value, not useful. *Worthless ideas.* **worthlessness** *noun*.

worthwhile *adjective* useful and important enough to spend time on.

worthy *adjective* good and deserving respect. **worthiness** *noun*.

wound (rhymes with sound) past tense of wind.

wound *noun* (say **woon**-d) an injury or bad cut, especially one caused by a knife or gun etc. **wound** *verb*. *They were badly wounded.*

wove, woven past tense and past participle of weave.

wrangler *noun* cowboy.

wrap (wraps, wrapping, wrapped) *verb* to put a cover around or to fold paper, cloth etc. around. *We wrapped up Dad's present.*

wrapping *noun* paper or other material put around something to cover or protect it.

wreath *noun* flowers and leaves arranged in a circle and tied together.

wreck *verb* to destroy or ruin something completely so that it is unusable. *Vandals wrecked the phone booth.*

An international team of aid workers helped clear up the wreckage after the flood.

AMAZING FACT

The opposite of 'worthless' is 'valuable' (meaning that it has worth) or 'priceless' (meaning so valuable that it is impossible to attach a price to it). Something may be priceless to us, not because it is worth a lot of money, but because it is something that cannot be replaced or has sentimental value.

He wrung out the washcloth and wiped her face.

SPELLING NOTE

Words that sound similar and should not be confused are: 'wrap' and 'rap', 'wring' and 'ring', 'write', 'right' and 'rite', and 'wrung' and 'rung'.

wreckage *noun* all the pieces that remain after something has been wrecked. *We cleaned up the wreckage after the flood.*

wren *noun* a very small brown bird with an upward-pointing tail.

wrench *verb* to twist something violently. **wrench** *noun* a tool used for gripping and twisting things such as nuts and bolts.

wrestle *verb* 1 to hold someone and try to throw them to the ground. 2 to struggle. **wrestler** *noun* somebody who wrestles as a sport.

wretched *adjective* 1 sad and very unhappy. 2 poor quality or unpleasant. *The situation after the drought was wretched for all the villagers.*

wriggle *verb* to twist and turn about. *Stop wriggling in your chair.*

wring (wrings, wringing, wrung) *verb* to force water out of a wet cloth by squeezing it. *He wrung out the wet dish cloth.*

wrinkle *noun* a crease or line in your skin or in cloth etc. **wrinkle** *verb*.

wrist *noun* the joint connecting your arm to your hand. *A limp wrist.*

write (writes, writing, wrote, written) *verb* 1 to form words, especially with a pen or pencil on paper. 2 to compose a book, piece of music etc. **writer** *noun* a person who writes books etc., usually to earn money.

writing *noun* 1 anything that has been written. Literature, poems etc. 2 handwriting *He has neat writing.*

wrong *adjective* 1 incorrect. The opposite is right. 2 bad and immoral. *It's wrong to lie.*

wrung past tense of wring.

wry *adjective* 1 twisted, bent. *She has a wry smile.* 2 slightly mocking. *A wry remark.*

WYSIWYG *abbreviation* what you see (on the screen) is what you get (when printed).

X Y Z

xenophobia *noun* a hatred of all foreigners.

Xmas *noun* a short informal spelling for Christmas. *Merry Xmas.*

X-ray *noun* 1 a kind of ray that can pass through solid things. 2 a photograph using x-rays of a part of the inside of your body. This enables doctors to see if anything is broken or diseased.

xylophone *noun* a musical instrument with wooden bars that you hit with small hammers to make notes.

Yy

yacht *noun* a boat, usually large and expensive, that is used for traveling for pleasure, sailing and racing.

yak *noun* a long-haired ox from Tibet and the Himalayas.

yam *noun* a tropical vegetable similar to a potato. *Yams are delicious in stews.*

Yamoussoukro *noun* the capital of the Ivory Coast.

yank *verb* to pull something suddenly and violently. **yank** *noun.*

Yaoundé *noun* the capital of Cameroon.

yap *noun* the short high-pitched bark of a small dog. **yap** (yaps, yapping, yapped) *verb. Their terrier yaps all day long.*

yard *noun* 1 the area round a house, usually covered in grass. *Our new dog has to learn to stay in our yard.* 2 a measure of length equal to 3 feet or 0.91 meters.

This X-ray of a human hand shows that no bones are broken.

yarn *noun* 1 wool or cotton spun into thread for sewing, knitting etc. 2 a long and often untrue story.

yasmak *noun* a veil worn by some Muslim women to cover all or part of their face.

Muslim women often wear a yasmak in public.

yawn *verb* to open your mouth wide and take in a deep breath because you are tired or bored. **yawn** *noun.*

year *noun* 1 the time it takes the Earth to travel once around the Sun – 365 days or 12 months or 52 weeks. 2 the period of time between 1 January and 31 December. **leap year** a year having 366 days, occurring every four years. In leap years February has 29 days.

yearly *adjective* 1 taking place once a year. 2 during or lasting a single year. *A yearly membership fee.* **yearly** *adverb.*

yeast *noun* a kind of fungus used in making bread rise and in brewing beer.

yell *noun* a loud shrill shout. **yell** *verb. He yelled above the noise of the traffic.*

yellow *noun* the color of ripe bananas and lemons. **yellow** *adjective. Yellow roses.*

yelp *noun* a sudden, sharp sound of pain or excitement. **yelp** *verb. The dog yelped when I stood on its tail.*

Yemen *noun* a country in The Middle East.

The main exports of Yemen are petroleum products, cotton and fish.

yen *noun* the main Japanese unit of money.

Yerevan *noun* the capital of Armenia.

yesterday *noun, adverb* the day before today. *Today is Monday, yesterday was Sunday.*

yew *noun* an evergreen tree with dark, needle-like leaves.

yield *verb* 1 to surrender, to give up and admit defeat. *He yielded under pressure.* 2 to produce. *How much wheat does this field yield?* **yield** *noun.*

yoga *noun* an Eastern system of meditation and self-control involving exercises to exercise and relax the body and the mind.

X
Y
Z

yogurt *noun* a thick, liquid food made from soured milk. *Strawberry yogurt.*

yoke *noun* a bar with two pieces that fit around the necks of a pair of oxen to keep them together so they can pull a plough etc. **yoke** *verb.*

yolk *noun* (rhymes with oak) the yellow part in the middle of an egg.

The yolk of an egg is its most nutritious part.

Yom Kippur *noun* a Jewish holy day at the start of the Jewish New Year in mid-September. It is a time of fasting and prayer.

yonder *adjective, adverb* (old-fashioned) over there. *The bench is under yonder tree.*

young *adjective* not old, having lived or existed for only a short time. **young** *plural noun* the offspring of animals. *The young of cows are called calves.*

youngster *noun* a young person.

youth *noun* 1 the time when a person is young. *He was a gymnast in his youth.* 2 a young man. 3 young people in general.

youthful *adjective* 1 young. 2 having the qualities of being young, relating to the young. *Youthful enthusiasm.*

yo-yo *noun* a toy made of two joined discs that you make run up and down a string that you hold.

Yugoslavia *noun* a country in Europe, made up of Serbia and Montenegro.

yule *noun* Christmas.

Zz

Zagreb *noun* the capital of Croatia.

Zambia *noun* a country in Africa.

Zambian *noun* a person who comes from Zambia. **Zambian** *adjective. Zambian copper mines also yield malachite.*

zany *adjective* funny in an odd kind of way. **zanily** *adverb.*

zap (zaps, zapping, zapped) *verb* 1 to strike or attack something suddenly in, for example, a computer game. 2 to keep changing quickly from one section of a tape, video, TV program etc.

AMAZING FACT

A zebra's stripes make them stand out in a zoo, but in their natural habitat, the grasslands of Africa, the stripes act as camouflage and help conceal them from predators.

DID YOU KNOW

The 12 signs of the zodiac are: Aries, Gemini, Taurus, Cancer, Leo, Virgo, Libra, Scorpio, Sagittarius, Capricorn, Aquarius and Pisces.

On the right are some of the signs of the zodiac as seen in the sky: Sagittarius, Gemini, Cancer and Scorpio.

WORD HISTORY

The shape of the letter Z developed from an ancient Egyptian symbol for an arrow. The Semites gave it the name 'zayin', their word for an arrow. The Greeks called it 'zeta'.

zeal *noun* enthusiasm, determined eagerness. *After their vacation, they approached work with renewed zeal.*

zebra *noun* An African animal like a horse with black and white stripes on its body.

zenith *noun* 1 the sky directly overhead. 2 the highest point, the peak or summit.

zero (zeros) *noun* nought, the name of the figure 0.

zest *noun* 1 enthusiasm, great enjoyment. *A zest for living.* 2 the outer peel of a lemon or orange.

zigzag *noun* a line that sharply bends one way then another like the letter Z. **zigzag** *verb. The path zigzagged up the hillside.*

Zimbabwe *noun* a country in Africa.

Zimbabwean *noun* a person who comes from Zimbabwe. **Zimbabwean** *adjective. Zimbabwean lakes.*

zinc *noun* a hard white metal used in alloys.

zipper *noun* a long narrow fastener with two rows of teeth that can be made to lock and unlock by sliding a tab up or down. *This sleeping bag has a double zipper.*

zither *noun* a ancient musical instrument with strings that are plucked.

zodiac *noun* (say **zoh-dee-ak**) a band in the sky through which the Sun, Moon and planets move and which astrologers divide into twelve sections each with its own symbol or sign and name. *Astronomers don't study the Zodiac.*

zombie *noun* 1 in stories, a dead body that is brought back to life. 2 a person who does not seem to be aware of what is going on and does things without seeming to think.

zone *noun* an area that is made separate for some special purpose. *We got a ticket because Mom parked in a no-parking zone.*

zoo *noun* a place where wild animals are kept for people to look at and study.

zoology *noun* (say zoo-ol-ogee) the scientific study of animals. **zoological** *adjective.* **zoologist** *noun.*

zoom *verb* 1 to move very quickly. 2 to focus a camera quickly from long distance to close up. **zoom lens** a camera lens that can be made to focus quickly on close-up things then far-away things.

What's wrong?

Try to correct the mistakes in these sentences.

1 Was you angry with me?

2 The cat is eating it's supper.

3 Im to busy to see you.

4 He drunk all the milk.

5 He dances good.

6 You could of said you wasn't coming.

7 Lie the book on the desk.

8 The cacti needs watering.

9 This is the widower of the late Mrs Jones.

10 Calm down and don't get so historical.

Answers 1 were 2 its 3 I'm 4 drank 5 well 6 have 7 lay 8 need 9 no late 10 hysterical.

Guess my definition

In this game you read out the definition of a word and ask your friends to say what the headword is. For example 'a soft yellow food made from cream and milk'. The answer is butter.

Matching sounds

Try to match the words that sound the same: beat him thyme cymbal steal knight meddle bear see two symbol steel beet bare time night sea medal.

Hidden words

Take a long word like 'drawing' or 'measurement' and see how many other words you can find in it. 'Drawing' contains draw, raw, win, wing, in.

Odd ones out

Which are the odd ones out in these groups:

Cod, trout, whale, herring, shark.

Car, lorry, van, airplane, motorbike.

Orange, apple, lamb, plum, cherry.

Backword

The word 'evil' becomes 'live' if you spell it backwards. Can you think of any other words that do this?

Code words

This code hides a simple sentence. All you have to do is read down the first column and then up the last column to find the message 'Thanks for the presents'.

TENS

HURT

AVON

NINE

KISS

SIDE

FOUR

OLOP

RISE

TOSH

In alphabetical order

Put these words in their correct alphabetical order:

Crown, cruise, crane, crow.

Live, lamb, loose, letter, likely.

Dragon, donkey, dust, dinosaur, deaf.

Sounds right

Think of a phrase or sentence using these words:

Roar, croak, neigh, bellow.

Crash, clang, bang, thud.

Kinds of

A crow is a kind of ?

A violin is a kind of ?

A beetle is a kind of ?

An apple is a kind of ?

Sets

Think of a single word for each of these sets of words:

Aluminium, brass, bronze, iron, zinc.

Plaice, cod, herring, trout.

Chair, sofa, bed, table.

Scrambled words

See if you can make new words from these words, e.g. the eyes—they see.

Angered, astronomers, evil, funeral, nameless, night, nuclear, orchestra, organ.

(Answers: enraged, moon-starers, veil, real fun, maleness/lameness, thing, unclear, groan.)

Changed

Take two words of the same length and link these two words together by putting in other words, each different from the next word by one changed letter. Here, for example, is how you could change 'head' into 'tail':
HEAD HEAL TEAL TELL TALL TAIL.

Guess words

Open the dictionary at any page with a friend and read out the first and last word on that page. Your friend must try to guess other words on that page.

Chain words

A game to play with several people. Using the last two letters of the previous word make another word, e.g. reserve vest street etiquette telescope pedal alone negligent entire and so on.

Months of the year

January was named after Janus, the Roman god of doors.

February comes from the Latin for a religious festival.

March is named after the Roman god of war. This was originally the first month of the year.

April comes from the Latin for 'to open' and refers to buds opening.

May is named after the Roman earth goddess, Maia.

June was named after Juno, the queen of the Roman gods.

July was named after Julius Caesar.

August was named after the emperor Augustus Caesar.

September was once the seventh month (after 'septem', Latin for seven).

October was the eighth month (after 'octem', Latin for eight).

November was the ninth month (after 'novem', Latin for nine).

December was the tenth month (after 'decem', Latin for ten).

Some general spelling rules

(But always remember there are lots of exceptions to most rules!)

Nouns

To make a noun plural you normally add 's' —road roads, cake cakes.

But if the noun ends in -ch, -s, -ss, -sh or -x you add -es—

Ass asses, church churches, bush bushes, bus buses, mix mixes.

Nouns ending in a consonant plus a 'y' lose the 'y' and add -ies—

Baby babies, copy copies.

Many nouns ending in 'o' generally add -es—Cargo cargoes, hero heroes.

Plurals that do not follow these rules are shown in the dictionary—

child children, mouse mice.

Some nouns that are always plural in form:

Scissors, shears, oats, clothes, pyjamas, trousers, measles, spectacles.

Some very irregular plurals:

Man men, mouse mice, woman women, goose geese, mouse mice, foot feet, tooth teeth, ox oxen.

Some nouns that are both singular and plural in form:

Fish, sheep, deer.

Adverbs

Adverbs are usually formed by adding -ly to the adjective—Odd oddly, amazing amazingly, quick quickly.

But if the adjective ends in -ll, just add -y— Dull dully.

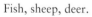

If the adjective ends in -le, drop the -le and add -ly—

Simple simply.

If the adjective ends in -ic, add ally— Historic historically.

(A notable exception is public publicly.)

Adverbs that do not follow these rules will be found in the dictionary.

Adjectives

To most adjectives of one syllable you normally add -er to make a comparative—

Near nearer, fast faster—Anne can run faster than her sister.

And you add -est to make a superlative— Nearest, fastest—Andy is the fastest runner in his class.

If the adjective ends in -e just add 'r' or 'st'—

Simple simpler simplest.

With some short adjectives ending with a consonant the consonant is doubled—

Red redder reddest.

With adjectives of more than two syllables use 'more' and 'most' for the comparative and superlative—

Careful, more careful, most careful. He's the most careful person I know.

Adjectives that do not follow these rules will be shown in the dictionary, for example—

Bad worse worst, good better best.

Verbs

To make the present participle, past tense and past participle to most regular verbs you add -ing, or -ed or -d—

Talk talking talked, pray praying prayed.

If the verb ends in 'e', the 'e' is dropped and -ing, or -ed are added—

Tame taming tamed.

The final consonant is doubled when a short word ends in a consonant—

Chat chatting chatted, slam slamming slammed.

I before E

'I before e except after c' is a good general rule, but only applies if the 'ie' in the word is pronounced like an 'ee'. So it is 'ie' in words such as field, believe and siege, and 'e' in words such as ceiling and receipt.

Some exceptions are: either, neither (which can be pronounced 'ee'), seize, weird, protein, and certain names such as Keith and Neil.

Words like eight, deign, reign and neighbor are spelled with 'ei' because they are not pronounced 'ee'.

Apostrophes

The possessive form of a noun is shown by writing ''s' at the end—

The boy's book.

The children's house.

Charles's bike.

When a noun is plural with the ending 's', add an apostrophe alone—

The girls' mother.

Each other or one another

Use 'each other' for two—

The two boys helped each other.

Use 'one another' for more than two.

All the children helped one another.

Double negative

'I never said nothing' is incorrect if what you want to say is 'I never said anything'. But it is correct if what you want to say is 'At no time did I ever say nothing'.

Aa Bb Cc

Gg Hh Ii Jj

Nn Oo Pp

Uu Vv Ww

Dd Ee Ff

Kk Ll Mm

Qq Rr Ss Tt

Xx Yy Zz

Acknowledgments

The publishers would like to thank the following
artists who have contributed to this book:

The Maltings Partnership
Andrew Clark
Julie Banyard
Gill Platt
Sally Launder
Wayne Ford
Guy Smith
Mike Saunders

All photographs supplied by Miles Kelly Archives.